Youth Crime and Youth Justice
Comparative and Cross-National Perspectives

Youth Crime and Youth Justice

Comparative and Cross-National Perspectives

Edited by
Michael Tonry
and Anthony N. Doob

Crime and Justice
A Review of Research
Edited by Michael Tonry

VOLUME 31

The University of Chicago Press, Chicago and London

The University of Chicago Press, Chicago 60637
The University of Chicago Press, Ltd., London

© 2004 by The University of Chicago
All rights reserved. Published 2004
Printed in the United States of America

ISSN: 0192-3234

ISBN: 0-226-80865-3 (cloth)
ISBN: 0-226-80866-1 (paper)

LCN: 80-642217

Library of Congress Cataloging-in-Publication Data

Youth crime and youth justice : comparative and cross-national perspectives / edited
by Michael Tonry and Anthony N. Doob.
　　p.　cm.—(Crime and justice : a review of research; v. 31)
　　Includes bibliographical references and indexes.
　　ISBN 0-226-80865-3 (cloth : alk. paper)—ISBN 0-226-80866-1 (pbk. : alk. paper)
　　1. Juvenile justice, Administration of—Cross-cultural studies.　2. Juvenile
corrections—Government policy—Cross-cultural studies.　I. Tonry, Michael H.
II. Doob, Anthony N.　III. Crime and justice (Chicago, Ill.); vol. 31.
HV9069.Y635　2004
364.36–dc22

2004000230
CIP

The paper used in this publication meets the minimum requirements of American National Standard for Information Sciences—Permanence of Paper for Printed Library
Materials, ANSI Z39.48-1984. ♾

Contents

Preface

Countries vary much more widely in juvenile than in adult justice systems. Although there are some institutional and cultural differences among Western countries in adult systems, particularly between civil law and common-law countries, the definitions of offenses, organizational arrangements, penalties available, and primarily retributive premises for the imposition of punishments are much the same. So, with differences only in detail, are the procedural and human rights protections accorded alleged offenders.

Juvenile systems, by contrast, vary widely in their structural details, age jurisdictions, and policy premises. This volume was conceived as an effort to document the range of variation in current and past practices and institutions in juvenile justice systems in selected Western countries and to attempt to determine what differences in practice and outcome those structural differences make.

The range of formal and purported normative differences is enormous. Some countries, such as the United States and England, operate juvenile justice systems that are, in effect, criminal courts for young offenders. Other countries—Scotland is a notable example—have systems based primarily on child welfare premises. Yet others—the Scandinavians, for example—have no special courts for handling offenses by young offenders: they are instead dealt with in adult criminal courts but under policies that produce less punitive dispositions than typically adults receive. New Zealand operates a youth justice system in which conferencing plays a major role and that because of its congruence with restorative justice ideals has attracted a great deal of attention around the world.

The preceding paragraphs describe structural and normative differences. There are many others. Age jurisdictions vary enormously between countries. In some countries, notably in Scandinavia, the age of criminal responsibility is fifteen, which means that intentional harms resulting from the actions of younger people are, as a legal matter, not crimes. Common-law countries have ages of criminal responsibility as young as seven. Other countries fall in between, with New Zealand again an outlier: its age of criminal responsibility is ten, but the minimum age of juvenile court jurisdiction is fourteen.

Likewise, countries vary substantially in the upper age jurisdiction of the juvenile court. In much of the United States, adult court jurisdiction begins at age eighteen, but there are other states in which it is as low as sixteen. In Scotland, children under sixteen are dealt with by children's hearings, and those sixteen and up by criminal courts.

The meaning of age limits varies enormously. In Canada, for example, recent changes have made it easier to transfer young offenders into adult courts, with the not entirely expected result that the number of children transferred has declined. In Germany, offenders eighteen and up are dealt with by the adult courts but transfer back into the juvenile court for sentencing is common. Conversely, in many American states in which adult court jurisdiction begins at eighteen, large numbers of younger offenders are transferred to the adult courts by judicial decision, or prosecutorial choice, or automatically when charged with designated serious offenses.

Whether any of this makes any difference to the experiences of young offenders, and, if so, how, in what ways, and to what degree, are not unimportant questions in an era when policy makers increasingly look across national boundaries in hopes of seeing better methods that might be imported, adapted, and implemented. These essays, we hope, shed some light on such questions.

This book is the eleventh thematic volume published as part of the *Crime and Justice* series. A planning session in Cambridge in October 2000 was attended by Anthony Bottoms, Jeffrey Fagan, Josine Junger-Tas, Lode Walgrave, and the two of us. At that session, a number of countries were specified whose systems seemed representative of distinctive approaches. A number of cross-cutting issues were identified, together with the names of scholars of appropriate expertise to write on each. Papers were commissioned, and a conference was convened in October 2001. It was attended by the writers, the planners, and the following: Richard Frase (Minnesota), Loraine Gelsthorpe (Cambridge), Nathan Harris (Cambridge), Amanda Matravers (Cambridge), Vincent Schiraldi (Center on Juvenile and Criminal Justice, Washington, D.C.), David J. Smith (Edinburgh), Jean Trépanier (Montreal),

Peter van der Laan (Netherlands Institute for the Study of Crime and Law Enforcement), Lorraine Waterhouse (Edinburgh), Janet Wiig (Minnesota), and Franklin Zimring (Berkeley).

After the conference, at which each draft paper was briefly presented and extensively discussed, additional critiques were sought from external referees. Enriched by all those reactions and all that advice, we then provided detailed sets of comments to each writer and invited revised versions of the essays.

We are enormously grateful to everyone who participated in this venture, whether as writer, planner, commentator, conference participant, or reviewer. In particular, of course, we appreciate the cooperation and good spirit of the writers. Preparation of *Crime and Justice* essays can be an arduous undertaking, and, to a person, writers responded with goodwill and enthusiasm.

This volume could not have been prepared without support from the Annie E. Casey Foundation, which awarded a grant to Castine Research Corporation in Castine, Maine, to support its preparation. Bart Lubow of the Annie E. Casey Foundation provided support and advice for which we are most grateful.

We are also grateful to Janet Wiig, director of the University of Minnesota's Criminal Justice Institute, which paid travel costs for American participants in the conference.

Michael Tonry
Anthony N. Doob

Anthony N. Doob and Michael Tonry

Varieties of Youth Justice

Like parents trying to figure how best to raise their children, countries have, in recent years, wrestled with the question of how to respond to youths who break laws. There are many different models. Few appear to work in a completely satisfactory manner from the perspective of those in each jurisdiction. There is not even consensus on what "youth justice systems" (where they exist) are trying to accomplish. Few decisions—other than that youths are different from adults—have been settled in the same way across jurisdictions. The manner in which each country has resolved the "youth justice" problem is almost certainly best understood within the broad context of that country's history and justice institutions. Hence it would be premature to carry out a true multicultural cross-jurisdictional study of youth justice systems without first attempting to understand each system within its own context. The essays in this volume represent an attempt to understand each system within the cultural context in which it exists.

Many jurisdictions are searching for new and better approaches for dealing with youth crime. It is as if, in the latter part of the twentieth century, many countries suddenly discovered that there was more than one way of responding to youths who offend. Principles, purposes, and procedures all changed, but the ambivalence within each community remained.

Anthony N. Doob is professor of criminology, the Centre of Criminology, University of Toronto, Canada. Michael Tonry is professor of law and public policy and director, Institute of Criminology, Cambridge University, and Sonosky Professor of Law and Public Policy, University of Minnesota Law School, and senior researcher, Netherlands Institute for the Study of Crime and Law Enforcement.

Approaches to youth justice are sometimes caricatured as falling at different points along a dimension of which one pole is a "pure" welfare model and the other is a "pure" criminal law or punishment model. Although this is an oversimplification, the tension that exists between responding to youths who have offended in terms of their social or psychological needs, and punishing them for what they have done, is part of the story of youth justice in many jurisdictions. Various essays in this volume illustrate that a criminal law approach need not be particularly punitive, nor a child welfare approach particularly effective.

Policy makers and practitioners often are not comfortable making clear distinctions between these two approaches. Snyder and Sickmund (1999, p. 87) suggest that most states in the United States have not been able to decide between them. Hence, they characterize thirty-two states as having both a "prevention/diversion/treatment" orientation and a "punishment" orientation in their legislated goals. The other eighteen jurisdictions are evenly split in their legislative goals between "punishment" and "child welfare" orientations. These stated goals are not unimportant, but seldom do they determine what actually happens.

This essay explores the variation that exists in the eight jurisdictions discussed in this volume. Section I describes one of the most important single facts about youth justice systems: a separate youth justice system is not necessary to ensure that youths are dealt with differently than are adults processed in the adult system. Section II outlines the complexity of the age limits of youth justice systems. Youth justice systems in many countries were quite stable until roughly 1970 or so. In the latter part of the twentieth century, however, many experienced changes, sometimes quite rapid, and often quite unprincipled. These changes are discussed in Section III. Section IV describes one aspect of the changes that took place in many countries—how various jurisdictions reconciled the tension between welfare principles and criminal law or punishment principles. Finally, in Section V, we note the contrasts between law in books and law in action. Understanding any youth justice system requires one to look not only at the formal legal structure but at how it operates in practice.

I. Separate Systems?

Youth justice systems vary much more between countries than do adult systems. Adult systems vary in many detailed ways but are broadly similar in most important respects. There is a good deal of consensus about what constitutes an offense. The exact nature of the prosecution process and court structures differs (especially between common-law and European countries), but there is widespread agreement that, at the end of the process, the sentence should, to a large extent, reflect the seriousness of the offense. Whatever else a sentence was said to accomplish, it would be seen unambiguously as punishment by the community and by the person subject to it. Sentencing systems in many countries have changed in the last thirty years—sometimes dramatically—but the focus of the sentence is more likely to be on the severity of punishment, rather than its purposes.

Youth justice systems do not have these same basic similarities. To give one illustration, what are commonly known as "status offenses"—behavior that is prohibited only because of a person's status as a youth (e.g., curfews, truancy) exist in some jurisdictions (e.g., in many U.S. states) but not in others (e.g., Canada, Denmark, or Germany).

Nor do all youth justice systems feature the same core features. In England and many U.S. states, youth justice systems closely resemble adult courts in their organization and their focus on punishment as a primary aim. In Scandinavian countries, people below age fifteen are legally incapable of committing crimes, and their serious misconduct is dealt with by social welfare agencies. At and after age fifteen, young offenders are processed by the same courts as process adults. In Scotland, a strong social welfare ethos dominates handling of young offenders. In New Zealand, nearly all cases are handled by conferences that many see as premised in part on ideas akin to those embodied in restorative justice.

The most notable aspect of the treatment of youths who offend in Western countries is that every country appears to have laws or policies reflecting the belief that youths should be treated differently from adult offenders. Exactly how they should be treated differently varies from country to country. What constitutes a "youth" also varies from country to country. And the rigidity of the demarcations between a child who is not criminally responsible and a youth who might be, and the demarcations between youthfulness and adulthood, also vary. But those responsible for criminal laws in all countries examined in this volume seem to agree that there should be some form of separation in how youthful and adult offenders are treated.

Accounts of juvenile justice history in the United States often focus on 1899 (the date of the founding of the first American separate court for juveniles in Chicago), just as Canadian juvenile justice is seen as dating from the first comprehensive "delinquency" legislation in 1908 or the first juvenile court in 1894. The experience of others, however, instructs that the formal beginnings of a "separate" youth justice system may not be especially important. The formal creation of a juvenile court is not necessary for there to be what is, from an operational standpoint, a separate youth justice system. Formal separation of juvenile from adult systems, exemplified by the "founding" of a juvenile court, may be no more than a North American idiosyncrasy and less important than the administrative structures and practices that determine a society's responses to youthful offending.

In Denmark, there is no formally separate system for young offenders. There are no special courts, and there are no special offenses (i.e., there are no status offenses). Denmark does not appear to have had a formally separate system (with distinct youth justice laws and a completely distinct set of youth justice institutions) for youths who offend. A naive American, therefore, might think that Denmark had not progressed even as far as reforms introduced in the early twentieth century in Chicago. As Kyvsgaard's essay in this volume demonstrates, however, that does not mean that Danish youths are treated as if they are adults. Clearly they are not.

The Swedish system of youth justice has similar characteristics. Early twentieth-century American reformers would be dismayed to find that those over the age of criminal responsibility (fifteen) in Sweden are dealt with in the criminal courts. The system that existed at the end of the twentieth century—with shared responsibility between the welfare system and the justice system—for those between ages fifteen and twenty—does not sound like a "separate justice system." Nevertheless, various rules identified by Janson in this volume differentiate the treatment of a sixteen-year-old from that of a twenty-one-year-old and add up to, in effect, a separate system. Youths between ages fifteen and seventeen, for example, cannot normally be sent to prison.

These two examples highlight the importance of looking at how youth justice systems work rather than exclusively at formal laws and institutions. Furthermore, it is well established that in the United States and Canada there were many aspects of a separate youth justice system, including separate custodial institutions and probation officers for juveniles, in place long before the establishment of the youth courts in Chicago and Toronto.

The tendency of most countries represented in this volume, however, was to establish some form of separate set of formal rules for youthful offenders. Beyond that, however, the similarity—at least at the level of the underlying operating theory—more or less disappears. It is difficult to find many similarities among England's preponderantly punitive system, the Scottish system of children's hearings, New Zealand's conferences, and the juvenile courts in the Netherlands.

Similarly, the influence of international conventions (the European Convention for the Protection of Human Rights and Fundamental Liberties and the United Nations Convention on the Rights of the Child) on European youth justice (see, in particular, Junger-Tas's discussion with respect to the Netherlands and Kyvsgaard's concerning Denmark) is not likely to have been anticipated by an American whose country is not even a signatory to the U.N. Convention.

But all of these "systems" have one important common element: all reflect the view that youths should be dealt with differently from adults. And, generally speaking, the assumption is that the youthfulness of an offender mitigates the punishment that youths should receive and that youths should be kept separate from adult offenders.

II. Age Limits

Many countries—Canada and Germany, for example—appear to have quite rigid demarcations between the system for dealing with youthful offending, the adult system of criminal justice, and the welfare system. One might suppose that these demarcations had meaningful referents—that youths are different the day after their eighteenth birthdays from the way they were the day before, or that the homeless seventeen-year-old who steals something to eat is different from the homeless seventeen-year-old who obtains food through some legal process. When the more fluid systems of Denmark and Sweden are compared to the more rigid systems of Canada or many American states, it is clear that there are advantages and disadvantages to each.

Countries vary widely in both minimum ages of criminal responsibility, before which a young person cannot be charged with a crime, and jurisdictional ages of youth courts. Snyder and Sickmund (1999, p. 93) present such data for the U.S. states that demonstrate wide variation. For example, the age of criminal responsibility is six in North Carolina and seven in Massachusetts, Maryland, and New York. The maximum ages of jurisdiction of the youth courts vary from fifteen (e.g., New York, North Carolina, and Connecticut) to seventeen (for

TABLE 1

Minimum and Maximum Ages of Youth Court Jurisdiction
by Country

Jurisdiction	Minimum Age	Maximum Age
Canada	12	17*
Netherlands	12	17
Germany	14	17
England	10	17
Scotland	8	15
United States (typically)	10	17
Sweden	15	Not relevant
Denmark	15	Not relevant
New Zealand	14	16

* This is the maximum age, meaning that the young person is a youth until the eighteenth birthday. Hence, "15" means up to the sixteenth birthday.

most states). Such data are useful for certain purposes, but can easily give a false impression of stability and certainty.

Table 1 shows maximum and minimum ages of youth court jurisdiction for the countries represented in this volume and the United States. Minimum ages vary widely, from eight to fifteen. In most countries adult court jurisdiction begins at age eighteen. Denmark and Sweden have no specialized youth court, so "adult" jurisdiction begins at age fifteen.

These data, then, would give an impression of similarity at the top age for five of the ten jurisdictions, and considerable variability at the bottom. They obscure, however, two phenomena. First, these ages have been, in some jurisdictions, unstable over time. These were the correct ages when these essays were written. In some jurisdictions, however, the ages have varied somewhat over time. More important, however, we see that the ages are not necessarily as firm as they might appear.

In Canada, the minimum age (twelve) was established in 1984. Prior to that, it had been seven. Until 1985, the maximum age had varied between provinces, with some provinces declaring youths to be adults at any age between sixteen and eighteen, or, in the case of Alberta, different ages had been set for girls and boys. Until April 2003, youths aged fourteen and above could be transferred into adult court. Indeed, presumptively they were to be transferred into adult court if they were at least sixteen years old at the time of the offense and were charged with certain serious violent offenses. If they were transferred, they would, for almost all purposes, be treated as if, by judicial decision, they had aged instantly into adulthood.

Since April 2003, youths charged with serious offenses remain youths for criminal justice purposes and remain in youth court but can, on application from the prosecutor, be sentenced as an adult if a judge determines that a proportionate youth sentence is not possible because the maximum permissible youth sentence is not long enough. Even then, the judge can sentence the youth to serve his or her sentence in a youth facility. To imply, then, that the juvenile justice law in Canada has always maintained jurisdiction over youths for six years beginning at the youth's twelfth birthday is an oversimplification, given that transfers were possible before April 2003 and adult sentences are permissible after that date.

The Netherlands' youth justice system, on the dimensions described in table 1, would appear to be very similar to Canada's. However, the apparent similarity of the age range of the two countries results more from coincidence than a similar development or similar principles. As Junger-Tas notes in this volume, the first formal criminal code in the Netherlands established, in 1809, that the minimum age of criminal responsibility was twelve, and youths up to age eighteen were liable to less severe sentences than were those ages eighteen and over. Only two years later, however, the French occupation resulted in the abolition of the minimum age, with judges having to decide on a case-by-case basis whether the youth should be held criminally responsible. In 1881, age fourteen became an important dividing point: those under age fourteen were, in effect, kept out of prisons but held in community facilities. In 1901, the maximum age was set at the eighteenth birthday, and the minimum age was again abolished.

Chronological ages are relatively easy to define. What become more murky, however, are situations where youths are deemed to be adults because of what they did. As Junger-Tas notes, the Netherlands' 1995 Juvenile Justice Act changed the manner in which sixteen- and seventeen-year-olds could be transferred into the adult system. Earlier, three conditions had to be met before a youth could be transferred: the offense had to be serious, there had to be aggravating factors such as the offense having been committed with adults, and the offender had to be seen as, effectively, having the maturity of an adult. The legislation that came into effect in 1995 changed this: only one of the conditions had to be present, and the "age" criterion apparently became more focused on the age of the offender at the time that the offense was committed rather than the youth's maturity. As an additional complication related to the issue of age, the maximum period of detention was changed with the new act so that those aged twelve through fifteen are liable to receive a maximum of a one-year sentence and those ages sixteen or seventeen at the time of the offense are liable to receive a two-year sentence.

The lower limit of criminal responsibility, on the surface identical to Canada's (age twelve), has become somewhat permeable. Junger-Tas describes a special project—called STOP—that focuses on minor infractions of the law by those under age twelve. Police are allowed to arrest these youths who, according to the "tabled" data, are below the age of criminal responsibility in the Netherlands. The police can propose an intervention by social workers, but formally this intervention requires parental approval. As Junger-Tas notes, increased transfer to adult court of those over age sixteen combined with increased use of STOP have the practical effect of lowering both of the age limits of the juvenile justice system. Said differently, these easy-to-define rigid dates have become less determinative.

The German Youth Court Law came into effect in 1923 and provided the framework for the state's response to offending by those between their fourteenth and eighteenth birthdays. Special courts and prisons for youths had existed before that time. Germany, Albrecht notes in this volume, has endorsed for approximately a century the idea that punishment is not the best approach to youthful offending. Nevertheless, in 1943, the Nazi government lowered the age of criminal responsibility to twelve and allowed the transfer to the adult system of offenders aged sixteen and over. These changes lasted only three years, however. But the age limits set out in the legislation are not quite as firm as would be implied by a table of minimum and maximum ages. Young adults, aged eighteen to twenty, can be prosecuted as if they were juveniles. In effect, there is the possibility of a transfer down because of variation in "maturation, social and moral development, and integration into the adult world" (Albrecht, in this volume). Germany's maximum age of seventeen is, then, very different from those ages found in American states.

The "age jurisdiction" for England appears to be fairly simple. However, within the range of juvenile jurisdiction, variation does exist. Until 1998 there were special restrictions on the use of custody for those under fifteen, but these restrictions were relaxed by the 1998 legislation. In addition, youths in England can be dealt with by the Crown (adult) Court rather than by the youth court. In serious cases, the youth is in jeopardy of receiving the same sentence an adult would receive. In the case of a homicide offense, committal to the Crown Court is mandatory. That is why probably England's most famous recent youth offense—the case involving two ten-year-old youths who killed James Bulger in 1992—was held in Crown Court and received full publicity. Interestingly, when the two youths found guilty of the offense were released as young adults, the government felt it necessary to protect their identities so that they could integrate into civil society.

But the lower age limit in England is being weakened in other ways. As Bottoms and Dignan note in this volume, children aged nine and under run the risk of formal intervention if they do something that could be considered criminal or if they misbehave in other ways. Though technically it is a civil proceeding, the child can be placed under the supervision of a social worker for what would otherwise be criminal behavior. Furthermore, the court is given powers to impose conditions designed to prevent future similar behavior. The difference between a criminal and a civil proceeding is probably somewhat obscure to the nine-year-old with restrictions on his freedom.

The age jurisdiction of the juvenile system in the United States varies from state to state, though the modal ages would appear to be similar to those in the United Kingdom. However, that is where the similarity ends. In particular, two factors must be considered. Even at the lowest age, in certain states, youths under twelve years old can be prosecuted as if they are adults.

More common is the ambiguity about the age jurisdiction at the top end. It is estimated that as many as 200,000 youths a year under the age of eighteen are processed in the adult courts in the United States as if they were adults.

In comparison, Canada, with about one-tenth as many youths as the United States, transferred fewer than 100 youths per year to adult courts even though the overall use of youth court appears to be relatively comparable in the two jurisdictions (Sprott and Snyder 1999). Most of the American youths who end up in adult court are not there as a result of judicially ordered waivers. In a few states (e.g., New York), there is no "judicial waiver" to adult court (Szymanski 2002).

Instead, two mechanisms account for most of these "instant adults." In many states, prosecutors have the power to decide that an offender should be dealt with as an adult. If the indictment is filed in the adult court, the youth is, then, for criminal justice purposes, an adult. Alternatively, some state legislatures have decided that, for certain serious offenses, a youth is to be considered to be an adult and the case is automatically processed through the adult criminal courts. The idea that the youth court jurisdiction is ages ten through seventeen, then, applies in many states only if the youth is lucky enough to avoid being deemed to be an adult for criminal justice purposes.

For someone from England, the United States, or Canada looking at youth justice systems, the idea of having a minimum age of criminal responsibility at age fifteen would almost certainly be seen as completely unrealistic. Sweden and Denmark, however, appear to survive quite well with such a system. When the youth is between the age of fifteen and his or her twenty-first birthday, sanctions are handed down by courts, but this period is described by Janson in this volume as part of the transition to adulthood. As he notes, prison for a youth below age eighteen requires "extraordinary" justification and between ages eighteen and twenty requires "special" justification. In any case, those under age twenty-one serve their time separately from adults. And, equally clearly, youth under age fifteen who offend are not completely ignored by the state.

If nothing else, the variation on what the upper and lower age limits mean should demonstrate the complexity and the interrelatedness of the various youth justice provisions that exist in Western countries. A seventeen-year-old would be a youth in five countries we have mentioned. But if that seventeen-year-old were to offend, he or she might well be treated in quite different ways—and decisions would be guided by quite different principles—depending on the country.

III. Stability and Change

Though the age jurisdiction is one tangible way in which youth justice systems in various countries have changed over the past 100 years, more profound changes have taken place in some, but not all, countries. There appears to have been stability in these systems up until the latter part of the twentieth century. Changes clearly occurred, but dramatic and rapid changes did not occur until the last few decades of the twentieth century.

In New Zealand, for example, the formal youth justice system brought to the country by its colonizers started off as might be expected: the values and practices of its original inhabitants were largely ignored in favor of a very British-sounding set of practices. From that time onward, there were many changes in how the justice system responded to youthful offenders. However, these changes were more evolutionary than radical. In the late nineteenth century, neglected children were sent to industrial schools, and youthful offenders could end up in prison or industrial schools. In 1925, children's courts were established, and the state's interpretation of the "best interests" of the child ostensibly defined what happened to youthful offenders. In the 1950s and 1960s some modifications were made—allowing for more punitive responses for older children and for the raising of the age of criminal responsibility from seven to ten.

Things began to change more radically in 1974 when, among other things, a distinction was made between those over and under age fourteen. In particular, the age of criminal responsibility (ten) and the age of prosecution (fourteen) were distinguished. This can be seen as an early sign of what New Zealand is today best known for—the involvement of families and local communities in decisions concerning youthful offenders. The legislative changes apparently did not have the impact expected, and the law itself was repeatedly amended over the next ten years. In 1989, the most radical change occurred when the youth justice legislation for which New Zealand is well known was introduced—a system that focuses, more than others described in this volume, on conferencing processes to decide how to deal with youthful offenders.

Canada's stability is easier to describe. The federal law that established a separate youth justice system in 1908 remained essentially untouched for seventy-six years. The 1984 law lasted only until 2003, but even that law was changed in symbolically important ways three times during its nineteen-year history. The changes that took place in the past twenty-five years, however, transformed Canada's youth justice system from a clearly welfare-oriented system (though technically under the federal government's criminal law jurisdiction) to a system based largely on accountability and responses proportional to the offense that was committed.

Scotland's history looks, on the surface, to be quite similar to Canada's in the sense that there was a period of long stability followed by change relatively late in the twentieth century. The Children Act of 1908 established a separate juvenile court that remained largely unchanged until 1968. At that point, the Social Work (Scotland) Act, which was fully implemented in 1971, set up a completely new system of "children's hearings." These remained largely intact until the early twenty-first century, though very recently changes again are being discussed.

England, as Bottoms and Dignan point out in this volume, had a history that appeared to be similar to that of Scotland until the 1960s. At that point, the two jurisdictions diverged dramatically. That divergence can be characterized on two dimensions: youth justice principles and the stability of the laws. The 1969 English legislation created what Bottoms and Dignan in this volume describe as a "radical shake-up of procedures, orders, and supporting service structures." The controversy around these changes resulted, beginning in the 1970s, in an "often bewilderingly rapid [set of] changes in the English youth justice system" from the mid-1970s to the late 1990s.

At the other extreme is Germany. As Albrecht notes in this volume, the notable characteristic of youth justice in Germany is its stability throughout the twentieth and early twenty-first centuries. There might be two reasons for this stability. First, the law was founded on clear criminal law principles; hence, the apparent disillusionment with social welfare interventions for offending youths that might be seen as characterizing other countries toward the latter part of the twentieth century was irrelevant in Germany. Second, there appears to have been a widely shared philosophical basis for the German juvenile justice system throughout the twentieth century: less criminal justice intervention is better than more.

It is not clear why stability seems to have characterized some systems and change has characterized others. To say that youth justice became politicized toward the end of the twentieth century in some countries but not others is only to restate the question.

IV. Welfare and "Justice"

The conflict between what are generally referred to as welfare principles and criminal law principles appears to have featured in at least some of the changes that have taken place in the latter part of the twentieth century. Criminal law, however, incorporates a number of quite independent concepts. As contrasted with welfare, criminal law can mean a greater focus on the offense rather than the offender, more focus on due process issues, proportional responses to offending, or a focus on punishment as a justification for intervention.

Every jurisdiction has had to grapple with this distinction in some way. Even Germany, which had a criminal law basis for its youth justice system throughout the twentieth century, had to consider whether social welfare concerns should be integrated into it. The prolonged consideration in the 1960s and 1970s of whether to "shift" delinquency into the welfare system, Albrecht notes, was never implemented and has since disappeared as an issue. Other countries—like Canada—have moved from a system that gave priority to one principle (welfare, under the law in effect from 1908 to 1984) to a law that came into effect in 2003 that focuses initially, and perhaps primarily in most cases, on the offense. Still others, as in many states in the United States, focus on welfare issues within the juvenile court, but focus on the offense (and criminal justice approaches) when dealing with relatively serious offenses.

Welfare issues played out in different ways in Denmark, a country with one of the more stable systems of dealing with youthful offenders. There is no formally separate juvenile justice system in Denmark. Kyvsgaard notes in this volume that Denmark's 1930 Criminal Code allowed a form of indeterminate sentence to be handed down to young offenders. These "youth prison sentences," which aimed at "educating and training juveniles with criminal proclivities," were abolished in 1973 in part because of concerns related to the indeterminacy of the sentence. Not until 2001 was a new special "youth sentence" reintroduced. Interestingly enough, the new youth sentence came about not because of concerns about education or welfare of youths but because of concerns about serious violent youthful offenders. Although not used very often (fifty times per year), it is notable that a type of special prison sentence that had been put in place seventy years earlier and abolished thirty years earlier was reincarnated (though in a somewhat different form) to accomplish the dual goal of rehabilitation and incapacitation. Even in relatively stable Denmark, there is tension between criminal law and child welfare.

The tension between a criminal law approach and a child welfare approach played out somewhat differently in the Netherlands. Although for centuries the history of juvenile justice predominately focused on the welfare tradition, more recently the system may have become more repressive. It is described, however, as a hybrid of punitive and welfare traditions. For most of the twentieth century, the system was largely oriented toward the welfare of young offenders, rejecting, therefore, the notion that the severity of the intervention or treatment should be proportional to the offense. This changed in the 1980s when, in a manner that was similar to that of other countries around this time, children's rights became an issue. Junger-Tas's characterization, in this volume, of the shift in approach is blunt, and her statement no doubt echoes in other countries: "The welfare approach to youth justice persisted until the 1980s, when it became obsolete. One reason was its excesses." She notes—again with words that could apply to many countries—that "a more general problem was that most interventions had no solid scientific basis. Far-reaching decisions taken on behalf of juveniles were based on shaky evidence and had a highly arbitrary quality." The result is that criminal law principles ascended in importance in 1995, and criminal law principles appeared, in the Netherlands, to be associated with more severe punishments for juveniles.

The association of welfare approaches to juvenile justice with leniency and criminal law or proportional sentencing with harshness is being challenged (or at least tested) by Canada's shift to a proportional (criminal law) model from a more mixed model of juvenile justice. Canada explicitly endorsed proportionality principles in sentencing in order to reduce the intrusion of the justice system into the lives of young people. Its 2003 legislation has specific prohibitions against the use of pretrial detention and prison for welfare purposes. The reasons for these provisions are clear: too many youths were being detained and sentenced to custody for welfare purposes. The preamble to the legislation refers to the goal of reducing the overreliance on incarceration for nonviolent offenses. It is impossible to know, however, whether this criminal law approach will result in reduced use of detention and custody.

Scotland's appears, on the surface, to be one of the apparently more "pure" welfare approaches. As Bottoms and Dignan note in this volume, the contrast between Scotland and England is particularly interesting because the two systems came out of the same legislative body, the U.K. Parliament. In comparing the decidedly more welfare orientation of the Scottish juvenile justice system to the more criminal law system that exists in the south, one important difference must be borne in mind. England's system deals with youths ages ten to seventeen (inclusive). In Scotland, an offender is no longer considered to be a youth after the sixteenth birthday, but eight-year-olds can be brought to the hearing as a result of an offense.

Hence a comparison of the welfare-oriented Scottish system with the more criminal English system is also a comparison of a system dealing with eight-to-fifteen-year-olds with a system dealing with ten- to seventeen-year-olds. The Scottish system, as Bottoms and Dignan point out, deals in the same way with cases involving matters of "care" as it does with offenses. In all cases, the children's hearing and the court are to deal with a child in such a way that "the welfare of that child throughout his childhood shall be . . . [the] paramount consideration" (Children [Scotland] Act 1995, sec. 16[1]). Indeed, the children's hearing—probably the most distinctive aspect of the Scottish system—is to be invoked not just when a child has committed an offense but when it is in the child's interest that there be some form of compulsory care. Compulsory outcomes, however, cannot be ordered unless they are in the child's interest; the commission of an offense is not sufficient cause for the state to intervene in the life of a young person.

But even in this welfare-oriented system, the threads of its welfare orientation are beginning to unravel. In 1995, the law was changed so that the primary role that welfare issues play in guiding outcomes can be reduced if it is necessary for public protection from serious harm. Apparently, this is rarely invoked. But even in Scotland, it seems, the notion that the youth justice institutions can protect the public from youth crime through the use of punishments has made its way into the legislation, though less so into practice.

England, as Bottoms and Dignan point out, presents a dramatic contrast. In 1991, the separation of the care and crime functions became complete. Crime was to be dealt with by the English youth court, and care was sent to the family court. This separation appears to be stable.

One of the less obvious shifts away from a welfare model occurred in New Zealand during the latter part of the twentieth century. The New Zealand youth justice system is notable in large part because of the emphasis that has been given, since 1989, to conferencing as a way of resolving cases involving youthful offenders. Though conferencing may not be seen as a "tough" response to youthful offending, its orientation is clearly some distance from a welfare-intervention model. The focus of a conference is more than simply a focus on the child.

We are not suggesting that a major focus on the welfare of children can be assumed in the long term to be in unrelenting decline in Western juvenile justice systems. However, as a generalization, its overall importance as an organizing principle in many (but not all) systems appears to be on the decline.

One reason may, of course, relate to the politicizing of youth justice in many countries. As Roberts points out in this volume, the belief in many countries that youth crime is increasing appears to fuel moves to "do something" about the problem. Moving away from a welfare orientation in dealing with youthful offenders may be one way of making the political point that a crime is a crime. Roberts quotes a former Canadian minister of justice as saying in 1997 that "if people think violent crime is an increasing problem, then there is a problem that we have to address," and "violent youth crime demands a strong response"—a statement that clearly is not likely to be interpreted as being supportive of a welfare orientation. Similarly, Roberts notes that mandatory sentencing laws in Australia were introduced in 1992 specifically to address concerns about leniency in the youth justice system.

Youth crime is an attractive territory for political opportunism since tough legislation (e.g., the automatic processing as adults of youths who murder, or mandatory sentences for very serious violent offenses) can be enacted with relatively few political or financial costs. Few people—or at least few of those who appear to influence political agendas—view tough youth crime measures as being tough on youths. Instead, they are seen as being tough on crime. But tough youth crime measures have another political advantage. Compared to legislative changes that affect sentencing generally (e.g., three-strikes laws for adult offenders), a shift from a welfare orientation to a tough offense-based system for the most serious offenders will not be likely to affect many youths and, therefore, will not cost a great deal.

V. Law in Books and in Action

Much of the toughening in youth justice systems came after apparent increases in youth crime leveled out. Much of the activity in the United States occurred in the mid-to-late 1990s, for example. Crime rates in the United States for adults and youths, including for violence, peaked in the early 1990s and then dropped off. Roberts suggests that extraordinary cases have sparked the moves in many countries toward toughness. One of the clearest examples of this—but at the same time one of the numerically least important—came in the mid-1990s in Canada. In 1991, Canada had changed the test for transferring youths to the adult justice system. It was a shift away from a balancing of the welfare needs of the youth and protection of society toward a clearer protection-of-society model. In 1995, legislation was once again introduced to change the rules on the transfer of youths. This was done at a time when there were no data on the effect of the earlier change, in large part because only a few cases had been handled under the 1991 rules. What is, perhaps, most important about these changes is that they had no apparent impact on the number of youth cases transferred to adult court. Few cases were transferred before the change, and the change in the legislation apparently had no effect on transfers.

The distinction between law as it is written and law as it is administered, then, is crucial in understanding a youth justice system. Canada, with a single youth justice law administered by thirteen different jurisdictions (ten provinces and three territories) demonstrates this: the manner in which youths are processed varies dramatically across jurisdictions. Furthermore, when legislation was enacted in the mid-1990s that, among other things, encouraged the use of alternatives to custody, there were no apparent changes in the high-rate use of custodial dispositions. Another broad, but little noticed, change that took place without new legislation was the dramatic increase in the use of short custodial sentences in the late 1980s in many provinces (Doob 1992). In the case of this increase, there not only was no legislative change but also little awareness, it seems, that this was occurring.

In Denmark, Kyvsgaard notes that between the 1950s and the 1990s there was a dramatic shift in the proportion of youth cases handled formally in the justice system. In the mid-1950s, only about 5 percent of youths apprehended for offenses were found guilty, but by 2000 this had increased to 77 percent. She notes that "this has not resulted from specific amendments or deliberate youth policy changes, but has resulted from general changes in legal usage and criticisms of withdrawals of charges for young offenders."

In Germany, for at least part of this period, the trend—again without legislative direction—was in the opposite direction. During the latter part of the twentieth century, there was increased diversion of youths from the formal system, which led to complaints by the police about underenforcement of the law.

In England during the latter part of 1980s, rates of formal processing decreased, though in this case the exact reasons are known. Other changes in the prosecution process—the establishment of the Crown Prosecution Service and greater use of informal warnings by the police—were responsible for the changes. However, why this trend apparently continued into the 1990s in periods of rising (the early 1990s) and then falling crime (mid-1990s onward) is somewhat mysterious. Some of this change at the end of the century, Bottoms and Dignan suggest, might be due to changes in offending (or at least apprehension) rates, but it is not clear how much can be attributed to this. In Scotland, by contrast, formal processing increased over the past twenty years.

The most interesting explanation for the variability in the United Kingdom is that there might be changes in confidence in the two jurisdictions in the manner in which youths are processed. If the system is trusted by the criminal justice community in Scotland, and youth justice officials (police, etc.) believe that youths will be handled appropriately, it makes sense that the system would be increasingly used. In England, Bottoms and Dignan suggest, the earlier days of minimum intervention and the "new youth justice" initiatives did not earn the confidence of the criminal justice community.

These are only a few examples of the large changes that occur in the youth justice system independent of formal policy and formal legislative actions designed to create changes. Whatever the reasons for the individual changes in specific countries, what is clear is that the modifications reflect complex interactions of the law, the community in which the law is being enforced, attitudes of justice officials and the public, and the operation of other related institutions. Nothing is simple in the field of youth justice.

The latter part of the twentieth century and the early part of the twenty-first century have been times when people in many countries have been searching for the "right" solutions to youth justice problems. Compromises abound. As Walgrave notes in this volume in his essay on one of the newest popular innovations in youth justice, restorative justice initiatives, there will always be tensions between the social welfare and social control approaches. More important, however, is his observation that "this tension is inevitable because juvenile justice jurisdictions try to combine what cannot be combined satisfactorily." Walgrave notes that the so-called Beijing rules expressed in the United Nations Declaration on the Rights of Children, which are meant to act as a guide to how young people are dealt with in all countries, "reflect a fundamental ambivalence" and, in attempting to combine approaches, might best be described as an attempt to sound good but gloss over basic incompatibilities between the approaches. The grafting of restorative justice principles onto the unresolved conflict between welfare and punishment goals obviously leads to other difficulties. Among them, Walgrave suggests that restorative approaches, when added to this mix of goals, may be vulnerable to all of the existing criticisms of punishment and treatment approaches.

The stories these essays tell will not provide the thoughtful reader with a simple solution to the fundamental problems of youth justice, just as reading about different methods of raising children will not help parents know with certainty how best to raise their own. Nevertheless, the stories about how these countries have developed and modified their approaches to youthful offending, along with the data they provide on youth crime and youth justice, provide a background against which all of us can learn more about the complexity of the problem.

The essays raise important questions about our youth justice systems. Youth justice systems, and changes in youth justice systems in particular, as Zimring (2002) suggests, need to be understood in the context of the criminal justice system that is in place for adults in each jurisdiction. In Sweden and Denmark, they are one and the same. But even in those jurisdictions that have formally separate justice systems, it is worth considering what the relationship is between changes in the two systems.

We tend to know less than we should about the involvement of the state in the lives of children during adolescence. Though we know that in some jurisdictions youths who are heavily involved in the youth justice system also are likely to have welfare needs, we know little about the decisions that are made which determine which system is invoked when both systems could be used and each might be seen as being relevant. Longitudinal studies of youths with representative samples are not terribly helpful in this regard because relatively few youths ever come in contact with the formal youth justice or child welfare systems. Although comparative data across jurisdictions on the relative use of the two systems do not exist (even where there are separate systems), these might be useful in understanding the ways in which states intervene in the lives of children. It might be, for example, that jurisdictions that have low rates of youth court, or criminal law, involvement have relatively higher rates of some form of state intervention into the lives of children for welfare purposes. Alternatively, it might be that the social policies that are likely to affect the level of welfare needs among children are the same as the policies that affect the level of involvement in offending. If this were the case, one could expect youth justice and child welfare rates to be positively correlated across jurisdictions.

In a similar vein, neither within jurisdictions nor across them do we know much about the reaction of youths to different types of interventions. Little is known about the relative efficacy of interventions in the two processes.

Nevertheless, the central lesson these essays offer is an important one: there is not likely to be a single best approach to responding to youthful offending. There is a good argument for seeing youthful offending and the youth justice system that responds to it as quite separate phenomena. Youthful offending may affect the youth justice system, but youth justice systems probably have very little impact on youthful offending. Some might see this hypothesis as a pessimistic one. Alternatively, it may free those who are responsible for modifying youth justice systems to focus more clearly on what is important about society's responses to crime. What is clear from the essays in this book, however, is that relatively similar Western countries have not arrived at a consensus on how best to respond to youth crime.

REFERENCES

Doob, Anthony N. 1992. "Trends in the Use of Custodial Dispositions for Young Offenders." *Canadian Journal of Criminology* 34(1):75–84.

Snyder, Howard N., and Melissa Sickmund. 1999. *Juvenile Offenders and Victims: 1999 National Report.* Washington, D.C.: Office of Juvenile Justice and Delinquency Prevention.

Sprott, Jane B., and Howard N. Snyder. 1999. "Youth Crime in the U.S. and Canada, 1991 to 1996." *Overcrowded Times* 10(5):1, 12–19.

Szymanski, Linda. 2002. "Judicial Waiver to Criminal Court (2001 Update)." *NCJJ Snapshot,* vol. 7, no. 6. Pittsburgh: National Center for Juvenile Justice.

Zimring, Franklin E. 2002. "The Common Thread: Diversion in the Jurisprudence of Juvenile Courts." In *A Century of Juvenile Justice,* edited by Margaret K. Rosenheim, Franklin E. Zimring, David S. Tanenhaus, and Bernadine Dohrn. Chicago: University of Chicago Press.

Anthony Bottoms and James Dignan

Youth Justice in Great Britain

ABSTRACT

The English and Scottish youth justice systems share a commitment to preventive as opposed to retributive goals, but pursue them in sharply contrasting ways. In Scotland, a unified welfare-based system, committed to the prevention of harm to children, encompasses children who offend and children in social jeopardy. It uniquely and radically separates functions between the courts as factual and legal arbiters and children's hearings as treatment tribunals. A correctionalist system, committed to the prevention of offending, has emerged in England. It repudiates earlier views that young offenders should be left to "grow out of crime" with minimal state intervention. Subsidiary goals include responsibilization (of offenders and parents), reparation, and case-processing efficiency. It is characterized by much institutional innovation, including introduction of multiagency youth offending teams. This "joined up" approach stops short of encompassing "care" and "offense" cases within the same jurisdiction as Scotland does. The systems' philosophical differences are reflected in many contrasting operational practices. Political devolution in Scotland has introduced turbulence into the Scottish system; that and the newness of the English system make it difficult to predict future developments.

In the constitutional law of the United Kingdom, the term "Great Britain" has a technical connotation, covering the countries of England, Wales, and Scotland.[1] However, within this geographical ambit,

Anthony Bottoms is Wolfson Professor of Criminology at the University of Cambridge and professorial fellow in criminology at the University of Sheffield. James Dignan is professor of criminology and restorative justice at the University of Sheffield. Some parts of the text of this essay, especially as they relate to Scotland, previously appeared in an article by Anthony Bottoms (2002).

[1] The fourth part of the United Kingdom is Northern Ireland, and the full formal title of the United Kingdom is The United Kingdom of Great Britain and Northern Ireland.

two almost completely separate legal jurisdictions operate. While Wales and England share basically the same law and legal procedures, by the terms of the Acts of Union of 1707, Scotland has retained its own legal system.[2] And in the field of youth justice, radically different systems now operate north and south of the border. What makes this situation especially intriguing is that until 1999 legislative proposals for altering the law in both England[3] and Scotland were processed by exactly the same body, the U.K. Parliament. Moreover—and somewhat paradoxically—the recent advent of a devolved Parliament for Scotland[4] seems to be creating some electoral pressures that could have the effect of lessening the differences between the two systems.

Historically, both England and Scotland trace the origins of their juvenile court systems—at least at a national level—to exactly the same legislative provision, the Children Act of 1908. However, these early juvenile courts were not the same as those that had been created in Illinois (and some other U.S. states) and in Norway a few years previously (see Dahl 1985; Tanenhaus 2002). In the terms of the helpful distinction drawn by Faust and Brantingham (1979, pp. 14–15), these North American and Scandinavian jurisdictions had set up socialized juvenile tribunals, based on what in the United States was called the *parens patriae* principle.[5] In such tribunals, there was a strong emphasis on the welfare of the child, a deliberate move away from formal crimi-

---

[2] Scotland and England were separate countries until 1707. In that year, both the Scottish Parliament and the English Parliament passed Acts of Union, abolishing themselves and creating a new United Kingdom of Great Britain.

[3] For simplicity, and following the usual convention, throughout this essay we often use the terms "England" and "English" instead of the more technically correct "England and Wales" or "English and Welsh."

[4] The new Scottish Parliament—the first since 1707—came into existence in 1999. From that date, responsibility for Scottish criminal justice, juvenile justice, and child protection has been transferred from the U.K. Parliament and the U.K. government to the Scottish Parliament and the Scottish Executive. These developments do not affect the key U.K. constitutional principle of the sovereignty of Parliament, since the U.K. Parliament has retained the formal power to abolish or suspend the new devolved machinery of government in Scotland.

[5] As Elizabeth Scott (2002, p. 116) puts it, under the *parens patriae* ("parenthood of the state") principle, the state "has the responsibility to look out for the welfare of children and other helpless members of society. Thus, parental authority is subject to government supervision; if parents fail to provide adequate care, the state will intervene to protect children's welfare." One consequence of this approach, when applied to children's courts, was the belief that—as an early twentieth-century Japanese scholar put it after a visit to the United States—"children's courts should not be an instrument to punish the child but one that protects and educates" (quoted in Morita 2002, p. 362). Or, as Ben Lindsey, an early judge of the Denver Juvenile Court, more bluntly stated, "our laws against crime are as inapplicable to children as they would be to idiots" (quoted in Scott 2002, p. 117).

nal procedures, and, conceptually, a "dematerialization of the offense" (Donzelot 1980, pp. 110–11) within the proceedings, so that—in the words of two early American commentators—"emphasis is laid, not on the act done by the child, but on the social facts and circumstances that are really the inducing causes of the child's appearance in court" (Flexner and Baldwin 1915, pp. 6–7). By contrast, in both England and Scotland the early juvenile courts were predominantly—in Faust and Brantingham's terminology—modified criminal courts. When dealing with allegations of offenses, in both jurisdictions, "the distinctive feature of the juvenile or children's courts introduced by the 1908 act was the fact that hearings had to be held in a separate building or at a different time from adult courts, and that public access was restricted. Apart from this they were criminal courts of due process, indistinguishable from other [lower] courts" (Ball, McCormac, and Stone 2001, p. 5).[6]

Additionally, however, the early twentieth-century legislation united within the new juvenile courts two jurisdictional strands, one relating to young offenders and the other to children "in need of care and protection." But in Great Britain—unlike many of the "socialized juvenile tribunal" countries—the so-called care jurisdiction of the juvenile court was always numerically and ideologically subordinate.[7]

Generalizing a little, and so ignoring some complexities of detail, the situation remained quite similar to that described above until the 1960s.[8] During that decade, however, there took place very intensive reexaminations of the juvenile justice systems in both England and Scotland, leading in both instances to major legislation that was intended to transform each system. In both jurisdictions, the dominant ideology underpinning the new legislation was similar—a significantly greater priority was to be given within the new systems to the overarching principle of the welfare of the child, even when dealing with

---

[6] However, because of the historically separate legal systems of the two countries, the nature of the lower criminal courts in England and Scotland differed significantly, and this affected to some extent the character and history of the early juvenile courts (for further details, see Bottoms [2002]).

[7] For example, in 1967 the Cook County Juvenile Court, covering the Chicago area, had a caseload that consisted of 54 percent offense-based cases, the remainder consisting of "runaways, truants, ungovernables . . . dependency, neglect" and so on (Morris and Hawkins 1970, p. 160). By contrast, in the same year, 81 percent of persons who were made the subject of orders by juvenile courts in England and Wales were dealt with for criminal offenses (see calculations in Bottoms [2002], n. 5).

[8] In the 1930s, England did move somewhat more fully than Scotland toward a more welfare-oriented philosophy, but still firmly within the framework of the "modified criminal court" tradition. For a fuller discussion, see Bottoms (2002).

allegations of crime. Ironically, all this took place just at the time that, in the United States, the first major legal challenges to the welfare-based *parens patriae* juvenile courts were being mounted, for example, in the landmark Supreme Court case of *In re Gault* (387 U.S. 1 [1967]).[9]

But although the 1960s developments were strongly underpinned by welfare principles in both England and Scotland, the reforms that were enacted led to very different results in the two jurisdictions. In Scotland, the new legislation—the Social Work (Scotland) Act 1968—was implemented in full in 1971. It abolished the former Scottish juvenile courts and set up in their place a new system of civil jurisdiction known as the children's hearings system, dealing both with children who had broken the law and those in need of care and protection. That system has remained in place, in a largely unchanged form, for over thirty years, and still commands widespread support in professional circles in Scotland (see further Sec. II below). It was given a new statutory framework by the Children (Scotland) Act 1995, but this did little to disturb either the principles or the institutions that had been established by the earlier legislation.

English experience has been much more turbulent. The Children and Young Persons Act of 1969 retained the outward form (and the personnel) of the preexisting English juvenile courts, but within that framework attempted to put in place a radical shake-up of procedures, orders, and supporting service structures (for details, see Bottoms, McClean, and Patchett [1970]). But, for complex reasons of domestic politics, the act was only partially implemented.[10] Moreover, even the parts that were implemented proved to be very controversial when they began to be put into practical effect. This resulted in some major within-system conflicts during the 1970s; these proved to be merely the first stage in a series of often bewilderingly rapid changes in the

[9] As Edelman (2002, p. 322) has noted, in this case "the Supreme Court recognized in strong language that the kind, paternalistic intent of the juvenile court's creators had mutated into an institution that, lacking due process and a guarantee of legal representation, was as likely to punish the innocent or overreact to minor offenders as it was to pursue a rehabilitative path."

[10] In the United Kingdom, acts of Parliament frequently contain a section to the effect that the act shall only come into force on a day specified by a government minister, and that the minister may specify different dates for the commencement of different sections of the act. The Children and Young Persons Act 1969 had been implemented only to a small extent when the Labour government that had piloted the act through Parliament lost power at a general election. Key sections of the act were then never brought into force either by the incoming Conservative government or by subsequent administrations.

English youth justice system, from the mid-1970s to the late 1990s (for an outline history of these developments, see Bottoms [2002]).

A new Labour government was elected in the United Kingdom in 1997 after a period of eighteen years out of power. Reform of the English system for dealing with youth crime was one of the principal policy priorities of the new administration. Legislation rapidly followed in the Crime and Disorder Act of 1998 and later in Part I of the Youth Justice and Criminal Evidence Act 1999. In each of these (separate) reforms, limited "piloting" of the new provisions has been carried out in selected local areas before the reforms were—in the approved jargon—"rolled out nationally." The reforms of the 1998 act were nationally implemented in June 2000, and the reforms of the 1999 act became operational nationally in April 2002. This new (post-1998) English youth justice system is significantly more interventionist and correctionalist than the approaches that immediately preceded it.

The preceding paragraph refers only to the "offense" side of the original dual jurisdiction of the English juvenile courts. The other element—the "care" jurisdiction—had, some years earlier, been completely remodeled by the Children Act 1989, which came into force in October 1991 (see Eekelaar [2002] for a brief history of child welfare and child protection legislation in England). Since that date, the care jurisdiction in relation to children has been handled in England by lower civil courts known as "family proceedings courts," a move that was welcomed by a leading academic commentator on child law as beneficial in removing such cases from "the criminal overtones associated with the juvenile court" (Bainham 1990, pp. 181–82). Thus, in England, for children and young persons coming before the courts there is now a deliberate institutional separation between the "care jurisdiction" (dealt with by the family proceedings court) and the "criminal jurisdiction" (dealt with by what is now called the Youth Court).[11] In Scotland, by contrast, the children's hearings system deals with both types of case, and many regard it as a major strength of the system that it does so.

Our task in this essay is to describe and comment on these two very different youth justice systems, operating side by side within the same nonfederal nation-state. One system is welfare based and combines

[11] In England, the maximum age of the juvenile criminal jurisdiction was raised from the seventeenth birthday to the eighteenth birthday by the Criminal Justice Act 1991, effective October 1992. As a consequence of this, juvenile courts were renamed as Youth Courts.

within it both offense and care cases; the other system deliberately splits offense and care cases, and, on the offense side, is explicitly correctionalist rather than welfare based. Some of the contrasts between the systems are of considerable interest to the academic or policy commentator, but the newness of the English system (on the crime side) also makes for significant difficulties for the analyst because at present there is necessarily very limited empirical evidence as to how the new system is working.

One final introductory comment must be made. Historically, it was difficult to compare crime rates in England and Scotland because of the different legal categories utilized in official criminal statistics. The advent of national crime victimization surveys in both countries from 1981 has made such comparisons much easier. We also know from detailed research analyses that the crime rates of the two countries were very similar in 1981 (Smith 1983; Mayhew and Smith 1985), so a good indication of crime trends can be gained by indexing the post-1981 official and crime survey data against a base, for each country, of 1981 = 100. When this is done (see fig. 1), it is clear that crime has risen more quickly in England than in Scotland in the last twenty years. A number of commentators have suggested that these differential crime trends might perhaps be related to the different juvenile justice systems in operation in the two countries, though exactly how is rarely specified.

Here is how this essay is organized. Appearing as it does in a volume of *Crime and Justice*, the chapter focuses principally on how the two systems deal with young offenders (although inevitably, given the contrasts highlighted above, the differential relationship of the crime and the care jurisdictions for children becomes a prominent theme). Section I provides details about the philosophies of the two different systems, including in the case of England some comments on why the present government was dissatisfied with some of the conceptual approaches prominent in the pre-1998 system. The lengthy Sections II and III describe, respectively, the Scottish and the English systems, with appropriate data on the workings of the systems where these are available. Section IV then provides data on differential trends in processing young offenders in the two countries, while Section V considers how the two juvenile justice systems relate to other, linked institutions—especially considering issues of minimum age and relationships with the child protection and adult justice systems. Section VI discusses some key current issues for the two systems, namely, the role of

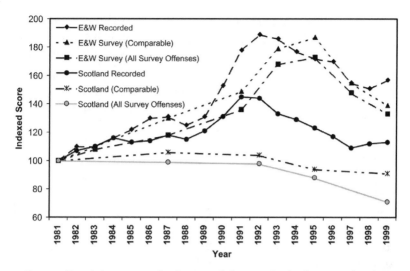

Fig. 1.—Trends in survey and police-recorded crime: Scotland compared with England and Wales, 1981–99 (indexed, 1981 = 100). Sources: Data have been drawn from official sources relating to recorded crime in the two countries: the British Crime Survey (which covers England and Wales only), and the Scottish Crime Survey. The most recent data from these sources can be found in Home Office 2000c; Kershaw et al. 2000; Scottish Executive 2000c, 2002d. Notes: The three main data sources utilized for each country are not directly comparable, but the use of indexation (1981 = 100) allows variation over time in each different data source to be plotted. "Recorded Crime" means, for England and Wales, notifiable offenses recorded by the police; for Scotland, where "crimes" and "offenses" are different legal categories, it means crimes recorded by the police. Data for both countries have been adjusted to take account of changes in recording procedures (in 1995 in Scotland and in 1998 in England and Wales). In both countries, "recorded crime" includes offenses against businesses and public bodies as well as against individuals and households; it also includes some victimless crimes. "Survey (Comparable)" means, for both countries, rates of victimization reported in nationally representative household crime surveys, but restricting the coverage to crimes that appear in the relevant country's statistics of police-recorded crime (i.e., excluding other, mostly minor, offenses). These data are nevertheless not directly comparable with the recorded crime data, because they are restricted to survey-reported victimizations involving individuals and households; crimes against business/public bodies, and victimless crimes, are excluded. In Scotland, the survey data cover only central and southern Scotland (the more populous parts of the country), because earlier sweeps of the Scottish Crime Survey were restricted to these areas. "All Survey Offenses" means, for both countries, rates of victimization for all offenses included in the respective national household crime surveys, whether or not the offense appears in the relevant country's recorded crime figures.

the police, publicly funded legal assistance, the use and nature of custodial provisions for young offenders, the treatment of ethnic minorities,
and policies for dealing with persistent offenders. Section VII describes
some (mostly embryonic, but potentially very important) moves toward principles of reparation and restorative justice in both England
and Scotland; finally, Section VIII offers some conclusions.[12]

I. Conceptual Frameworks

In considering the conceptual frameworks of the two systems, it is appropriate to begin with Scotland, since its system was established
nearly thirty years before the current English system.

A. Scotland

The principal source of the principles underlying the Scottish juvenile justice system is now section 16 of the Children (Scotland) Act
1995, which expresses in fresh language some concepts that have been
fundamental to the system since its inception in 1971 while also introducing an important new exception to one of these principles. Collectively these foundational values are usefully described as "the section
16 principles" (Kearney 2000, p. 23).

The most important of the section 16 principles is that of the paramountcy of the welfare of the child, expressed by saying that when a
children's hearing or a court decides or determines "any matter with
respect to a child, the welfare of that child throughout his childhood
shall be their or its paramount consideration" (sec. 16[1]). This "welfare principle," like the other section 16 principles, is applied without
differentiation to offense cases and to care cases. Hence, in offense
cases, it is this goal, and not punishment, that is sought by the system,
and children's hearings are—in the normal case—required to use the
welfare principle as the key test in deciding the extent of any compulsory intervention in the child's life. All this is highly congruent with the
"child conservationist" type of philosophy that is characteristic of most
welfare-oriented juvenile justice systems, as articulated by Alder and
Wundersitz (1994, p. 3): "The 'welfare model' is associated with . . .

---

[12] Because of the recency and the extent of the post-1998 reforms, youth justice research is currently a rapidly evolving field in England, and youth justice policy has recently become the subject of high-level political activity in Scotland (see Sec. II). We
have attempted to provide a thorough survey of both countries up to the end of the
calendar year 2002; but given the current volatility of the field, there will almost certainly have been further developments by the time this volume is published.

protectionist policies. . . . From this perspective, because of their imma-
turity, children cannot be regarded as rational or self-determining
agents, but rather are subject to and are the product of the environment
within which they live. Any criminal action on their part can therefore
be attributed to dysfunctional elements in that environment. The task
of the justice system, then, is to identify, treat and cure the underlying
social causes of offending."

"Child conservationist" philosophies, when applied to juvenile justice systems, have in the past had a distinctly mixed track record. One
of their problems has been a tendency to display an excessive zeal to
"save" the child, so leading to the taking of extensive powers over his
or her life, ostensibly in the interests of the child's welfare, but often
doubtfully so to neutral observers.[13] The Scottish system has, from the
outset, sought to avoid this kind of difficulty. Thus, the Kilbrandon
Committee of 1964—from whose report the present Scottish juvenile
justice system directly emanates—argued that "referral should be
made to juvenile [treatment tribunals] for one reason only, namely that
prima facie the child is in need of [compulsory] special measures of education and training" (Scottish Office 1964, para. 138). This basic approach was subsequently incorporated into the Scottish legislation,
where it is now framed as the principle that no requirement or order
shall be made with respect to a child unless "it would be better for the
child that the requirement or order be made than that none should be
made at all" (Children [Scotland] Act 1995, sec. 16[3]); or, in short-
hand, the "no non-beneficial order principle" (Kearney 2000, p. 25).

The importance of this philosophical approach, when applied to offense-based cases, can be illustrated from a case example in a 1998 volume on European juvenile justice systems (Mehlbye and Walgrave
1998). As one way of highlighting differences between the systems in
different countries, the editors of this volume requested each national
contributor to provide a narrative explaining how their jurisdiction
might deal with a fifteen-year-old boy with two previously proved offenses of burglary, now arrested again for breaking into a private house
(acting alone) and stealing a videocassette recorder, some jewelry, and

---

[13] See n. 9 above. Note also, for example, the 1960s research by Wheeler et al. (1968)
on juvenile court judges in Boston. In this study, judges with more liberal social and
political attitudes and a "humanistic, social welfare ideology" (p. 55) ordered a greater
degree of intervention into the lives of those adjudged delinquent than did more socially
conservative judges because they thought that in so doing they were acting in the best
interests of the juvenile offenders.

some money, to a total value of about £500. In the chapter on Scotland, the author (Stewart Asquith) imagines that "Hamish, a fifteen-year-old Scottish boy" would in these circumstances be referred to the children's hearing. However, Asquith is at pains to point out that the fact that Hamish has committed an offense is not enough in itself for him to be referred to a hearing, since the referring official ("the reporter") must also be persuaded that Hamish is probably in need of compulsory measures of care, in the interests of his own welfare, before a referral may properly be made.[14] Moreover, Asquith points out that when Hamish reaches the children's hearing, if the tribunal decides "that [his] parents have control of the situation and there is evidence that compulsory measures of care are not needed, *then the case, notwithstanding the amount involved in the theft, could be discharged*" (Asquith 1998, pp. 425–26, emphasis added). In other words, in Kilbrandon's conceptual framework, now embodied within Scottish legislation, although the commission of an offense is one of the possible so-called grounds that constitute a necessary precondition for compulsory measures of care, in itself an offense is not a sufficient basis for ordering compulsory measures of care. We shall examine in the next section how this approach, and the welfare principle more generally, has worked out in practice in Scotland.

Supplementing the paramountcy of welfare and the "no non-beneficial order" principles, section 16 of the 1995 act also contains a third main principle, namely, that before taking a decision with respect to a child, a children's hearing or court shall so far as practicable (and taking into account the age and maturity of the child) give that child the opportunity to express his or her views. Moreover, if any views are expressed, the tribunal must "have regard to such views" when taking its decision.

Section 16 has one further provision, sometimes described as the "derogation from the paramountcy principle" (Kearney 2000, p. 24). This is a new provision, enacted for the first time in 1995, which states that a children's hearing or court may set aside the principle of the paramountcy of welfare if it is considered necessary to do so "for the purpose of protecting members of the public from serious harm (whether or not physical harm)" (Children [Scotland] Act 1995, sec.

---

[14] As Kearney points out, the Scottish legislation (and the rules made under that legislation) do not expressly guide a reporter in this respect, but the paramountcy principle "in effect must govern the approach of the reporter whose task it may be to bring a child before" a children's hearing (Kearney 2000, p. 23).

16[5]). The limitation of this exception to cases involving potentially serious harm is important (though the term "serious harm" is not further defined in the statute), and in practice it seems that the derogation from paramountcy principle has rarely been invoked. Hence, for example, in the imaginary case of "Hamish" (see above), it has been assumed that the paramountcy of welfare principle applies.

There is one final key principle of the Scottish system that needs to be described, though it is not a "section 16 principle"; we will call it the "adjudication/treatment distinction." The Kilbrandon Committee argued that many of the shortcomings of the pre-1971 Scottish juvenile courts arose from the fact that, although the system attempted (at least to an extent) to consider the welfare of the juvenile at the sentencing stage, this was done within the framework of a court of criminal law. This was considered unfortunate because the criminal context was thought to affect, to its detriment, "the entirely separate stage of the proceedings at which, the issue of [guilt] having been resolved, the question of practical action in the form of training measures appropriate to the needs of the offender falls to be resolved" (Scottish Office 1964, para. 71). Since the Kilbrandon Committee was chaired by a very senior Scottish judge, it had, as one might expect, no hostility to courts as such; indeed, the committee considered that the courts remained the best forum for the fulfillment of certain functions within the juvenile justice system, such as adjudication on disputed guilt for an alleged offense (or the equivalent of this for "care and protection" cases). But the committee was convinced that, when considering treatment in the child's best interests, "on a preventive and educational principle" (para. 71), a criminal court was not the best forum. Hence, what the Kilbrandon report recommended, and what has existed in Scotland since 1971, is a dual system where there exist side by side both courts (dealing with disputes of fact on alleged grounds for compulsory intervention) and lay tribunals (dealing with the treatment of the child after an offense or other ground for intervention has been admitted or proved). Twenty years after the introduction of this principle, this approach received strong endorsement from a senior Scottish judge in a leading case:[15] "The genius of [the Kilbrandon] reform, which has earned it so much praise . . . was that the responsibility for the consideration of the measures to be applied was to lie with what

[15] Lord President Hope, giving judgment in the high-profile "Orkney case" on alleged satanic sexual abuse of children, Sloan v B, 1991 SLT 530 at 548E.

was essentially a lay body, while disputed questions of fact as to the allegations made were to be resolved by the sheriff sitting in chambers as a court of law."

B. England

When we turn to the conceptual foundations of the post-1998 English youth justice system, we are immediately in a different world. We are also to some extent in a contested world, since some commentators have used phrases about the foundations of the new system that seem to us to be unwarranted (e.g., John Muncie [1999] has described the post-1998 system as based on "institutionalized intolerance"). It is therefore necessary to choose words with some deliberation and care.

In our view, to understand the conceptual foundations of the new English system, one needs to go back to the mid-1990s, when the new philosophy began to be enunciated. We will therefore first describe three features of the mid-1990s landscape in English youth justice, and we will argue that two of these (the so-called minimum intervention principle and an emphasis on procedures) were consciously disavowed in the new youth justice philosophy, while the third (a clear split between criminal and care jurisdictions) was tacitly accepted. Then, turning to the principles that the new system positively espouses, we shall argue that four are of special importance, namely, the primacy of offending prevention, reparation, efficiency, and responsibilization.

1. *Influences from the Mid-1990s.* Three aspects of English youth justice in the mid-1990s that influenced the new philosophy are the youth justice movement, an emphasis on procedures, and the separation of the criminal and care jurisdictions.

a) The "Youth Justice Movement." One cannot understand the present English youth justice system without also understanding the dominant ideological approach taken by most English youth justice workers in the period 1985–97.[16] This ideology, known variously as the "new orthodoxy" and the "philosophy of the youth justice movement," had quite complex origins and development, which need not be discussed here (see Bottoms [2002]; and, more fully, Bottoms et al. [1990]; Nellis [1990]). It is crucial to appreciate, however, that the youth justice movement had highly significant on-the-ground effects on youth justice practice in most parts of England and Wales, even though it flour-

---

[16] By "youth justice workers" we mean professionals who serviced the juvenile court either as probation officers or (especially) as social workers working for local authority social services departments (for further details, see Bottoms et al. [1990]).

ished when the national government was Conservative, and the main principles of the movement were the opposite of those of traditional conservatism.

Two of the key conceptual foundations underpinning the approach of the youth justice movement were as follows: First, it was argued that the so-called age-crime curve (well known to all students of criminology) shows that the great majority of the children who offend will eventually "grow out of crime"; and, second, it was suggested, following labeling theory, that all official processing of juvenile delinquents is potentially harmful to them, with placement in an institution the most harmful of all possible interventions.[17] Hence, the youth justice movement adopted a philosophy of "minimum intervention," akin to that of so-called radical nonintervention (Schur 1973). The central policy prescription of the movement was to "hold" a juvenile offender in a not too intensive (and, therefore, in its view, not too damaging) environment until he or she had grown out of crime. In more detail, the principal tenets of the "new orthodoxy" have been summarized as follows (Bottoms et al. [1990], pp. 3–4, modifying a characterization originally produced by Pitts [1988], pp. 90–93):

(i) The helping professions are sometimes a major source of hindrance to young offenders, because they pathologise them, intervene in their lives too readily and too intensively, and may therefore unwittingly encourage courts to use institutional disposals if and when welfare-based community treatments eventually fail;

(ii) Placing young offenders in residential or custodial institutions is to be avoided whenever possible, because such institutions have an adverse effect on the criminality and social development of these offenders;

(iii) Placing young offenders in community-based alternatives is clearly to be preferred to institutional sentencing;

(iv) Minimum intervention is the best approach, if practicable, given magistrates' sentencing philosophies and other constraints of

---

[17] Of course, neither of these propositions is unassailable. The allegedly deleterious effects of official interventions predicted by labeling theory by no means always occur (see, e.g., Sherman 1993), and criminal career researchers have shown that there are important differences between "adolescent-limited" offenders, who have a short crime career in their teen years, and some persistent offenders who begin their criminal careers early and then persist (see, e.g., Moffitt et al. 2001). These complexities were rarely recognized by the youth justice movement.

the system; hence, among other things, cautioning young offenders is clearly to be preferred to taking them to court;

(v) Welfare considerations should not be predominant in criminal proceedings in the juvenile court (e.g., re sentencing/ remand decisions), or in decisions whether to caution or prosecute;

(vi) Research and monitoring of local juvenile justice systems is vital in order to discover, for example, what kinds of cases have recently been sent to custody, what recommendations were made by social workers/probation officers in court reports in those cases, etc.; when the information from this monitoring has been absorbed, social workers can target the need for appropriate further action in pursuit of "minimum intervention" goals.

For reasons other than those advocated by the youth justice movement, Conservative governments in the 1980s supported an increase in the use of formal police cautioning as an alternative to the prosecution of young offenders in the juvenile court.[18] Members of the youth justice movement enthusiastically endorsed this approach and indeed proselytized for it with local police forces (for a description of this philosophy in action in a local area, see Davis, Boucherat, and Watson [1989]). This advocacy included pressure for so-called multiple cautioning, that is, repeated cautions for relatively persistent offenders, on the grounds that more formal interventions—such as prosecution— might push such offenders "further into the system" (as indicated in the philosophy outlined above). The consequence of all this, nationally, was a marked increase in the cautioning rate (see table 1A); thus, for males aged fourteen to sixteen the cautioning rate more than doubled in the twelve-year period 1980–92 (from 34 percent in 1980 to 73 percent in 1992), and there were similar though less extreme increases for all other age/gender groups.[19] In addition to this, during

---

[18] Until very recently, "police cautions" had no statutory basis, and they arose out of the traditional common law discretion of the police officer in English law. By the 1960s, however, statistics on formal police cautions were nationally collected, and a caution was citable in court as a previous crime, in the event of a further offense by the cautioned offender. Conservative governments encouraged cautioning in the 1980s first in a 1980 white paper and then in formal national guidance circulars to local police forces in 1985 and 1990 (for further details, see Bottoms [2002]). Procedurally, formal police cautions for juvenile offenders in England were always administered in person at a police station by a police officer, with a parent or parents accompanying the young offender.

[19] Table 1 also shows that there are consistent differences in the cautioning rate by age (younger offenders receive more cautions) and gender (females receive more cautions). By way of caveat, it should be noted that table 1 does not include data on police "informal warnings," which also increased in the late 1980s and 1990s; informal warnings are discussed in Sec. IV.

TABLE 1

Cautioning Rates for Young Offenders for Indictable Offenses in England and Wales, 1970–2001

	Age 10–13		Age 14–16	
	Males	Females	Males	Females
A. 1970–92:*				
1970	50	66	24	39
1975	63	83	33	57
1980	65	85	34	58
1985	79	93	51	78
1990	90	96	69	86
1992[†]	91	97	73	90

	Age 10–11		Age 12–14		Age 15–17	
	Males	Females	Males	Females	Males	Females
B. 1992–2000:[‡]						
1992[†]	96	99	86	96	59	81
1993	96	99	83	95	59	80
1994	95	100	81	94	56	77
1995	94	99	79	93	54	76
1996	94	99	77	91	51	72
1997	93	98	74	89	49	68
1998[§]	91	97	72	88	48	67
1999[§]	87	96	69	87	45	64
2000[§]	86	95	68	86	43	63
2001[§]	86	95	66	85	42	64

Source.—Annual volumes of *Criminal Statistics, England and Wales.*

Note.—All data shown are the cautioning rates for the year, age group, and gender in question. The "cautioning rate" is the number of persons cautioned, divided by the number of persons found guilty or cautioned, multiplied by 100.

* For the period 1970–92 (i.e., before the raising of the maximum age of the juvenile justice system from the seventeenth to the eighteenth birthday, effective October 1992).

[†] The raising of the maximum age of the juvenile justice system occurred in October 1992; data for that year are therefore given (with different age breakdowns) in both parts of the table.

[‡] For the period 1992–2000 (i.e., after the raising of the maximum age of the juvenile justice system to the eighteenth birthday, effective October 1992).

[§] "Reprimands" and "final warnings" (under the Crime and Disorder Act, 1998) have been counted as cautions in calculating data for these years. Reprimands and final warnings were available only in a few pilot areas from October 1998 to May 2000. From June 2000 onward, reprimands and final warnings are available nationally, and the power to caution juvenile offenders has been withdrawn.

the late 1980s and early 1990s, members of the youth justice movement used several so-called gatekeeping tactics to try to reduce rates of custody and residential care for young offenders, a campaign that was in general extremely successful (see Tutt and Giller 1987; Bottoms et al. 1990, chap. 1; Allen 1991).

Some backlash against the "minimum intervention" philosophy was probably inevitable. When it arrived, it came from both nonpolitical and political sources. The politically independent Audit Commission (1996), in a review of the English youth justice system, pointed out, first, the very high rates of cautioning that had developed in the English system by the early 1990s (shown in table 1), with very little use of the so-called caution-plus option (in which a caution could be followed up with some voluntary intervention with the offender, designed to reduce reoffending). Hence, almost all cautioned offenders simply received a verbal warning; there was very little positive preventive action. Second, the Audit Commission drew attention to the relatively high use of conditional discharges by the youth courts in the early 1990s, for offenders of all ages (see table 2).[20] This was despite the fact that these were prosecuted cases where, by definition, the cautioning option had not been pursued by the police. In the Audit Commission's (1996, p. 35) phrase, therefore, in the mid-1990s it could be said that, adding together police cautions and court discharges, "little or nothing" happened to the great majority of children and young people formally processed by the English youth justice system.[21]

Prior to the Audit Commission's report, there was also evidence of a more explicitly political rejection of some of the youth justice movement's preferred policies—not least because the early 1990s was a period of increasing public anxiety about crime in general, and juvenile crime in particular, in the wake of the tragic murder of a young child

[20] In England, convicted offenders may be sentenced to a "conditional discharge" for a stated period of not more than three years. The offender so discharged leaves the court with no obligations except to refrain from reoffending. If he or she reoffends within the operational period of the conditional discharge, then he or she may be sentenced for the original offense as well as for the fresh offense. The "discharge" column in table 2 includes not only conditional discharges but also absolute discharges; in practice, however, absolute discharges are rare.

[21] In 1995, the national criminal statistics in England and Wales recorded a total of 132,800 "known young offenders" (i.e., persons under eighteen found guilty of or formally cautioned for an indictable offense). Of these, 14,000 were discharged by the courts, and a reasonable estimate would be that 87,000 were cautioned with no caution-plus component. Hence, the proportion of known young offenders to whom "nothing happened" was approximately 75 percent.

(James Bulger) in 1993.[22] Hence, in 1994 the Conservative government issued new national cautioning guidelines (see n. 18), designed particularly to reduce the use of "multiple cautioning" by the police, and the cautioning rate for all age/gender groups of juveniles thereafter receded (see table 1*B*). But this political mood was not confined to one parliamentary party, and the Labour Party, in an important 1996 document that prefigures most of its post-1997 reforms of the new youth justice system, stated bluntly that the analysis it had conducted "casts considerable doubt on whether we can continue to rely on the belief underpinning the current youth justice system that young men grow out of offending behaviour quickly. We believe the time has come for fundamental changes to be made" (Straw and Michael 1996, p. 1).

b) An Emphasis on Procedures. As part of the analysis in its 1996 report, the Audit Commission pointed out that refinements introduced to the English system of criminal justice in general in the previous twenty years—such as the growth of state-aided legal representation for defendants and advance disclosure of the prosecution case—had slowed down the procedures of the Youth Court (Audit Commission 1996, p. 26). Studies suggested that the average number of times a prosecuted young person made an appearance in front of the Youth Court, up to and including the final sentence, was as high as four occasions (Audit Commission 1996, p. 29; O'Mahony and Haines 1996, pp. 42–43). But court appearances, the Audit Commission insisted, were expensive, each involving the presence of at least five persons paid for from public funds. Therefore, the commission argued, there should be a transfer of emphasis within the public funds devoted to the youth justice system, away from processing and toward more effective remedial action with young offenders.

Independently of the Audit Commission's work, the Labour Party had reached similar conclusions. Long processing times from offense to sentence were highlighted. It was argued in the Labour Party document that "the scope for getting young offenders and their parents to face up to the offending behaviour" was being compromised, first by

---

[22] James Bulger was a two-year-old child who was led away from a shopping center by two boys age ten, taken to a railway track, and then killed. Images of the toddler hand-in-hand with the offenders and being led quietly away were captured on the shopping center's CCTV system and replayed to horrified audiences on national television. Understandably, this event led to a massive national debate about dealing with juvenile crime. We deal with a subsequent court decision relating to James Bulger's killers later in this chapter.

TABLE 2
Sentencing of Children and Young Persons for Indictable Offenses, England and Wales, 1992–2001 (Percent)

	Discharge	Fine	Community Orders*	Custodial Orders	Other	Total	N (Thousands)
A. Males age 10–11:†							
1992	61	5	33	...	—	100	.2
1993	58	1	37	...	2	100	.2
1994	65	2	29	...	3	100	.3
1995	66	5	28	...	1	100	.3
1996	65	4	29	...	1	100	.2
1997	58	5	35	...	1	100	.3
1998	61	2	34	...	2	100	.4
1999	54	4	37	...	5	100	.6
2000	38	3	54	...	4	100	.5
2001	19	3	71	...	6	100	.5
B. Persons age 12–14:							
Males:							
1992	47	8	41	3	2	100	4.7
1993	44	6	49	0	2	100	5.3
1994	45	6	47	0	1	100	6.6
1995	44	6	48	1	1	100	6.8
1996	43	5	49	1	1	100	6.4
1997	43	5	49	2	1	100	6.8
1998	42	5	49	2	2	100	7.7
1999	39	6	48	3	5	100	8.3
2000	28	6	56	6	3	100	8.2
2001	17	5	65	7	5	100	8.5
Females:							
1992	64	7	26	0	2	100	.6
1993	60	6	32	0	2	100	.6
1994	64	5	30	0	1	100	1.0
1995	60	7	32	0	1	100	1.0

1996	56	5	37	1	1	100	1.0
1997	56	4	38	1	2	100	1.0
1998	55	6	37	0	1	100	1.3
1999	51	6	38	1	4	100	1.4
2000	35	7	51	2	4	100	1.4
2001	24	6	60	3	7	100	1.6

C. Persons age 15–17:

Males:

1992	29	19	37	11	2	100	28.8
1993	30	12	43	14	2	100	26.2
1994	29	13	42	14	2	100	28.6
1995	28	12	43	15	2	100	30.1
1996	27	12	43	16	2	100	32.5
1997	26	12	43	17	2	100	33.6
1998	26	13	41	16	2	100	35.0
1999	24	14	43	16	3	100	35.0
2000	20	14	48	15	3	100	33.9
2001	15	14	52	15	4	100	34.3

Females:

1992	53	16	27	2	3	100	3.6
1993	50	13	33	3	1	100	3.1
1994	50	10	34	4	1	100	3.8
1995	48	11	35	4	1	100	4.0
1996	46	10	39	4	1	100	4.2
1997	42	10	41	6	1	100	4.6
1998	41	10	40	6	2	100	5.1
1999	39	11	39	6	2	100	5.2
2000	30	11	48	7	3	100	5.2
2001	22	10	57	7	5	100	5.3

Source.—Annual volumes of *Criminal Statistics, England and Wales.*

* There are a variety of community orders (see table 8 for a breakdown of this total). For present purposes, the reparation order (available to the youth court from 1998) has been counted as a community order, although in law this is not a technically accurate characterization.

† Data on females age ten to eleven are omitted because of small numbers (there was a total of only 252 females of these ages sentenced in the ten years shown).

the excessive procedural delays, and second by the so-called "theatre of the court processes," which was seen as unhelpful (Straw and Michael 1996, p. 5; see further discussion in Sec. III). In the authors' view, "the purpose of youth courts must change from simply deciding guilt or innocence and then issuing a sentence to one in which an offence triggers a wider enquiry by the court into the circumstances and nature of the offending behaviour leading to a plan of action for changing that behaviour" (Straw and Michael 1996, p. 10).

c) Separation between the Criminal and Care Jurisdictions. A fundamental change in English youth justice took place in 1991, though this point is often insufficiently commented upon in accounts of the English system. As indicated in the introduction to this chapter, from October 1991 the Children Act 1989 came into force, and from that date the dual care/crime jurisdiction of the English juvenile courts, dating back to the early twentieth century, came to an end. Instead, the 1989 act created a separate care jurisdiction in the family proceedings court, leaving the juvenile court—soon to be known as the Youth Court (see n. 11)—to deal exclusively with criminal cases.[23] Congruently with the (later) Scottish 1995 act, within the English care jurisdiction, the Children Act 1989 (sec. 1[1]) declared that, save in exceptional circumstances, "the child's welfare shall be the court's paramount consideration."

The English youth justice reforms of the late 1990s have essentially taken for granted this marked institutional separation between the criminal and the civil jurisdictions for dealing with children in need of official attention. None of the key documents leading to the 1998 reforms sought to revisit the principles or the detail of the Children Act, and in these documents the relationship between the criminal and the care jurisdictions for children has received very little attention. All this is so notwithstanding the fact that arrangements are so very different in Scotland and that, in the Labour Party's 1996 document (Straw and Michael 1996), some aspects of the Scottish system (such as the dialogue within a children's hearing) were seen as superior to those then operating in England.

---

[23] The Children Act 1989 was the product of extensive prelegislative consultation with all relevant parties. It extensively remodeled the English law on the care of children; it has subsequently attracted very wide support among relevant professionals and has been politically uncontroversial. For a full commentary on the act in its original form, see Bainham (1990); for analyses of the operation of the act, see the annual reports published by the Department of Health (the responsible government department), the latest of which is Department of Health (2001).

2. *A New Direction.*   The Crime and Disorder Act 1998 changed the direction of English youth justice in a number of fundamental ways, including the following four key principles.

a) The Primacy of Offending Prevention.   Section 37 of the Crime and Disorder Act 1998 boldly states that the principal aim of the English youth justice system shall henceforth be "to prevent offending by children and young persons." The same section further provides that "in addition to any other duty to which they are subject, it shall be the duty of all persons and bodies carrying out functions in relation to the youth justice system to have regard to" the new principal aim.

Technically speaking, it could be argued that the new principal aim provides only limited guidance, at least to some participants in the system. Take sentencers, for example. Under other statutory provisions, they are at present required—in the normal case—to decide between custodial and noncustodial sentences and to fix the length of any custodial sentence that is passed by asking themselves the question whether the proposed sentence is commensurate with the seriousness of the offense (with some additional provisions concerning the weight to be given to previous convictions, and so forth).[24] Sentencers are further required, in all decisions relating to juveniles, to "have regard to the welfare of the child or young person, and [they] shall in a proper case take steps . . . for securing that proper provision is made for his education and training."[25] In addition to these "commensurability" and "welfare" factors, sentencers must now additionally have regard to the new "principal aim," though it is not at all clear how, for them, given the other statutory obligations to which they are subject, it really is the principal aim. Moreover, they are given no guidance as to how, in individual cases, they should balance the potentially conflicting claims of commensurability, the welfare of the young person, and the prevention of offending.

But, in another sense, all this is to take too formal and legal an approach to the "primary aim." It is clear that the new legislation, by enacting the "primary aim," intends principally to signal a significant symbolic shift of direction for the English youth justice system, characterized by the government in the language of effectiveness: "We need a more effective system of justice for young offenders . . . [focused on]

---

[24] Powers of Criminal Courts (Sentencing) Act 2000, secs. 35, 79, 80, 151, etc.

[25] Children and Young Persons Act 1933, sec. 44(1). This long-standing statutory provision has never been repealed, and remains part of English law relating to youth courts.

prioritising cost-effective early intervention and intensive community supervision to nip offending in the bud" (Straw and Michael 1996, p. 18).

The key features of the new preventive approach are, as largely prefigured in the above quotation, effective early intervention and the intensive supervision of persistent offenders. As table 2 shows, and as we shall consider more fully later, the emphasis on early intervention has also led to a marked reduction in the youth courts' use of the conditional discharge since 1998.

b) Reparation. In addition to the primary aim of prevention, the new youth justice system has, from its inception, sought to ensure that, as Straw and Michael (1996, p. 12) put it, "Greater attention should be given . . . to ensuring an element of reparation in sentencing and enabling young offenders to understand the harm done to victims and communities." While there were some reparative features in the pre-1998 youth justice system, the new system aims to advance reparation very significantly.

c) Efficiency. We have seen that Labour Party commentators in the mid-1990s were skeptical about delays in the system and about what they (and the Audit Commission) saw as an overemphasis on procedures at the expense of effective action to prevent offending. They accordingly expressed a determination "to make far better use of the resources currently wasted within the youth justice system" (Straw and Michael 1996, p. 18). In pursuing this aim of efficiency,[26] particular emphasis was placed on the speeding up of case processing. In addition, and in order to try to give greater national leadership and direction to the system, a new national Youth Justice Board was created.

d) Responsibilization. This rather unlovely word has been usefully coined by John Muncie (1999, p. 169) to describe an important feature of the new youth justice system. It has a double connotation: first, it emphasizes that young offenders are now to a greater extent being required to take responsibility for their own actions; second, it highlights the Labour Party's view that there was a need to change the previous situation whereby "too often parents [were] not made to face up to their responsibilities for the young person's offending behaviour" (Straw and Michael 1996, p. 1).

In the official policy paper immediately preceding the Crime and

---

[26] Note that the Labour Party document explicitly endorsed the two main aims of what has been called "the new public management": cost efficiency (output for a given unit cost) and demonstrable service effectiveness (performance measured against publicly stated goals and targets; see James and Raine 1998, pp. 33–34).

Disorder Act 1998, the new Labour government set out many of the details of its proposed youth justice reforms. In a hard-hitting preface to this document, the then home secretary (Jack Straw)[27] by implication referred to several conceptual aspects of the new system and also emphasized the intended decisive break with the philosophy of the former youth justice movement, which he branded as an "excuse culture." His words are worth quoting in full: "An excuse culture has developed within the youth justice system. It excuses itself for its inefficiency, and too often excuses the young offenders before it, implying that they cannot help their behaviour because of their social circumstances. Rarely are they confronted with their behaviour and helped to take more personal responsibility for their actions. The system allows them to go on wrecking their own lives as well as disrupting their families and communities" (Home Office 1997a, preface). It is the practical outworking of this "post-excuse culture" policy approach that we must focus on in our subsequent discussion of the new English youth justice system.

C. *Assessment*

It will be clear from the preceding discussion that there are significant differences in philosophy between the Scottish and the English juvenile justice systems. Of particular importance is the paramountcy, in the Scottish system, of the welfare of the child, a feature that is replicated in England in the care jurisdiction for children, but not in the criminal jurisdiction. Linked to this point is the priority that is given in Scotland to treating young offenders and children in need of care within the same legal framework, operating on unified principles; by contrast, England has chosen to adopt a deliberate institutional separation between criminal and care cases and to apply different principles in the two subsystems.

Other important differences concern reparation and efficiency, both now prominent in the English system for dealing with criminal cases, but traditionally very little emphasized in Scotland (though there are now distinct signs of change in this regard, as we note later). The responsibility of the child for his or her offenses is also differently

[27] Within the U.K. government, the home secretary is in charge of the Home Office and has responsibility for the safety and security of citizens "at home," i.e., when not abroad. Some of the home secretary's functions are United Kingdom–wide (e.g., passports, immigration, and asylum). However, his criminal justice responsibilities relate only to England and Wales, and this was also the case prior to Scottish devolution (see n. 4 above), at which time the responsible minister for Scottish criminal justice and child care within the U.K. government was the Secretary of State for Scotland.

treated; this principle is now strongly emphasized in England, but in Scotland, while not disavowed, it is set firmly within a child-conservationist conceptual approach.

For criminal cases, England has recently set its face firmly against the "minimum intervention" philosophy that tended often to prevail before 1998. Scotland, by contrast, still espouses the Kilbrandon principle of "no non-beneficial order"; and, as we will see later, this makes for some interesting differences in practice from England. However, it is important to draw attention to the fact that there were always important differences of emphasis between the English youth justice movement's approach to "minimum intervention" and the Scottish "no non-beneficial order" principle. As previously indicated, the English youth justice movement's conceptual approach was hostile to the incorporation of welfare principles into juvenile justice systems, and its version of "minimum intervention" was akin to a philosophy of "radical nonintervention." By contrast, the Scottish philosophy, from the Kilbrandon report onward, is explicitly welfare based and espouses the "no non-beneficial order" principle only within that framework.[28]

Despite the very important differences between the philosophies of the English and Scottish juvenile justice systems, the two jurisdictions do have some common features. Most notably, both now explicitly adopt a preventive principle as a primary aim, though the focus of the preventive effort is different (the prevention of crime in England; the prevention of harm to the child in Scotland, though this might often include measures designed to prevent further offending). The shared emphasis on prevention marks out the two British juvenile justice systems as being importantly different from those systems elsewhere in the world that, in the wake of the revolt against the original child-welfare-oriented juvenile court systems, have adopted philosophies of just deserts, leading in some cases to a questioning of the validity of the case for a separate juvenile jurisdiction.

II. The Current Systems in Outline: Scotland

Before describing the two British youth justice systems in detail, an important preliminary point must be made about the different age ranges that they deal with. In the United Kingdom, the age of majority

---

[28] At one point, a notable clash of philosophies took place in one region of Scotland (Fife), when some English youth justice workers moved north and attempted to impose their "radical nonintervention" approach on the Scottish children's hearing system in that area. The result was a major conflict, leading to a lengthy official report known as the Fife Report (Kearney 1992). For a brief account, see Bottoms (2002, pp. 460–61).

(for the purposes of voting, making valid contracts, etc.) is eighteen. The scope of the English youth justice system has, since 1992 (see n. 11), been extended up to the age of majority. The minimum age of criminal responsibility in England is ten; therefore, the English youth justice system deals with persons aged ten to seventeen inclusive alleged to have committed criminal offenses. In Scotland, however, both the maximum and the minimum age limits are lower. The children's hearing system deals with fresh cases only up to the sixteenth birthday, an age roughly equivalent to the end of compulsory schooling.[29] Additionally, the age of criminal responsibility in Scotland remains at present at its historically low level of eight; hence the hearings system deals with persons aged eight to fifteen inclusive alleged to have committed offenses, as well as with children from birth to age fifteen who are thought to be potentially in need of special measures of care. Given the existence of the children's hearing system, there is an element of legal fiction about the concept of "the age of criminal responsibility" in Scotland, and there are also recent proposals for change in this area. However, the fact that the English youth justice system deals with sixteen- and seventeen-year-olds, while the Scottish system does not, is a major point of difference between the two jurisdictions. Indeed, in the year 2001, there were 51,000 persons aged sixteen and seventeen in England and Wales who were formally identified as having committed an indictable offense, and they constituted 45 percent of the total number of known indictable offenders under eighteen in the jurisdiction in that year (Home Office 2002a, table 5.24). In Scotland, most of these persons would be outside the ambit of the juvenile justice system, a fact that has led to some significant recent policy discussions north of the border.

In describing the two British youth justice systems, in each case we provide a formal "process" description of the system and also offer evidence (from official data and from research) as to how the systems are operating in practice. As in the previous section, we begin with the more well established of the two systems.

A. Formal Description

A flowchart of the Scottish system is provided in figure 2. It is fundamental to the philosophy of the Scottish system that cases involving

[29] However, children's hearings also have a continuing jurisdiction (or review jurisdiction) over children who have been made the subject of a supervision requirement; this continuing jurisdiction can under certain circumstances extend up to the child's eighteenth birthday. For further details, see later discussion.

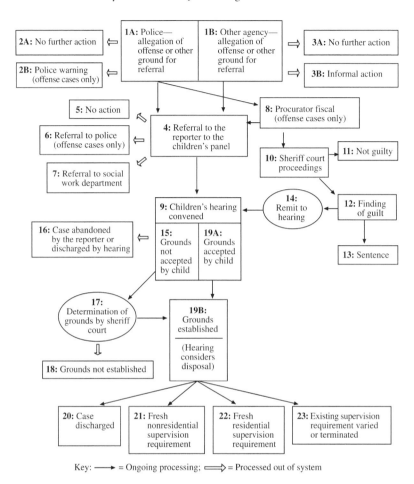

Key: ⟶ = Ongoing processing; ⟹ = Processed out of system

FIG. 2.—The Scottish juvenile justice system in outline

allegations of offenses are to be treated in a similar manner to other types of cases that might cause the state to decide to take compulsory measures of care in the interests of a child's welfare (such as the child being beyond the control of his or her parents, the child's health and development being placed at serious risk because of parental neglect, and so on). Hence, the system outlined in figure 2 applies both to offense-related and to other cases, but, because our focus is on offense-based cases, we describe the system principally as it applies to them.

The great majority of offense-based cases are initially reported to the police (fig. 2, box 1A). If the police decide that an offense has been committed and that a particular child is responsible, they then have four options: they may take no further action (box 2A); officially warn the child (box 2B); refer the child to an official called the "reporter to the children's hearing" (box 4); or, in a restricted range of cases, refer the child to the state prosecutor (known in Scotland as the "procurator fiscal") with a view to possible prosecution (box 8). The second of these options is by far the most commonly chosen.[30]

The reporter to the children's hearing occupies a pivotal gatekeeping role in the Scottish system, as can be seen from the centrality of box 4 in figure 2. On receiving a referral, the reporter is first expected to satisfy himself or herself (seeking additional information if that seems necessary) that there is evidence to support the so-called ground on which the case was referred (e.g., that an offense really has been committed by this child, that he or she really is beyond parental control, etc.). If this test is not satisfied, the reporter takes no action with regard to the referral (box 5). If a ground is believed to exist, then the reporter must further assess—again seeking additional information if necessary—whether the child is potentially in need of compulsory measures of care (as discussed in the case of "Hamish," described above); only if the reporter's answer to this further question is also affirmative should the case be referred on to the children's hearing (box 9). (If the answer to the second question is negative, the reporter may, but is not obliged to, take no action [box 5]; he or she may also refer the case to the local social work department who may assist the child informally [box 7], or, in offense cases, the reporter may refer the child back to the police with a view to a formal police warning or similar procedure [box 6].)

Data on reporters' decision making in offense-based referrals for the years 1980–2000 are presented in table 3. The table shows an increasing willingness by reporters to use options other than referrals to a hearing: in 1980, nearly 50 percent of offense referrals were sent on to a hearing, but by 2000 this figure had reduced by half. Among the three nonhearing (diversionary) options, referrals to the police for a warning diminished (8 percent to 2 percent), referrals to the social work depart-

---

[30] The year 1989 is the last for which we have full national figures for this stage of the process (excluding "no further action" cases). In that year, there were 26,300 cases in which the police took some formal steps in relation to acknowledged or alleged offenses by children under sixteen. Of these cases, 76 percent were forwarded to reporters, 11 percent were given a police warning, and 13 percent were reported to the procurator fiscal (Scottish Office 1991, p. 5). More recent data on police warnings in five of the eight Scottish police forces are given in Audit Scotland (2002, p. 14).

TABLE 3

Initial Action by Reporters in Scotland on Alleged Offense Referrals, Males and Females Combined, 1980–2000 (Percent)

	No Action	Referred to Social Work Department	Referred to Police	Referred to Hearing	Total	N
1980	39	4	8	48	100	22,303
1985	49	4	7	39	100	25,144
1990	56	6	4	33	100	24,694
1995	61	6	3	30	100	27,606
1996*	64	6	3	26	100	28,105
1997*	65	6	3	26	100	27,562
1998*	67	7	3	24	100	28,213
1999*†	71	6	2	20	100	36,133
2000*	66	10‡		24	100	26,766

Source.—Annual volumes of the Scottish Office Social Work Services Group Statistical Bulletin entitled *Referrals of Children to Reporters and Children's Hearings* (to 1995); annual *Statistical Bulletins of the Scottish Children's Reporter Administration* (from 1996).

* Data for 1996 onward are for the last nine months of the calendar year stated, plus the first three months of the next year.

† The data for the year 1999 are clearly aberrant, if one looks at the N column, although surprisingly this point is not discussed in the original published data source. It would appear from table 4 that the probable main reason for the aberration is double counting of referrals that included both offense and nonoffense grounds. This emphasizes the fact that the data in this table relate to referrals, rather than to children, and one child can be the subject of multiple referrals on different grounds or from different agencies, or both.

‡ The data source in 2000 no longer separated these two types of referral.

ment increased only a little, and the proportion of "no action" cases rose markedly (from 39 percent to 66 percent). On the face of it, these data contrast rather interestingly with the parallel English data, which similarly show a marked increase in the use of a diversionary measure (police cautioning) in the 1980s, but where this was followed by a reduction of cautioning in the 1990s as political skepticism about the "minimum intervention" philosophy increasingly had an effect (see table 1). However, English-Scottish comparisons in this area are complicated by the nature of the Scottish system. For example, if a child is placed under supervision by a hearing after an offense-related referral and then commits a further minor offense, the reporter may well feel there is little purpose to be served in referring the child back to a hearing (they would probably take no action, in view of the existing supervi-

TABLE 4

Breakdown of Reasons for "No Action" Decisions by Reporters in
Offense Cases, 1980–2000 (Percent)

	Insufficient Evidence	Action on Other Grounds of Referral	Under Current Supervision	Compulsory Care Unnecessary	Total
1980	4	1	11	23	39
1985	4	1	12	32	49
1990	3	1	18	35	56
1995	4	1	19	36	61
1996*	4	1	21	38	64
1997*†	4	2	17	43	65
1998*	3	2	18	43	67
1999*‡	3	17	16	36	71
2000*	3	. . .	20	43	66

Source.—Annual volumes of the Scottish Office Social Work Services Group Statistical Bulletin entitled *Referrals of Children to Reporters and Children's Hearings* (to 1995); annual *Statistical Bulletins of the Scottish Children's Reporter Administration* (from 1996).

* See note to table 3.
† Estimate because of change of statistical database.
‡ See note to table 3 on the apparently anomalous nature of the data for 1999.

sion requirement). To throw further light on this issue, table 4 provides a breakdown of the main reasons for reporters' "no action" decisions (in effect producing a disaggregation of col. 1 in table 3). Since 1980 there has been an increase in "no action" decisions because the child is already under supervision, but decisions on the basis that "compulsory care is unnecessary" have also risen steadily during this period. We may therefore reasonably conclude that reporters have indeed pursued an increasingly diversionary approach during the last two decades, a matter to which we return below.

Now let us move on to the next stage of the system, referring again to figure 2. Suppose that a reporter has referred an offense-based case to the children's hearing, but the referred child denies involvement in the alleged offense. It is at this point that the adjudication/treatment distinction in the Scottish system (described in Sec. I) becomes especially apparent. Asquith (1998, pp. 425–26) explains the procedures, again with reference to the imaginary case of "Hamish":

At the Children's Hearing, Hamish is there with his mother and father. The others present are the Reporter, the panel members and a Social Worker. There are no police (who do not attend Children's Hearings) and there are also no members of the public. Hamish denies the charge when it is read to him and the hearing cannot proceed because it has no jurisdiction over the establishment of the facts of the referral. Hamish has to go to court, the sheriff court, where the facts of the case will be established or not. If they are then Hamish will go back to the Children's Hearing, where the need for compulsory measures of care will be considered.

These procedures are shown in figure 2 at boxes 9, 15, 17, 18, and 19B. They might seem quite cumbersome, but it must be remembered that a division of functions between the courts and the children's hearings was central to the thinking of the Kilbrandon Committee, which established the hearings system. Some procedures of this kind are in fact the necessary consequence of the fact that the children's hearing, being solely a treatment tribunal, is structurally precluded from considering any dispute of fact or law pertaining to the alleged "grounds" of the hearing, while the sheriff court, being a court of law (and therefore in the Kilbrandon report's thinking an inappropriate tribunal to decide upon treatment issues for a juvenile), is structurally precluded from considering issues of appropriate treatment if the grounds of referral are held to be established.

It should be added that this adjudication/treatment distinction does not exhaust the "dual system" features of Scottish juvenile justice in offense-based cases. The police may, in a restricted range of cases, refer a case to the procurator fiscal (box 8); and in such circumstances the procurator fiscal may, at his or her discretion, prosecute the case in the sheriff court (box 10). The two parallel systems (reporter → children's hearing; procurator fiscal → sheriff court) are nevertheless linked in that either the procurator fiscal or the court may refer or remit a case into the children's hearing system (boxes 4, 14). However, it is very important to note that while the adjudication/treatment distinction (and the dual system features that flow from it) are integral to Kilbrandon's core philosophy, the "fiscal route" cases (boxes 8, 10, 11, 12, 13), while also originally created on the recommendation of the Kilbrandon Committee, can only properly be regarded as a quite deliberate exemption or exclusion of certain cases from the reach of that philosophy, on the grounds (principally) of the nature (especially the serious nature) of the offense alleged. We consider these "fiscal route" cases more fully in Section V.

Let us now return to the main system and consider finally the children's hearing itself, on the assumption that the ground for the hearing has been accepted by the child or established by the sheriff court (boxes 19A, 19B). Each local area in Scotland has a so-called children's panel, which is made up of lay members of the public who have been appointed by a government minister as being suitable people to officiate at children's hearings. When a children's hearing is called, arrangements are made to select three members of the children's panel to preside over the case (of the three, at least one must be female, and one male). In offense-based cases, it is of course quite common for adolescents to commit crimes as a group, but because the focus of children's hearings is not upon the offense but upon the child and his or her needs, in such circumstances if the reporter refers all the children to the children's hearing, a separate hearing will be held for each child.

A children's hearing is a private occasion (the public are not admitted and the press hardly ever attend);[31] it must take place in a building other than a court building or a police station. The hearing is focused on the child's needs, and, in offense-based cases, neither the police nor the victim attends. The reporter, however, does attend, and, in offense-based cases, holds all relevant police reports. A social worker from the local authority's social work department also attends. The intention of the system is that the child, the parents, the social worker, and the members of the children's panel who are conducting the hearing will have ample opportunity, within an informal atmosphere, to explore carefully in discussion not only the circumstances that gave rise to the ground for the hearing (e.g., an offense or persistent truancy) but also all other relevant aspects of the child's social and family situation. Given this intention, it is usual for all the participants to sit around a single table during the hearing.

The rules for the conduct of children's hearings provide that the child and his or her parents may, at their discretion, bring someone to the hearing to speak on their behalf during these discussions (a "representative"), and this representative may be a lawyer. However, representatives are not permitted to act as agents, in the sense of being permitted to speak instead of the parties they represent (in other words, even if a representative is present, the hearing may still directly ques-

---

[31] Bona fide representatives of the media may attend, but identifying details of the child or his or her address or school may not be disclosed, and the hearing also has power to exclude the media in the interests of the child's welfare (for details, see Kearney [2000], p. 255); hence, there is little incentive for the media to attend.

tion the child and the parents). But despite the fact that representatives are permitted to attend, there has until very recently been no provision for publicly funded legal assistance at a children's hearing (although such representation is available in the sheriff court if the grounds of the hearing are contested; boxes 15, 17).[32] The absence of public legal aid in children's hearings has been a matter of long-standing controversy on which there have been important recent developments. The traditional justification for the absence of legal aid is that the routine provision of legal representation would change the atmosphere of hearings by making them more adversarial, and it would also discourage parents and children from expressing their own views, thus inhibiting constructive discussion.

At the end of the discussion in the children's hearing, the hearing members must decide on the appropriate disposal for the child. In the case of a child attending a hearing for the first time, they have only three choices. First they may, to use the official terminology, discharge the case (box 20), which simply means that no compulsory measures of care are ordered. As the imaginary case of Hamish illustrates, such a step may be taken by the hearing because they are satisfied that informal supervision or help is available to the child and therefore that compulsory measures are unnecessary. Second, the children's hearing may make a nonresidential supervision requirement, allowing the child to remain in his or her home under the supervision of a social worker (box 21); or, third, a residential supervision requirement (box 22) may be made, placing the child in a specified kind of residential establishment, such as a hostel, a local authority home, or a residential school. If a residential supervision requirement is made, the children's hearing may additionally, if specified criteria are met, make a "secure accommodation authorization," which permits senior social work staff to place the child in secure accommodation for such period as they con-

---

[32] The Children (Scotland) Act 1995, sec. 41, does, however, provide that a children's hearing shall, if it is considered "necessary" to do so in order "to safeguard the interests of the child in the proceedings," appoint a person to perform that safeguarding function "on such terms and conditions as appear appropriate" (see further Kearney [2000], chap. 17). Such "safeguarders" may be, but are not necessarily, lawyers. In the years 1998–2000 inclusive, safeguarder appointments were much more likely to be made in non-offense-based cases (12 percent of such cases had safeguarders) than in offense-based (2 percent) or mixed-offense- and non-offense-based cases (4 percent) (Scottish Children's Reporter Administration 2002, table 15). Note also that safeguarder appointments are made at the discretion of the children's hearing, so there is no right to receive such assistance.

sider necessary.[33] Finally, in the case of a child already under a supervision requirement who again appears before a hearing on a fresh ground or a review (see n. 29 on the "continuing jurisdiction" of the hearing), the hearing has the additional option of varying or terminating the supervision requirement (e.g., a nonresidential supervision requirement might be varied to become a residential supervision requirement [box 23]). Given the statutory "no non-beneficial order" principle, a supervision requirement—residential or nonresidential—may normally only be made by the hearing if they consider that it would be "better for the child that the requirement or order be made than that none should be made at all" (otherwise they should discharge the case). These principles hold even if a fairly serious offense has been committed (as Asquith's [1998] commentary on the case of "Hamish" illustrates), unless the so-called derogation from the paramountcy principle is applicable.

The restricted range of disposals available to the children's hearing is worthy of brief comment. Some might be surprised at the absence of measures such as the fine, or "community service" (unpaid work), or compulsory measures of reparation or compensation to victims of offenses. But such omissions are, in the Scottish system, quite deliberate. Since the children's hearing system is welfare based, with no conceptual distinction between offense based and other cases, it is said to follow, first, that all disposals should in principle be equally available in all types of case, and, second, that measures such as the fine cannot form part of the system since they are explicitly punitive rather than welfare based. A limited exception to these principles is, however, the use of secure accommodation within a residential supervision order (see above).

---

[33] A children's hearing may authorize placement in secure accommodation where one of the following criteria is satisfied: either that the child, having previously absconded, is likely to abscond unless kept in secure accommodation, and, if he absconds, it is likely that his physical, mental, or moral welfare will be at risk; or that the child is likely to injure himself or some other person unless he is kept in secure accommodation (Children [Scotland] Act 1995, sec. 70[10]). The reference to injuring another person in the second of these criteria is an apparent derogation from the paramountcy-of-welfare principle, though this may be "more apparent than real" (Kearney 2000, pp. 289–90) because it could be said to be in the child's long-term interests that he be prevented from injuring others. Even when a secure accommodation authorization is made, it is not necessarily acted upon; actual placement in secure accommodation, and decisions as to its duration, are left to the director of social work for the relevant area and the person in charge of the relevant residential establishment (Children [Scotland] Act 1995, sec. 70[9]).

In any case where a supervision requirement is made (whether residential or nonresidential), the children's hearing has a continuing jurisdiction over that case. Supervision requirements remain effective for one year and must be reviewed by a full children's hearing at the end of that period. At any such review, the supervision requirement may only be continued (either in its original or in a varied form) if special compulsory measures of care are still adjudged to be necessary in the interests of the child's welfare (or if the "derogation from the paramountcy principle" applies). Subject to that important criterion, however, a supervision requirement can in principle be continually renewed (and, if judged appropriate, amended) until the child reaches his or her eighteenth birthday.

The annual published data on the Scottish children's hearing system does not differentiate, at the hearing decision stage, between the making of nonresidential and residential supervision requirements. Data on hearings' decisions in offense-based cases where the child is not already under supervision are shown in table 5.[34] These data show, perhaps surprisingly, that throughout the 1990s less than two-thirds of such cases have been placed under supervision, the remaining one-third being discharged by the hearing. In interpreting this figure it should be recalled that all cases that are sent to a hearing are, in principle, cases where a reporter has already adjudged that there are prima facie grounds for compulsory measures of care; clearly, in about a third of offense cases not already under supervision, the hearing takes a different view.[35] What therefore begins to become apparent at this point is the considerable use of noninterventionist disposals in offense-based cases within the Scottish system, both at the reporter stage (tables 3 and 4) and at the hearing stage (table 5). As we have already noted, noninterventionism was the subject of criticism in the Audit Commission's (1996) review of the English system in the 1990s. In Scotland,

[34] The data on decisions relating to children already under supervision are not very helpful for present purposes, since the main categories are simply "supervision requirement varied" and "supervision requirement continued without variation." In the year 2000, hearings dealt with 1,170 offense-based cases where the child was not already under supervision and 1,606 cases of children under supervision referred by reporters on fresh offense-based grounds.

[35] Comparison of the N's in tables 3 and 5 seems at first sight to reveal a sharp discrepancy. The principal explanation is that table 3 concerns referrals, while table 5 is based on a total of children sent to a hearing. In the system as a whole, including nonoffense cases, the average number of referrals per child in 2000 was 1.5 (see table 7); it is possible that the figure is higher for offense-based referrals. For the N of offense-based hearing cases where the child is already under supervision, see n. 34 above.

TABLE 5

Disposals by Hearings in Offense-Based Cases, 1987–2000: Persons
Not Already under Supervision, Males and Females Combined
(Percent)

	Supervision Requirement	Discharge or Other Disposal*	Total	N
1987†	54.3	45.7	100	2,984
1990	62.0	37.9	100	2,552
1995	64.6	35.4	100	1,730
1996‡	63.9	36.1	100	2,102
1997‡	63.6	36.3	100	1,498
1998‡	58.9	41.1	100	1,480
1999‡	58.4	41.6	100	1,092
2000‡	61.0	39.0	100	1,170

SOURCE.—Annual volumes of the Scottish Office Social Work Services Group Statistical Bulletin entitled *Referrals of Children to Reporters and Children's Hearings* (to 1995); annual *Statistical Bulletins of the Scottish Children's Reporter Administration* (from 1996).

* According to a leading legal authority, when a hearing decides not to make a supervision requirement, "they shall discharge the referral" (Kearney 2000, p. 296). However, in recent years the relevant Scottish statistics record a growing percentage of "other" cases, stated to include "cases where no order was made by the Hearing." The apparent distinction between "discharge" and "no order" appears to be legally doubtful and to have no practical effect.

† This is the first year for which data are available in these categories.

‡ Data for 1996 onward are for the last nine months of the calendar year stated, plus the first three months of the next year.

of course, "no action" decisions can be formally justified through the "no non-beneficial order" principle, but at least one leading commentator on the Scottish system has recently questioned whether the high use of "no action" decisions is truly in the long-term welfare-based interests of children: "no action may simply be delaying a child's entry into the system following subsequent referrals" (Waterhouse 2002). Moreover, she comments, the "significant reliance on no action decisions" in offense-based cases could have the danger that, politically, "youth crime might be seen not to be taken seriously" (Waterhouse 2002). This is indeed a real danger in the current context.

The available data make no differentiation between cases of residential and nonresidential supervision at the hearing decision stage. It is, however, possible to obtain data about the numbers and proportion of children under current supervision following an offense-based referral,

TABLE 6

Children under a Current Supervision Requirement Who Were
Originally Referred on Offense Grounds, Showing Nature of
Current Placement, Scotland, 1980–99 (Percent)

	Nonresidential Placement	Residential School	Other Residential Placement	Total and (N)
1980	67	20	13	100 (4,634)
1985	72	15	12	100 (3,409)
1990	75	13	11	100 (2,917)
1995	75	14	11	100 (2,926)
1996*	76	14	10	100 (2,810)
1997*	81	11	8	100 (1,624)
1998*	79	13	8	100 (1,397)
1999*	78	13	9	100 (1,204)
2000*	75	14	10	100 (1,902)

Source.—Annual volumes of the Scottish Office Social Work Services Group Statistical Bulletin entitled *Referrals of Children to Reporters and Children's Hearings* (to 1995); annual *Statistical Bulletins of the Scottish Children's Reporter Administration* (from 1996).

Note.—Data given are for males and females combined, showing the nature of the current placement on June 30 in the year shown.

* Data for 1996 onward are for the last nine months of the calendar year stated, plus the first three months of the next year.

distinguishing between residential and nonresidential placements (see table 6). These data show that, since 1980, there has been a slightly declining proportion of children currently under supervision who are placed residentially, within a declining total number of children currently under supervision of any kind (see the "N" column). The total number of children in residential placements following offense-based referrals has therefore declined significantly over the last twenty years.

B. An Overview of a Welfare System in Action in Offense-Based Cases

Many people, when they hear about the Scottish system, are intrigued. How could it possibly be the case that a relatively serious offense—such as the burglary in the imaginary case of Hamish—can be decided purely on grounds relating to the offender-child's welfare? Do the various actors in the system really adhere strictly to the formal principles of the system, or do they in practice operate on more familiar, punitive criteria?

These questions have been central to empirical research on the Scottish system and are addressed utilizing the findings of that research. But since the research base is not extensive, and the main studies have been conducted at very different times, a brief initial description of the principal research contributions is appropriate.

A very early project was conducted by Allison Morris and Mary McIsaac (1978), based on fieldwork in two areas in 1972–73. The authors' interpretation of their data has proved to be controversial, but their research has remained as a continual reference point for later studies. A larger and more nationally representative research project was then carried out by Martin, Fox, and Murray (1981), with fieldwork in 1978–79, and until very recently this was universally regarded as the benchmark study of the Scottish system. Two years later, Stewart Asquith (1983) published his doctoral dissertation, based on fieldwork conducted in the mid-1970s. This was a small study, but it is of special interest because, uniquely in the published literature, it provides a direct empirical comparison of the Scottish and the then-English systems, based on fieldwork in two local areas, one on each side of the border.

There was then a long hiatus, during which a few papers on particular aspects of the Scottish system were published, but no major research was attempted. This fallow period finally ended when the U.K. Scottish Office commissioned two linked research projects that were carried out during the years 1994–97. One of these, based at the University of Stirling, focused on process-based aspects of the children's hearing system (Hallett and Murray 1998), while the other, based at Edinburgh University, consisted primarily of a thorough statistical description of a representative sample of cases dealt with by reporters and hearings, including some data of a longitudinal character (Waterhouse et al. 2000).

1. *Reporters' Decision Making.* The reporters to children's hearings in Scotland hold a very special place in this mixed juvenile justice and child-care system. Initially employed by local government, since the late 1990s reporters have been grouped together into a national service. Their numbers, however, are small; in the mid-1990s there were only 140 reporter posts in the whole of Scotland (Kuenssberg and Miller 1998, p. 173). Their tasks are also challengingly diverse. Some aspects of reporters' functions have an inescapably legal aspect—for example, formally referring a case to a children's hearing, citing the appropriate grounds; or, in the event of a remit or reference from the sheriff court to the hearing, explaining to the panel members exactly

what are the respective legal powers and duties of the hearing and the court. At other times, however, reporters are required to make judgments that are delicately personal (e.g., assessing whether, in the case of a child suffering from parental neglect, the additional guidance that seems needed would, from the perspective of the child's best interests, be optimally provided on a voluntary or a compulsory basis). Given this diversity of tasks, it is not surprising that reporters have been recruited from varied professional backgrounds: in the mid-1990s, half were lawyers, one-third from a background in professional social work, and the remainder from other professions including teaching and nursing (Kuenssberg and Miller 1998, p. 174). Interestingly, the fifty-four reporters in Hallett and Murray's (1998) nationally representative sample were predominantly female (63 percent) and young (70 percent were less than forty-five years of age).[36]

Martin, Fox, and Murray (1981) studied reporters' decision making in offense-based cases, using a multivariate statistical technique. In cases where the child had been referred for the first time on offense grounds, when other factors were held constant, the variables that were significantly associated with reporters' decisions to send the child to a hearing were the number of offenses alleged within the referral, known family problems, poor school attendance, and behavior problems at school. For the "recidivist" sample, all these factors were again significant (though with the "family problems" variable showing a weaker association within this group); additionally, however, the seriousness of the main offense alleged was highly significant. The researchers therefore concluded that reporters seemed to display, in offense-based cases, a "constant attempt to balance . . . the seriousness of the offence or offences committed against an inevitably subjective and indirect estimate of the strengths and weaknesses of the child's home and school situation. Neither set of considerations has an overall dominance" (Martin, Fox, and Murray 1981, p. 91).

Fifteen years later, in offense-based cases, Hallett and Murray's (1998, chap. 2) research similarly showed the influence of a mixture of offense-related and social factors on reporters' decisions, with school-related issues again prominent. However, these researchers' rather different (more qualitative) methodology highlighted the considerable importance of one factor that had not been included in Martin, Fox,

---

[36] In the larger urban areas, reporters' offices will typically contain several appointed reporters who will normally have a mix of different professional backgrounds and skills and can share and allocate these skills to the tasks in hand.

and Murray's statistical analysis, namely, the cooperation or otherwise of families. Cooperation or noncooperation was not of great significance in cases where reporters decided to take no further action, such cases being generally governed by other criteria. However, parental cooperation was a factor of often crucial importance where reporters had to decide between referral to a hearing and referral to the social work department for voluntary advice and guidance: if parents were cooperative, voluntary advice was more likely to be the outcome. Even here, however, there was a complication in offense-based cases, because "referrals of a serious nature usually led to a hearing [since seriousness] outweighed other considerations," including that of parental cooperation (Hallett and Murray 1998, p. 38). This last finding, taken together with the other research results summarized above, highlights a pervasive apparent tension within the Scottish children's hearing system as it deals with offense-based cases, a tension between the system's official ideology (which strongly prioritizes the child's welfare needs) and the seemingly commonsensical requirement of taking some notice of the offenses that have brought the child to official attention.

The very recent Audit Scotland (2002) report on youth crime has added to our understanding of reporters' decision making by highlighting—for the first time in the literature—considerable disparity between different areas. In 2000–2001, in Scotland as a whole, 24 percent of offense referrals were sent on to a children's hearing (see table 3), but in the forty-seven reporter practice areas, previously unpublished data showed that the rate varied between 10 percent and 47 percent. The report comments that the "test of compulsion" that reporters are required to apply (i.e., whether the child is prima facie in need of compulsory measures of supervision) appears from these data to be "very much an individual decision, and these vary considerably across the country" (Audit Scotland 2002, p. 24). This disparity, the report concluded, was partly caused by the fact that "there is no standard assessment tool that reporters use to guide their decision making process" (Audit Scotland 2002, p. 24).

2. *Children's Hearings.* The second key decision point in the system is the children's hearing itself. In Hallett and Murray's (1998) study, the median duration of a hearing was between thirty-one and forty-five minutes, and Asquith (1983, p. 185) reported that in his study areas the average hearing took significantly longer than the average case in the English juvenile court.

The children's panel members who conduct hearings are lay members of the public. In this regard, the children's hearing, although not a court, is continuous with the tradition in Britain whereby the lower criminal courts have often been presided over by laypeople. However, children's panel members are recruited specifically to deal with children, within an overtly welfare-based system; hence it is not surprising that Asquith (1983, p. 134) found in the 1970s that panel members were, by comparison with English magistrates, more likely to have an occupational background in the spheres of health, education, and welfare.

Lay tribunals, of course, may from time to time require expert assistance or prompting on points of law or procedure, a function that is exercised within the English Youth Court by an official known as the "clerk to the justices." In the Scottish children's hearing system, surprisingly, no one explicitly occupies such a role, though in practice the reporter is usually expected to do so, and it can be argued (see Kearney 2000, p. 21) that "it is implied throughout [the legislation]" that he or she should fulfill these functions. Martin, Fox, and Murray (1981, p. 277), in their early research study, expressed disappointment that reporters were not more proactive in keeping hearings in line with prescribed legal and procedural standards. Fifteen years later, hearings' adherence to procedural rules, such as informing parents and children of their rights, had generally improved by comparison with the earlier findings, yet the research data still indicated that there was significant room for improvement (Hallett and Murray 1998, p. 124); and "while some reporters did contribute to hearings by prompting or correcting panel chairmen about families' rights, there were many instances in which they did not" (Hallett and Murray 1998, p. 52). Inevitably, findings such as these strengthen the case of those who have argued for greater legal (or other) representation within the hearings.

Over the years there have been a number of interesting observational studies of children's hearings. Martin, Fox, and Murray (1981, chap. 8) attempted to characterize styles of dialogue in 301 observed hearings. They found that while in over 90 percent of cases there were some passages of dialogue that were "encouraging [and] non-directive," the hearings also contained some exchanges where panel members demonstrated attitudes or behavior such as "shocked [or] indignant, [trying] to elicit guilt [or] shame" (present in 36 percent of cases), "interrogating [or] demanding" (44 percent), "exhorts to shape up [or] threatens with legal consequences" (35 percent), and even "sarcastic [or] contemptuous" (22 percent). A consumer study of 105 children undertaken as part of the Martin, Fox, and Murray study (but published separately) suggested that these dialogue styles were directly related to children's immediate reactions to the hearing; for example, those exposed to the "sarcastic/contemptuous" style were more likely to expect the police subsequently to hold their appearance at a hearing against them, while anticipation of stigma from potential employers was associated with having been on the receiving end of the "exhorting/threatening" approach (Erickson 1982). The author of this study accordingly suggested in her conclusions that "while the potential of Hearings to socialise children in a positive, integrating way to community values was realised to some extent, the capacity to instil or reinforce feelings of rejection or alienation in youthful offenders was also documented" (Erickson 1982, p. 104).

As Erickson admitted, her study would have been stronger had it contained an element of follow-up; but her explicit reference at one point (1982, p. 94) to clients' perceptions of legitimacy and fairness anticipates a literature that has richly elaborated such themes in the years since her study was conducted (see esp. Tyler 1990; Sparks, Bottoms, and Hay 1996; Paternoster et al. 1997; Tyler and Huo 2002).

Later studies of dialogue in hearings are broadly consistent with the findings of Martin, Fox, and Murray's research. Alison Petch (1988), for example, conducted a consumer study of parents' reactions to 100 children's hearings. Before interviewing the parents, she first attended the relevant hearings and classified them according to the "dominant characteristics" of the proceedings. On this basis, twenty-five were rated as "supportive, encouraging" and six as constituting an "open exchange" between panel members and parents and children; but sixteen were rated as "formal [or] ritual," eleven as "indecisive [or] amateur," eleven as "challenging [or] humiliating," and nine as "probing." In the most recent research, Hallett and Murray (1998, chap. 3) counted all speech acts in a sample of sixty observed hearings; this analysis showed that panel members spoke most frequently, followed in descending order by children, mothers, and social workers, with reporters and fathers (often absent) as the least frequent contributors. However, the high ranking of children in this "contribution count" should not be misunderstood, for in no less than three-quarters of all their contributions children actually spoke one line or less (e.g., a monosyllabic response). Underlying these figures is the important fact that the typical dialogue in a children's hearing is not a naturally flowing discussion between equals; rather, "the contribution of panel members was characterised far more by questions (to families and professionals), and the contribution of children and young people (and to a lesser extent, parents) far more by answers" (Hallett and Murray 1998, p. 47).

Some data from Asquith's (1983, chap. 8) research enable us more clearly to understand the character of the dialogue in children's hearings by comparison with English juvenile courts in the 1970s. In the Scottish hearings observed by Asquith, there were (overall) slightly more oral statements made by panel members than by others to panel members (3,118 to 2,815), and—a point of special significance—over 90 percent of the dialogue in each direction was made between panel members, children, and parents. Taken together with the Hallett and Murray results, this suggests an inquisitorial, interrogatory procedure in the Scottish hearings, with panel members taking a very active role and the dialogue focused firmly around the panel member/child/parent nexus. By contrast, in the English juvenile court that Asquith studied, the magistrates were much more passive: 915 oral statements were made to them, but only 159 statements were made by them (an imbalance of nearly six to one). Most of the statements made to magistrates (over three-quarters) were made by those representing the prosecution and (if the defendant was legally represented) the defense; parents and children contributed only one-sixth of these statements. When magistrates did speak, it was predominantly (68 percent) to parents or children, but, in general, magistrates were neutral receivers of information, not taking a very proactive role. In an accusatorial, court-based criminal justice system, none of this is actually very surprising, but the data do point up quite sharply the markedly different character of the dialogue in the more inquisitorial Scottish children's hearings.

Asquith's data also suggested that the average Scottish hearing takes longer than the average English court case, a point that is reflected in the markedly different N's of the statement counts above.[37] Since parents and children contribute more often, within hearings that are longer, it is obvious that they participate more in Scottish hearings than in English court cases, even if much of their participation is very brief. Moreover, we must remember that hearings do routinely "provide an *opportunity* for families to contribute if they wish to and feel able to" (Hallett and Murray 1998, p. 47), an opportunity that a minority of families take up to such an extent that Petch (1988) described

---

[37] Especially as Asquith observed slightly more English court cases (thirty-five) than Scottish children's hearings (thirty) (Asquith 1983, p. 157).

the main characteristic of six of her observed hearings as "parent-dominated." Less positively, however, the recent Audit Scotland (2002, pp. 21–22) report shows that recommended time periods for various stages of the processing of offense-based cases are frequently exceeded, and the average time that children and parents have to wait from initial police contact to the start of a children's hearing is as long as 5.5 months.

What might be described as the "staccato participation" of children in the dialogue of hearings is not necessarily seen as a problem by the children themselves. Indeed, in Erickson's (1982) study, the great majority of interviewed children expressed satisfaction with their participation levels, regardless of whether this participation was rated by independent observers as "high," "medium," or "low." In the same research, half the children expressed the view that their input had had some effect on the decision (p. 98), and three-quarters said they had understood everything that had gone on (p. 96), a finding that notably contrasted, to the advantage of the Scottish system, with the few consumer studies of English juvenile courts at that date (e.g., Morris and Giller 1977). Where children did not understand, it was generally because panel members either used "big words" or adopted a style in which "interjections were delivered rapidly, with panel members interrupting the child or each other" (p. 96). From these findings, Erickson generalized by saying that hearings were best understood when both the pace and the content of the dialogue were controlled, with proceedings conducted in "a relaxed and orderly fashion . . . with clear and precise vocabulary" (1982, p. 97).

Both Hallett and Murray (1998, chap. 4) and Waterhouse et al. (2000, chap. 6) carried out consumer studies of parents and children, but in each case with very small samples. The main results are by now familiar: the system was seen as generally fair; the sense of being a participant was valued; both parents and children felt they were listened to; participation was sometimes inhibited by nervousness, or by some panel members seeming to be intimidating or antagonistic; understanding was generally good but panels' language style could be a problem; and parents and children were not always informed about their legal rights.

What, finally, of the position of social workers in children's hearings? Their role is to provide formal written reports on the child's social background, to speak to these reports at the hearing, and thereafter to participate in the dialogue, as they consider appropriate, in the child's best interests. Social workers' written reports normally contain formal recommendations about the future treatment of the child, and over the years research has consistently shown that such recommendations are usually accepted by the hearing (Hallett and Murray [1998], p. 57, citing also earlier research studies). Yet despite this congruence of view on the outcomes of cases, relationships between social workers and panel members are not always good. Indeed, Hallett and Murray (1998) reported that social worker/panel member relationships were, in their research study, more problematic than any other professional relationships within the hearings system (p. 78) and were characterized by "a considerable degree of conflict" (p. 123). There were indications of these tensions in many of the observed hearings, with panel members "holding social workers to account, who were in turn defensive" (p. 123). Using other data from their observational study, Hallett and Murray further reported that "social workers more frequently told Panel members what the families' views were than facilitated families' participation in the hearings" (p. 51).

It is clear from Hallett and Murray's study, and from other sources, that in part the reported conflicts between social workers and panel members focus on the question of resources. In this context, it is important to note the rapidly growing workload placed on the children's hearing system in recent years; 21,000 children were referred to the system in 1985, but this had risen to 33,000 in 2000, a growth of over 50 percent in fifteen years (table 7). Much the fastest-growing element within this trend has been the rapid expansion of "care and protection" referrals (table 7). Inevitably, growth of this rapidity, especially in care and protection referrals, places strain on social work departments, and one consequence of this is that voluntary supervision by social workers (in principle, in the Scottish system, to be preferred to compulsory measures of care) becomes increasingly difficult to deliver within the available resources. Hallett and Murray found that, in such circumstances, panel members sometimes used compulsion (i.e., a supervision requirement) simply as a means to gain access to scarce resources (and notwithstanding the niceties of the "no non-beneficial order" rule). As one panel member put it, "if you're really stuck you would say to yourself, well it can't do much harm to impose a supervision order on this child, but it may do harm not to" (Hallett and Murray 1998, p. 74).

Indeed, even the imposition of compulsory measures of supervision does not necessarily guarantee the resources that panel members hope for. In the cohort study by Waterhouse et al. (2000), while standard

TABLE 7

Alleged Grounds in Referrals to Reporters to Children's Panels in Scotland, 1975–2000

	Care and Protection Referral*	Nonoffense Behavioral Referral†	School Attendance Referral	Alleged Offense Referral	Total	N (000s)		Average Referrals per Child
						Referrals	Children	
1975	4	2	6	88	100	30.0	22.2	1.4
1980	9	3	10	79	100	29.0	19.0	1.5
1985	10	5	10	74	100	34.2	21.1	1.6
1990	28	5	8	59	100	37.3	24.3	1.7
1995	29	5	9	57	100	42.9	26.8	1.6
1996‡	28	5	9	58	100	46.5	26.9	1.7
1997‡	30	6	8	55	100	47.5	27.8	1.7
1998‡	34	8	7	51	100	51.9	30.2	1.7
1999‡	41	8	7	45	100	63.9	33.8	1.9
2000‡	41	8	6	45	100	60.2	32.7	1.8

SOURCE.—Annual volumes of the Scottish Office Social Work Services Group Statistical Bulletin entitled *Referrals of Children to Reporters and Children's Hearings* (to 1995); annual *Statistical Bulletins of the Scottish Children's Reporter Administration* (from 1996).

NOTE.—Data given in the first four columns are percentages of all alleged "grounds for referral" for males and females together. Where a single referral includes more than one ground, both grounds are counted separately for the purposes of this table; hence, the total of "grounds for referral" is larger than the total number of referrals. Columns 6–8 give numerical data on numbers of referrals and of children to whom those relate.

* "Care and protection" referrals include children alleged to be "suffering by neglect or lack of parental care"; being the victim of an offense, or being a member of a household of a child offended against; being or likely to become a member of a household of a child offender; and "falling into bad associations or exposure to moral danger."

† "Nonoffense behavioral" referrals include children allegedly beyond the control of their parents; (from 1983 onward) those alleged to have "misused a volatile substance by deliberately inhaling"; and (from 1997 onward) those alleged to have misused alcohol or drugs.

‡ Data for 1996 onward are for the last nine months of the calendar year stated, plus the first three months of the next year.

social work placements were normally available, special placements such as foster care in a family context, or hostel accommodation, were frequently not immediately available to children's hearings.

Looking back over the research findings reported in this subsection on children's hearings processes, three points perhaps stand out. One is the issue of participation, which is clearly valued by children and parents, even if actual participation is frequent rather than extensive. This is a theme that is highly congruent with the research literature on legitimacy and procedural justice: generally speaking, if participants feel they have had an opportunity to have their say, and have been treated with respect in the procedures, they are more likely to regard the whole process as fair, even if the outcome is not wholly to their liking (see generally Tyler 1990; Tyler and Huo 2002). But, second, it seems "respect" is not in fact always delivered in the Scottish juvenile system, perhaps principally because the interrogatory, inquisitional format of the hearings system can too easily result in panel members adopting, on occasion, intimidatory styles or inappropriately complex language, or neglecting to tell parents and children about their assigned rights within the system. Moreover, since reporters are essentially passive within hearings, social workers are quite often on the defensive vis-à-vis panel members, and legal or other representation has up to now been, for all practical purposes, nonexistent, there may be few countervailing forces that can be mobilized to restrain panel members on the minority of occasions when they may seem to exercise their powers or presence too forcefully or weightily.

The above two conclusions focus on the processes of the children's hearings, but it is important also to consider the outcomes of hearings, and here the question of adequate back-up social work resources in the field seems to be an increasingly important issue as the workload of the hearings system expands. For example, resource issues may have an effect on the proportion of cases where the hearing discharges the referral on the grounds that informal social work help is available. Resource issues can also have some effect on the process of children's hearings, playing out sometimes in tensions between what panel members want and what social workers can deliver.

C. Deeds in a Needs-Based System

It is time to consider more fully the central conceptual dilemma, previously highlighted, about the way that offenses are considered within the Scottish system. In theory, a criminal offense is simply one of the possible grounds that, if proved or accepted, might bring a child before a hearing; once a child is before a hearing, the paramount consideration for the members of the panel is (in the usual case) his or her welfare need. This approach therefore seems, on the face of it, to place almost no emphasis on the criminal act (of theft, violence, or whatever) in offense-based cases. That is in one sense unsurprising: the welfare-oriented tradition in juvenile justice has always tried to place emphasis "not on the act done by the child, but on the social facts and circumstances that are really the inducing causes of the child's appearance in court" (Flexner and Baldwin 1915, p. 6). But is such an approach really sustainable in practice?

Morris and McIsaac's (1978) early research caused controversy in Scotland by delivering a robustly negative answer to this question. With the benefit of hindsight, their analysis can be seen to have been partly wrong and partly right.

One claim that these authors made was that "the type of tribunal (juvenile court or welfare tribunal) is largely unimportant. What is crucial is the philosophy underlying that tribunal and the ideology of its practitioners" (Morris and McIsaac 1978, p. 111). One can see how such a comment might come to be made. Both England and Scotland staff their juvenile justice tribunals with laypersons, who adjudicate on a part-time basis and who inevitably bring to their adjudications some aspects of their ordinary, everyday experiences as citizens. It might appear, therefore, not to make a great deal of difference whether these laypeople are assembled together as a juvenile court or as a children's hearing, especially if they are dealing with offense cases where some kind of response by the tribunal to the child's delinquent act might seem necessary. Indeed, Allison Morris herself developed such a claim about the Scottish system (in a later publication with other coauthors), arguing that, notwithstanding the Kilbrandon philosophy, in practice the Scottish system had delivered "the re-emergence of the principle of the offence as the primary criterion of intervention. . . . Although treatment was the *official* goal priority, control of the child's behaviour became the *operational* goal priority. Research suggests that the hearings, in fact, operate on tariff principles just as in the juvenile courts. . . . What is promoted, therefore, as a welfare jurisdiction is no more than a replication of the practice south of the border" (Morris et al. 1980, p. 67).

This line of thinking, at least in the bold form encapsulated in Morris et al.'s (1980) quotation, was convincingly refuted by Asquith's

(1983) small comparative study of the English and Scottish systems. The selection processes for magistrates and panel members attracted different kinds of applicants in the two countries, particularly because the tasks of Scottish panel members are, while those of English magistrates are not, confined to juvenile cases. Moreover, the postselection training and experience were different, with magistrates' training and experience not only obliging them to consider how to adjudicate on issues of guilt or innocence (an issue reserved, in Scotland's "dual system," for the sheriff court, not the children's hearing), but also placing more emphasis on factors such as how to "think judicially." The net result was that the type of the tribunal was in practice not at all irrelevant for the laypeople who presided at the adjudications; indeed, the type of the tribunal actually helped to shape "the philosophy . . . and the ideology of its practitioners," as Morris and McIsaac had themselves put it. Asquith (1983) further demonstrated that what he called the attitudinal "frames of relevance" of Scottish panel members' thinking were substantially more welfare-oriented than were those of English juvenile magistrates, and there was also more internal agreement among the Scottish sample than among the English sample about the importance of welfare factors. In dealing with offense-based cases, Asquith's small empirical study of actual decisions also suggested that issues such as the imputed intentionality of the offender and the assessed seriousness of the child's delinquent act were of substantially greater direct significance in decision-making thought processes for English magistrates than for Scottish panel members (Asquith 1983, p. 167). Clearly, therefore, Morris et al.'s claim that the children's hearing system is "no more than a replication of the practice south of the border" cannot be seriously sustained.

But what about the further (and arguably more important) claim that the Scottish system in practice endorses, in offense-based cases, "the principle of the offence as the primary criterion of intervention" (Morris et al. 1980, p. 67; see also Morris and McIsaac 1978, p. 136)? Or, to put the matter another way, has the Scottish system, in offense-based cases, in effect adopted a tariff principle, notwithstanding the official ideology of "need, not deed"?

The evidence on this point is both complex and intriguing. For example, Asquith (1983) found that, notwithstanding the attitudinal differences between his English magistrates and Scottish panel members, when it came to actual decision making, in offense-based cases there were relatively few differences in the way that magistrates and panel members operated.[38] Moreover, for the Scottish panel members "social protection and seriousness [of offense] were in fact significantly more important for decision-making in relation to cases with more than one [criminal] charge than for those with only one" (p. 168). Asquith's explanation for these various findings is that offense factors are in practice relevant in both English and Scottish decision making, but in Scotland they are reinterpreted within a "frame of relevance" that is "predominantly derived from welfare considerations" (p. 211).

Other researchers have reached broadly similar conclusions. In the most recent research study, Hallett and Murray (1998, p. 36) comment that "whether [Scottish juvenile justice] has been operating a tariff system" has been a widely discussed issue for twenty-five years. They divide their own discussion of this point between reporters' and hearings' decision making. As to the former, there was clear evidence of the importance of offense-based factors, but there were "many exceptions" to this generalization, and in any event reporters often explained the apparent tariff system using a "best interests" justification. As one reporter put it, "I know we're not supposed to consider the child's deeds, but it's also in the child's interests to be, to feel, responsible for taking serious actions" (Hallett and Murray 1998, p. 19).

When it came to the observed hearings in Hallett and Murray's study, in just under a third of all cases (which included care and protection as well as offense-ground cases), "much of the 'talk' was about issues more readily associated . . . with the criminal justice system," such as the seriousness of the offense, the protection of the public, warnings, and tariffs (p. 53). However, the authors comment that when such discourse was in evidence, it was "almost invariably mixed with welfare talk" (p. 53). Hallett and Murray thus endorsed the view of an earlier (and less empirical) researcher: "In offence and truancy cases, there is a constant balancing of the non-punitive and the punitive. Help is offered, advice given, but 'the consequences' of non-co-operation are constantly emphasized" (Adler 1985, p. 93).

In conclusion, then, it seems clear that "deeds" are in practice by no means irrelevant within the Scottish welfare-based system of juvenile justice. The principle that the welfare of the child is paramount is wholeheartedly endorsed by most official participants in the system, but in offense-based cases they do not usually ignore the child's of-

---

[38] This was after the type of offense, the number of crimes currently before the tribunal, and the number of previous offenses had been held constant.

fense. Often, they reinterpret offense-related factors into welfarist language, but not infrequently more overt comments about the delinquent act may be made, or the adverse consequences of further offending may be explicitly threatened. There are real tensions here, and they seem to be tensions inherent within the welfare model of juvenile justice itself when dealing with offense-based cases. The Scottish system has grappled seriously with the tensions, but it has not overcome them.

D. A Sample Study

The most recent large-scale research study of the Scottish system, by Lorraine Waterhouse and colleagues (2000), provides the first empirical data on a representative sample of children passing through the hearings system (both for offense and nonoffense reasons). Within this research, some special attention was paid to children who were referred to the children's hearings system for their offending behavior (Waterhouse et al. 2000, chap. 5). Many of the results of this research will surprise no one who is familiar with the literature on longitudinal studies of criminal careers and on youth offending more generally (for a summary, see, e.g., Farrington [1997]). For example, the study found that the social characteristics of the children referred for offending reasons were "broadly similar" to the research sample of children in need, and the social background of the child offenders was frequently characterized by "family poverty, disruption, and difficulty," with many also having "experience of public care and poor educational experience." Many of the children were considered to have broader and major care needs in addition to offending (Waterhouse et al. 2000, p. 95), and it was found that many of the children eventually referred to the system—perhaps in their teens—for offending behavior had initially been referred at a younger age for reasons other than offending. Findings such as these do, of course, tend to provide empirical support for juvenile justice systems such as that in Scotland that offer close integration between the mechanisms for dealing with offenders and those for dealing with children in social need.

Consistently with much other criminological research, Waterhouse et al. (2000, p. 83) also found that a smallish group of offenders in the Scottish system is responsible for a disproportionate percentage of all the offenses known to have been committed by the cohort. Disturbingly, however, in the concurrent process-based research by Hallett and Murray (1998), many professionals involved in the children's hearing system (reporters, panel members, and police officers), while very supportive of the hearings system in general, expressed little confidence in the system's capacity to deal well with those older juveniles who are persistent offenders. There seemed to be several reasons for this low confidence level, including (again) a lack of appropriate resources to deal with this group, "a reluctance on the part of some Panel members directly to address in hearings the offences which constituted the grounds of referral" (Hallett and Murray 1998, p. 93), and a feeling by some that the system is not philosophically well geared to deal with persistent offenders because there is too much stress on voluntary participation and cooperation and not enough on discipline and punishment where that seems needed. These broad conclusions have been repeated in the recent Audit Scotland (2002, p. 32) report, where a lack of specialist training for panel members in dealing with persistent offenders was also highlighted.

We have previously noted that the upper age limit for the initial jurisdiction of the children's hearings system is the child's sixteenth birthday. The difficulties reported in the previous paragraph suggest that any higher upper age limit for the children's hearing system might be difficult to sustain. Yet there has also for some time been widespread anxiety among relevant professionals in Scotland about the present arrangements whereby young persons aged sixteen and over are routinely dealt with in the adult criminal justice system,[39] and anxiety has also been expressed about the apparently high rates of custodial sentencing for young adults, including those ages sixteen and seventeen. These concerns are given weight by some findings in the research by Waterhouse et al. (2000). As part of this study, a representative sample of children referred to reporters in 1995 (for any reason, offense-based or otherwise) was followed up statistically for a period of two years. Of those age sixteen or over by 1997, and for whom matching identifiers could be provided, over half had a conviction in an adult criminal court by 1997; and, of those acquiring one or more such convictions, no fewer than 28 percent had received a custodial sentence.[40] The evidence seems to suggest, therefore, that while the very close in-

[39] As previously noted, young offenders ages sixteen or seventeen who are already the subject of a supervision requirement may still be dealt with by the children's hearing under its "continuing jurisdiction," and this can include a hearing to consider a fresh offense that such a young person has committed since his sixteenth birthday. In practice, however, almost all such fresh offense cases are prosecuted in the adult courts.

[40] However, because of technical problems of matching identifiers experienced by the researchers, it is not clear that this is based on a wholly representative sample of cases.

terrelation of the mechanisms for dealing with offense-based and other referrals at younger ages is a major strength of a welfare-based system such as that in Scotland, by the time the child reaches older adolescence, a straightforwardly welfare-based system for dealing with offenders carries less confidence among professionals in the system and can perhaps (although this point is not definitively established) lead to especially severe interventions in the adult system for those who are seen to have "failed" in the juvenile system.

E. Postdevolution Policy Developments

A major new chapter in Scotland's political history opened in 1999 with the creation of the devolved Scottish Parliament sitting in Edinburgh—the first such Scottish national assembly since the Acts of Union in 1707 (see nn. 2 and 4). As part of the new devolution arrangements, a new Scottish Executive has also been created, and day-to-day policy responsibility for the children's hearings system has been devolved from the U.K. Scottish Office to the Scottish Executive.[41]

At the new Scottish cabinet's very first strategy meeting in 1999, the subject of youth crime was discussed. This led to the creation of an Advisory Group on Youth Crime, whose short report—with the Scottish Executive's response—was published the following year (Scottish Executive 2000a, 2000b). It is worth noting at once that the subject of this report was youth crime, and not the children's hearing system as a whole; this in itself was an innovation in recent Scottish policy, and one that has subsequently been strongly maintained.

The advisory group proposed no fundamental changes to the children's hearing system, but it did highlight two matters of particular policy concern, both of which had been clearly identified by previous research. The first of these was the need for an improved handling of persistent young offenders, which the advisory group hoped could be achieved by an expansion of "the range and availability of effective, quality assessed, community-based interventions and programmes" (Scottish Executive 2000a, p. 3), requiring substantial extra resources. Second, the advisory group noted that there were "widespread criti-

[41] Responsibility for policy and administration in the children's hearing system belonged before 1999 to the Secretary of State for Scotland in the U.K. government (see n. 27 above). However, as the title implies, this minister had responsibility for a huge range of policy issues, including health, education, and transport, as well as criminal justice and social services. Ministers in the devolved Scottish Executive have more manageable briefs. The principal minister now responsible for the children's hearing system is the Minister for Education and Young People.

cisms" of the existing procedures across the transition from the children's hearing system to the adult criminal justice system, a transition that the report characterized as "too abrupt." In particular, the advisory group commented, "The criminal justice system is described as too focused on adults and unable to deal with the particular aspects of youth offending. The Children's Hearings system is described as too focused on welfare issues and unable to address the particular aspects of youth offending" (Scottish Executive 2000a, p. 4).

Among other recommendations arising from its report, the advisory group proposed the development of a national strategic framework "to define objectives, mechanisms, functions and resources needed to address youth crime" (2000a, p. 6). This would be backed up by local "multidisciplinary teams" that would operate at a strategic level, draw up a youth crime plan for the local area, and then oversee its implementation. "Youth crime," in this context, was firmly conceived as relating both to crimes committed by children under sixteen years of age and those committed by young persons age sixteen to twenty.

All the recommendations of the advisory group were accepted by the Scottish Executive (2000b), and in June 2000 the Executive announced a four-year, £23.5 million investment in preventing youth crime. Central to this program was the formal creation of new strategic youth crime bodies in every local authority area in Scotland, to be known as youth justice teams. Each team is expected to include "senior representation from [all] relevant agencies involved in youth justice" (Scottish Executive 2002c, p. 5).

The Executive followed up its 2000 announcements by publishing an action plan to reduce youth crime (Scottish Executive 2002c) early in 2002 (and this included a commitment to encourage "the extension of restorative justice approaches across Scotland" [p. 9]). However, this relatively routine activity was suddenly upstaged a few months later by a flurry of high-level political activity, apparently embarked upon in anticipation of the parliamentary election in Scotland in 2003.[42] With

---

[42] It is possible that these events were influenced by the work of Audit Scotland, a postdevolution official audit and accounts body in Scotland. In June 2001, Audit Scotland (2001) published a report on *Youth Justice in Scotland* that was described as a "baseline report," to be followed by a more comprehensive study. The more comprehensive study was eventually published in December 2002 (Audit Scotland 2002) and contained a number of criticisms of the youth justice system, some of which have been highlighted in the text. Opposition political parties (the Conservatives and the Scottish National Party) had given various indications, well before the publication of the second report, that they would use it for the purposes of political criticism; it may well be that this caused the Scottish Executive suddenly to give youth crime a higher policy profile.

appropriate publicity, the Scottish first minister set up an "Ad Hoc Ministerial Group on Youth Crime," chaired by himself and comprising four other ministers. This group first met on May 22, but already by June 26 it had reported formally to the Scottish cabinet, which (unsurprisingly, given that the group was chaired by the first minister) accepted its recommendations.

The ministerial group put forward ten principal proposals (Scottish Executive 2002*a*), of which the four most important, for present purposes, were as follows:

1. The creation of a pilot scheme of so-called Specialist Children's Hearings, which would "fast-track persistent offenders under 16" (p. 3). This would include special training for panel members "to enable them to respond in a more targeted way to the complex issues raised by persistent offenders" (p. 3).

2. A "youth court feasibility project" to determine the feasibility of setting up special youth courts for sixteen- and seventeen-year-olds, "with some flexibility to include 15 year olds" (p. 3).

3. Consideration of a national scheme of police warnings, "which the Lord Advocate would be able to endorse"[43] (p. 4), including the possibility of introducing "restorative cautions similar to those run by Thames Valley police in England" (p. 4) (on which see Sec. VII).

4. Creation of a set of national standards to operate between local authorities, the criminal justice system, and children's hearings, covering "issues such as reporting, timescales, quality of intervention programmes to reduce offending, and follow-up on Hearings' decisions" (p. 4).

In the second half of 2002, very rapid action was taken to try to drive forward these proposals. In particular:

1. It has been announced that three areas of Scotland have been chosen as pilot areas for the new fast-track specialist children's hearings, the pilots to begin in early 2003. Announcing this on October 23, 2002, the Minister for Education and Young People (Cathy Jamieson) said that a disproportionate amount of youth crime was carried out by a "hard core of persistent offenders," and that "these young tearaways cause misery for communities

---

[43] The Lord Advocate is the senior law officer in the Scottish government, equivalent to the Attorney General in most English-speaking jurisdictions.

throughout Scotland"; the new schemes would "deal with them quickly" and "make them face up to their actions" (BBC News Scotland 2002, p. 1).

2. A working party on the feasibility of a youth court was established in August 2002 and published its report in January 2003 (Scottish Executive 2003b). Its conclusion was that a youth court was feasible under existing legislation, and that a pilot project should take place in one area (Hamilton). The youth court should be available only for sixteen- and seventeen-year-olds who were persistent offenders, defined as "at least three separate incidents of offending which have resulted in criminal charges within a six months period" (Scottish Executive 2003b, p. 2). Other than in exceptional circumstances, "fast-tracking" should ensure that potential youth court defendants should make their first appearance in court within ten days from the date of the charge. At the time of publication of the working party's report, it was announced that ministers in the Executive had committed themselves to establishing the youth court, in line with the recommendations in the report, before the next Scottish parliamentary election in May 2003.

3. In the second half of 2002 a report was published by the Improving the Effectiveness of the Youth Justice System Working Group, creating what were described as National Standards for Scotland's Youth Justice Services (Scottish Executive 2002b).

4. The Scottish Executive has committed itself to a target of reducing the number of persistent young offenders by 10 percent by 2006.

At the time of writing, it is obviously unclear what the final results will be from this very recent flurry of political activity. A few comments of an interim nature can be made, however. First, virtually the whole thrust of postdevolution policy-making in this area has focused exclusively on youth crime, with very little reference to the wider care agenda of the children's hearings system (notwithstanding that in recent years much of the fastest growth in referrals to that system has been in care and protection cases; see table 7). Some aspects of this recent policy-making also seem somewhat alien to the post-1971 traditions of the children's hearing system, notably the pilot scheme of specialist children's hearings, which is expected to deal exclusively with, and "fast track," persistent offenders (described by the relevant minister as "young tearaways"). Second, there is an increasing tendency to cast policy, conceptually, across the age-sixteen-to-seventeen divide and to "bridge the gap" (Scottish Executive 2000*a*, p. 9) between what are now described as "two parallel systems for dealing with young offenders in Scotland" (Scottish Executive 2002*a*), namely, the children's hearing system for those under sixteen and the adult courts for those sixteen and over. Third, there is an increasing sense of a national plan for youth crime, a development that is also very evident in England. Fourth, and perhaps more surprising, within this national plan there is a revival of interest in the police warning.

Over and above the technicalities, however, what seems clearly discernible in all this activity is a definite politicization of debates on youth justice in Scotland. Prior to devolution, youth justice policy was managed at the U.K. Scottish Office, and very rarely indeed did it feature in policy debates in the U.K. parliament at Westminster. The children's hearing system was the subject of a good deal of interest among relevant professional groups, the civil service, and some social elites in Scottish society (see generally Lockyer and Stone [1998]), but knowledge of it outside these circles was limited (Hallett and Murray 1998). Devolution has changed all this. It has set up a national assembly in Scotland, with elected members responsible directly to local electorates who are—if opinion polls are to be believed—worried about crime, and especially youth crime, as one of the key public service or "quality of life" issues, along with health services, education, transport, and so on.[44] Child-care policy does not feature as one of these populist issues, so devolution has changed the conceptual framework of juvenile policy discussions in Scotland away from a holistic welfare-based approach and toward a "youth crime" approach (a change that has been aided by research-based demonstrations of the difficulty of the transition, at age sixteen, from the children's hearing system to the adult criminal justice system). The net effect of these changes is to begin to push the Scottish system in some respects closer to the English.

III. The Current Systems in Outline: England
As with our discussion of the Scottish system, we begin by providing a formal "process" description of the post-1998 English youth justice

[44] Of course, Scottish members of the U.K. Parliament were and are also responsible to local electorates. However, since in population terms England is a much larger country than Scotland, issues such as crime and justice, when dealt with in U.K. elections, inevitably focus mainly on the English system. Members of the new Scottish Parliament, by contrast, are elected in special Scotland-only elections where specifically Scottish quality-of-life issues feature much more prominently.

system, and then outline some preliminary research findings on the new system in operation.

A. Formal Description

A key feature of the recent English youth justice reforms is the adoption of a statutory "principal aim" for the entire youth justice system, namely, to prevent offending by children and young persons. All agencies and individuals with responsibilities for youth justice are now required by statute to have regard to this aim, which is, according to the Home Office (2000a), to be achieved with regard to the following six key objectives: the swift administration of justice; ensuring that young people face up to the consequences of their offending, ensuring that the risk factors associated with offending are addressed in any intervention,[45] delivering punishment that is appropriate for the offense and proportionate to the seriousness and frequency of offending, encouraging reparation by young offenders to their victims or the wider community, and reinforcing parental responsibility.

In the initial statute setting up the new system (Crime and Disorder Act 1998), local government authorities were given significant additional responsibilities relating to crime prevention and youth justice, including (and most importantly in the present context) the duty to draw up annual "youth justice plans" (which are intended to be based on the authority's wider local "crime and disorder audit" and strategy),[46] to provide comprehensive youth justice services for their localities, and to establish new multiagency "youth offending teams" (or YOTs, as these teams have become colloquially known) that will cover the local authority area. The principal duty of the YOTs is to coordinate and provide youth justice services to "all . . . who need them" and to carry out functions assigned to the team by the local youth justice plan.[47] The composition of the YOTs is partially prescribed by statute

[45] The Youth Justice Board has developed a formal risk and need assessment instrument known as ASSET to assist with this task.

[46] The Crime and Disorder Act 1998 also contains wider provisions—not solely focused on youth—that require the local government authority and the police in each local area in England and Wales to convene a multiagency, crime-prevention partnership aimed at the reduction of crime in the area. Such partnerships are required to carry out a local "crime and disorder audit" and to develop strategies of crime reduction. For a discussion, in an international context, see Crawford and Matassa (2000, chap. 5).

[47] It is important to emphasize that the intended role of YOTs is extremely wide-ranging and embraces not only "frontline" operational responsibilities, but also significant strategic functions, for example, in helping to formulate the local authority's annual youth justice plan.

in that each local team must include at least one of each of the following: social worker from the local authority social services department (SSD), probation officer, police officer, person nominated by a health authority within the local authority area, and person nominated by the local authority's chief education officer.[48]

Another very important new organizational feature within the recently transformed youth justice framework is the Youth Justice Board (YJB) for England and Wales, also created by the 1998 act (sec. 41). This is a so-called nondepartmental public body (i.e., a public body that is not an integral part of a government department) whose members are appointed by the home secretary (see n. 27), and it now has strategic responsibility for the youth justice system as a whole, plus oversight of the operation of the new youth offending teams.[49] Its specific functions include advising the home secretary on how the principal (preventive) aim of the youth justice system might most effectively be pursued, setting national standards and promoting good practice, and monitoring the operation of the youth justice system and the provision of youth justice services.[50] In addition, since April 2000 the Youth Justice Board has been given responsibility for commissioning custodial and other secure facilities (now known collectively as the "juvenile secure estate") for young people under eighteen and for allocating young offenders to such facilities.

The changes that have been made to the youth justice system in England and Wales have not been confined to institutional reforms and responsibilities but also extend to the youth justice process itself. Indeed, the system as a whole has been so significantly altered since 1998 that it is often referred to as the "New Youth Justice" (e.g., Goldson 2000). Although there are some important points of continuity between the "new" youth justice system and the one it replaces, much of it is barely recognizable. A flowchart of the new English youth justice system is provided in figure 3. As well as setting out the key stages in

[48] The inclusion of the health and education agencies reflects a deliberate attempt to require YOTs to attend not only to the offenses committed by young people but also to the factors that might have precipitated them.

[49] The Youth Justice Board's first chairman was Lord Warner, who had advised the Labour Party's Home Office spokesman (Jack Straw) while in opposition, and who therefore had a significant input into the Labour Party's 1996 document on the youth justice system (Straw and Michael 1996). The board's first chief executive was Mark Perfect, who had been the lead author of the Audit Commission's (1996) report.

[50] It also has grant-making powers to promote the development and evaluation of new and innovative practice, which it has used, inter alia, to fund projects to develop restorative justice, mentoring, and cognitive behavioral programs.

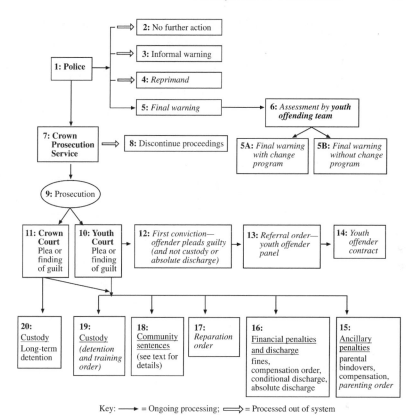

Key: ——→ = Ongoing processing; ⟹ = Processed out of system

FIG. 3.—The English youth justice system in outline. Italics indicate new or radically reformed aspects of the system.

the youth justice process, this diagram also attempts to indicate the scale of the recent changes by printing in italics those aspects that are either completely new or have been radically reformed.

An important preliminary observation in considering figure 3 is that the system that is portrayed relates only to the way that offense-based cases are dealt with, and this is immediately a crucial contrast with the Scottish system (see fig. 2). The links (such as they are) between the criminal youth justice system and the child protection system in England and Wales are dealt with in a subsequent section.

Where a case involving an alleged offense by a young person is reported to the police (box 1), they have a number of "diversionary" options available to them (rather than proceeding toward a possible prosecution), though their room for maneuver is now much less extensive than it was before the recent youth justice reforms. Thus, the police may simply decide to take no further action (NFA), which effectively means that the case is dropped (box 2), or they may informally warn the young suspect, in which case no formal record is kept and the incident cannot be mentioned in court in the event of any future prosecution (box 3). Informal warnings are now discouraged by the Home Office.

Under the pre-1998 youth justice system the main precourt diversionary alternative to prosecution consisted of a fairly permissive nonstatutory cautioning system covering both young and adult offenders, which resulted in the offender being given a "formal caution" (see n. 18) that was citable in court in any later proceedings. With regard to young offenders under the age of eighteen, however, this old-style system of formal cautioning has now been replaced by a more restrictive statutory regime comprising the distinct categories of "reprimands" and "final warnings" (Crime and Disorder Act 1998, secs. 65–66). Under this new system, reprimands (box 4) are only supposed to be given to first offenders, and even then only if the offense is not very serious. In the event of a further offense after a reprimand (or a more serious initial offense) a young offender may expect at best to receive a single statutory warning (frequently referred to as a "final warning") or, if the offense is more serious, a prosecution. The pre-1998 practice of repeat, or multiple cautioning—much favored by adherents of the "minimum intervention" philosophy of the youth justice movement—is no longer permitted.[51] The best a young offender can usually now hope for is a single reprimand, followed by a single final warning, and then prosecution.[52]

---

[51] Although the present government (and its predecessor) has frequently castigated the practice of multiple cautioning, it is worth noting that this practice was relatively uncommon. Research by the Home Office (1994) found that only 8 percent of a sample of offenders who had been cautioned in 1991 had already received two or more cautions, and other evidence around the same time (Evans 1994, p. 569) suggested that the proportion of young offenders in receipt of three or more cautions was less than 4 percent. Nor was it common for young offenders to be cautioned for very serious offenses, since only 1 percent of all cautions issued in 1994 were for "indictable-only" offenses (Home Office 1995).

[52] The first national circular that disapproved of multiple cautioning (issued by the Conservative government in 1994) explicitly left open the possibility of informal warnings (on which see above). The Labour government has formally discouraged informal warnings in its new preferred progression of reprimand/final warning/prosecution. However, constitutionally the Home Secretary has no powers to direct a local police authority on matters of this kind, only to issue "guidance," and it is known that at least one of the forty-two local police forces in England and Wales is continuing to utilize informal warnings on a fairly regular basis.

Where an offender is to be issued with a final warning (box 5), the police are required to refer the case to the local youth offending team (box 6). The YOT is then expected to assess the offender's suitability for a compulsory "rehabilitation" or "change" program (boxes 5A and 5B), using the "ASSET" instrument (see n. 45). Consistently with the policy of early intervention strongly embodied in the new youth justice system, the aim of the "change program" is to confront and address the offender's behavior. Moreover, the clear expectation in the official Home Office guidance that accompanied the national implementation of the new youth justice system was that virtually all offenders in receipt of a final warning would be expected to participate in a change program of this sort (Home Office 2000a).

One important aspect of the post-1998 youth justice system that appears to have been overlooked by many commentators relates to a significant change in the pretrial decision-making process. For at least a decade prior to the mid-1990s, the decision whether to prosecute offenders or divert them was in many parts of England shared between the police and a multiagency panel that was variously known as a "cautioning panel" or "juvenile liaison bureau."[53] These panels exercised a very important gatekeeping function with respect to decisions to prosecute or divert from prosecution, and they have been credited, in part, with contributing to the very rapid growth of cautioning in England and Wales from 1980 onward that is illustrated in table 1. Doubts were cast, however, on the continued viability of this system by the 1994 guidance circular discouraging multiple cautioning. When the Labour government set up its new youth justice system, including the multiagency YOTs with their diverse memberships and responsibilities, it might have been expected that among the tasks of the YOTs would be the offering of preprosecution advice to the police, along the lines of the old-style multiagency cautioning panels. Conspicuously, however, this is explicitly not among the functions of the new YOTs, presumably largely because of the association of the old cautioning panels with the "culture of excuses" and the "minimum intervention" philosophy that the government is so keen to extirpate (though the potential for delays in making a referral to a multiagency body will also not have

[53] Such panels usually comprised nominated police officers and representatives from the local authority social services department, but often also included representatives from probation, education, and youth services. Technically, the decision at the end of the panel meeting was that of the police, but in practice it was normally a collective decision.

escaped attention in a government very keen to shorten processing times). Instead, responsibility for the initial "prosecution/diversion" decision has been allocated exclusively to the police—although, as we have noted, their powers of discretionary diversion have also been curtailed by the new "two-strikes-only" approach that is embodied in the system of reprimands and final warnings.

If the police decide to prosecute an offender, the case is then referred to the Crown Prosecution Service (CPS; box 7), which has the final say over whether a prosecution proceeds to court or is discontinued (box 8; discontinuations may occur either because the available evidence is not considered sufficiently strong or because the CPS considers for some reason that it is not in the public interest to pursue the prosecution).[54] If it is decided not to prosecute on public interest grounds, the CPS may refer the case back to the police with a recommendation that they reprimand or warn the offender, although in practice such references back appear to be rare. If, on the other hand, the CPS decides to prosecute, the case then normally proceeds to the Youth Court (box 10), which is a specialized and somewhat modified division of the so-called magistrates' court. To explain more fully, in England there are two tiers of criminal courts. The lower tier comprises magistrates' courts, which are normally presided over by a group of three lay (non-legally qualified) members of the community known as "magistrates" or "justices of the peace" (the two terms are interchangeable). The upper tier of the criminal court system is provided by the so-called Crown Court, which is presided over by a professional judge. Offenders who are under the age of eighteen are normally tried and sentenced in the Youth Court (see n. 11), but a small proportion may exceptionally be tried and sentenced in the Crown Court (box 11).

Lay magistrates are ordinary members of the public, selected by a government minister to act as a magistrate on a part-time basis. Youth Court magistrates are (except in London) not directly appointed to that court; rather, they are initially appointed simply as local magistrates, sitting in the adult magistrates' court. Then, each year, some magistrates in each area are selected by their peers to form the Youth

[54] The Crown Prosecution Service in England has a more restricted role than that of public prosecution agencies in many countries. At present it acquires responsibility for a case only when the police have recommended the case for prosecution, and it therefore has no jurisdiction or oversight over earlier stages of the process, including police decisions to reprimand or issue a final warning. There are currently legislative proposals to alter the relationship between the police and the CPS, but they will probably have only a limited impact on youth justice cases.

Court Panel, eligibility for which is nominally confined to those who are felt to be "specially qualified" for dealing with young offenders (Children and Young Persons Act 1933). However, as one commentator pointed out when this system was first introduced seventy years ago, "the degree to which special qualifications are in fact obtainable depends on the extent to which they are to be found among the local justices" (Elkin 1938, pp. 66–67). As with Scottish children's hearings, the trio of Youth Court magistrates in any given case must include members of both sexes.

The Youth Court (and the juvenile court before it) has, since its inception, differed from the adult magistrates' court in the extent to which it is open and accessible to those not directly involved in the case. Thus, no one is allowed to be present unless specifically authorized by the court, except for the members and officers of the court, parties to the case (including parents or guardians), their legal representatives, witnesses, and bona fide representatives of the media. Although the proceedings may be reported in the press, the identity of the young defendants may not normally be disclosed, with the result that such cases are generally given a fairly low profile in the media. These restrictive attributes prompted the former home secretary, Jack Straw (in a speech to the Labour Party conference, Oct. 2, 1997), to describe the Youth Court, rather unflatteringly, as a "secret garden." These restrictions apart, proceedings in the Youth Court have traditionally been modeled on those to be found in adult courts, with all that that entails by way of formality, scope for delay, and lack of a formal role for the victim; the physical layout of the court, while often less formal than that of an adult magistrates' court, is usually significantly more formal than the roundtable discussion format of a Scottish children's hearing. There is a right to legal representation in Youth Court proceedings, and (except in minor cases) this will normally be paid for by the publicly funded system of criminal legal aid. The proportion of young defendants who received legal representation paid for by the criminal legal aid system rose from 3 percent in 1969 to 40 percent in 1984 (Allen 1991) and is almost certainly much higher now, though strangely no national statistics are available on this point. The formality and the extent of legal representation in the Youth Court do tend to restrict constructive dialogue between magistrates and the defendant and his or her parents. The present government has commissioned research and introduced measures that are intended to alter many of these traditional characteristics of the Youth Court.

However, the government's reforming zeal to change the settings in which criminal justice is administered extends beyond the Youth Court itself and has resulted in the insertion of a radically new forum for dealing with certain young offenders, namely, those who are prosecuted before the Youth Court for the first time, who plead guilty on that occasion, and who in the opinion of the court should not receive either a custodial sentence or an absolute discharge (both of which disposals are rare for first-time defendants). In such circumstances the Youth Court is now (from April 2002)[55] normally mandatorily required[56] to deal with the case by passing a sentence known as a "referral order" (box 12). This order requires the young offender to attend a meeting of another newly created body known as the "youth offender panel" or "YOP" (box 13). The YOP is convened by the local youth offending team (YOT), which also supplies one member of the three-person YOP panel, the other two being laypersons drawn from an approved list. In addition to the offender and his or her parents, any victim of the offense is also invited (but not obliged) to attend the panel meeting; but, controversially, although the offender may be accompanied by an adult "friend," publicly funded legal aid is not available to defendants in YOP proceedings (see further discussion in Sec. VI). The purpose of the panel meeting is to conclude a contractual agreement (box 14) known as a "program of behavior," the principal aim of which must be the prevention of reoffending. The duration of the program of behavior will have been fixed by the Youth Court at the time of making the referral order: it can be from three to twelve months, and the expectation is that the length will be proportionate to the seriousness of the offense(s). If no agreement can be reached in the YOP on a program of behavior, or if a contract is made but subsequently breached, the young offender will be returned to court to be sentenced for the original offense. If an agreement is reached, however, the YOP is responsible for monitoring it and, provided the offender complies with it, the referral order is then discharged. Before leaving the referral order, however, we should draw attention to one very unusual feature that it embodies: the referral order is a sentence, but, uniquely in En-

---

[55] This new measure was not—like most of the youth justice reforms—contained in the Crime and Disorder Act 1998, but in the later Youth Justice and Criminal Evidence Act 1999. Like the earlier reforms, the referral order provisions were piloted in a small number of local areas before national implementation in April 2002.

[56] The making of a referral order is compulsory where the young offender pleads guilty to all offenses charged. If he or she pleads guilty to some and not guilty to other charges, the Youth Court may at its discretion make a referral order.

glish law, it is a sentence that is available only to defendants who plead guilty. This unique feature opens up the tactical possibility of avoiding the referral order by deliberately pleading not guilty, and there have been some anecdotal accounts—not yet substantiated by research—of maneuvers of this kind being deployed in some cases.[57]

For offenders who are prosecuted and sentenced in the normal way, the range of disposals available to the Youth Court was, even before 1998, already wide in comparison with the measures available to the Scottish children's hearings; and, as we will now describe, it has been significantly extended by the recent youth justice reforms. Available lower-level disposals include the fine and compensation orders (box 16)—both of which may be imposed either on young offenders themselves or their parents—and the various kinds of discharge. Prior to 1998 the conditional discharge was a very popular way of dealing with young offenders, particularly where the offense was not a very serious one. However, this measure was tainted in the eyes of the new Labour government by its association with the so-called excuse culture. Accordingly, the Crime and Disorder Act 1998 provided that, where a young person is sentenced within two years of receiving a final warning, the conditional discharge is not available as a sentence unless there are "exceptional circumstances" relating either to the offender or the offense; the Youth Courts' use of the conditional discharge has subsequently dropped sharply (see table 2).

In place of this measure the government has introduced a new "entry-level" disposal for less serious offenses, known as the reparation order (box 17). Such orders require young offenders to make reparation either to the victim of the offense (provided the victim consents) or to the community at large (e.g., by doing unpaid work), and courts are required to give reasons for not imposing such an order where they have the power to do so. Reparation orders are intended to help young offenders understand and face up to the consequences of their actions (in accordance with the "responsibilization" ethos outlined earlier) and to offer some practical recompense to victims. The reparation that is imposed must be proportionate to the seriousness of the offense and may not exceed twenty-four hours in total. The YOTs have an impor-

---

[57] There seem to be two main reasons why defendants might employ a tactic of this kind: first, because publicly funded legal representation is available at the Youth Court but not at the YOP proceedings, and second, because of fears that the package of activities constructed under the program of behavior might be disproportionate to the seriousness of the current offense(s). We discuss both of these issues in later subsections.

tant part to play with regard to reparation orders—they are responsible for identifying offenders for whom such an order might be suitable; communicating with victims; preparing reports for the Youth Court to offer advice on what kind of reparation might be appropriate; and, if an order is made, supervising the implementation of the required reparation.

Slightly higher up the tariff come what are known in law as "community sentences" (box 18).[58] A new community sentence for juveniles was introduced by the 1998 act, namely, the "action plan order," which is designed to provide a short but intensive and individually tailored intervention in a young offender's life, focused on addressing the factors that might have been responsible for the offense. The order requires the offender to comply with the requirements of a three-month action plan, which may also include reparation to the victim (provided the latter consents) or the community, if that is considered appropriate. As with the reparation order, YOTs are also involved in advising the Youth Court about the possible content of the action plan order, coordinating arrangements and supervising the young offender while on the order.

Most of the community sentences that are currently available to the Youth Courts are, however, not new; they include the supervision order, the probation order, the community service order, the combination order (community service order plus supervision), the attendance center order,[59] and the curfew order (curfew plus electronic tagging).[60] Among these we wish to make particular mention of supervision orders, since they are quite similar to action plan orders except that they last longer; their length can be anything between three months and three years. In terms of their effect, they require young offenders be-

[58] Since the Criminal Justice Act of 1991, sentencing disposals for both adult and young offenders in England have been ranked according to their severity into three principal bands: custodial penalties; "community sentences"; and other sentences, including fines, warning penalties, and, now, reparation. Courts are required to ensure that the sentence that is imposed is appropriate (proportionate) to the seriousness of the offense according to statutory "threshold criteria" (see Cavadino and Dignan [2002] for further details).

[59] "Attendance centre orders" require a young offender to attend at a center run by police officers, where he or she will engage in various activities such as sports and craft work and attend talks on matters such as drug and alcohol abuse. The length of the order varies by age but is normally not less than twelve hours, with a maximum of thirty-six. Attendance is for short periods, normally on Saturdays.

[60] We are using pre-2000 legislative language in this sentence, and in table 8. Several names were changed by an act of Parliament in 2000, but are likely soon to change again, so we have omitted the complexities. In addition to the community sentences listed here, the 1998 act created a new "drug treatment and testing order."

tween the ages of ten and seventeen to be supervised by a YOT member (formerly a social worker or probation officer), with whom they are expected to meet at regular intervals. Offenders under supervision may also be required to undertake certain "specified activities" to help them address their offending behavior. Given the existence of this order, it might be thought strange that the action plan order was added to the armory of the Youth Court in the 1998 reforms, but the government was anxious to provide what it saw as a new and more focused short-duration intervention for those who were not too far advanced in their criminal careers.[61]

Some have noted that a consequence of this total set of reforms is that a young offender could easily receive, in succession, a "change" package attached to a final warning, a program of behavior under a referral order contract, and (by which stage the offender has reached the Youth Court for final disposal) either a reparation order (that could well include, inter alia, a "victim awareness" component) or an action plan order. Critics fear that these various packages might well seem indistinguishable to young offenders and thus be of diminishing effect, and possibly also to Youth Court sentencers, who might conceivably be reluctant to continue administering "more of the same" to offenders who are perceived to have been given too many bites at the cherry. Since referral orders were only introduced nationally in April 2002, it is at present unclear whether there is any justification for such foreboding.

Although the supervision order has been available for many years, its discretionary "specified activity" provision has been associated with two recent attempts to strengthen its bite. First, supervision orders can now include a requirement to make reparation either to the victim of the offense or the community at large. Second, and more important, since the autumn of 2001 new community-based Intensive Supervision and Surveillance Programmes (ISSPs) have been introduced, which can be attached to supervision orders.[62] They are intended to be targeted on persistent offenders who have been charged or warned at least four times within a twelve-month period and who have previously been

---

[61] The Youth Justice Board for England and Wales (2002) has recently called for action plan orders to be extended to up to twelve months, which would further erode the distinction between these two penalties. See also n. 63 below.

[62] They may also be attached to probation orders or bail supervision packages, and, in addition, they may also form part of the postcustodial supervision arrangements for those given detention and training orders (on which see later discussion).

subject to a custodial sentence or community order. The ISSPs involve intensive monitoring of the young offender's movements and whereabouts by means such as electronic monitoring and telephone monitoring using voice verification technology. They also include highly structured, individually tailored packages of measures that are intended to address the young person's offending behavior (e.g., training and education programs lasting up to five hours per day), and they are also intended to encourage the performance of reparation (Home Office 2001*a*). These programs are the subject of a research evaluation, although the final report is not due until March 2004.[63]

So far the orders we have been considering are all targeted on the young offenders themselves.[64] Among the new measures introduced by the Crime and Disorder Act, however, was a power for the courts to impose a "parenting order" (box 15) on the parents (or guardians) of children who commit offenses or behave antisocially. Parenting orders may consist of two elements. The first requires parents to attend counseling or guidance sessions, which can last for up to three months. The second may require parents (or guardians) to exercise a measure of control over their child (e.g., by ensuring that the child attends school or avoids certain people or places) for a period of up to twelve months. Failure to comply with the order (which is supervised by YOT workers) constitutes a criminal offense that is punishable with a fine of up to £1,000. The order was inspired by the connection that has been well established in criminological research studies (see, e.g., Farrington 1997) between poor parenting skills and the development of criminal careers, and it is another clear example of the "responsibilization" ethos we referred to earlier. (For the sake of completeness, we should also make brief reference at this point to a number of other ancillary measures that can be imposed by the court, including parental "bindovers" or sureties, and also compensation payments; box 15.)

With regard to custodial options (box 19), previous restrictions on

[63] The Youth Justice Board has called for the ISSP approach to be made available to the courts in a separate statutory order that would last for up to twelve months instead of the present six-month maximum. The board hopes that the courts would be more likely to use such sentences as an alternative to short custodial sentences, which the board believes are ineffective. The government indicated in a white paper (Home Office 2002*b*, para. 5.53) that it intended to make such programs available as part of an extended action plan order (see n. 61 above), the maximum duration of which would be increased from three to twelve months.

[64] See Cavadino and Dignan (2002, chap. 9) for details of the other community orders, including the curfew order, attendance center order, and drug treatment and testing order.

the availability of custody for young offenders aged twelve and under fifteen have been deliberately relaxed as part of the package of reforms in the "new youth justice," and yet another new sentencing disposal has also been introduced. Under the new arrangements, young people under eighteen cannot be sentenced to adult imprisonment, but, from the age of twelve upward, they may in certain circumstances be given a "detention and training order" (DTO) for a period of between four and twenty-four months.[65] The first half of a DTO is served in custody, while the second half is served under supervision in the community. The aim of these new custodial arrangements is to create what is described as a "seamless sentence" (enabling the young offender to move "seamlessly" from custody to the community). The focus is intended to be on clear "sentence planning," to ensure that the time in custody is spent constructively, and is then followed up by effective supervision and support on release. The detention and training order is apparently relatively inflexible with regard to length, however, since it may be imposed only for specified periods of four, six, eight, ten, twelve, eighteen, or twenty-four months.[66] Moreover, the scope for early release is also limited, since the release date can either be brought forward or put back (depending on progress made against the objectives specified in the "training plan") for a period of up to two months, but only in respect to orders of eight months or longer.

The DTO replaces two former custodial measures: the "secure training order" (available for offenders aged twelve to fourteen) and "detention in a young offender institution" (available for offenders aged fifteen to seventeen).[67] The secure training order was introduced by the Criminal Justice and Public Order Act 1994 and was intended to close a supposed gap in the law concerning offenders who were below the normal age for custodial sentences (which was then fifteen) and whose offenses were not sufficiently serious for them to be sentenced to long-term detention (see below). However, whereas the secure

---

[65] The legislation also provides for detention and training orders to be available for "persistent" young offenders as young as ten or eleven, but this provision is not currently in force. For offenders ages twelve to fourteen, this sentence can also only be imposed on those considered to be "persistent offenders." See further below.

[66] However, the court of appeal has reduced this apparent inflexibility by ruling that it applies only to a sentence for a single offense; where an offender is convicted for two or more offenses, consecutive periods can be imposed that total to numbers of months other than those prescribed in the statute.

[67] Detention in a young offender institution is, at the time of writing, still available as a sentence for offenders age eighteen and under twenty-one, though it is likely soon to be brought within the ambit of adult imprisonment.

training order could only be imposed where the young offender satisfied certain restrictive statutory criteria relating to persistence, the DTO may be imposed on any young offender under the age of fifteen where the court is "of the opinion that he is a persistent offender" (Powers of Criminal Courts [Sentencing] Act 2000, sec. 100[2]; see generally Ball, McCormac, and Stone 2001, chap. 28), and in practice the courts (including the court of appeal) have interpreted this provision very broadly.[68]

Finally, we turn to the arrangements for the sentencing of young offenders whose cases are, exceptionally, dealt with in the Crown Court instead of the Youth Court (box 11). In addition to all the sentencing powers available to the Youth Court, the Crown Court also has additional powers relating to custodial sentences. If the offense for which the young person is convicted is one of murder, the appropriate measure is a mandatory indeterminate sentence of long-term detention (Powers of Criminal Courts [Sentencing] Act 2000, sec. 90). For other serious offenses, the maximum penalty that the court may impose on a young person is the same period of determinate custody that would apply in the case of an adult offender (Powers of Criminal Courts [Sentencing] Act 2000, sec. 91). This sentence is known as "long-term detention" to distinguish it from the detention and training order (see box 20).

Young offenders who are held in custody (whether on remand or after sentencing, and whether sentenced to a DTO or to long-term detention), are held in a variety of facilities that are collectively known as the "juvenile secure estate." It is a statutory duty of the Youth Justice Board to commission places in these facilities from the relevant managing authorities, and subsequently to allocate individual young offenders to a particular institution. There are three types of juvenile secure facilities, each of which has different historical antecedents and different managing authorities. The most numerous are the juvenile Young Offender Institutions, managed by the Prison Service. Historically, these derive from the sentence of "detention in a young offender institution," available for offenders age fifteen plus before the 1998 reforms; they currently provide 2,870 places for boys under age eighteen in thirteen discrete units and 100 places for girls under age eighteen

---

[68] For a review of case law, see Stone (2001*b*). The most striking case is perhaps R v. Smith (2000) Crim LR 613, where an offender before the court for the first time was deemed by the court of appeal to be a "persistent offender" because he had committed a spate of offenses in a two-day period.

in four units that are located within adult prisons. A second type of facility consists of local authority secure units, which are operated by local authority social service departments and provide places for 316 boys and girls in twenty-eight such units. They trace their origins to an earlier and more welfare-orientated phase in English juvenile justice history, and they house not only young offenders but also some young people in need of care and protection who require secure accommodation in their own best interests. The third type of institution comprises a small number of secure training centers that are operated by the private sector. They provide places for 130 boys and girls in three separate units and owe their origins to the "secure training order," introduced in 1994 but now abolished. In deliberately merging these types of facilities within a single "juvenile secure estate," and the single sentence of the "detention and training order," the government attempted to simplify and unify the law and policy relating to juvenile custody. However, in significant ways the historical antecedents of the three kinds of facilities continue to exercise an important (and somewhat inflexible) set of constraints, not least because the managerial arrangements are so different in the three kinds of facilities.

B. A Preliminary Assessment of the New Youth Justice Reforms in Operation

In spite of their very recent introduction, most of the new youth justice reforms have been piloted—in keeping with the government's ostensible commitment to an "evidence-led approach" to its reform program[69]—and some preliminary research findings from these pilots are now available (see, e.g., Hine and Celnick 2001; Holdaway et al. 2001; Newburn et al. 2001*a*, 2001*b*, 2002; Shapland et al. 2001). These provide the first—albeit highly tentative—indications of the possible impact of the reforms once they have been "rolled out" nationally.[70] Us-

---

[69] The government originally signaled its intention to evaluate the research evidence from the 1998 Crime and Disorder Act pilot before ordering the national policy implementation. This would have enabled lessons to be learned, and possible modifications made, in the light of the experience gained. However, this sequence of events did not materialize, presumably because of political imperatives.

[70] The YOT-related reforms that were introduced by the Crime and Disorder Act 1998 were implemented on a nationwide basis in June 2000, following an eighteen-month pilot period. The second wave of reforms (relating to the introduction of referral orders and youth offender panels) began with the enactment of the Youth Justice and Criminal Evidence Act 1999; an eighteen-month piloting phase then began in March 2000, and national roll-out commenced in April 2002. On the piloting of so-called statutory time limits, see n. 87 below.

ing these and other preliminary sources—including national statistical data for 2000 and 2001—we comment briefly on a number of aspects of the new youth justice system in practice, while emphasizing that the reforms are still too recent for definitive assessment.

1. *Organizational Changes.*   The two principal organizational changes in the new youth justice system are the creation of the YOTs and the advent for the first time of a national supervisory agency, the Youth Justice Board. It is fair to say that, between them, these new bodies have dramatically reconfigured the landscape of English youth justice. To begin with the YOTs, there are now 154 such multiagency teams in existence, though the process of establishing these teams and implementing the various new measures under the Crime and Disorder Act has been far from straightforward, with many implementational problems experienced in the early days of the YOT pilots. The research into the pilot area YOTs showed that, in terms of their composition, the field of recruitment into the YOTs did clearly conform to a multi-agency pattern (Holdaway et al. 2001, pp. 57–59). Social services staff comprised under half (43 percent) of the YOT staff membership (compared with around 80 percent in the SSD-led "youth justice teams" of pre-YOT days), with significant representation also from probation (14 percent), the police (11 percent), education (7 percent), and health (5 percent). Moreover, just under one in five YOT staff appeared to have been recruited from agencies and positions that have not traditionally been associated with youth justice work. This broader occupational composition may provide an early indication of the potential for the reforms to achieve at least a degree of cultural change on the part of youth justice workers.

However, the evaluation study of the pilot areas (Holdaway et al. 2001) highlighted a number of developmental problems relating to YOTs. In the first place, it is important to emphasize that many (though not all) members of youth offending teams are seconded from other agencies to work within the YOTs. These staff members retain their employment status with their parent agency, which means that those working within the YOTs have very disparate pay scales and conditions of service. Second, research in the pilot areas suggested that not all partner agencies were equally committed to the new multi-agency approach, and problems were experienced within the pilot YOTs with regard to securing staffing and financial commitments from health and education departments in particular. Funding for YOTs has also proved to be a highly contentious issue, and progress toward the introduction of "pooled budgets" (described by Holdaway et al. as a "litmus test of multi-agency co-operation" [2001, p. 55]) has been patchy and slow. Parochialism on the part of contributing agencies has by no means been eliminated and appears at present to pose limits on the extent to which YOTs might be capable of influencing the routine work and approaches of partner agencies, notwithstanding their own multiagency status. Very possibly this will improve with time, though the Youth Justice Board has recently indicated that "there are still some clear lessons that need to be heeded by all partners" (Youth Justice Board for England and Wales 2002, p. 2).

Although YOT staff in the pilot areas appeared to approve of the idea of multiagency working and were generally enthusiastic about the impact of the new (1998) legislation, there were also clear signs of cultural resistance toward at least some aspects of the "new youth justice." Thus, in the second staff survey undertaken as part of the pilot evaluation, over half (61 percent) of YOT workers believed that the 1998 act contained contradictions, and fewer than half (only 44 percent) approved of the "single reprimand," suggesting that the noninterventionist ethos that was associated with the old juvenile justice movement might still be prevalent among YOT staff,[71] though again this might alter as the YOTs become better established. Another significant finding is that a significant proportion of YOT staff (45 percent) felt that too little attention is paid to young offenders' welfare needs.

Another interesting finding of the pilot research, this time from the YOT staff "activity analysis" that was undertaken as part of the pilot evaluation, was that only 12 percent of YOT staff time was devoted entirely to the "new" crime and disorder work, the rest being spent on more traditional work in preparing reports, servicing the Youth Court, and working with offenders on supervision orders. Of course this traditional work will itself have altered in significant respects—for example, preparing reports and servicing the Youth Court necessarily requires YOT members to take account of the new context. But the finding does emphasize the fact that although much of the English youth justice system has indeed radically changed since 1998, in terms of day-to-day "on the ground" routine activities, there is also a significant degree of continuity.

---

[71] There were also clear signs of resistance, on the part of some YOT workers at least, with regard to the idea of working with victims, which suggests that not all are wedded to the "restorative justice" elements in the new legislation (see Sec. VII).

As for the Youth Justice Board, this has swiftly established itself as a key player within the youth justice arena, alongside the more established criminal justice agencies, or "fiefdoms" as Shapland (1988) has perceptively referred to them. As such, it has been charged with responsibility for promoting and pursuing the government's youth justice reform agenda in the direction that has been set out in the legislation and policy documents to which we have already referred. It is too soon to pass judgment on how successful the Youth Justice Board is likely to be in attaining its ambitious program.[72] At this stage we confine ourselves to three preliminary observations.

The first is that the creation of such a powerful new agency, with its own very clearly mapped out agenda and set of priorities, gave rise to an awkward transitional phase during the period in which responsibility for formulating (and also evaluating) youth justice policy was being transferred from the Juvenile Offenders' Unit at the Home Office to the new body. Whereas the piloting program concerning the 1998 Crime and Disorder Act reforms and their evaluation had been established under the "old regime," the Youth Justice Board quickly established (and funded) its own "pathway YOTs," whose work was unrelated to that in the pilot areas. This occurred partway through the original piloting process, and without waiting for the outcome of the independent evaluation of the Home Office's selected pilot areas. To some extent, the creation of a group of separate pathway sites, with the aim of formulating and disseminating good practice lessons for others, was seen by the original pilot YOTs as a wasteful duplication of effort and resources, and was felt (with some justification) to have diminished their own profile as pilots (Holdaway et al. 2001, p. 48). It also, inevitably, focused attention away from the lessons that could be learned from the independently evaluated piloting exercise and, to that extent at least, was somewhat at odds with the government's repeatedly stated commitment to an "evidence-led" approach.

The second observation is that the creation of a powerful new agency has—perhaps predictably—resulted in a degree of "competitive jousting" between the newly created Youth Justice Board and some of the longer-established criminal justice "fiefdoms" with regard both to the "terrain" over which they each claim control and also their

---

[72] The breadth and scale of this agenda are set out in the Youth Justice Board's own Corporate and Business Plan, together with a set of targets and an assessment by the board of the main risks to the attainment of its core objectives (Youth Justice Board for England and Wales 2001a; see also Youth Justice Board for England and Wales 2002).

formal processes of cooperation. As examples of this element of competitive jousting we would cite the Youth Justice Board's success in wresting away from the prison service control over a significant part of the juvenile secure estate, to which we have already referred, and also its (so far unsuccessful) bid to extend its sphere of responsibility to encompass the custodial arrangements relating to young adult offenders (between eighteen and twenty-one years of age).[73] A further example concerns relations between the Youth Justice Board and the recently revived national Correctional Services Strategy Board, which will bring together representatives from the prison service and the National Probation Directorate as well as the Youth Justice Board itself. The strategy board is one of a number of recent initiatives designed by the government to secure improved coordination with regard to the aims and activities of key criminal justice agencies, on this occasion in the correctional sphere. However, while the Youth Justice Board is keen to participate in this national strategy forum, it has been much more reluctant to join forces with the prison and probation services in the key area of the accreditation of effective treatment programs. In this sphere, the YJB has decided not to participate in the recently revamped joint Correctional Services Accreditation Panel, preferring instead to undertake its own accreditation processes. The YJB has justified its stance in this respect on substantive grounds, but others have interpreted the move in more overtly political "competitive jousting" terms.

Our third and final observation relates to the role of the Youth Justice Board within the overall youth justice planning process and also, indirectly, to its accountability. As we have seen, the YJB is responsible for monitoring the activities of youth offending teams,[74] though it also has the power to promote and fund additional initiatives. One well-publicized example of the board's willingness to exercise this latter power

[73] This is an unusual bid, and one that has caused considerable controversy. Those opposed to the bid point out that the Youth Justice Board has no other responsibilities with regard to offenders age eighteen-plus; hence, they argue that this is a clear case of the board straying outside its terms of reference. The board, by contrast, points to the improvements its commissioning regime has brought about in juvenile young offenders institutions (see Sec. VI) and argues that it could achieve similar improvements for eighteen- to twenty-one-year-olds if granted a similar role in respect to them.

[74] Rather unusually within the criminal justice system, until very recently YOTs were not liable to any other form of inspection, though it had originally been suggested that they should be (Leng, Taylor, and Wasik 1998). However, in December 2002 it was announced by the government that henceforth YOTs were to be subject to inspection by joint teams representing several inspectorates (social services, probation, police, education, etc.).

relates to its funding of and support for a series of so-called Youth Inclusion Programmes (YIPs), which are intended to steer young people away from a life of crime.[75] These programs are initially funded (and largely controlled) by the YJB, which proclaimed (in a press release dated October 21, 2002) that "Youth Inclusion Programmes remain at the heart of our prevention strategy," even though there were only seventy such programs in existence at the time, and despite the fact that statutory responsibility for coordinating the provision of youth justice services locally had initially been firmly vested in local YOTs. Although there are some promising initial research findings relating to YIPs, the YJB's strong financial and political support for such discrete, separately funded, short-term local initiatives, catapulted into the sphere of mainstream youth justice programs, raises important questions about the political and policy accountability of the Youth Justice Board, particularly in view of its somewhat free-floating status as a nongovernmental public body.[76]

2. *Pretrial Processes, Especially Final Warnings.*   At the time of writing, it is too soon to be able to make any definitive assessment of the new pretrial processes, including notably the new and more structured system of reprimands and final warnings. At the level of overall national statistics, it is important to note, however, that the cautioning rate was already in decline during the period leading up to the implementation of the new system, as table 1 shows. Early indications from the first data that are available following the national implementation of the new system in June 2000 suggest that this decline is set to continue. Thus, counting reprimands and final warnings together, the "cautioning" or "diversion" rate continued its steady decline of recent years for both male and female juveniles. In the case of males ages twelve to fourteen, for example, the rate fell from 74 percent in 1997 (the year when the new Labour government was elected) to 66 percent in 2001 (table 1). Despite this decline, however, it is important to em-

---

[75] The board has also established a variety of other crime prevention initiatives, including "splash" schemes to provide activities for young people during school holidays and "positive futures" programs that are designed to use sport to divert young people from crime.

[76] On the question of accountability, it should also be noted that the Youth Justice Board has now taken over from the Home Office the responsibility for commissioning and publishing governmental research into the functioning of the youth justice system. However, in the view of some observers, including ourselves, the board's presentation of research findings is inclined to be partisan rather than dispassionate; we give some examples of this tendency in later subsections.

phasize that these police-based disposals continue to play a very large role in the reformed English youth justice system: for all age/gender groups except males ages fifteen to seventeen, more than half of all identified offenders are still dealt with by way of reprimand or final warning (table 1).

The proportion of diverted young offenders who received reprimands (68–70 percent) as opposed to final warnings (30–32 percent) in the first nineteen months of national implementation of the new youth justice system (June 2000–December 2001) is broadly in line with the findings of the pilot evaluation, which recorded proportions of 75 percent and 25 percent, respectively (Holdaway et al. 2001). As was to be expected, however, the ratio of reprimands to warnings is higher among younger defendants, who typically commit less serious crimes, and among whom there is a higher proportion of first offenders (Home Office 2002a, p. 31).

A more surprising finding from the pilot evaluation research showed that the proportion of offenders in receipt of a final warning who were recommended as being suitable for a change program (43 percent) was much lower than might have been expected in view of the official guidance emanating from the Home Office. In many cases in which a change program was recorded as being inappropriate, this was because of a belief that there was little risk of reoffending, and therefore no need for further intervention.[77] Once again, this suggests that the ethos of active prevention and early intervention that has imbued much of the recent youth justice legislation may not have resonated so positively among YOT workers themselves, many of whom might have been more used to working within a "minimum intervention" philosophical context. The proportion of final warnings supported by intervention programs has, however, been rising: it was slightly higher (52 percent) immediately after national implementation and has now increased still further, to 70 percent in 2001 (Youth Justice Board for

---

[77] There is some empirical evidence to support the view that the risk of reoffending is not especially high among those likely to receive final warnings. National data for persons of all ages given a caution in 1994 and having no previous convictions and one previous caution show a subsequent two-year conviction rate of 30 percent (Home Office 2001b, p. 108). (Most but not all juveniles receiving final warnings will have received a previous reprimand, so these data are—excepting the age factor—approximately equivalent.) Hine and Celnick's (2001) research, discussed later, showed a 30 percent one-year conviction rate for a sample of young offenders receiving final warnings in the pilot areas.

England and Wales 2002, p. 5).[78] But the issue is not simply one of numbers. Doubts were raised by the researchers in the pilot evaluation about the extent to which the activities undertaken within change programs would effectively address the offender's behavior, since many of these activities seemed "tokenistic." (As an example, YOTs sometimes simply required offenders to write a letter about their impression of the effect their offense might have had on a victim, even though in many cases the letter was not sent to the victim.) How far this also will change as the system becomes more established remains to be seen; on the face of it, however, the Youth Justice Board's recent linking of intervention numbers to funding (see n. 78) seems likely to encourage rather than discourage tokenism.

Research into the pre-1998 juvenile cautioning system produced, consistently over many years, evidence of two rather disturbing features of precourt practice. They were, first, that the cautioning rate varied quite markedly in different police force areas, in ways that could not be accounted for by different youth crime profiles, and therefore reflected divergent policy or practice among police forces; and, second, that the formal preconditions of a caution (which include an admission of guilt and evidence sufficient to support a prosecution if the case were taken to court) were not always met in practice (see, e.g., Evans and Wilkinson 1990; McConville, Sanders, and Leng 1991; Evans and Ellis 1997). Preliminary evidence suggests that both of these features might have been carried over into the new reprimands/final warning system. In 2001, for example, for indictable offenses the "diversion" (or "cautioning"; see table 1) rate for twelve- to fourteen-year-old males varied from a high of 85 percent diverted in Northamptonshire to a low of 50 percent in Merseyside (Home Office 2002a, p. 40), a degree of variation that is unlikely to be attributable to different underlying crime/offender profiles. Recent research for the Youth Justice Board by Holdaway (2002) also uncovered several cases of final warnings where the legal preconditions for such a warning had seemingly not been met.

Holdaway's (2002) important research contributes to our understanding of final warnings in at least four ways. First, before deciding upon a warning, police services must carry out a formal assessment of the seriousness of the offense and any previous offending (using a pre-

---

[78] The Youth Justice Board has set a target of 80 percent of all final warnings to be accompanied by intervention programs by 2003, and funding is to be withheld from YOTs that fail to meet the target.

scribed "gravity assessment instrument" that produces simple scores from 1 to 4). Home Office guidance indicates that only those who score 3 should be formally warned, others being reprimanded (those with scores of 1 or 2) or recommended for prosecution (score 4). In Holdaway's research, 20 percent of final warnings were outside these guidelines (6 percent had scores of 1 or 2; 14 percent scored 4).

Second, the intervention programs delivered under a final warning have a curious legal status. Unlike the pre-1998 "caution plus" packages, they are not purely voluntary; but, unlike formal "conditional diversion" schemes in many other jurisdictions, a simple failure to complete the program cannot result in prosecution.[79] The compromise position adopted for the final warning is that those constructing the intervention program have to specify in advance "citable elements" of the package; in the event of a further offense, failure to complete a citable element (but not failure in other parts of the program) may then be formally adduced in evidence in subsequent court proceedings. However, whereas the decision whether to warn (rather than reprimand or recommend for prosecution) is for the police alone, the identification of citable elements of the program is a matter for the YOT. Clearly, there is scope for considerable discretion in this regard. In Holdaway's research, two-thirds of the final warnings had no citable elements, largely because, in the researcher's assessment, "many YOT workers were uneasy about a compulsory view of the intervention programme, and equally uneasy about non-attendance being cited in a subsequent court hearing" (Holdaway 2002). Findings such as these once again suggest a degree of on-the-ground cultural resistance to the official policies being pursued in "the new youth justice."[80]

Third, Holdaway's research suggests that, as final warning practice has developed, two distinct models of working have been established in different police force areas. In the first type, the offender is warned by the police and then referred to the YOT for assessment for a "change package." In the other model, the referral to the YOT takes

[79] A "conditional cautioning" system for adults in England was recommended in an official review of the criminal courts (Auld 2001), and at the time of writing this has been included in a bill recently presented to Parliament. However, there are no plans to extend this to juveniles.

[80] Holdaway's (2002) research also demonstrated that risk factors identified in the ASSET instrument (see n. 45 above) were frequently not addressed in final warning change programs, especially in the areas of education and parenting. Interviews with YOT workers suggested a number of reasons for this, e.g., that the problem was considered too complex or entrenched to be dealt with within the limits of a short intervention program.

place before the warning is delivered, so that at the subsequent oral delivery of the warning explicit links can be made between the warning and the intervention package (including, ideally, ensuring that persons who will be delivering the intervention are present at the formal oral warning). Holdaway regards this second model as preferable, and in terms of the aims of the new English youth justice framework, that seems clearly to be the case. However, one can also understand how the first model might attract some police services by its speed and bureaucratic efficiency.

Fourth, Holdaway's research suggests that, at least in some areas, YOTs are struggling to deliver the whole range of new tasks that have been allocated to them. According to this research, where such circumstances exist there is a tendency to prioritize court and postcourt work rather than the final warning interventions.

Another important, and more statistical, piece of research into the final warning system predates Holdaway's latest findings. This study, by Jean Hine and Anne Celnick (2001), was undertaken as a follow-up to the national evaluation of the pilot YOT projects. It compared one-year court conviction rates in, first, a sample of young offenders in the pilot areas who received a final warning between February and September 1999, and, second, in a comparison group derived from a national sample of young offenders who were given cautions during 1998 (i.e., immediately prior to the introduction of the new reprimand and final warning procedures). Using a multivariate analysis on data for the comparison group, the researchers were able to calculate an expected rate of further offending for the final warning group, thus taking account of underlying differences in the composition of the two samples.[81] On this basis, the study found that the final warning sample had outcomes that were six percentage points better than expected (a 30 percent actual rate of court convictions compared with an expected rate of 36 percent), a difference that was statistically significant.

Although the authors of the study themselves concluded (Hine and Celnick 2001, p. 36) that "there is no data to suggest how much of this improvement is a result of the deterrence effect of the new procedures and how much is a consequence of the intervention work by the [pilot] youth offending team," elsewhere the report presents evidence that

---

[81] Independent variables included in the regression analysis were sex, age group (<13, 13–15, 16+), and none/some previous criminal proceedings (of any kind, including formal cautions).

supports a somewhat different—albeit rather more negative—inter-pretation. The crucial data are contained in a table (Hine and Celnick 2001, table 12) that compares the proportions of finally warned offenders who were subsequently convicted according to whether or not they were assessed as appropriate for a change program.[82] The subsequent court conviction proportions were virtually identical for those who had been assessed as appropriate for a change program (30 percent) and for those in respect of whom such a program was considered to be inappropriate (29 percent), and this lack of difference remained when the controls based on the multivariate analysis were applied. It is therefore a reasonable conclusion that, at least in the aggregate, change programs made no difference to the better-than-expected outcome for the 1999 final warning sample,[83] and that some other factor must therefore have been responsible for the measured improvement.[84] A plausible alternative explanation for this finding is that the improvement in the conviction rate could have been the result of the greater deterrent impact of the new final warning procedure (where "next time you will definitely go to court" messages are clearly delivered), compared with the less decisive old-style police cautioning system. This "deterrent" interpretation cannot be confirmed without further research, but it is consistent with some of the qualitative data in Holdaway's research, where deterrence seemed to be the principal message received by offenders and their parents during the final warning process.[85]

The Hine and Celnick study is the most statistically rigorous assess-

---

[82] Eleven percent of the final warning sample were excluded from this analysis—4 percent because of unclear data on assessment of appropriateness for a change program and 7 percent because no YOT member met the offender, hence no such assessment could take place.

[83] Two caveats are relevant: first, the data distinguished only between those assessed as appropriate/not appropriate for a change program, and there is no information on who actually received such a program (though this must have been substantially higher in the "appropriate" group), and, second, as with any aggregate evaluation, it is possible that some positive and some negative findings with regard to subgroups are masking each other.

[84] It also remains possible, of course, that the quality of final warning change programs has improved since the pilot period and that a different result on the change program question would be obtained if the Hine and Celnick research were to be replicated today. However, it should also be noted that the Youth Justice Board for England and Wales (2002) continues to place greater emphasis on the proportion of final warnings that are accompanied by change programs than on the content of those programs.

[85] Other interpretative possibilities on the results of the Hine and Celnick study include possible complications arising from the fact that the control sample was taken from an earlier year than the final warning sample. This type of issue is more fully discussed below in relation to the later study by Jennings (2003).

ment currently available on the success of the final warning scheme. It is therefore rather surprising that the Youth Justice Board's Annual Review for 2001–2002 fails to mention this research, but nevertheless claims that final warnings "have proved effective, particularly where they are associated with an intervention programme" (Youth Justice Board for England and Wales 2002, p. 5). No convincing evidence for this last assertion is provided.[86]

3. *The Youth Court.*   A prominent feature of the new youth justice reforms has been the attempt to speed up the prosecution process, particularly with regard to the time taken to deal with young recidivists. In the wake of criticisms made by the influential official report into the operation of the pre-1998 youth court system (Audit Commission 1996), the Labour Party committed itself, at the 1997 general election, to halving the average time from arrest to sentence for persistent young offenders. Following its electoral victory, the Labour government then issued national guidance and set up various local pilot projects with the aim of developing "fast-tracking" initiatives. The electoral pledge on persistent offenders was successfully achieved by the autumn of 2001, and more generally during the period 1998–2001 there has been much emphasis on speeding up youth justice processes in all types of cases, in a process known as the "Narey reforms" after the author of a key report (see Home Office 1997*b*; Narey 1997). The experience in the pilot areas was that the issue of speeding up Youth Court processes was one of the most easily understood features of the whole package of reforms, and also one that was widely endorsed and acted upon. However, the researchers also found evidence, in all the pilot areas, that, on occasion, speed "was being treated as an end in itself," which "was having the unintended consequence of jeopardising the attainment of other important objectives" (Holdaway et al. 2001, p. 25). The most serious problem in this regard concerned the issue of victim consultation.

In addition to these general fast-tracking initiatives, the Crime and Disorder Act 1998 also introduced more specific statutory time limits

---

[86] The main evidence offered (Youth Justice Board for England and Wales 2002, pp. 5, 10) is, first, that in Devon 96 percent of final warnings now have a change program, and in a fifteen-month period there was "a 22 percent reduction in recorded youth crime" in that county (but no threats to the validity of this inference are discussed), and second, that, using the ASSET instrument, there was a "measurable improvement" nationally in 80 percent of cases of final warnings with intervention programs (but reliability and validity issues with regard to the completion of ASSET forms are not discussed, nor is any control group utilized).

for young offenders, the effect of which is to prescribe maximum periods between the date of arrest and first appearance in court (known as the "initial time limit," or ITL, which is set at thirty-six days), between the date of first court appearance and first day of trial (known as the "overall time limit" or OTL, set at ninety-nine days), and between conviction and sentence (known as the "sentencing time limit" or STL, set at twenty-nine days). Each limit applies to every charge or summons separately, and the potential penalty for breaching the ITL or the OTL is the staying of the case. Like other initiatives in the English youth justice reforms, statutory time limits were initially piloted in a small number of areas.[87] The interim evaluation report on these pilots (Shapland et al. 2001) found that very few cases were in breach of the ITL or the OTL, that the STL "did not seem to be impacting on courts' or agencies' patterns of work," and that "YOTs were not very aware of the STL" (p. vii). Criminal justice agencies generally supported the national roll-out of statutory time limits for all youth cases, though the STL, which has no penalty attached to it, was seen as "toothless." However, at the time of writing (early 2003), the final report of this research, although completed, had not been published by the Home Office, and national roll-out of statutory time limits has not taken place.

Turning to the procedures of the Youth Court itself, we described this earlier as being only a slightly modified version of an adult magistrates court, and thus still continuous with the 1908 "modified criminal court" approach. As part of the ongoing youth justice reform program, however, attempts have recently been made to change the culture of the Youth Court in several important respects. For example, research was commissioned in 1998 to set up a "Demonstration Project" in two court areas, which ran from October 1998 to March 2000 (Allen, Crow, and Cavadino 2000). The aim of the project was to devise and demonstrate ways of effecting cultural changes within the court that—independently of legislative and structural changes in the youth justice system—might be used to support the new statutory provisions and also to promote greater confidence in the system. This was followed by the publication of formal guidance that was issued to all courts (Home Office and Lord Chancellor's Department 2001). Among the recommendations of the guidance document are changes in the court-

[87] Time limit pilots commenced on November 1, 1999, in six areas, with a view to national implementation in 2002, subject to the results of the pilots, which took place over an eighteen-month period.

room layout to encourage and facilitate better communication;[88] the promotion of more effective engagement between magistrates and defendants and their parents with a view to probing the reasons for offending, and encouraging plans to change the defendant's offending behavior; making the court process more open by inviting victims (and others, including members of the public) to attend;[89] and encouraging courts to consider lifting reporting restrictions by the media in appropriate cases. Thus, this guidance shows the government's continuing commitment to changing what it had earlier described as the "secret garden" culture of the Youth Court.

Attempts to alter the functioning of Youth Courts have, however, been somewhat patchy. In general, it would be true to say that relatively little attempt has been made to "bring sentencers on board" with regard either to the new multiagency YOT environment or to the new sentencing disposals and, in particular, the elements of restorative justice that some of them (e.g., the reparation order and the referral order) entail. For example, very little attention has been given to the need to provide training for magistrates on these issues, in stark contrast with the intensive and expensive training program that accompanied an earlier phase of sentencing reforms that were associated with the Criminal Justice Act 1991 (Holdaway et al. 2001). The uneven attention that has been given to the need for cultural change in the Youth Court may in turn have contributed to some of the tensions that have arisen in implementing the new youth justice measures. One obvious example relates to the potential for conflict between the "speeding up" of the processing of young offenders (see above) and the need to allow sufficient time for sensitive victim consultation. Another example was provided in 2001, with a public clash between the Youth Justice Board and the Youth Court magistrates on the question of the use of custodial disposals.

4. *Youth Offender Panels.*   As with the YOT and final warning evaluations, the findings from the various evaluation reports on youth offender panels and the associated introduction of referral orders (Newburn et al. 2001*a*, 2001*b*, 2002) show a mixture of successes and

---

[88] For example, arranging for parents to sit next to their children, and placing magistrates in the well of the court so that they are at or near the same level as defendants instead of sitting at a raised bench.

[89] For example, in cases where the nature of the offending is persistent or serious, or has affected a number of people or the local community in general, or where it is felt that alerting others to the young person's behavior would help to prevent further offending by him or her.

disappointments. On the "credit" side of the balance sheet, it appears that YOTs within the pilot areas have successfully established the institutional infrastructure for YOPs by recruiting and training sufficient numbers of community panel members.[90] Both young people and their parents also compared the panel process favorably with the Youth Court in terms of their levels of understanding of the process, their opportunities to participate, the perceived fairness of the proceedings, and their ability to comprehend the impact of the offense (Newburn et al. 2002, p. 36); the first three of these points show similarities with the findings from research into the Scottish children's hearings. Finally, Youth Courts are reported to have taken a generally positive view of the new referral orders, though the take-up across the eleven pilot sites appears to have been very uneven, with very low numbers of referral orders being made in the West London sites. (A similar pattern of uneven implementation, with particularly poor take-up in the London area, was also a feature of the 1998 sentencing changes.) However, one anxiety expressed by Youth Court magistrates concerned the "automatic" nature of the referral order system. After a final warning, any fresh offense should, according to official guidance, lead to a prosecution, and if the offender then pleads guilty (see n. 57), a referral order is (in most circumstances) mandatory for the Youth Court. But, magistrates complained, this could result in rather elaborate "behavior contracts" being constructed by YOPs for trivial offenses; these could be disproportionate to the seriousness of the offense, and perhaps not really needed in "risk of re-offending" terms (Newburn et al. 2002, p. 21). These complaints are, of course, not unfamiliar; they are the kind of apparent dysfunction that has often been seen to arise in criminal justice systems where mandatory decision-making outcomes are specified in legislation.[91]

5. *Sentencing Patterns.*   For technical reasons (relating to Home Office data coding), it was not possible for those researching the pilot

[90] Ninety-one percent of whom were white, and 69 percent of whom were female. Over two-thirds (68 percent) were over the age of forty, and exactly half were employed in professional or managerial occupations. A further 14 percent described themselves as retired or semiretired, and only 4 percent described themselves as having manual occupations (Newburn et al. 2001*b*, p. 78; see also Newburn et al. 2002, p. 9).

[91] Concerns of a similar kind had been raised during the parliamentary debates on the introduction of referral orders, focusing on a hypothetical offender jumping a red traffic light. But the government "stood firm, convinced that all young offenders on first conviction, including red light violators (whose recklessness was seen as eminently suitable for panel attention) require to be challenged about their behaviour rather than to be simply processed as defendants" (Ball, McCormac, and Stone 2001, p. 230).

areas to determine precisely the proportionate use of each of the new Crime and Disorder Act disposals relative to existing sentencing options (Holdaway et al. 2001, p. 65). However, it was possible for the researchers to determine the approximate combined "market share" for three of the new disposals (reparation orders, action plan orders, and parenting orders). This analysis showed that there were striking variations in the level of take-up for the new orders, which in three of the pilot areas fluctuated between 25 percent and as high as 50 percent of all sentences imposed on offenders within the relevant age groups, while they scarcely made any impact at all in the three London YOT areas.

Whether this geographical variation has continued since national implementation is not certain, but we do now have national data on sentencing covering the first nineteen months of the new system (June 2000–December 2001; see tables 2 and 8). This shows that the Youth Courts have, for the most part, been implementing the new system in ways intended by the government. Conditional discharges have decreased markedly, especially for younger sentenced offenders (a higher proportion of whom have no previous court appearances; table 2). By contrast, community orders (including, for this analysis, the reparation order) have increased markedly for younger offenders, and significantly in all age groups (table 2). Taken together, "market share" of the main two new orders, the reparation order and the action plan order (both "entry-level" sentences), is very large among offenders ages ten to eleven (40 percent for males), gradually decreasing as one goes up the age range, and more persistent offenders are included among those sentenced (table 8). When the data for these two orders are considered separately, reparation orders slightly outnumber action plan orders among the youngest offenders, but this is reversed for those age twelve and over. The community orders that have declined in proportionate use are the supervision order (predictably losing ground to the action plan order) and, perhaps more surprisingly, the attendance center order. The reason for the latter development seems to be that time at an attendance center can now be ordered as part of an action plan order, and the action plan is being "perceived by sentencers to occupy the same tariff niche but with greater flexibility in responding to offence and offender" (Ball, McCormac, and Stone 2001, p. 277).

The sentencing data in tables 2 and 8 are, however, in an important sense interim data only. The overall package of reforms in the new English youth justice system has been implemented in two principal stages. The second of these stages, introducing the referral order and the YOP, was not implemented nationally until April 2002. Since the referral order is a sentence of the Youth Court, mandatorily applied to large numbers of first-time defendants in that court, it is inevitable that its arrival will alter the noncustodial sentencing patterns shown in tables 2 and 8, but in exactly what ways cannot be predicted at present.

To turn finally to custodial sentencing, there was a marked increase in the proportionate use of custodial sentences for persons age fifteen plus during the 1990s, but since 1998 the rate for this age group has stabilized for males, though it shows some continuing increase for females. For offenders ages twelve to fourteen, however, the introduction of more permissive custodial sentencing powers in the Crime and Disorder Act 1998 has resulted in very sharp increases in the proportionate use of custodial sentences for both boys and girls (table 2). Overall, during the first year of the new detention and training order the number of custodial orders imposed increased by 10 percent, despite a 12 percent reduction in number of recorded offenses in the eight categories of offenses most likely to attract a custodial sentence (Youth Justice Board for England and Wales 2001b). Since the increase in the number of girls who are given custodial sentences has been higher than that for boys, by the end of March 2002, 7 percent of the juvenile population in custody was female, compared with just 3.9 percent in April 2000.

The Youth Justice Board has expressed disquiet about these trends in custodial sentencing, which it sees as making it difficult to deliver appropriate provision for juveniles in custodial institutions. In 2001 it took the unusual step of writing to all youth courts about this matter, an action that was resented by some magistrates, who saw this action as an attempted executive interference in judicial functions. In 2002, further concern was expressed by the YJB in the wake of an increase in the total juvenile custodial population following a high-profile court of appeal case on the sentencing of street robberies (including mobile phone robberies) (Youth Justice Board for England and Wales 2002, pp. 6, 15). The board has expressed particular concern about the use of short DTOs, arguing that "it is difficult to reconcile short periods in custody with the principal youth justice aim of preventing offending" (Youth Justice Board for England and Wales 2002, p. 19). The board has also drawn attention to a striking variation in custodial usage between different courts: between October 2000 and September 2001, the ratio of custodial to community sentences ranged from one to three in some parts of the country to one to twenty-six in another,

TABLE 8

Percentage of Young Offenders Convicted of Indictable Offenses Who Were Sentenced to Different Kinds of Community Order, England and Wales, 1997–2001

	Supervision or Probation Order	Attendance Center Order	Community Service or Combination Order	Reparation Order	Action Plan Order	Other	Total Community Orders
A. Males age 10–11:*							
1997	23	12	†	†	†	...	35
1998	24	11	†	(P)‡	(P)	...	34
1999	30	7	†	(P)	(P)	...	37
2000	24	8	†	12	11	...	54
2001	22	8	†	22	18	1	71
B. Persons age 12–14:							
Males:							
1997	30	19	†	†	†	...	49
1998	31	18	†	(P)	(P)	...	49
1999	30	18	†	(P)	(P)	...	48
2000	26	13	†	7	10	...	56
2001	23	9	†	14	17	2	65

Females:							
1997	25	12	†	†	†	⋯	38
1998	28	9	†	(P)	(P)	⋯	37
1999	27	10	†	(P)	(P)	⋯	38
2000	26	7	†	8	10	⋯	51
2001	21	4	†	15	20	1	60
C. Persons age 15–17:							
Males:							
1997	21	10	12	†	†	⋯	42
1998	21	9	12	(P)	(P)	⋯	43
1999	20	10	13	(P)	(P)	⋯	43
2000	17	8	13	4	5	1	47
2001	17	6	11	7	9	2	52
Females:							
1997	28	6	6	†	†	⋯	41
1998	29	5	6	(P)	(P)	⋯	41
1999	28	5	6	(P)	(P)	⋯	40
2000	24	5	7	5	6	1	48
2001	24	4	6	10	12	1	57

Source.—Annual volumes of *Criminal Statistics, England and Wales*.
Note.—See table 2 for data on the overall distribution of sentences.
* Data on females age 10–11 are omitted because of small numbers.
† Sentence not legally available.
‡ (P) indicates that sentence available only in pilot areas.

a difference that could not be accounted for by seriousness of the offenses concerned (Youth Justice Board for England and Wales 2002, p. 19; see also Bateman and Stanley 2002).

6. *Parenting Orders.*   Research into the operation of parenting programs has been undertaken by the Policy Research Bureau (Ghate and Ramella 2002), which examined thirty-four parenting projects between spring 1999 and the end of 2001.[92] The final report showed that two-thirds of parents attended the programs on a voluntary basis, while one in six was on a statutory parenting order, usually but not always in respect of a criminal offense committed by a child.[93] Attendance rates were reported to be high, and by the time they left the projects most parents were said to have reported significant positive changes in parenting skills and competencies. Despite initial hostility expressed by many of those who came via the compulsory route, only 6 percent of the "exit ratings" were negative or indifferent about whether the programs had been helpful, and over nine in ten would recommend the program to other parents in their situation. These positive attitudinal changes were not matched to anything like the same extent by their children, however; they showed only mild indications of any improvement in the way they perceived their relationships with their parents.

The study also sought to measure changes in young people's offending behavior, using both official and self-report data. Most young people in the one-year reconviction study were prolific offenders: 89 percent had been convicted during the year before their parents were referred to the program, and the average number of recorded offenses committed during this period was 4.4 per offender. During the follow-up period, 61.5 percent were reconvicted, which is a statistically significant reduction from the preprogram rate, and the average number of offenses committed was only 2.1 per offender. Although these findings have been heralded by the Youth Justice Board and the government as evidence of the parenting order's potential to reduce short-term reconviction rates, they should be interpreted with great caution, as Ghate and Ramella (2002) themselves acknowledge. The most obvious ground for caution relates to the absence of a control group, which

---

[92] Parenting orders were first evaluated as part of the national evaluation of the youth justice pilot reforms introduced by the Crime and Disorder Act (Holdaway et al. 2001, pp. 43 ff., 99 ff.). This research found that they were slow to develop and experienced variable rates of take-up; there was also a marked degree of professional resistance on the part of YOT staff to the compulsory aspects of the order itself.

[93] Parents may also be required to attend parenting classes for failure to ensure that their children attend school regularly.

makes it impossible to say whether the changes in offending rates before and after the program would have been different in the absence of a parenting program.[94] The need for caution is further underlined by the results of the self-report study, which presents a very different picture to that based on official reconviction data. When asked how many offenses they had committed in the four weeks immediately prior to their parents' first contact with the parenting program, and also in the four weeks just prior to their parents leaving the program, the average number reported was virtually identical in each case (4.04 and 4.12, respectively). Clearly, therefore, much firmer evidence is needed before we can be confident that parenting programs really have the beneficial impact on offending behavior that an uncritical reading of the preliminary evaluation findings might suggest.

7. *Evidence of Overall Effectiveness?*   Given that the primary aim of the reformed English youth justice system is the prevention of (re)offending, it is perhaps not surprising that a number of research studies to date (such as those of Hine and Celnick and the Policy Research Bureau, discussed above) have focused on the impact that recent reforms might have had on reoffending rates. It is equally unsurprising, in view of the short period of time that has elapsed since the implementation of the "new youth justice system," that such evidence as there is to date is very tentative. To conclude this section, however, we examine a study that appears (at least at first sight) to provide considerable evidence of overall success for the new system.

This research was conducted by a Home Office researcher, Debbie Jennings (2003), and it compares the one-year reconviction rates of a general cohort of young offenders dealt with in the first quarter of 2001 (by way of a reprimand, final warning, or court disposal, excluding custody)[95] with an intendedly equivalent "baseline" sample dealt with in the first half of 1997, before the new youth justice reforms were promulgated. Thus, the research design has similarities to that of Hine and Celnick (see above), but its post-1998 sample includes the full range of new youth justice disposals (except custody), unlike Hine and Celnick's study, which was restricted to final warnings.

[94] Earlier research by Bottoms (1995) with different samples of English juvenile offenders (undergoing custody, intensive community supervision, and ordinary supervision) found that all samples showed a reduction in official criminality from the twelve months before a court appearance to the twelve months after it.

[95] Convictions resulting in custodial sentences were excluded because of the delaying effect that custody has on the commencement of the period during which the offender is at risk of a further conviction.

Jennings's research is based on the use of a predictive model that makes use of logistic regression analysis on the "prechange" group to calculate expected reconviction rates for the "postchange" group. If expressed in the same way that Hine and Celnick express their findings (which is the conventional way of presenting such reconviction data), the study shows a reduction in the expected rate of reoffending in the 2001 sample by 7.7 percentage points.[96] However, the "headline" claim in Jennings's report is for a 22.5 percent reduction in reoffending, a figure that has been obtained by expressing the actual reduction in the expected rate as a percentage reduction on the predicted rate.[97]

Moving beyond the headline claim, an appendix table in Jennings's report provides data on the "percentage improvement over the adjusted predicted rate" for each separate method of dealing with young offenders (pp. 10–11, table A1). According to this table, one disposal in particular had an exceptionally high percentage improvement in performance from 1997 to 2001, namely, the reprimand. This finding is not specifically highlighted in Jennings's text,[98] but the result makes the policy analyst immediately wary, for the reprimand is one element of the English youth justice system that has changed very little from 1997 to 2001.[99] The implication of the data, if taken at face value, is therefore that a virtually unchanged disposal has contributed particularly greatly to a very significant overall reduction in reoffending rates since the new youth justice system came into effect. Obviously, the face

[96] This is an adjusted figure, to take account of the speeding up of court processing from 1997 to 2000, consequent upon the "Narey reforms" discussed earlier.

[97] That is, the (adjusted) expected reconviction rate was 34.1 percent, and the actual rate was 26.4 percent (7.7 percentage points less). Expressing 7.7 as a percentage of 34.1 yields the figure of 22.5 percent.

[98] As indicated in the text, for the whole 2001 sample the percentage improvement over the adjusted predicted rate was 22.5 percent. For cases reprimanded, the figure was 47 percent. The next highest improvement reported was much lower: it was for the final warning (at 19.3 percent). The research report states that the two precourt disposals "show particularly marked falls in reconviction rates relative to the predicted rates" (Jennings 2003, p. 7), but it does not draw attention to the large difference between the results for the reprimand and the final warning in this regard.

[99] The reprimand has, of course, changed its name from the caution, and it is now set within the new reprimand/final warning system. But, unlike the final warning and like the old caution, it carries no expectation of a "change program" with it, nor is a court appearance automatically threatened for the next offense. As we show in Section VII, there has been some government encouragement of "restorative reprimands," following the example of practice in the Thames Valley police force; but in early 2001 (the processing date of the cohort studied by Jennings [2003]) the take-up of this suggestion was slight, with most police restorative work with juveniles focusing on the final warning stage.

validity of such a statement is not transparent, and the analyst necessarily wonders whether other factors might be in play.

Jennings provides data on the numerical distribution of her 1997 and 2001 samples on certain key variables (age, sex, principal current offense, etc.), and, from these data, proportions can easily be calculated. Two points in particular arise from such an analysis. First, the proportion of the 1997 sample who were cautioned was 65 percent, but in the 2001 sample those reprimanded or finally warned constituted 76 percent of the total. Thus, within the research samples, the "cautioning rate" actually rose from 1997 to 2001 in the research samples, contrary to the national trend (see table 1).[100] Second, for the variable "current principal offense" the proportion listed as "other offense" rose from 10.5 percent in 1997 to 30 percent in 2001—a very large increase. Both these reported trends suggest that there might well have been a significant change in the nature of the juvenile cases included within the utilized data source (data extracted from the police national computer) between 1997 and 2001.[101] The possibility of any such change is not, however, considered in Jennings's report, and the issues remain unclear at the time of writing.

What are the implications of these matters for the claimed overall reduction in reoffending from 1997 to 2001? The key questions here seem to be, first, whether or not there has been a significant shift in the composition of the police national computer samples from time 1 to time 2, and, second, whether any such changes are adequately controlled for within the multivariate model utilized in the research study.[102] These issues have been raised with the Home Office and should become clearer in due course. For the moment, however, it

[100] This increase in police-based disposals is highlighted in the report (Jennings 2003, p. 6), but the contrast with the nationally published data is not mentioned. Table 1 gives the relevant national data for indictable offenses. For summary nonmotoring offenses, the cautioning rates also declined: for example, using the same calculation methods as in table 1, for these offenses for twelve- to fourteen-year-olds, the cautioning rate fell (between 1997 and 2001) from 77 percent to 67 percent for males and from 78 percent to 75 percent for females (Home Office 2002a, p. 53). For the distinction between indictable and summary offenses, see n. 103 below.

[101] Both samples were drawn randomly from the Police National Computer records for juvenile offenders dealt with at the relevant dates. The national cautioning rate data, reported annually in the Home Office *Criminal Statistics* (see table 1 and n. 100), are derived from different data sources.

[102] Details of the multivariate controls utilized in the analysis are given in Jennings (2003). The main variables included in the multivariate model were "the number of offence categories at the current appearance or in the previous criminal career; the length of the criminal career; age of offenders at the current instance; and previous cautions, previous convictions and combinations of the two" (p. 8).

seems most appropriate to remain agnostic on the question as to whether Debbie Jennings's report provides solid evidence for the overall success of the new youth justice policies in preventing reoffending.

8. *Concluding Observations.*   Looking back over the research findings reported in this section, a number of themes stand out. The first is that the English youth justice system remains in a state of considerable flux, and although certain aspects appear to be changing, doubts linger as to the extent to which all of the latest reforms will fully "take root." Second, it appears to be easier to bring about organizational than cultural change within a youth justice context, particularly where the changes "go against the grain" of some established working practices, and also where they are inadequately resourced. Third, the evidence to date suggests that government attempts to promote changes in youth justice have been uneven, with greater emphasis being placed on "efficiency" goals such as fast-tracking than on those that require a change of outlook and ethos on the part of sentencers and youth justice practitioners. But even here, there are differences in the level of commitment to different aspects of the reform program, with greater emphasis being placed on the principles of prevention (especially among persistent offenders) and early intervention than those relating to victim involvement and restorative justice. Finally, it is too early to say conclusively whether any of the reforms are delivering the improvements in reoffending rates that they are designed to achieve (though the overall results of Hine and Celnick's final warning reconviction study seem encouraging). The evidence that is available on reoffending is mostly tentative and needs to be treated with considerable circumspection, notwithstanding some enthusiastic claims from official sources.

IV. Differential Processing of Young Offenders in England and Scotland

Having now outlined the youth justice systems in both England and Scotland, we may briefly consider some interesting data comparing rates of processing in the two countries (for children under sixteen only). Of course, this can only be done within the limitations of the available published data sources. Two key concepts are therefore used in this brief section: first, "final processing" refers in England to being found guilty of an indictable offense[103] at the Youth Court, and in Scot-

---

[103] The main categories of indictable offenses are violence against the person, sexual offenses, burglary, robbery, theft and handling stolen goods, fraud and forgery, criminal

land to making an appearance before a children's hearing on an offense ground (whether or not other grounds are also alleged); second, "initial processing" refers in Scotland to being referred to a reporter on an offense ground (whether or not also on other grounds), and in England to being officially processed for an offense to the minimum extent of being formally cautioned for an indictable offense.[104]

We have already noted the time-trend contrast in England and Scotland, whereby the previous acceleration of formal cautioning was halted and reversed in England in the 1990s, while in Scotland reporters' "no action" decisions continued to rise (tables 1, 3, 4). A further very interesting English-Scottish contrast is seen when one examines the detailed age distribution of diversionary approaches. As shown in table 9A (using 1999 data), in England for both males and females there is a steady stepwise increase in the proportionate use of prosecution (as opposed to formal cautioning) as one ascends the age range, while in Scotland reporters' referrals to the children's hearing show a much flatter age pattern. The reasons for this contrast have not been investigated empirically, but it seems likely that the difference may have its roots in the contrasting philosophical bases of the two systems. In England, an explicitly criminal-justice-based system, prosecution is an obviously more severe decision than cautioning, so it is understandable if it is used less often the younger the child. Similar considerations apply to some extent in the Scottish system, but the welfare orientation of the system probably flattens the trend. Additionally, as we have already seen, in Scotland a prior hearing appearance leading to a supervision requirement may in itself be a reason for a reporter to decide on a "no action" approach, whereas in England (especially post-1998) prior crimes mean increased probabilities of prosecution—and older children have more prior crimes than do younger ones.

The data in table 9A also show an interesting gender contrast between the two countries. Males have a lower rate of diversion (i.e., a

damage, and certain drugs offenses. Nonindictable ("summary") offenses are divided into summary motoring offenses, and other summary offenses (which include some minor offenses of violence, offenses against public order including prostitution offenses and drunkenness, offenses against the social security legislation, some drugs offenses, etc.).

[104] In Scotland, "initial processing" can easily be shown statistically because of the initial sieve provided by the reporter: data on referrals to reporters are routinely available. In England there are no readily available inclusive data at an early stage in the process; therefore, the concept in the text ("officially processed for an offense to the minimum extent of being formally cautioned") has had to be operationalized by adding together those formally cautioned and those eventually found guilty (all of whom will at an earlier point have been through a stage of initial processing).

TABLE 9

Comparisons of Children and Young Persons Initially and Finally
Processed on Offense Grounds (Scotland) or for Indictable Offenses
(England), 1999, by Age-Specific Categories

	Males		Females	
Age	England	Scotland	England	Scotland
A. Persons finally processed as a proportion of persons initially processed:*				
11 and under	14	13	†	9
12	21	19	5	17
13	27	20	11	18
14	37	21	17	19
15	46	16	28	12
16	55	. . .	35	. . .
17	61	. . .	46	. . .
B. Persons finally processed per 10,000 in the age group:*				
11 and under	9	18	†	2
12	32	75	3	18
13	68	121	13	40
14	150	193	26	61
15	244	140	45	35
C. Persons initially processed per 10,000 in the age group:*				
11 and under	60	145	16	28
12	151	411	59	123
13	247	638	109	234
14	401	920	152	304
15	530	945	164	286

* "Final processing" means, in England, found guilty of an indictable offense; in Scotland, referred to a children's hearing on offense grounds. "Initial processing" means, in England, cautioned for or found guilty of an indictable offense; in Scotland, referred to a reporter on offense grounds.

† Figures cannot be accurately computed.

higher proportion of cases finally processed) in both countries, but the male/female contrast, for most ages, is much more pronounced in England. The reasons for this difference are unclear and would repay detailed study.

The differential age distribution of diversionary usage (shown in table 9A) has direct effects on rates of final processing in the two systems. Here comparisons are not exact, because in Scotland the national data refer to all offense referrals, while in England detailed data are available only for indictable offenses (see n. 103). On this basis, however, rates of final processing (as defined above) are higher in Scotland for the younger age groups, but this reverses sharply at age fifteen, especially for males (table 9B). It is nevertheless very interesting that Scottish rates of offense-based processing as far as a hearing are, for children aged thirteen or less, so much higher than English final processing rates that they would remain higher even if one made an appropriate statistical allowance for the absence of nonindictable offenses from the English data.[105] Moreover, this is so despite the fact that diversion has continued to rise in Scotland in the 1990s.

Overall rates of initial processing of children for offenses by the two systems in 1999 are shown in table 9C. Here Scottish rates are—interestingly—uniformly higher, and this would remain the case for all age groups even if one made an appropriate allowance for the absence of nonindictable offenses from the English data.[106]

This in turn naturally leads to an exploration of whether such differences have remained constant over time. Table 10, updated from a previous analysis by Bottoms (2002, pp. 482–84), attempts to examine this question, using data similar to that in table 9C but extended back to 1980. The results are surprising, especially when read in conjunction with the data in figure 1 about trends in crime in the two countries over the same period.

In England, despite the greater rises in the crime rate (fig. 1), rates of official processing of twelve- to fifteen-year-olds have fallen (sharply for males, marginally for females). This pattern is first discernible in the second half of the 1980s, at which date it is known to be attributable to two special factors operating at that time, namely, the creation of the Crown Prosecution Service[107] and the greater adoption of informal warning policies by police forces (informal warnings, unlike formal cautions, are not recorded in national databases).[108] However,

---

[105] In 1999, 8,900 offenders ages ten to fourteen inclusive were found guilty of indictable offenses, and 5,000 were found guilty of summary offenses. Thus, for offenders finally processed, a roughly appropriate statistical allowance for the inclusion of summary offenses would be +56 percent above the rate for indictable offenses.

[106] For initial processing, an appropriate corrective factor for 1999, calculated in the same way as in n. 105 above, would be +54 percent.

[107] The Crown Prosecution Service was created in 1986. An unpublished Home Office paper in 1993 revealed that the "discontinuance rate" (discontinuation of prosecution proceedings that the police had initiated) rose overall for indictable offenses from 7 percent in 1985 to 22 percent in 1991. Rates of increase in discontinuations were higher for juveniles than for adults. For further details, see Bottoms 2002 (p. 494, n. 47).

[108] The practice of informal warning was boosted by guidance given in a Home Office circular on cautioning in 1985. However, police forces varied greatly in their take-up of the suggestion about informal warnings (Evans and Wilkinson 1990). For police services that promoted informal warnings seriously, the effect on the local statistics of offenders could be considerable (Farrington and Burrows 1993, p. 67).

TABLE 10

Selected Indexes of Offense-Based Formal Processing of Young Persons per 1,000 Population in the Age Group, England and Scotland, 1980–2001

	England: Males				Scotland: Males				England: Females				Scotland: Females			
	12*	13	14	15	12	13	14	15	12	13	14	15	12	13	14	15
1980–82	34	48	67	82	31	48	73	82	11	16	18	17	5	10	16	17
1983–85	34	51	70	85	35	56	82	91	11	17	20	19	5	10	16	18
1986–88	27	42	61	76	36	59	94	110	8	12	17	18	6	13	21	23
1989–91	23	36	53	68	36	57	91	115	6	11	16	17	6	13	22	24
1992–93	22	33	49	64	34	57	85	103	8	15	21	20	8	16	23	28
1994–96	18	30	45	60	38	59	87	103	8	15	19	17	10	19	28	30
1997–99	16	25	40	54	40	63	92	94	6	11	16	16	11	22	31	28
2000	14	23	36	51	39	59	88	89	6	11	17	15	11	18	31	28
2001	13	23	36	50	N.A.	N.A.	N.A.	N.A.	6	12	17	15	N.A.	N.A.	N.A.	N.A.
(Rate change, 1980/82–2000)	(−20)	(−25)	(−31)	(−31)	(+8)	(+11)	(+15)	(+7)	(−5)	(−5)	(−1)	(−2)	(+6)	(+8)	(+15)	(+11)

NOTE.—The chosen indexes of offense-based processing are England—annual average of persons found guilty or formally cautioned for indictable offenses per 1,000 population in the age group, and Scotland—annual average of persons referred to a reporter on offense grounds per 1,000 population in the age group.

* Age.

the decline in English rates of per capita official processing of juveniles for offenses has continued throughout the 1990s, both in periods of rising recorded crime (to 1993) and falling crime (1994 onward). It has continued further into 2000 and 2001 after the national implementation of the new English youth justice system, notwithstanding that there is at least impressionistic evidence that the creation of the new reprimands/final warning system has led some police services to substitute formal reprimands for informal warnings. But if reprimands are replacing informal warnings, and the former are recorded while the latter are not, why are rates of processed offenders continuing to fall (table 10)? The core of the answer must lie in the recent fall in the crime rate, but whether this is itself a full explanation remains unclear.[109]

By contrast with the English trends, in Scotland rates of formal processing of juveniles have risen in the last twenty years (table 10). Thus one is faced with a fascinating statistical paradox: in the jurisdiction where crime has risen less sharply (fig. 1), rates of official processing have risen (table 10), while in the jurisdiction with faster crime increases, rates of official processing have fallen. Why is this so?

One possible reason focuses on the details of the processing mechanisms in the two countries. At least part of the reason for the decline in English initial processing rates from the mid-1980s onward was the growth of informal warnings, which do not appear in the statistics of official processing. By contrast, in Scotland there is no evidence of a similar tendency—indeed, some observers believe (though there is no adequate national data) that police warnings have declined and a higher proportion of cases have been passed to the reporter. In the light of this background, the data in table 10 could be regarded as at least partly artifactual. Yet the data also apparently say something about differential confidence in the two systems. In Scotland, it would seem, confidence in the reporter/children's hearing system is high enough for participants not to want to seek diversion from it by informal processing. In England, at least in the days of the "minimum intervention" philosophy, that was not the case in many areas—and it is not

---

[109] Rates of processed offenders have fallen slightly less sharply for juveniles than for older persons in the period since the national introduction of the new youth justice system (1999–2001), which would be consistent with a switch away from informal processing and into reprimands and final warnings for juveniles. However, the age group difference is not marked, and it is possible that there is still in place a more widespread use of informal warnings than the government would wish to see.

obvious that the "new youth justice" has yet wholly succeeded in changing this cultural view.

Finally, one should note that it is theoretically possible that the data shown in table 10 and figure 1 are causally connected. Important cross-national research work on crime trends by Farrington, Langan, and Wikström (1994), covering the United States, Sweden, and England, showed that the strongest negative correlation in the analysis "was between changes in the survey crime rate and changes in the probability of an offender being convicted" (p. 127). This strong correlation does not, of course, in itself point to the existence of any causal link, but the authors' data are consistent with a hypothesis that crime rates are inversely related to the probability of sanctioning, for reasons of deterrence. (For a fuller discussion of this research, and of the many pitfalls in seeking to establish valid inferences of deterrent effects in criminological analysis, see von Hirsch et al. [1999].)

The data in table 10 and figure 1 are consistent with this line of reasoning in that rates of crime (committed, of course, by persons of all ages) are inversely correlated with the rates of official processing of adolescents for criminal activities. One could therefore perhaps develop a complex hypothesis to the effect that the existence in Scotland of a welfare-based system of juvenile justice, which has been widely supported by influential voices in Scottish communities, has encouraged the official processing of juveniles through that welfare-based system, that this relatively high rate of official processing has had a deterrent effect on potential offenders, and that similar processes have not occurred in England. The very simple data in figure 1 and table 10 do not begin to substantiate such a hypothesis. But they can, we believe, reasonably be said to raise the hypothesis.

V. System Links: Youth Justice in Relation to Other Formal Systems of Social Control

In this section we turn our attention to some ways in which the two British youth justice systems relate to other formal mechanisms of social control. Specifically, we consider the following three issues, in each case considering the two systems side by side: the thresholds that determine the age at which young offenders may become liable to formal interventions based on an allegation of crime, the relationship between the youth justice institutions and those relating to social welfare (and especially to child protection), and the minority of cases where young offenders are dealt with by the adult courts.

A. Age Thresholds Regulating Entry to the Juvenile Justice System in Crime-Related Cases

Policy questions relating to the age of entry to the juvenile justice system are complex, and it is important to note from the outset that they encompass two distinct sets of issues. The first relates to the age at which children are deemed to have the mental capacity to commit a crime; the second relates to the age at which it is considered appropriate to render them liable to prosecution and formal sanctions.[110] We begin by briefly tracing the evolution of the age thresholds in the two jurisdictions before turning, separately, to examine some key contemporary developments.

At common law, children who were under the age of seven were regarded as incapable of knowing the difference between right and wrong and therefore not having the capacity to commit a crime—a doctrine known as *doli incapax* ("incapable of evil"). In both jurisdictions, the minimum age at which a child could be prosecuted and punished was raised from seven to eight in 1932, and, in England and Wales only, this age threshold was further raised in 1963 from eight to ten. Additionally, in England and Wales (but not Scotland) there was for many years a rebuttable presumption that children under the age of fourteen were *doli incapax:* that is to say, the case against an alleged child offender could not proceed until the prosecution had proved in court that the defendant was capable of appreciating the difference between right and wrong.

Since 1998, however, the degree of protection that is afforded to English children below the age of fourteen who may commit an act which is, in law, an offense has been altered in two important respects. In both instances, the change reflects the "responsibilization" element of the new youth justice philosophy. First, the rebuttable presumption of *doli incapax* for defendants aged ten and under fourteen has been abolished (Crime and Disorder Act 1998, sec. 34), thereby increasing the likelihood that offenders of this age may be successfully prosecuted. The practical importance of this change should not be overstated, since it seems clear that most youth courts were not "assiduous in applying the presumption prior to abolition" (Ball, McCormac, and

---

[110] Somewhat confusingly, this distinction is not always observed in practice, and the same term—"age of criminal responsibility"—is often used to cover both sets of issues (or even the age at which a person becomes liable to the full penalties that are prescribed by the ordinary criminal law, though the latter threshold is more accurately referred to as the "age of criminal majority").

Stone 2001, pp. 20–21). However, the change was of considerable symbolic significance in emphasizing the government's insistence that young offenders should be made responsible for their actions, and as such it attracted some negative comment from those anxious to avoid any reduction in the degree of legal protection that is afforded to juvenile defendants in England (Bandalli 1998, 2000; Fionda 1999).

Second, as a result of the Child Safety Order, which was also introduced by the Crime and Disorder Act 1998 (sec. 11), children below the age of ten are now exposed to the risk of formal intervention in what might be described as quasi-criminal proceedings. Child safety orders may be imposed on children who have committed an act for which they might have been prosecuted if over the age of ten, or if they have acted in an antisocial manner that is likely to cause harassment, alarm, or distress to others, or if they are in breach of a local child curfew.[111] The order may be imposed by a magistrates' family proceedings court (which is a civil court, and indeed is the court that now deals with the noncriminal "care" jurisdiction relating to children), but only on the application of a local authority social services department. The effect of the order is to place the child under the supervision of a social worker or YOT worker (normally for three months, but exceptionally for up to twelve months) and to require the child to comply with specific requirements made by the court. For example, the court may impose requirements to ensure that the child receives appropriate care, protection, and support and is subject to proper control, or to prevent any repetition of the kind of behavior that resulted in the order being made.

Only two such orders were imposed in the seven pilot areas during the eighteen-month piloting period of the reforms contained in the Crime and Disorder Act 1998 (Holdaway et al. 2001, pp. 44–45, 108–9), and, it would seem, there have also been very few since then. One reason for the virtual nonuse of this new measure was felt (in the pilot research) to be that social services department staff believed there were very few children for whom such an order might be appropriate. In part this could reflect a degree of cultural resistance on the part of so-

---

[111] Provisions were introduced (in sec. 14 of the Crime and Disorder Act) enabling local authorities to introduce child curfew schemes, the effect of which is to ban children below the age of ten from streets and other public places at night unless accompanied by a responsible adult. The provision has subsequently been extended in scope to children under the age of sixteen (in the Criminal Justice Act and Police 2001) despite a continuing reluctance on the part of the local authorities to invoke the original powers. By the end of 2002, not a single child curfew order had been applied for.

cial workers and YOT staff to an order that is widely considered to be extremely interventionist. There may also be practical problems stemming from the fact that children as young as this have not routinely been featured in police records in the past. A third factor, which we discuss more fully in the next subsection, is that such cases may often be thought to be more appropriately dealt with within the essentially separate English child protection system.[112]

Although there have been no parallel moves toward greater "responsibilization" of younger children in Scotland, there have been recent proposals to amend the current age thresholds. Until now, as we have seen, Scotland has retained its historically very low age (eight) of criminal capacity. Although this sometimes attracts adverse comments by outside observers, in reality it is not an issue of very great practical significance. Recall that, in the children's hearing system, reporters do not refer a child to a hearing merely on the grounds of an offense having been committed; recall also that a hearing is unable to make an order or requirement unless this would be better for the child than making no order. The offense is simply an initial "ground" presaging possible intervention, if such intervention is subsequently deemed necessary in the interests of the child's welfare. There are other initial grounds that can be used in the case of young children with behavioral difficulties, such as the ground of being beyond parental control. (No child under eight can be reported to the system on an offense ground, but such children may be—and are—reported on other grounds.) Whether a nine-year-old child is reported on offense or other grounds might seem, therefore, of not very great significance, except in the rare cases where either a child is prosecuted rather than brought before a children's hearing, or denies the "offense ground" in the children's hearing and must then, in effect, be found either guilty or not guilty in a quasi-criminal trial before a sheriff in chambers. The theoretical possibility of such appearances, however, is a feature of the Scottish system that would certainly be deemed unacceptable by many observers.

In October 2000, the Scottish Law Commission (2002) was asked by

---

[112] The effect of a child safety order—placing a child under supervision—is much the same as might be achieved by an order intended to protect the child's welfare. However, the ground for making the order is different, and the "paramountcy of welfare" principle set out in the Children Act 1989 does not apply to child safety orders. These observations were prompted by a comment made by Tony Doob and have drawn on and developed remarks made by Tim Newburn (2002, p. 563).

the Scottish Executive to examine a range of issues relating to the age of criminal responsibility in Scotland, and in January 2002 it published its recommendations. The commission approached its task by differentiating—we believe, quite correctly—between the minimum age at which a child should be exposed to a possible criminal prosecution and the minimum age of criminal capacity. As to the former, its recommendation was that this should be raised from the current age of eight to twelve; that is, the commission proposed that the "fiscal route" cases (see fig. 1, boxes 8, 10) should be restricted to persons age twelve or above. However, on the second question (of criminal capacity), the commission made the unorthodox suggestion that this concept should be completely abolished. The implication would be that a child below the minimum age for prosecution (of whatever age) who commits an offense would be liable to be referred to the children's hearing system on offense-based grounds and not simply on other grounds such as "beyond parental control." Both of these principal recommendations, but especially the second, are potentially controversial.[113] It is unclear, at the time of writing, whether the Scottish Law Commission's recommendations will be accepted.

B. Relationship between Youth Justice and Social Welfare Systems

As we have noted previously, the differing structural relationship between what used to be called the "criminal" and the "care" jurisdictions is now probably the most profound way in which the systems in England and Scotland diverge. In Scotland, except for the very small number of cases in which a prosecution is mounted, what would in other juvenile justice systems be "criminal" cases have been entirely subsumed into the institutions of the children's hearing system, and the proceedings in a hearing, even where they involve an offense-based case, are unambiguously civil proceedings. Reporters, social workers and children's panel members all become completely accustomed to dealing with both offense-based and other cases, and, while they may alter their approach to a degree when handling the different types of

---

[113] The commission justified its second recommendation by referring to the reasoning of the Kilbrandon Committee that, in the context of a welfare system that deals with the vast majority of children, there is no need for a rule on the age of criminal responsibility in the sense of capacity to commit crime. Nevertheless, this single-minded attempt to eliminate what the commission referred to as "a confusing anomaly in our law" would mean, if it were enacted, that even a six-year-old child accused of an offense could theoretically be obliged to appear before a sheriff in chambers to deny, for example, that he or she had intended to steal goods found in his or her possession.

cases, they are nevertheless working within what is universally acknowledged to be a unified system, in which an allegation of an offense is merely one of the several ways that a child or young person may be referred for official attention. Indeed, some children themselves become aware of the unified character of the system; in the statistical study by Waterhouse et al. (2000) of children's case histories, it was found (consistently with much other research on criminal careers) that many offenders had "broader and major care needs, in addition to offending" (p. 95), and that many of the children referred to the system for offending behavior had at an earlier age been referred for reasons other than offending.

All this is in stark contrast to the situation in England, where we find different courts (the Youth Court and the family proceedings court), different operating philosophies in those two courts, different bodies bringing cases before the respective courts (the Crown Prosecution Service, of course, deals only with the criminal jurisdiction), and different supporting social agencies (the youth offending team for the Youth Court and the local authority social services department for the family proceedings court). The only point of commonality here is that the local authority social services department (SSD) is also a contributor to the YOT, but in practice, within most SSDs, the YOT members and the child protection team work almost completely independently.

There is, nevertheless, at least one interesting organizational interface between the two jurisdictional systems, concerning the recently introduced child safety order for children under the age of ten. And for that reason it may be instructive to examine more closely the experience of this order during the pilot phase of the youth justice reform process. The introduction of child safety orders was in line with the Labour government's "early interventionist" philosophy, specifically with regard to the disorderly and "criminal" behavior of children below the age of criminal responsibility. However, unlike most of the other interventions introduced by the Act, child safety orders could be made only on the application of a local authority social services department to the family proceedings court. All the youth justice pilot areas developed a similar assessment and referral process for handling such cases; these processes involved multiagency checks including an assessment of the child and family and also a multiagency forum for decision making that incorporated clear routes for diverting potentially eligible children into the child protection system or to other specialist services, if that were considered appropriate (Holdaway et al. 2001, p. 109).

This fairly elaborate gatekeeping mechanism in many ways resembles the multiagency decision-making structure that was frequently used before 1998 to determine whether young offenders were prosecuted or diverted from prosecution. The existence of the mechanism may help to explain why the number of child safety orders made during the pilot phase of the reforms was so small. Children involved in minor incidents, and those whose parents were prepared to take responsibility for their children, were likely to be screened out, but children for whom there was evidence of significant harm were likely to be diverted into the child protection system. Children who were most likely to be seen as suitable for child safety orders included those who were not themselves at risk of harm, but whose parents condoned their behavior, or in respect of whom there was a lack of parental responsibility, supervision, or interest. But in cases such as these, a parenting order could conceivably offer a more appropriate alternative than a child safety order.

The obvious difficulty of differentiating between children who should be referred to the child protection system and those for whom a child safety order might be felt appropriate points to one of the key weaknesses of the new English youth justice reforms. It seems clear that those who developed the child safety order had not sufficiently considered the interface between this new measure and the child protection system, probably because the whole thrust of the 1998 reforms is focused on the crime side, with very little reference to the parallel child welfare and child protection system.

The difficulties of the interface between offense-based and care-based jurisdictional systems can also be acute with regard to those over the age of ten who commit offenses, but who also have clear welfare needs. Such persons are not subject to the same assessment and referral process as are under-tens considered for child safety orders, and these older children may find themselves in the strange position of being dealt with separately by the YOT and the child protection team, within institutional frameworks that find it hard to connect with each other. There is limited systematic evidence on this point to date, but some researchers have produced depressing case examples of children with significant welfare problems who are dealt with by YOTs within the formal logic of the reprimand/final warning/prosecution system, with limited consultation with colleagues in child-care teams.

One particularly problematic area in this regard concerns the welfare of children who find themselves in custody as a result of offenses they may have committed, and the allocation of responsibility among the various relevant agencies (which include the YOTs, local authority social services, and the prison service). A recent joint chief inspectors' report (Chief Inspectors, England and Wales 2002, chap. 8) highlighted the very serious risks to the welfare of young people held in Young Offender Institutions, pointing out that they include those who experience the greatest harm from bullying, intimidation, and self-harming behavior. More generally, however, the report made the following rather sharp comment on the work of the YOTs: "The work of the YOTs was detached from other services, and there was only limited evidence that they were addressing [issues connected with the safeguarding of children]. The focus of their work with young offenders was almost exclusively on their offending behaviour, and did not adequately address assessing their needs for protection and safeguarding" (Chief Inspectors, England and Wales 2002, para. 8.20).

To the outside observer it seems strange that the 1998 legislation, which imaginatively and innovatively brought the health and education agencies together in a multiagency partnership approach to youth offending, should nevertheless have perpetuated a continuing sharp divide between the activities of the YOTs and the child protection teams—especially as the same children may well, at different points in their lives, be dealt with by both teams. Since the local authority social services department is centrally involved in both of these service delivery teams, it is not impossible to envision a radical improvement in the present situation—although if this is attempted it will certainly need to take fully into account the differing demands of the different courts and agencies involved in England's deliberately constructed twin-track system.[114]

C. Juveniles Prosecuted in the Adult Courts

Both the Scottish and the English systems allow limited numbers of juveniles to be prosecuted in adult courts. In this subsection, we consider how these procedures work in practice.

[114] One possible source of optimism in this regard is that the government in 2002 created a new Children and Young Persons Unit, located within the Department of Education and Skills, which is intended to fulfill a key coordinating function across government departments, seeking to bring a greater element of "joined-up government" to the whole area of services for children (including education). In October 2002, the government announced a "new direction for children's services" whereby local authorities, the health service, the police, and key criminal justice agencies would agree on local preventive strategies focused on young people facing difficulties, and also on their families. It was further indicated that this initiative would be complemented in 2003 by a green paper dealing with longer-term prevention of youth crime and youth exclusion.

In Scotland, the police may report a juvenile alleged to have committed an offense to the procurator fiscal for possible prosecution. The Lord Advocate has for many years issued guidance to chief constables on the categories of offenses that they may properly report to procurators fiscal in this way, and the latest (1996) guidance includes two principal such categories for children under sixteen (see Kearney 2000, pp. 14–16).[115] These are: very serious crimes,[116] and crimes or offenses alleged to have been committed by a child age fifteen or over which in the event of a conviction may result in a disqualification from driving (but only if the procurator fiscal considers that it would be in the public interest to obtain a disqualification which would probably still be in force when the child becomes sixteen).

The rationale for these two categories is as follows. First, very serious offenses are thought to be so societally important that they must be deliberately exempted or excluded from the children's hearing procedures, notwithstanding that this exclusion is, in conceptual terms, an admitted anomaly (i.e., there is no intrinsic reason why treating an offense as a presenting problem for a welfare-based approach is less conceptually valid just because the offense is serious). Second, the children's hearing—being a child welfare tribunal—has no power to order a driving disqualification, so if such an order is thought by the procurator fiscal to be in the public interest, then the fifteen-year-old should be prosecuted.

In addition to these two principal categories for potential prosecution, the Lord Advocate's 1996 guidance advises chief constables that they may report to procurators fiscal "any other offences, alleged to have been committed by children, where you are of the opinion that, for special reasons (which must be stated in the report) prosecution might be considered" (see Kearney 2000, pp. 15–16).

Data on children under sixteen prosecuted in Scottish courts in the years 1994–99 (inclusive) are contained in the Scottish Law Commission's (2002) report on the age of criminal responsibility. Two key aspects of these data are shown in table 11.[117] The first shows a declining

---

[115] The guidance also allows chief constables to report any person over sixteen who is still technically a child within the jurisdiction of the children's hearing (because he or she is under eighteen and still subject to a supervision requirement made by a hearing). Thus, there is in Scotland no restriction on the prosecution in the adult courts of any alleged offender age sixteen or over.

[116] Specifically, crimes "which require by law to be prosecuted on indictment or which are so serious as normally to give rise to solemn proceedings on the instructions of the Lord Advocate in the public interest" (Kearney 2000, p. 14).

[117] A further important matter is age. Of the 1,165 cases of under-sixteens prosecuted between 1994 and 1999 (see table 11), no fewer than 83 percent were of fifteen-year-olds, and only 5 percent involved children age thirteen or less.

TABLE 11

Children under Age Sixteen Prosecuted in the Scottish Courts,
1994–99

A. By Year

Year	N
1994	246
1995	243
1996	203
1997	189
1998	179
1999	105
Total	1,165

B. By Type of Offense (Data for 1994–99 Combined)

	N	Percent
Homicide	11	.9
Violent crimes* (including robbery)	182	15.6
Offenses of violence* (simple assault, breach of the peace)	168	14.4
Sexual crimes	31	2.7
Housebreaking, and theft by opening lock-fast places	121	10.3
Theft and fraud (including shoplifting)	129	11.1
Fire raising and damage	95	8.2
Theft and unlawful taking of motor vehicles	291	25.0
Other motor vehicle offenses	32	2.7
Other offenses (including drug offenses)	105	9.0
Total	1,165	100.0

SOURCE.—Scottish Law Commission 2002.

* For certain purposes, Scottish law distinguishes between "crimes" and "offenses," the former being the more serious.

number of these cases in recent years, consequent in part upon the fact that the Lord Advocate's 1996 guidance was more stringent than previous circulars. Second, however, when one considers the kinds of offenses for which prosecution was allowed to proceed, it seems clear that by no means all of these fall within the Lord Advocate's two principal 1996 categories since the offenses prosecuted include not only serious offenses and motor vehicle–related offenses, but also such matters as simple assault, breach of the peace, and shoplifting.

The explanation for this apparent anomaly probably centers on the discretionary "special reasons" category that the Lord Advocate allows to chief constables and on the now widespread perception in Scotland that the children's hearing system does not necessarily deal well with persistent offenders. Although hard evidence on the matter is lacking, it seems likely that most of those prosecuted for nonmotoring offenses that do not come within the "very serious" category are persistent offenders whom the police would like to see prosecuted rather than brought again before the hearing. That said, however, it must also be noted, first, that the total number of these prosecutions is small,[118] and, second, that of those who were found guilty of an offense when prosecuted,[119] no fewer than 30 percent were then remitted by the court to the children's hearing for disposal rather than being sentenced by the court.

Indirect evidence in support of the possibility that persistent offenders might be being reported to procurator fiscals comes from the study by Waterhouse et al. (2000, pp. 86–90). These authors collected data on a small special sample ($N = 113$) of so-called jointly reported children and young people, that is, those reported by the police both to the reporter and to the procurator fiscal. Some of these young people were sixteen or seventeen and already under a supervision requirement made by a children's hearing; others were under sixteen (exact age breakdown not given). The authors report that none of the jointly referred sample referrals was a first referral for offending, that only nineteen of 113 had not previously been the subject of a supervision requirement, and that two years after their initial joint referral this small sample had a total of 1,870 offenses (including presample offenses) recorded against them in official police records (pp. 87, 89). They were also from particularly disadvantaged social backgrounds, even by comparison with the generality of children referred to the reporter for offending (p. 88). Additionally, in interviews conducted as part of the research, two procurators fiscal commented that in principle children under the age of sixteen would be dealt with by the children's hearing system unless the offense merited otherwise, but in practice there was "a 'grey area' when children were within months of their sixteenth birthday" (p. 93).

Before leaving the Scottish system, it is important to recall that the very great majority of sixteen- and seventeen-year-old offenders are

---

[118] In 1998, for example, 179 children under sixteen were prosecuted in the Scottish courts (table 11), compared to 2,614 children under sixteen who were referred to a hearing on offense grounds, or 11,426 who were referred to a reporter.

[119] A surprisingly high proportion (22 percent) of the 1,165 cases shown in table 11 had their charges found not proven.

prosecuted in the adult criminal courts. This has recently led to some sharp criticisms of the system; for example, one leading commentator has argued that "graduation to adult criminal processes at around sixteen is low by European standards . . . and marks Scotland out as possibly the only country in western Europe dealing routinely with sixteen- and seventeen-year-olds in adult criminal courts" (Whyte 2001, p. 81). This line of criticism, initially accepted by the Advisory Group on Youth Crime (Scottish Executive 2000a), has now after various political mutations led to the announcement of a pilot project of special youth courts for persistent offenders in this age group—though we will have to wait to see what the longer-term consequences of this initiative might be.

We turn now to England and to the arrangements for the trial and sentencing of young persons whose cases are, exceptionally, dealt with in the Crown Court instead of the Youth Court.[120] Cases in this category include those who are charged with homicide (where committal to the Crown Court is mandatory), and those who are jointly charged with a person age eighteen or over (where a committal may be made if the Youth Court considers it necessary in the interests of justice to commit both the older and younger offender to the Crown Court). In addition, young offenders who are charged with offenses for which, as an adult, they could be imprisoned for at least fourteen years, or are charged with indecent assault or causing death by dangerous driving, may also be committed to the Crown Court for trial if magistrates decide that the appropriate sentence is likely to be greater than they are empowered to impose.

Total numbers of defendants under eighteen sent for trial in the Crown Court since 1991 are shown in table 12.[121] As will be seen, the figures show a marked drop in the period 1991–93. This was directly attributable to the raising of the maximum age of the youth (formerly juvenile) court from the seventeenth to the eighteenth birthday from October 1, 1992. Traditionally, juvenile courts had always sent fewer

---

[120] Juveniles (under eighteen) may also in some circumstances appear in adult magistrates' courts when they are jointly charged with a person age eighteen or over. For further details, see Ball, McCormac, and Stone (2001, chap. 7).

[121] It should be noted that until 2000, Youth Courts also had a right to commit for sentence to the Crown Court after a conviction in the lower court. This was abolished by the Crime and Disorder Act 1998 consequent upon the creation of the new detention and training order (which is available in the Youth Court). However, use of this power was in any case numerically small (in 1999, 4,900 persons under eighteen appeared for trial in the Crown Court [see table 12], but the corresponding figure for those appearing for sentence only was much lower—900).

TABLE 12

Juveniles under Age Eighteen
Appearing at the English Crown
Court for Trial, 1991–2001

Year	N
1991	5,200
1992	4,700
1993	2,700
1994	2,700
1995	3,300
1996	4,300
1997	5,200
1998	5,000
1999	4,900
2000	5,000
2001	4,600

SOURCE.—Annual volumes of *Criminal Statistics, England and Wales.*
NOTE.—Data given to nearest hundred.

cases to the Crown Court than had adult magistrates' courts, so the assimilation of seventeen-year-olds into the Youth Court in 1992 meant that they benefited from the former juvenile court ethos in this respect. From 1994 to 1997, however, there was a steady rise in the number of persons committed to the Crown Court, with a slight fall from this level more recently.

Until recently, juvenile defendants who were tried in the Crown Court were exposed to exactly the same level of formality and exactly the same procedures—including trial by judge and jury—as those in a normal adult trial. Moreover, they were not entitled to the protection afforded by the restrictions on publicity that normally apply to those who are tried in the Youth Court. Protection from publicity in the Crown Court was dependent instead on a specific order from the court restraining publication by the media, if the court felt that this was appropriate in the instant case.

The use of substantially unmodified adult criminal proceedings for cases involving very young defendants was challenged in the European Court of Human Rights in 1999, following a highly publicized trial in which two very young children were tried in the Crown Court for the murder of a toddler when the defendants were just ten (see also n. 22).

Although the procedure in this case was modified to a certain extent in view of the defendants' age,[122] the trial was nevertheless conducted in most respects with all the formality of an adult criminal trial, including wigs and gowns for judge and counsel, and with the child defendants required to be present throughout the proceedings. The European Court of Human Rights held that the two defendants were unable to participate effectively in the court proceedings because of the adult nature of the court environment (*Cases of V. and T. v. the United Kingdom* [2000] 30 EHRR 121). This, it was held, amounted to a breach of Article 6(1) of the European Convention on Human Rights (concerning the right to a fair trial).

The government accepted this judgment, and on February 16, 2000, the Lord Chief Justice, Lord Bingham, issued a practice direction entitled *The Trial of Children and Young Persons in the Crown Court* ([2000] 2 All ER 285). The practice direction provides guidance for the conduct of such proceedings, the aim of which is to further reduce the level of formality in an attempt to make the proceedings less intimidating, humiliating, and distressing for young defendants and so improve their level of understanding and ability to participate. More recently, a review of the criminal courts conducted by Lord Justice Auld (2001) has recommended that young defendants who are accused of "grave crimes" should be tried by a specially constituted Youth Court,[123] comprising a judge and at least two experienced youth panel magistrates. This proposal, if implemented, would have the controversial effect of removing altogether the entitlement of such defendants to have their cases tried before a jury, whereas this safeguard would continue to be available for adult defendants charged in identical circumstances.

As regards sentencing, three related sets of concerns have been raised regarding the differential sentencing powers that are now available respectively in the Youth Court and the Crown Court. First, the coexistence of two sets of custodial provisions for different categories of offenders in different courts has created the potential for some anomalies with possibly unjust outcomes (Bateman 2001; Stone 2001*a*). For example, a first-time offender age twelve to fourteen (of-

---

[122] The defendants were seated next to social workers in a specially raised dock, with parents and lawyers seated nearby. Moreover, the hearing times were modified to reflect the school day, and additional ten-minute intervals were taken every hour.

[123] Unless the charges facing the young defendants are inextricably linked to those against adult defendants with whom they are jointly accused of committing the offenses in question.

fender A) whose offense is felt to be too serious to be dealt with by means of a community sentence might well be sent for trial in the Crown Court in order to "qualify" for a custodial sentence in the form of longer-term detention (since a detention and training order would only be available to the Youth Court in the case of a "persistent offender"). Conversely, offender B, an offender of the same age, who was deemed to be "persistent," would be liable to be sentenced on conviction by the Youth Court to a detention and training order of up to two years. Consequently, offender B might well be tried and sentenced in the Youth Court, even where his offense is more serious than that committed by offender A.

A second concern relates to the frequency with which the "grave crime" custodial provisions have been invoked in recent years. This has had the consequent effect of exposing significant numbers of young defendants not only to the rigors of a quasi-adult criminal trial process, but also to the full range of sentencing powers that are normally only available in respect of adult offenders. For many years the "grave crimes" provisions were resorted to very rarely. Thus, in 1970, only six sentences were imposed under section 53 of the Children and Young Persons Act (the precursor to section 91 of the Powers of Criminal Courts [Sentencing] Act 2000). A decade later, in 1980, the number had risen to sixty-five, and by 1985 it had reached 154. In the period 1996–2001, however, the annual average number was 620, with a record 748 sentences in 1997.[124]

The third concern stems from research suggesting that children who commit "grave crimes" are themselves among the most vulnerable in society. A study of 200 children and young people sentenced under section 53 of the Children and Young Persons Act 1933 showed that over 90 percent had been victims of childhood trauma, and that 74 percent had experienced some kind of abuse (e.g., emotional, sexual, physical, or organized/ritual abuse; Boswell 1996, p. 89). This has prompted further doubts as to the appropriateness, both of the rigors of an adult trial and also the "punitive" nature of the sentencing and custodial regimes to which such offenders are likely to be exposed.

In summary, therefore, while the Scottish and English systems have markedly different provisions relating to the use of adult courts for ju-

---

[124] An important reason for this increase was the widening of the categories of offense eligible for longer-term detention by the Criminal Justice and Public Order Act 1994 (passed when a Conservative government was in power).

venile defendants, in both jurisdictions there are difficulties that have led to significant comment.

VI. Key Contemporary Issues

Having examined some of the ways in which the core institutions of youth justice relate to other formal social control mechanisms in England and Scotland, we now discuss a number of key contemporary issues for the two systems, specifically, possible changes in the role of the police, the right to and availability of publicly funded legal assistance, the use and quality of residential and custodial provision for young offenders, the treatment of ethnic minority young offenders, and policies for dealing with persistent offenders.

A. An Altered Role for the Police?

One noteworthy aspect of the recent English youth justice reforms is that they appear to herald a significant and potentially controversial shift in the traditional roles and responsibilities of the police. Until recently these were mainly confined to the tasks of recording and detecting criminal offenses, plus the apprehension and questioning of suspected offenders and assisting in their prosecution by assembling evidence and relaying this to the Crown Prosecution Service. Although the increasing involvement of the police in the nonstatutory practice of cautioning offenders who admitted their offenses represented something of a departure for them, this could still reasonably accurately be characterized as a diversion from prosecution and the rest of the formal system of social control based on the use of "penal" sanctions of one form or another.[125]

Now, however, the police's increasingly proactive involvement in the administering of reprimands and final warnings with "change programs"—particularly where these take the form of Thames Valley–style "restorative" reprimands and conferences—is beginning to look more like a supplement to the regular system of social control, and one that involves the active penalization of minor offenders by the police themselves, without a judicial hearing (and, in the English system,

---

[125] The police have also for many years been involved in the running of attendance centers (see n. 59). However, the young offenders who attend such programs are ordered to do so by the court after they have been tried and convicted; moreover, by an administrative anomaly, the management of attendance centers is not part of regular police duties but is done under special license from the Home Office.

without reference to the Crown Prosecution Service).[126] Moreover, the active involvement of police officers who have been seconded to youth offending teams in virtually all aspects of their wide-ranging responsibilities[127] has resulted in a further blurring of the traditionally distinct lines of demarcation between "policing," "prosecutorial," "judicial," and, finally, "executive" functions with regard to the application and delivery of penal sanctions. One reason why these developments are likely to prove controversial is that the checks and balances that are conventionally thought to be safeguarded by a system based on a "separation of powers" may be far less effective in a system in which a single agency such as the police appears to combine such a wide range of functions. One traditional safeguard, whose role within this reshaped criminal justice landscape now looks much more problematic, relates to the right to legal representation, which we discuss further in the next subsection.

It is particularly noteworthy that, in the English reforms, this more proactive executive-style role for the police has been developed simultaneously with the dismantling of the former multiagency juvenile liaison panels, in which social workers and others advised the police on the exercise of their prosecution/caution decision (and, in the era of the dominance of the "minimum intervention" philosophy, their advice was almost always slanted in a particular direction; see Davis, Boucherat, and Watson 1989). The government's message, in the post-1998 reforms, therefore seems to be: we trust the police (and the CPS), but not others, at the prosecution stage, and we also trust the police to play an enhanced role at later stages of the process.

In Scotland, there were until recently no similar developments, but now the decision of the 2002 Ad Hoc Ministerial Group on Youth Crime to develop a national strategy on police warnings (with a specific mention of Thames Valley–style restorative warnings) is perhaps in-

---

[126] However, it has been established that the practice of police cautioning is subject to judicial review, though within rather narrow limits: R v. Chief Constable of Kent, ex parte L (1993) I All ER 756. This must apply also to reprimands and final warnings.

[127] In many of the pilot YOTs, police officers were mainly involved in the assessment of offenders for, and delivery of, "change programs" in connection with final warnings, and as members of "reparation" or "short-term intervention" teams. However, in some of the pilots they were also seconded to court teams and given responsibilities for report writing, and, in at least one of the pilots, a police member was appointed as a unit manager with overall responsibility for one of the area-based offices within the youth offending team. Although referral orders were not in operation at the time of the pilot YOT evaluation, there is also nothing to prevent police officers from attending YOPs as the YOT team member on the panel.

dicative of a parallel governmental approach. If this policy does develop in the way the Scottish Executive apparently intends, this will reverse the previous tendency for the police to report the overwhelming majority of offense-based cases to the reporters and, once again, will bring the police into greater prominence within the system.

All the signs are that the U.K. government and the Scottish Executive will be untroubled by criticisms of such developments on "separation of powers" grounds. The defense of the developments is likely to be along these lines: "this will help reduce youth crime; the police are in the front line in the fight against crime, and they have the support of the great majority of the public in this fight; leave them alone to get on with the job." In other words, in the government's thinking, the "statutory principal aim" of the English youth justice system (the reduction of crime) is, in a rapidly changing and anxious society, much more important than the worries of liberal intellectuals about erosions of the separation of powers. It will be very interesting, in the coming years, to see whether the proactive role of the police in English and Scottish youth justice develops further, and also whether other countries appear to move in a similar direction.

B. The Right to Publicly Funded Legal Assistance

We have already made the point that Scotland's adoption of a welfare-based juvenile justice system in the late 1960s was out of line with developments in many other jurisdictions—including, notably, jurisdictions in the United States—in which a retreat from welfare-based approaches was accompanied by moves to strengthen due process safeguards. One such safeguard relates to a recognition of children's and young people's entitlement to publicly funded legal assistance, including a right to legal representation and advocacy. Support for such a right is contained in a number of international instruments that have been promulgated in recent years, and this has raised concerns that the Scottish children's hearings system (and, more recently, the new youth offending panel that has been introduced in conjunction with the referral order in England and Wales) may not be fully compliant with international standards and conventions.

The most important of these international instruments are the United Nations Convention on the Rights of the Child, which was promulgated in 1989, and to which the United Kingdom acceded in 1992, and the European Convention on Human Rights, which the United Kingdom ratified in 1950. The two key provisions of the

United Nations Convention in the present context are, first, Article 12, which stipulates that a "child shall . . . be provided with the opportunity to be heard in any judicial and administrative proceeding affecting the child, either directly or through a representative of an appropriate body, in a manner consistent with the procedural rules of international law." A second provision, dealing specifically with detained children, further stipulates that "every child deprived of his own liberty shall have the right to prompt access to legal or other appropriate assistance, as well as the right to challenge the legality of the deprivation of his or her liberty before a court or other competent independent and impartial authority, and to a prompt decision on any such action" (Article 37[d]). As for the European Convention on Human Rights, the most important provision is Article 6, which guarantees the right to a fair trial.

In the Scottish context, these international conventions present two main difficulties. The first is that, as we have previously explained, although children attending hearings have a right to be accompanied by a "friend," who may be a legal representative, public funds have traditionally not been available for this purpose. Consequently, very few children are in practice legally represented at children's hearings (Cleland 1996; Gordon 1996), though legal representation is available with regard to the minority of cases in which children are tried in the sheriff court, at hearings held before the sheriff where the grounds of referral to a hearing are contested, and also in appeals against the decision of a hearing.[128] The second difficulty is that children may be deprived of their liberty at a children's hearing, in cases where a residential supervision requirement is imposed, and some (e.g., Lockyer 1994, p. 129) have suggested that other compulsory measures of care, including home supervision, also entail a loss of liberty. Since children who are made the subject of residential supervision requirements are usually not legally represented, the United Kingdom's ability to comply with Article 37(d) of the United Nations Convention on the Rights of the Child seemed doubtful. Accordingly, the U.K. government, on signing the U.N. Declaration, entered a reservation in which it drew attention to the existence of children's hearings, asserted that they have "proved over the years to be a very effective way of dealing with problems of

---

[128] As previously noted (see n. 32), the children's hearing may also appoint a safeguarder, though this is rare in offense-based cases. However, safeguarders do not take instructions from the child, and therefore do not act as advocates in a conventional sense.

children in a less formal, non-adversarial manner," and therefore reserved the right to continue operating with the current system.[129]

In the English context, the issue of legal representation has not until recently presented any difficulty, since defendants are entitled to publicly funded representation and assistance in connection with criminal court (including Youth Court) proceedings irrespective of their age. However, the situation has now significantly changed following the introduction of youth offending panels (YOPs) in conjunction with referral orders, which are now mandatory for most young offenders who plead guilty on being prosecuted for the first time. When introducing the concept of YOPs in the relevant Parliamentary debate, the government repeatedly stressed that it was drawing on the experience with Scottish children's hearings. It had also already made clear, in the White Paper *No More Excuses* (Home Office 1997*a*, para. 9.37) that it intended "no legal representation at the youth panel stage," pointing out in this connection that a plea of guilty would already have been entered at the Youth Court, the length of referral would have been determined by the court, and a custodial disposal was not an available option. The depth of the government's hostility toward the idea of permitting legal representation at YOP hearings was made very clear by the following remarks, which were made in Parliament by Paul Boateng, a government minister and a lawyer with experience of practice in youth courts: "I can think of nothing more destructive to the objectives of the Bill than involving lawyers in youth offender panels. That would add nothing to their operation and would seriously obstruct the panels' objectives. The panels should be seen in terms of those objectives: they are designed to reduce the barriers between a young person and his or her offending. After years of practice . . . I can say that the role of the defence lawyer is to be such a barrier between young people and their offending" (Boateng 1999, col. 36).

Opposition MPs were not convinced, and expressed concern that the bill might be incompatible with Article 6 of the European Convention on Human Rights (ECHR) since a lack of legal representation could mean that the process of drawing up a contract for a "programme of behaviour" would be coercive. The government rejected these concerns, though it stopped short of banning legal representation at YOP

---

[129] The reservation also stated, incorrectly, that legal representation "is not permitted" at such hearings, when in fact the position is that lawyers are allowed to attend and participate but only in the capacity of advisers to, rather than advocates for, the child, and (crucially) even then not at public expense.

hearings. The final legislation allows young defendants to nominate an adult (who may be a lawyer) to accompany them to any meeting of the panel, though this is subject to the agreement of the panel and, as in Scotland, no public funding is available for this purpose.

The first judicial ruling on the extent to which the United Kingdom's practice with regard to the issue of legal representation for proceedings involving children is compliant with its international obligations was delivered on August 7, 2001, in the important Scottish case of *S. v. The Principal Reporter and Lord Advocate*.[130] The case was brought under the Human Rights Act 1998, which extends to the whole of the United Kingdom and which came into force on October 2, 2000. The most important effect of the act is to incorporate the ECHR into U.K. law, which means that the Convention is now directly binding in both English and Scottish domestic law.[131] Moreover, the courts are not only obliged where possible to interpret English and Scottish law so that it is compatible with the Convention, they also have the power, in cases where such an interpretation is not possible, to issue a formal "declaration of incompatibility." When such a declaration is issued, the government has the power to "fast-track" legislation through Parliament to remove the incompatibility.

The case of *S. v. The Principal Reporter and Lord Advocate* involved a referral by a sheriff court to the Court of Session (the supreme civil court in Scotland). The question that the Court of Session was asked to address was whether or not the children's hearing system complied with the requirements of Article 6 of the ECHR, given that publicly funded legal representation could not be made available to a child even where he was not able to represent himself properly and satisfactorily. At a preliminary hearing, the Court indicated that it was contemplating making a declaration of incompatibility (on grounds that we will specify shortly). In the end, however, the Court did not make such a declaration, since it was persuaded that Scottish ministers had the power under existing legislation to make regulations to provide for

---

[130] The case is not reported as such, but a summary of the relevant extracts from the final judgment can be found on the internet at the Scottish Court Service's website at the following location: http://www.scotcourts.gov.uk/opinions/A2730.html.

[131] Previously, litigants who believed that their human rights had been violated by virtue of the United Kingdom's failure to respect and abide by the provisions set out in the Convention could only gain redress by means of the long and expensive procedure of petitioning the European Court of Human Rights in Strasbourg. The Strasbourg procedure is not available until all possible avenues to redress within domestic law have been exhausted.

representation before a children's hearing—even though they had not, as yet, exercised that power.

In response to this case, Scottish ministers introduced new statutory regulations relating to legal representation at children's hearings.[132] Under these regulations, a children's hearing may (either at a prehearing "business meeting" or at the hearing itself) appoint a legal representative for a child either if it appears that such representation is required in order "to allow the child to effectively participate at the hearing" or if it is thought that it may be necessary to make a supervision requirement with a secure accommodation authorization.[133] Any such representative has to be drawn from one of two existing panels— the appointed panel of "safeguarders" (see n. 32) or the panel of curators ad litem and reporting officers. The purpose of this restriction appears to be to ensure that appointed legal representatives understand (from prior experience) the subtle dynamics of the children's hearing process and therefore, while properly representing their client's interests, do not do so in an overly adversarial or confrontational manner.

Within the United Kingdom, there are a number of tribunals which, while not courts, nevertheless fulfill formal adjudicatory functions that are of great importance to some citizens.[134] Such tribunals are subject to inspection and oversight by a body known as the Council on Tribunals, and the children's hearings are one of the institutions overseen by the council.[135] In a report on the hearings system published soon after the new regulations on legal representation had been promulgated, the Scottish Committee of the Council on Tribunals (2002, chap. 3), while welcoming the recent developments, nevertheless commented that "we are concerned that the criteria [of eligibility for publicly funded representation] are limited."[136] The council formally recommended that the Scottish Executive "keep under review" the new

---

[132] The Children's Hearings (Legal Representation) (Scotland) Rules 2002 (Scottish Statutory Instrument 2002 no. 63).

[133] The children's hearing is also empowered to make such appointments "notwithstanding that an appointment [as a safeguarder] may be made . . . under the Act" (Rule 3 of the 2002 Rules).

[134] For example, employment tribunals, social security tribunals, and immigration tribunals.

[135] For example, the newly promulgated rules on legal representation (n. 133 above) could not, by law, be finalized until the Council on Tribunals had been formally consulted.

[136] Although this point was not spelled out by the council, one obvious way in which the new rules are limited is that they do not explicitly cover residential supervision cases where a secure accommodation authorization is not contemplated—which is arguably still in breach of Article 37(d) of the United Nations Convention.

regulations, and commented that "this particular tribunal system requires skilled and appropriate representation" (para. 57), an issue on which "a full debate" would be beneficial.

What are the implications of these Scottish developments for the English YOP system? In the Scottish case, the Court of Session took the view that although the children's hearing comes within the general protections of Article 6 of the ECHR (concerning the right to a fair trial), nevertheless, even when dealing with offense grounds for referral, the hearing remains a civil proceeding. The children's hearing is not determining a criminal charge, and accordingly it is not a criminal process to which the additional safeguards specified in Articles 6(2) and 6(3) of the ECHR apply. In the Scottish context of a tribunal that does not determine guilt and whose principal function is to decide on the disposal that will be in the best interests of a child, such a finding is relatively uncontentious. Whether the same conclusion would necessarily be reached in respect to the English youth panel procedure is, however, debatable. It could be argued that the English referral order resembles the Scottish procedure insofar as the young person has already pleaded guilty; hence the YOP hearing is not "determining a criminal charge" and is therefore not a criminal process to which the additional safeguards contained in paragraphs 2 and 3 of Article 6 should apply. It could be argued, however, that the English referral order is, in comparison with the Scottish procedure, more akin to a sentencing procedure, albeit one in which the young person is invited to participate and which cannot result in a custodial disposal. On this basis it might be argued that the young person should be entitled to safeguards in addition to those available in children's hearings, particularly since one of the functions of a legal representative in a criminal trial is to address the court on matters relating to the sentence that might be imposed even after the defendant has pleaded guilty. For example, one issue that could arise relates to the "punitive burden" that might be imposed on offenders who are dealt with by youth offending panels—particularly for relatively minor offenses—and how this compares in terms of proportionality with comparable offenders who are dealt with by the Youth Court.[137] However these particular

---

[137] In the English legislation, the intention is that issues of "punitive burden" and "commensurability" are dealt with by the Youth Court in fixing the length of the referral order. However, within a referral order of a fixed period (say six months), the punitive burden of the elements of a "programme of behaviour" fixed by the YOP could obviously vary considerably.

arguments might finally be resolved, it seems now very unlikely, in the light of Scottish developments, that the English YOP system will be able to retain its present policy of allowing no publicly funded legal representation of any kind, in any type of case.

C. *Usage and Quality of Custodial Provision for Young Offenders*

Concerns have been raised in both England and Scotland with regard to the extent to which custodial punishments are imposed on young offenders, and also the nature of the custodial conditions in which they are held (though on the second of these points, the concerns focus very predominantly on England). This is another issue in respect of which critics maintain that neither jurisdiction conforms to relevant international standards and conventions, notably the U.N. Convention on the Rights of the Child 1989.

If we consider first the extent of the use of custody, Article 37(b) of the U.N. Convention stipulates that the detention of a child should be used "only as a measure of last resort and for the shortest appropriate period of time." Comparative data on the age profile of prison populations for various member states of the Council of Europe (2001), however, show that in 1998 (the most recent year for which such data are available) England and Scotland were among the European countries whose prison populations contained the highest proportion of prisoners under the age of eighteen, being exceeded in this respect only by Greece and Ireland (see table 13). At 3.5 and 3.6 percent, respectively, the Scottish and English percentages were six times as large as those recorded by countries such as Denmark, Finland, the Netherlands, Spain, and Sweden. Such figures have fueled the concerns of those who believe that the detention of juveniles in Great Britain is neither used as a measure of last resort nor for the shortest appropriate period of time.

In England and Wales the number of juvenile offenders under the age of eighteen (sentenced and remanded) in custodial facilities of all types increased by 10 percent, from 2,753 in April 2001 to 3,034 in April 2002, while the average length of sentence also increased over the same period, from four months to 4.8 months (Youth Justice Board for England and Wales 2002, p. 15). According to a survey conducted by the Youth Justice Board, the great majority of juvenile offenders (87 percent) served their sentences in Young Offender Institutions (commissioned by the YJB from the prison service), while a small number (7 percent and 6 percent, respectively) were placed in Secure Training

TABLE 13
Young Offender Profile of Prison Populations within the Council of Europe at September 1, 1998

Country	Median Age*	Prisoners Age under 18 Years[†]	
		N	Percent
Germany	N.A.	N.A.	N.A.
Austria	N.A.	199	2.9
Belgium	31	187	2.3
Bulgaria	N.A.	143	1.2
Croatia	38	31	2.8
Cyprus	25	0	.0
Czech Republic	31	342	1.5
Denmark	N.A.	15	.4
Finland	34	7	.3
France	32	822	1.5
Greece	45	387	7.3
Hungary	32	148	1.0
Ireland	24	126	4.8
Italy	34	N.A.	N.A.
Latvia	34	394	4.1
Lithuania	31	441	3.4
Malta	N.A.	5	1.9
Moldova	31	225	2.2
Netherlands	30	59	.5
Norway	35	12	.5
Poland	N.A.	N.A.	N.A.
Portugal	33	243	1.7
Romania	N.A.	2,327	4.5
Slovakia	34	90	1.4
Slovenia	32	15	1.9
Spain	32	163	.4
Sweden[‡]	34	10	.2
Turkey	54	2,188	3.4
United Kingdom:			
England and Wales	28	2,353	3.6
Scotland	28	215	3.5

Source.—Council of Europe 2001, p. 62, table 2.

* Median age of prison population (only) includes pretrial detainees.

[†] Prisoners under eighteen years of age includes pretrial detainees (but not those in civil detention).

[‡] Data relate to convicted and sentenced prisoners only.

Centres or Local Authority Secure Units. According to figures published by the Home Office, the largest age group among the juvenile sentenced population in prison service custody (males and females combined) was seventeen-year-olds, who accounted for 56.5 percent of the total population, followed by sixteen-year-olds (32.1 percent) and fifteen-year-olds (11.4 percent).

In Scotland, as we have seen, juveniles (those under sixteen) may find themselves in detention by one of two principal routes: as a result of a secure accommodation authorization made by a children's hearing or as a result of a custodial sentence that is imposed by a sheriff court following a decision by the procurator fiscal to prosecute the case. However, the numbers involved in the second of these possible routes is small, and the main reason for Scotland's high position in the European custodial comparison (table 13) relates to the considerable use of custodial sentences among sixteen- and seventeen-year-olds processed through the adult courts, a point which as we have seen has exercised a number of Scottish commentators. There is also little room for complacency with regard to the use of secure accommodation for under-sixteens in Scotland. An official report by the Social Work Services Inspectorate (1996) estimated that, at that date, Scotland had proportionately 30 percent more secure places in local authority accommodation than England,[138] and the review explicitly conceded that Scotland was in breach of the requirement of the U.N. Convention that secure detention should be used "only as a measure of last resort." This led one influential Scottish commentator to ask why the Scottish youth population, which showed "no distinctive features from other countries," required so many containment facilities (Whyte 1998). His answer, derived from comments in the 1996 Inspectorate report, was that the decline over the years in residential school places in Scotland (see table 6, second column), coupled with the general competition for scarce resources in Scottish child care (including the hearings system), had had the unintended consequence of an increased resort to secure care for more difficult children, even though they had not reached the stage of requiring secure care as a "last resort." Interestingly, however, since the Inspectorate's 1996 report, secure accommodation authorizations have increased, especially for boys.[139]

---

[138] Note, however, that this comparison is restricted to local authority accommodation, so it excludes the fifteen-year-olds in prison service accommodation in England.

[139] Fresh secure accommodation authorizations have been made as follows from 1992 to 2000: 1992, 104; 1993, 130; 1994, 120; 1995, 147; 1996, 110; 1997, 177; 1998, 189;

Turning from the scale on which custodial punishments are inflicted to the conditions in which young offenders are held in captivity, Article 37(c) of the United Nations Convention on the Rights of the Child stipulates that "every child deprived of liberty shall be treated with humanity and respect . . . and in a manner which takes into account the needs of persons of his or her age. In particular, every child deprived of liberty shall be separated from adults unless it is considered in the child's best interest not to do so and shall have the right to maintain contact with his or her family through correspondence and visits."

In the view of many commentators, the English system too often fails to meet these standards. The position is complicated by the fact that, as noted above, the juvenile secure estate consists of three different types of secure accommodation, which are governed by different sets of regulations. There is, however, widespread consensus among informed commentators in England, first, that many young people in custody are themselves very vulnerable,[140] and, second, that of the three kinds of institution within the "secure estate," prison service establishments are the least suitable for more vulnerable children. Despite this, a recent report (Hazel et al. 2002) found that, apart from the youngest children, the Youth Justice Board had in general been unable to ensure that "vulnerable" trainees were placed outside of prison service institutions.

Until very recently it was thought that, within the juvenile secure estate, only children in local authority secure accommodation were covered by the welfare provisions of the Children Act 1989, which offer a degree of support and protection since the children concerned are subject to monitoring and assessment that is carried out by local authority social service departments. However, a high court case brought in 2002 by a nongovernmental campaigning organization (the Howard League) has now been successful in establishing that the duties of local authority social services departments under the Children Act (e.g., to safeguard children against abuse) do also apply to children in the prison service's Young Offender Institutions.[141] This decision could have important implications for the future.

1999, 137; 2000, 194 (data from annual volumes of statistics published by the Scottish Children's Reporter Administration).

[140] A study of a sample of young people who were sentenced to detention and training orders showed that two-thirds had been excluded from education, four in ten had been looked after by the local authority, and 17 percent has been on the child protection register at some point in their lives (Hazel et al. 2002).

[141] R. v. Secretary of State for the Home Department, ex parte Howard League for Penal Reform and the Department of Health (interested party), (2002) EWHC 2497 (Admin).

Successive chief inspectors of prisons (H.M. Chief Inspector of Prisons for England and Wales 1997, 2002) have voiced serious concerns that the conditions in which children are held in prison service establishments do not conform to any reasonable interpretation of the U.N. provisions referred to above.[142] Indeed, such conditions were among the main reasons why budgetary and commissioning responsibility for the custodial care of such juveniles was transferred from the Prison Service to the Youth Justice Board in 2000. However, as we noted in a previous section, a recent joint chief inspectors' report (Chief Inspectors, England and Wales 2002) has raised serious doubts as to the adequacy of this reform from a welfare perspective. Another report on Young Offender Institutions that brings together the key concerns and recommendations of thirty-one prisons inspectorate reports between January 1988 and October 2001 was published in November 2002. In a foreword to the report, the former chief inspector of prisons, Sir David Ramsbotham, wrote, "I hope that the report will, at last, prick the conscience of the nation. It is a national disgrace that the United Kingdom, the fourth richest country in the world, a nation known for the civilisation it has spread round so much of the world, should have remained silent when confronted with evidence of how its children are treated in prison" (Hodgkin 2002, p. 4).

The latest chief inspector's report, by Sir David Ramsbotham's successor (H.M. Chief Inspector of Prisons for England and Wales 2002), fully acknowledges the considerable injection of resources into juvenile prison service establishments that has taken place since the advent of the new youth justice system and also the setting of much more rigorous targets and standards following the transfer of commissioning functions to the Youth Justice Board. But although in these respects progress has been made in improving outcomes for children held in prison service custody, the report also points out that there is a long way to go before the level of provision is compatible with current international stipulations. One particularly acute remaining problem relates to girls under the age of eighteen, including a small number of unsentenced female prisoners who should not, by law, be remanded to the prison service, and conditions for whom were described as deplorable. Another problem relates to the difficulty in maintaining contact between young offenders and their families, since the location of several of the establishments selected for young prisoners is far from ideal, and lengthy travel is often necessitated.

[142] Reports published by the Scottish Chief Inspector of Prisons have been far less damning in comparison.

Although the principal concerns about custodial conditions in England have focused on prison service accommodation, there are also significant difficulties with regard to local authority secure accommodation. Paradoxically, in a system such as England's, with (generally speaking) a rather rigid separation between the criminal and the care jurisdictions, these systems nevertheless come together at this ultimate point (for under-fifteens) because both systems need some locked accommodation, of which there is a shortage. However, the side-by-side placement of offenders and those in secure accommodation for their own protection creates some difficulties of bullying and intimidation (Goldson 2002), and there is also a significant gender issue in play because most boys are in local authority secure units for offense reasons, while most girls are admitted through the welfare route (O'Neill 2001). Additionally, some have expressed concern that "paramountcy of welfare" considerations for care cases can, given side-by-side living with a larger number of offenders, become easily diluted, a situation that is further complicated by the very significant purchasing power of the Youth Justice Board (who deal with offenders only) in the post-1998 commissioning arrangements (Goldson 2002). Thus, this small segment of the overall youth justice system contains several important tensions.

D. Treatment of Ethnic Minority Young Offenders

The treatment of ethnic minority defendants by the juvenile justice system has long been a matter of concern throughout Great Britain, though the most vigorous debates on the issue have occurred in England and Wales, which has a higher proportion of ethnic minority residents than Scotland, and which is also where most of the relevant empirical research has been undertaken. Statistics relating to the ethnic composition of the juvenile prison population (Home Office 2000*b*, p. 44) graphically highlight the overrepresentation of prisoners from ethnic minority backgrounds. Whereas white prisoners ages fifteen to seventeen comprised 76 percent of prisoners within this age bracket, black inmates accounted for 19 percent, even though black people only account for around 2 percent of the general population age ten and over in England. (Asian-origin prisoners made up a further 3.3 percent of the juvenile prison population, and those of other ethnic backgrounds the final 1.6 percent.) Official estimates suggest that only around 7 percent of the general population is of nonwhite ethnic origin, so even allowing for the fact that minority ethnic groups tend to have a younger age structure than the white population,[143] the degree of over-representation of black young prisoners is large.

In seeking empirical evidence that might help to account for this ethnic imbalance, we must emphasize that much of the voluminous literature on ethnicity and criminal justice relates to adult or young adult age groups (see Bowling and Phillips [2002] for a full recent review of this literature). In this section we provide only a brief overview of the much more limited research evidence that relates specifically to juveniles, though even here it should be noted that all of this predates (in some instances by nearly two decades) the recent youth justice reforms in England and Wales. Landau and Nathan (1983) found that white juveniles in London were significantly more likely to be cautioned than their black counterparts, even when previous record, offense type, and seriousness were controlled for. It has been suggested that one factor that might help to explain these findings relates to known differences in the propensity of defendants from different ethnic backgrounds to admit their offenses, but research by Phillips and Brown (1998) suggested that black juveniles were less likely to have their cases referred to pre-1997 cautioning panels than white or Asian juveniles even after controlling for their lower admission rates.

One of the most comprehensive studies of race and juvenile justice processing was undertaken by Mhlanga (1997), who used multivariate analysis in order to investigate whether a defendant's ethnic background was likely to have influenced outcome decisions relating to diversion as opposed to prosecution and sentencing to various measures. He found that young African/Caribbean defendants were significantly less likely than their white counterparts to be subject to police diversionary measures, more likely to have been prosecuted at court, and more likely to be sentenced to custody, though he also found that there was a greater likelihood for such defendants to be acquitted at court due to insufficient evidence.

More recently, the main focus of the debate over the treatment of ethnic minority suspects has switched from factors that might affect the decision making of individual officials within criminal justice agencies to more collective failings on the part of those agencies themselves. In 1999, a public inquiry into the way the police dealt with the

---

[143] Whereas under-sixteen-year-olds make up only 20 percent of the white population, minority ethnic groups tend to have a younger age structure: for Indians it is 23 percent, for all black groups it is 34 percent, for those of Pakistani or Bangladeshi origin it is 37 percent, and for all other groups it is 30 percent.

racist murder in London six years previously of a black teenager, Stephen Lawrence, concluded that the flaws in the police investigation were the result of "professional incompetence, institutional racism and a failure of leadership by senior officers" (Macpherson 1999, p. 137). This was followed in November 2000 by the launch of a formal investigation on the part of the Commission for Racial Equality (CRE) into allegations of racist bullying, harassment, and violence within the prison service, including well-publicized incidents at Feltham and Portland Young Offenders Institutions.[144] Even before the CRE announced its inquiry, the director-general of the prison service had openly admitted that the prison service suffered from institutional racism, and that a minority of prison staff were blatantly racist. Four prison officers were subsequently dismissed for overtly racist behavior and belonging to racist organizations. Overall, therefore, there is much disturbing evidence, and certainly no room for complacency about the way in which the English youth justice system treats black suspects, offenders, and victims.

E. Persistent Offenders

It is highly appropriate that we should conclude this section of our review—entitled Key Contemporary Issues—with the subject of persistent offenders. This is because, as earlier sections have shown, special policy prominence is now given, in both England and Scotland, to the question of how to reduce offending rates among this difficult group. Unfortunately, however, there are limits to what can be said about these policies in a research-based paper of this kind, since the Scottish focus on persistent offenders has only recently been formulated, and in England the research on the very important Intensive Supervision and Surveillance Programmes is not due to be delivered until March 2004 (see Sec. III).

We can, however, usefully draw attention to two research evaluations. In Scotland, the most frequently discussed program for youthful persistent offenders is the Freagarrach project in the central region; for example, the recent Audit Scotland (2002, p. 3) report comments that local authorities outside the central region have been "slow to replicate successful intensive services such as Freagarrach." An evaluation of this project by researchers from Lancaster University was published in

---

[144] The two-year-long investigation had still not reported at the time of writing, despite recriminations by the former director-general of the prison service who claimed that this had hindered attempts to tackle racism in prisons (*The Guardian*, June 14, 2002).

2001 (Lobley, Smith, and Stern 2001). It is a community-based project, which reportedly managed to secure engagement and trust among the young offenders it dealt with, notwithstanding that their offending behavior was very prolific.[145] Thus, the researchers commented that staff "communicated an attitude of respect and care, which many young people—and their parents—contrasted favourably with their experience of other adults in positions of authority" (p. 2), and parents of young offenders praised the staff "for their insight, their persistence, and above all for their willingness to accept young people who had been rejected by most adult institutions" (p. 4). Evaluation of the effectiveness of the program in terms of subsequent criminality was, however, not straightforward (Lobley, Smith, and Stern 2001, chap. 5). The researchers identified a clear reduction in offending rates from the year before attending Freagarrach to the year after, but they appear to be unaware that such findings are common in many samples of young offenders.[146] Other less than ideal features of the formal evaluation relate to the nature of the control groups used,[147] and the way that the reoffending data are presented.[148] The most persuasive data for the success of Freagarrach are found in relation to the apparently relatively low proportion of posttreatment offenses requiring a residential or custodial commitment.[149] In general, however, it would be fair to say that while the evaluation suggests many positive features of service delivery in Freagarrach, the performance of the project in relation to offending reduction is not definitively established by the research evaluation.[150]

[145] Of the ninety-five young people on whom follow-up data were available, two-thirds had been first identified as having committed an offense at an early age (under twelve), and the average number of officially recorded offenses in their police records in the year before attending Freagarrach was 17.7.

[146] See Bottoms (1995), discussed in note 94 above. For a more statistical discussion of this phenomenon, see Maltz (1984, pp. 30–40).

[147] Two control groups were used, but on average neither was as criminal as the Freagarrach group, and multivariate statistical techniques were not utilized to control for the differences in background characteristics.

[148] Follow-up periods ranged from six months to four years, but reoffending data are given discretely for each group (i.e., those with six months follow-up, one year follow-up, etc.), with no aggregation. Thus, although eighty-one young people had a follow-up period of twelve months or more, the data as presented do not enable one to calculate the twelve-month reoffending rates for this whole group.

[149] A higher proportion of young people in the two control groups were sentenced to custody in a two-year follow-up period than was the case for the Freagarrach group, notwithstanding that the control groups had less serious previous criminality (Lobley, Smith, and Stern 2001, p. 69). However, this finding is based on relatively small numbers.

[150] It should also be noted that the researchers considered that the reductions in known offending that they identified in the Freagarrach sample might have constituted

The second evaluation is focused on the English Youth Inclusion Programmes (YIPs). These are local community programs, initially funded from the center by the Youth Justice Board but subject to local managers matching the YJB grant. The rationale of the programs is said to be principally "to include socially excluded young people in mainstream society." To this end, YIPs have been aimed at the fifty most "at risk" children ages thirteen to sixteen in seventy of the most deprived (and high crime) local housing areas in England and Wales. The provision offered on programs is said to be distinct from general youth work because of the focus on crime and offending; thus, programs must offer targeted assistance to those in the core group of fifty. However, the actual activities undertaken are sometimes not very different from those in general youth work; for example, in the second quarter of 2002 the largest single activity undertaken in the YIPs was "sport," which accounted for nearly a quarter of all activities.

The YIPs are being evaluated by a team lead by John Burrows, a senior ex-Home Office researcher. The research report was due to be released in 2002, but this has now been postponed because central funding for the YIPs has recently been extended to 2006. A YJB briefing note on the evaluation has, however, provided the following information:[151] The average number of the "top fifty" young offenders in each local area who were engaged in activities by the YIP was, in the first two quarters of 2002, respectively, nineteen and twenty-six. (No information is provided about the range.) The average number of young people engaged in activities per YIP was, in the same two quarters, respectively, seventy-two and ninety-six. (Again, there is no information about the range.) There has been "a very substantial reduction—of some 66 percent—in arrest rates" for those members of local "top fifties" who were engaged in activities by YIPs in the second quarter of 2002.

These data are apparently promising, but it would be premature to reach any final conclusions until the full research results are available, especially as the stated results vary markedly by quarter. We can be certain, given the strong policy focus on prolific offenders in both England and Scotland, that the research base in this field will be substantially stronger in three or four years' time.

"a relatively brief 'containment' effect rather than a long-term change" (Lobley, Smith, and Stern 2001, p. 65).

[151] Unpublished briefing note dated October 24, 2002, kindly made available to the authors by Matthew Anderson of the Youth Justice Board.

VII. Restorative Justice Initiatives

In our final main section, we turn to the nascent subject of restorative justice, where the main focus again is on developments in England.

A. Restorative Justice Initiatives in England and Wales

Compared with many other jurisdictions, the concept of restorative justice has been relatively slow to take root in England, at least at the level of mainstream developments that are intended to operate as an integrated part of the regular criminal justice system.[152] But there has been a rather longer history of "stand-alone" initiatives, most of which have comprised small-scale, local, experimental projects that have been established with the aim of developing different forms of restorative justice processes (on such processes, see Marshall [1999]; Dignan and Lowey [2000]). We here briefly summarize the main types of stand-alone initiatives before going on to assess the restorative justice impact of the more recent mainstream developments, all of which have been associated with the post-1998 phase of youth justice reforms.

1. *Victim-Offender Mediation and Reparation Schemes.* Some of the earliest English developments took the form of victim-offender mediation and reparation schemes, a number of which were established during the mid-1980s, and some of which received short-term financial support from the Home Office (for details, see Davis, Boucherat, and Watson [1987]; Marshall and Merry [1990]; Davis [1992]). One group of projects (mostly targeted on juvenile offenders) operated at the pre-court stage, often in conjunction with a police caution as an alternative to prosecution.[153] A second group of projects was court-based, and either operated on adjournment between conviction and sentence, or offered mediation and/or reparation as part of a sentence. A small number of projects accepted referrals at all stages of the criminal justice process from caution to postsentence, including the period prior to an imprisoned offender being released from custody. Although these early initiatives reported a number of successes, not least in demonstrating

---

[152] It is worth noting, however, that there is an older tradition of court-ordered "reparative" penalties, such as the compensation order and the community service order, that goes back to the 1970s (see Cavadino and Dignan [2002], chap. 5, for details).

[153] Although most schemes of this type were relatively short-lived and at best enjoyed a somewhat precarious existence on the margins of the regular criminal justice system, they are of historical interest since they helped to develop and popularize the concept of "caution plus," which was commended by the influential Audit Commission (1996). Thus, they may well have helped to inspire the somewhat similar "change program" component of the final warning scheme that we described earlier.

the potential viability of a restorative justice approach within a criminal justice context, most of them also experienced difficulties in securing funding and institutional support, and some of them found it hard to recruit sufficient numbers of cases from the regular criminal justice agencies. English victim-offender mediation projects have also tended to rely much more heavily on indirect mediation than the face-to-face encounters that are more commonly used in North America and elsewhere (see, e.g., Umbreit and Roberts 1996; see also Miers et al. 2001). Moreover, government support for the initiatives evaporated after a brief period of interest during the mid-1980s and was not rekindled until the emergence of the current youth justice reform program in 1998.

Since the reawakening of official interest in restorative justice initiatives, however, the Home Office commissioned a fifteen-month retrospective evaluation of the effectiveness of seven different stand-alone restorative justice projects in England, two dealing principally with adult offenders and the other five with juveniles (Miers et al. 2001). Although the study concluded that one of the adult schemes had had a significant impact on reoffending rates (in comparison with a control group) and was cost-effective in reducing further offending, the juvenile stand-alone schemes did not have any significant impact on reconviction rates and were not cost effective in terms of reconvictions.

2. *Family Group (or Community) Conferences.* The development of New Zealand–style family group conferencing in England and Wales has been much more recent and does not date back much before the late 1990s (for a fuller discussion, see Dignan and Marsh [2001]). Unlike victim-offender mediation, however, the family group conferencing model has been adopted, not only in a criminal justice context but also within a child protection setting.

Within a criminal justice context, the early experience of conferencing has followed a broadly similar pattern to the one just outlined for victim-offender mediation, with a very limited number (twelve to fifteen) of small-scale pilot projects operating on the margins of the regular criminal justice system. Some successes have been reported, particularly with regard to high levels of participant satisfaction. But similar developmental problems have also been encountered, including difficulty in attracting high numbers of referrals, tensions between projects and mainstream criminal justice agencies, and, in the case of at least one of the projects, difficulties in securing participation on the part of victims.

Within the child protection field, family group conferences have established a more secure footing, and it has been estimated that around half of the 100 or so social services departments in England have had some experience with conferencing (Challiner, Brown, and Lupton 2000). There are several reasons why conferencing seems to have developed a firmer footing in a child protection setting than in the criminal justice arena, including a higher level of institutional support and a more secure funding environment. Also, because there is no involvement by victims in child welfare conferences, the potentially problematic issue of resolving the conflicting needs of the victim and the offender at the conference (Maxwell and Morris 1993) does not need to be addressed. Moreover, in the child welfare field there was already a well-established ethic that developing a sense of partnership between professionals and service users was likely to provide the most effective way of working. There was also a good degree of professional freedom, with less possibility of conflict with other professions, and somewhat less control by the courts. Despite all these advantages, however, the development of child protection conferencing has been a relatively slow process.

3. *Police-Led Conferencing.*   A third form of restorative justice process that has also become established in England and Wales in recent years involves the police-led variant of the conferencing model that was originally pioneered in Wagga Wagga in New South Wales. This has subsequently spread to a number of other Australian sites—notably Canberra and Sydney—and also to the United States, Canada, and, in England, the Thames Valley police force, which covers the counties of Oxfordshire, Berkshire, and Buckinghamshire.[154] The Thames Valley police began to introduce the "scripted conferencing" model in the mid-1990s (see Pollard 2000; Young 2001) as the standard way of dealing with "low tariff" offenses that would previously have been dealt with by means of a police caution. The approach is now used across the force in three different contexts: when administering "restorative cautions" (which are attended by the offender and usually his or her parents), in "restorative conferences" (at which victims and possibly their supporters may also be present), and also in "community conferences" (which are attended by members of the wider public). Following the election of the Labour government in 1997, the Thames Valley

---

[154] A small number of other police forces in England and Wales adopted the same model soon afterward, but the Thames Valley initiative was the first and remains the best known.

approach attracted the interest of the then Home Secretary, Jack Straw, and it has subsequently influenced the development of some of the more recent "mainstream" restorative justice initiatives in England and Wales.

The Thames Valley initiative is also of interest because it has been independently evaluated (Hoyle, Young, and Hill 2002), using an "action research" model that was designed to improve the quality of the process. The evaluation also incorporated a one-year reconviction study,[155] the results of which were compared by the authors with baseline data obtained by Hine and Celnick (2001) as the control group for their study. Whereas Hine and Celnick found that 29 percent of their sample of juveniles who received a caution in 1998 had a subsequent court conviction within one year, the comparable figure for the Thames Valley sample was 14 percent, and, despite the very small size of the latter sample ($N = 56$), the difference in resanctioning rates was found to be statistically significant (at $p < .05$). The two samples appeared to be broadly similar in terms of demographic variables such as gender and mean age, and also offense-related variables such as the proportion with previous cautions or convictions.[156] However, as the authors of the Thames Valley evaluation report themselves point out, the small sample size necessitates treating their findings with caution. So, although the research does appear to provide very encouraging tentative evidence that certain kinds of restorative justice interventions might result in a reduction in reoffending rates, there is clearly a need for a larger-scale evaluation before any firm conclusions can be drawn.

Since the original emergence of these "stand-alone" initiatives, several elements of a restorative justice approach have been introduced by the post-1998 youth justice reforms, and they now form part of the mainstream response to youth offending in England and Wales. These developments relate to three distinct phases of the criminal justice process: preprosecution, the first court appearance, and sentencing options following subsequent convictions.

---

[155] Although the evaluation report ranges far more widely than this, we will concentrate here on the measure that is likely to be of most interest to policy makers.

[156] Moreover, although the Thames Valley restorative cautioning sample was processed before the full implementation of reforms associated with the introduction of youth offending teams, action had already been taken to speed up the processing of youth justice cases. The authors suggest that "all other factors being equal," this could have resulted in a worse resanctioning rate over a twelve-month follow-up period because of the increased likelihood of cases coming to court if processing times are faster. It will be recalled that Jennings (2003) produced adjusted reoffending rates to take account of this phenomenon (n. 96 above).

4. *Restorative Justice Interventions at the Preprosecution Stage.* Under the Crime and Disorder Act 1998 and the original accompanying Home Office guidance, little was said initially about the content and format of the reprimand, beyond stressing the need to make clear the implications for the young person. As for the final warning, the main emphasis was on the need to address the offender's behavior and prevent any future offending, through the "change program." However, pilot areas were also advised of the importance of contacting victims, where possible, to establish their views about the offense and to assess the nature and significance of any harm or loss that might have resulted from it. They were also instructed to consider whether or not some form of direct contact with, or reparation to, the victim would be appropriate, and a number of different forms of possible reparation were identified. The evaluation of the pilot areas highlighted a number of shortcomings in the way that final warnings were being implemented (summarized in Holdaway et al. [2001], pp. 72–80;[157] see also Evans and Puech [2001]), and new, much more detailed, guidance was then issued in April 2000, which sought to address some of these deficiencies (Home Office 2000*a*).

The most important change, for present purposes, was explicitly to encourage the use of restorative justice principles and practice in the delivery of both reprimands and final warnings, drawing directly on the Thames Valley police model of restorative cautioning and restorative conferencing. It is too soon to say what effect the revised guidance may have, and the guidance makes clear that it is still open to police forces to deliver "standard" reprimands and final warnings. But the letter that accompanied the circular stressed that "Ministers and the Youth Justice Board consider strongly that the restorative approach will make final warnings more meaningful and effective" and urged all forces to give "careful consideration to the restorative justice principles, and [to] apply them wherever possible." Moreover, the Youth Justice Board is making available training for police officers, YOT workers, and others to facilitate restorative warnings and conferences. Further guidance was issued in November 2002, which largely consolidated the original version, though it also included further encouragement to adopt a re-

---

[157] In brief, the evaluation found that victims were contacted in just 15 percent of cases, and only 7 percent of victims were involved in any kind of mediation or reparative activity (4 percent in direct reparation, which included mediation, and 3 percent in indirect reparation). Concerns were also raised about the relevance of the change program in relation to the nature of the offense that had been committed.

storative approach "to make final warnings more effective and meaningful" (Home Office/Youth Justice Board 2002, p. 6).

5. *Restorative Justice Interventions at the Point of First Conviction.*   In Section III we briefly outlined the new referral order, which was "rolled out" nationally in April 2002. How might we assess the potential impact of this new measure from a restorative justice perspective? One of the most significant and radical aspects of the new procedure relates to the process itself, since this involves a switch in the primary decision-making forum from a traditional court-based judicial model to a potentially much more inclusive and informal "conferencing" forum. The YOT, which is responsible for setting up the panels and convening meetings, is not only given power to require attendance on the part of the young offender and his or her parents, but may also invite victims (who should be routinely consulted as to whether they might wish to attend), supporters of both victims and offenders, anyone else who has been affected by the offense, and, where considered appropriate, a representative of the community at large. The work of the new panels is also intended to be governed by the three principles that were considered by the Home Office (1997*a*, pp. 31–32) to underlie the concept of restorative justice: responsibility, restoration, and reintegration.[158]

With respect to outcomes, the content of any agreement that may be made as a result of a referral order is restricted, in the main,[159] to three principal types of measures: first, those that are designed to secure "restorative" outcomes—including financial or other kinds of reparation for the benefit of the victim of an offense, mediation, or "community reparation" (unpaid work on behalf of the community); second, those that are intended to address the young person's offending behavior or assist with his or her rehabilitation (e.g., participation in programs offering education and training or which aim to tackle drugs or alcohol abuse); and, third, restrictive measures that are

---

[158] The "reintegrative" potential of the new measure was underlined by the 1997 white paper entitled *No More Excuses* (Home Office 1997*a*), which anticipated that once a contract had been successfully completed and discharged by the panel, the effect would be to "purge" the offense, in the sense that it would be regarded as immediately spent for the purposes of the Rehabilitation of Offenders Act 1974, thereby removing the continuing stigma that is normally associated with a conviction. However, this aspect of the order was not included in the subsequent legislation.

[159] Youth Justice and Criminal Evidence Act, sec. 8; see now Powers of Criminal Courts (Sentencing) Act 2000, sec. 19. Agreements that might entail the imposition of any other physical restrictions on a young offender's movements, or that require the electronic monitoring of the offender's whereabouts, are specifically prohibited.

intended to reduce the likelihood of further offending (e.g., requiring the offender to be at home at specified times [analogous to a home curfew] or to stay away from specified persons or places or both).

However, the Youth Court retains (somewhat illogically) the power to impose ancillary orders on offenders who receive referral orders; they may thus be ordered to pay compensation and costs by the court in addition to any obligations they may assume as part of the youth offender contract. This new English procedure therefore falls short of the rigid distinction between adjudication and disposition that is one of the hallmarks of the Scottish system of juvenile justice. Nor is this just a theoretical point: the pilot evaluation found that courts in the pilot areas were actually making greater numbers of ancillary compensation orders than in nonpilot comparator areas (Newburn et al. 2002). One possible explanation for this is that courts in the pilot areas were being reminded of the reparative potential of the referral order and were keen to be seen to be "playing their part." However, the imposition of a compensation order by a court is conceptually very different from a mutual agreement on the part of victim and offender that some form of financial reparation should form part of the outcome following a restorative process. The courts' apparent enthusiasm for court-ordered compensation could also have the effect of both reducing the incentive for victims to participate and limiting the scope for the parties themselves to determine the most appropriate restorative outcomes.

It is too soon to predict how the work of the YOPs might work out in practice, particularly since the evaluation of the pilot phase has only recently been completed (Newburn et al. 2002).[160] However, one notable and somewhat disappointing feature of the pilot evaluation was the very low rate of victim participation. Victims attended panel hearings in only 13 percent of cases in total, and in only 28 percent of cases was there any form of victim involvement, for example, in the form of a statement to be relayed to the offender or consent to personal reparation (Newburn et al. 2002, p. 41). Moreover, in contrast to the early experience of family group conferencing in New Zealand (Morris, Maxwell, and Robertson 1993, p. 309), this does not appear to be because of inconvenience in the timing of the panels, since almost two-

---

[160] See, in addition, Newburn et al. (2001a, 2001b) for interim reports from the pilot evaluations. See also Crawford (2003), who has identified a number of possible unintended consequences that could undermine the restorative impact they might otherwise have.

thirds were held after 5 p.m. and over one-third were scheduled to begin after 6 p.m. Rather, the relative absence of victim participation
would appear to have more to do with difficulties encountered in identifying, contacting, and consulting with victims and persuading them
to participate.[161]

It is not clear at this stage to what extent these findings may be the
result of temporary implementation problems (connected, e.g., with
the development of new protocols and procedures) as opposed to more
structural problems having to do with unresolved tensions within the
legislation itself. One major problem relates to the Data Protection
Act, which was passed in 1998, the same year as the Crime and Disorder Act. Although it was initially believed that this legislation would
not apply to the YOTs, the Home Office later adopted a much more
restrictive interpretation, insisting that initial contact with victims
could only be undertaken by the police as "authorised data holders."
The problem with this approach is that other YOT workers may be
better qualified, more highly motivated, and more experienced than
the police when it comes to consulting with victims on matters relating
to reparation and mediation.

Of the three rather different types of mainstream restorative justice
interventions that have been introduced as part of the recent youth justice reforms, the referral order potentially goes furthest in the direction of establishing a participatory, inclusive, and consensual way of
responding to youth crime. But so far, as we have seen, its scope is
restricted solely to those offenders who are convicted for the first time
of offenses to which they have pleaded guilty.[162] Moreover, the extremely low levels of victim participation in and attendance at panel
hearings during the pilot phase raise serious doubts about the extent
to which the interests of victims are likely to be represented within the
new forum, and this—if sustained in the longer term—could significantly undermine the restorative potential of the panels themselves.

6. *Restorative Justice Interventions as Optional Sentencing Measures for
"Multiply-Convicted" Young Offenders.* Elements of a restorative justice approach also feature in a number of the recently introduced (or
amended) sentences that are now available to youth courts, including

[161] This was clearly the view of panel members themselves, the great majority of
whom "agreed" (40 percent) or "strongly agreed" (45 percent) that "more should be
done to encourage victims to attend" (Newburn et al. 2001*b*, p. 79; 2002, p. 32).
[162] The home secretary has power to amend the categories of offenders who may be
eligible for the referral order procedure, subject to formal Parliamentary approval.

reparation orders and action plan orders, and as an additional condition that may be attached to a supervision order. The emphasis, in all of these measures, is on making offenders accountable for what they have done by requiring them to undertake some form of reparation for either their victim or the community. However, the Crime and Disorder Act also stipulates that before any reparative interventions—of whatever kind—are imposed, the views of the victims should be sought and relayed to the court, and offenders can only be ordered to make direct reparation to victims who have consented to this (which amounts, in effect, to a limited veto). As for the content of any reparative interventions, there is scope for victim-offender mediation to take place, though the main emphasis is on practical reparative activities[163] that should, if possible, be related to the offense, and also letters of apology.

The evaluation of the youth justice pilots showed that victims were contacted in around two-thirds of cases in which there was an identifiable victim, and, of those who were contacted, exactly half consented to some form of reparation being made by their offender. The pilot study also showed that the great majority (80 percent) of reparation orders imposed by the court involved indirect reparation, and in 63 percent of cases reparation was ordered to be made to the community. Only 9 percent of cases resulted in mediation between victim and offender, though victims received some form of direct reparation in a further 12 percent of cases (Holdaway et al. 2001; Dignan 2002, pp. 79–80). However, the study also identified a serious source of tension between the requirement of victim consultation and pressure on the pilot YOTs to speed up the processing of young offenders through the courts, and it is possible that this tension may in part account for the relatively small proportion of cases involving direct reparation (Holdaway et al. 2001, p. 88). Thus, the emphasis on fast-tracking largely precluded contact with victims before an offender was convicted, and a number of magistrates were reluctant to adjourn cases to enable victims to be consulted before sentencing the offender. In the opinion of the researchers, victim consultation was too often seen as an optional extra that need only be undertaken when it does not hold up proceedings.

7. *Restorative Justice Initiatives in England and Wales: Concluding Re-*

---

[163] Offenders cannot be ordered to make financial compensation as part of a reparation order, though this can be ordered separately as an ancillary order.

marks. Elements of a restorative justice approach have featured reasonably prominently in a range of recent youth justice reforms and have now been introduced at various stages in the criminal justice process. Consequently, restorative justice initiatives of one kind or another do now form part of the mainstream response to youth offending in England and Wales, at least in the sense that they are no longer confined to "marginal, irregular and highly localised activities" (Dignan 1999, p. 53). However, two important caveats are in order in assessing the current situation.

The first is that, as we have seen, the initiatives themselves draw on an eclectic mixture of approaches that not only emanate from a variety of different jurisdictions but are also derived from a range of different philosophical and practice-based assumptions about restorative justice and the way it should be implemented. Thus, there are clearly major differences between the three main types of restorative justice initiatives we have outlined.

The police-led and facilitated scripted conferencing model that is now being encouraged at the preprosecution stage draws consciously on an explicit "crime control" perspective that is associated both with John Braithwaite's (1989) theory of reintegrative shaming and with Donald Nathanson's (1992) work on shame and pride within the context of his "affect theory." As for the reparative interventions that are available under the Crime and Disorder Act, these draw in part on the principle of "coerced restitution" that has given rise in the past to the principle of court-ordered compensation orders and community service orders.[164] But they also draw to a lesser extent on the more recent development of extrajudicial forms of offense resolution that have come to be associated with the (ostensibly voluntary and noncoercive) practice of victim-offender mediation. It is possible that the tensions resulting from these partially conflicting conceptions of reparative justice may have accounted for some of the difficulties identified during the evaluation of the 1998 YOT pilot reforms. For example, interviews with magistrates suggested that they were more likely to subscribe to

---

[164] The "coerced restitution" component of the reparation order was strengthened in April 2001 by the launch of a "community payback" initiative, which will require all youth offending teams to develop standardized packages of structured activities that may be offered to courts in cases where victims do not wish to receive direct reparation. This has generated concerns that the "mediation" component may be further marginalized, partly because of the problems over victim consultation to which we referred earlier and partly because the courts may prefer the more predictable (and "punitive") outcomes that are likely to result from the community payback scheme.

the principle of "coerced reparation," while those with YOT workers and members of not-for-profit organizations responsible for delivering reparative interventions suggested a strong tendency to equate reparation almost exclusively with mediation and to resist the notion of community reparation. This suggests a possible partial explanation for the low take-up of reparation orders in the London area (though other factors, such as a traditionally high reliance on financial penalties, may also have played a part). For it is at least possible that YOT staff may have been reluctant to recommend a reparation order unless it involved an element of mediation between victim and offender, while magistrates may have felt unenthusiastic about ordering an offender to make reparation unless it involved some form of work-based activity.

Both of the above sets of initiatives may be contrasted in turn with the potentially much more inclusive and consensual decision-making processes that might be expected to form part of the youth offender panel proceedings. But while these proceedings represent a clear departure from the traditional modified criminal court model that combines adjudicatory and dispositional functions, the new forum also appears to draw on a range of disparate precursors. The use of community volunteers in an extrajudicial forum for determining dispositional outcomes is somewhat reminiscent of both the Scottish children's hearings system and the Community Reparative Boards that have been developed in Vermont (see Dooley 1995, 1996; Bazemore and Umbreit 1998, p. 3; Dignan and Lowey 2000, p. 30). However, the panels differ from both of these other forums by including provision for victim participation from the outset. This particular aspect of the youth offender panel more closely resembles the New Zealand family group conference procedure; however, the latter does not involve members of the community in its conferencing process, whereas the non-YOT members of the youth offending panel are explicitly intended to provide a community dimension, and there is also the possibility of including other members of the community in the panel discussion.

The eclectic mixture of restorative justice approaches that has informed recent developments in England poses potentially awkward questions as to their compatibility. It also raises serious doubts about the underlying coherence of the government's overall approach to restorative justice issues.

A second important caveat is that these disparate approaches have been introduced in the context of a wider set of youth justice reforms, not all of which are easily compatible with the restorative justice ethos of "repairing the harm" that has been brought about by the offense. One very obvious example relates to the desire to speed up the youth justice process, in the interests of both efficiency and also to increase the effectiveness of any intervention by reducing the delay between the commission of an offense and its consequences for the offender. It is extremely difficult to reconcile the constant emphasis on fast-tracking and the use of statutory time limits with the need for patience and sensitivity if victims are also to be consulted and enabled to participate in restorative justice processes without being pressured or excluded by time constraints. Such tensions might be expected to result in major implementation difficulties, and it may be instructive that both the evaluation of the 1998 youth justice pilots and the more recent 1999 youth offender panel pilots have raised very serious concerns about the scope for meaningful victim participation in the new restorative justice processes (Holdaway et al. 2001; Newburn et al. 2001*a*, 2001*b*).[165]

B. Restorative Justice Initiatives in Scotland

Even by comparison with England, restorative justice initiatives have barely taken off in Scotland. There are a few stand-alone mediation and reparation schemes operating in specific localities, some of which receive referrals direct from the procurator fiscal, provided both parties consent (Young 1997, p. 66).[166] Such schemes depend on the discretionary powers of the prosecutor to divert cases from prosecution. In 1997 the Scottish Office funded eighteen pilot schemes to social work and other service agencies, though one aspect of the social work intervention was the facilitation of mediation and/or reparation to identifiable victims.

Although from a restorative justice perspective the Scottish children's hearing system shares some features that are also to be found in mediation and (especially) conferencing models—notably a procedure that is based on intentionally informal and inclusive discussion involv-

[165] Indeed, the same may also be true of the Thames Valley–style police-led conferencing model since the level of victim participation in police-led conferencing again appears to be closer to those encountered in other restorative justice processes in England and Wales than in other police-led conferencing procedures elsewhere in the world (Hoyle, Young, and Hill 2002, p. 9). Thus, victims participated in just over 11 percent of cautions with some restorative element (i.e., excluding "instant cautions"), though it is not clear how many of the latter involved cases in which there was an identifiable victim.

[166] At least one family group conferencing initiative has recently been launched in Scotland, again on a stand-alone basis (personal communication from Keith Simpson of SACRO).

ing the child and his or her family—victims are conspicuous by their absence. Nor is there any obligation (or expectation) that hearings will facilitate or encourage the production of "restorative outcomes." So, even though some (e.g., Mackay 1997; Marshall 1999) have suggested that the children's hearing system could fairly easily be adapted to serve restorative ends, it would require a fairly major modification of the process and, more to the point, a significant change of ethos to effect such a change. Since there does not appear to be any strong appetite in Scotland for making such a change (at least for the present), the prospects for the further development of restorative justice initiatives in the immediate future do not seem particularly auspicious.

Nevertheless, two other developments may also be worth mentioning as signs of a possible quickening of interest in restorative justice approaches even north of the border. The first relates to an experimental Young Offenders' Mediation Project established by a voluntary organization (Safeguarding Communities and Reducing Offending in Scotland [SACRO]), within the context of the Scottish children's hearings system (Sawyer 2000). This multiagency project is based in Fife, and brings together representatives from SACRO, Fife Council's Children's Reporter, Fife Social Work Department, and the police. Three key aspects of the scheme are the principles of early intervention, the inclusion of a victim perspective, and support for voluntary reparation to the victim or the community. One distinctive feature is the target population for the scheme, which is aimed at young offenders (ages eleven to sixteen) who show signs of developing a pattern of offending behavior. However, an evaluation report (Sawyer 2000) disclosed that referrals were by no means confined to this category, and that many victims and also offenders' parents felt that the scheme was a more appropriate response for first-time offenders than a police warning. Although most of the offenders referred to the SACRO project felt positively about the interventions in which they were engaged,[167] there was no difference between the reconviction rates—as measured by those who were referred to the children's reporter over a twelve-month follow-up period—of those who had and those who had not been referred to the program.

The second development relates to the important new policy pro-

---

[167] Similarly positive findings were reported by the evaluation of the Scottish Office's pilot program operated by procurator fiscals. Most of those participating in the mediation and reparation schemes indicated that they had a better understanding of the impact of their offending on their victim (Barry and McIvor 2000, p. 4).

posals emanating originally from the report of an advisory group on youth crime that was published by the Scottish Executive in July 2001. In the context of a report that was particularly focused on the problems posed by persistent young offenders, this group also included among its objectives the need for "greater emphasis on prevention, diversion and the concept of restorative justice." Early the next year, the Scottish Executive (2002c) published an Action Programme to Reduce Youth Crime. This action program set out a number of commitments covering four key areas where, in the words of the Executive, "we will make progress in 2002." They included, inter alia, "giving victims an appropriate place in the youth justice process" and "supporting the extension of restorative justice approaches across Scotland." More specifically, the program announced that a review of restorative justice schemes would be commissioned to help identify "what works." Moreover, as we mentioned earlier, the Scottish Executive Ministerial Group announced later in 2002 that consideration would be given to the introduction of a national scheme of police warnings, including the possibility of introducing "restorative cautions" similar to those run by the Thames Valley police in England.

In February 2003, a progress report on the strategy for victims was published (Scottish Executive 2003a). The report referred to consultations on the introduction of a "victim statements scheme," which is intended to facilitate greater participation on the part of victims. It also announced, without giving details, that it would "improve the position of victims in children's hearings." However, there were no references to restorative justice initiatives, nor does there appear to have been much progress with regard to the introduction of restorative cautioning for juveniles. All of this is in marked contrast with the extremely rapid developments we have referred to earlier with regard to other changes to the youth justice system including, notably, the introduction of fast-track children's hearings for persistent offenders, the pilot establishment of a Youth Court for sixteen- and seventeen-year-olds, and the development of national standards. The apparent reluctance to prioritize restorative justice reforms in Scotland with the same degree of enthusiasm that has been shown for some of these other developments is, of course, consistent with some earlier experience in England. While restorative justice is clearly now on the agenda for Scottish youth justice, it would be rash to suggest that its prospects north of the border look particularly auspicious in the immediate future.

VIII. Conclusion

In Section I of this essay, we set out the principal conceptual underpinnings of the English and Scottish youth justice systems. For under-sixteens in Scotland, there is a clear official commitment, in the majority of cases, to the paramountcy of the principle of the welfare of the child. England's more correctionalist agenda has prioritized the prevention of offending by young people as the principal aim of the system, with secondary commitments to responsibilization, reparation, and efficiency (including speed of processing). Both systems have therefore committed themselves primarily to preventive (or consequentialist) goals, in contradistinction to the more retributive approaches apparent in some other jurisdictions in the wake of the due process youth justice reforms of the 1960s and thereafter.

In drawing the essay to a close, it is appropriate briefly to review the strengths and weaknesses of the two systems, bearing in mind their own explicit goals, and taking account of the detailed analyses of earlier sections. Within the overall context of the history of juvenile justice, the post-1971 Scottish children's hearing system can legitimately lay claim to three rather special achievements. First, it is a clearly welfare-based system, but unlike many welfare-based systems in the first two-thirds of the twentieth century, it cannot be claimed of Scottish juvenile justice that the "kind, paternalistic intent" of its founders has "mutated into an institution that . . . [is] as likely to punish the innocent or overreact to minor offenders as it [is] to pursue a rehabilitative path" (Edelman 2002, p. 322).[168] Second, and quite possibly related to the first point, the Kilbrandon report (Scottish Office 1964), which led to the creation of the Scottish system, pioneered a unique and radical separation of functions between the courts (as institutions dealing with due process issues, including appeals) and the children's hearing as a treatment tribunal. This separation of functions has been widely praised in Scotland, and it appears to constitute a structural arrangement that has contributed greatly to overall confidence in the system.

The third special achievement in Scotland has been to hold together, in a unified system, children who offend and children who are in need of care because of their social circumstances. Criminal career research has consistently shown that many young offenders suffer from

---

[168] Indeed, as seen in Sec. III, Waterhouse (2002) has recently questioned whether the Scottish system might be making too great a use of "no action" decisions, and whether a higher level of intervention might be more truly in the long-term welfare-based interests of the children concerned.

considerable parenting deficits, schooling difficulties, and social disadvantage (Farrington 1997); they can therefore often reasonably be described as "social victims" as well as "young offenders." It follows that in any given jurisdiction there may be significant overlap between the children dealt with as juvenile offenders and those dealt with by the child protection system, and this crossover has been demonstrated empirically in Scotland. Given such an overlap, there is clear policy merit in holding closely together the institutions and the supporting social services that deal with youth crime and with child protection, especially for younger children, as Scotland's unified system has demonstrated.

But research-based and other analyses of the Scottish system show also that it suffers from some significant difficulties; four may usefully be highlighted here. First, the whole purpose of defining an act as a crime in any given society is to indicate that it is worthy of censure (Sumner 1990; von Hirsch 1993), and there is inevitably some tension in practice between the implications of the respective concepts of censure and of the paramountcy of the child's welfare. This does not mean, as was once claimed, that practice in the Scottish children's hearings is "no more than a replication of" what goes on in England's more criminal-justice-oriented system (Morris et al. 1980, p. 67), but it does mean that something resembling a tariff approach can at times be discerned within Scottish practice, notwithstanding its official welfare ideology.

Second, research has shown that for a variety of reasons the welfare-based children's hearing system does not deal well with persistent offenders, especially as they approach the upper age limit of the system's jurisdiction (the sixteenth birthday). This suggests that any attempt to sustain a welfare-based system of this kind with a higher age range could run into difficulties.

Third, once they have progressed beyond age sixteen, the Scottish system deals with young offenders wholly within the adult criminal justice system. (Scotland is thus, in a sense, simultaneously a rare example of a surviving welfare-based juvenile justice system and, for older children, an exemplification of what might ensue if one abolishes completely a specialist juvenile jurisdiction.) This part of the Scottish system is underresearched, but experience of day-to-day practice has left many informed observers unhappy with the sharp transition from a juvenile to a fully adult system at age sixteen and uneasy also about the apparently high rates of custody for adolescent offenders.

Fourth, the welfare-oriented nature of the Scottish system for under-sixteens has rendered it suspicious of the involvement of lawyers in the children's hearings themselves (though lawyers are freely allowed in the sheriff court within Scotland's "twin-institutional" system; see fig. 2). This suspicion has not been shared by all supporters of the children's hearing system, but it has been widespread (see, e.g., the contributions in Lockyer and Stone [1998]). Some change in this respect has recently been forced on the system in the wake of human rights challenges, but more challenges, and probably more concessions, can be expected in this area.

Over and above these particular issues, the recent advent of devolved government in Scotland has of late made youth crime a much more overtly political issue than it was previously. This new context is potentially of huge importance, and its arrival makes it particularly difficult to predict future developments in Scotland.

If the post-1971 Scottish system is a fascinating example of late-twentieth-century experimentation with a welfare-based juvenile justice system, then the post-1998 English system is an equally fascinating twenty-first-century foray into correctionalism for juveniles. Central to the whole system is the repudiation of the previous view, very widely held by youth justice workers in the 1980s and 1990s, that young offenders could safely be left to "grow out of crime" with minimal intervention from official agencies (who, it was thought, often produced deleterious consequences when they attempted to intervene).

The post-1998 English system undoubtedly has some significant strengths. Terrie Moffitt (1993; see also Moffitt et al. 2001) has suggested a very useful "developmental taxonomy" for young offenders, separating them into "adolescence-limited offenders" and "life-course-persistent offenders." Utilizing the language of this taxonomy, it can be said that the English youth justice workers of the 1980s and 1990s made the mistake of assuming that the vast majority of young offenders were of the "adolescence-limited" type.[169] The new system has therefore supplied an important corrective to this view, not least in its special focus on persistent offenders and on early intervention where that seems needed.

Other strengths of the "new youth justice" should be noted. Given its consequentialist emphasis, it has prioritized a focus on the effective-

---

[169] Moreover, the minority of life-course-persistent offenders contribute very disproportionately to the total number of offenses by young people.

ness of the system (and particularly on the reduction of reoffending), which was largely absent in the 1980s and early 1990s (see, e.g., the evidence in Bottoms et al. 1990). It has also prioritized efficiency, attempting to focus—and to use wisely—the limited resources of the system on the primary consequentialist goals, rather than merely on the formal processing of young offenders. Hence, for example, there is a strong new emphasis on "fast-tracking," which reduces the number of interim court appearances prior to the final disposal of the case. It has placed a bold and potentially very imaginative emphasis on active multiagency joint working (both at the strategic and operational levels) through the new local youth offending teams, which embrace agencies concerned with health and education as well as traditional criminal justice agencies for juveniles such as social services, the police, probation, and so on. It has created much more of a sense of a national plan for dealing with youth justice issues, not least through the creation of a powerful new central body, the Youth Justice Board, and through the board's monitoring of performance at the local level (e.g., through the use of the ASSET risk and needs assessment [see n. 45] and through its attempts to raise standards in custodial provision via its new commissioning powers vis-à-vis the prison service). Finally, it has attempted to place significantly greater emphasis than did the pre-1998 system (or the Scottish system) on the needs of victims and on the desirability of bringing home to offenders the adverse impact that crime can have upon victims.

In addition to these positive features of the "new youth justice," there are also some enduring strengths of the English youth justice system that date from an earlier era. Among these we may single out, by contrast with Scotland, first, a more gradual transition from the juvenile to the adult jurisdictions, with a higher age for the commencement of full exposure to the adult criminal justice system (the eighteenth rather than the sixteenth birthday), and, second, the retention (alongside the principle of prevention) of pre-1998 provisions relating to proportionality in sentencing, a concept that is (officially at least) wholly absent from the Scottish system.

The reformed English youth justice system is still in its developmental stages, and research into its functioning is therefore still very limited, especially on the key question of effectiveness (reduction of reoffending). On a tentative basis, however, a number of more negative points of assessment can already be identified, and six may be mentioned here.

First, the system strongly emphasizes the responsibility of young offenders for their actions and the responsibility of parents for the proper upbringing of their children. In theory, this emphasis is set within a context where the social causes of offending (including poverty, poor educational provision, and social exclusion) are also fully recognized, but in practice it sometimes seems that "responsibilization" has been prioritized in relative isolation from these wider social factors.[170]

Second, and in sharp contrast to the Scottish system, there is a marked institutional separation between the structures and systems for dealing with youth offending and with child care/child protection. This has led, for example, to recent sharp criticism in a joint Inspectorates report (Chief Inspectors, England and Wales 2002) that youth offending teams are paying insufficient attention to the welfare needs of the offenders with whom they deal. The paradox of an imaginative multiagency youth offending team structure (see above) that has, in general, weak links with child protection colleagues and a weak commitment to child welfare issues is one of the strangest features of the new English youth justice system.

Third, in rightly repudiating (as a universal nostrum) the "grow out of crime/leave the kids alone" philosophy, the new English youth justice system might have gone too far in the opposite direction. To return to Moffitt's (1993) developmental taxonomy, adolescence-limited offenders do indeed exist, and do not necessarily require (in crime-preventive terms) much in the way of official intervention. The new English youth justice system is tending to emphasize early intervention as a desirable goal for all (or nearly all) offenders (see, e.g., n. 78), and in so doing it might be overreacting to the weaknesses of the pre-1998 system. A more discriminating approach, based on careful risk and need assessment, might be preferable, even strictly within the new system's own emphasis on crime prevention and the efficient use of resources.

Fourth, there are some signs of danger that the new English system, with its relatively automatic progression from reprimand to final warning to (if one pleads guilty) a referral order, can on occasion run into

---

[170] The Labour Party has become famous in the United Kingdom for a slogan ("tough on crime, tough on the causes of crime") that encapsulates a dual emphasis on responsibilization and on taking seriously the social causes of crime. But, in adult as in youth justice policy, it has proved to be much easier in policy terms to address the first half of this slogan than the second.

the kinds of difficulty that are by now familiar in criminal justice systems that attempt to prescribe mandatory processes and outcomes. In brief, the automatic progression can seem very heavy-handed if the next offense in the sequence is trivial.

Fifth, while the system is indeed attempting to address the needs of victims, there is on occasion a real tension between this goal and other goals of the new system (such as speed of processing and correctional interventionism). There is also some tension between the centralizing requirements of the new national plan for youth justice and the decentralizing tendencies of a restorative justice approach (on issues of this kind, see Braithwaite [2000]). Linked to these issues, the new English interest in victim-oriented approaches has drawn on an eclectic mixture of policy traditions that is not yet fully consistent or coherent (see Sec. VII).

Sixth, and on a more political note, there appears to be some tendency toward defensiveness among those who are driving the new youth justice policy. Achievements are strongly emphasized, but criticism—even constructive criticism based on research findings—seems to be less welcome, notwithstanding the government's official commitment to an evidence-led policy approach. This defensive tendency is of course understandable, particularly in the early years of a system that has promoted radical change. But if the tendency remains unmodified, it could in the future significantly inhibit the new system's ability to adapt in the light of research evidence and changing circumstances.

This brief concluding assessment of the English and Scottish youth justice systems perhaps allows one to develop some kind of provisional template against which preventively focused youth justice systems might be measured. Such a template might include factors such as an administratively unified approach to offense-based and child protection cases among younger children; a graduated age transition to the adult system; an appropriate emphasis on the censure of wrongful acts, but set sensitively within frameworks that truly take account of the relevant social contexts; a proper emphasis on the human rights of offenders, but not in a way that allows lawyers to sabotage the preventive or restorative focus of the system; a strong emphasis on joint inter-agency working, at both the strategic and operational levels; the development of appropriate risk and needs assessments to differentiate properly between categories such as adolescence-limited and life-course persistent offenders; the development of effective programs of intervention, with early intervention in the lives of genuinely high-risk children; and the development of services for victims and programs to bring home to offenders the sufferings of victims, without major tension with other goals of the system (such as correctional effectiveness and efficient service delivery). Such a template provides a challenging agenda for any preventively oriented youth justice system. It will be very interesting to see how the English and the Scottish systems will be measured against it in ten years' time.

REFERENCES

Adler, Ruth M. 1985. *Taking Juvenile Justice Seriously*. Edinburgh: Scottish Academic Press.

Alder, Christine, and Joy Wundersitz, eds. 1994. *Family Conferencing and Juvenile Justice: The Way Forward or Misplaced Optimism?* Canberra: Australian Institute of Criminology.

Allen, Charlotte, Iain Crow, and Michael Cavadino. 2000. *Evaluation of the Youth Court Demonstration Project*. Home Office Research Study no. 214. London: Home Office.

Allen, Rob. 1991. "Out of Jail: The Reduction in the Use of Penal Custody for Male Juveniles 1981–88." *Howard Journal of Criminal Justice* 30:30–52.

Asquith, Stewart. 1983. *Children and Justice: Decision-Making in Children's Hearings and Juvenile Courts*. Edinburgh: Edinburgh University Press.

———. 1998. "Scotland." In *Confronting Youth in Europe: Juvenile Crime and Juvenile Justice*, edited by Jill Mehlbye and Lode Walgrave. Copenhagen: AKF Forlaget.

Audit Commission. 1996. *Misspent Youth: Young People and Crime*. London: Audit Commission.

Audit Scotland. 2001. *Youth Justice in Scotland: A Baseline Report*. Edinburgh: Audit Scotland.

———. 2002. *Dealing with Offending by Young People*. Edinburgh: Auditor General for Scotland and the Accounts Commission.

Auld, Robin Ernest, Right Honourable Lord Justice. 2001. *Review of the Criminal Courts of England and Wales: Report*. London: Stationery Office.

Bainham, Andrew. 1990. *Children, the New Law: The Children Act 1989*. Bristol: Jordan & Sons.

Ball, Caroline, Kevin McCormac, and Nigel Stone. 2001. *Young Offenders: Law, Policy and Practice*. 2d ed. London: Sweet & Maxwell.

Bandalli, Sue. 1998. "Abolition of the Presumption of *Doli Incapax* and the Criminalisation of Children." *Howard Journal of Criminal Justice* 37:114–23.

———. 2000. "Children, Responsibility and the New Youth Justice." In *The New Youth Justice*, edited by Barry Goldson. Lyme Regis, Dorset: Russell House.

Barry, Monica, and Gill McIvor. 2000. *Diversion from Prosecution to Social Work and Other Service Agencies: Evaluation of the 100% Funding Pilot Programmes: 1999.* Crime and Criminal Justice Research Findings no. 37. Edinburgh: Scottish Executive, Central Research Unit.

Bateman, Tim. 2001. "A Note on the Relationship between the Detention and Training Order and Section 91 of the Powers of Criminal Courts (Sentencing) Act 2000: A Recipe for Injustice." *Youth Justice* 1(3):36–41.

Bateman, Tim, and Chris Stanley. 2002. *Patterns of Sentencing: Differential Sentencing across England and Wales.* London: Youth Justice Board.

Bazemore, Gordon, and Mark S. Umbreit. 1998. *Conferences, Circles, Boards and Mediations: Restorative Justice and Citizen Involvement in the Response to Youth Crime.* Washington, D.C.: Department of Justice, Office of Justice Programs.

BBC News Scotland. 2002. "Fast Route for Young Offenders." BBC online news release, October 28, 2002, at www.news.bbc.co.uk.

Boateng, Paul. 1999. Speech in Standing Committee E, June 8, 1999. *Parliamentary Debates: House of Commons Official Report, Standing Committees, Session 1998–99*, vol. 6.

Boswell, Gwyneth. 1996. *Young and Dangerous: The Background and Careers of Section 53 Offenders.* Aldershot: Avebury.

Bottoms, Anthony E. 1995. *Intensive Community Supervision for Young Offenders: Outcomes, Process and Cost.* Cambridge: University of Cambridge, Institute of Criminology.

———. 2002. "The Divergent Development of Juvenile Justice Policy and Practice in England and Scotland." In *A Century of Juvenile Justice*, edited by Margaret K. Rosenheim, Franklin E. Zimring, David S. Tanenhaus, and Bernadine Dohrn. Chicago: University of Chicago Press.

Bottoms, Anthony E., Phillip Brown, Brenda McWilliams, William McWilliams, and Michael Nellis. 1990. *Intermediate Treatment and Juvenile Justice.* London: H.M. Stationery Office.

Bottoms, Anthony E., J. David McClean, and Keith W. Patchett. 1970. "Children, Young Persons and the Courts: A Survey of the New Law." *Criminal Law Review* (July), pp. 368–95.

Bowling, Benjamin, and Coretta Phillips. 2002. *Racism, Crime and Justice.* Harlow: Longman.

Braithwaite, John. 1989. *Crime, Shame and Reintegration.* Cambridge: Cambridge University Press.

———. 2000. "The New Regulatory State and the Transformation of Criminology." *British Journal of Criminology* 40:222–38.

Cavadino, Michael, and James Dignan. 2002. *The Penal System: An Introduction.* 3d ed. London: Sage.

Challiner, V., L. Brown, and C. Lupton. 2000. *A Survey of Family Group Conference Use across England and Wales.* Portsmouth: University of Portsmouth Social Services Research and Information Unit and University of Bath Department of Social and Policy Studies.

Chief Inspectors, England and Wales. 2002. *Safeguarding Children: A Joint*

Chief Inspectors' Report on Arrangements to Safeguard Children. Joint report by the Chief Inspector of Social Services; the Director for Health Improvement, Commission for Health Improvement; H.M. Chief Inspector of Constabulary; H.M. Chief Inspector of the Crown Prosecution Service; H.M. Chief Inspector of the Magistrates' Courts' Service; H.M. Chief Inspector of Schools; H.M. Chief Inspector of Prisons; and H.M. Chief Inspector of Probation. London: Department of Health.

Cleland, Alison. 1996. "The Child's Right to Be Heard and Represented in Legal Proceedings." In *Children's Rights in Scotland,* edited by Alison Cleland and Elaine E. Sutherland. Edinburgh: W. Green/Sweet and Maxwell.

Council of Europe. 2001. *Penological Information Bulletin no. 22.* Strasbourg: Council of Europe.

Crawford, Adam. 2003. "The Prospects for Restorative Justice in England and Wales: A Tale of Two Acts." In *Criminology, Conflict Resolution and Restorative Justice,* edited by Kieran McEvoy and Tim Newburn. Basingstoke: Palgrave.

Crawford, Adam, and Mario Matassa. 2000. *Community Safety Structures: An International Literature Review.* Review of the Criminal Justice System in Northern Ireland, Research Report no. 8. Belfast: The Stationery Office.

Dahl, Tove Stang. 1985. *Child Welfare and Social Defence.* Oslo: Norwegian University Press.

Davis, Gwynn. 1992. *Making Amends: Mediation and Reparation in Criminal Justice.* London: Routledge.

Davis, Gwynn, Jacky Boucherat, and David Watson. 1987. *A Preliminary Study of Victim Offender Mediation and Reparation Schemes in England and Wales.* Home Office Research Study no. 42. London: H.M. Stationery Office.

————. 1989. "Pre-Court Decision-Making in Juvenile Justice." *British Journal of Criminology* 29:219–35.

Department of Health. 2001. *The Children Act Report 2000.* London: Department of Health.

Dignan, James. 1999. "The Crime and Disorder Act and the Prospects for Restorative Justice." *Criminal Law Review* (January), pp. 48–60.

————. 2002. "Reparation Orders." In *Reparation and Victim-Focused Social Work,* edited by Brian Williams. London: Jessica Kingsley.

Dignan, James, with K. Lowey. 2000. *Restorative Justice Options for Northern Ireland: A Comparative Review.* Review of the Criminal Justice System in Northern Ireland, Research Report no. 8. Belfast: The Stationery Office.

Dignan, James, and Peter Marsh. 2001. "Restorative Justice and Family Group Conferences in England: Current State and Future Prospects." In *Restorative Justice for Juveniles: Conferencing, Mediation and Circles,* edited by Allison Morris and Gabrielle Maxwell. Oxford: Hart.

Donzelot, Jacques. 1980. *The Policing of Families.* London: Hutchinson.

Dooley, M. J. 1995. *Reparative Probation Program.* Waterbury: Vermont Department of Corrections.

————. 1996. *Restoring Hope through Community Partnerships: The Real Deal in Crime Control.* Lexington, Ky.: American Probation and Parole Association.

Edelman, Peter. 2002. "American Government and the Politics of Youth." In *A Century of Juvenile Justice*, edited by Margaret K. Rosenheim, Franklin E. Zimring, David S. Tanenhaus, and Bernadine Dohrn. Chicago: University of Chicago Press.

Eekelaar, John. 2002. "Child Endangerment and Child Protection in England and Wales." In *A Century of Juvenile Justice*, edited by Margaret K. Rosenheim, Franklin E. Zimring, David S. Tanenhaus, and Bernadine Dohrn. Chicago: University of Chicago Press.

Elkin, Winifred. 1938. *English Juvenile Courts*. London: Kegan Paul.

Erickson, Patricia. 1982. "The Client's Perspective." In *The Scottish Juvenile Justice System*, edited by F. M. Martin and Kathleen Murray. Edinburgh: Scottish Academic Press.

Evans, Roger. 1994. "Cautioning: Counting the Cost of Retrenchment." *Criminal Law Review* (August), pp. 566–75.

Evans, Roger, and Rachel Ellis. 1997. *Police Cautioning in the 1990s*. Home Office Research Findings no. 52. London: Home Office.

Evans, Roger, and Kyela Puech. 2001. "Reprimands and Warnings: Populist Punitiveness or Restorative Justice?" *Criminal Law Review* (October), pp. 794–805.

Evans, Roger, and Christine Wilkinson. 1990. "Variations in Police Cautioning Policy and Practice in England and Wales." *Howard Journal of Criminal Justice* 29:155–76.

Farrington, David P. 1997. "Human Development and Criminal Careers." In *The Oxford Handbook of Criminology*, 2d ed., edited by Mike Maguire, Rod Morgan, and Robert Reiner. Oxford: Clarendon.

Farrington, David P., and John N. Burrows. 1993. "Did Shoplifting Really Decrease?" *British Journal of Criminology* 33:57–69.

Farrington, David P., Patrick A. Langan, and Per-Olof Wikström. 1994. "Changes in Crime and Punishment in America, England and Sweden in the 1980s and 1990s." *Studies in Crime and Crime Prevention* 3:104–31.

Faust, Frederic L., and Paul J. Brantingham, eds. 1979. *Juvenile Justice Philosophy: Readings, Cases, and Comments*. 2d ed. St. Paul, Minn.: West.

Fionda, Julia. 1999. "New Labour, Old Hat: Youth Justice and the Crime and Disorder Act 1998." *Criminal Law Review* (January), pp. 36–47.

Flexner, Bernard, and Roger N. Baldwin. 1915. *Juvenile Courts and Probation*. London: Grant Richards.

Ghate, Deborah, and Marcelo Ramella. 2002. *Positive Parenting: The National Evaluation of the Youth Justice Board's Parenting Programme*. London: Youth Justice Board.

Goldson, Barry. 2002. *Vulnerable Inside: Children in Secure and Penal Settings*. London: Children's Society.

———, ed. 2000. *The New Youth Justice*. Lyme Regis, Dorset: Russell.

Gordon, A. 1996. "The Role of the State." In *Children's Rights in Scotland*, edited by Alison Cleland and Elaine E. Sutherland. Edinburgh: W. Green/ Sweet and Maxwell.

Hallett, Christine, and Cathy Murray. 1998. *The Evaluation of Children's Hear-*

ings in Scotland. Vol. 1, *Deciding in Children's Interests.* Edinburgh: Scottish Office, Central Research Unit.

Hazel, N., A. Hagell, Mark Liddle, Deborah Archer, Roger Grimshaw, and J. King. 2002. *Detention and Training: Assessment of the Detention and Training Order and Its Impact on the Secure Estate across England and Wales.* London: Youth Justice Board.

Hine, Jean, and Anne Celnick. 2001. *A One Year Reconviction Study of Final Warnings.* Sheffield: University of Sheffield. Available online on the Home Office website at http://www.homeoffice.gov.uk/rds/pdfs/reconvictstudy warn.pdf.

Hodgkin, R. 2002. *Rethinking Child Imprisonment: A Report on Young Offender Institutions.* London: Children's Rights Alliance for England.

H.M. Chief Inspector of Prisons for England and Wales. 1997. *Young Prisoners: A Thematic Review by H.M. Chief Inspector of Prisons for England and Wales.* London: Home Office.

———. 2002. *A Second Chance: A Review of Education and Supporting Arrangements within Units for Juveniles Managed by H.M. Prison Service: A Thematic Review by H.M. Chief Inspector of Prisons for England and Wales Carried Out Jointly with the Office of Standards in Education.* London: Home Office.

Holdaway, Simon. 2002. "A Study of the Final Warning Scheme Operating in 30 Youth Offending Teams." Unpublished research report prepared for the Youth Justice Board.

Holdaway, Simon, Norman Davidson, James Dignan, Richard Hammersley, Jean Hine, and Peter Marsh. 2001. *New Strategies to Address Youth Offending: The National Evaluation of the Pilot Youth Offending Teams.* Research, Development and Statistics Occasional Paper no. 69. London: Home Office.

Home Office. 1994. *The Criminal Histories of Those Cautioned in 1985, 1988 and 1991.* Home Office Statistical Bulletin no. 8/94. London: Home Office.

———. 1995. *Cautions, Court Proceedings and Sentencing, England and Wales 1994.* Home Office Statistical Bulletin no. 18/95. London: Home Office.

———. 1997a. *No More Excuses: A New Approach to Tackling Youth Crime in England and Wales.* Cm. 3809. London: The Stationery Office.

———. 1997b. *Tackling Delays in the Youth Justice System: A Consultation Paper.* London: Home Office.

———. 2000a. *Circular Introducing the Final Warning Scheme: Revised Guidance.* London: Home Office. Also available online at www.homeoffice.gov.uk/yousys/youth.htm.

———. 2000b. *Statistics on Race and the Criminal Justice System 2000.* London: Home Office.

———. 2000c. *Criminal Statistics, England and Wales 1999.* Cm. 5001. London: The Stationery Office.

———. 2001a. *Criminal Justice: The Way Ahead.* Cm. 5074. London: The Stationery Office.

———. 2001b. *Criminal Statistics, England and Wales 2000.* Cm. 5312. London: The Stationery Office.

———. 2002*a*. *Criminal Statistics, England and Wales 2001.* Cm. 5696. London: The Stationery Office.

———. 2002*b*. *Justice for All.* Cm. 5563. London: The Stationery Office.

Home Office and Lord Chancellor's Department. 2001. *The Youth Court 2001: The Changing Culture of the Youth Court—Good Practice Guide.* London: Home Office.

Home Office/Youth Justice Board for England and Wales. 2002. "The Final Warning Scheme: Guidance for the Police and Youth Offending Teams." Issued November 2002. London: Home Office.

Hoyle, Carolyn, Richard Young, and Roderick Hill. 2002. *Proceed with Caution: An Evaluation of the Thames Valley Police Initiative in Restorative Cautioning.* York: Joseph Rowntree Foundation.

James, Ann, and John Raine. 1998. *The New Politics of Criminal Justice.* London: Longman.

Jennings, Debbie. 2003. "One Year Juvenile Reconviction Rates: First Quarter 2001 Cohort." Home Office Online Report no. 18/03. London: Home Office Research, Development and Statistics Directorate.

Kearney, Brian. 1992. *The Report of the Inquiry into Child Care Policies in Fife.* Edinburgh: H.M. Stationery Office.

———. 2000. *Children's Hearings and the Sheriff Court.* 2d ed. Edinburgh: Butterworths.

Kershaw, Chris, Tracey Budd, Graham Kinshott, Joanna Mattinson, Pat Mayhew, and Andy Myhill. 2000. *The 2000 British Crime Survey: England and Wales.* Home Office Statistical Bulletin 18/80. London: Home Office.

Kuenssberg, Sally, and Alan Miller. 1998. "Towards a National Reporter Service." In *Juvenile Justice in Scotland: Twenty-Five Years of the Welfare Approach*, edited by Andrew Lockyer and Frederick H. Stone. Edinburgh: T&T Clark.

Landau, Simha F., and Gad Nathan. 1983. "Selecting Delinquents for Cautioning in the London Metropolitan Area." *British Journal of Criminology* 23: 128–49.

Leng, Roger, Richard Taylor, and Martin Wasik. 1998. *Blackstone's Guide to the Crime and Disorder Act 1998.* London: Blackstone.

Lobley, David, David Smith, and Christina Stern. 2001. *Freagarrach: An Evaluation of a Project for Persistent Young Offenders.* Edinburgh: Scottish Executive, Central Research Unit.

Lockyer, Andrew. 1994. "The Scottish Children's Hearings System: Internal Development and the U.N. Convention." In *Justice for Children*, edited by Stewart Asquith and Malcolm Hill. Dordrecht: M. Nijhoff.

Lockyer, Andrew, and Frederick H. Stone, eds. 1998. *Juvenile Justice in Scotland: Twenty-Five Years of the Welfare Approach.* Edinburgh: T&T Clark.

Mackay, R. 1997. "Restorative Justice and the Scottish Children's Justice System." Paper presented to the International Conference on Restorative Justice for Juveniles, Leuven, Belgium, May 1997.

Macpherson, William. 1999. *The Stephen Lawrence Inquiry: Report of an Inquiry by Sir William Macpherson of Cluny.* Cm. 4262. London: The Stationery Office.

Maltz, Michael D. 1984. *Recidivism*. Orlando, Fla.: Academic Press.

Marshall, Tony F. 1999. *Restorative Justice: An Overview*. London: Home Office Research Development and Statistics Directorate.

Marshall, Tony F., and Susan Merry. 1990. *Crime and Accountability: Victim/Offender Mediation in Practice*. London: H.M. Stationery Office.

Martin, F. M., Sanford J. Fox, and Kathleen Murray. 1981. *Children Out of Court*. Edinburgh: Scottish Academic Press.

Maxwell, Gabrielle, and Allison Morris. 1993. *Family, Victims and Culture: Youth Justice in New Zealand*. Wellington: Victoria University Social Policy Agency and Institute of Criminology.

Mayhew, Pat, and Lorna J. F. Smith. 1985. "Crime in England and Wales and Scotland: A British Crime Survey Comparison." *British Journal of Criminology* 25:148–59.

McConville, Mike, Andrew Sanders, and Roger Leng. 1991. *Case for the Prosecution*. London: Routledge.

Mehlbye, Jill, and Lode Walgrave, eds. 1998. *Confronting Youth in Europe: Juvenile Crime and Juvenile Justice*. Copenhagen: AKF Forlaget.

Mhlanga, Bonny. 1997. *The Colour of English Justice: A Multivariate Analysis*. Aldershot: Avebury.

Miers, David, Mike Maguire, Shelagh Goldie, Karen Sharpe, Chris Hale, Ann Netten, Steve Uglow, Katherine Doolin, Angela Hallam, Jill Enterkin, and Tim Newburn. 2001. *An Exploratory Evaluation of Restorative Justice Schemes*. Crime Reduction Research Series Paper 9. London: Home Office.

Moffitt, Terrie E. 1993. "Adolescence-Limited and Life-Course-Persistent Adolescent Behavior: A Developmental Taxonomy." *Psychological Review* 100:674–701.

Moffitt, Terrie E., Avshalom Caspi, Michael Rutter, and Phil A. Silva. 2001. *Sex Differences in Antisocial Behaviour: Conduct Disorder, Delinquency, and Violence in the Dunedin Longitudinal Study*. Cambridge: Cambridge University Press.

Morita, Akira. 2002. "Juvenile Justice in Japan: A Historical and Cross-Cultural Perspective." In *A Century of Juvenile Justice*, edited by Margaret K. Rosenheim, Franklin E. Zimring, David S. Tanenhaus, and Bernadine Dohrn. Chicago: University of Chicago Press.

Morris, Allison M., and Henri Giller. 1977. "The Juvenile Court—the Client's Perspective." *Criminal Law Review* (April), pp. 198–205.

Morris, Allison M., Henri Giller, Elizabeth Szwed, and Hugh Geach. 1980. *Justice for Children*. London: Macmillan.

Morris, Allison M., and Mary McIsaac. 1978. *Juvenile Justice?* London: Heinemann.

Morris, Allison, Gabrielle M. Maxwell, and Jeremy P. Robertson. 1993. "Giving Victims a Voice: A New Zealand Experiment." *Howard Journal of Criminal Justice* 32:304–21.

Morris, Norval, and Gordon Hawkins. 1970. *The Honest Politician's Guide to Crime Control*. Chicago: University of Chicago Press.

Muncie, John. 1999. "Institutionalized Intolerance: Youth Justice and the 1998 Crime and Disorder Act." *Critical Social Policy* 19:147–75.

Narey, Martin. 1997. *Review of Delay in the Criminal Justice System.* London: Home Office.

Nathanson, Donald L. 1992. *Shame and Pride: Affect, Sex and the Birth of Self.* New York: Norton.

Nellis, Michael. 1990. "Intermediate Treatment and Juvenile Justice in England and Wales 1960–1985." Ph.D. thesis, University of Cambridge.

Newburn, Tim. 2002. "Young People, Crime and Youth Justice." In *The Oxford Handbook of Criminology*, 3d ed., edited by Mike Maguire, Rod Morgan, and Robert Reiner. Oxford: Oxford University Press.

Newburn, Tim, Adam Crawford, Rod Earle, Shelagh Goldie, Chris Hale, Angela Hallam, Guy Masters, Ann Netton, Robin Saunders, Karen Sharpe, and Steve Uglow. 2002. *The Introduction of Referral Orders into the Youth Justice System: Final Report.* Home Office Research Study no. 242. London: Home Office.

Newburn, Tim, Guy Masters, Rod Earle, Shelagh Goldie, Adam Crawford, Karen Sharpe, Ann Netten, Chris Hale, Steve Uglow, and Robin Saunders. 2001a. *The Introduction of Referral Orders into the Youth Justice System: First Interim Report.* RDS Occasional Paper no. 70. London: Home Office.

———. 2001b. *The Introduction of Referral Orders into the Youth Justice System: Second Interim Report.* RDS Occasional Paper no. 73. London: Home Office.

O'Mahony, David, and Kevin Haines. 1996. *An Evaluation of the Introduction and Operation of the Youth Court.* Home Office Research Study no. 152. London: Home Office.

O'Neill, Teresa. 2001. *Children in Secure Accommodation: A Gendered Exploration of Locked Institutional Care for Children in Trouble.* London: Jessica Kingsley.

Paternoster, Raymond, Robert Brame, Ronet Bachman, and Lawrence Sherman. 1997. "Do Fair Procedures Matter? The Effect of Procedural Justice on Spouse Assault." *Law and Society Review* 31:163–204.

Petch, Alison. 1988. "Answering Back: Parental Perspectives on the Children's Hearing System." *British Journal of Social Work* 18:1–24.

Phillips, Coretta, and David Brown. 1998. "Entry into the Criminal Justice System: A Survey of Police Arrests and Their Outcomes." Home Office Research Study no. 185. London: Home Office.

Pitts, John. 1988. *The Politics of Juvenile Crime.* London: Sage.

Pollard, Charles. 2000. "Victims and the Criminal Justice System: A New Vision." *Criminal Law Review* (January), pp. 5–17.

Sawyer, B. 2000. *An Evaluation of the SACRO (Fife) Young Offender Mediation Project.* Crime and Criminal Justice Research Findings no. 43. Edinburgh: Scottish Executive.

Schur, Edwin M. 1973. *Radical Nonintervention: Rethinking the Delinquency Problem.* Englewood Cliffs, N.J.: Prentice-Hall.

Scott, Elizabeth S. 2002. "The Legal Construction of Childhood." In *A Century of Juvenile Justice*, edited by Margaret K. Rosenheim, Franklin E. Zimring, David S. Tanenhaus, and Bernadine Dohrn. Chicago: University of Chicago Press.

Scottish Children's Reporter Administration. 2002. *Statistical Bulletin no. 25: Referrals of Children to Reporters and Children's Hearings.* Stirling: Scottish Children's Reporter Administration.

Scottish Committee of the Council on Tribunals. 2002. *Special Report on the Children's Hearing System.* Edinburgh: Scottish Committee of the Council on Tribunals.

Scottish Executive. 2000*a. It's a Criminal Waste: Stop Youth Crime Now.* Report of the Advisory Group on Youth Crime. Edinburgh: Scottish Executive.

———. 2000*b. Scottish Executive Response to the Advisory Group on Youth Crime Review.* Edinburgh: Scottish Executive.

———. 2000*c. Recorded Crime in Scotland 1999.* Statistical Bulletin, Criminal Justice Ser. CrJ/2000/2. Edinburgh: Scottish Executive.

———. 2002*a. Executive's Youth Crime Review: Report and Statement on Recommendations.* Edinburgh: Scottish Executive.

———. 2002*b. National Standards for Scotland's Youth Justice Services: A Report by the Improving the Effectiveness of the Youth Justice System Working Group.* Edinburgh: Scottish Executive.

———. 2002*c. Scotland's Action Programme to Reduce Youth Crime 2002.* Edinburgh: Scottish Executive.

———. 2002*d. The 2000 Scottish Crime Survey: Overview Report.* Edinburgh: Scottish Executive.

———. 2003*a. Scottish Strategy for Victims Progress Report.* Edinburgh: Scottish Executive.

———. 2003*b. Youth Court Feasibility Project Group Report.* Edinburgh: Scottish Executive.

Scottish Law Commission. 2002. *Report on Age of Criminal Responsibility.* Scottish Law Commission Report no. 185. Edinburgh: The Stationery Office.

Scottish Office. 1964. *Report of the Committee on Children and Young Persons Scotland.* Cmnd. 2306 (the "Kilbrandon Report"). Edinburgh: H.M. Stationery Office.

———. 1991. *Children and Crime, Scotland 1989.* Statistical Bulletin Criminal Justice Series. Edinburgh: Scottish Office.

Shapland, Joanna. 1988. "Fiefs and Peasants: Accomplishing Change within the Criminal Justice System." In *Victims of Crime: A New Deal?* edited by Mike Maguire and John Pointing. Philadelphia: Open University Press.

Shapland, Joanna, Jennifer Johnstone, Angela Sorsby, Tamsin Stubbing, and John Jackson, with Jeremy Hibbert and Marie Howes. 2001. "Evaluation of Statutory Time Limit Pilot Schemes in the Youth Court: Interim Report." University of Sheffield. Available online on the Home Office website at www.homeoffice.gov.uk/rds/pdfs/interim.

Sherman, Lawrence W. 1993. "Defiance, Deterrence and Irrelevance: A Theory of the Criminal Sanction." *Journal of Research in Crime and Delinquency* 30:445–73.

Smith, Lorna J. F. 1983. *Criminal Justice Comparisons: The Case of Scot-*

land and England and Wales. Research and Planning Unit Paper no. 17. London: Home Office.

Social Work Services Inspectorate. 1996. *A Secure Remedy: A Review of the Role, Availability, and Quality of Secure Accommodation for Children in Scotland*. Edinburgh: Scottish Office.

Sparks, Richard, Anthony E. Bottoms, and Will Hay. 1996. *Prisons and the Problem of Order*. Oxford: Clarendon.

Stone, Nigel. 2001*a*. "Legal Commentary—Custodial Sentencing: Aims and Principles in Youth Justice, Disparity and Other Complexities." *Youth Justice* 1(3):42–46.

———. 2001*b*. "Legal Commentary—Detention and Training Orders for under 15 Year Olds: The Problem of Persistence." *Youth Justice* 1(1):53–55.

Straw, Jack, and Alan Michael. 1996. *Tackling Youth Crime, Reforming Youth Justice: A Consultation Paper on an Agenda for Change*. London: Labour Party.

Sumner, Colin, ed. 1990. *Censure, Politics and Criminal Justice*. Milton Keynes: Open University Press.

Tanenhaus, David S. 2002. "The Evolution of Juvenile Courts in the Early Twentieth Century: Beyond the Myth of Immaculate Construction." In *A Century of Juvenile Justice*, edited by Margaret K. Rosenheim, Franklin E. Zimring, David S. Tanenhaus, and Bernadine Dohrn. Chicago: University of Chicago Press

Tutt, Norman, and Henri Giller. 1987. "'Manifesto for Management': The Elimination of Custody." *Justice of the Peace* 151:200–202.

Tyler, Tom R. 1990. *Why People Obey the Law*. New Haven, Conn.: Yale University Press.

Tyler, Tom R., and Yuen J. Huo. 2002. *Trust in the Law: Encouraging Public Cooperation with the Police and Courts*. New York: Russell Sage.

Umbreit, Mark S., and Ann Warner Roberts. 1996. *Mediation of Criminal Conflicts in England: An Assessment of Services in Coventry and Leeds*. St. Paul: University of Minnesota Center for Restorative Justice and Mediation.

von Hirsch, Andrew. 1993. *Censure and Sanctions*. Oxford: Clarendon.

von Hirsch, Andrew, Anthony E. Bottoms, Elizabeth Burney, and Per-Olof Wikström. 1999. *Criminal Deterrence and Sentencing Severity: An Analysis of Recent Research*. Oxford: Hart.

Waterhouse, Lorraine. 2002. "The Scottish Children's Hearings in Perspective." Paper delivered at the University of Cambridge Institute of Criminology, summer 2002.

Waterhouse, Lorraine, Janice McGhee, Bill Whyte, Nancy Loucks, Helen Kay, and Robert Stewart. 2000. *The Evaluation of Children's Hearings in Scotland*. Vol. 3, *Children in Focus*. Edinburgh: Scottish Executive.

Wheeler, Stanton, Edna Bonacich, M. Richard Cramer, and Irving K. Zola. 1968. "Agents of Delinquency Control." In *Controlling Delinquents*, edited by Stanton Wheeler. New York: Wiley.

Whyte, Bill. 1998. "Rediscovering Juvenile Delinquency." In *Juvenile Justice in Scotland: Twenty-Five Years of the Welfare Approach*, edited by Andrew Lockyer and Frederick H. Stone. Edinburgh: T&T Clark.

———. 2001. "Reviewing Youth Crime in Scotland." *SCOLAG Legal Journal* 283:80–82.

Young, Peter. 1997. *Crime and Criminal Justice in Scotland*. Edinburgh: Stationery Office.

Young, Richard. 2001. "Just Cops Doing 'Shameful' Business? Police-Led Restorative Justice and the Lessons of Research." In *Restorative Justice for Juveniles: Conferencing, Mediation and Circles*, edited by Allison Morris and Gabrielle Maxwell. Oxford: Hart.

Youth Justice Board for England and Wales. 2001*a*. *Corporate Plan 2001–02 to 2003–04 and Business Plan 2001–02*. London: Youth Justice Board.

———. 2001*b*. "Curb Short Term Custody—End Justice by Geography." Press release, Oct. 9, 2001. London: Youth Justice Board.

———. 2002. *Building on Success: The Next Steps, Youth Justice Board Review 2001–02*. London: Youth Justice Board.

Anthony N. Doob and Jane B. Sprott

Youth Justice in Canada

ABSTRACT

Starting in 1908 with a law based on welfare principles and finishing in 2003 with a law based on criminal law principles and proportionality, successive changes in Canada's youth justice legislation have provided additional structure in governing the key decisions involving youths. While criminal law in Canada, including youth justice laws, is a federal responsibility, the provinces administer the law. Interestingly, there are very large differences in the manner in which the provinces administer the single (federal) criminal law. Although most Canadians believe that the youth justice system is too lenient, the data show that many of the cases being processed through Canada's youth courts and many of the cases resulting in imprisonment for youth involve very minor offenses. Federal government concerns about the provincial overuse of the youth justice system and about the high rates of custodial sentences for minor offenses were important determinants of the shape of the most recent youth justice legislation—the Youth Criminal Justice Act (YCJA), which came into effect in 2003. For political reasons, these concerns were "balanced" with symbolically tough, but practically inconsequential, measures. It remains to be seen what the effects of the new law will be.

In the past century, Canada has had three quite different laws governing the manner in which young offenders are handled. The shift, over time, has been from a law based on welfare principles toward legislation that focuses more on criminal law principles and proportionality. In addition, successive changes in legislation have provided more structure in governing the key decisions that are made in the youth justice system. Finally, the legislation has, over time, shifted away from the assumption that the reduction of offending by youths can best be accomplished within the formal youth justice system.

Anthony N. Doob is professor of criminology, the Centre of Criminology, University of Toronto, Canada. Jane B. Sprott is assistant professor, Department of Sociology and Anthropology, University of Guelph, Guelph, Ontario, Canada.

In the past twenty years, youth justice issues in Canada have been important politically for various reasons. People believe that youth crime has been increasing, though the evidence, especially in the past ten years, does not support this conclusion. The public assumes that the youth justice system controls the level of youth crime in our communities, and people believe that the youth justice response has been too lenient. At the same time, there is evidence that many of the cases being processed through Canada's youth courts and many of the cases resulting in imprisonment for youth involve very minor offenses.

Canada is a federal state. Criminal law, including youth justice laws, is a federal responsibility, though the administration of justice is a provincial responsibility. The result of this split in responsibility is that there are very large differences in the manner in which the single (federal) criminal law is administered. Federal government concerns about provincial overuse of the youth justice system and about high rates of custodial sentences for minor offenses were important determinants of the shape taken by the most recent youth justice legislation—the Youth Criminal Justice Act (YCJA) passed in 2002. Politically, however, these concerns were "balanced" with symbolically tough measures. Based on Canada's experience with similar "tough" sounding changes, it appears likely that these tough changes will have no impact in practice. It remains to be seen whether the new law will result in fewer cases going to court and fewer youths going to prison.

The history of youth justice in Canada is the story of two parallel, but separate, youth justice systems: the political youth justice system (the system as it is seen and discussed in the political realm) and the operational youth justice system (the system as it operates on a daily basis). The political youth justice system itself is not coherent. There are substantial pressures to "get tough" on young people who have offended. At the same time, there are political concerns about too many youths who have apparently committed minor offenses being brought into the formal system and too many youths being incarcerated.

This essay explores the manner in which these conflicting tendencies have played out in the past 100 years on questions such as the age of youths under the jurisdiction of the youth court, decisions on whether a case should be brought to court, "transferring" youths to adult court, and principles of sentencing, including the use of "custodial" sentences. These policy issues can be seen as ways of understanding Canada's youth criminal justice system.

Canada's youth justice system, since 1908, has changed in at least three ways. In the first place, there has been a very clear move from a "child welfare" approach to youthful offending toward a "criminal law," or accountability-proportionality, response to youthful offending. Whereas Canada's first youth justice law, the 1908 Juvenile Delinquents Act (JDA; R.S.C. 1970, chap. J-3), saw all offenses as symptoms of an underlying "delinquent" state, Canada's newest step on this path, the 2002 YCJA, sees offenses as something that the state has an obligation to respond to in a measured, proportional manner.

The second major shift that has occurred over the past century is a move toward more structure in the laws. The JDA said, in effect, that almost any bad behavior on the part of a youth made that youth subject to being defined as delinquent. And this 1908 legislation allowed almost any disposition or sentence to be imposed to address the problem. The most recent legislation provides not only principles (e.g., in terms of what goes to court and how sentences are handed down) but also "hurdles" that must be overcome (e.g., in determining that a youth should be held in pretrial detention or in sentencing the youth to custody).

Finally, the law has shifted away from the optimistic view that crime can be addressed effectively with youth justice interventions. The 1908 legislation required the judge to act like a sensible parent. The legislation passed by Parliament in 2002 requires the judge to hand down the most rehabilitative and reintegrative sentence within the requirement that the sentence be proportional to the seriousness of the offense. These shifts have taken place within a context of contradictory political pressures both to be tough with young offenders and to use the youth justice system parsimoniously.

We argue that many of the problems that Canada faced in the operation of its youth justice system during the latter part of the twentieth century come from an inability or unwillingness to make difficult decisions about what the goals are of the youth justice system. This led to an apparent ambivalence about what the youth justice system should look like. At the same time, structural concerns arise as a result of an unusual constitutional division of responsibilities for youth justice matters: criminal law, including young offender legislation, is a federal responsibility, but Canada's ten provinces and three territories are responsible for the administration of justice. The result is that the provinces and territories, with different political climates, ideologies, and administrative practices, administer the same youth justice legislation in quite different ways (Doob and Sprott 1996).

Recent legislative changes by the Canadian federal government appear to be addressing some of the fundamental problems of youth justice. Whether many of the explicit and progressive goals of the legislation are accomplished will be determined by administrative policies that are largely the responsibility of provincial governments whose focus is largely on the "political youth justice system" rather than the "operational youth justice system."

Section I outlines the constitutional context for youth justice legislation in Canada. We then describe the first two pieces of federal youth justice legislation—the 1908 JDA, which had a clear "child welfare orientation," and the 1984 Young Offenders Act (YOA; R.S.C. 1985, c. Y-1), which moved Canadian youth justice legislation a large step closer toward criminal law principles. Both reflected values and approaches that were consistent with approaches and concerns elsewhere in North America. Section II describes the pressures, which started almost immediately after the YOA was passed, to change this law. This pressure is discussed in the context of concern about crime and the justice system as well as the pressure to look "tough." Section III describes the problem faced by the Liberal government after its return to power in 1993 in looking and sounding as if it were "tough on crime" while still remaining liberal. Section IV focuses on the four-year period beginning in 1998 in which the third of Canada's youth justice laws developed. The conflicting concerns and political realities during this period are described. Finally, the legislation and the political process of selling it are discussed in Section V. In Section VI, we speculate about the possible impact of the new legislation.

I. History of Canadian Youth Justice from 1908 to 1984

Canada is a federal country, consisting of ten provinces and three territories. The division of responsibility between these two levels of government is important in many areas, including youth justice. In order to understand the nature and problems of youth justice in Canada, it is first important to look at the constitutional arrangements in the country. We briefly describe the first of three sets of legislation that have operated during the past century. The history is important because today's issues reflect the problems and models of youth justice that Canada has experienced over the past century.

A. Constitutional Arrangements

Under the Canadian constitution, the responsibility for the criminal justice system is what is typically referred to as a "shared responsibility" between the federal and provincial governments.[1] The federal government has responsibility for legislation on criminal law, whereas the provinces have responsibility for the administration of the criminal law.[2] However, welfare legislation, including child welfare legislation (and its administration), is a provincial responsibility. Thus there are different child welfare laws in each province. These laws cover children who are neglected, abused, or otherwise in need of state protection. In addition, youths who are seen as being in need of apprehension for offending but who are under twelve years old (the current age of criminal responsibility) can usually be apprehended under child welfare legislation.

Canadian youth justice laws have always allowed, or encouraged, discretion in responses by police and others to offending. Canadian provinces vary dramatically across time and space in the political orientation of their governments. These governments also vary in the way in which they apparently view youths generally and young offenders in particular. The result is that there is considerable variation in the manner in which the system deals with youths (Doob 1992; Carrington and Moyer 1994; Doob and Sprott 1996), as we discuss in more detail in Section IV.

Canada, since 1982, has had a "Charter of Rights and Freedoms" (pt. I of the Constitution Act, 1982; enacted by the *Canada Act 1982*, [U.K.] c. 11), which, not surprisingly, governs youth justice matters along with all other laws. For the most part, Charter issues do not have much impact on youth justice legislation. The exception is a requirement that any person facing a penalty lasting five years or more must have the option of a trial by jury. This leads to the otherwise inexplicable maximum sentence of five years less a day for youths tried for homicide offenses between 1992 and 1995. In addition, a complex set of

---

[1] Canada has ten provinces and three territories (in which the federal government assumes some of the powers that otherwise would go to the provinces). The three territories combined constitute 40 percent of the landmass of Canada but have a combined population of only 99,200, which is roughly 0.3 percent of the total population (Statistics Canada 1996). For ease of presentation, when we refer to "the provinces," we will mean the provinces and territories unless we state otherwise.

[2] An issue that we do not discuss further is the constitutional anomaly that Newfoundland, which joined Canada in 1949, did not operate under Canada's youth justice laws until 1984, when the 1908 JDA was replaced with the YOA.

notice and "election" provisions (choice of mode of trial) became necessary as penalties for youths tried in youth court broke through the five-year barrier in 1995. The requirement of a uniform age of youth court jurisdiction also flows from concerns raised by Canada's Charter of Rights and Freedoms.

B. An Overview of the Move toward Criminal Law Principles

Until 1908, there were no separate criminal laws dealing with young offenders. Youths over age seven could be charged criminally and dealt with under the same laws as adults. They were often, however, imprisoned separately from adults.

In 1908, after a good deal of debate (See Leon [1977] for a discussion of the development of Canada's first juvenile offending law), the Parliament of Canada enacted, under its criminal law powers, the JDA, an act that would remain, essentially unchanged, until 1984, when it was replaced with the YOA. The JDA had jurisdiction over youths who offended who were at least seven years old. The maximum age varied from sixteen to eighteen across provinces. In one province, Alberta, the maximum age was, for most of this period, sixteen for boys and eighteen for girls. Although the JDA was a criminal law—creating a single offense of delinquency—it was consistent with the child-saving period in which it was enacted (Leon 1977; Platt 1977). Three sets of provisions support this assertion.

First of all, the scope of the JDA was broad. A youth who committed any criminal offense, breached any provincial law or municipal bylaw, was liable to be placed in a provincial training school or reformatory for any reason, or was engaged in "sexual immorality or any similar form of vice" (JDA, sec. 2[1]) was guilty of a single offense: that of delinquency. All "offenses" then were symptoms of a single underlying problem: delinquency.

Second, the principles of the JDA emphasized "welfare" principles. The direction to those working in the system was that the juvenile delinquent "shall be dealt with not as an offender, but as one in a condition of delinquency and therefore requiring help and guidance and proper supervision" (JDA, sec. 3[2]). Furthermore, "the care and custody and discipline of a juvenile delinquent shall approximate as nearly as may be that which should be given by his parents, and that as far as practicable every juvenile delinquent shall be treated, not as a criminal, but as a misdirected and misguided child, and one needing aid, encouragement, help, and assistance" (JDA, sec. 38). Although it was criminal law, one of the choices available to the judge was to commit the youth to the child welfare system (JDA, sec. 20[1][h]).

Third, sentences under the JDA were indeterminate. In fact, the court could order the youth back to court for a review of the sentence at any time up until the youth had turned twenty-one. An important complication, however, created tension between the parts of the system. The act contemplated two different types of custodial dispositions: commitment of the youth to the local Children's Aid Society or commitment of the youth "to an industrial school." Industrial schools were defined as including a "juvenile reformatory or other reformative institution or refuge for children" (JDA, sec. 2[1]). These came to be known as "training schools" in most parts of Canada and were, for the most part, secure institutions. Once a youth was committed to an industrial school or a children's aid society, however, "the child may thereafter be dealt with under the laws of the province in the same manner in all respects as if an order had been lawfully made in respect of a proceeding instituted under authority of a statute of the province; and from and after the date of issuing of such order except for new offenses, the child shall not be further dealt with by the court under this Act" (JDA, sec. 21[1]).

In effect then, and in reality as soon as a youth had been committed to training school, the juvenile court lost all control. The youth could be released whenever the (provincial) training school authorities deemed it to be appropriate under provincial laws. As the federal government pointed out during the process of changing the laws in the early 1980s, "In keeping with the [JDA's] treatment oriented approach, the dispositions which a juvenile court judge may give are frequently open-ended, on the grounds that when the juvenile is sufficiently 'treated' the authorities will terminate the disposition" (Canada 1981, p. 2). In addition, "Under the [JDA] once a juvenile court has pronounced a custodial sentence, jurisdiction of the case is usually transferred to the provincial authorities. In theory the provincial authorities can then unilaterally alter the juvenile court's decision in any direction which might offer, in their opinion, more 'aid encouragement, help and assistance'—even if it means the premature release of a juvenile whom the court has sentenced to custody" (Canada 1981, p. 11).

Juvenile courts could be held "in the private office of the judge or in some other private room in the courthouse or municipal building" (JDA, sec. 12[2]) and, therefore, could be closed to the public. The separation from the adult system was meant to be complete. If the trial were held in a regular courtroom, half an hour "shall be allowed to elapse between the close of the trial . . . of any adult and the beginning of the trial of a child" (JDA, sec. 12[2]). More important was the provision that the identity of the young person be kept private, and no identifying characteristics be published (JDA, sec. 12[3]).

The JDA survived essentially without changes until 1984. However, in 1961, the federal Department of Justice started a process of examining the need for change by setting up a committee to examine the youth justice system. It is important to recall that it was during the 1960s that "rights-oriented" issues (culminating in such cases as *In re Gault*, 387 U.S. 1 [1967]) were having their influence on youth justice in the United States. The principles contained in those cases were part of the debate in Canada throughout this reform period (1961–84). During this period of discussion, there was a government committee report in 1965 (Department of Justice Committee on Juvenile Delinquency 1965), a bill introduced in Parliament in 1970 (the Young Offenders Bill [C-192]) that was not enacted before the Parliamentary session ended in 1972, another federal government committee report with draft legislation in 1975 (Solicitor General Canada 1975), a set of "highlights" of proposed legislation from the (Liberal) federal minister responsible for youth justice law in 1977 (Canada 1981), another set of "legislative proposals" in 1979 (Solicitor General Canada 1979; from the Conservative government that was in power for seven months beginning in mid-1979), and, finally, a bill introduced into Parliament in 1981 by the Liberal government that became law in 1984 (the YOA, R.S.C. 1985, c. Y-1).

These various reports and pieces of draft legislation created a process that, at least for the final fifteen years (1969–84), kept "youth justice" on the policy agenda. In addition, however, these various documents created a forum for debate and discussion that forced those interested in youth justice policy to consider carefully what they thought legislation should look like. The 1975 report, for example, proposed an elaborate structure to screen cases out of the court and back into the community (Solicitor General Canada 1975). It also recommended a minimum age of criminal responsibility of fourteen and jurisdiction until a youth turned eighteen. Finally, it recommended that youths should not be transferred to adult court until they turned sixteen.

In 1977 when the Liberal government released its set of "highlights" of youth justice legislation (Solicitor General Canada 1977), the proposed minimum age of criminal responsibility was twelve. Two years later, in the midst of a seven-month Conservative reign, the government's proposed minimum age was also twelve. As that report stated, "It was universally agreed that under the current Juvenile Delinquents Act the age of seven years was too young for criminal proceedings" (Solicitor General Canada 1979). The maximum age was another matter. The Liberal government in 1977 had indicated that it would prefer a uniform age of eighteen across the country but had not achieved a consensus with the provinces and, therefore, would maintain provincial choice. The Conservatives, two years later, indicated their law would have a uniform maximum age. Their preferred maximum age was sixteen, but they were flexible if the provinces agreed, instead, on allowing a uniform maximum age of seventeen or eighteen.

For the most part, the 1979 Conservative legislative proposals were the same as the 1977 Liberal proposals. The legislation (as the proposed YOA) that was introduced into Parliament in 1981 by the Liberal government after it regained power in 1980 would have allowed provinces to choose the maximum age (sixteen, seventeen, or eighteen). However, only slightly more than a year later and two years before the bill became law, Canada acquired a Charter of Rights and Freedoms, which, among other things, guaranteed "equal protection and equal benefit of the law" (Charter of Rights and Freedoms, sec. 15[1]). The bill was amended during the legislative process such that a uniform maximum age of eighteen was set for the whole country.

That age range—the twelfth to the eighteenth birthday—still stands. It was set as a result of a combination of political necessity (the perception or assumption of a newly established constitutional requirement) and political compromise. There is, however, still pressure to lower both ages.

C. The Young Offenders Act: A Shift of Principles and a Set of Compromises

The 1984 YOA moved a good distance away from "welfare" principles toward criminal law principles.[3] Due process rights (e.g., the right to a lawyer, rights of appeal, definite sentences, and a hint of proportional sentencing) were all part of the act. In addition, however, the

[3] The law came into effect in 1984, but the implementation of the uniform maximum age of eighteen did not come into effect until 1985.

YOA had a definite treatment orientation. The principles placed in the act in the legislative process in the early 1980s illustrate the tension between a welfare and a criminal law orientation. For example, the YOA states that:

3 (1) It is hereby recognized and declared that
  (*a*) while young persons should not in all instances be held accountable in the same manner or suffer the same consequences for their behaviour as adults, young persons who commit offences should nonetheless bear responsibility for their contraventions;
  (*b*) society must, although it has the responsibility to take reasonable measures to prevent criminal conduct by young persons, be afforded the necessary protection from illegal behaviour;
  (*c*) young persons who commit offences require supervision, discipline and control, but, because of their state of dependency and level of development and maturity, they also have special needs and require guidance and assistance.

The YOA is, however, unambiguously, criminal law. Though carefully referred to throughout the act as "dispositions," sentences under the YOA are definite sentences. Clearly this was an important change and a change that the government described in part in terms of public safety: "The new Act recognizes that the youth court is the authority that should decide the extent to which custody and other dispositions are used to ensure the safety of Canada's communities and people. It would therefore be inconsistent if such decisions could be unilaterally altered by provincial authorities without reference back to the court" (Canada 1981, p. 11).

Proportionality entered the new act but was not part of the language. The maximum length of a custodial sentence was normally two years, but for the most serious offenses (those that would put an adult in jeopardy of a life sentence), the maximum sentence for a youth was three years. The use of "secure" custody (as contrasted with "open" custody) originally had offense-based restrictions. As Trépanier concluded five years after the act was implemented, "The Young Offenders Act and the interpretation given it by the courts have introduced proportionality as one of the considerations that must guide the judge in his choice of a measure" (1989, p. 33).

Criminal law principles, however, do not necessarily imply harsh treatment. One of the most broadly recognized failures of the YOA was the tendency to bring large numbers of cases into the court system. This failure, however, was not the result of criminal law principles within the act. For example, the declaration of principle made it clear that young offenders need not be brought to court: "Where it is not inconsistent with the protection of society, taking no measures or taking measures other than judicial proceedings under this Act should be considered for dealing with young persons who have committed offenses" (YOA, sec. 3[1][d]).

Keeping youth out of the court system had become a priority in Canada during the 1970s. During this period, concern about the labeling of young persons as offenders was part of youth justice culture. Not surprisingly, the 1975 federal committee report (Solicitor General Canada 1975) recommending new youth justice legislation referred to youth who had offended as "young persons in conflict with the law" presumably to avoid labeling them as "juvenile delinquents" (the term in use at that time) or "young offenders," the term that would come into effect in 1984. This set of proposals included

> a mechanism to screen cases prior to court action over and above the present informal exercise of discretion. This mechanism would provide the opportunity to screen cases on a uniform basis to determine if a more appropriate alternative to formal court proceedings is available. This reflects an ever-growing body of opinion that holds that an appearance in court often may be unnecessary and perhaps even harmful to some young persons. Therefore, if intervention in the life of a young person is justified on the basis of the alleged commission of an offence, then the option should be available to deal with a young person without the necessity of resorting to the court process. . . . [The] primary function [of the screening mechanism] would be to consider the feasibility and possibility of diverting the young person from the court process to other resources that are better able to deal with him having regard to all the circumstances at hand. (Solicitor General Canada 1975, p. 10)

This issue—the failure of the youth justice system to screen out cases that were seen as inappropriate for the youth court—is an issue that has not yet been solved. Part of the problem then—in the 1970s—and now is that there appears to be substantial provincial (and municipal) variation in the proportion of those youths who come to the attention of the police who are taken to court. In one study (Conly 1978), the "charge rate" (proportion of youths taken to court in relation to those who were apprehended by the police for an apparent offense) varied across twelve metropolitan areas in Canada from 17 percent to 96 percent. The variation was not simply provincial. Cities within some provinces showed dramatic differences as well.

This issue was clearly salient to the drafters of the 1984 YOA. The official book of "highlights" from the act released by the office of the federal minister responsible for the act noted that "one of the underlying principles of the new Act is that, for less serious offenses, alternative measures to the formal court process might be used. It has been recognized for some time that many young people are brought to court unnecessarily, when other effective means to deal with them already exist in some provinces. These programs, called *diversion programs*, may entail community service, involvement in special education programs, counseling or restitution agreements; their common characteristic is that they are all voluntary" (Canada 1981, p. 6).

In other words, the minister responsible for the act made it clear that it is not in the public interest to invoke the criminal law for all young people who commit criminal offenses. Our point is not that such an approach is unusual. It is not. But the fact that Canada's law is "criminal" does not mean that it is meant to be invoked in a harsh manner.

Symbolically, one of the important changes that were brought about by the proclamation of the YOA was the end of the ability of the court to turn a criminal matter into a child welfare matter. As we have pointed out, under the earlier legislation (the 1908 JDA) the court, after finding a young person to be a delinquent, could "commit the child to the charge of any children's aid society" (JDA, sec. 20[1][h]). This was no longer possible after the 1984 YOA became law. At least in theory, there were two separate approaches: the provincial child welfare laws or the federal (criminal) young offender laws. The YOA made no reference to the provincial child welfare laws. Presumably it was left to those administering the law to determine into which stream a child should be thrown.

Quebec addressed this decision quite explicitly in its 1977 Youth Protection Act (YPA; Quebec: Loi sur la Protection de la Jeunesse, Chapitre P-34 [1977, c. 20, a146]). A case involving a young person who apparently committed an offense would go to a provincial administrative official who would decide whether the case should go to youth court or be dealt with outside of the youth (criminal) court structure. Although some serious due process concerns were raised about the particular approach used in the late 1970s and early 1980s to screen youths out of the youth court system in Quebec (see, e.g., Trépanier 1983), the more generally applauded tradition of Quebec's keeping youth out of the formal youth (criminal) court system has been maintained to the present day, as is described in Section IV below.

The shift to definite sentences was an important change from the previous legislation. Most offenses were punishable by a term in custody of no more than two years. For the most serious cases (including murder up until 1992), the maximum legal (aggregate) length of any sentence was three years. Although some suggested that three years was too little, the argument was that if three years was not sufficient to accomplish whatever it was that the youth justice system was supposed to accomplish, the youth (if he or she was at least fourteen years old) could be transferred to adult court. Once a youth was committed to custody, the expectation was that he or she would spend that full sentence in custody, though temporary absences could be granted administratively. Transfer was always seen as a type of "safety valve" for those cases where the youth justice system did not appear to be adequate. The theory was that the maximum sentence length in the youth court could be kept relatively low because the transfer provisions allowed exceptional cases to escape these limits.

One symbolically important acknowledgment of rehabilitation principles in the YOA is the provision that allow reviews of sentences— including custodial sentences—by a youth court judge. The application for a review can come from provincial officials or from the youth. Thus a young person with a relatively long sentence (over six months) can apply for a review of the sentence. The judge can leave the sentence as it was or can reduce its harshness (e.g., move the youth from a secure to an open custody facility, or from a custodial facility into the community, or shorten the length of time in custody). Probation conditions can also be altered, but the length of the sentence cannot be extended. Judges appear to see reviews as being an important part of individualized justice. Most judges (80 percent in a recent survey) believe that the original sentencing judge should carry out the review presumably because they believe that the sentencing judge has a unique ability to assess the changed circumstances (Doob 2001). Unfortunately, little is known about the frequency of reviews or their impact on custodial (or other) sentences. It would appear from survey data of

judges (the only data currently available) that the proportion of sentences receiving reviews varies considerably across the country (analysis by the authors of data reported in Doob [2001]).

D. Transfers of Youths into the Adult Criminal Justice System

Throughout Canada's youth court history (i.e., 1908 to the present),
youths age fourteen and older have been in jeopardy of being "transferred" out of the youth justice system into the adult system. The
transfer takes place in the youth court after the first appearance in that
court. A youth can be transferred for all but the most trivial of offenses.
From 1908 to 1984, the test for transfer was fairly simple sounding: if
the court is of the opinion "that the good of the child and the interest
of the community demand it," that youth could be transferred to adult
court (JDA, sec. 9[1]). Courts obviously "sharpened" this test somewhat. It remained clear, however, that transfers were meant to be rare.

The consequences of being transferred in Canada are serious. First
of all, for most criminal law purposes, the fourteen-year-old who is
transferred to adult court is deemed to be a full adult. This means that
they have the rights of an adult (e.g., a choice of a jury trial) but could
also be sentenced as an adult. In the case of murder, for example, this
meant, after 1977 (and until 1992), that a youth over age fourteen
could, if transferred and subsequently found guilty of murder, be sentenced to imprisonment for life without parole eligibility for twenty-
five years. For more mundane cases, the consequences are also important: when a case is transferred to the adult court, the youth can be
named publicly by the mass media as soon as the transfer is "complete"
(i.e., all appeals have been disposed of). Normally, youths are not in
jeopardy of being identified in the mass media at any stage of youth
court proceedings or after conviction.

As one might expect, with the shift toward a more legal orientation,
the initial "test" for transfer was also more explicit under the YOA
than it had been previously. It was still possible to transfer almost any
youth over age fourteen who was charged with almost anything other
than the most trivial of offenses. In deciding whether a case should stay
in the youth court or be transferred to the adult court, a judge had to
consider the seriousness of the offense, and the age, maturity, and
criminal record of the youth. Then the judge had to consider which
system—the youth system or the adult system (including the correctional facilities of the two systems)—"in the interest of society and
having regard to the needs of the young person" (YOA, sec. 16[1])

could best "meet the circumstances of the case" (YOA, sec. 16[2][c]). Judges found this a challenging task, in part, of course, because they were making decisions about which of two systems could best deal with a case before any of the facts of the case had been established. The notion that the judges were to "balance" the interests of society and those of the young person was consistent with the rest of the act. When judges were confronted with a fork in the road to justice, the YOA instructed them to take it.

E. Conclusion: A New Youth Justice Law, 1984–85

In summary then, the changes that took place in Canada's youth justice laws in 1984 tended to focus on "criminal law" principles. These changes took place as a result of a process that began in 1961 and ended in April 1985 when a uniform maximum age of eighteen was implemented across Canada. This overall "criminal law" or "due process" orientation of the law included the following elements: an explicit acknowledgment of due process rights (rights of appeal, special restrictions on the use of statements by accused youth, and rights to counsel); a restriction of the jurisdiction of the act to federal (criminal) acts; a change in the age of jurisdiction (from a minimum age of seven to twelve, and to a uniform maximum age of the eighteenth birthday); definite sentences with relatively short maximum sentences; a hesitant first start at acknowledging the importance of proportionality (e.g., in maximum sentence length, in the availability of secure custody as a sentence option, and in the criteria for transfer to adult court); and the enshrining of the principle that "the rights and freedoms of young persons include a right to the least possible interference with freedom that is consistent with the protection of society, having regard to the needs of young persons and the interests of their families" (YOA, sec. 3[1][f]). These changes created a system in Canada where youths were (and still are) being dealt with in a separate system from adults, but in a system where the justification for them being there and the principles that govern the manner in which they are treated are clearly "criminal law" principles.

It is worth noting, in this context, that according to survey evidence (Doob 2001) most judges in Canada who hear youth court matters also hear (adult) criminal court matters. The vast majority of youth court judges (84 percent across in all provinces) who responded to this survey indicated that they also hear adult criminal cases as part of their regular work. For 37 percent of the respondents to this survey, youth court matters are mixed in with adult criminal cases in the normal daily docket.

F. The Other Youth Justice System: The Child Welfare System

As we have pointed out, the full legislative and administrative responsibility for the child welfare system lies with the provinces. The importance of provincial laws increased in 1984 for two reasons. First, the scope of behavior falling under the YOA included only those behaviors that were violations of federal law. Provincial and municipal laws were no longer included, and there was no longer a "catchall" category of behavior like "sexual immorality or similar form of vice." Second, what otherwise would be offenses by those eleven years old and younger were no longer under criminal law control.

Generally speaking, the provincial legislation focuses on traditional child welfare issues—children suffering or at risk of physical or sexual harm, neglect, and so on. The Ontario law—the Children and Family Services Act (R.S.O. 1990 c. C. 11) that came into effect in 1984—covers all children in the province under the age of sixteen. In part because of the void left in the criminal law for youths under age twelve who might commit offenses, a "youth in need of protection" typically includes a broad definition of harms from which provinces wish to protect children. Thus, in Ontario the child can be found in need of protection if

> the child is less than twelve years old and has killed or seriously injured another person or caused serious damage to another person's property, [and] services or treatment are necessary to prevent a recurrence and the child's parent or the person having charge of the child does not provide, or refuses or is unavailable or unable to consent to, those services or treatment; or the child is less than twelve years old and has on more than one occasion injured another person or caused loss or damage to another person's property, with the encouragement of the person having charge of the child or because of that person's failure or inability to supervise the child adequately. (Children and Family Services Act, Ontario, secs. 37[2][j] and [2][k])

The Ontario child welfare law is not dramatically different from other provincial laws. And, like the federal (criminal) legislation, it has an explicit, but not very strong, statement endorsing the principle of minimal interference. Under "purposes" it states that "so long as they are consistent with the best interests, protection, and well being of children," there is the necessity "to recognize that the least disruptive course of action that is available and is appropriate in a particular case to help a child should be considered" (Children and Family Services Act, Ontario, sec. 1[2][2]). "Considering" a course of action does not, obviously, require that it be chosen.

If a youth is found to be in need of protection, there is, again, a presumption in favor of the least disruptive intervention or a community placement (e.g., with a relative, neighbor, etc.; Children and Family Services Act, Ontario, sec. 57). Nevertheless, the fact remains that, on the balance of probabilities, youths can be placed into the care of the state if they have committed offenses and the parents appear to a court to be unable to supervise them adequately. Hence, although Canada's criminal law does not address the offending of youths under age twelve, the state can and does apprehend and hold in secure settings youths under age twelve who commit offenses.

The separation of the "welfare" system from the "youth [criminal] justice system" became clearer with the YOA than it had been under the JDA. As the youth justice system became more clearly focused on criminal behavior, the pressures to move toward a harsher system became more focused.

II. Pressure for Change

When it received its final vote in Canada's (federal) House of Commons, the YOA received all parties' support. It is unusual for all major political parties in Canada to agree on anything. Agreeing on youth justice legislation would not, therefore, be expected. Perhaps the more than twenty years of discussion was responsible for this.

Soon after the YOA came into force (in April 1984), however, controversy returned. There were a number of technical problems that occurred almost immediately (e.g., in a few of the provisions having to do with records of youth justice matters). But there were also substantive concerns. A new offense—failure to comply with a disposition (largely a breach of a probation order)—was introduced into the YOA in 1986. Fourteen years later, this single offense would be responsible for 23 percent of the custodial sentences handed down in the country. For the first two years of the act's operation, if a young person breached a condition of a probation order, the breach could result in a resentencing of the youth for the original offense. The amendments that came

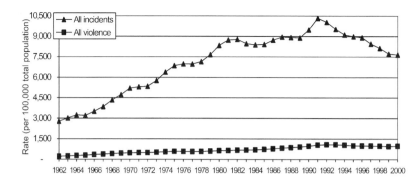

FIG. 1.—Rate (per 100,000) of all criminal code incidents and all violence (Canada), 1962–2000. Source: Canadian Centre for Justice Statistics, Statistics Canada 1962–2001.

into force in 1986 were the first of three sets of amendments that attempted to "look tough" on youth crime (R.S.C. 1985, c. 24 [2d Supp.]). In 1992 and again in 1995, the maximum sentences for murder were increased, and the rules for transfer to adult court were changed. These are described in Section II.B.

A. Crime Trends and Public Perceptions

Youth justice laws in Canada have been shaped since 1984 by an intensely political process. Although it could be argued that the change from the welfare-oriented JDA to the more "legally" oriented YOA developed as a result of principled debate, it would be hard to argue that the debate during the latter part of the 1980s and the 1990s was as principled.

Canadians have, for years, reported to pollsters that they believe that sentences for adults are too lenient. A Province of Ontario poll found that 77 percent of residents thought that adult sentences were too lenient. The corresponding figure, from the same survey for youth court sentences was 86 percent (Doob et al. 1998). The difficulty is that part of the belief that sentences are too lenient is based on the incorrect assumption that harsher sentences will lead to a safer community (Doob et al. 1998).

To understand what happened to youth justice legislation during this period, we need to look at what was happening to measures of crime at this time. As shown in figure 1, "crime" as measured by incidents reported to the police increased quite regularly from 1962 until the early 1980s. During the 1980s, however, overall crime incidents reported to the police did not go up dramatically, and certainly there was no sustained increase during the 1990s. Violence, as a proportion of all incidents, was never very large.

A more careful look at the curve for violence, however, is important. Clearly the rate of violent incidents reported to and by the police increased between 1962 and the early 1990s. But the increase in "crime" was not driven, in large part, by the increase in the number of reported violent incidents.

The only measure that exists at a national level of official responses to youth crime comes from police reports of the number of "youths charged" from aggregate (Uniform Crime Reports) data. Because these are aggregate data (reported centrally only in terms of the number of "youths," not their ages), it is impossible to compare data from before April 1985 with data after this date. On April 1, 1985, the provinces adopted a uniform maximum age of eighteen. Prior to that, as we have pointed out, whether a sixteen- or seventeen-year-old was a youth or adult depended on the province (and to a lesser extent, on gender). There are serious concerns, as well, with the accuracy of the data on "youths not charged" such that the Canadian Centre for Justice Statistics, Statistics Canada, no longer routinely reports these data.

The result is that "youths charged" from 1986 onward constitutes the best available data on what was happening in youth justice in the early years of the YOA (1986–91). More important, for our purposes here, "youths charged" is often cited, incorrectly, as a good measure of "youth crime."

These data show a rather dramatic increase in youths charged for any violent offense. These are often cited by the police and others as an indication that "the youth violence problem" is getting worse. This increase, however, is disproportionately driven by increases in the low-end violent cases. As an illustration, we have included, in figure 2, the relevant rates for the three levels of assault in Canadian law. Level-1 assault ("common assault") accounts for dramatically more of the increase than does either level 2 ("assault causing bodily harm or assault with a weapon") or level 3 (aggravated assault). It was not until the mid-1990s that evidence could be found to suggest that "violent youth crime" had leveled off.

Youth court data show similar patterns—suggesting that it is largely minor violence that accounts for the increase. By the mid-1990s, when the numbers of violent cases going to court leveled off, the suggestion was often heard that although the number of violent cases was not in-

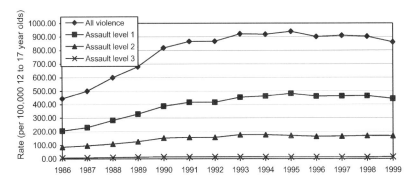

Fig. 2.—Rate (per 100,000, twelve- to seventeen-year-olds) of charging youths (all violence and selected violent offenses, Canada). Source: Canadian Centre for Justice Statistics, Statistics Canada 1986–2000.

creasing, the "quality" of youth violence was changing—toward more serious, brutal incidents. The available data do not support this assertion (see Doob and Sprott [1998]; for an opposing view, see Gabor [1999]; then see Doob and Sprott [1999]).

Carrington (1995, 1998, 1999) suggests that much of the apparent increase in youth crime or youth violence during the 1980s was illusory. His analysis suggests that the police, under the new act, tended to charge youths whom previously they would have cautioned or dealt with informally. Thus, increased youth crime—as measured by changes in the number of youths charged by police—appeared to have had less to do with changes in the behavior of youths than with changes in police decision making. The "youth crime wave" was, then, probably police induced.[4] Nevertheless, the public's most accessible proxy for serious youth crime—the youths charged with violent offenses—went up every year from 1986 to about 1993 before leveling off in the mid-1990s.[5]

Even though Canada has relatively few youths accused of homicide

[4] This interpretation is not universally accepted; see, e.g., Corrado and Markwart (1994); Markwart and Corrado (1995).

[5] Unfortunately, Canada does not have very useful measures of youthful offending that are independent of the justice system. One longitudinal study (Statistics Canada's National Longitudinal Survey of Children and Youth) of a representative sample of Canadian children is currently being conducted, but to date there are only two waves (collected in 1994 and 1996) of data publicly available, and self-report data at these two points in time are available only for ten- to eleven-year-olds. Nevertheless, ten- to eleven-year-olds at these two points in time did not differ appreciably in their level of self-reported offending. For details of the survey and of the results of this analysis, see Sprott, Doob, and Jenkins (2001).

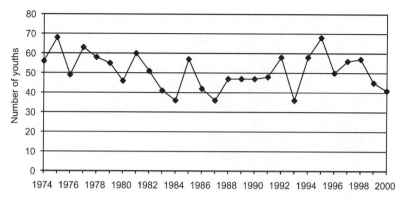

Fig. 3.—Number of youths named as suspects for homicide cases (Canada). Sources: Data provided to the authors by Canadian Centre for Justice Statistics, Statistics Canada; Feodorowycz 2001.

offenses each year and, as shown in figure 3, there is no evidence of a consistent trend, most Canadians probably believe that homicides involving youths are increasing. Seventy-nine percent of adult residents of the Province of Ontario thought, in 1997, that youth homicides were increasing, a proportion that is significantly higher than the 66 percent who believed, incorrectly, that the overall Canadian homicide rate was increasing (Doob et al. 1998).

Between 1984 and 1995, the YOA was amended three times. As we have seen, these were times when, except for homicides, there was a good deal of public evidence supporting the belief that crime generally and violent youth crime in particular were increasing. With these data as the background, it would not be surprising if Canadians perceived increasing crime to be a problem. And it would not be surprising if the governments in power felt pressure to do something. The governments, however, appeared to have listened somewhat selectively to the public. Getting tough on crime is not seen by a majority of Canadians as the best way to address crime generally or youth crime in particular (Doob and Roberts 1988; Doob et al. 1998). And many respondents, when faced with specific cases, were not as punitive as their general attitudes might suggest (Sprott 1998).

B. The Changes Begin in Earnest: Sentences for Murder and Transfers to Adult Court

Canada has not been immune to the practice of assuming that crime levels in a society are a direct function of criminal justice policies. A spectacular case helped tie up the loose strings in the package of beliefs suggesting that the YOA was too lenient. A youth charged with the murder of three people in Toronto was found guilty in youth court and sentenced to the maximum custodial sentence of three years. No attempt to transfer the youth had been made, apparently because there had been an agreement between the Crown and defense that the youth would be found not guilty by reason of insanity. However, the youth court judge, after hearing the submissions from both sides, determined that although there was sufficient evidence to find the youth guilty of murder, there was insufficient evidence to find him not guilty by reason of insanity. When, in the late 1980s, the youth was released from custody, the tabloid press in Toronto saw this case as evidence of the leniency of the YOA. The fact that the prosecutor had not applied to transfer the youth and that the "consensual insanity defense" was procedurally flawed did not enter into the debate.

Politically, this and other cases, as well as the apparent increase in violent youth crime, set the scene for something to be done. A government focused on a quick solution to a youth crime problem can look to youth crime legislation as a solution to its political problems. In 1992, the YOA was amended again. This time the move toward tough-sounding dispositions focused largely on serious violent cases, and in particular, not surprisingly, on homicide. Clearly there was no evidence that homicides involving accused youths were a particular problem. And there was no evidence that there were any special problems involving cases that "should" have resulted in a transfer to adult court but that had such a transfer denied by a judge.

The Progressive Conservative government that was in power from 1984 to 1993 did not invariably take a hard-line view about crime. In 1993, for example, a Conservative-dominated Parliamentary committee looking into crime prevention focused almost exclusively on the social causes of crime and on noncriminal justice approaches to reducing crime (Standing Committee on Justice and the Solicitor General 1993). It noted that "the United States affords a glaring example of the limited impact that criminal justice responses may have on crime" and that "evidence from the U.S. is that costly repressive measures alone fail to deter crime" (Standing Committee on Justice and the Solicitor General 1993, p. 2). Nevertheless, the apparent problem of relatively short sentences for murderers was not examined within this context. A three-year sentence for a multiple murdering youth was a political problem and, perhaps, a problem of proportionality, notwithstanding the fact that almost all youths charged with homicide offenses in Canada are eligible for transfer to adult court. For example, thirty-five of thirty-nine youths in 1998–99 and sixty-three of the sixty-seven youths in 1999–2000 facing a murder or manslaughter charge were in jeopardy of being transferred since they were over age fourteen at the time of the offense. Nevertheless, only seven youths (out of a possible thirty-five) in 1998–99 and twelve youths (out of a possible sixty-three) in 1999–2000 who were over fourteen at the time of the homicide incident were transferred to adult court. In the fiscal year 1991–92, the first year in which complete national data were available on the operation of the YOA, forty-nine of the fifty-one youths in court for homicide offenses were in jeopardy of being transferred. Only eight youths were, in fact, transferred (Canadian Centre for Justice Statistics, Statistics Canada 1992). Nevertheless, the law was changed in 1992 to increase the maximum sentences available in youth court for murder.

As shown in table 1, the maximum sentences in youth court increased considerably. Receiving less publicity was the fact that if a youth were to be transferred into the adult system and found guilty of murder, the minimum time of parole ineligibility was reduced considerably.

Thus, moving more toward a proportionality model of sentencing, there were, after 1992, three bands of offenses: those offenses with maximum sentences of two years, three years, and (for murder) five years less a day. The lowering of the parole ineligibility period for murder for those cases where the youth was transferred to adult court obviously reduced the discontinuity between the two systems. For a youth in jeopardy of a conviction for murder, the choice until 1992 had been a three-year sentence (in the youth system) or a life sentence with no possibility of parole for ten to twenty-five years.

The changes in the transfer provisions were also important from a political perspective. Originally, as we have noted, the court was required to balance the protection of society and the needs of the young person. After years of perceived increases in youth crime and statements linking levels of youth crime to youth justice policies, the "test" for transferring a youth to adult court changed in such a way that priority was given to "protection" of society: "The youth court shall consider the interest of society, which includes the objectives of affording protection to the public and rehabilitation of the young person and determine whether those objectives can be reconciled by the youth remaining under the jurisdiction of the youth court, and if the court is

TABLE 1

Penalties for Murder by Youth, 1984 to the Present

Period	Maximum Sentence in Youth Court	Mandatory Sentence in Adult Court, Ages Fourteen to Fifteen at Time of the Offense	Mandatory Sentence in Adult Court, Ages Sixteen to Seventeen at Time of the Offense
1984–92	Maximum of three years	Mandatory life, no parole for twenty-five years (first degree), ten to twenty-five years (second degree)	Mandatory life, no parole for twenty-five years (first degree), ten to twenty-five years (second degree)
1992–96	Maximum of three years custody, plus two-years-less-a-day of "conditional supervision in the community"	Mandatory life, no parole eligibility for five to ten years	Mandatory life, no parole eligibility for five to ten years
1996–2003	Maximum of six years custody plus four years conditional supervision in the community (first degree) and four plus three years (second-degree murder)	Mandatory life, no parole eligibility for five to seven years	Mandatory life, no parole eligibility for ten years (first degree) or seven years (second degree)
2003 onward (YCJA)	Maximum of six years custody plus four years conditional supervision in the community (first degree) and four plus three years (second-degree murder)	Mandatory life, no parole eligibility for five to seven years ("adult sentence")	Mandatory life, no parole eligibility for ten years (first degree) or seven years (second degree; "adult sentence")

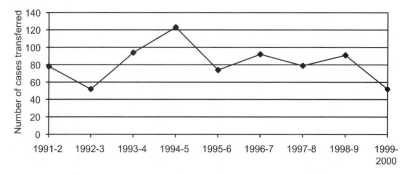

Fig. 4.—Total number of transferred cases (Canada, 1991–2000). Source: Canadian Centre for Justice Statistics, Statistics Canada 1991–2000.

of the opinion that those objectives cannot be so reconciled, protection of the public shall be paramount and the court shall order that the young person be [transferred to adult court]" (YOA, sec. 16[1.1]).

Clearly the goal was either to make it easier—or to make it be perceived to be easier—to transfer youths suspected of offending to adult court. However, when examining trends in the use of transfers over the years, there appears to be no evidence of an increase. Figure 4 shows the total number of transfers in Canada each year since 1991 when national data were first available. The data show that there are fluctuations each year in the number of cases transferred to adult court, but there appears to be no meaningful increase. This suggests that although legislation was enacted in 1992 (and again in 1995 as described in Sec. III) with the apparent intent of making it easier to transfer youths to adult court, there was no overall increase in the number of children transferred to the adult system. This figure also reminds us of another fact: very few cases have ever been transferred into the adult system.

Looking at the overall number of cases transferred obscures some interesting provincial variations. Figure 5 shows the rate of transferring cases in the four largest provinces in Canada over the past decade. The denominator in these figures is the population of youths in the province. Because provinces bring cases into court at very different rates, we decided that "cases in court that are eligible for transfer" in a province was a less useful denominator.[6] Clearly the rate of transfer-

[6] We have expressed these "transfers to adult court" rate figures in terms of rates per 100,000 youths in the province rather than per 1,000 cases to court. The reason for this is simple: if some provinces, such as Quebec, bring few cases to court, it would make sense that they would transfer a higher portion of these cases to adult court than a prov-

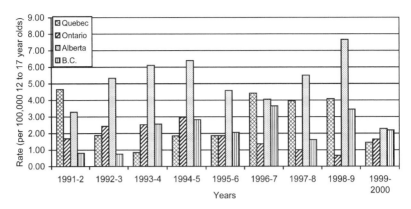

Fig. 5.—Rate (per 100,000 twelve- to seventeen-year-olds) of transferring cases, four largest provinces. Source: Canadian Centre for Justice Statistics, Statistics Canada 1991–2000.

ring youths to adult court varies across provinces and over time. There is considerable volatility in the rates of transfers. However, transfers, until recently, appeared to be more likely to occur in some provinces (e.g., Quebec and Alberta) than in others (e.g., Ontario and British Columbia; see fig. 5).

Although national data exist on the number of youths who are actually transferred to adult court, no data exist on the number of times transfer applications are brought to the court. Provincial court judges in early 2001 were asked how many transfer hearings they had heard in the previous five years (51 percent of the judges had heard no transfer hearings) and how many were successful. From these very rough estimates, it appeared that about 60 percent of the transfer applications were successful. Hence, even if every application were successful, there would be few youths transferred to adult court.

III. Balancing Youth Justice

A Liberal government was elected in the 1993 federal elections on a platform that included "toughening up" the YOA. Interestingly, the Liberal platform document (Liberal Party of Canada 1993) included

---

ince like Alberta or Ontario, which have large numbers of very minor cases coming to court. Expressing "transfers" as a function of the number of youths in the province, then, is a measure of how eager or reluctant a province is to exclude its most difficult youths from childhood.

errors about the YOA that made the actual law look more lenient than it was.[7] The stage was set for additional changes that were not necessarily "needed" from anything but a political perspective. The 1995 amendments (R.S.C. 1985, C. Y-1, amended 1995, chap. 19) were a combination of changes, most of which appeared to be part of a "balanced approach" to youth justice. Tough approaches were paired with "lenient" approaches. The changes on the "liberal" side of the ledger tended to be rather weak, and therefore ineffectual, in their wording. Those on the tough side tended to be weak, and therefore irrelevant, in their impact.

The "liberalizing" 1995 amendments included a statement in the declaration of principle that "the protection of society, which is a primary objective of the criminal law applicable to youth, is best served by rehabilitation, wherever possible, of young persons who commit offences, and rehabilitation is best achieved by addressing the needs and circumstances of a young person that are relevant to the young person's offending behaviour" (YOA, sec. 3[1][c.1]). The amendments also added some admonitions designed to limit the use of custodial sentences for youths: "An order of custody shall not be used as a substitute for appropriate child protection, health and other social measures. . . . A young person who commits an offence that does not involve serious personal injury shall be held accountable to the victim and to society through non-custodial dispositions whenever appropriate; and . . . custody shall only be imposed when all available alternatives to custody that are reasonable in the circumstances have been considered" (YOA, sec. 24[1.1]).

There are two points that need to be made about these changes. First, there was not much debate about them. Second, they are weak.

---

[7] The Liberal platform stated that they would address the current law on criminal records, which they described as follows: "Currently an eighteen-year-old could land in adult court with no criminal record despite a number of prior convictions in youth court. Regardless of the severity of the offense charged, or the number of previous youth court convictions, he or she is treated as a first-time offender in adult court" (Liberal Party of Canada 1993). In fact, the law in Canada has never been that youth court records are automatically "cleared" as an eighteenth birthday gift to the youth. A youth court record cannot be disclosed if five years without a finding of guilt has elapsed since the end of a sentence (YOA, secs. 45[1][f]–[g]). In other words, the record could only disappear on the eighteenth birthday if the offending took place when the youth was twelve years old and the sentences (including any time on probation) were completed on the youth's thirteenth birthday. It seems rather implausible that a twelve-year-old could acquire a serious record of violent offending and complete all sentences before she or he turned thirteen. Even if this were to happen, it is a different kind of case from that conjured up by the Liberal Party election rhetoric.

Note that phrases like "where possible," "where appropriate," and "reasonable in the circumstances" are used rather than strong admonitions.

The prohibition on using custody for child welfare purposes is, obviously, the strongest of the provisions we have mentioned. These provisions came into effect in 1996. Five years later when youth court judges were surveyed, 37 percent of the judges indicated that in half or more of the cases, "the youth's home (and/or parents) or living conditions were such that there was a need to get him or her into a more stable environment," and this was a relevant factor in the decision to impose custody (Doob 2001). Only 27 percent of respondents indicated that this was a factor in none or almost none of the cases in which they imposed custody (Doob 2001). It seems unlikely that the other provisions designed to reduce the use of custody would have had much impact, since the one provision that was a clear prohibition was ignored by substantial numbers of judges.

The main tough-on-crime amendments in 1995 had to do with transfers and the maximum sentences for homicide offenses. Clearly, the "need" to change these aspects of the law was political, not substantive. The government had absolutely no evidence that there were any problems in these two parts of the law that might not have already been "fixed" by the amendments that went into effect in 1992.

As summarized in table 1, the government in 1995 increased (from five years less a day to seven to ten years) the maximum length of sentences for murder. And, interestingly, they reduced somewhat the parole ineligibility period for those fourteen- and fifteen-year-olds transferred to adult court for murder. These amendments create procedural complexities for the youth courts since Canada's constitution requires that the accused have an option of a jury trial if he or she is in jeopardy of imprisonment for five years or more (Charter of Rights and Freedoms, sec. 11[f]). Until 1995, jury trials had not existed in youth courts. If a youth were transferred to the adult system, he or she would have the same access to jury trials as adults. But "youth court" jury trials were new. In any case, however, these changes came before there had been any possibility of evaluating the impact of the 1992 amendments. A need to "look tough" was, apparently, the dominant motivation for change.

Perceptions were also the basis of another 1995 innovation. Sixteen- and seventeen-year-old youths charged with any of four very serious violent offenses (murder, manslaughter, attempted murder, and aggravated sexual assault)[8] would be "presumptively" transferred to adult court unless they successfully argued that the transfer should not take place. Interestingly, however, the "test" as to whether a transfer should take place was the same as it had been. Not surprisingly, there seems to be no evidence that the change in law had any impact. Data for six-teen- and seventeen-year-olds alone (without including the twelve- to fifteen-year-olds) are not easily available. However, looking at all of the cases coming to court for one of these four presumptive offenses during the 1990s, it is clear that the number transferred seems to have been unaffected by the change in the law. It seems that during the 1990s, Canada transferred at most 10–19 percent of the sixty-five to ninety-four serious violent cases involving sixteen- and seventeen-year-old accused youths that came to court each year. The data in table 2 do not appear to support the notion that creating "presumptive" trans-fers to adult court (fully in effect from 1997–98 onward) had any im-pact.

The changes appear to have been designed to placate public opinion by being able to point to tough measures that had been taken against young offenders. The minister, however, had another problem. He had promised a full review of the YOA. In fact, two parallel reviews took place after the government had legislated these changes. These two re-views—one by a "federal-provincial-territorial task force" (Federal-Provincial-Territorial Task Force on Youth Justice 1996) and the other by the Standing Committee on Justice and Legal Affairs of the House of Commons (Standing Committee on Justice and Legal Affairs 1997)—carried out their responsibilities, reporting in 1996 and 1997, respectively. The necessity for the federal-provincial-territorial review derived from the fact that the provinces and territories administer the law and would have been left out of the review by the House of Com-mons committee.

Soon after these bodies reported, a federal election took place (1997), and a new minister of justice was appointed. Again, the govern-ment had promised to respond to the House of Commons committee reports and to change the YOA. As the government's response, the minister, in May 1998, released a "white paper" entitled "A Strategy for the Renewal of Youth Justice," which contained broadly written outlines for proposals that responded to two things: the political im-

---

[8] The most serious of three levels of sexual assault in the Canada's Criminal Code (R.S.C., 1985, chap. C-46).

TABLE 2

Total Number of Cases in Youth Court, Number of "Presumptive"
(Serious Violent) Cases in Youth Court, and the Number of
"Presumptive" Cases That Are Transferred to Adult Court (Canada)

Year	Total Number of Cases in Youth Court	Number of Presumptive Cases to Youth Court (Sixteen- and Seventeen- Year-Olds Only)*	Number of Presumptive Cases Transferred to Adult Court (All Ages)[†]	Percent of Presumptive Cases Transferred to Adult Court (All Ages)
1991–92	116,397	65	8	12
1992–93	115,187	83	11	13
1993–94	115,949	74	14	19
1994–95	109,743	91	14	15
1995–96	111,027	87	9	10
1996–97	110,065	80	12	15
1997–98	110,883	89	13	15
1998–99	106,665	69	12	17
1999–2000	102,061	94	13	14

Source.—Canadian Centre for Justice Statistics, Statistics Canada, 1992–2001, and data purchased by the authors from Statistics Canada.

* Presumptive offenses include murder, manslaughter, attempted murder, and aggravated sexual assault.

[†] The number of sixteen- and seventeen-year-olds actually transferred is not available. The figures reported here of actual transfers includes all those transferred, regardless of their ages. Overall, those under sixteen and, therefore, not presumptively transferred account for only 14 percent of all cases transferred. These figures and, therefore, the proportion transferred (in the final column of this table) are likely to be slightly inflated.

perative and the policy imperative (Department of Justice, Canada 1998).

The political imperative is simple to describe. As various commentators (e.g., Cullen, Wright, and Chamlin 1999; Tonry 1999; Doob 2000) have pointed out, it is easier to be "tough on crime" than to be smart about crime. Hence, there were the necessary tough elements. Among them was the proposal that the category of "presumptive offenses" would be broadened in two ways: by lowering the age at which a youth would be presumptively treated as an adult from age sixteen to age fourteen and by creating a new category of "presumptive adults": those youths who had established a pattern of violent offending.

In addition, a symbolic thorn in the side of some police officers was removed. The YOA had special restrictions on the admissibility of statements from accused youths. These were not easy to follow, but competent police forces had developed protocols for taking statements from youths that apparently overcame the procedural hurdles while respecting the requirements of the act. Nevertheless, the admissibility of confessions by accused youths was made easier as a way of signaling that the government was on the side of the police, not accused youths.

On the other side, there were acknowledgments of a number of serious problems with the operation of the YOA. The most important of these had to do with the overreliance on youth court and imprisonment as solutions to youth crime. As discussed earlier, the overreliance on youth court had been identified as a problem twenty-five years earlier. It has never been successfully addressed. In addition, by the end of the 1990s, notwithstanding political pressure to be tough, there seemed to be some consensus that custody as a sentence for youths was being overused. The House of Commons committee, on the basis of unpublished data, suggested that Canada uses custody at a higher rate than it is used in the United States. A study published subsequently (Sprott and Snyder 1999) confirmed this estimate for certain classes of offenses. More generally, however, there was the feeling that the YOA was not operating properly.

IV. The End of the Young Offenders Act

When the government of Canada released its "strategy" white paper in the spring of 1998, it noted that Canada used the youth justice system and youth custody for many very minor offenses (Department of Justice, Canada 1998). This is quite easily documented.

A. The Use of Court and Custody

Using the most recent data available, it appears that the minister of justice's concern was well founded. Table 3 shows the types of cases that come into Canada's youth courts as well as the cases that end up with youths being sentenced to custody.[9] Theft of goods valued at less than $5,000 accounts for roughly 14 percent of all cases going to youth court. Adding in three other relatively minor offenses—possession of stolen property, failure to appear in youth court, and failure to comply with a disposition—one finds that these four offenses account for

[9] A "case" consists of one or more charges against a single young person that all have their first appearance in the same court on the same day. Cases going to court are described by the single most serious charge that the youth is facing.

TABLE 3

Cases (Principal Charge) in Youth Court and Sentenced to Custody
(Canada, 1999–2000)

	Cases in Court		Cases Sentenced to Custody	
	Total Number of Cases	Percent	Total Number of Cases	Percent
Theft under $5,000	14,514	14	2,005	9
Possession of stolen property	4,738	5	1,411	6
Failure to appear	11,078	11	2,579	11
Failure to comply with a disposition	13,517	13	5,234	23
Subtotal of minor offenses	43,847	43	11,229	48
Other thefts	4,536	4	1,011	4
Mischief/damage	5,103	5	726	3
Breaking and entering	10,285	10	2,853	12
Minor assault	10,235	10	1,521	7
Subtotal: sum of eight less serious offenses	74,006	73	17,340	75
All other violence	12,702	12	2,595	11
Drug possession	3,779	4	282	1
All other drug offenses	1,615	2	312	1
All other offenses	9,959	10	2,686	12
All cases	102,061	100	23,215	100

Source.—Statistics Canada 1998–2001, Youth Court Data Tables, 1999–2000, tables 3 and 8.

roughly 43 percent of all cases going to youth court. This proportion varies a bit from province to province and from year to year. But it is safe to suggest that somewhere between one-third and one-half of the cases going to youth court from any province in any year have as their most serious charge one of these four offenses.

When one adds in other thefts, mischief or damage to property, breaking and entering, and minor assaults, we find that these eight sets of offenses account for close to three-quarters of all cases in youth court. Given that court is cumbersome, slow, expensive, and probably counterproductive, it is not surprising that the Canadian government questioned the utility of bringing these cases to court. Those same eight offenses also account for the majority (75 percent) of cases sentenced to custody in Canada.

Other cases—including all other violence and drug cases—constitute a small portion of the court workload and, interestingly enough, a small portion of the cases where the youth is sentenced to custody. Drug offenses, for example, are the most significant charge in only about 2.6 percent of the custodial sentences.

Canada tends to rely on custody for relatively minor offenses. Compared with other countries, Canada appears to have a relatively high rate of youth incarceration. For example, Canada has a similar or slightly higher rate than the United States in its use of custody for violence and property offenses (Sprott and Snyder 1999). However, the majority of custodial sentences in Canada are relatively short. In 1999–2000, for example, 34 percent of custodial sentences in Canada were for less than one month, and another 43 percent of custodial sentences were for from one to three months. Thus, 77 percent of custodial sentences in Canada are for three months or less.

These short sentences are seen by judges as accomplishing a variety of different things. In a recent survey of judicial attitudes across Canada (Doob 2001), judges were asked to indicate the importance of each of nine different factors in the decision to hand down a short period of time in custody. The most important factor was the need—because of the seriousness of the offense—to place the youth in custody. Hence, the offense "required" custody, but the period of time it required was not very long. One wonders why noncustodial sentences could not have been found as substitutes for these short periods of custody. The second and third most important factors were both "future" oriented: the judges indicated their belief in the rehabilitative impact of sentences by giving relatively high ratings to the reason "the youth had been given non-custodial sentences in the past and did not stop offending," and by also endorsing the importance of "short sharp shocks" (Doob 2001).

As would be expected, their offense records affect the likelihood that youths will be sentenced to a period in custody. Table 4 shows the effect of criminal record on two offenses (minor assault and assault causing bodily harm) for the four largest Canadian provinces. There is, not surprisingly, considerable variation in the proportion of cases from each offense-record combination that receives custody in the four provinces. For example, 3.3 percent of minor assaults with no previous convictions are sentenced to custody in Alberta, while 11.8 percent of minor assaults with no previous convictions are sentenced to custody in Ontario. In general, however, the more previous convictions the youth has, the more likely it is the youth will be sent to custody. In

TABLE 4

Percent Receiving Custody as a Function of the Number of Previous
Findings of Guilt (Selected Offenses, Four Largest Provinces,
1996–97)

| | Number of Previous Findings of Guilt | | | |
Province	None	One	Two	Three or More
Minor assault:				
Quebec	7.9 (392)	20.7 (92)	52.8 (36)	78.6 (14)
Ontario	11.8 (2,196)	38.7 (506)	62.0 (216)	70.6 (180)
Alberta	3.3 (423)	13.7 (168)	26.5 (83)	38.6 (88)
British Columbia	6.3 (457)	23.1 (104)	44.6 (56)	75.0 (32)
Assault with a weapon or causing bodily harm:				
Quebec	13.3 (263)	28.3 (46)	57.9 (19)	64.7 (17)
Ontario	26.0 (500)	51.9 (129)	75.9 (58)	82.5 (57)
Alberta	14.1 (135)	37.2 (43)	42.1 (19)	67.9 (28)
British Columbia	15.6 (109)	46.7 (30)	75.0 (16)	81.3 (16)

SOURCE.—Data provided to the authors by Canadian Centre for Justice Statistics, Statistics Canada.

NOTE.—Numbers in parentheses indicate the number of cases on which each percent is based.

this respect it is interesting to note the lack of differentiation of offense seriousness. Thus, a youth with a criminal record who is found guilty of a minor offense often has a considerably higher likelihood of receiving a custodial sentence than does a youth without a record who is found guilty of a more serious offense. In Ontario, for example, 38.7 percent of minor assaults with one previous conviction receive a custodial disposition, while 26 percent of assaults causing bodily harm with no previous convictions receive a custodial disposition.

B. Provincial Variation

Another concern about the use of youth court is the variability, across provinces, in the use of court and custody. Given that it is the provinces that administer the YOA, it is not surprising that there are some differences in the ways that it is administered. However, the variability that does exist is dramatic, especially when it seems that levels of offending by youths across provinces are fairly similar (Sprott,

TABLE 5

Variation in Rate of Bringing Cases to Court and Sentencing to
Custody (Canada and Selected Provinces, 1999–2000)

	Rate of Bringing Cases into Youth Courts*	Percent of Guilty Cases Sentenced to Custody	Rate of Sentencing Cases to Custody*
Canada	41.67	34.0	9.48
Nova Scotia	41.16	35.7	10.56
Quebec	19.59	27.4	4.37
Ontario	42.75	39.8	10.17
Saskatchewan	94.12	33.8	20.91
Alberta	61.43	28.1	12.24
British Columbia	36.42	33.7	8.52

SOURCE.—Canadian Centre for Justice Statistics, Statistics Canada, 1999–2000.
* Rate is per 1,000 youths (twelve to seventeen years old) in population.

Doob, and Jenkins 2001). As shown in table 5 (for the four largest
provinces and two of the smaller provinces), the rates of bringing cases
into court and of the use of custody differ dramatically across provinces
(see also Doob and Sprott [1996] for a more detailed analysis). What
we see, then, are large provincial differences in the rate of taking
youths to court; some variability in the rate at which youths are placed
in custody once found guilty; and, when these are combined, substantial interprovincial differences in the number of youths, per 1,000 in
the population, who are placed in custody each year.

The decision to bring cases to court may relate in some cases to explicit policies at the provincial level. Quebec, as we have pointed out,
has a policy (and a law to implement that policy) of keeping youths out
of the youth justice system. Ontario, by contrast, appears to have a policy to require youth court for many youths who commit minor offenses. In 1994, the provincial left-of-center New Democratic Party
developed a "Violence Free School Policy" (Ministry of Education and
Training, Province of Ontario, Canada 1994) that directed school officials to call the police whenever there was anything more serious than
the most minor school violence.

Many judges believe that there are many cases that come before
them that could have been dealt with outside of the court. Twenty-
seven percent of Quebec judges responding to a survey thought that
half or more of the cases they were seeing could have been dealt with
adequately outside of the court; the comparable figure for Ontario was

55 percent (Doob 2001). Generally speaking, large numbers of judges, particularly outside of Quebec, thought that many of the cases they were seeing in court could have been dealt with outside of court. The variability between the views of Quebec judges and those in the rest of Canada appears to result from perceived differences in the adequacy of community programs for dealing with youths who offend (Sprott and Doob 2002).

C. The Case of Quebec

As shown in table 5, Quebec has the lowest use of youth court and custody when compared with all the other provinces. Quebec has a unique history that sets it apart from other provinces in terms of the treatment of juvenile offenders. This difference in the rate of bringing youths into youth court is not surprising given that Quebec implemented a form of formal diversion of young people from the youth justice system long before the YOA was made law (Trépanier 1983). As mentioned earlier, in the 1970s Quebec passed legislation—the Youth Protection Act—to divert children from the youth justice system. Therefore, even though a young person may be brought to the attention of the police because of an offense, such a youth would be diverted from the criminal justice stream if it was felt that, in essence, the case could best be handled other than in youth court. In contrast, Ontario fought the necessity of having "alternative measures" programs for youths up to the Supreme Court of Canada (*R. v. S.* [S] [1990] *Supreme Court Reports* 254). Hence, given the legislated provincial policy that youths who offend should not necessarily be brought to court, it is not particularly surprising to find variation between Quebec and the rest of Canada in youth court caseloads.

The lower rate of taking youths to court appears to be the largest difference between Quebec and the rest of Canada. When one looks at indicators of what actually happens in court, the data tell a somewhat different story. Tables 4 and 5 suggest that Quebec judges are not sentencing dramatically differently from judges elsewhere in Canada. And when one looks at transfers to adult court (fig. 5), it would appear that in some recent years Quebec prosecutors and judges have been transferring more youths into the adult system than have prosecutors and judges in some other provinces. The more noticeable effect, however, is that since the mid-1990s, as far as transfers to adult court go, the "Quebec system" did not appear to be more "child centered" than the "systems" in place in Ontario and British Columbia.

largely elderly people who are appointed for life to act as the "upper" legislative body, sent the YCJA back to the House of Commons. This was accomplished by adding an amendment to the sentencing principles that essentially incorporated the adult sentencing provision quoted above. Hence, this section created a legislative snag between the two houses of the Parliament of Canada. In the end, the House of Commons accepted the Senate amendment. The requirement that "all available sanctions other than custody that are reasonable in the circumstances should be considered for all young persons, with particular attention to the circumstances of aboriginal young persons" (YCJA, sec. 38[2][d]) is now part of the law.

It is, however, almost certainly more important for aboriginal youths, and for others who might be in jeopardy of being sentenced to custody, that there are stronger prohibitions against the indiscriminate use of custody for youths contained in the YCJA than in the YOA or in the (adult) criminal code. These provisions are described in Section V.

E. Conclusion: The End of an Era

The YOA had few friends when the minister of justice announced, in May 1998, that she would soon bring in a new youth justice law. It gathered some friends shortly thereafter, however, when the Quebec government used its apparent support for the YOA as a demonstration of Quebec's distinctiveness within the Canadian federation. The YOA, therefore, became a tool for separatists in Quebec to argue that the Canadian federation does not serve Quebec's interests. The argument was simple: Canada was forcing the YCJA onto an unwilling Quebec. Quebec would prefer to maintain its distinct youth justice system under the YOA.[12] But generally, the YOA did not have much public or political support. The minister's justification for having a new law, rather than amendments to the old law, was that it would "send a clear signal to Canadians of all ages that a new legal framework is in place" (Department of Justice, Canada 1998, p. i).

She attempted, in her white paper outlining her plans (Department of Justice, Canada 1998), to differentiate changes in the youth justice laws from other policies aimed at the problem of youthful offending.

---

[12] Part of Quebec's opposition to the bill may have derived from the way it was described by the minister's office in the initial press release (Department of Justice, Canada 1999) (see Sec. V.A. in this essay). By describing the bill largely in terms of its tough-sounding provisions, the minister's office gave the impression that the bill would automatically lead to tough outcomes in all provinces.

Her strategy, she argued, had three complementary parts: first, "prevention"—this was largely the focus of activity outside the formal justice system (crime prevention programs, a "National Children's Agenda" focusing on such strategies as support for low income families); second, "meaningful consequences for youth crime"—proportional responses were emphasized ("The consequences for the crimes will depend on the seriousness of the offense and on the particular circumstances of the offender" [p. 13])—it was noted, however, that "community-based penalties are often more effective than custody and will be encouraged for lower-risk, non-violent offenders" (p. 13). And, third, "rehabilitation and reintegration"—the document suggested that rehabilitation and reintegration are "particularly important for serious, violent offenders, including those youth receiving adult sentences" (p. 14).

The document, like many before it, stated that it was not necessary or desirable, often, to bring youth to court for offenses (Department of Justice, Canada 1998, p. 5). It noted that youths were incarcerated more often than adults tended to be under certain circumstances. And it cited the 1997 Parliamentary committee report (Standing Committee on Justice and Legal Affairs 1997) for the assertion that "the rate of youth incarceration in Canada is much higher than that of many Western countries, including the United States, Australia, and New Zealand" (Department of Justice, Canada 1998, p. 7). Many of the provisions that, eventually, would be contained in the law were mentioned, in general terms.

The bill introducing the new law was first presented to Parliament in March 1999. A new session of Parliament, followed by a federal election in the fall of 2000, meant that the bill had to be reintroduced two more times before it finally passed the House of Commons in the spring of 2001. The Senate, an appointed body analogous to the British House of Lords, typically, after debate, passes government bills. In this case, as described in Section IV.D., the Senate instead amended the bill forcing it back to the House of Commons for another vote. The bill passed was again approved by the House of Commons in February 2002 and received royal assent shortly after. It was proclaimed into force in April 2003. The new law is, in fact, very different from the YOA.

V. The Youth Criminal Justice Act

As we have pointed out, there are two substantial problems with the YOA on which almost all policy and academic observers agreed: the youth justice system is being overused for minor offenses, and too many youths are going to custody, especially for relatively minor offenses. We have noted that the YOA has "admonitions" not to use custody when other sanctions are plausible and that it allows police and others to keep youths out of the formal court system. The biggest single change that came into force with the YCJA is that the degree of directness of the "guidance" has increased considerably. What are admonitions under the YOA have turned into formal "tests," or hurdles, that need to be overcome in the YCJA. It is not that these hurdles—or guidelines, to use a more common word—cannot be surmounted or avoided. In many cases, however, it will be clear what decision was contemplated by the new act. It would appear that the government of Canada has decided that if it has legal responsibility for young offenders, it should make policy on how young offenders should be handled.

The law was, however, created in an intensely political climate. The government could appear to be responding to public concern about crime by bringing in a harsh law. Hence, the government attempted to do the impossible: be sensible but seem tough. It is not clear that they succeeded, at least with their political goals. Although there was pressure to lower the minimum and maximum ages that define who is a "youth," the government did not appear interested in the suggestion. There existed at the time data suggesting that such changes were not a political necessity since the public could easily be persuaded to be content with other approaches to dealing with youths under age twelve who offended (see Sprott and Doob 2000).

Furthermore, the liberalizing impact of the separatist Quebec provincial government cannot be ignored. Youth justice laws provided the government of Quebec with an ideal political tool. Quebec has traditionally been more child centered in its orientation to youth justice laws. If the federal government were to force Quebec to do something that it could not avoid through administrative procedures (e.g., deeming sixteen- or seventeen-year-olds to be adults for all criminal law purposes), it would be a perfect—and accurate—example of how Quebec was different and, within Canada, was being forced to do something regressive that it would not have done on its own.

These age limits, therefore, remained. The acts that could bring a youth in contact with the youth justice system—violations of criminal and other federal laws—also did not change. What changed is what happens to a youth when apprehended.

The preamble to the bill noted, among other things, that "Canadian society should have a justice system . . . that reserves its most serious intervention for the most serious crimes and reduces the over-reliance on incarceration for non-violent young persons" (Bill C-7, House of Commons, First Session, Thirty-Seventh Parliament, 49–50 Elizabeth II, 2001 [as passed by the House of Commons May 29, 2001]). It also acknowledges that Canada is a party to the United Nations Convention on the Rights of the Child. But "saving the most serious intervention for the most serious crimes" is a principle that would appear in a number of places in the new act.

An important change in orientation in the act is that the "protection of the public" is not to be interpreted as meaning either deterrence or incapacitation. The YCJA states that the youth justice system does various things—addressing the circumstances underlying offending, rehabilitating and reintegrating offenders, and ensuring meaningful consequences—"in order to promote the long-term protection of the public" (sec. 3[1]). Thus, the words "protection of the public" appear. The underlying theory, however, appears to be that ensuring meaningful consequences along with rehabilitation and reintegration are means to accomplish long-term protection. The focus on long-term protection rather than the short-term protection afforded by short sentences is also important.

Along with these general statements are the principles designed to address the need to screen cases out of the court system. Measures outside of the formal court system ("extrajudicial" measures) such as warnings, referrals to community programs, and so on, are "presumed to be adequate to hold a young person accountable for his or her offending behaviour if the young person has committed a non-violent offence and has previously not been found guilty of an offence" (YCJA, sec. 4[d]). The Canadian youth justice system has tended to focus on the youth's background of offending at least as much as the offense. Thus it is important that the new law states that noncourt alternatives can be used even if they have been used before, and even if the youth has been found guilty on a previous occasion (YCJA, sec. 4[d]). If the offense is minor and noncourt approaches "are adequate" to hold the youth accountable, then they should be used.

Police are told that they "shall" in all cases consider noncourt approaches in all cases before starting judicial proceedings (YCJA, sec. 6[1]). However, perhaps because of the provincial, rather than federal, responsibility for the administration of justice, the failure of a police officer to consider noncourt approaches does not invalidate any charge that is laid against the youth (YCJA, sec. 6[2]).

Canada does not have complete data on the number of youths detained before trial. This number is, however, seen as being higher than it need be. Generally speaking, there are two main legal justifications in Canada for detaining a person before trial: that the accused will not show up for trial and that the accused is likely to commit an offense or interfere with the administration of justice. In an attempt to limit the use of pretrial detention under this second justification, the YCJA states that "in considering whether the detention of a young person is necessary [because there is thought to be a substantial likelihood that the youth will commit an offense or interfere with the administration of justice while on release] a youth justice court . . . shall presume that detention is not necessary . . . if the young person, could not, on being found guilty, be committed to custody [under the sentencing provisions of this Act]" (YCJA, sec. 29[2]).

In other words, a youth who would not be sentenced to custody for the offense should not be detained in custody while awaiting trial for that same offense. Many judges under the YOA (30 percent in a survey of youth court judges; Doob 2001) indicated that at least half of the youths whom they detained awaiting trial were detained only because of welfare considerations. The YCJA explicitly forbids this practice (sec. 29[1]).

When a youth has been found guilty, judges are told that "the purpose of sentencing . . . is to hold a young person accountable for an offence through the imposition of just sanctions that have meaningful consequences for the young person and that promote his or her rehabilitation and reintegration into society, thereby contributing to the long-term protection of society" (YCJA, sec. 38[1]). More specifically, "the sentence must be proportionate to the seriousness of the offence and the degree of responsibility of the young person for that offence" (YCJA, sec. 38[2]). Furthermore, subject to the proportionality requirement, "the sentence must be the least restrictive sentence that is capable of [holding the youth accountable]" and must be "the one that is most likely to rehabilitate the young person and reintegrate him or her into society" (YCJA, sec. 38[2]).

While the proportionality principle sets the rules by which the relative severity of sentences are determined, the actual sentence (within the limits set by proportionality) must be the most likely sentence to rehabilitate or reintegrate. As various commentators (e.g., von Hirsch

1976) have pointed out, a proportionality principle on its own defines the relative severity of punishments. It does not, however, define on its own the level of punishments that should be given. Perfect proportionality, therefore, could be achieved by giving all young persons custodial sentences as long as their length was proportional to the seriousness of the offense. Thus, it is necessary to set at least some standards within the proportionality framework. The YCJA chose to focus on the decision of whether a youth receives a custodial sentence.

Custodial sentences can only be imposed if one or more of four conditions are met: it is a violent offense; the youth has previously failed to comply with noncustodial sentences (i.e., more than one sentence); the youth has been found guilty of a moderately serious offense and has a history of findings (i.e., more than one) of guilt; or, "in exceptional cases where the young person has committed an . . . offence, such that the imposition of a non-custodial sentence would be inconsistent with the purpose and principles [of sentencing]" (YCJA, sec. 39[1]).

Furthermore, in cases where custody is imposed, the judge is specifically required in section 39(9) "to state the reasons why it has determined that a non-custodial sentence is not adequate to achieve the purpose [of sentencing] including, if applicable, the reasons why the case is an exceptional case" (i.e., those cases where the youth was sentenced to custody on the basis of the "exceptional case" criterion in sec. 39[1]). The point of these, and other similar requirements, is clear: judges are forced to think about whether custody is really necessary.

In 1996, the traditional purposes of sentencing (individual and general deterrence, incapacitation, rehabilitation, and denunciation) were added as explicit "objectives" of the sentencing laws for adults (Criminal Code of Canada, sec. 718). The judge, when sentencing an adult, is supposed to impose "just sanctions that have one or more of [these] objectives" but is to do so within the principle that "a sentence must be proportionate to the gravity of the offence and the degree of responsibility of the offender" (Criminal Code of Canada, sec. 718.1). Generally speaking, these sections have been criticized as being too vague and contradictory (Roberts and von Hirsch 1999). There is no evidence that we are aware of that codifying these sections had any impact on sentencing above and beyond what had been common practice before these changes (Roberts and von Hirsch 1999, p. 53; Doob 2000, pp. 326–27).

There are two notable differences between the YCJA sentencing provisions and the adult criminal code provisions. First, the YCJA provisions are clear in their intent. They are designed to limit the use of custody. The mechanism to limit the use of custody is that one or more of four explicit criteria must be met before a youth can be placed in custody. Explanations for the decision must be given.

Second, the YCJA contains no references to general or specific deterrence or to incapacitation in the context of sentencing. Canadian judges have tended to interpret the "protection of society" as being accomplished in part through deterrence and incapacitation. In the YCJA, however, sentencing contributes to the long-term protection of the public by "hold[ing] a youth accountable for an offence through the imposition of just sanctions that have meaningful consequences and that promote his or her rehabilitation and reintegration into society" (YCJA, sec. 38[1]). Although there is no section that specifically says that deterrence and incapacitation have no place in the sentencing of youths, there is a section that indicates that the adult sentencing provisions do not apply (YCJA, sec. 50[1]) except when an adult sentence is being imposed on a youth (YCJA, sec. 74[1]).

When determining the severity of the sentence, proportionality principles are obviously meant to dominate. However, in the choice of the exact sanction that is to be imposed, the judge is required to choose the sentence that is the least restrictive possible, that is most likely to rehabilitate and reintegrate, and that promotes a sense of responsibility and acknowledgment of the harm done (YCJA, sec. 38[2]). But if a custodial order is imposed, there are additional changes. In order to accomplish "reintegration," a "custody" sentence has been transformed into a "custody and supervision" order whereby a fixed portion (one-third) of the sentence is normally served in the community after the custodial portion. Reviews of dispositions by the court are also still possible.

One difficulty for the federal government is that it has little direct power to force provincial governments to provide noncustodial sanctions. Many judges (29 percent), particularly those judges outside of Quebec and in smaller communities, indicate that they do not have an adequate range of sanctions available to them at sentencing (Doob 2001). The YCJA provides possibilities for additional noncustodial sanctions, but provinces make their own decisions on whether to provide an adequate range of noncustodial choices to judges.

These two parts of the new law—strengthened principles to attempt to reduce the use of youth court, and more explicit sentencing principles—are undoubtedly the most important potential changes in youth justice law. The intent of both parts of the law is clear. The issue, of course, is whether the intent of the law will be followed. When one looks at the cases that are coming to court or are ending up in custody (see table 3), it is clear that thousands of cases presently ending up in custody should not be there under the YCJA. First-time shoplifters, for example, will be exceedingly difficult to place in custody. Whether the law will be successful in accomplishing its stated goals (e.g., reducing the use of youth court and of custody) is, of course, not certain.

A. Political Reality Steps In: Selling the New Law

The YCJA was first introduced into Parliament and to the Canadian public in March 1999. In the week before the bill was introduced, stories appeared in some of the larger Canadian newspapers under headlines like, "Youth-Crime Bill Aims to Aid Prosecutors" (Anderssen 1999); "New Act Would Jail Parents for Children's Crimes: New Youth Criminal Justice Act to Be Introduced" (Ovenden 1999); "Youth Crime Laws Get Tough: Young Offenders' Criminal Records No Longer Secret" (Tibbetts 1999); and "New Law to Get Tough on Youth: Harsher Penalties for Violence, Age of Adult Trials Drops to 14, New Repeat Offender Category" (MacCharles 1999).

It appears that these stories were the result of motivated "leaks" from the government. Whether these stories were, in effect, planted by the government, it is clear that the government was successful in priming the public to expect a tough bill. The news coverage after the release of the bill was slightly more "balanced," but, nevertheless, the tough parts of the bill dominated discussion. This was not surprising when one looks at the description of the bill released by the minister's office to the press on March 11, 1999, the day that the bill was released. The first four bullet points in the press release (Department of Justice, Canada 1999) indicated that the YCJA would include provisions that "allow an adult sentence for any youth 14 years old or more . . . ; expand the offenses for which a young person convicted of an offense would be presumed to receive an adult sentence . . . ; lower the age for youth who are presumed to receive an adult sentence . . . ; permit the publication of names of all youth who receive an adult sentence. Publication of the names of [serious violent offenders over age fourteen] will also be permitted" (pp. 1–2).

To the uninitiated, these provisions could be seen as indications that the new law was going to be tough on youth crime. The first of the points listed by the minister's office is noteworthy because it is a statement of the law as it has always been in Canada. It is about as meaningful as a statement that murder, under the YCJA, will be an offense. The last two of the thirteen points describing the new legislation was that the YCJA would "allow for and encourage the use of a full range of community-based sentences and effective alternatives to the justice system for youth who commit non-violent offenses; and recognize the principles of the United Nations Convention on the Rights of the Child" (Department of Justice, Canada 1999, p. 2).

It is not surprising, therefore, that the bill was labeled as being largely tough. The first eleven points in the press release all sound tough. The bill itself is long and complex. For reporters who have deadlines and who know nothing about what might be buried in complex legal language, the press release may be both the starting point and the end point of their knowledge of the bill.

Only those who had access to data on Canada's youth justice system would be able to know that these tough provisions were numerically unimportant. Few, if any, cases would be affected by them.

The most extreme of the irrelevant points is the one listed as number ten. It states that the new law would "permit tougher penalties for adults who willfully fail to comply with an undertaking made to the court to properly supervise youth who have been denied bail and placed in their care" (Department of Justice, Canada 1999, p. 2). Although clearly this change was incorporated into the law, relatively few people would know that it is possible that no adult has ever gone to prison for this offense. Published statistics for 1999–2000 suggest that no person even went to court for this offense.[13] Raising the hypothetical maximum sentence from six months in prison to two years in prison is hardly newsworthy, since almost nobody even gets charged for this offense, let alone goes to prison for it. It is a bit like claiming to be tough on crime by threatening the death penalty for whistling under water. Nevertheless, this provision got higher billing than the changes

---

[13] The statistics are not absolutely clear on this. There were three "cases" (a basket of one or more charges against a single accused appearing together for the first time in court on the same day) involving accused people age eighteen or older for "failure to comply with an undertaking." Most such accused are, of course, the youths themselves who fail to comply with undertakings they have made. Turning to the data on persons (all of the charges a person faced during the twelve-month period), there were no persons age eighteen or over who had this charge as their most serious charge in youth court (where such a charge would appear, no matter what the age of the accused). It seems likely, therefore, that no adult was charged with this offense in 1999–2000.

that could result in thousands of youths not going to court or to custody. Clearly the intended message was that the YCJA is tough legislation.

B. Other Changes to Canada's Youth Justice Legislation

As we have already pointed out, Canada transfers very few youths to adult court. The procedure by which youths are transferred has been a source of criticism for some time (Beaulieu 1994; Standing Committee on Justice and Legal Affairs 1997). The YCJA, instead of having "transfers" to adult court, would have a procedure where the youth would stay in youth court and be dealt with as a youth. However, for serious offenses (where proper notice had been given), the prosecutor could ask, at the sentencing hearing, for an adult sentence. The test as to whether an adult sentence should be given is fairly simple: if a youth sentence "imposed in accordance with the purpose and principles [of sentencing in the YCJA] would have sufficient length to hold the young person accountable for his or her offending behaviour," the youth shall be sentenced as a youth (YCJA, sec. 72[1][a]). If not, the youth shall be sentenced as an adult. In other words, the test is whether a proportionate sentence can be given in the youth system within the maximum sentences laid out in the act (two or three years of custody and supervision for all offenses other than murder). If a youth is sentenced as an adult, the judge then decides whether it is appropriate for the youth to start serving the sentence in a youth or an adult facility. The name of the youth who is sentenced as an adult can be published. Normally, the identity of accused (or convicted) youths cannot be published.[14]

It is impossible to know for certain whether many adult sentences will be imposed on youths. In 1999–2000, however, there were only eighteen custodial sentences handed down in youth court that exceeded twenty-four months out of 23,215 custodial sentences imposed. Even if all of these were, instead, given adult sentences and all of those transferred received adult sentences, one would expect only about 70 or so adult sentences to have been awarded that year.

Another tough-sounding measure contained in the new act is the

---

[14] One exception is in the case of a youth charged with a very serious violent offense (one of the "presumptive offenses") but given a youth sentence rather than an adult sentence; a judge may allow the identity of the convicted youth to be published "if the court considers it appropriate in the circumstances, taking into account the importance of rehabilitating the young person and the public interest" (YCJA, sec. 75[3]).

provision that anyone over the age of fourteen who was found guilty of one of the four presumptive offenses (murder, manslaughter, attempted murder, or aggravated sexual assault) or who had a history of serious violent convictions would be "presumptively" sentenced as an adult. Two factors make it unlikely that this will be very important. First, as we discussed earlier, the 1996 "presumptive transfer" provisions had no apparent impact on transfer rates. Second, the test of whether a person should be sentenced as a youth or as an adult is the same: can a youth sentence be crafted that meets the "proportionality" test?

In order to emphasize the distinction between criminal and child welfare law and to facilitate child welfare intervention where it is appropriate, the YCJA allows judges at any stage of the proceedings to refer a case to a child welfare agency "to determine whether the young person is in need of child welfare services" (sec. 35). In a tentative acknowledgment of developments in many parts of Canada and as an encouragement for the expansion of such activities, "a youth justice court judge, the provincial director [of youth services, or, if delegated, a probation officer], a police officer, a justice of the peace, a prosecutor or a youth worker may convene or cause to be convened a conference for the purpose of making a decision required to be made under this Act" (YCJA, sec. 19[1]). In addition, courts are reminded of this ability to refer matters to conferences "for recommendation to the court on an appropriate youth sentence" (YCJA, sec. 41). Conferences are essentially undefined ("conference means a group of persons who are convened to give advice in accordance with Section 19"; YCJA, sec. 2[1]). Effectively this means that various forms of less formal community forums can be deemed to be conferences. In sentencing and in other judicial functions, they would provide advice rather than make decisions. By contrast, if the decision was being made outside of the judicial setting (e.g., on how to hold a youth accountable for an action that was not going to court), the conference could, it would appear, have authority.

C. The Legislative Process

As described earlier, the Canadian Senate has a tradition of criticizing government legislation but, in the end, passing it. In the case of the YCJA, the Senate raised issues that had not received much attention. One of these was that there was no provision requiring that the YCJA be interpreted in light of the United Nations Convention on the Rights of the Child. Canada, like all countries other than the United

States and Somalia, is a signatory to this convention. The concern that was expressed by government officials about the convention is that Article 40 defines proportionality in a way that is quite different from the way in which the term is used in the section 38 of the YCJA. The YCJA indicates that sentences must be "proportionate to the seriousness of the offence and the degree of responsibility of the young person for that offence" (YCJA, sec. 38). The UN Convention, by contrast, states that "a variety of dispositions . . . shall be available to ensure that children are dealt with in a manner appropriate to their well-being and proportionate both to their circumstances and the offense" (United Nations Convention on the Rights of the Child, 1989, Article 40[4]). According to senior government officials, two problems were seen with this formulation. First, there is obvious concern that "appropriate to their well-being" is set as an equal requirement to proportionality. Hence, one could argue that this would allow youths to be imprisoned "for their own good" even if the offense were minor. Second, it is not clear what it means to be "proportionate" to two different factors. For example, what would it mean to be "proportionate" to a youth's circumstances if the youth were without resources or support and had committed either a very serious or a very minor offense. Thus there was concern that this could be interpreted as undermining the basic proportionality model since "who" the youth was and "what" the youth had done were to determine jointly the severity of the intervention. Youths who commit minor offenses, under the UN Convention, could be placed in custody for social welfare reasons because this could be seen as being "proportionate" to their circumstances.

Canada has never endorsed the requirement in Article 37(c) of the UN Convention on the Rights of the Child that "every child deprived of liberty shall be separated from adults unless it is considered in the child's best interest not to do so." Under the YOA, for example, a young person can be detained prior to trial in a place that is not separate and apart from adults if it is necessary "for the safety of others," or there is no other place of detention available within a reasonable distance (YOA, sec. 7[2]). This latter problem is not trivial in some remote parts of Canada where there are seldom separate detention facilities. A more "principled" situation involving youths in adult facilities occurs in those cases where young people are transferred to the adult system for trial and then found guilty. In these cases, the youth can be ordered by the court to serve the sentence in a youth facility or an adult facility (YOA, sec. 16.2). In the YCJA, the placement of the youth who receives an adult sentence is still a judicial decision. However, if the youth, at the time of sentencing, is under age eighteen, the youth is presumptively sentenced to serve the sentence in a youth facility (YCJA, sec. 76[2]). Hence, the YCJA does not bring Canada into strict compliance with Article 37(c) of the UN Convention but is closer than is the YOA.

As has been pointed out elsewhere in this essay, the desire to lock up youths for therapeutic reasons is quite popular in Canada. In a brief to the Senate of Canada, one Quebec organization that represents youth correctional facilities noted with dismay that with the YCJA, "what we see is an automatic escalation of measures based on the nature of the offence and the degree of the young person's involvement in the commission of that offence. For example, it will become almost impossible for a youth court judge to commit a young person to custody for property crimes even if, in the opinion of experts, that young person is engaged in a trajectory of delinquency, being a member of a criminal gang for example" (Association des Centres Jeunesse du Quebec 2001).

The Senate committee that held hearings on the YCJA recommended a number of amendments to the YCJA, including the proposal that the act should be interpreted in such a way as "best assures" compliance with the UN Convention. It is difficult to know whether such an amendment would have made any difference, since the UN Convention is certainly much less definite than the YCJA about most things, including the meaning of proportionality.

In the end, as described in Section IV.D., the Senate focused more on local aboriginal people than on UN conventions. It expressed its concern about the bill on one dimension only: the failure of the YCJA to focus explicitly on the need to consider punishments other than custody for aboriginal youths in particular.

D. Summary

The YCJA has been criticized from both the criminal justice "right" and the criminal justice "left" for being too complicated.[15] The ideological critics have also criticized it for being too tough on youths (the

---

[15] Clearly there are many other changes in the law, and many of the provisions are, undoubtedly, complex. The YCJA is 157 sections long, compared with 70 sections for the YOA and 45 sections for the JDA. Much—but probably not all—of the escalation in size relates to the decision to be much more explicit about the manner with which cases are dealt.

view of many academics and members of helping professions, and the Province of Quebec) and for being too soft on offending youths (the view of most politically conservative provincial governments and some conservative writers). These are not, however, the most important aspects of the legislation.

What is most noteworthy about this piece of legislation is its attempt, for the first time in Canadian history, to draft criminal legislation that explicitly and implicitly describes what it is trying to accomplish and that lays out a policy for the manner in which it should be administered. In the area of criminal law, it contains provisions that are as close as Canada is likely to get for quite some time to a form of sentencing guidelines.

Judges and others are told what to expect (e.g., proportionality) and are told what not to expect (minor cases ending up in custody or very serious cases ending up with what would appear to be a light sentence because of the needs of the child). At the same time, enormous power is left with those who administer the law. The tough-sounding provisions—adult sentences for youths being the most obvious—clearly do not need to be imposed if a province wishes otherwise. There are procedural disincentives for a province that wishes to impose an adult sentence since, among other complexities, a youth in jeopardy of receiving an adult sentence would have the right to a jury trial. A province such as Quebec that has principled objections to these provisions can, therefore, choose not to ask for adult sentences. But achieving the intent of the law requires an educated and alert defense bar and judiciary. In some provinces, such as Ontario, youths are often represented by counsel whose main activities involve other areas of law. To the extent that they assume that there are few substantive differences between the YCJA and the criminal code, the intent of the new law will not be fulfilled. In other parts of Canada, where most young offenders' cases are handled by specialized legal aid lawyers, there is more reason to believe that change will occur. Judges, as well, vary in terms of how focused they are on "youth" matters. The judge who hears only the occasional young offender matter paired with a lawyer who is not knowledgeable about the YCJA does not sound like a winning combination.

VI. Conclusions

If the political process by which the YCJA became law is predictive of the process by which it will be administered by the provinces, there is reason for concern. The process of passing the bill began with a promise by the minister of justice in 1994 to do a major overhaul of youth justice legislation. Parliamentary and federal-provincial-territorial examinations of the system then followed. A policy paper describing the government's intentions was released in May 1998. The bill itself was introduced into the House of Commons in three different legislative sessions before it received final House of Commons approval in May 2001. Then Canada's Senate, in a very rare move, defied the elected chamber of Parliament and amended the bill with a controversial, and almost certainly ineffectual, provision. By amending the bill, the Senate required the House of Commons to review and approve, yet again, a bill that it had been considering, in one form or another, for almost three years. The bill's final legislative approval on February 4, 2002, marked, then, the end of a prolonged gestation period and a very difficult birth.

There are some data that suggest that difficult prenatal periods and difficult childbirths combined with lack of resources and social disadvantages during the period of early development are likely to lead to life-course persistent antisocial behavior in boys (Tibbetts and Piquero 1999). One can hope that the analogous difficult early experiences of this legislation will not also lead to life-course persistent difficulties.

There are signs that attempts are being made to get beyond the problems that the new law faced during the legislative process. For example, as discussed in Section V of this essay, police officers are told that they are required to consider noncourt approaches to holding youths accountable for their offenses. A number of police forces in Canada, most notably the Toronto Police Service, Canada's largest municipal police force, have, in anticipation of the implementation of the new act, started programs within their forces to encourage police officers to use the court more sparingly. The federally funded National Judicial Institute is organizing a large training program for judges. Much of this program focuses on the need for judges to sentence differently under the YCJA than they have been doing under the YOA. If either or both of these (and other similar) programs are effective, the types of cases coming into the youth justice system under the YOA and going into custody (described in table 3) could change dramatically. The federal government department responsible for youth justice matters has initiated a research program designed to monitor various aspects of the operation of the youth justice system in a sample of communities in order to be able to identify problems of implementation.

At the same time, some aspects of the new legislation, designed largely to placate the provinces, will be interesting to monitor. For example, the general principle limiting disparity in sentencing was modified during the legislative process to require that "the sentence must be similar to the sentences imposed in the region on similar young persons found guilty of the same offence committed in similar circumstances" (YCJA, sec. 38[2][b]). Quebec, in particular, argued that it did not want its judges to be required to sentence in the same way as judges in other regions.[16] Under the YOA, the level of custody—"secure" or "open"—is determined by the youth court judge. Under the YCJA, the legislation presumes that the decision on the "level of custody" will be left to the provincial correctional authorities, but provinces can opt to have it decided by the youth court judge as a sentencing decision. Provinces can also decide whether the "presumptive adult sentence" provisions, described in Section V, apply at age fourteen, fifteen, or sixteen. These changes—clearly designed to suggest to provinces that the federal government would not interfere with the administration of justice—are unlikely to increase the already large amount of provincial variation. They deal with issues where there is already considerable variability, or they deal with issues that are likely to occur only rarely in any province. Nevertheless, they do signal a small amount of deference to provincial sensibilities.

One unfortunate aspect of the untidiness of the legislative process between 1998 and 2002 is that one of the original purposes of bringing a completely new youth justice act—to rehabilitate public confidence in youth justice legislation—seems to have been compromised by the legislative process. As we pointed out in Section V.A., the minister of justice, in introducing the first version of her legislation, contributed to the public's confusion about the legislation. With politicians—including the minister of justice who introduced the legislation and her successor, who was named just as the legislative process was ending—being unwilling to appear enthusiastic about the new legislation, one might expect that public support for the legislation will not come quickly or easily.

What will change, however, is that decisions—and aggregate data such as sentencing patterns—will be able to be evaluated against the

---

[16] The term "region" is an interesting one in this context since some provinces (Quebec, Ontario, and British Columbia) are regions, whereas the other seven provinces are divided into two regions (the Prairies, and the Atlantic Provinces). The territories are not normally considered to be part of any region.

provisions of the legislation. The YOA appears to have been designed to support Yogi Berra's observation that "if you don't know where you are going, you may not get there." The YCJA, on the other hand, may not get Canada's youth to the place that the legislation proposes, but at least we will know that they are not there.

REFERENCES

Anand, Sanjeev. 2000. "The Sentencing of Aboriginal Offenders, Continued Confusion and Persisting Problems: A Comment on the Decision in *R. v. Gladue.*" *Canadian Journal of Criminology* 42:412–20.

Anderssen, Erin. 1999. "Youth-Crime Bill Aims to Aid Prosecutors." *Globe and Mail* (March 11), p. A4.

Association des Centres Jeunesse du Quebec. 2001. "Comments on Bill C-7, the Proposed Youth Criminal Justice Act." Written brief submitted to the Senate Committee on Legal and Constitutional Affairs, Ottawa, October.

Beaulieu, Lucien A. 1994. "Youth Offenses—Adult Consequences." *Canadian Journal of Criminology* 36:329–42.

Canada. 1981. *Highlights of the Young Offenders Act.* Ottawa: Minister of Supply and Services, Canada.

Canadian Centre for Justice Statistics, Statistics Canada. 1962–2001. *Canadian Crime Statistics.* Ottawa: Canadian Centre for Justice Statistics, Statistics Canada.

———. 1992–2001. *Youth Court Statistics.* Ottawa: Canadian Centre for Justice Statistics, Statistics Canada.

Carrington, Peter J. 1995. "Has Violent Youth Crime Increased? Comment on Corrado and Markwart." *Canadian Journal of Criminology* 37:61–73.

———. 1998. "Changes of Police Charging of Young Offenders in Ontario and Saskatchewan after 1984." *Canadian Journal of Criminology* 40:153–64.

———. 1999. "Trends in Youth Crime in Canada, 1977–1996." *Canadian Journal of Criminology* 41:1–32.

Carrington, Peter J., and Sharon Moyer. 1994. "Trends in Youth Crime and Police Response, Pre and Post-YOA." *Canadian Journal of Criminology* 36: 1–28.

Conly, Dennis. 1978. *Patterns of Delinquency and Police Action in the Major Metropolitan Areas of Canada during the Month of December, 1976.* Ottawa: Solicitor General Canada.

Corrado, Raymond R., and Alan Markwart. 1994. "The Need to Reform the YOA in Response to Violent Young Offenders: Confusion, Reality or Myth?" *Canadian Journal of Criminology* 36:343–78.

Cullen, Francis T., John Paul Wright, and Mitchell B. Chamlin. 1999. "Social

Support and Social Reform: A Progressive Crime Control Agenda." *Crime and Delinquency* 45:188–207.

Department of Justice, Canada. 1998. *A Strategy for the Renewal of Youth Justice.* Ottawa: Department of Justice, Canada.

———. 1999. "Minister of Justice Introduces New Youth Justice Law." Press release, March 11. Ottawa: Department of Justice, Canada.

Department of Justice Committee on Juvenile Delinquency. 1965. *Report: Juvenile Delinquency in Canada.* Ottawa: Queen's Printer.

Doob, Anthony N. 1992. "Trends in the Use of Custodial Dispositions for Young Offenders." *Canadian Journal of Criminology* 34:75–84.

———. 2000. "Transforming the Punishment Environment: Understanding Public Views of What Should Be Accomplished at Sentencing." *Canadian Journal of Criminology* 42:323–40.

———. 2001. *Youth Court Judges' Views of the Youth Justice System: The Results of a Survey.* Toronto: Centre of Criminology, University of Toronto.

Doob, Anthony N., and Julian V. Roberts. 1988. "Public Punitiveness and Public Knowledge of the Facts: Some Canadian Surveys." In *Public Attitudes to Sentencing: Surveys from Five Countries,* edited by Nigel Walker and Mike Hough. Cambridge Studies in Criminology no. 59. Aldershot Hants, England: Gower.

Doob, Anthony N., and Jane B. Sprott. 1996. "Interprovincial Variation in the Use of the Youth Court." *Canadian Journal of Criminology* 38:401–12.

———. 1998. "Is the 'Quality' of Youth Violence Becoming More Serious?" *Canadian Journal of Criminology* 40:185–94.

———. 1999. "The Pitfalls of Determining Validity by Consensus." *Canadian Journal of Criminology* 41:535–43.

Doob, Anthony N., Jane B. Sprott, Voula Marinos, and Kimberly N. Varma. 1998. *An Exploration of Ontario Residents' Views of Crime and the Criminal Justice System.* Toronto: Centre of Criminology, University of Toronto.

Federal-Provincial-Territorial Task Force on Youth Justice. 1996. *A Review of the Young Offenders Act and the Youth Justice System in Canada.* Ottawa: Department of Justice, Canada.

Fedorowycz, Orest. 2001. "Homicide in Canada—2000." *Juristat,* vol. 21, no. 9. Ottawa: Canadian Centre for Justice Statistics, Statistics Canada.

Gabor, Thomas. 1999. "Trends in Youth Crime: Some Evidence Pointing to Increases in the Severity and Volume of Violence on the Part of Young People." *Canadian Journal of Criminology* 41:385–92.

LaPrairie, Carol. 1990. "The Role of Sentencing in the Over-Representation of Aboriginal People in Correctional Institutions." *Canadian Journal of Criminology* 32:429–40.

Leon, Jeffrey S. 1977. "The Development of Canadian Juvenile Justice: A Background for Reform." *Osgoode Hall Law Journal* 15:71–106.

Liberal Party of Canada. 1993. "A Liberal Perspective on Crime and Justice Issues." Election document. Released April 1993, updated August 1993. Ottawa: Liberal Party of Canada.

MacCharles, Tonda. "New Law to Get Tough on Youth: Harsher Penalties for Violence, Age of Adult Trials Drops to 14, New Repeat Offender Category." *Toronto Star* (March 11), p. A1.

Markwart, Alan, and Raymond R. Corrado. 1995. "A Response to Carrington." *Canadian Journal of Criminology* 37:74–87.

Ministry of Education and Training, Province of Ontario, Canada. 1994. *Violence-Free Schools Policy.* Toronto: Government of Ontario.

Ovenden, Norm. 1999. "New Act Would Jail Parents for Children's Crimes: New Youth Criminal Justice Act to Be Introduced." *National Post* (March 6), p. A1.

Platt, Anthony M. 1977. *The Child Savers: The Invention of Delinquency.* 2d ed. Chicago: University of Chicago Press.

Roach, Kent, and Jonathan Rudin. 2000. "*Gladue:* The Judicial and Political Reception of a Promising Decision." *Canadian Journal of Criminology* 42: 355–88.

Roberts, Julian V., and Andrew von Hirsch. 1999. "Legislating the Purpose and Principles of Sentencing." In *Making Sense of Sentencing,* edited by Julian V. Roberts and David P. Cole. Toronto: University of Toronto Press.

Solicitor General Canada. 1975. *Young Persons in Conflict with the Law: A Report of the Solicitor General's Committee on Proposals for New Legislation to Replace the Juvenile Delinquents Act.* Ottawa: Ministry of the Solicitor General.

———. 1977. *Highlights of the Proposed New Legislation for Young Offenders.* Ottawa: Ministry of the Solicitor General.

———. 1979. *Legislative Proposals to Replace the Juvenile Delinquents Act.* Ottawa: Ministry of the Solicitor General.

Sprott, Jane B. 1998. "Understanding Public Opposition to a Separate Youth Justice System." *Crime and Delinquency* 44:399–411.

Sprott, Jane B., and Anthony N. Doob. 2000. "Bad, Sad, and Rejected: The Lives of Aggressive Children." *Canadian Journal of Criminology* 42:123–33.

———. 2003. "Two Solitudes or Just One? Provincial Differences in Youth Court Judges and the Operation of Youth Courts." *Canadian Journal of Criminology and Criminal Justice* 45(1):73–80.

Sprott, Jane B., Anthony N. Doob, and Jennifer M. Jenkins. 2001. "Problem Behaviour and Delinquency in Children and Youth." *Juristat*, vol. 21, no. 4. Ottawa: Canadian Centre for Justice Statistics, Statistics Canada.

Sprott Jane B., and Howard N. Snyder. 1999. "Youth Crime in the U.S. and Canada, 1991 to 1996." *Overcrowded Times* 10(5):1, 12–19.

Standing Committee on Justice and Legal Affairs. 1997. *Reviewing Youth Justice.* Thirteenth Report of the Standing Committee on Justice and Legal Affairs, Shaughnessy Cohen, M.P., Chairman. Ottawa: House of Commons.

Standing Committee on Justice and the Solicitor General. 1993. *Crime Prevention in Canada: Toward a National Strategy.* Twelfth Report of the Standing Committee on Justice and the Solicitor General, Dr. Bob Horner, M.P., Chairman. Ottawa: House of Commons.

Statistics Canada. 1996. *Canada Year Book, 1997.* Ottawa: Statistics Canada.

———. 2000. *1999 General Social Survey, Cycle 13: Victimization. Public Use Microdata File Documentation and User's Guide.* Ottawa: Statistics Canada.

Statistics Canada. 1998–2001. *Youth Court Data Tables*. Ottawa: Canadian Centre for Justice Statistics.

Stenning, Philip, and Julian V. Roberts. 2001. "Empty Promises: Parliament, The Supreme Court, and the Sentencing of Aboriginal Offenders." *Saskatchewan Law Review* 64:137–68.

Task Force Established to Study the Administration of the Young Offenders Act in Quebec. 1995. *In the Name of . . . and Beyond the Act*. Michel Jasmin, Chairman. Quebec City: Minister of Justice, Quebec.

Tibbetts, Janice. 1999. "Youth Crime Laws Get Tough: Young Offenders' Criminal Records No Longer Secret." *Ottawa Citizen* (March 7), p. A3.

Tibbetts, Stephen G., and Alex R. Piquero. 1999. "The Influence of Gender, Low Birth Weight, and Disadvantaged Environment in Predicting Early Onset of Offending: A Test of Moffitt's Interactional Hypothesis." *Criminology* 37:843–77.

Tonry, Michael. 1999. "Why Are U.S. Incarceration Rates So High?" *Crime and Delinquency* 45:419–37.

Trépanier, Jean. 1983. "The Quebec Youth Protection Act: Institutionalized Diversion." In *Current Issues in Juvenile Justice*, edited by Raymond R. Corrado, Marc Le Blanc, and Jean Trépanier. Toronto: Butterworths.

———. 1989. "Principles and Goals Guiding the Choice of Dispositions under the YOA. In *Young Offender Dispositions: Perspectives on Principles and Practice*, edited by Lucien A. Beaulieu. Toronto: Wall & Thompson.

United Nations. 1989. "Convention on the Rights of the Child." Available at http://www.unicef.org/crc/crc.htm (last accessed May 9, 2003).

Von Hirsch, Andrew. 1976. *Doing Justice: The Choice of Punishments*. Report of the Committee for the Study of Incarceration. New York: Hill & Wang.

Allison Morris

Youth Justice in New Zealand

ABSTRACT

The Children, Young Persons and Their Families Act 1989 incorporated
family group conferences into New Zealand's youth justice system.
Though not premised on restorative justice ideas, New Zealand's system
is broadly compatible with them. Alleged offenders under age fourteen
may not be criminally prosecuted (except for murder or manslaughter),
and offenders from fourteen to seventeen years old must be referred to a
family group conference either before formal charges or before
sentencing. Conferences include the offender and family members, the
victim and supporters, and others and are chaired by a youth justice
coordinator (often these are social workers). Outcomes must be accepted
by all participants. Offenders, their families, and victims are more satisfied
with conferences than with justice system processes. Victims are least
satisfied, however, and least willing to participate. Implementation failures
may partly explain this. Court referral rates and institutional placements
have fallen sharply. Reconviction data are tentative, but offenders' positive
conferencing experiences may predict lower recidivism. Some police
remain negative or skeptical. Recent government decisions to build youth
penal facilities and rely more heavily on actuarial risk prediction may be
inconsistent with conferencing. Overall, though, accomplishments have
been substantial, and the future looks promising.

The New Zealand youth justice system—and family group conferences
in particular—has been the center of international interest since it was
introduced in 1989, and family group conferences have since been imi-
tated by a number of other countries (Hudson et al. 1996).[1] Maxwell

Allison Morris is former professor of criminology, Victoria University of Wellington, New Zealand.

[1] Various versions of conferencing have been developed or tried in countries as diverse as Australia, Belgium, Canada, England, Ireland, Singapore, South Africa, Sweden,
and the United States.

and Morris (1993), on the basis of research carried out in the early 1990s, were critical of some aspects of the practice but stressed the potential of the objects and principles underlying the new system and suggested that it was probably just a matter of time before this potential was realized: poor practice would be eradicated through training and better resourcing, and the objects and principles would flourish.

Now, more than ten years later, I am less sure of this potential, and the main purpose of this essay is to consider whether family group conferences in New Zealand have, in practice, realized their potential. Another purpose is to try to understand why New Zealand now deals with young offenders in the way that it does. McDonald (1978, p. 45) wrote that "social forces act to adjust the rights and obligations of childhood to be congruent with the times." Thus, he suggested that, from 1840 to 1899 in New Zealand, children were seen as chattels; from 1900 to 1944, children were seen as social capital; from 1945 to 1969, they were seen as psychological beings; and, from 1970, as citizens. There is some truth in this, although I doubt that the boundaries are so clear-cut. The very existence of a separate youth justice system makes it clear that children are not yet seen as full citizens.

In Section I, I look briefly at how young offenders were dealt with in New Zealand in the past. It is difficult to be precise about the period prior to colonization by Europeans, primarily the British, as much of what is written dates from the middle of the nineteenth century. In the first part of this story, however, there is little that is unique to New Zealand: changes there mirror changes elsewhere, and the parallels in ideology are striking.[2] In 1989 in New Zealand, however, legislation was passed (the Children, Young Persons and Their Families Act) that introduced, at that time, a unique, innovative, and radical way of dealing with young offenders that has captured the world's attention. In Section II, I describe the factors leading to this change and, in Section III, I describe briefly what this legislation sought to achieve and place particular emphasis on those principles that reflect restorative justice values. In Section IV, I describe more fully the practice of youth justice in New Zealand and, in Section V, I examine the extent to which key objects and principles of the act have been realized. In Section VI, I briefly respond to some of the theoretical objections that have been

---

[2] See, e.g., Platt's (1969) account of developments in the United States, Stang Dahl's (1974) account of developments in Norway, and Morris and Giller's (1987) account of developments in England.

made about family group conferences and, in Section VII, I reflect on future prospects.

I. Describing the Past

In traditional Maori society, there were clear rules about behavior that was acceptable and that was not acceptable, and, according to Jackson (1987, p. 26), Maori recognized a distinction between sharing property with *whanaunga* (relatives) and taking from a stranger. He refers there to written records that document a thief being ordered by his chief to forfeit all his goods to a *Pakeha* (European) from whom he had stolen a rope. Jackson (1988, p. 40) also recounts examples of the payment of a *taonga* (gift of something precious) by an offender's *whanau* (family) to the *whanau* of the victim, and of large *muru* (exacting compensation) parties that sought recompense from whole villages. In each case, he says, the *utu* (price of compensation) was mediated through ritualized *korero* (discussion).

Thus, Maori shared with *Pakeha* a clear code of right and wrong behavior, but "its philosophical emphasis was different." By this, Jackson (1988, p. 36) means that "the system of behavioural constraints implied in the law was interwoven with the deep spiritual and religious underpinning of Maori society so that Maori people did not so much live under the law, as with it. It was part of everyday existence." He highlights the differences in the following way: "Under Pakeha notions of criminal jurisprudence, the objectives are to establish fault or guilt and then to punish. The sentencing goals of retribution, revenge, deterrence, and isolation of the offenders are extremely important, although the system often plays lip service to the idea of rehabilitation as well. A Maori system would endeavour to seek a realignment of those goals to ensure restitution and compensation rather than retribution; to mediate the case to everyone's satisfaction rather than simply punish" (1988, p. 277).

Whether or not any distinction between adults and young people was made in the Maori system of justice is unclear, but it seems unlikely. Responsibility for wrongdoing was placed on the family of the offender, not just on the individual, and sanctions were aimed at restoring balance. Thus, according to Jackson (1988, pp. 43–44): "The *whanau* of the offender was made aware of its shared responsibilities, that of the victim was given reparation to restore its proper place, and the ancestors were appeased by the acceptance of the precedents which they had laid down. . . . It provided a sense of legal control which was effective because it had a unifying base that recognised the need for social order and the value of balance in community affairs."

The underlying philosophy, therefore, was very different from the English law and jurisprudence brought to New Zealand by the colonizers. However, by the 1870s, the laws of England applied in New Zealand. In line with English practice at that time, the age of criminal responsibility was set at seven.[3]

This meant that young offenders in New Zealand were, around the middle of the nineteenth century, not recognized as a distinct group of offenders. Adult and young offenders were sanctioned in much the same way, and it was not uncommon for children and young people to be imprisoned for quite minor offenses. Pratt (1992) cites the example of two boys aged between seven and eight who ran away from Auckland City Mission in clothes belonging to it, for which each received a three-months prison sentence. Young offenders, like adult offenders, could also be whipped; Pratt (1992) refers to a boy of eight being whipped for committing a burglary. The primary intention was to deter individual offenders and others from crime, and that the offender was a young person made little difference. This reflected no more than the belief that young people were little different from adults in their daily lives.[4]

The first break in dealing with juvenile and adult offenders in the same ways was the result of the appearance of a large number of destitute or neglected children, especially children of mixed ethnicity, created largely by the pauperism and breakup of families. The industrial school—a combination of a school and an orphanage—was developed by private organizations, particularly by churches, and was a direct response to this new problem. Barrington and Beaglehole (1990, p. 170) quote one minister in the mid-1850s saying that half-caste children should be taken into the church boarding schools that were attached

[3] This age of criminal responsibility was first set out in statute in sec. 176(5) of the Justice of the Peace Act of 1882. It states there that "any child who is not, in the opinion of the Court . . . above the age of seven, and of sufficient capacity to commit a crime" is not punishable. This was repeated in sec. 22 of the Criminal Code Act of 1893 and again in sec. 41 of the Crimes Act of 1908. The age of criminal responsibility remained seven until 1961.

[4] As in England, the child immigrant was expected to work alongside his or her family, and the state did not interfere with this or with the selling or farming out of children when families were destitute. Even after children began working in New Zealand factories and mills, the state was slow to act, and some of the early legislation passed in England was not adopted in the colonies until some time later. Children under age fourteen remained in the workforce until late into the nineteenth century despite acts (from 1877 onward) that made schooling free and compulsory (McDonald 1978).

to the mission stations at that time to rescue them from "poverty, ig-
norance, and vice, and from the degradation of being brought up as
Maoris."

Importantly, the first national statute—the Neglected and Criminal
Children Act 1867—like its English counterpart, distinguished between neglected and criminal children: industrial schools were intended to hold neglected children, and reformatories were intended to
hold criminal children.[5] However, only industrial schools were built
(by 1876, there were ten institutions for "orphaned, criminal, or destitute children") and so neglected and criminal children were, in practice, held together.[6] These institutions were described as bleak, and the
avowed intent was as much to contain the children as to train them
(McDonald 1978; May 1997).

For the main part, therefore, the distinction between the two categories of children continued to be blurred on pragmatic (cost) if not
ideological grounds, so much so that the Industrial Schools Act 1882,
which repealed the 1867 act, made no mention of reformatories. Instead, this act allowed the managers of the industrial schools to classify
children and to separate the neglected from the criminal. This act also
made it no longer mandatory to first punish (imprison) the criminal
child before committing him or her to the industrial school. However,
children continued to be held in prison until late into the nineteenth
century.[7] At the same time, the number of children committed to industrial schools increased dramatically (Dalley 1998a).[8]

Conceptions of children and young people gradually changed. According to McDonald (1978, p. 47), bringing up children began to be

---

[5] There was power to send a child who had offended to an industrial school if two
justices thought it appropriate given the child's age and the circumstances of the case.
Also, as in the equivalent statute in England, a child who offended had first to serve the
appropriate prison sentence for the offense; placement in the reformatory was intended
to follow this.

[6] Holding the two groups of children together was not without opposition, however:
some thought that "unfortunate yet honest and respectable children" should not be
mixed with those "inured to crime" (quoted by Seymour 1976, p. 11), who were seen
as more difficult to manage and as tending to corrupt the others.

[7] Seymour (1976, p. 15) quotes the inspector of prisons who frequently referred in
the 1880s and early 1890s to the "scandal" of the imprisonment of children even though
by then they would have been held separately from adult prisoners where possible. The
number of children in prison did not decline significantly until 1896 (for data, see Seymour 1976, p. 16, n. 75). Many of these children would have been serving very short
sentences or awaiting transfer to an industrial school.

[8] This was due primarily to moral panics about what was termed the "larrikin nuisance": gangs of children wandering the streets harassing others and creating a public
nuisance (Dalley 1998a, p. 17).

seen as too important to be left to families, and "society's social capital was related directly to the degree of care given to children." From the beginning of the twentieth century, therefore, the health, welfare, and education of children became a matter of public concern and political action.[9] Conceptions of how children's offending should be responded to changed too, as in other countries at this time. In part, this was due to the emergence of the new sciences of psychiatry and psychology and, later, of positivist criminology. Offending began to be seen as a symptom of various causes, and the appropriate response to offenders began to be seen as treatment—preferably involving early and indeterminate detention—and not punishment. Young people were a prime target: first through the industrial and reformatory schools but later through probation,[10] probation homes, and, for more hardened juvenile offenders, Borstals.[11] Similar thinking about the distinctiveness of juvenile offenders led to modifications in court procedures for children from around 1865 onward, culminating in the Juvenile Offenders Act of 1906 that provided for magistrates to hear cases involving children under age sixteen at different times from adults.[12]

The international "child saving" or reform movement is usually seen as having its roots in the general humanitarianism and philanthropy of the nineteenth and early twentieth centuries, but these reforms are also acknowledged to have grown out of nineteenth- and early twentieth-century fears as well as aspirations (Platt 1969; Morris and Giller 1987). This was true of New Zealand, too. Reforms might have sought to advance the welfare of children through removing them from adult courts and prisons, but they also grew out of concerns about

[9] McDonald (1978, p. 48) gives us some flavor of this in his reference to a health department report from 1922 that stated that "in one city school thirty-three out of fifty-eight children showed physical deformity." More generally, developments in New Zealand, especially with respect to health and welfare, were far advanced for the times. Dalley (1998a, p. 14) described New Zealand then as having "an international reputation as a 'social laboratory.'"

[10] Probation was first introduced in statutory form in the First Offenders' Probation Act. Supervision was carried out at that time by jailers or senior police officers and so was not seen as entirely appropriate for young offenders. It was not until the beginning of the twentieth century that probation was more widely used for them. Juvenile probation officers were introduced in 1917 (Statute Law Amendment Act, sec. 10). This set the way for child welfare officers, who were introduced in 1925.

[11] Invercargill prison took such boys from 1909 onward and was first designated a Borstal in 1918. Legislative recognition of such an institution did not occur until 1924 with the passing of the Prevention of Crime (Borstal Institutions Establishment) Act.

[12] The provisions of this act were subsequently incorporated into part III of the Justices of the Police Act of 1908.

the number of children growing up on the streets or without "adequate" parental control, and about their unacceptable behavior. The reforms, therefore, promised more humane responses to young offenders and, at the same time, more effective control. These promises, however, were not really fulfilled, and procedures and practices for dealing with young offenders were described in 1920 as "somewhat haphazard" (quoted in Seymour 1976, p. 31).

The next main event in the story of youth justice in New Zealand is the passing of the Child Welfare Act of 1925.[13] This signified two changes intended to create special provision for young offenders: the formation of the child welfare branch (which became responsible for the supervision and care of child offenders as well as of neglected children), and the creation of the children's court. This involvement of the child welfare branch with young offenders led to an increasing focus on the "needs" or "best interests" of the child.

What "best interests" meant in practice, however, was the processing through the courts of young people, especially young Maori, for quite minor offenses, and their placement in institutions indeterminately (in practice, this would be for any time up until the age of twenty) "for their own good." Thus, the 1925 act can be seen as finally eradicating the distinction between offending and neglected children. Court practices themselves did not change much as a result of the 1925 act—children's cases were still mainly heard in the adult court, and only a few magistrates were appointed who were specially qualified because of their knowledge of children.[14] Indeed, Seymour (1976, p. 37) states that these new courts were not special tribunals for children but were adult courts "clumsily modified."

The police in New Zealand have always exercised a wide discretion in dealing with young offenders, especially with respect to minor crime (Seymour 1976, p. 47). As early as the 1930s, they began to consult with child welfare officers about how young offenders should be dealt

[13] Dalley (1998a, p. 8) describes this as New Zealand's first major child welfare legislation, and, although it was based on practices overseas, "its implementation was viewed with interest around the globe." She suggests that this was a typical pattern in the development of New Zealand social policy: "picking up some ideas, rejecting others, and devising indigenous programmes to meet child welfare needs particular to this country" (Dalley 1998a, p. 8).

[14] A 1927 amendment (Child Welfare Amendment Act of 1927) in fact removed the requirement that the children's court should sit in a different building; it was considered enough for the young offenders attending the children's court not to have contact with those attending other court sittings.

with. Their main emphasis was on preventing youth crime and responding to the welfare of those young people who offended.[15]

Post World War II, New Zealand experienced a period of social and economic change, including mass migration from rural to urban communities, particularly by Maori, with the resulting loss of support from *whanau*, and a rapid growth in the population. Perhaps not unrelated, there also emerged concerns about young people as demonstrated through moral panics about juvenile crime (especially by Maori) and adolescent sexual behavior (or "moral delinquency" as it was called then).[16] It is from this period that the psychological and child guidance services grew rapidly in New Zealand. But it is also from this period that Maori began to argue that they were best suited to deal with their own children. For example, in some areas in the 1950s, tribal committees heard charges against Maori children (Dalley 1998*b*, p. 205). However, no state resources were allocated to allow Maori to do this.

During this period, consultations between the police and child welfare officers about how best to deal with minor crime committed by young people became formalized with the development of the juvenile crime prevention section of the police in 1957. Rusbatch (1974, p. 34), citing police general instructions, says that the underlying purpose was "to keep the welfare of the children to the forefront when dealing with delinquency." In an attempt to reduce the number of young people prosecuted, the juvenile crime prevention section was required to make background inquiries about the young offenders coming to their notice, to carry out home visits, and to liaise with other departments. The expectation was that the power to prosecute would be used sparingly and that other methods of dealing with young offenders—such as warning or social welfare follow-up—would be considered and used wherever appropriate.

In the 1950s and early 1960s, new punitive powers became available

[15] Seymour (1976, pp. 47–48) refers to the annual report of the education department for 1931 that states that, after consultation between the police and the child welfare officer, a number of children whose offenses were "of insufficient importance to warrant court action" were "adequately" dealt with "otherwise, usually by being regarded as preventive cases under the supervision of a Child Welfare Officer."

[16] McDonald (1978, p. 49) describes the incidence of juvenile delinquency then as "alarming," but, interestingly, the method chosen to forestall this was ensuring children's "psychological adjustment" through providing good preschool experiences and play centers. A special investigative committee set up to examine "moral delinquency" in children and adolescents, which reported in 1954, was, according to McDonald (1978, p. 50), "largely ignored and quickly became stamped as the moralists' credo." He describes "the prevailing climate towards youngsters" as looking "more to the origins of behaviour rather than means of repressing it" (1978, p. 50).

for young offenders: sixteen-year-old boys could be sentenced to detention centers;[17] boys aged fifteen and sixteen could be sentenced to periodic detention;[18] boys and girls aged fifteen and sixteen were eligible for Borstal training;[19] and, in exceptional circumstances, children could be sentenced to imprisonment.[20] The age of criminal responsibility was raised from seven to ten in 1961 (sec. 3 of the Crimes Act).

And there the story remains more or less until the 1970s despite dissatisfaction with the 1925 act. According to Seymour (1976, p. 45), new legislation dealing with young offenders had been promised in 1966, but a bill was not introduced until November 1973. This was heralded by the then minister of social welfare as a "completely new approach" (quoted by Seymour 1976, p. 45). The Children and Young Persons Act of 1974 made a distinction, in section 2, between children (those under age fourteen) and young persons (those aged fourteen or over but under age seventeen).[21]

Offenses committed by those under age fourteen became the concern of newly created children's boards. These consisted of a police officer, a social worker, a representative of the Department of Maori and Island Affairs, and a local community member. They had jurisdiction only where the child admitted the offense and there were no outstanding issues with respect to reparation. Children and their parents were able to attend the children's board's meetings (but they could not be compelled to attend), and the children's board's powers were fairly limited: they could take no action, warn the child, counsel the child (or the parents), refer them to another agency for counseling or help (provided the child and parents agreed), or, as a last resort, refer the case back to social welfare with a recommendation that proceedings be brought in court, but, as we are about to see, these could not be criminal proceedings. The children's boards could also arrange other measures such as community work on an informal basis, but they had no power to enforce these measures. The children's boards were intended to keep children under fourteen years out of the courts, to encourage families to discuss their difficulties and to participate in decisions about how best to deal with their children's offending, and to provide families with support.

[17] See secs. 15–17 of the Criminal Justice Act of 1954 (inserted in 1960).
[18] See secs. 2–23 of the Criminal Justice Amendment Act of 1962.
[19] See secs. 18–20 of the Criminal Justice Act of 1954.
[20] See sec. 14 of the Criminal Justice Act of 1954.
[21] In terms of state intervention on the basis of offending, this distinction remains valid.

Section 25(2) of the Children and Young Persons Act of 1974 made it impossible to bring criminal proceedings against a child. Under section 27(2)(f), a child whose offenses warranted court action had to be made subject to a complaint that he or she is "in need of care, protection, or control." This section also made it clear that the commission of an offense per se was not sufficient to warrant such action; the child's offending had to be of a "number, nature, or magnitude" that indicated that the child was "beyond the control" of his or her parents or that it was "in the interests of his future social training or in the public interest" that such a finding be made.

The Children and Young Persons Act of 1974 also gave statutory recognition, in section 26, to the practice already described of specialist police officers and social workers (and sometimes a representative of the Department of Maori and Island Affairs) meeting together (in what were called conferences) to discuss together whether prosecution was necessary for those aged fourteen but under age seventeen who had not been arrested.[22] They then made recommendations about the need for prosecution to a senior police officer who, in turn, decided whether or not the young person should, in fact, be prosecuted. The intention here, too, was to keep young persons out of the courts.

Most of the other provisions in the Children and Young Persons Act of 1974 simply clarified existing practice. The children's court was renamed the Children and Young Persons Court, but this seems to have been no more than a change in name. However, the then minister of social welfare said that it was hoped not only that magistrates would be appointed to this court "with experience in dealing with young people," but also that they would "exercise jurisdiction solely in a children and young persons court" (quoted by Seymour 1976, p. 52). The 1974 act also gave legal rights greater priority through, for example, allowing young offenders' families (and, on occasion, the young persons themselves) access to, and the right to rebut, the reports written about them by social workers and through providing legal representation to children who were subject to complaint (care and protection) proceedings.[23]

---

[22] By now the juvenile crime prevention section was called the police youth aid section.

[23] According to McDonald (1978, p. 52), the mid-1970s saw the birth of the children's rights movement in New Zealand, and he claims it reached a peak in 1979 with the International Year of the Child. However, as we will see, a concern for children's rights has continued to exert an influence, as demonstrated by New Zealand's ratification of the United Nations Convention on the Rights of the Child in 1993.

The Children and Young Persons Act of 1974 continued to make available the same measures that were available under the 1925 act (discharges, admonitions, fines, restitution, supervision, committal to the care of the director-general of social welfare, and, in certain situations, the various punitive and custodial measures outlined previously), but it provided some new measures—counseling or other assistance for parents and the possibility of attaching two new conditions to a supervision order: a semicustodial measure and community work.[24]

It had always been possible under the 1925 act to transfer certain children from child welfare supervision to (adult) probation and from child welfare institutions to Borstals. But the Children and Young Persons Act of 1974 went further: it provided, in section 36(1)(j), that young persons who were aged fifteen and older for whom adult measures were thought appropriate could be convicted and transferred to the magistrate's court for sentencing.

In many of these changes and consolidations of existing practice, New Zealand was influenced to some extent by debates and developments overseas. The ideas underlying diversion and early intervention or prevention were highly influential in most youth justice systems from the 1970s onward. Also influential in the 1970s were concerns about the excesses of "welfare" and the need to substitute more "justice," and the need to both provide support to parents to bring up their children and, at the same time, to make them more responsible for their children's offending. In addition, ideas around the punishment and control of certain children and young persons were never truly absent from debates about youth justice.

The 1974 Children and Young Persons Act also, however, went further than developments overseas: it tried to involve families and local communities more in decisions about young offenders through the introduction of the children's boards, a move that was specifically New Zealand in its origins and that marks the beginning of the much more radical changes to come in the late 1980s. Children's boards were one of the first attempts to more fully involve Maori in decisions affecting their young.

However, research carried out on the youth justice system in New Zealand in the mid-1980s by Morris and Young (1987) confirmed that

[24] Seymour (1976, p. 52) quotes the then minister who describes this measure as paving the way for "forms of treatment which are halfway between the relatively unrestricted freedom under a supervision order at present while the young person is in the community and the extreme alternative of custodial care 7 days a week."

practice had changed little. Frontline police still arrested large numbers of young people so that they would have to appear in court and would not be the subject of consultation processes between the police and social workers about whether prosecution was necessary. When frontline police referred young people to the youth aid section of the police for action, most of them were then dealt with by police warning, and very few were referred on by youth aid for consultation about prosecution. In effect, it had already been decided that most of these young people did not warrant prosecution.

The consultation process itself was clearly "managed" by the police: their introductory remarks defined the parameters and set the tone for the discussion, and they clearly dominated the meetings both formally and informally—social workers and other participants were often unprepared, contributed little to the discussions, and, in the main, endorsed the police recommendation. Indeed, for certain offenses, the consultation process was viewed by the police, according to Morris and Young (1987), as a legal requirement that had to be gone through to enable a prosecution to occur rather than acting as a barrier to prosecution.

With respect to the children's boards, they referred very few children back to social welfare for consideration of complaint proceedings, but this was because, in the main, the police initiated such proceedings themselves without recourse to the children's boards. Most cases referred to the children's boards were routinely dealt with by way of a token disposition—mainly a warning—often after what Morris and Young (1987, p. 95) describe as wide-ranging and rambling discussions. Referrals for specialist help or counseling rarely occurred. Discussions at children's boards were dominated by board members. Children participated to a very limited extent, and parents contributed only a little more so. Thus, according to Morris and Young (1987), the children's boards were not generally effective in achieving their goals of diverting children from courts, providing social welfare and other support to children or their parents, or enabling families to participate in decisions about their children.

II. Shaping the Present

The Children and Young Persons Act of 1974 was repeatedly amended over the next ten years, and both policy makers and practitioners working with young offenders were concerned about the practices mentioned above—the overreliance on arrest, courts, and institutions.[25] The report of the Advisory Committee on Youth and the Law in our Multi-Cultural Society (1983) was highly critical of practices under the 1974 act.[26] In addition, an increasing number of young offenders were sent to the adult courts for sentencing: a clear indication of the perceived failure of the youth justice system to deal with them (Doolan 1993).

It was time for change and, in the future direction of youth justice, New Zealand was clearly influenced by the continuing international debates about the potentially harmful effects of court appearances and institutions, the perceived failure of "welfare," and the need to provide more "justice" for children and young people who committed offenses. However, other changes were thought necessary, too. Mike Doolan, a senior public servant, conducted a study tour in the mid-1980s of various countries (Scotland, England, Canada, and the United States) with the brief to bring back the best of international practice, but he concluded that the answer to New Zealand's particular "problems" did not lie overseas (Doolan 1988).

In the 1980s also, New Zealand experienced an economic recession, high public expenditure, and a huge national debt that resulted in a program of radical structural changes, including the move in many arenas from state responsibility to family and community responsibility. Maori also began to demand change, especially with respect to young Maori offenders, and one of the changes promised by the 1984 (Labour) government was to honor the Treaty of Waitangi, the treaty signed in 1840 that sets out relationships between Maori and the Crown. Any new youth justice legislation would have to take Maori demands into account.[27]

[25] There was also concern about what was happening in social welfare homes. For example, a complaint was made in 1979 to the Human Rights Commission by the Auckland Committee on Racism and Discrimination after an inquiry by it in 1978. It believed that the treatment that young people were receiving in social welfare homes violated the United Nations Covenant of Civil and Political Rights that New Zealand had ratified in 1978. The Human Rights Commission (1982) subsequently recommended the need for minimum standards of care, for better staff training, and for the outlawing of certain practices (such as the testing of girls in social welfare homes for venereal disease).

[26] Its terms of reference (Advisory Committee on Youth and the Law in Our Multi-Cultural Society 1983, p. 9) were to examine current legislation, practices, and procedures about children and young people coming to official notice as the result of offending; to identify any areas of "inappropriateness, confusion or misunderstanding"; and to recommend changes "which may be more appropriate and effective having regard to [young offenders'] cultural background."

[27] The claim that Maori were, throughout this period, overrepresented in institutional populations is commonly promoted, but Dalley (1998b, p. 190) questions this and sug-

Two influential documents added force to these demands. First, the report of the Ministerial Advisory Committee on a Maori Perspective for the Department of Social Welfare called *Puao-Te-Ata-Tu* (Daybreak) published in 1986 called for more culturally appropriate ways of dealing with Maori juvenile offenders. This report, based on extensive consultation with Maori, was an indictment of both the policy and delivery of social welfare services to Maori.

The committee (Ministerial Advisory Committee 1986, p. 17) referred to the "messages of frustration, anger, and alienation" that it had heard from Maori, though it acknowledged that these were "flavoured with hope, unfulfilled expectations, pride, and *aroha*" (love), and believed that "the angry sense of powerlessness is not matched with a sense of hopelessness." It described the operation of the law since 1840 as "largely inimical to the interests of the Maori people" and as having "defeated the maintenance of the Maori way of life" (Ministerial Advisory Committee 1986, p. 18); it also described the department of social welfare as institutionally racist and as having acted in discriminatory ways against Maori (p. 24). To remedy this, the committee argued that biculturalism—"the essential prerequisite to the development of a multi-cultural society" (p. 19)—was the appropriate policy direction. It also argued for strategies "for rebuilding the basis of independent Maori society" (p. 24). In particular, these included giving Maori resources to develop their own programs.

Second, a two-volume report by Moana Jackson for the then department of justice called *The Maori in the Criminal Justice System: A New Perspective: He Whaipaanga Hou* (1987, 1988) also pointed to "institutional racism." Jackson convened a number of *hui* (a gathering of people for a discussion) with Maori throughout New Zealand and argued for a return to the Maori justice practices of the past. The following quote from a participant at one of these *hui* gives some flavor of Maori feelings at that time: "Of course we had a *ture*, a law, and when we lost that we were a wayward people. If our *rangatahi* (youth) are wayward today, you go back to the loss of our *ture* to know why" (Jackson 1988, p. 34).

---

gests that official policy from the 1920s onward was to place Maori children with their *whanau*, in their tribal areas, or with other Maori families. She documents (1998*b*, p. 192) that between 1925 and the 1970s, less than 10 percent of the children in care were placed in institutions and that most children remained in residences for less than two years. However, she also documents (1998*b*, p. 194) that from the 1940s to the early 1970s, Maori were three times as likely as *Pakeha* children to appear in the youth justice or care and protection systems.

Specifically, and more controversially, Jackson advocated an autonomous system for dealing with Maori offenders that would exist alongside the conventional criminal justice system. However, he also argued for a more holistic response to Maori offending and cautioned that remedying it would require "social and racial equity rather than mere administrative reform" (Jackson 1988, p. 163). The then minister of justice rejected the possibility of a separate parallel justice system, but the case for giving more attention to the rights of the *tangata whenua* (people of the land) and making the legal system more sensitive to Maori values was accepted, as were Jackson's suggestions about the need to move toward biculturalism and to a greater sharing with Maori of resources, responsibilities, and decision making.

In addition, two international instruments seem to have influenced the emerging changes. The United Nations Convention on the Rights of the Child was cosponsored by New Zealand and was adopted by the United Nations in November of 1989. It sets out the responsibilities of the state toward young people and makes clear that, while the primary responsibility for young people resides with their families, the state also has obligations to them, especially when their families are disadvantaged or unable to provide adequate care and support. Article 12 states that children's views should be taken into account in any judicial or administrative hearing affecting them and was clearly influential in shaping the procedures introduced in New Zealand in 1989. So were Article 30, which places a value on maintaining children's cultural roots, and Article 40, which gives children involved in offending certain rights. Of specific interest are statements that children should be treated with dignity, should be reintegrated into society, and should be dealt with so far as possible without resorting to judicial proceedings provided their rights are safeguarded. The New Zealand Government signed the convention in 1990.[28]

The United Nations Declaration of Basic Principles for Victims of Crime was influential in the passing of the Victims of Offences Act of 1987 in New Zealand. Both state, among other requirements, that victims of crime should have access to welfare, health, and legal services; that they should be treated with dignity, courtesy, and compassion; and that they should be informed about criminal justice processes and outcomes. This act also set up the Victims Task Force to monitor compli-

---

[28] It ratified it in 1993, and I will discuss in Sec. V the implications and consequences of this ratification.

ance with the act, to assess the adequacy of services for victims, and to make suggestions for change. Though there was no explicit discussion of victims having an active role in decisions about how best to deal with offending, the time was ripe to take more account of victims' views and interests.

Collectively, then, there were a number of influences on the eventual content of the Children, Young Persons and Their Families Act 1989. International debates about youth justice, acceptance of the need to protect children's rights, an awakening acknowledgment of victims' interests, and, above all, the need to create a system of youth justice that was not monocultural but that reflected the diversity of the New Zealand population and, in particular, the *mana* (prestige) of the *tangata whenua*. Family group conferences—the special innovation of the 1989 act—are said to have their roots in the *whanau hui* (family meetings) of Maori.

III. Introducing the Children, Young Persons and Their Families Act 1989 and Restorative Values

The Children, Young Persons and Their Families Act 1989 sets out a number of general objects and principles in sections 4 and 5 and also sets out in section 208 a number of principles that relate specifically to youth justice. In general terms, the act encourages diversion[29] and moves some way toward a justice approach[30] without abandoning the desire to achieve positive outcomes for young people who offend.[31]

However, the act also reflects certain innovative strategies: it emphasizes the provision of culturally sensitive and appropriate procedures

[29] Section 208(a), e.g., refers to the principle that, unless the public interest requires otherwise, criminal proceedings should not be instituted against a child or young person if there is an alternative means of dealing with the matter. Section 208(d) refers to the principle that a child or young person who commits an offense should be kept in the community as far as practicable, and sec. 208(f)(ii) states that any sanctions imposed should take the least restrictive form that is appropriate in the circumstances.

[30] Section 4(f)(i), e.g., refers to ensuring that, where children or young persons commit offenses, they are held accountable and encouraged to accept responsibility for their behavior; sec. 208(b) refers to the principle that criminal proceedings should not be instituted against a child or young person solely in order to provide any assistance or services needed to advance the welfare of the child or young person.

[31] Section 4(a), e.g., refers to the object of promoting the well-being of children and young persons by having appropriate services, sec. 4(b) refers to assisting families, and sec. 4(f)(ii) specifically states that young offenders should be dealt with in a way that "acknowledges their needs" and that gives them the opportunity to develop in "responsible, beneficial and socially acceptable ways."

and services for young offenders,[32] and it introduces procedures (family group conferences)[33] to encourage young offenders,[34] families,[35] and victims to come to an agreement about how offenses should be dealt with. These agreements are expected to have due regard to the interests of any victims as well as to the well-being and accountability of offenders.[36]

The phrase "restorative justice" did not feature in the New Zealand debates about youth justice at this time, but the youth justice system generally, and family group conferences in particular, are now commonly presented as an example of restorative justice in practice, since the values underlying family group conferences are seen as reflecting restorative justice values (see, e.g., NACRO 1997; Dignan 1999).[37] Both family group conferences and restorative justice give a say in how the offense should be resolved to those most affected—victims, offenders, and their "communities of care"—and both give primacy to their interests. Thus, the state no longer has a monopoly over decision making. In a sense, the state's role—or the role of its representatives—is redefined: as information giver, as facilitator, as deliverer of services, and as provider of resources. Both family group conferences and restorative justice processes also emphasize addressing the offending and its consequences in meaningful ways; reconciling victims, offenders, and their communities through reaching agreements about how best to deal with the offending; and trying to reintegrate or reconnect both victims and offenders at the local community level through healing the harm and hurt caused by the offending and through taking steps to prevent its recurrence.

---

[32] See sec. 4(a)(i) and (iii).

[33] See secs. 245 to 271.

[34] This sentiment is inferred from sec. 5(d) of the 1989 act, which refers to the principle that consideration should be given to the wishes of the child.

[35] Section 5(a) refers to the principle that, wherever possible, a child's or young person's family—including *whanau, hapu* (subtribe), *iwi* (tribe), and family group—should participate in the making of decisions affecting their children; sec. 208(c)(ii) refers to the principle that the ability of families to develop their own means of dealing with their children's offending should be fostered.

[36] See sec. 208(g).

[37] Although restorative justice values, processes, and practices have been around for a long time (Jackson 1988; Consedine 1995; Braithwaite 1999), there was a resurgence of interest in them internationally in the 1990s (see, e.g., Zehr 1990; Van Ness and Strong 1997), in part as a response to the perceived ineffectiveness and high cost (in both human and financial terms) of conventional justice processes and in part as a response to the failure of conventional systems to hold offenders accountable in meaningful ways or to adequately respond to victims' needs and interests.

IV. Conferencing in Practice

Since enactment of the Children and Young Persons Act of 1974, New Zealand has distinguished between the age of criminal responsibility (ten) and the age of prosecution (fourteen).[38] It also distinguished between children (those aged less than fourteen years) and young persons (those aged fourteen and under seventeen) and used different procedures for these two groups when they committed offenses. Children who commit offenses are now dealt with under the care and protection provisions of the 1989 act, and young persons who offend are now dealt with under the youth justice provisions of the 1989 act. This essay relates primarily (but not solely) to those aged fourteen and under seventeen, but first I provide a brief description of what happens to children under the age of fourteen.

Section 14 of the 1989 act defines the range of situations in which a child or young person is in need of care and protection and includes the child who has committed an offense or offenses "the number, nature and magnitude of which is such as to give serious concern for the well-being of the child" (sec. 14[e]). The type of interventions such children can experience are similar to those that young persons who offend might experience—for example, a police warning, police diversion, or referral to a family group conference. And so what I say later about each of these applies to children who offend as well as to young persons who offend. However, the focus of this intervention tends to be different: where children are involved, the focus is intended to be the child's welfare rather than the child's accountability. As a last resort and if lesser forms of intervention fail, an application can be made to the family court for a declaration that such a child is in need of care and protection. This has the effect of placing the child in the state's care.

From the age of seventeen, young people who commit offenses are dealt with in the same manner as adults, that is, in the district court or, if the offense is serious, in the high court. The youth court can transfer other cases involving serious offenses (e.g., arson and aggravated robbery) to the high court. There is also provision for the youth court to transfer offenders to the district court, depending on the seri-

---

[38] As a result, those aged ten to fourteen who commit offenses cannot be prosecuted in the adult criminal courts or in the youth court, except when they commit murder or manslaughter, in which case, they can be prosecuted and, like young persons who commit such offenses, will be dealt with in the adult criminal courts (the high court or the district court).

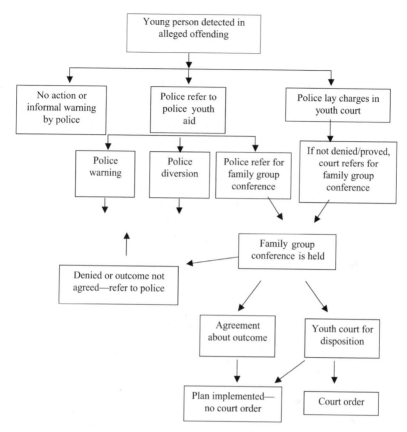

Fig. 1.—Pathways through the New Zealand youth justice system

ousness of the offense and the previous offending history of the young person. However, the vast majority of offending by young persons—including such serious offenses as rape, robbery, and assault—are dealt with under the procedures described briefly in the following paragraphs and summarized in figure 1. I then describe more fully three key points—police responses to young offenders, family group conferences, and the youth court.

A. Police Responses to Young Offenders

For most young people in New Zealand, the police are their first point of contact with the youth justice system. Frontline police determine whether to deal with the young person informally, by warning, by arrest, or by referral to police youth aid (as noted previously, a

TABLE 1

Main Outcomes of Police Decisions by Age: Percentages

Outcomes	Under 10	10–14	14–17	All under 17
Warning	58	57	35	43
Diversion	37	37	29	32
Family group conference	3	3	10	8
Youth court	0	0	25	17

SOURCE.—Maxwell, Robertson, and Anderson 2002.

branch of the police who specialize in working with children and young people) who will in turn decide whether to warn, to divert (this involves some action in addition to a warning and will be explained below), or to refer the young person to a family group conference.[39] The police, therefore, stand as gatekeepers to the youth justice system and, for most young offenders, the police are their only point of contact with the New Zealand youth justice system.

Table 1, based on a recent survey of a number of New Zealand police districts by Maxwell, Robertson, and Anderson (2002), shows how the police dealt with almost 1,800 children and young persons with whom they came into contact in 2000–2001. Overall, three-quarters of the young offenders in this sample were dealt with solely by the police, and only a small proportion were referred directly for a family group conference. However, it is also clear from table 1 that those aged fourteen and under seventeen are much more likely than younger age groups to be dealt with by referral for a family group conference and, of course, only this age group can be dealt with in the youth court.

Closer examination of the data pointed to fairly extreme variations in the different police districts: figures for the various police districts in the sample ranged from 69 percent to 23 percent for young people being warned, from 53 percent to 12 percent for young people being diverted, from 22 percent to 1 percent for young people being referred to family group conferences directly by the police, and from 24 percent to 4 percent for young people being arrested and charged in the youth court.

[39] A child or young person may be arrested in New Zealand only in certain statutorily defined situations: to ensure their appearance at the youth court, to prevent the commission of other offenses, to prevent the loss or destruction of evidence or interference with witnesses, when it is required in the public interest, and when the offense is "purely indictable."

There are no legislative criteria for police decision making, and they have wide discretion. Maxwell, Robertson, and Anderson (2002) conducted three stepwise regression analyses in an attempt to explain these variations in police districts. First, the seriousness of the offense committed by the young person, previous offending, committing more than one offense, and being older primarily determined the choice among these four main outcomes—warning, diversion, referral to family group conferences, and being charged in the youth court. Second, the young person's age and the police district involved primarily determined whether the young person was charged in the youth court or was referred to a family group conference. Third, whether a young person was diverted or warned was primarily determined by the seriousness of the alleged offense, the young person committing more than one offense, and the police district involved in the decision. Overall, Maxwell, Robertson, and Anderson (2002) concluded that the age of the offender was the most important factor, followed by differences in police practices across districts.

With respect to diversion, almost two-thirds of the young people in Maxwell, Robertson, and Anderson's (2002) sample made apologies to victims (usually in writing but sometimes in person), a third agreed to do community work, and just over a fifth made reparation. Thus, in large measure, diversion can be seen as reflecting restorative values, too, by attempting to make amends to victims where possible. In addition, almost a fifth of the young people in this sample attended some kind of program (this can be seen as reflecting welfare or rehabilitative values), and more than a tenth were made subject to a curfew or some other restriction (this can be seen as reflecting crime-control values).

Maxwell, Robertson, and Anderson (2002) found that there was considerable variation across the police districts: for example, apologies were made by less than a fifth of offenders diverted in one police district compared with 93 percent in another; reparation was made by almost half of the offenders diverted in one police district compared with just 7 percent in another; and curfews and other restrictions were not used at all in some police districts but were used for two-fifths of the offenders diverted in another.

Maxwell, Robertson, and Anderson (2002) conducted a regression analysis to distinguish between decisions by the police about what they called "accountability" measures (work in the community of a general nature, curfews, restrictions, and donations to charity) and "restorative" or "rehabilitative" measures (apologies, reparation, work of an offense-related nature, and attendance at a program). They concluded that variables associated with the police districts "were definitely of greater importance" than variables associated with offenders "in the extent of use of relatively punitive responses" (2002, p. 72).

B. Family Group Conferences

As figure 1 demonstrates, the family group conference operates at two distinct and key points: as an alternative to courts (for young people who have not been arrested), and as a mechanism for making recommendations to judges before sentencing (for young people who have been arrested). This means that the police cannot refer young offenders who have not been arrested to the youth court without first having a family group conference; most of these conferences end in an agreement that does not involve a court appearance. It also means that judges cannot sentence young offenders who have been arrested without first referring them to a family group conference and taking into account its recommendations. This key positioning of family group conferences is consistent with the restorative justice value of empowering young people, families, and victims by giving them a role in the decisions about how best to respond to offending and thereby reducing the powers of professionals who must take these parties' views into account.

A family group conference involves the young person, members of his or her family, *whanau* (family group), and whoever they invite (e.g., friends, teachers, youth club organizers, and the like), the victim or victims or their representative, victims' support persons, the police, the young person's lawyer (usually only in court referred cases), and, sometimes, a social worker. They are facilitated by the youth justice coordinator.

Coordinators are mainly social workers by training and are located within and supervised by managers from the Department of Child, Youth and Family Services.[40] Coordinators are key individuals in this process in that they are, in a sense, the guardians of the objects and principles of the act. Their duties are set out in the act (sec. 426) and include meeting with the police to explore alternatives to the instigation of criminal proceedings, preparing the parties for the family group conference, convening the conference, recording any decisions made, notifying appropriate people of the outcome of the conference, and,

---

[40] This service also deals with care and protection issues, and most of its resources have been devoted to these.

on occasion, monitoring compliance with the conference's decisions (though, more commonly, social workers or family members are meant to do this). Coordinators are also charged with keeping to the time frames set out in the 1989 act.[41]

The family group conference takes place wherever the family wishes, provided the victims agree. This means that conferences can take place in the family's home or at a *marae* (meeting house)—though both of these are, in practice, not common venues. More usual are community rooms or rooms in buildings managed by the Department of Child, Youth and Family Services. Meetings take much longer than the few minutes that judges routinely take to deal with young offenders in conventional criminal justice processes.

The family group conference considers only cases in which the young person admits the alleged offense or has already been found guilty in court, and all the participants in family group conferences contribute to the discussions and to decisions about the eventual outcome. One feature—relatively distinctive to New Zealand—is that the family and the young person are meant to be given the opportunity to discuss privately at some point how they think the offending should be dealt with. When the conference reconvenes with all the participants present, this plan is then discussed, and everyone's agreement is sought, or amendments are made.

The intended focus of the discussion and the resulting outcomes are the young person's offending and any matters related directly to the circumstances of that offending. However, as noted earlier, section 208(g) of the 1989 act states that, in determining outcomes, due regard should be paid to the interests of the victim. This invites consideration at the conference of apologies, reparation, and community work. Other outcomes (or recommendations) can include donations to a charity, involvement in a training program, supervision by a social worker or community organization, a residential placement (for a short time),[42] and, occasionally, a period in custody.[43] Outcomes are limited

---

[41] In police-referred cases, the family group conference needs to be convened within twenty-one days, and, in court-referred cases, the family group conference needs to be convened within fourteen days.

[42] Supervision in a residence requires a court order. Such orders allow young people to be placed in a residence for up to three months (reduced to two months if they do not abscond or commit further offenses), and the period in the residences is followed by a period of supervision of up to six months.

[43] Periods in custody (corrective training or imprisonment) also require a court order, but they also require the young person to be transferred from the youth court to the district or high court. Certain conditions must be met before such a transfer can occur.

only by the imagination of the parties, though parsimony (rather than proportionality) is intended to be a limiting factor.[44]

The plans and decisions reached at the family group conference are binding if all those present at the conference agree to them (and, where relevant, once they are accepted by the youth court judge). Each party to the conference, at least in theory, has a veto and can register their disagreement. If participants cannot reach an agreed outcome or recommendation, the police in police-referred (nonarrest) conferences then have to decide whether or not and how to proceed, and the judge in court-referred (arrest) conferences has to make the decision about the appropriate sentence. With respect to police-referred conferences, the conference can be reconvened at the request of any of the parties (e.g., if the young offender does not comply with the agreement), and a date can be included in the agreement for a review of the plan. With respect to court-referred conferences, judges sometimes adjourn cases for the completion of the plans before sentencing and, in all cases other than those withdrawn or discharged, are provided with a report on the young offender at the completion of the conference plan or court order.

Maxwell et al. (2003) report on recommendations made at family group conferences with respect to two samples of young offenders. The "retrospective" sample was approximately 1,000 young offenders who were referred to family group conferences in certain areas in 1998 and who were age sixteen at that time; the "prospective" sample was around 100 young offenders who were referred to family group conferences in some of the same areas in 2001 or 2002.

Table 2 presents these data. For both samples, an apology was the most common recommendation. Some kind of community work was the next most commonly agreed recommendation, followed by reparation for the retrospective sample, and some kind of program for the prospective sample. Restrictions such as curfews were relatively common for both samples. Overall, relatively few recommendations were made for young offenders in the retrospective sample to have some kind of court order, and there were no such recommendations in the prospective sample. Conference recommendations (and plans), therefore, frequently reflected restorative values but also at times reflected rehabilitative, reintegrative, and crime-control values.

---

[44] Section 208(f)(ii) states that any sanction should take the least restrictive form that is appropriate in the circumstances.

TABLE 2

Recommendations of Family Group
Conferences for Retrospective and
Prospective Samples: Percentages

Recommendations	Retrospective	Prospective
Apologies	76	83
Community work	67	63
Reparation/donation	53	45
Restrictions	38	42
Programs	24	47
Court orders	14	0

Source.—Maxwell et al. 2003.

C. The Youth Court

Only a minority of young offenders in New Zealand (those arrested and charged) experience a court process. The youth court, which replaced the Children and Young Persons Court in 1989, is a branch of the district court and deals only with young offenders. Its procedures and practices are modified somewhat, but generally speaking it is run in much the same way as the adult criminal court except that it is closed to the public. All young people appearing in the youth court are represented by a lawyer (youth advocate), and, as noted above, judges cannot sentence young offenders without referring them first to a family group conference. In accordance with the philosophical underpinnings of the 1989 act, judges are expected to endorse the recommendations of the family group conference wherever possible. They are also expected to try to involve young people and their parents in the court processes and decisions, and to avoid the use of court orders unless absolutely necessary (McElrea 1993). Their role, therefore, is very different from that of judges in conventional adult and youth courts.

Where cases are referred to the youth court, the possible outcomes are as follows in order of severity: transfer to the district court; supervision with residence;[45] supervision with activity; community work; supervision; fine, reparation, or restitution; forfeiture; to come up if called upon within twelve months (a type of conditional discharge); admonition; discharge from proceedings; and police withdrawal of the

[45] Supervision with residence orders, as the name implies, involves residence in an institution, but these cases are managed by the Department of Child, Youth and Family Services and not by the Department of Corrections.

charge. In addition, it is possible to order the disqualification of a driver involved in a traffic offense.

Maxwell et al. (2003) state that, in 2001, less than two-fifths of cases dealt with in the youth court resulted in court orders; the remainder were withdrawn or discharged after the completion of the plans agreed to at the family group conference. National data are not available on the specific nature of the orders made in the youth court, but data on Maxwell et al.'s (2003) retrospective sample indicated that 10 percent were made the subject of a supervision order, 4 percent were made the subject of a supervision with activity order, and 3 percent were made the subject of a supervision with residence order.

Transfer to the district court can take place at two different stages of the process. First, it can occur when the young offender first appears in the youth court if he or she is at least fifteen years of age and the offense is either purely indictable (the most serious offenses) or is punishable by imprisonment for a term exceeding three months and the young person elects trial by jury under section 66 of the Summary Proceedings Act. Second, it can occur at sentencing when the nature or circumstances of the offense are such that, if the young person were an adult, he or she would be sentenced to custody, and the court is satisfied that any order of a noncustodial nature would be inadequate. Data from the retrospective sample indicated that only 7 percent of these young people were transferred to the district or high court, and only 5 percent received a custodial sentence.

V. Achieving the Objects and Principles of the Children, Young Persons and Their Families Act 1989

This section examines six key aims: diversion from courts, residences, and custody; participants' involvement in and satisfaction with family group conferences; the protection of young offenders' rights; holding offenders accountable for their offending; enhancing offenders' well-being; and the cultural appropriateness of family group conferences. Implicit in much of this discussion is an assessment of the extent to which family group conferences reflect restorative justice values. In addition, I examine data on the extent to which family group conferences reduce reoffending, although this was not an explicit object of the 1989 act. At most, it is implicit if—and arguably only if—all the other objects and principles in the act are achieved. And, finally in this section, I examine data on the extent to which youth justice in New Zealand meets key articles of the United Nations Convention on the Rights of the Child.

Maxwell and Morris (1993) carried out the first evaluative research on the New Zealand youth justice system, but, given that their field-work was carried out more than ten years ago, care needs to be taken in assuming that their findings remain valid. Maxwell et al. (2003) carried out a more recent evaluation (drawing data from 1998 and from 2001–2), and this offers both some more recent information and the opportunity to assess practice over this period. Changes made since the implementation of the 1989 act are also noted.

A. Diversion from Courts and Custody/Residences

I have already described the significant role currently played by the police in New Zealand in diverting young people from courts; table 1 showed that three-quarters of young offenders were dealt with by the police in 2000–2001. I now turn to describe the impact that this has had on the number of young offenders appearing in the youth court.

In the three calendar years prior to the introduction of the Children, Young Persons and Their Families Act 1989, the average rate of youth court appearance for young people aged fourteen and under seventeen was 630 per 10,000. However, the passing of the 1989 act resulted in an immediate drop, to 160 per 10,000 young people in this age group in 1990 (Department of Statistics 1991). By 1998, the rate of youth court appearances had gradually risen again to 230 per 10,000, and the rate for 2000–2001 is 240 per 10,000.[46] This is still substantially lower than in the years prior to the 1989 act. Figure 2 (adapted from Maxwell et al. 2003) shows the changing rates of youth court appearances from before the introduction of the Children, Young Persons and Their Families Act up to 2001.

Not only has there been marked decline in the number of young people appearing in the youth court, but there has also been a decline in the use of custody in institutions managed by the department of corrections. In 1987, 295 young people received a custodial sentence in the adult courts. This dropped to 104 in 1990. Since then, it rose to a high of 143 in 1997 but has since decreased again so that, by 2001, only 73 young people had received a custodial sentence in the adult courts. These data are shown graphically in figure 3.

---

[46] These figures have been derived from data supplied by the Ministry of Justice and Statistics New Zealand and are cited in Maxwell et al. (2003).

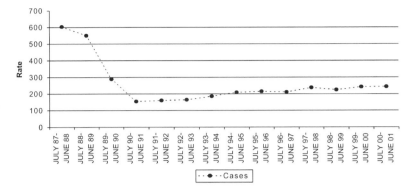

Fig. 2.—Rates per 10,000 aged between fourteen and seventeen years of distinct cases in the youth court for the June/July years 1987 to 2001. Source: Adapted from Maxwell et al. 2003.

This overall downward trend in the use of custody could reflect the decline in the number of young people appearing in the youth court, but it seems rather to reflect a decline in the number of young offenders convicted and transferred to the district or high courts for sentencing as an adult and an increase in the number of young offenders dealt

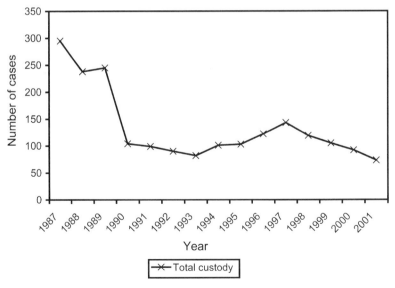

Fig. 3.—Custodial sentences for cases transferred from the youth court from 1987 to 2001. Source: Adapted from Maxwell et al. 2003.

with within the community. Convictions and transfers to the district or high courts decreased from nearly 1,500 per year prior to the 1989 act to less than 200 per year since then.

It appears, therefore, that the 1989 act has been remarkably successful at reducing the number of young people appearing in courts and being sentenced to custody. However, there are grounds for concern. The government's 1999 budget envisioned establishment of seven youth units in prisons to get young men (under age twenty) out of adult prisons and that, over the next three years, almost $18 million (New Zealand) would be spent on building the first four units. By January 2003, four specialist youth units, managed by the department of corrections, were open with accommodation for 143 offenders.

Those under the age of seventeen sentenced to imprisonment are now sent to these units rather than to adult prisons, and it is estimated that around twenty-five to thirty sixteen-year-old boys and a few fifteen-year-old boys will be held in them. Eventually there are to be 220 places in youth units, although, as I note later, it is expected that most of these places will be taken by those aged seventeen to nineteen. However, it is at least possible that more boys under the age of seventeen will be sentenced to imprisonment as a result of the existence of these units.

Data from Maxwell et al.'s (2003) retrospective sample showed that less than a third of those given some kind of supervision order had supervision with residence orders, or, put another way, only twenty-one of the 696 young offenders in this youth court sample received orders of supervision with residence. Maxwell et al. (2003) also cite data for 2000 that indicate that there were 115 supervision with residence orders that year. This translates into less than 4 percent of the young offenders appearing in the youth court. In October 2001, seventy-five young offenders were in social welfare residences.

This means that the number of young offenders in residences has declined markedly since 1989. We can attribute this decline in part to the 1989 act.[47] However, again, there are grounds for concern, as the

[47] In fact, the decline in the number of children placed in residences began before 1989. Dalley (1998a, p. 314) refers to the closure of five institutions in 1977 and writes that, by late 1989, there were only nine residences with places for 300 compared with twenty-six residences with places for 900 in 1979. She also reports (1998a, pp. 314–15) that, during 1989, the average number of admissions to institutions dropped from 202 per month to seventy-five; that, in 1990, five more residences were closed so that only four, with 83 places, remained; and that twelve of these were for care and protection cases, and only thirty-nine were for secure care. Dalley further reports (1998a, p. 316)

number of places available in residences is set to increase. The residential services strategy is intended to increase the number of beds in residences to 166 by 2002–3. Separate residences are being built for children in the care and protection and youth justice systems, and there are currently four youth justice residential centers (although, importantly, most of the young people currently being held in these centers are on remand rather than under sentence). The availability of specialist treatment places for young offenders has also increased. For example, a new residential unit for boys who have committed sex offenses (*Te Poutama Arahi Rangatahi*) was opened in 1999 and can take up to twelve boys.[48]

Overall, it appears that the gains made immediately after the implementation of the 1989 act in terms of reducing the number of young offenders appearing in courts and being sentenced to custody or placed in residences have been maintained. However, the number appearing in courts has increased again steadily from 1990–91 to 2000–2001 by more than 60 percent, and the availability of custodial and residential places for young offenders has increased, too.

B. Involving Participants

Decision making in conventional justice systems is hierarchical in that the decisions are imposed, and they are imposed by "others": they are not made by offenders, victims, and their families, and they do not have to be agreed to by them. In contrast, it is clear from what has already been said that all the participants in family group conferences can contribute to the discussions and to the eventual outcome.

1. *Young Offenders.*   Young offenders are expected to participate actively in discussions about how best to deal with their offending, and they in turn can expect their views to be taken into account in this decision. Maxwell and Morris (1993) found that most young people felt involved in the decision-making process at least partially and that most were satisfied with the outcomes reached. However, at that time, Maxwell and Morris (1993) also found that some young people remained uninvolved. They speculated that this was likely to be due to families' and professionals' unwillingness or inability to hear and value

---

that the number admitted to residences declined from 1,295 in 1989–90 to 655 in 1992–93.

[48] This unit is in Christchurch in the South Island but takes boys from all over New Zealand.

young people's views, especially when these young people were offenders.

More recent data (Maxwell at al. 2003), based on interviews with 520
young offenders who were involved in family group conferences in
1998 (the retrospective sample) and with just over 100 young offenders
who were involved in family group conferences in 2001–2 (the prospective sample), show that around half of both groups said they felt
involved in making decisions at the family group conference. Also,
two-thirds of the retrospective sample and three-quarters of the prospective sample said they had the opportunity to say what they wanted
to at the conference. Almost all the young offenders in both samples
said that they understood the decision, and the majority (61 percent of
the retrospective sample and 73 percent of the prospective sample) said
that they agreed with it. The following two quotes provide some sense
of the positive nature of most young offenders' experiences of family
group conferences: "It was good having my parents there and having
support from them," and "It was good—just saying my side and saying
sorry and being able to have a say in the plan" (Maxwell et al. 2003).

However, it is also clear that a significant proportion of young offenders felt differently: over two-fifths of the retrospective sample and
more than a quarter of the prospective sample did not feel involved in
making decisions at the conference; a quarter of the retrospective sample (but less than a tenth of the prospective sample) said that they did
not have the opportunity to say what they wanted to at the conference.
Just over two-fifths of the retrospective sample and almost a third of
the prospective sample said that they felt too intimidated to say what
they wanted to at the conference. More than a quarter of the retrospective sample and 15 percent of the prospective sample did not agree
with the decisions reached. Although these figures have to give some
cause for concern in terms of whether family group conferences are
fully meeting their objects and principles and whether they are realizing their restorative potential, they should perhaps not be read too pes-
simistically. The overall picture is more positive than that which
emerges in comparisons with how young offenders feel about their
involvement and treatment in conventional courts or similar decision-
making forums. Even in New Zealand, where efforts have been made
to transform the youth court by encouraging offenders' participation
and by simplifying language, only a third felt involved in the decisions
there, and only a half felt able to say what they wanted to the judge
(Maxwell et al. 2003).

2. *Families.*   Most families who participated in Maxwell and Morris's (1993) research felt that they had been involved in the decision-making process; only a fifth said that they had not felt involved. Almost half the parents said that they had decided how the offending should be dealt with and nearly two-thirds felt the family had been involved in the decision, at least in part; only a fifth identified the professionals alone as the decision makers. There was also little doubt that those families who had experienced both conferences and courts preferred family group conferences. Their comments highlighted the participatory nature of the family group conference and the greater degree of support available to them in contrast to the stress that often accompanied a court appearance. As well as feeling more comfortable at the family group conference, families also understood more of what had happened and believed that it provided a more realistic forum for decision making. However, Maxwell and Morris (1993) found that some families were not well prepared for what was expected of them, and that families were not always provided with the information they needed to come up with good outcomes. In a few cases, professionals (particularly the police) took over the process and, in the families' view, dictated outcomes.

The families of the prospective sample were asked for their views on family group conferences, and these again were mainly positive: almost all understood what was happening at the conference, 88 percent felt treated with respect, 85 percent agreed with the decisions made, and 80 percent said that they were able to express their views and felt involved in the decisions made. In the words of one family member: "It was a very open sharing. It dealt with the anger and hurt experienced by the victim but in a non-threatening manner and we [the young person and the family] were able to respond by apologising to her and her family" (Maxwell et al. 2003).

However, one in ten families did not feel able to express their views at the conference, and one in ten did not feel involved in the decisions made. Indeed, 70 percent said they felt that they were treated like a "bad person." It is difficult to know just how to treat these more negative findings as, although indicative of some failures in practice and failure to reach restorative ideals, they may nevertheless be "better" than the findings that would emerge if families involved in conventional courts or similar decision-making forums were asked similar questions. Certainly, Maxwell and Morris's (1993) early research supports this claim. Maxwell et al. (2003) do not present more recent New Zealand data on families' views of courts.

3. *Victims.* Maxwell and Morris (1993) commented that victims were present in less than half of the family group conferences they observed in 1990–91 and that the principal reason for this was poor practice: the victims had been invited late in the process, or the time for which the conference had been set was inconvenient for them. Maxwell et al.'s (2003) analysis of just over 750 family group conferences held in 1998 in which a victim could have attended shows that a victim was present in just over two-fifths of the conferences, and that, if victims' representatives are added to this figure, just under half of the conferences had some "victim" presence: hardly any change from the situation described by Maxwell and Morris (1993) in 1990–91. For the hundred or so family group conferences Maxwell et al. (2003) observed in 2001–2, victims were present for half, and, if victims' representatives are added to this figure, just over half of the conferences had some "victim" presence—again, hardly any difference from the situations just described for 1990–91 or for 1998.

Maxwell and Morris (1993), on the basis of their early research, suggested that ensuring victims' attendance at family group conferences had not been given enough of a priority and that, as was noted above, practice was poor in this respect.

Maxwell et al. (2003) asked the forty-two victims who had not attended the family group conferences that they observed in 2001–2 why they had not attended. By far the most common reason (given by 45 percent) was that they did not want to meet the young offender or his or her family. The next most common (given by almost a third) was that they would have liked to attend but were unable to. Both of these reasons could still be linked to poor practice—for example, victims may not want to meet the offender if the process or potential benefits to them are not adequately explained, or if they do not feel well enough prepared for such a meeting. However, victims' unwillingness to meet offenders also may strike more fundamentally at the ability of family group conferences to fully meet restorative justice aspirations and ideals. The objects and principles of the Children, Young Persons and Their Families Act 1989, however, may still be met, since it requires only that the victim's interests are given "due regard."

The major reasons given by the fifty-eight victims who did attend the family group conferences observed by Maxwell et al. (2003) were to tell the young offender how they felt (this was said by more than half) and to express their views on what should happen (this was said by more than two-fifths). Almost a third wanted to find out more about the young offender, and more than a fifth wanted to obtain reparation.

All of these motivations reflect what we know about victims' interests (or what victims want out of meetings with offenders) and are embedded in restorative values. Indeed, most of the victims who attended said they were able to express their views at the conference and were given a chance to explain the impact of the offending on them. As one victim put it: "I do think conferences are a good thing. They allow people to get things off their chest. A victim like myself finds out more and it gives you a better understanding to see the offending face to face. I saw the young person showing respect, listening and contributing" (Maxwell et al. 2003).

Maxwell and Morris's (1993) early research found that 60 percent of victims who participated in conferences thought them helpful and felt better as a result of their involvement. However, around a quarter of victims felt worse as a result of attending, and only around a half were satisfied with the outcomes reached. Maxwell and Morris (1993) again speculated that most of the reasons for this were poor practice: at that time, victims were not able to have support people with them, and they could feel quite isolated and vulnerable when confronted with the offender and his or her family and family support; they also speculated that much of the dissatisfaction about agreements stemmed from the lack of knowledge about the completion of the agreed outcome rather than objections to the agreement itself.

There seem to have been some significant changes here. Eighty-one percent of the victims who attended the family group conferences observed by Maxwell et al. (2003) said that they felt better as a result of attending, and only 5 percent said that they felt worse. Indeed, 90 percent said that they felt treated with respect, and almost three-quarters said that their needs had been met at the conference. Also, most victims who attended the family group conference agreed with the decision, and more than two-thirds said that it had helped put matters behind them. In addition, more than two-thirds of the victims who had not attended had been told about the outcome reached, and more than half felt that the outcome was "about right."

However, Maxwell et al. (2003) also noted some more negative findings: for example, victims who attended the family group conference did not always feel involved in making the decision—only about half of them reported this.[49] Also, more than two-fifths of the victims

[49] This finding is perhaps explained by the fact that families are allowed and encouraged to deliberate privately about possible outcomes to try to ensure that they take own-

who had not attended the family group conference thought that the decision reached was "too soft." Overall, however, the findings on victims' experiences of family group conferences are reasonably favorable, particularly when contrasted with their almost total lack of involvement in conventional courts (other than as witnesses) or similar decision-making forums.

C. Protection of Young Offenders' Rights

The major area of controversy with respect to the protection of young offenders' rights in New Zealand has centered around their interactions with police officers. Young offenders who appear in the youth court are represented by court-appointed youth advocates.[50] These lawyers are specially selected for their personality, cultural background, training, and experience as being suitably qualified to represent young people (sec. 323 of the Children, Young Persons and Their Families Act 1989). They provide the young person with legal advice generally, represent him or her in court, and can attend the young person's family group conference. A survey by Morris, Maxwell, and Shepherd (1997) found that not all youth advocates felt it appropriate to attend their client's family group conference, and a few of those who did attend seemed to act in a way that was at odds with the principles of the act (e.g., they spoke for the young persons rather than allowing or encouraging them to speak for themselves).

The Children, Young Persons and Their Families Act 1989 sets down the rights of children and young persons who are arrested or stopped and questioned by the police. Specifically, and most controversially, section 215 of the act gave young people being questioned by the police certain rights—for example, the right to have a lawyer present and to withdraw their consent to making a statement. The New Zealand Police Association claimed that the requirements were cumbersome, made it more difficult for police officers to question young people, and took up time that was better spent in other police duties. They pressed early on for some amendment to the act. And so, as early as 1991, it was decided that the act needed to be reviewed. A review

---

ership of them. There is a tension here between empowering the family and the young offender and empowering victims.

[50] Young people who attend police-referred family group conferences are not generally entitled to free legal representation, although families may invite (and pay for) a lawyer to attend, and in exceptional (and undefined) circumstances, youth justice coordinators may be able to fund the attendance of a lawyer in police-referred conferences through the Department of Child, Youth and Family Services.

team chaired by a retired judge, Judge Mason (hence its colloquial name, the Mason Report), was appointed. It reported in 1992 (Ministerial Review Team to the Minister of Social Welfare 1992).[51]

The majority of the submissions made to the ministerial review team were against making any changes in the law. However, the police wanted it changed, and there had recently been a case in which a young person charged with murder had been discharged because the statement he had made was not in compliance with section 215. There was considerable media (and consequently public) concern about this. The ministerial review team accordingly recommended changes that allowed the police to make general inquiries before explaining the rights set out in section 215, and the Children, Young Persons and Their Families Act 1989 was amended accordingly in 1994.

It is said by the police that this change was in line with the original intention of the section but, if so, it means that this amended section is out of line with the New Zealand Bill of Rights Act of 1990 and the United Nations Convention on the Rights of the Child (which at that time New Zealand had signed but not ratified). It also did not adequately recognize the vulnerability of children and young people in their interactions with the police. This vulnerability to abuse was apparent in Maxwell and Morris's (1993) early research. They found breaches in the procedural safeguards and misunderstandings by police about what was expected of them with the result that young people who were arrested were not always informed fully of their rights before being questioned, and that questioning sometimes started before the adult of the young person's choice was present, and sometimes when no adult was present at all. Thus, the police were breaching the act but were effectively "rewarded" by changes in the legislation to meet some of their demands.

Despite this legislative change, frontline police continue to view the 1989 act quite negatively. Potaka's (1997) small-scale survey of forty frontline police officers in Wellington showed that they responded to questions about the 1989 act negatively more often than positively. Most felt unable to deal with offenders under the act. Almost three-quarters felt the grounds for arresting young people were insufficient. Almost half felt unhappy about informing young people of their rights in all situations. More than half felt it time consuming to contact parents or adults.

---

[51] Although it commented critically on the management of some family group conferences, it declined to suggest any amendments to this part of the act.

These negative attitudes among police officers may have wider implications for policing young people. Research in Australia and the United Kingdom has shown that young people are frequently stopped on the street by the police, that they are often unaware of their rights when this happens, and that, even when they are aware of their rights, they are often reluctant to enforce them because of power differentials between them and the police (see, e.g., Alder et al. 1992; Anderson et al. 1994). Claims by Maori who participated in research by Te Whaiti and Roguski (1998) on Maori perceptions of the police point to a similar situation in New Zealand. Te Whaiti and Roguski wrote that all the participants in their *hui* believed that the police harassed young Maori under the pretext of "criminal suspicion," that young Maori were stopped and questioned on the street "for no apparent reason," and that young Maori were "targeted in a specific way." In the words of one participant: "My experiences are to do with harassment and young people being searched and badly handled, and handled in a racist way. But I'm not talking about once or twice, I'm talking about every time they went out the gate. . . . So there were a couple of years there where all the young people coming in and out of that gate were being searched" (cited in Te Whaiti and Roguski 1998, p. 30).

This perceived harassment and overpolicing were seen as having detrimental effects on relationships between Maori young people and the police. The vulnerability of young people generally to police actions was recognized in the 1989 act in its original form but was diluted by subsequent amendment. This seems likely to exacerbate any tensions between the police and young people and, in particular, between Maori and the police.[52]

D. Holding Offenders Accountable

Involving young offenders in a family group conference in a direct way is a potentially effective mechanism for holding them accountable for their offending and for encouraging them to accept responsibility for their behavior. Young people in family group conferences (unlike in conventional criminal justice processes) are expected to speak and to participate in discussions, and to some extent, as noted earlier, this happens. That most young people agree to apologize and carry out

[52] The research on police attitudes to Maori by Maxwell and Smith (1998) produced evidence that about a fifth of police officers in New Zealand responded differently (negatively) toward certain ethnic groups. This, too, does not bode well for interactions between the police and young Maori.

some reparative, rehabilitative, or restrictive sanction is also indicative of their acceptance of responsibility for the offending.

However, in 1998, the then principal youth court judge (Young 1999, p. 238) complained that "too often there is no monitoring of sentences with the result that judges and the community have no idea whether or not sentences are completed." Maxwell and Morris (1993) had noted earlier that one of the main reasons for attending victims' dissatisfaction with the process was that they did not know whether the agreement reached at the conference had actually been carried out. If these concerns remain relevant, it means that some young offenders are avoiding accountability.

Maxwell et al. (2003) examined around 860 cases in files of the Department of Child, Youth and Family Services where some information on the plans made at family group conferences in 1998 was available. In a quarter of these cases, there was no specific mention of who was to monitor the plan. Monitoring arrangements were fully described in only a third of cases. They also attempted to assess whether or not the agreements or plans made at family group conferences were actually carried out. However, examination of a subsample of 252 of their 1998 sample of conference cases showed that these data were missing or recorded as not applicable for a third. On the other hand, for most of the 170 cases where data were available, the plans were recorded as having been completed either fully or mainly.

More complete information comes from the 520 young offenders in the retrospective sample who were interviewed by Maxwell et al. (2003). Around two-thirds of these said that they had completed at least part of the plan agreed to at the family group conference. Thus, the failure to monitor the plans agreed to at family group conferences (or at least the failure to record whether or not they were monitored and by whom) and the failure of young offenders to complete all elements of the plans remains a matter of concern. The remedy is, however, relatively simple. A good family group conference should identify who is to monitor the completion of the different elements of the conference's outcome and should also set a review date to check whether the agreements have been completed. Where there is a failure to complete the agreement, the conference should then be reconvened.

E. Enhancing Offenders' Well-Being

Early comments on the extent to which the outcomes of family group conferences were able to enhance offenders' well-being were quite critical (Maxwell and Morris 1993, p. 179). In practice at that time, not many young people were provided with services or programs as a result of a family group conference. This was not the result of poor decision making by conferences but, rather, a reflection of the fact that New Zealand had few specialist services or programs for young people, especially for those who have been involved in repeat or serious offenses. There was also criticism (Young 1999, p. 238) that outcomes from conferences were often "nothing more than apologies and purposeless community work."

There are now more programs available than ten years ago for young offenders and for those at risk of offending. For example, the family start program provides intensive support and early intervention services for "at risk" families at birth, wraparound programs provide tailored and individualized services and support for older "at risk" children, and the social workers in schools program provides early intervention to children in primary schools.[53]

In late 1998, the government made funding available to the Department of Child, Youth and Family Services to develop a strategy (the youth services strategy) aimed at providing better ways of recognizing and meeting the needs of young people who continue to offend and who are viewed as being at high risk of developing criminal lifestyles.[54] More recently, in 2002, the government published the youth offending strategy aimed at preventing and reducing offending and reoffending by children and young people (Ministry of Justice and Ministry of Social Development 2002).[55] It made four key recommendations, three of

[53] Not all of these initiatives have been evaluated, but Shepherd and Maxwell (1999) evaluated three demonstration projects that were intended to identify children at risk and to seek to improve their behavior, including their offending. They showed that the children's behavior at school improved, and that their involvement in offending declined.

[54] Three screening tools are now meant to be used by social workers to achieve this. These are: CAGE (Cut down, Annoyed, Guilty, and Early morning consumption), a short screen for alcohol and drug use that focuses on the negative effects of usage; the six-item Kessler screening tool, which is aimed at identifying psychological distress; and a suicide screen. The CAGE and Kessler screens were both developed overseas and not for this age group. However, the Department of Child, Youth and Family Services maintains that they are relevant tools. If the young person appears suicidal, the suicide risk assessment framework is applied. If any other risks are identified, referrals are made for specialist assessment and, once the young person's immediate needs are addressed, the well-being assessment tool is applied, and a well-being plan is formulated. Depending on the results of this assessment, the social worker may access specialist family homes, one-to-one care, or specialist rehabilitation programs. These screening and assessment tools are meant to inform discussions at family group conferences, and conferences' outcomes are meant to reflect the well-being plan.

[55] This strategy should be read alongside the report of the Ministerial Taskforce on Youth Offending (2002) and *The Youth Justice Plan for Child, Youth and Family Services* (Department of Child, Youth and Family Services 2002).

which are relevant here: a new delivery mechanism to achieve this goal of reducing offending and reoffending,[56] a range of measures to improve the delivery of youth justice services, and the development of new comprehensive and intensive interventions for serious young offenders (such as day reporting centers that will rely on "multisystemic therapy") (Ministry of Justice and Ministry of Social Development 2002, pp. 38–40).[57] This strategy also endorses the use of risk identification and assessment tools.

Overall, the range of programs available for young offenders has increased over the past ten years. However, there are no data, as yet, on the effectiveness of the youth services strategy in either meeting the needs of young offenders or reducing their reoffending. And any impact from the youth offending strategy will take some time to emerge.

F. Cultural Appropriateness of Family Group Conferences

One aim underlying the Children, Young Persons and Their Families Act 1989 was to encourage responses to young offenders to be more culturally appropriate and sensitive. However, Maxwell and Morris (1993, p. 186) suggested that family group conferences in the early 1990s "often failed to respond to the spirit of Maori or to enable outcomes to be reached which are in accordance with Maori philosophy and values." However, they went on to say that, at times, conferences did transcend tokenism and embodied Maori *kaupapa* (spirit and values) and that there was "at least, the *potential* for FGCs [conferences] to be more able to cope with cultural diversity than other types of tribunals" (1993, p. 187, emphasis in the original).

Since 1999, the government has been committed to strategies aimed at "closing the gap" between Maori and *Pakeha*. Though this phrase is no longer in vogue, the policy continues, and the aim is to address the socioeconomic inequalities that Maori experience. Part of this has involved devolution of services to Maori, and there are now more than twenty *iwi* (tribes) providing social services through contracts with the Child, Youth and Family Services department. There are also now a small number of Pacific Island social services providers to provide services for young people from Pacific nations.

---

[56] This will rely on local youth offending teams (comprised of key practitioners from the police, social services, health, and education), oversight by ministers and senior public servants, and an independent advisory council.

[57] The final recommendation related to measures to improve the quality and robustness of information about offending by children and young people in New Zealand.

Tauri (1998) has argued that rather than empower Maori, the 1989 act signified the "indigenisation" of New Zealand's youth justice system. He also argued that the state has disempowered Maori by employing their justice processes while denying them jurisdictional autonomy. He dismissed the consequences of the state's attempt to endorse biculturalism as no more than tokenism.[58] In a later paper, Tauri suggested that the family group conference "represents little more than an extension of the State's biculturalism . . . onto the arena of criminal justice, that has done little to adequately address criticisms made by some Maori of the justice system itself" (1999, p. 159).

He examined two key areas—the cultural appropriateness of conferences and the exclusion of Maori cultural expertise—to show that family group conferences had failed to empower Maori. It is true that *marae* are rarely used as conference venues. However, interviews with Maori young offenders and their families in both 1990–91 (Maxwell and Morris 1993) and in 2001–2 (Maxwell et al. 2003) seem to indicate that Maori young offenders and their families do not have a problem with the venue of conferences—even when the conference is held in a building managed by the Child, Youth and Family Services department. It is also true that in the early days of conferencing, social workers were too commonly present at conferences, but this has certainly changed. More important, what Tauri ignored was that many social workers (and coordinators) are themselves Maori.

Love (2000, p. 26) acknowledged that many Maori offenders, Maori victims, and their *whanau* have found family group conferences beneficial and preferable to the previous court-based system. She also, however, acknowledged a number of problems: insufficient resources have, at times, had the effect of placing even more responsibilities onto struggling Maori families; the overinvolvement of professionals in decision making can disempower Maori; *Pakeha* professionals lack understanding of cultural knowledge and cultural systems; and, most important, the "real" power remains with state representatives. Thus, Love (2000, p. 29) argues that

It may . . . serve only to provide a brown veneer for a white system that has historically contributed to state run programmes of cultural genocide and *whanau* dismemberment. It may also serve to

[58] This amounts, according to Tauri (1998), to no more than the presence of Maori advisors or Maori units within government departments, the adoption of Maori names and Maori motifs or letterhead, cultural sensitivity training, and the like.

undermine Maori systems and institutions and to co-opt Maori people and cultural forms as agents in our own oppression. . . . In some ways, family group conferences as practiced with Maori *whanau* represent an attempt to merge two systems of power relations, communications and world views. The result is sometimes productive, but at least as often it results in a clash of the two systems, and the misappropriation and misinterpretation of Maori cultures, systems and values . . . the result has often been a token acknowledgement of minority Maori culture, and the continued imposition of dominant Western perspectives.

Overall, therefore, Maori commentators are suspicious of the changes that have occurred and certainly do not see them as having transferred power to Maori. However, that was not really the 1989 act's intent; this would require much more government action.[59] At the same time, it does seem that the current youth justice system, and family group conferences in particular, offer more to Maori than past systems that were monocultural and reflected the values of a *Pakeha* criminal justice system.

G. *Reducing Reoffending*

Many young offenders who come into the youth justice system, in New Zealand as elsewhere, have disadvantaged and deprived backgrounds (see, e.g., Fergusson, Horwood, and Lynskey 1992; Maxwell and Robertson 1995), and section 4 of the 1989 act can be read as trying to address this by indicating a preference for reintegrative and rehabilitative strategies as part of an attempt to reduce reoffending.

Analysis of the convictions of almost 1,000 young offenders dealt with by family group conference in 1998 and who were sixteen-year-olds at that time (Maxwell et al.'s [2003] retrospective sample) showed that more than two-thirds of these young people were reconvicted and more than a fifth were sentenced to imprisonment within three years of entering the adult criminal justice system. These statistics do not make very encouraging reading. However, it is not possible to say whether these are "better" or "worse" than the situation before the introduction of the 1989 act as there are no comparable reconviction statistics. It is also not possible within New Zealand to match these young offenders with a sample of young offenders who are being dealt

---

[59] The issue of Maori sovereignty is the subject of ongoing debate but is unlikely to be conceded by the New Zealand government.

with in a different way. By definition, those dealt with solely by the police are less serious and less persistent offenders. Overseas comparisons would also not be particularly helpful because of difficulties of matching.

Instead, Maxwell et al. (2003) examined the correlates of reoffending and attempted to identify the variables that were most useful in predicting reoffending through a series of regression analyses. Though they found that negative factors in young offenders' background were important, they also found that family group conferences could make a contribution to preventing reoffending despite these negative background factors and irrespective of the nature of the offending.

In particular, Maxwell at al. (2003) stressed good preparation of young offenders before the family group conference and emphasized, at the family group conferences, the importance of young offenders feeling supported, understanding what is happening, participating in the decisions, and not feeling stigmatized or excluded. They conclude that conferences that generate feelings of remorse and enable young offenders to repair the harm they caused their victims, to feel forgiven, and to form the intention not to reoffend are likely to reduce the chances of further offending.

H. Meeting Key Provisions of the United Nations Convention on the Rights of the Child

Ratification of the United Nations Convention on the Rights of the Child in 1993 meant that New Zealand agreed to report on its implementation of the convention and to ensure that its legislation and practice are in accordance with it. New Zealand first reported to the United Nations on its compliance with the convention in 1995. The government, of course, claimed that to a large extent New Zealand does comply, though it entered three reservations. Only one concerns us here: the government reserved, at that time, the right to mix young people with adult prisoners where there was a shortage of suitable facilities, where it was in the interests of other young people in an institution to have the young person removed, and where it was in the young person's interests or to his or her benefit to be held with adults in prison.

The government's report was scrutinized within the United Nations and was later commented on by it. It identified a number of positive factors, and there is no doubt that New Zealand has been reasonably successful at meeting certain international standards.[60] For example, it has been effective at diverting young people from courts, custody, and residences. It has also been reasonably successful—or at least more successful than jurisdictions that continue to rely on conventional criminal justice processes—at involving young offenders in decisions and attempting to make processes more culturally responsive.

But the United Nations did list thirteen concerns. Of relevance here is the broad nature of the reservation entered about imprisoning young people with adults.[61] However, as noted earlier, there has been some shift in policy about this since then, and young men under the age of seventeen sentenced to imprisonment are now placed in the new youth units instead of in adult prisons. But so, too, are vulnerable male prisoners under the age of twenty, and it is estimated that the majority of the offenders in these units will be aged seventeen to nineteen.[62] This means that the New Zealand government is still in breach of the UN convention by holding boys under age seventeen with young men under twenty and by making no provision at all for girls.

VI. A Brief Note on Theoretical Objections to Family Group Conferences

Warner (1994) argued that the sanctions agreed to at family group conferences are unlikely to be proportionate to the severity of the offense and are unlikely to be consistent. She further claimed that family group conferences can infringe legal rights. There may be some truth in both of these claims: offenders involved in similar offending may end up with different outcomes, and, although certain procedural safeguards must be followed within family group conferences, young people's lawyers do not always attend. However, both criticisms are examples of using conventional criminal justice values as a measure of performance in a youth justice system that prioritizes quite different

[60] It welcomed the introduction of the Domestic Protection Act of 1995 that provides greater protection against domestic violence than previously and which, in particular, extends these protections to children. It also welcomed the procedure by which all proposed legislation is assessed to evaluate its impact on children. And it welcomed the fact that the Human Rights Act applies to children and that the Human Rights Commission can receive complaints from children.

[61] Other concerns were the fragmented nature of the government's approach to children's rights; the low minimum age for charging children with serious offenses; the authorization in sec. 59 of the Crimes Act to use physical force in the family against children for disciplinary reasons provided it is reasonable; and the high youth suicide rate in New Zealand.

[62] Prisoners under the age of twenty are screened for their risk of suicide, self-harm, and being bullied.

objectives. Within a conferencing framework, inconsistencies between outcomes that are the result of genuine agreements between offenders and victims, and that take into account the needs and wishes of those most directly affected by the offense, are desired outcomes. And, in family group conferences, the intention is for offenders to speak for themselves, rather than to have lawyers speak for them, and for dialogue to take place between offenders and victims, rather than discouraging the offender and the victim from talking directly with each other.

The conclusion of critics like White (1994) and Polk (1994) is that family group conferences are simply an extension of state control that is made more effective by co-opting families (and perhaps by co-opting victims, too, but they do not mention this). While some state control is undeniable, the significance of the beliefs expressed by many families and young offenders (and some victims) that they feel involved in the process and in the determination of outcomes is also undeniable and has to be given some weight. Overall, a process that involves many victims, offenders, and families and has resulted in fewer young people ending up in courts, in residences, or in custody cannot simply and lightly be dismissed as a mechanism for extending state control.

VII. Prospects for the Future

I have raised some concerns about the extent to which all of the objects and principles of the Children, Young Persons and Their Families Act 1989 and the core values of restorative justice have been realized in the practice of youth justice in New Zealand. I have also drawn attention to what I see as some worrying trends. It is possible that the recommendations in the youth offending strategy will address these concerns and correct these trends. One certainly cannot challenge proposals to develop high-quality interventions for young offenders or to "ring-fence" budgets to be used specifically on implementing the plans agreed to at family group conferences. However, the strategy seems, at least in part, to have been captured by the promises of risk identification and assessment tools "as a way of targeting interventions and scarce resources in the most effective and efficient manner" (Ministry of Justice and Ministry of Social Development 2002, p. 16). Where this fits with empowering offenders, families, and victims is unclear. There also seems to be a subtle shift occurring with respect to the role of family group conferences. The youth offending strategy specifically states that family group conferences "are particularly appropriate for those youth who need to be held accountable for their offending, *but who are succeeding in other parts of their lives and have few other problems that require any intervention*" (Ministry of Justice and Ministry of Social Development 2002, p. 35; emphasis added). Only time will tell whether or not this, in reality, signifies a return to reliance on decision making by professionals and a change in the role and influence of family group conferences.

The youth justice system in New Zealand and family group conferences in particular have attracted considerable international attention. It has been remarkably successful at diverting young people from courts, custody, and residences, and it has been reasonably successful at involving offenders, victims, and their families in key decisions about how best to deal with offending, in holding young offenders accountable for their actions, and in enabling victims to put matters behind them. However, despite rhetoric to the contrary, victims are not much more involved in family group conferences now than they were ten years ago. Similarly, not enough progress has been made in empowering Maori (and Pacific peoples) to deal with their own young people. And there are worrying trends: the number of young offenders appearing in courts is increasing, as is the number of places in residences and prisons, and this is not occurring against a backdrop of dramatic changes in youth crime.[63] The youth offending strategy set out in 2002 contains some important recommendations aimed at improving practice in youth justice and in family group conferences. However, in my view, some of its recommendations are themselves a matter for concern. Only time will tell. But there is a risk that youth justice practices in New Zealand will become a poor vision of what might have been.

REFERENCES

Advisory Committee on Youth and the Law in our Multi-Cultural Society. 1983. *Report.* Auckland: Office of the Race Relations Conciliator.
Alder, Christine, Ian O'Connor, Kate Warner, and Rob White. 1992. *Perceptions of the Treatment of Juveniles in the Legal System: A Report to the National Youth Affairs Research Scheme.* Hobart: National Clearinghouse for Youth Studies.

---

[63] Young people continue to make up about a fifth of known offenders—a picture that has remained unchanged for many years. Youth crime has increased, but this increase is not out of line with increases in crime generally (Maxwell and Morris 2000).

Anderson, Simon, Richard Kinsey, Ian Loader, and Connie Smith. 1994. *Cautionary Tales: Young People, Crime and Policing in Edinburgh.* Aldershot, England: Avebury.

Barrington, John, and Timothy Beaglehole. 1990. "'A Part of Pakeha Society': Europeanising the Maori Child." In *Making Imperial Mentalities: Socialisation and British Imperialism,* edited by J. A. Mangan. Manchester: Manchester University Press.

Braithwaite, John. 1999. "Restorative Justice: Assessing Optimistic and Pessimistic Accounts." In *Crime and Justice: A Review of Research,* vol. 25, edited by Michael Tonry. Chicago: University of Chicago Press.

Consedine, Jim. 1995. *Restorative Justice: Healing the Effects of Crime.* Lyttelton: Ploughshares.

Dalley, Bronwyn. 1998*a. Family Matters: Child Welfare in Twentieth Century New Zealand.* Auckland: Auckland University Press in association with the Historical Branch, Department of Internal Affairs.

———. 1998*b.* "Moving Out of the Realm of Myth: Government Child Welfare Services to Maori, 1925–1972." *New Zealand Journal of History* 32:189–207.

Department of Child, Youth and Family Services. 2002. *The Youth Justice Plan for Child, Youth and Family Services.* Wellington: Department of Child, Youth and Family Services.

Department of Statistics. 1991. *Justice 1990.* Wellington: Department of Statistics.

Dignan, Jim. 1999. "The Crime and Disorder Act and the Prospects for Restorative Justice." *Criminal Law Review* (January), pp. 48–60.

Doolan, Mike. 1988. "From Welfare to Justice (towards New Social Work Practice with Young Offenders): An Overseas Study Tour Report." Unpublished manuscript. Wellington, New Zealand.

———. 1993. "Youth Justice: Legislation and Practice." In *The Youth Court in New Zealand: A New Model of Justice,* edited by B. J. Brown and F. W. M. McElrea. Auckland: Legal Research Foundation.

Fergusson, David, John Horwood, and Michael Lynskey. 1992. "The Childhoods of Multiple Problem Adolescents: A 15 Year Longitudinal Study." *Journal of Child Psychology and Psychiatry* 35:1365–74.

Hudson, Joe, Allison Morris, Gabrielle Maxwell, and Burt Galaway, eds. 1996. *Family Group Conferences: Perspectives on Policy and Practice.* Annandale, N.S.W., Australia: Federation Press.

Human Rights Commission. 1982. *Report on Representations by the Auckland Committee on Racism and Discrimination: Children and Young Persons Homes Administered by the Department of Social Welfare.* Wellington: Human Rights Commission.

Jackson, Moana. 1987. *The Maori and the Criminal Justice System: A New Perspective, He Whaipaanga Hou.* Wellington: Policy and Research Division, Department of Justice.

———. 1988. *The Maori in the Criminal Justice System: A New Perspective, He Whaipaanga Hou.* Pt. 2. Wellington: Policy and Research Division, Department of Justice.

Love, Catherine. 2000. "Family Group Conferencing: Cultural Origins, Sharing and Appropriation—a Maori Reflection." In *Family Group Conferencing: New Directions in Community-Centered Child and Family Practice*, edited by Gale Burford and Joe Hudson. New York: Aldine de Gruyter.

Maxwell, Gabrielle, and Allison Morris. 1993. *Families, Victims and Culture: Youth Justice in New Zealand.* Wellington: Social Policy Agency and Institute of Criminology.

———. 2000. "Young Offenders." *New Zealand Law Journal* (February), pp. 28–32.

Maxwell, Gabrielle, and Jeremy Robertson. 1995. *Child Offenders: A Report to the Ministers of Justice, Police and Social Welfare.* Wellington: Office of Commissioner for Children.

Maxwell, Gabrielle, Jeremy Robertson, and Tracy Anderson. 2002. *Police Youth Diversion: Final Report.* Wellington: Crime and Justice Research Centre.

Maxwell, Gabrielle, Jeremy Robertson, Venezia Kingi, Allison Morris, and Chris Cunningham. 2003. *Achieving Effective Outcomes in Youth Justice Research Project: Final Report.* Wellington: Ministry of Social Development.

Maxwell, Gabrielle, and Catherine Smith. 1998. *Police Attitudes to Maori.* Wellington: Institute of Criminology.

May, Helen. 1997. *The Discovery of Early Childhood: The Development of Services for the Care and Education of Very Young Children, Mid Eighteenth Century Europe to Mid Twentieth Century New Zealand.* Wellington: Auckland University Press, Bridget Williams Books.

McDonald, Dugald. 1978. "Children and Young Persons in New Zealand Society." In *Families in New Zealand Society*, edited by Peggy G. Koopman-Boyden. Wellington: Methuen.

McElrea, Frederick. 1993. "A New Model of Justice." In *The Youth Court in New Zealand: A New Model of Justice*, edited by B. J. Brown and F. W. M. McElrea. Auckland, New Zealand: Legal Research Foundation.

Ministerial Advisory Committee on a Maori Perspective for the Department of Social Welfare. 1986. *Puao-Te-Ata-Tu (Daybreak).* Wellington: Department of Social Welfare.

Ministerial Review Team to the Minister of Social Welfare. 1992. *Review of the Children, Young Persons and Their Families Act 1989.* Wellington: Department of Social Welfare.

Ministerial Taskforce on Youth Offending. 2002. *Report of the Ministerial Taskforce on Youth Offending.* Wellington: Ministry of Justice and Ministry of Social Development.

Ministry of Justice and Ministry of Social Development. 2002. *Youth Offending Strategy: Preventing and Reducing Offending and Re-offending by Children and Young People: Te Haonga.* Wellington: Ministry of Justice and Ministry of Social Development.

Morris, Allison, and Henri Giller. 1987. *Understanding Juvenile Justice.* London: Croom Helm.

Morris, Allison, Gabrielle Maxwell, and Paula Shepherd. 1997. *Being a Youth Advocate: An Analysis of Their Role and Responsibility.* Wellington: Institute of Criminology.

Morris, Allison, and Warren Young. 1987. *Juvenile Justice in New Zealand: Policy and Practice.* Wellington: Institute of Criminology.

NACRO (National Association for the Care and Resettlement of Offenders). 1997. *A New Three Rs for Young Offenders.* London: NACRO.

Platt, Anthony M. 1969. *The Child Savers: The Invention of Delinquency.* Chicago: University of Chicago Press.

Polk, Kenneth. 1994. "Family Conferencing: Theoretical and Evaluative Questions." In *Family Group Conferencing and Juvenile Justice: The Way Forward or Misplaced Optimism?* edited by Christine Alder and Joy Wundersitz. Canberra: Australian Institute of Criminology.

Potaka, Lynn. 1997. "Police Views on the Children, Young Persons and Their Families Act." *Criminology Aotearoa/New Zealand* (Newsletter of the Institute of Criminology, Victoria University of Wellington, New Zealand) 8(September):6–7.

Pratt, John. 1992. *Punishment in a Perfect Society: The New Zealand Penal System, 1840–1939.* Wellington: Victoria University Press.

Rusbatch, S. 1974. "The Youth Aid Section of the New Zealand Police: Its Justification, Performance and Future Development." Unpublished dissertation, Diploma in Public Administration, Victoria University of Wellington, Wellington.

Seymour, John. 1976. "Dealing with Young Offenders in New Zealand: The System in Evolution." Occasional Pamphlet no. 11. Auckland: Legal Research Foundation.

Shepherd, Paula, and Gabrielle Maxwell. 1999. *Evaluation of the Child and Young Person's Support Worker Demonstration Project.* Wellington: Institute of Criminology.

Stang Dahl, Tove. 1974. "The Emergence of the Norwegian Child Welfare Law." In *Scandinavian Studies in Criminology*, vol. 5, edited by Nils Christie. London: Martin Robertson.

Tauri, Juan. 1998. "Family Group Conferencing: A Case-Study of the Indigenisation of New Zealand's Justice System." *Current Issues in Criminal Justice* 10(2):168–82.

———. 1999. "Explaining Recent Innovations in New Zealand's Criminal Justice System: Empowering Maori or Biculturalising the State?" *Australian and New Zealand Journal of Criminology* 32(2):153–67.

Te Whaiti, Pania, and Michael Roguski. 1998. *Maori Perceptions of the Police.* Wellington: New Zealand Police.

Van Ness, Daniel W., and Karen Heetderks Strong. 1997. *Restoring Justice.* Cincinnati: Anderson Publishing.

Warner, Kate. 1994. "The Rights of Young People in Family Group Conferences." In *Family Group Conferencing and Juvenile Justice: The Way Forward or Misplaced Optimism?* edited by Christine Alder and Joy Wundersitz. Canberra: Australian Institute of Criminology.

White, Rob. 1994. "Shaming and Reintegrative Strategies: Individuals, State Power and Social Interests." In *Family Group Conferencing and Juvenile Justice: The Way Forward or Misplaced Optimism?* edited by Christine Alder and Joy Wundersitz. Canberra: Australian Institute of Criminology.

Young, Ron. 1999. "Youth Justice in New Zealand: Some Problems." In *Youth Justice in Focus,* edited by Allison Morris and Gabrielle Maxwell. Wellington: Institute of Criminology.

Zehr, Howard. 1990. *Changing Lenses: A New Focus for Crime and Justice.* Scottdale, Pa.: Herald Press.

Josine Junger-Tas

Youth Justice in the Netherlands

ABSTRACT

Youth justice in the Netherlands has been riven with ambivalences since
the early 1980s. Juvenile involvement in property crime has been stable
and in violent crime has increased somewhat, though less than is shown
by police data. Nonetheless, the public and politicians respond as if the
problems were worse. Policies and laws have shifted toward greater
emphasis on young offenders' rights and on more use of repressive
measures than earlier when welfare values were more dominant. In
practice, however, commitment to welfare values remains strong, and
welfare institutions play active roles responding to young offenders.
Changed criteria make waiver of young offenders to adult courts easier,
but the numbers waived have fallen, and most who are waived receive
community penalties. Statutes have authorized longer confinement terms
for young offenders, but the use of long sentences has declined. There has
been a substantial increase in the use of community penalties, including
community service and victim compensation, and new programs have
given the police greater powers to take action against alleged offenders.
International conventions and treaties are taken seriously in the
Netherlands and have affected the youth justice system in important ways.

The Netherlands is a small country in northwest Europe, lying on the
border of the North Sea and facing England. Although its land area
may be compared to that of countries such as Belgium and Switzerland, the country has a relatively large population of 16 million inhabitants, making the Netherlands the most densely populated country of
the European Union. Ten percent of the population belongs to an eth-

Josine Junger-Tas is visiting professor, Institut de Police Scientifique et de Criminologie, Université de Lausanne, SUISSE, and visiting professor, University of Utrecht
Faculty of Law, Willem Pompe Instituut, Utrecht, the Netherlands.

nic minority, the most sizable being from Surinam, Turkey, and Morocco. Other growing groups include people from Asia (China, Afghanistan, Iraq), Africa (Ghana, Somalia), and the former Yugoslavia. Most live in one of the four big cities, where half of young people below age fifteen belong to a minority group. The Dutch population is somewhat younger than in the rest of the European Union, with the exception of Ireland. This is because its birthrate is higher, resulting in population growth since 1990 of 6.4 percent, with 19 percent of the population under age fifteen. This is surpassed only by Ireland, where 23 percent of the population is under age fifteen (Social and Cultural Planning Office 2001). However, the youth population is declining: 1.5 million were aged twelve to eighteen in 1980, and only about 1.1 million in 2000.

To understand Dutch juvenile justice, its origins, and how it has changed, one must understand the origins of the social welfare system, which forms the essential background. Two main factors have determined how the Dutch state, and its social welfare and child-care systems, developed. First, from very early on, (local) government was composed of rich merchants instead of an aristocratic class, contrary to most of Europe. The Netherlands never had extensive nobility, and beginning in the Middle Ages many prosperous cities achieved great independence. Although there have been fierce conflicts between Holland's bourgeois rulers and the House of Orange, particularly in the seventeenth century, the country has long been characterized as a republic accommodating a constitutional monarchy. Second, the historic power battle between the church and the state over responsibility for poor relief, child care, and juvenile justice has continued to the twentieth century. It is against this backdrop that the development of social welfare, child care, and juvenile justice must be understood. A number of different religious denominations and the state claimed to have special responsibility for social welfare, child care, and education, which led to a system of social and economic "pillars," each striving for autonomy. However, the need for unity and for coherent national policies forced authorities to develop a decision model based on consultation, negotiation, and consensus. This exists to this very day as the "polder model."

Two more preliminary observations. First, the Netherlands was never merely an island in the European ocean. Of course, the country was affected by influences from abroad, from the humanitarian ideas of the French Enlightenment to the writings of John Howard in England, and later by the influence of the United States. However, in this essay the emphasis is on the distinctiveness of the Dutch evolution in respect to social welfare and juvenile justice policies. Second, changes in juvenile justice are not independent of changes in adult criminal justice. One author describes penitentiary youth care as part of both the adult prison system and the system of residential care for children (Leonards 1995). Similarly, the curtailment of the social welfare system in the 1980s and the 1990s had considerable influence on juvenile justice policies.

Several conclusions may be drawn about the Dutch juvenile justice system. A predominant characteristic is the influence of the welfare tradition. From the sixteenth century onward, a welfare system developed that played an important role in child care and concerning juvenile delinquency. In the nineteenth century, institutions for abused, neglected, and delinquent children became increasingly common. Juvenile justice developed into essentially a welfare and protective system in the twentieth century. Most juveniles are kept outside the system. The police deal informally with large numbers of cases. Only a small minority of young offenders are taken to court, and in the 1960s a number of institutions were closed. However, in the 1980s the mood changed toward a system that allocated more individual rights to juveniles but became more repressive. This led to an increase in youth institutions to house a growing population. An important element in European juvenile and adult justice, setting it apart from that in the United States, is the influence of international standards, including the European Convention for the Protection of Human Rights and Fundamental Liberties, to which all legislation in Europe must conform, and the UN Convention on the Rights of the Child.

Juvenile justice in the Netherlands, including new (preventive) measures and sanctions, is a hybrid. Although some features are undoubtedly more punitive than before, many elements—especially in practice—maintain the welfare tradition. For example, in cases of child abuse and "problem" behavior, every effort is made to persuade parents to accept services voluntarily so that there is no need to take the case to court. A network of social agencies helps parents solve debt problems and offers treatment in cases of substance use, health problems, and parenting problems. A recent proposal to parliament would, in every geographical region, combine child welfare services, psychosocial services, child care, and probation into one central office in an effort to act more quickly and improve services. The changes in juvenile delinquency since 1980, as shown in police records, are shown in figures 1 and 2. Figure 1 shows absolute figures, suggesting large fluctuations in juvenile contacts with the police, and figure 2 shows rates per 1,000 juveniles. The number of young people aged twelve to seventeen interrogated by the police for a delinquent act about doubled between 1960 and 1980 (see fig. 1).[1]

Between 1980 and 2000, however, there are fluctuations due, among other causes, to the 27 percent decline in the youth population aged twelve to seventeen. So looking at absolute figures suggests a decline after 1980. However, the rates per 1,000 juveniles aged twelve to seventeen shown in figure 2 indicate that rates between 1980 and 2000 were broadly stable. Police figures show considerable stability between 1982 and 1990, and some increase in property crime and vandalism. Violence is the exception; between 1994 and 1998 there is a definite increase. Although theft with violence seems to have declined by about 20 percent, violence against persons increased by 60 percent. The causes of this change are multiple, and I return later to this issue. Most violent offenses are assaults, and some are robberies (purse snatching or threatening someone to get money).

Children interrogated by the police increased on an annual basis from 3.5 percent to 4.4 percent of the youth population aged twelve to eighteen. Girls form only one-tenth of those interrogated. Table 1 summarizes what happens once young people are taken to the police station for interrogation. Many more youth are dealt with by social agencies than by police, because it is assumed that problems can be best dealt with by welfare services on a voluntary basis. However, given the number, nature, and size of most of these (private) services, and their insistence on privacy for their clients, we do not know how many young people receive their services. Moreover, in many cases, several social agencies assist one family at the same time and sometimes for a very long time before a case ends up in court.

Although the absolute number of juveniles taken into the juvenile justice system is low, public opinion surveys show widespread worry about increasing crime, in particular youth crime. In the Netherlands—as in many countries in Europe—fear and xenophobia have increased in the last years. Ethnic minorities serve as scapegoats in this respect. A number of factors might help to explain this trend, expressed

---

[1] A juvenile may be interrogated by the police at the police station if he is suspected of having committed an offense.

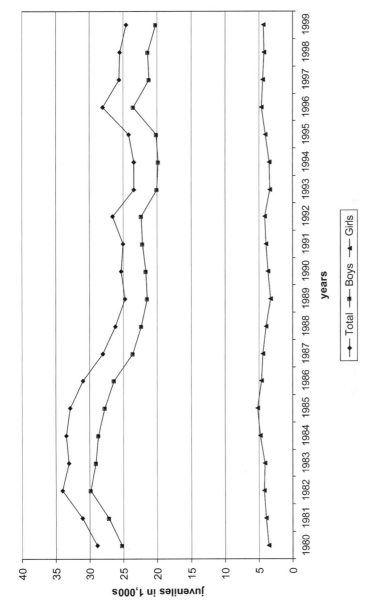

Fig. 1.—Juveniles aged twelve to seventeen interrogated by the police, 1980–99. Source: Huls et al. 2001, p. 363.

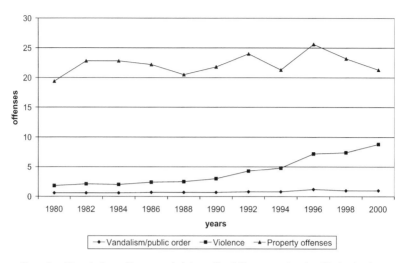

Fig. 2.—Trends in police-recorded juvenile delinquency in the Netherlands per 1,000 population ages twelve to seventeen, 1980–2000. Source: Huls et al. 2001, p. 365.

TABLE 1

Juvenile Cases Handled in the Netherlands in 1999

	Percent
Juveniles interrgated by the police	
N = 47,900 (4.4 percent of youth population):	
Diverted by the police	47.5
Cases taken to court	
N = 25,400 (2.3 percent of youth population):	
Dealt with by prosecutor	65
Dealt with by juvenile judge	35
Convicted	
N = 8,000 (.7 percent of youth population):	
Alternative/community sanctions	43
Fine	7
Youth detention	36
Of which:	
Unconditional	1
Conditional (+alternative sanctions or fine)	35
Other	14

Source.—Huls et al. 2001, p. 150.

among other ways in the emergence of right-wing parties.[2] One is on-going immigration, a phenomenon that is very hard to control and which creates social instability. Another is changes in, and insecurity of, the market economy, combined with a gradual weakening of state-supported social welfare services and support.

Here is how this essay is organized. Section I describes briefly the development of the social welfare system, and Section II examines the origins of child care and juvenile justice. Section II also describes the introduction of the *Code Pénal*, which determined criminal and juvenile justice legislation during the nineteenth century, and Section III reviews the first civil and penal Children's Acts, which laid the ground-work for Dutch child care and juvenile justice. Section IV deals with juvenile delinquency in the last forty years of the twentieth century, and Sections V and VI examine changes in criminal and juvenile justice in the last twenty years. Section VII reviews the new juvenile justice act of 1995. Section VIII discusses the most recent trends in juvenile justice, while Section IX examines the influence of international stan-dards. In Section X, an attempt is made to offer some hypotheses for the new approach to juvenile justice that appears to be emerging in many countries. The final section considers briefly what the future might look like.

I. The Establishment of a Social Welfare System

The medieval view of poverty was that the poor were free people and poverty was a test imposed by God. Rich people were expected to sup-port the poor, and by their charitable works could obtain letters of in-dulgence freeing them from their sins so that they would not burn in hell. Poverty was not considered a social problem, and the poor were allowed to beg in the church, on the streets, or by knocking on the doors of private homes (Groenveld 1997*a*; Vlis 2001).

These views changed all over Europe in the first half of the sixteenth century. City authorities banned begging, introduced the obligation to work for those in good health, and established an apprenticeship sys-tem for orphans (Groenveld 1997*b*). As a form of child care, small chil-dren were placed with a wet nurse, and children—from age eight on—were supposed to provide for (part of) their subsistence by working. Some specialization in institutions was gradually introduced. People

---

[2] In general, though, these parties lose support as soon as they participate in govern-ment, as may be seen in Austria, the Netherlands, and local government in France.

slowly realized that the apprenticeship system often led to considerable exploitation and maltreatment of children. Taking care of vulnerable children, such as foundlings and orphans, in specialized institutions seemed a better solution.

In the seventeenth and eighteenth centuries, the Dutch Republic passed through a period of great prosperity, and a real social welfare system was created in most Dutch cities. No doubt the elite also considered poor relief as a control strategy to maintain its hold over the community, while the poor accepted relief as a kind of survival strategy. Political power was in the hands of bourgeois citizens. Most merchants and artisans realized how uncertain their own fates were and how close poverty might be. Moreover, rich and poor lived in the same neighborhoods and frequently interacted. This no doubt colored their views and attitudes toward the poor.

At the beginning of the seventeenth century, more than 15 percent of Delft's population received poor relief. Even in hard times, poor relief was kept going, if only to prevent unrest and uprising. Support was often generous and flexible: although meant only for citizens, assistance was extended to immigrants and refugees as well. Support was differentiated and assistance was given according to the needs of the poor, bereft, or sick. Special care was given to lone mothers and the elderly. The city supplied free housing for homeless people and, in the event of death, money was supplied to insure a decent funeral. Of course, some abused the system. For example, some of the poor had other sources of income and sold what they received. Support was then withdrawn, but when their personal situation deteriorated, they were often readmitted into care. Family abandonment, begging, theft, and prostitution were criminal acts but did not necessarily lead to loss of relief. That depended on the seriousness and persistence of the behavior. However, most of the poor were very careful because the detection rate was high; they had to report weekly to the "charity chamber," and there were regular home visits.

In the nineteenth century, views on what caused misery and crime changed: unlike in the sixteenth and seventeenth centuries, the discrepancy in income and status between the rich and the poor was extreme, which contributed to the view that poverty was essentially a consequence of an irregular, sloppy, and failing family life of irresponsible and ignorant people. One response was a middle-class "civilizing campaign" to reform the lower classes. Middle-class worries materialized in societies against alcohol abuse and the maltreatment of animals, for educational reform, child care, and female emancipation. Much was expected of sanctions to get the poor in line. In the nineteenth century, the Dutch population doubled, but the number of policemen grew tenfold.

At the end of the century, militant socialism pushed for reform. Because poverty was still widely seen as a product of bad morals and the poor were considered lazy and inclined to evil, a system of poor visitors was established. This was a first step toward the professionalization of social work, embodied in the first School for Social Work in 1899.

The social welfare system as it has developed since the sixteenth and seventeenth centuries has special features. It is based on compulsory insurance provided either by the state (old age provisions) or by premiums paid by employers and employees. It includes an extensive healthcare system, covering the life span, free education to age twelve, and state provision for all citizens aged sixty-five and over. Although important financial cutbacks occurred in the 1970s and 1980s, the system has not collapsed. Some claim that socialism has had decisive influence, but historical studies show that the system had its origin in earlier times. Its essential characteristic is that many misfortunes that befall individual persons, such as unemployment, sickness, and invalidity, are not considered solely as personal failures but are felt as a collective responsibility. However, adequate functioning of the system requires solidarity between citizens and a fair degree of social cohesion, qualities that are under increasing threat.

II. Origins and Development of Child Care and Juvenile Justice

In the sixteenth and seventeenth centuries, orphanages housed orphans and abandoned children in—for that time—reasonable conditions: the children were clothed, ate three meals a day, received schooling, and, when reaching majority, left the home with some funds. Excavations have discovered toys but also wooden straps for punishment (Vlis 2001).

Orphanages dealt with criminality of pupils. The children lived in very cramped conditions with strict and rigid institutional rules. Delinquent behavior included fighting, vandalism, maltreatment of personnel, theft, sale of orphanage property (such as food, clothes, or tools), refusing to study or disturbing Bible study, "immoral" behavior, and running away. Punishments included beatings with a wooden strap, a whip, or on a whipping post, public display, being put on bread and water, and being put in the stocks. In extreme cases, young persons could be evicted, but the charity board preferred sending difficult older boys with the merchant navy to the colonies. The boys tried to escape because conditions on the ships were awful and only 50 percent of them survived (Schegget 1976).

Juvenile delinquents were punished in ways that we would today consider barbaric, although several documents—as early as the sixteenth century—show that the courts took children's ages into account. A study of sixteenth-century Utrecht shows that court documents do not mention children below age twelve (Penders 1980). Such children either did not appear in court or were punished too lightly to justify registration. This suggests that children below age twelve were not considered criminally responsible. The documents mention them only as witnesses or victims. Children aged twelve to fifteen received milder punishment than adults. For example, they were often convicted to floggings "in the presence of the court," meaning behind closed doors, in order to avoid public humiliation. Above age fifteen, there were no differences in treatment between young people and adults.

The eighteenth and nineteenth centuries saw important changes in the conception of childhood and adolescence. Growing emphasis was placed on the preparation of children for responsible adulthood.[3] There was growing opposition to corporal punishment, which was rejected not only because of its cruelty but also because public executions were distasteful to many and felt to be increasingly intolerable. In addition, it was widely felt that behavioral change cannot be achieved by harsh coercive measures but only by the force of internal norms of behavior. Corporal punishment was considered both barbaric and ineffective. New ideas of rehabilitation developed, and psychological interventions became preferred over physical punishment (Rothman 1990, 1998). The new rationalism looked for interventions that would have greater effect on children and be more humane. It was based on two notions. The first is that deviance and delinquency are not so much caused by the innate wickedness of a child as by the environment in which the child is raised. Poverty, neglect, and abandonment would lead to vagrancy, deviance, and delinquency. The second is the opti-

---

[3] This is related to social change, such as a decrease of infant mortality, better knowledge about hygiene, breast-feeding, and bacteria as carriers of disease.

mistic illusion that antisocial behavior can be eliminated if correct measures are taken.

Meanwhile the first steps in developing a full-fledged child protection system were taken. Orphans and foundlings were separated and had their own institutions. The church was most active in child care. Shock at complaints about the low quality of care in overpopulated institutions and about the exploitation of children by foster families prompted a number of initiatives. Two associations were founded, one for improving institutional care and one for improving foster care. Gradually the emphasis shifted toward institutional care. It was felt that well-designed institutions would offer security and form an educational and training environment for increasing groups of children: not only for orphans, but also for poor, abandoned, and neglected children, and for those roaming the streets "looking for mischief and delinquency." Although the reformers' intentions were undoubtedly sincere, their definition of "children threatened by physical and moral danger" was extraordinarily elastic. It is as if the middle classes were at the same time alarmed by the social upheaval of the time and optimistic about successful remedies. Recognizing that the causes of misery were in society itself, they did not plead for social reform but chose instead to isolate children from the sinful, corrupt, and criminal cities. A labor division was established: neglected and abandoned children were placed in the care of private charity organizations, and criminal youth were the business of the state. This led to a great number of child-care homes and institutions financed by private organizations and by state subsidies.

The first criminal code for the Netherlands was introduced in 1809. It was fairly liberal, establishing the minimum age of penal responsibility at age twelve; children between ages twelve and fifteen would be liable for a maximum of two months of prison; those aged fifteen to eighteen would receive lighter sentences than adults. However, the French occupation imposed the French *Code Pénal* in 1811, which, despite some adaptations, remained in force up to 1868. This was considerably stricter and did not reflect prevailing Dutch norms and values: the code allowed life sentences, the death penalty for many crimes, forced labor, and deportation. As for children, the minimum age disappeared: under age sixteen the principle of *incapacitas doli* prevailed; the judge had to decide case by case whether the child was able to distinguish right from wrong. Those considered not competent were sent to a house of correction where they could be held to age twenty, while most sentences for others were halved and the death penalty was converted into ten to twenty years of prison.

Several attempts were later made to amend the criminal code, but these failed. However, an act of 1854 abolished the gallows, branding, and the pillory, and sentences to the death penalty were considerably restricted. More important, the act introduced the principle of mitigating circumstances, in particular for juveniles. Reconviction was considered as an aggravating circumstance. These principles gave large discretionary powers to judges, which continue to characterize Dutch sentencing to this day. After 1860, the death penalty was no longer applied. In 1870 it was abolished, and the principle is now rooted in the constitution.

A new criminal code was adopted in 1881. The only sanctions were prison and the fine. Children under age fourteen were to be placed in a communal regime; over age fourteen, they were to be placed in individual cells, similar to adult prisoners. Those deemed *incapacitas doli* were sent to a state correctional institution. This system prevailed until 1915, when the conditional sentence was introduced (Leonards 1995, p. 36).

In the second half of the nineteenth century, special youth prisons were created in order to avoid mixing adult prisoners and minors. The residential sector, which housed abandoned and neglected children but often included petty delinquents, also increased considerably following the French and German examples (Dekker 1985). These institutions were dominated by a pedagogical ideal: education, not punishment, was to be their central concern. Residential care was considered a social intervention, undertaken by enlightened citizens and religiously inspired movements. Their objective was to restore social order (Dekker 1985). The reformers' influence was so great that even those who wanted to create youth prisons acknowledged the importance of a pedagogical orientation for penal institutions. Although high reconviction figures discredited the system, the faith in institutional education was unshakeable, and ever-longer sentences were imposed to enable the institution to realize its educational mission.

One result of the new criminal code was an enormous increase in the number of institutions for children, from eleven in 1850 to 106 in the period 1874–1914. The number of available places increased from 465 in 1800 to about 12,000 in 1914, the increase being primarily accounted for by private institutions (see table 2). Given that in 1869 the Dutch population included only 3,500,000 inhabitants, compared to

TABLE 2

Number of Youth Institutions according to Denomination and
Capacity, 1800–1915

Period	1800–1830	1830–50	1850–74	1874–96	1896–1905	1905–15
Protestant	4	7	16	20	25	39
Roman Catholic	2	4	19	41	47	54
State	0	0	3	2	3	7
Other	0	0	3	2	3	7
Capacity	465	876	4,067	7,504	8,857	11,998

Source.—Leonards 1995, p. 52.

about 16,000,000 in 2003, the number of institutional places was indeed considerable (Woude 1985).

III. The Children's Acts

In the family economy of premodern society, cruelty and child abuse were private matters and of no concern to authorities. When children started to work in factories, however, the conditions of child labor became a public matter and were perceived as a problem. Many parliamentary and other surveys looked into the working conditions of children, finally leading to protective legislation for children and women (Smelser 1959). In addition, if parents abused their power or neglected their children, it was felt that the state should intervene and take over the parental role. A firm belief in education and rehabilitation and the growing role of the state in social, economic, and judicial matters set the stage for creation of a separate jurisdiction for children, including both children in need of protection and juvenile delinquents.

In 1901 parliament adopted a child care law dealing with child protection issues, and a children's penal law creating a specific system for dealing with a perceived increase in juvenile delinquency (Dekker, Dankers, and Leonards 1997). Two principles dominated the children's acts. First, in child protection, parental authority was restricted, so that parents could no longer remove their children from the institution when they were of age to be employed. Second, with respect to delinquency, delinquent children were to be reeducated and not punished. If punishment was deemed necessary, it should have an educative character.

As a first step, the civil code was changed. Parental rights could be taken away temporarily if parents were incapable of raising their children adequately or removed permanently if they were guilty of neglect or maltreatment. A guardianship council was created, which had to be heard by the court in all child care cases and provided for guardians when needed. Private organizations were authorized to appoint guardians. This reinforced the dominant position of church-affiliated organizations in child care.

The Penal Children's Act was also enacted in 1901. The act abolished the principle of *incapacitas doli*, according to which the judge had to decide whether a child under the age of ten—the minimum age for penal intervention at that time—could be held responsible for his criminal behavior. The minimum age disappeared, but the jurisdiction of the act was extended to age eighteen. The act did not specify different punishments, nor the length of the education process. It was up to the judge to decide whether the child should be punished or educated and for how long. Sanctions included reprimands, fines, and reform school. Those under fourteen could be sentenced to the reform school for a maximum of six months; for those aged fourteen to eighteen this was twelve months. In addition, and this was an innovation in Dutch juvenile justice, a term in a reform school could be imposed as a conditional sentence. In penal proceedings, a preliminary inquiry had to establish the family's socialization capacity, and the child's development, character, and behavior, in order to allow the judge to decide whether to return the child to the family or place it in a state or private reeducation establishment. The guardianship society, later the Council of Child Protection, was charged to make these inquiries. Children were accorded the same procedural rights as adults. Lawyers were appointed for those under age eighteen to defend the child or make appeals.

With its comprehensive set of children's acts, abolishment of *incapacitas doli*, the discretionary power given to the judge, and the association of support and assistance with the judicial process, the Netherlands had one of the most progressive children's acts in Europe at that time (Rooy 1982). Modernization led to increasing paid employment of professionals, and to appointment of professional and specialized juvenile judges, introduced by the act of 1921. The law gave large discretionary powers to the juvenile judge. The prosecutor's power was reduced (he had to consult the judge before taking any decision about minors), and the juvenile judge had authority to act as an examining judge. Although, now as then, juvenile judges had responsibility for civil and penal matters, the judge remained rooted in the culture and structure of the criminal law. For example, the distinction between children in need of protection and delinquent children was retained, the judicial principles of criminal law were preserved, and the juvenile judge remained part of the regular judiciary (Bac 1997). The juvenile judge was considered a specialist in specific matters of criminal law. In 1961, the powers of the juvenile judge were enlarged, allowing him to act also in execution of sanctions.

The 1921 act established the supervision order, a new measure that could be imposed both in civil proceedings and in penal matters "when a child, for whatever cause, is raised in such a way as to threaten him with moral or physical ruin" [Indien een kind, uit welke oorzaak ook, zodanig opgroeit dat het met zedelijken of lichamelijken ondergang bedreigd wordt] (*Wet op de Invoering van den Kinderrechter en van de Ondertoezichtstelling van Minderjarigen* [Introduction of the juvenile judge and of the supervision order for minors] 1921, art. 373, *Staatsblad* no. 834). Social workers were appointed as family guardians and had considerable power. They had to assist and guide parents but could advise the juvenile judge to restrict or to remove parental authority and to place the child in an institution.

IV. Juvenile Delinquency, 1980–2000

To understand recent changes in Dutch juvenile justice, it is useful to consider developments in juvenile delinquency during this period. Public opinion and the opinion of many of those working in the police, the prosecutor's office, and the juvenile court is that delinquency increased, became more serious, and changed in nature. Youth violence is widely believed to have increased, girls to have become more involved in delinquency, and ethnic minorities to have become more active in offending.

What does available evidence tell us? Rates of recorded property offenses clearly stabilized, particularly for boys. There has been some increase in recorded delinquent behavior of girls between 1980 and 2000 (fig. 1), but this is only somewhat true for property crime rates (see fig. 3).

The same trend is apparent for vandalism and public order offenses. Girls commit little vandalism or offenses against public order (see fig. 4). These figures show an unexpected increase in 1996. This peak and the ensuing higher level of juvenile delinquency are partly related to the introduction of a new juvenile justice act in 1995. Under it, the former police practice of dropping petty offense charges was aban-

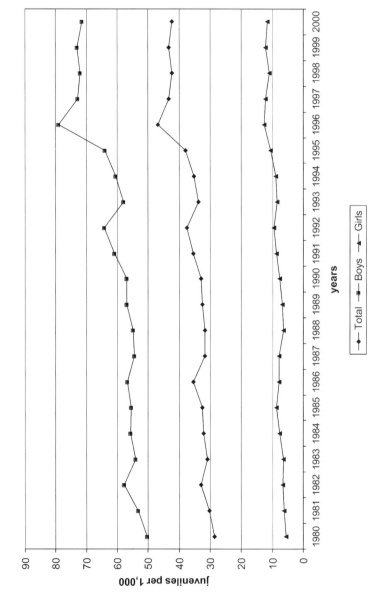

Fig. 3.—Police-recorded property offenses per 1,000 juveniles ages twelve to seventeen, 1980–2000. Source: Huls et al. 2001, p. 364.

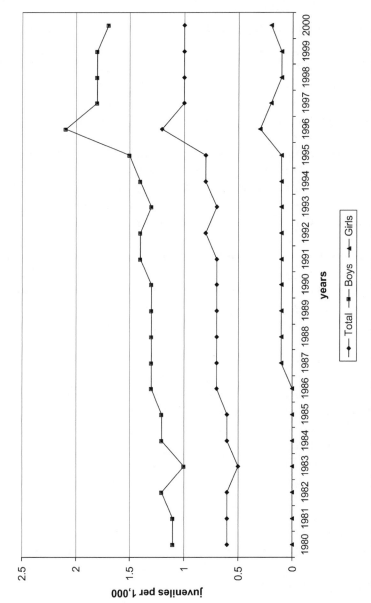

Fig. 4.—Police-recorded vandalism and public order offenses per 1,000 juveniles ages twelve to seventeen, 1980–2000. Source: Huls et al. 2001, p. 364.

doned and replaced by a policy of prosecution followed by diversion. One consequence is that from that date petty offenses are counted in police statistics.

Vandalism and public order offenses among girls are rather rare, but there appears to be an increase in violent acts in recent years, mainly relating to fighting or minor assaults. Overall, the level of girls' delinquency remains considerably lower than that for boys.

The steep increase in recorded violent offenses is controversial. Juvenile delinquency receives increasing attention from the public, in parliament, and in the media, and for most people delinquency equals violence. Both the police and the juvenile justice system are focusing on all forms of violent acts, and there is an increasing tendency among the general public to report such offenses (Kester and Junger-Tas 1994). Just how much of the apparent rise in rates results from changes in citizen reporting and police recording and how much from a real increase in violence is hard to know.

Property offenses form the bulk of delinquent acts for both sexes. This is true for the Netherlands as it is true for other countries in Europe (Junger-Tas, Marshall, and Ribeaud 2003). The general stability of property rates for boys is clear, whereas girls show some increase. However, figures 3 and 5 show that most of the increase in girls' delinquency is due to a rise in violent behavior. This is similar for boys, with most of the increase in delinquency due to a rise in violence, consisting mainly of minor assaults and, to a lesser degree, theft with violence. The latter is often committed by members of ethnic minority groups (Haan 1993). Finally, vandalism and offenses against public order are rare among males and practically nonexistent among females. How do youth crime rates compare to adult rates? Table 3 gives some details of the overall crime picture according to degree of urbanization.[4] Young people to fourteen years old form about 19 percent of the total population, and 44 percent of the population is aged fifteen to forty-four.

Most crime occurs in highly urbanized areas; crime rates in rural areas are about one-quarter of those in the big cities. Even more so than for juveniles, the majority of recorded crime is property crime. Violent offenses constitute only a minor part, even in the big cities. Vandalism and public order offenses are considerably more frequent than are violent crimes, and this is also true in moderately urbanized areas.

[4] Unfortunately, the Centraal Bureau voor de Statistiek only calculates rates for the whole criminally responsible population.

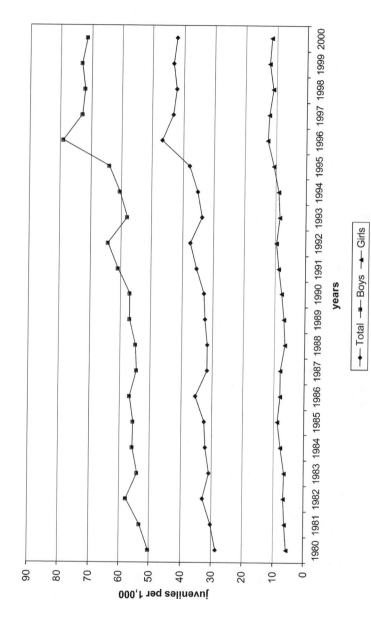

FIG. 5.—Police-recorded violent offenses per 1,000 juveniles ages twelve to seventeen, 1980–2000. Source: Huls et al. 2001, p. 363.

TABLE 3

Recorded Crime per 1,000 Population Ages 12–79, according to
Degree of Urbanization

	1995	1996	1997	1998	1999
Big cities					
(population >100,000):					
Recorded crime	157.8	142.7	155.0	153.7	170.8
Property crime	123.9	106.9	115.0	114.3	124.3
Violence	10.4	10.0	10.7	11.1	13.0
Vandalism/public order	13.1	13.8	14.6	14.2	16.7
Middle-sized cities:					
Recorded crime	94.4	94.6	92.3	93.0	93.5
Property crime	67.6	64.4	62.1	61.4	60.7
Violence	4.6	4.9	5.3	5.5	5.8
Vandalism/public order	13.9	16.1	16.6	16.4	16.8
Rural areas:					
Recorded crime	43.1	43.1	44.0	44.4	45.3
Property crime	30.0	28.6	27.9	27.0	27.3
Violence	1.8	1.9	2.5	2.7	2.9
Vandalism/public order	6.7	7.8	8.4	8.8	8.8

SOURCE.—Huls et al. 2001, p. 325.

Comparing youth rates with total rates reveals some interesting differences. First, violence forms a considerably larger part of juvenile delinquency rates than of total crime rates. Second, vandalism and public offenses are not as frequent among juveniles as among the entire (adult) population.

Another question is whether juvenile delinquency starts at ever-younger ages, a claim often made by police and juvenile judges. There is very little evidence in support of this. Repeated studies of police figures do not substantiate these claims (Kruissink and Essers 2001; Boerman, van Tilburg, and Grapendaal 2002). One problem, of course, is that penal responsibility starts at age twelve and there are no delinquency statistics before age twelve. Table 4 sheds some light on the earliest police contacts according to age (Boerman et al. 2002).

Three percent of Dutch, 7 percent of Moroccan, and 5 percent of Turkish juveniles have their first official police contact at age twelve. Furthermore, 7 percent of Dutch, 11 percent of Moroccan, and 10 percent of Turkish juveniles have their first contact with the police at age thirteen. These figures suggest two things. First, juvenile delinquency before age twelve seems to be rare, and, second, juvenile of-

TABLE 4

Age at First Police Contact, Young People Ages 12–24 of Three
Ethnic Groups, 1999

Age	Dutch (Including Second Generation) (N = 38,321)	Moroccan (N = 5,121)	Turkish (N = 2,148)
12	3	7	5
13	7	11	10
14	11	15	13
15	12	16	12
16	12	12	13
17	11	10	9
18	10	7	7
19	9	5	7
20	7	4	6
21	5	3	5
22	4	3	4
23	4	3	4
24	3	2	4

SOURCE.—Boerman, Tilburg, and Grapendaal 2002, p. 169.

fending among Turkish and Moroccan children starts somewhat earlier than among Dutch children.

Data collected by prosecutors show that the number of children aged twelve dealt with by the prosecutor increased by 30 percent in the period 1995–2000 and the number of thirteen-year-olds increased by 25 percent in the same period (Minister of Justice 2002). This suggests a shift toward an earlier onset of delinquent behavior than was usual in the 1980s.

There is some self-report data on delinquency of young children, but the samples are generally limited to particular areas and are not representative of the country. A study on bullying in schools of children aged eleven to fifteen living in a large and a middle-sized city included some questions on delinquent acts committed in the last twelve months (Junger-Tas and van Kesteren 1999). In the elementary schools, vandalism was reported by about 5 percent, graffiti by 6.5 percent, and shoplifting by 7.5 percent of eleven- and some twelve-year-old children, while violence was reported by only 3 percent. This does not point to an early onset of delinquency in general, but admittedly the indications are sketchy.

TABLE 5

Percentage Pupils (Ages 12–24) Reporting to Have Committed an
Offense in the Preceding Twelve Months, 1992–99

Offenses	1992 (N = 15,245)	1994 (N = 17,770)	1996 (N = 10,352)	1998 (N = 17,005)
Violence:				
Participation in serious fight in school	. . .	6.7	6.6	7.3
Participation in serious fight outside school	. . .	11.7	13.1	12.2
Causing injury to another requiring medical attention	8.0	8.6	8.0	8.1
Theft:				
Bicycle theft	6.4	6.0	5.5	6.2
Shoplifting	8.7	9.8	11.4	8.2
Other theft <fl. 50	6.3	7.3	7.7	6.4
Other theft >fl. 50	2.9	3.4	3.1	3.6
Vandalism:				
Vandalism of school property	5.4	6.4	6.6	6.9
Vandalism of objects in street	9.5	10.6	10.9	10.7
Police contacts	12.3	12.9	12.9	11.8

Source.—Huls et al. 2001, p. 143, presenting weighted data from the NI BUD/SCO National School Survey, 1992–99.

Returning to the question of increasing juvenile violence, self-report figures indicate some increase in violence against persons, although mainly with respect to less serious offenses (Schreuders et al. 1999). It might be useful to compare police figures with the latest self-report data, which are based on surveys of random samples of the Dutch youth population (age twelve to eighteen) every two years by the research and documentation center of the Dutch ministry of justice (Wetenschappelijk Onderzoek– en Documentatie Centrum [WODC]).

A drawback is that ethnic minorities, who are concentrated in the big cities, are not well represented. Since delinquency rates of minority youth tend to be higher than those of indigenous youth (Junger 1990; Etman, Mutsaers, and Werdmölder 1993; Hulst and Bos 1993; Junger-Tas 1997), this may result in underestimation of the level of delinquency. According to table 5 and looking at property offenses over the years, there appears to be some increase in fencing, but that is about all. Overall, the rates show much stability. With respect to violence the only increase seems to be in "wounding someone with a weapon," where a weapon is mainly some sort of knife. However, taking into account the extremely low violence rates, the reliability of this result is questionable. The other violent acts also show great stability and, consequently, do not confirm the alarming police figures on violent offending.

A recent study of violent crime trends in the Netherlands compared police statistics and victimization data, finding very different trends. Although police data show violent crime increasing, victimization surveys show a decrease since the 1990s. Other sources, such as hospital records, do not show an increase either. These data suggest that the increase in violent crime as shown in police figures is partly due to better recording, increased computerization, and greater willingness of the population to report crimes to the police. The recorded increase in violent crimes appears to be real but much lower than police figures suggest (Junger-Tas 1996; Wittebrood and Junger 1999).

Caution is required in drawing conclusions. Property offenses have stabilized since the 1980s, and vandalism and public order offenses show hardly any increase. There is indeed a rise in violent acts among young people. According to victimization and self-report data, however, the rise is not as steep as police statistics indicate, police action toward young people being influenced by pressures from public opinion and politics. Female delinquency has increased, but despite some rise in violence since the 1990s, it remains at a low level, and the increase is largely limited to property offenses. In addition, despite repeated claims from the police and judiciary that there is an increase in offending by children under age twelve, no firm evidence of this has come forward. Finally, self-report studies confirm earlier studies and show higher involvement in delinquent behavior in some ethnic minorities in comparison to Dutch juveniles (Junger-Tas et al. 2003).

V. Dutch Juvenile Justice before 1995

The characteristics of juvenile justice in the Western world in the first half of the twentieth century are broadly similar, whether it includes a separate juvenile court, a juvenile judge, or a welfare board, such as in Scandinavian countries. First, large discretionary powers were based on the notion of *parens patriae*. All agents of the system, including the juvenile judge, the police, and the public prosecutor, were supposed to act "in the best interest of the child." Second, the principle that the punishment should be proportional to the offense was rejected. The interest of the individual child predominated, making it possible to impose a civil measure, such as a supervision order, in penal cases. This placed juvenile delinquents and children "threatened by physical or moral danger" into one category. Third, there was heavy emphasis on treatment instead of punishment. Later, this led to extrajudicial practices to avoid court proceedings, by both the police and the public prosecutor. Fourth, considerable efforts were made to reduce the formal character of court procedures. Hearings were not public; procedures had an informal and confidential character; and the privacy of the juvenile was protected. Fifth, in view of the principles of treatment, rehabilitation, and protection in the child's best interest, the need for legal procedural rights, such as they exist for adults, was not felt.

The ideal was that the juvenile judge—like a medical doctor or a psychologist—would diagnose the problem and the child's needs and then take actions tailored to those needs. The separate juvenile justice system was based on humanitarian concerns. It symbolizes increased consideration for the well-being of children and more respect for their individual personality. It had its heyday through much of the twentieth century, and its philosophy remained practically unchanged until the 1980s.

Statutory changes in 1961 introduced some modifications in Holland but did not change the fundamentals of the system. Instead of considering children as less responsible and accountable than adults, the new act justified a special juvenile justice system by stating that young people are developing human beings and in consequence all measures taken in their respect should have an educative character (Bartels 1983), a statement figuring more than twenty years later in the Preamble of the Recommendation No. R (87) 20 of the Council of Europe's Expert Committee on Juvenile Delinquency (1989). The age of twelve was established as the minimum age of criminal responsibility, although delinquent children below age twelve could be referred to the juvenile judge under child protection legislation.

The police had large discretionary powers; they could take "no further action," dismiss the case after speaking with the parents, or send a report to the prosecutor. Although not expressly stipulated in Dutch criminal law, police dismissal policy has gradually become institutionalized. Frequency of offending and the nature and seriousness of the offense are overriding factors in determining police decisions (Junger-Tas et al. 1983). The old law provided for regular three-party consultations: prosecutor, juvenile judge, and the council for child protection decided together whether a case would be prosecuted or dismissed with an unofficial reprimand, a procedure that—although rather efficient—would later be banned by the European court, emphasizing the need for independence of the juvenile judge. After the juvenile penal law was revised in 1995, new consultations developed between police, the council for child protection, and the prosecutor in order to speed up procedures and take immediate action when necessary. The prosecutor independently dismissed a large number of cases, and in the 1980s only about 15 percent of children coming into contact with the police appeared before the juvenile judge.

Three comments are in order. First, as in many European countries, Dutch law does not recognize so-called status offenses, such as truancy, running away, incorrigibility, or alcohol use; these may be considered as problem behaviors that could eventually lead to a child protection measure. Second, petty offenders are often referred to the child protection system, since such referrals do not create a criminal record and are considered less stigmatizing. Third, in the 1970s there were only seven state institutions and about 300 private homes, which were financed by the ministries of justice and welfare. Half of the children in these homes were there on a court order, and half were placed by welfare, school, or medical authorities. The latter were voluntary placements to which parents agreed. So within residential homes there was no distinction between children with petty delinquent behavior, children in need of protection, and children with other kinds of disturbances. One paradox, however, was that a sentence of the juvenile judge could lead to a maximum of six months detention, but a child protection measure could be extended to two years and could be renewed. As a consequence, many youths preferred to be punished rather than to be treated. Another paradox was the problem of a residual group of serious delinquents who had repeated contacts with the juvenile justice system. The solution was pretrial detention, which increased from 1 percent of all criminal cases of minors in 1965 to 8 percent in 1972 (Junger-Tas and Zee-Nefkens 1980).

In the 1980s, the first voices were raised to urge consideration of the child as a subject of rights instead of as a helpless being (report of the Wiarda commission 1971), followed by a proposal for revision of the juvenile sanctioning system in 1982.[5]

VI. Changes since the 1980s

The welfare approach to youth justice persisted until the 1980s, when it became obsolete. One reason was its excesses. The policy of placing

[5] However, the proposals did not trigger legal change.

as few children as possible in institutions was, of course, reasonable. Beneficial effects of institutional treatment on children could not be demonstrated. Given the negative consequences for children's lives of such an experience, however, it is wise to use restraint. The problem was that no adequate alternative residential or ambulatory services were created. Moreover, because social workers wanted "clients" to accept and be motivated for intervention, whether in welfare or judicial settings, they were not able to reach the really difficult kids, including serious delinquents. A more general problem was that most interventions had no solid scientific basis. Far-reaching decisions taken on behalf of juveniles were based on shaky evidence and had a highly arbitrary quality. Moreover, important social changes in Western society, such as higher levels of education, technological change, and emancipation movements touching women, youth, homosexuals, mental patients, and prison inmates, meant that families no longer accepted the absolute authority of a paternalistic judge over the lives of their children.

The United States was the first country to change the system, through the famous decision in *In Re Gault* (387 U.S. 1 [1967]), granting juveniles due process rights, such as notice of charges, rights to counsel, confrontation, and cross-examination, and the privilege against self-incrimination. The *Gault* decision had far-reaching consequences. Although the Supreme Court did not challenge the separateness of the juvenile court, this was the starting point for a gradual blurring of the distinctions between criminal court and juvenile court.

That meant the disintegration of an essentially protective system, based on the idea that the delinquent is mainly a victim of circumstances and environment, in favor of a system that stressed free will and reaffirmed young people's responsibility for their actions. In addition, disappointment with treatment results in general and with institutional treatment in particular (Martinson 1974) undermined confidence in therapeutic interventions and prepared minds for renewed emphasis on retribution and punishment.

Neoclassical retributive principles, expressed by von Hirsch (1976) in *Doing Justice: The Choice of Punishments*, also penetrated Dutch criminal justice. The principles of "just deserts," according to which the convicted person should receive the punishment he deserves; of proportionality, which requires that the punishment should be directly proportional to the seriousness of the crime; and equality, requiring that like cases should be treated alike, were adopted in Dutch criminal law. Von Hirsch and his colleagues aimed to achieve a fairer, more just, and more lenient sentencing system. They presented numerous examples of how this could be achieved, including the use of imprisonment for the most serious criminals only, and presented a number of alternatives to incarceration.

In practice in the United States and also in many European countries, theory and policy moved independently. Von Hirsch's ideas were used by policy makers to justify considerably harsher policies. Why first in the United States and later also in Europe did the criminal justice and juvenile justice systems change so radically? This question is taken up in Section X below, after discussion of changes that have occurred in Dutch juvenile justice leading to the adoption of new legislation in 1995.

Usually in Holland, many informal new practices are introduced, preparing the ground, before laws are changed. Police interventions changed first. The traditional options were to take no further action, to drop the charges, to refer the child to child-care authorities, or to send an official report to the prosecutor. It was now felt desirable to reduce use of the standard practice of dropping charges in cases of petty offenses. This was done on the basis of a stepping-stone theory, according to which immediate penal intervention was required to prevent the development of a criminal career. Thereafter, charges could be dropped only on condition of the offender paying compensation to the victim or attending a diversion program, called HALT (Het AL-Ternatief). The latter program, of which sixty-five now exist all over the country, is financed by the ministry of justice and the municipality, and is run by social workers. The intervention, which takes at most one free Saturday, includes reparative work and payment of damages to the victim. The program was started in Rotterdam in 1982, its objective being to reduce vandalism. Since then it has spread all over the country: 1,184 children were referred to HALT in 1987, but in 1999 that number was 22,756 (fig. 6). The program deals with offenses such as damage to property, simple theft, fencing, and disorderly conduct in public places (fig. 7).

Most HALT referrals are for minor property offenses, such as shoplifting. To assure a more uniform police approach, prosecutorial guidelines were issued in the 1990s specifying the limits of police discretion in this field. For example, young persons can be admitted to the program on the condition that they have confessed and have not participated in two such projects before. If the young person performs his

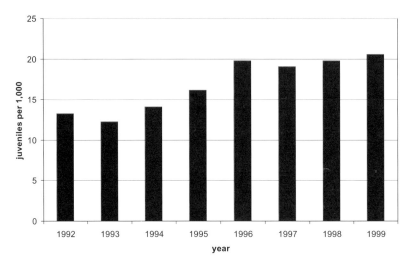

Fig. 6.—Number of HALT referrals per 1,000 juveniles ages twelve to seventeen, 1992–99. Source: HALT Nederland 2000.

tasks as agreed upon, the charges will be dropped. If he does not, prosecution will be started. In adult criminal justice, the police have similar powers. They can offer a so-called transaction (a fine) as a condition for dismissing the case.

The role of the prosecutor is central. He is the key figure in the

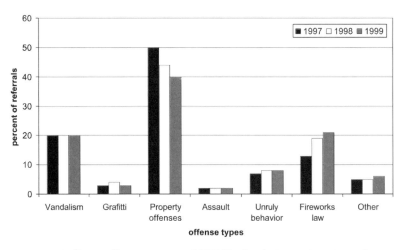

Fig. 7.—Different offense types in total HALT referrals (percent), 1997–99. Source: HALT Nederland 2000.

Dutch justice system and has very large powers. The prosecutor is responsible for all investigating activities of the police. He prosecutes and deals with a growing number of different types of penal cases. If he refers the case to court, he is responsible for the indictment and for recommending a specific penalty. Since the 1980s, prosecutors have been subjected to growing pressures from government and from the general public in favor of harsher penalties for criminals. More emphasis has recently been placed on instrumental aspects of the prosecutor's work, such as responsibility for police investigation practices and for efficient and expedient procedures.

The principle of expediency is an important prosecuting tool. The prosecutor has power to dismiss a case when prosecution is not in the public interest or is not required by public order. Both in juvenile and adult cases, the prosecutor may drop the case with or without any notification. With adults, the prosecutor may impose fines in more serious cases than the police are allowed to do. In 1983, that power was greatly expanded, and the prosecutor may now offer a transaction by fine in cases subject to up to a maximum penalty of six years imprisonment. Recent changes allow the prosecutor to impose a short community sanction in the form of a transaction, as in juvenile justice. This has been introduced to improve the system's efficiency. The prosecutor may see the juvenile in his office and impose a conditional dismissal, the conditions being an apology or payment of compensation to the victim, and may impose a community service sanction of a maximum of forty hours.

The principle of expediency gives the prosecutor considerable powers to deal quickly with a host of less serious offenses. Until 1980, three-quarters of all recorded offenses were dealt with by a technical dismissal, based on a lack of evidence, or by a policy dismissal, based on discretionary authority. In 1983, 15,000 of 40,000 cases of vandalism and simple theft were dropped without any condition on the basis of the "dismiss, unless . . ." principle.

In the 1980s, prompted by the increased volume of recorded cases and by a radical change in views on crime and punishment, the expediency principle was changed into "do not dismiss, unless. . . ." This had far-reaching consequences: the number of cases where the charges were simply dropped declined drastically, and the number of transactions (and thus recorded offenses) increased considerably. Figure 8 shows the inflow of cases and the number of cases dealt with by prosecutors and judges between 1995 and 1999.

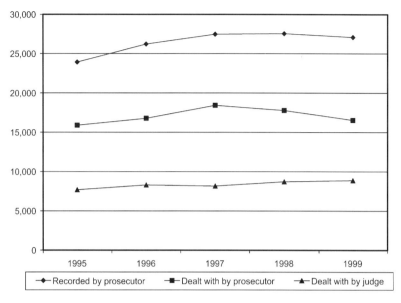

Fig. 8.—Inflow of juvenile court cases and number of cases dealt with by prosecutor and judge, 1995–99. Source: Huls et al. 2001, p. 367.

The majority of cases dealt with by the prosecutor are property offenses (53 percent), followed by damage of property (23 percent), and violence (20.5 percent). In the adult system, the prosecutor usually imposes large fines in the form of a transaction. In the juvenile justice system, the prosecutor may impose a fine, payment of damages, community service of forty hours, or youth probation for a term of six months.

Community service was a major innovation. Inspired by the English model of community service, it was first introduced for adults in 1981 in eight experimental court districts. Community service slowly spread across the country and generated successive evaluations (Bol and Overwater 1984; Spaans 1994, 1995). A 1989 law made it official sentencing policy.

The successful introduction of community service for adults had a strong effect on those working in the juvenile justice field. Because community service was believed to have many advantages over prison, such as a less criminogenic environment, better opportunities for rehabilitation, and reparation to the victim or the community, it was seen as particularly appropriate for juveniles. In 1983, community service was introduced for juveniles along with another sanction modeled on the English intermediate treatment order (Junger-Tas 1989; Laan 1991). The latter consisted of a structured and strict three-month training program, based on behavioral techniques, social skills training, and vocational training. It was used in serious cases as an alternative to pretrial detention (Laan 1987; Laan and Essers 1990). Both sanctions, however, were welcome additions to the limited sanctioning options that juvenile judges had, instead of substitutes for institutional placements. Since these beginnings, the popularity of community sanctions has been overwhelming. Of all juvenile sentences in 1996, 60 percent were alternative sanctions. In 1998, that proportion increased to about 70 percent. In 1983, juvenile judges imposed 298 community service orders (CSOs) and six training orders. In 1995, there were roughly 3,000 community service orders and 1,500 training orders. Juvenile judges were willing to experiment with training orders, although this was something entirely new in juvenile justice. Training orders may vary from six meetings to a three-month program and are still mainly imposed on juveniles. Following positive evaluations (Laan and Essers 1990), the more intrusive orders, combining training with intensive supervision, were extended to young adults.

Community sanctions for adults are mainly imposed in cases of theft, assault and battery, vandalism, and social security fraud. They serve as a substitute for short prison sentences in only half of the eligible cases, and in the other half as a substitute for fines or suspended sentences (Spaans 1995). Suspects charged with sexual or firearms offenses are generally not eligible; nor are drug addicts, repeat offenders, and offenders without a fixed address. Over the years, successful completion is achieved in a high 85 percent (adults) to 89 percent (juveniles) of cases. Figure 9 shows the increase in community sanctions in the juvenile justice system.

Up to 2000, community sanctions could be imposed only by a judge in adult cases. New laws in 2000 also gave the prosecutor such authority. Figure 10 shows the main dispositions taken by judges between 1995 and 1999, showing the share of community service in the total number of dispositions. Although about 30 percent of all sentences are prison sentences, nearly half (45 percent) are fully or partly conditional. In many of these cases, judges will impose probation with a community service order as a condition. However, the number of CSOs is smaller than in juvenile justice. If the police diversion program HALT (since 1995) is seen as part of the official sanctions pack-

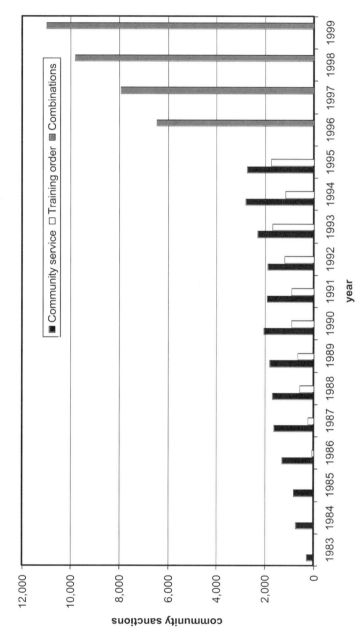

Fig. 9.—Trends in community sanctions for juveniles, 1983–99. Sources: Huls et al. 2001, p. 382; Ministry of Justice 2002.

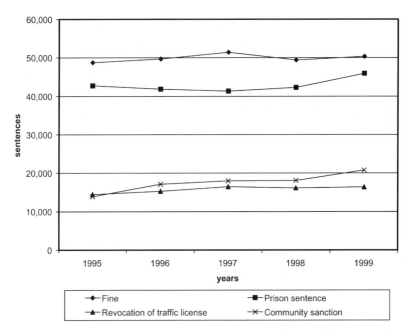

FIG. 10.—Sentences imposed by judges on total criminally responsible population ages twelve to seventy-nine, 1995–99. Source: Huls et al. 2001, pp. 369–70. Since the Centraal Bureau voor de Statistiek collects data on all persons criminally responsible, sentences of juveniles are included. However, fines are rare among juveniles (a community sanction is preferred) and the rare prison sentences refer only to juveniles ages sixteen to eighteen.

age, community sanctions constitute the vast majority of all sanctions imposed on juveniles. A study of reconviction data, conducted about ten years after the introduction of the community sanctions scheme, confirmed earlier studies showing that recidivism rates are related primarily to the criminal records of the target groups and not to the type of intervention (Pease, Billingham, and Earnshaw 1977; Petersilia and Turner 1990, 1991; Spaans 1995).

VII. Juvenile Justice 1995 Act

The act of 1995 introduced numerous changes that affect the police, prosecutor, juvenile judge, and council for child protection. In addition, criminal procedures have changed, emphasizing the increased maturity of young people (*Wet voor de Herziening van het Jeugdstrafrecht en procesrecht* [Revision of penal justice and procedural justice for juveniles] 1995, *Staatsblad* art. 528). A number of procedures that were distinctive to juvenile justice were abolished, and the sanctioning system has been modified. Although juveniles have obtained more due process rights, this was deemed necessary because punishments have become more severe. The juvenile justice system has also been simplified, and differences between adult criminal justice and juvenile justice procedures have been drastically reduced.

The changes have not lacked critics. The Dutch Society for the Administration of Justice and Child Protection, an independent body controlling the preservation of inmates' rights within penal institutions, and including membership of both prosecutors and judges, suggested that the ostensible increase in youth maturity might have to do more with the ways adults view minors than with the behavior of young people.

HALT. HALT was originally informal, based on voluntary collaboration between the police, the program, and juveniles and their parents. It has now been adopted in law as an official transaction offered by the police. At the same time, the existing prosecutorial guidelines have been incorporated in the law, thereby tightening prosecutor control and changing HALT into a de facto penal sanction.

The prosecutor. The new law gives the prosecutor authority to offer an alternative sanction up to forty hours as a transaction. Where the proposed sanction will be more than twenty hours, the juvenile is entitled to legal counsel. However, by far the most important change relates to waiver of juveniles aged sixteen to eighteen to the adult court. Formerly, three conditions had all to be met: the committed offense had to be serious, there had to be aggravating circumstances, such as the commission of the offense with adults, and the offender had to have an adult or mature personality. Under the new law, any one of these conditions is sufficient for transfer to adult court. With respect to the age limits, what counts is the age of the youngster at the moment he committed the act.

The juvenile judge. The three-party consultations between juvenile judge, prosecutor, and the council for child protection, in which the parties examined all cases and decided together what further action to take, what inquiries to make, and whether there had to be prosecution, became controversial. These consultations, threatening the independence of the different partners, could no longer be defended. This was also the case for the requirement that the prosecutor had to consult the judge before prosecuting a case. These practices were abolished, and the juvenile judge is no longer allowed to intervene in the execution of the sanction.

However, Dutch judges have maintained considerable power, in particular in the use of aggravating and mitigating circumstances when sentencing. This continues to be the case in both juvenile and adult criminal justice. Furthermore, in serious cases where the maximum detention penalty exceeds six months, the trial can no longer be held by the juvenile judge alone. Three judges, one of whom is a juvenile judge, are required (Koens 1995).

Legislators wanted to abolish the old requirement for juveniles to be present at the trial, to parallel adult criminal law, where this was not required. The Society of Family and Juvenile Law protested and claimed that appearance at the trial had a pedagogical effect. This requirement was preserved.

Sanctions. There are now only two main sanctions for young offenders: the fine and youth detention. In addition, three types of alternative sanctions are available. These are community service for the benefit of the community, compensation or reparation of damage caused to the victim, and the training order. The maximum term of detention, which was six months, has been doubled to twelve months for juveniles aged twelve to sixteen, and quadrupled to twenty-four months for those aged sixteen to eighteen. In addition, penal treatment measures in special institutions have been introduced for serious, violent, and sexual offenders needing treatment; these may extend to six years. However, this measure applies to a limited number of young people. There has been a great concern that in the first years the new rules facilitating waiver led to an increase in sixteen- to eighteen-year-olds in adult prisons. Average detention periods in juvenile institutions increased, and a sizable state building program for more secure places took place.

The following figures on sentences to (partly) unconditional detention compare the age group of twelve to seventeen with young adults (eighteen to twenty-four)—the largest age group in prison—according to the length of the unconditional part of the sentence, as sentencing developed after 1995. Figure 11 shows that use of short sentences (under one month and 1–3 months) declined drastically after the change of the law in 1995 but stabilized from 1997 onward at a considerably lower level. This pattern is even stronger for sentences of 3–6 months. Sentences of six months or more—although at a higher level—also de-

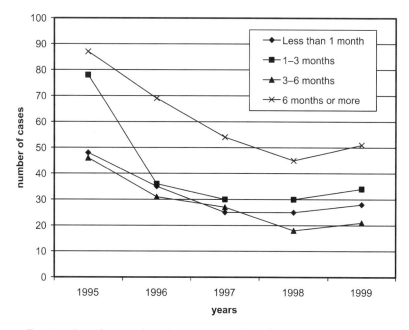

Fig. 11.—Juvenile court detention sentences of juveniles ages twelve to seventeen, according to length of detention, 1995–99. Source: Huls et al. 2001, p. 376.

clined between 1995 and 1998 but have increased slightly since. The data suggest that short sentences for juveniles have become rare, while those of six months or more have become more frequent. As for young adults, figure 12 indicates that sentences both of 3–6 months and of six months or more declined steadily between 1995 and 1999, while at the same time and after a decrease, there has been an increase in sentences of less than one month and 1–3 months. This does not suggest that judicial decision making has become much more punitive since 1995, although there is evidence that between 1985 and 1995 sentence lengths increased for both adults and juveniles (Grapendaal, Groen, and Heide 1997). In neither case does there seem to be a continuing trend to an ever more repressive approach. Sentencing practices seem to have stabilized.

In addition to juveniles in youth detention, the Netherlands has a great number of children over and under age twelve in child-care homes as a child protection measure. Most are in open institutions, although there are also some secure places for extremely damaged and difficult children. Figure 13 shows the number of children in child-care homes and in penal institutions.

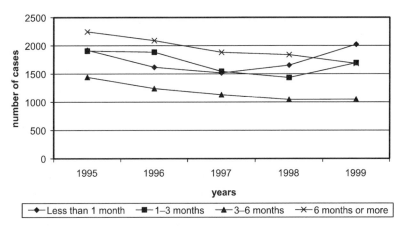

Fig. 12.—Criminal court prison sentences for young adults ages eighteen to twenty-four according to length of detention, 1995–99. Source: Huls et al. 2001, p. 376.

One striking pattern in figure 13 is the high number of ethnic minorities in the penal youth institutions. Although there has been a rise in the number of Dutch juveniles in recent years, the number of minority entries is more than twice that of Dutch youngsters. This contrasts starkly with child care, where both the number and the increase

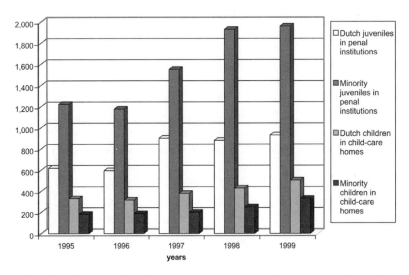

Fig. 13.—Number of juveniles (ages twelve to seventeen) entering penal institutions and children (ages zero to seventeen) entering child-care homes, 1995–99. Source: Huls et al. 2001, p. 381.

among minority children placed in child care are lower than for Dutch children. The data suggest that minority juveniles come to the attention of authorities on the basis of delinquent behavior to a much larger degree than as a consequence of child abuse or neglect. This may mean that minority families are less troubled than Dutch families, but it may also indicate that authorities have little idea what happens in minority families. Comparing these domains, it should be recalled that the length of stay in child care is usually far longer than in penal institutions and may take at least two years.

A worrying trend is the new focus on children below age twelve, based on claims that there is an increase in delinquency in that age group. In May 1999 a special project called STOP, for children aged twelve and under, was introduced on an experimental basis in all court districts. Police officers, in case of a minor infraction of the law, such as vandalism or shoplifting, could arrest the children, then contact the parents and propose educative intervention by social workers. In cases where a problematic situation is suspected, the police may refer the child to the council for child protection. In the experimental period, 1,700 children were referred to one of the fifty-three HALT agencies charged with the execution of this measure. Most referred youngsters were aged ten and eleven, and 88 percent were boys. Most infractions were vandalism, small thefts, and shoplifting. Interventions include offering apologies, writing a story, making a drawing, and viewing an educative video film. The intervention still requires the parents' voluntary acceptance, but it is unclear how long or whether this will continue. Most parents accept the police proposal, in particular if support and assistance in other domains is offered. However, nothing can be said about STOP's effectiveness at reducing renewed contacts with the police. On the basis of a superficial process evaluation, based mostly on professionals' opinions, the deputy minister of justice informed parliament that STOP will be introduced on a national level, although the deputy minister pleaded for the authority to offer assistance when approaching parents. Increased transfer of juveniles to adult court and STOP tend in practice to lower penal responsibility from age twelve to age ten, and to lower penal majority from eighteen to sixteen.

To summarize the main characteristics of the juvenile justice system as it has developed in Holland and elsewhere in much of the Western world since the 1980s, the following elements are of central importance: the offender is viewed as a rational being with a free will and is seen as fully and individually responsible for his actions; one consequence is more severe penal interventions at the expense of protection and treatment; the victim becomes a central figure in legal procedures, leading to an emphasis on restitution and reparation of harm done; due process rights for juveniles have led to considerably more formal justice proceedings than was the case before; possibilities of transferring juveniles from juvenile to adult court are increased; differences between the adult criminal justice system and the juvenile justice system have been greatly reduced; and, because of increasing use of incarceration for more serious offenders, extrajudicial procedures and community sanctions tend to be limited to nonserious offenders.

The flowchart in table 6 shows how all cases and, in particular, juveniles, are handled by the system, from the estimate of total victimization by the Dutch population to the number of people involved in the justice system. Comparing juveniles with the total picture of cases recorded at the level of the prosecution service, two things stand out: one is the number of juvenile cases that are joined to others and the second is the number of charges dropped. Both are higher for juveniles. However, the total number of transactions, most of which concern adults, is higher than for juveniles. This is probably related to the high number of transactions with respect to traffic offenses.

Another difference is the low number of fines imposed on juveniles. Juvenile judges feel that fines are not an adequate sanction because in most cases parents pay the fine. In addition, the number of unconditional detentions is small—3 percent of all sentences to detention—most being conditional and combined with a community sanction. This is in contrast to the adult pattern, where more prison sentences are pronounced and most are unconditional. It is difficult to know how many conditional prison sentences involve community service because adult CSOs, unlike in juvenile justice, are not "main sanctions," but additional sanctions, and do not figure in the statistics.

From table 6 we may conclude that despite a recent more punitive approach, there still is a strong tradition of emphasizing the educative character of juvenile justice and a firm belief in the malleability of the young. This may explain both the search for more effective interventions and the tendency to intervene earlier with light measures and support and assistance. Secular traditions of social welfare and paternalistic but benevolent attitudes toward the young are deeply rooted in Dutch juvenile justice and in the minds of many practitioners.

TABLE 6

Total Juvenile Cases Dealt with by Police, Prosecutors, and Juvenile Judges in 1999

	Number
Estimated number of victimizations:	
Estimated number of offenses against citizens	4.8 million
Of which reported to police	1.6 million
Recorded offenses:	
Number of official reports	1,284,300
Number of suspects heard by the police	267,200
Juvenile cases:	
Number of minors heard by the police	47,900
Of which diverted (HALT)	22,800

Court Cases (Total 25,400)			
Prosecutor: 16,500 cases (percent)		Judge: 8,900 cases (percent)	
Charges dropped	31	Joinders	7
Transaction	41	Acquital	4
Joinders	29	Findings of guilt	89 (±8,000)

Sentences (percent)	
Youth detention	33*
Fine	7
Alternative sanction	43
PIJ measure**	2
Other	15

Source.—Huls et al. 2001.

* Approximately 2,700 sentences, of which 70–80 are unconditional, and the rest are conditional plus an alternative sanction or fine.

** PIJ = Placement in an institution. It is a penal measure implying long-term treatment with a maximum of six years, in contrast to the penal sanction of custody, which carries a maximum term of one year for those under age sixteen and two years for those ages sixteen and seventeen.

VIII. Some Recent Trends

Will Dutch juvenile justice policy continue to become increasingly repressive or will it pause and reflect on what juvenile justice is about and what we want it to be? There are some hopeful signs.

First, the youth police, a long-time specialty that had been abolished, is being reintroduced. Some police departments employ an educator or social worker to assist them in youth cases. A government doc-

TABLE 7

Sentencing by the Juvenile and Criminal Courts of Juveniles
Aged 12–17, 1995–99 (Percent)

	1995 (N = 7,687)	1996 (N = 8,297)	1997 (N = 8,154)	1998 (N = 8,714)	1999 (N = 8,869)
Juvenile court	84	94	96	97	97.5
Criminal court	16	6	4	3	2.5

Source.—Huls et al. 2001, p. 375.

ument recently submitted to parliament recognizes the importance of youth specialists in the police, the prosecution system, and juvenile court. Second, the personal circumstances and personality of the offender continue to be taken into account in the sentencing process, both in criminal and in juvenile justice. Third, despite legal dispositions making transfer of young delinquents to adult court a lot easier, the latest statistics show that youth prosecutors are increasingly reluctant to do this: in 1995, the year of the introduction of the new legislation, 16 percent (1,194) of cases submitted to juvenile judges were transferred. This had fallen to 2.5 percent (223) in 1999 (see table 7). The new law, in cases where the maximum penalty may be more than six months detention, requires a trial of three judges, one of them a juvenile judge. Because the maximum length of detention for juveniles has increased and the number of youth institutions has multiplied, the need for the transfer of serious cases to the adult court has diminished. Moreover, of the 1999 transfers, seventy were sentenced to a suspended sentence, fifty to community service, fifty to a fine, and only fifty to a prison term.[6]

Fourth, the Dutch tradition can be seen in considerable financial investments in youth institutions and involvement of institutional treatment staff with the young people in their care. While in most establishments treatment still is haphazard, based on good intentions and vague ideas about providing security, structure, and discipline, there is increasing awareness of the requirements of program effectiveness and thorough evaluation of results. Treatment interventions that have been shown to be effective are slowly being introduced in a number of institutions. More emphasis is also placed on adequate aftercare, and several institutions follow up with those who leave for periods ranging

[6] Personal communication by Dutch Central Bureau of Statistics Voorburg (2000).

from six to twelve months. Community sanctions, whether work projects or training orders, are popular among juvenile judges, but training orders are now also being introduced in adult justice, showing again the connectedness of the two systems.

A new law on penitentiary principles was enacted in parliament in 1998, and a similar one was adopted for youth institutions in 2001. Both introduced the option of the young person's spending the last part of the detention period outside the institution. Juveniles who have served at least half of their term may spend their last three months of detention in employment or following a vocational training course. The requirements for Schooling and Training Projects (STPs) are as follows:[7] the maximum length is three months and the program is delivered twenty-six hours a week; activities include social skills training, (vocational) education, and preparation for the labor market; services have to be provided in case of drug addiction and psychosocial problems, including consultation, treatment, and educational measures aiming at the rehabilitation of the juvenile. Although options are limited, the combination of a controlled and gradual transition to liberty with an introduction to the labor market seems very useful.

Finally, restorative justice has been introduced as a new form of sanctioning. Particularly interesting is the renewed focus on the individual offender and victim, which is quite in opposition to neoclassical principles. The term "restorative justice" covers many types of intervention, from mediation to reparative activities in the community (Leest 2001, p. 64). A limited number of mediation pilot programs are under way in which offenders in serious crimes, having been punished, meet with their victim(s). The objective is to "restore" the relationship between these individuals. In another pilot program, family group conferences are being conducted in which juvenile offenders meet the victim and his family. Special mediation sessions are being developed in schools to resolve conflicts between pupils, as well as in neighborhoods where citizens are assisted by mediator-volunteers to solve conflicts and avoid escalation.

Another related development is the establishment of local prosecution offices (a project known as Justice in the Neighborhood and based on a French model). Of course, this is mainly done to deal quickly and informally with petty offending, but prosecutors are increasingly be-

---

[7] In *Regulations Judicial Youth Institutions*, the ordinances establishing rules for practical application of the act (Deputy Minister of Justice, 2002, the Hague, Ministry of Justice).

coming involved in solving local problems. They meet with citizen associations and in schools in their area, and they tend to have a mediating role in maintaining social peace and good community relations.

Many prevention initiatives are also undertaken by the ministry of justice in collaboration with the ministries of welfare, education, internal affairs (responsible for minority policies), and municipalities. These include parent training courses in child protection and in persistent truancy cases, financing four pilot programs of the strategic model and the social intervention program Communities That Care (Hawkins and Catalano 1992), and setting up pilot programs in schools to improve school achievement and social competence of children from deprived families.

One consequence of the increasing number of prevention programs, child protection measures, and juvenile justice interventions is the creation of a "program" market in which numerous private commercial agencies offer such programs, emphasizing the need for some form of impartial judgment of what is valid and what is not. Following the English model of a correction treatment accreditation commission, efforts are under way to introduce a similar commission in the Netherlands. The aim of the English accreditation commission is to develop a core curriculum of programs that ensure that offenders in the prison and probation system will be dealt with according to "what works" principles (Lewis 2001). The theoretical bases of particular programs, program designs, program implementation, and program effectiveness are examined and may lead to full acceptance of the program, to its rejection, or to possible acceptance after having met certain criteria. Members include independent (academic) experts, representatives of the Home Office, and inspectors of the prison and probation services. This is suited to all types of penal interventions, although the ministry of justice will probably start with institutional treatment programs and community sanctions. However, at some point early intervention and social competence programs are also likely to have to meet tests of effectiveness and program delivery quality.

IX. International Standards

Several international organizations have issued recommendations, rules, and standards for criminal justice and juvenile justice. For Europe, the most important has been the Council of Europe, created in 1949 to increase collaboration between member states. The council can formulate recommendations but cannot impose them on member states. Started with ten member states, the council now has forty members, but its influence is dwindling in favor of the European Union. The council's most important achievement was preparation of the European Convention for the Protection of Human Rights and Fundamental Liberties (ECHR), which was adopted in 1950 and is enforced by the European Court of Human Rights in Strasbourg. Because international jurisdiction supersedes national jurisdiction, the European court's influence on the member states, which have all adopted the convention, is considerable. National legislation is continually tested against ECHR provisions and the court's jurisprudence. For example, Article 6 of the ECHR requires that a trial be held by an "impartial tribunal" and does not admit an exception in juvenile cases. In the *de Cubber* case (see Bac 1995), a young Belgian man was tried by several judges, one of whom had also been the examining judge. The European court ruled that these two functions were incompatible. Although Dutch judges and prosecutors felt that the Netherlands' situation was not strictly comparable to the Belgian one, it became standing practice to appoint a different judge at the trial in cases where the juvenile judge had conducted the judicial inquiry. The 1995 law abolished the double role of the juvenile judge. The judge can no longer simultaneously examine the case and be judge at the trial.

Another important question is whether juvenile proceedings should be open to the public and the media. According to Article 6 of the ECHR, this would generally be required, but exception may be made in the interest of the juvenile. Moreover, Article 40 of the UN Convention on the Rights of the Child (CRC) requires that the privacy of the child be safeguarded at all stages of the penal process. As a consequence, the Netherlands' parliament decided that in juvenile justice the whole penal process would take place behind closed doors.

The United Nations is also influential with respect to youth policies, child care, and juvenile justice. The UN Convention on the Rights of the Child was established in 1989 by the General Assembly and has been ratified by 191 states. The UN commission supervising its implementation does not have individual complaint procedures, and therefore violations of the convention cannot be brought to an international court. However, there is a supervision procedure in the form of a UN reporting committee, which assesses every five years the measures taken by states to implement the convention's provisions as well as the progress made in respect of these provisions. In addition, pressures are exercised on states by nongovernmental organizations, such as

UNICEF, Defense for Children, and Amnesty International. For example, the Netherlands has been criticized for not providing sufficient information to children about their rights, for policy in child abuse cases, and for policy toward lone minors seeking asylum (Defence for Children International 2000).

Articles 37, 39, and 40 of the convention have a direct effect on juvenile justice, meaning that the convention's norm should be formulated in a way that does not imply a need for new legislation and that national law should make it possible for this norm to affect the system of law directly (Mijnarends 2001). Article 37 guarantees the rights of the child in the case of deprivation of liberty; Article 39 emphasizes the duty of authorities to rehabilitate and reintegrate young people after detention; and Article 40 guarantees the establishment of a juvenile justice process that is respectful of a juvenile's rights.

The critical question is whether the convention will be observed by the UN member states that have ratified it. Since there are no sanctions attached to nonobservation, it is to be expected that in nondemocratic countries with an underdeveloped judicial system this will not be the case. One may, however, expect that efforts to observe the provisions will be strongest in Western democracies where the legal profession and the media play an important role. The convention's main importance lies in the values it represents and its moral appeal to realize these values in practice.

In addition, five-yearly UN congresses have adopted *Standard Minimum Rules for the Administration of Juvenile Justice* (the Beijing rules) in 1985, and *Rules for the Protection of Juveniles Deprived of Their Liberty* (the Havana rules) in 1990. Both instruments reflect Western values and were prepared by European lawyers. The Beijing rules were originally designed and formulated by a committee chaired by Professor Horst Schüler-Springorum from the University of Munich. The Beijing rules include formal criminal procedures around notions such as the well-being of juveniles, proportionality of the penalty to the act, taking into account mitigating circumstances, and the minimum age for criminal responsibility. The Havana rules are concerned with juveniles in detention, specifying the reintegration of the juvenile as an objective, and his right to adequate treatment and contacts with his family (Mijnarends 1999).

The impact of the UN Convention on the Rights of the Child will probably grow over the years, at least in Europe. However, because of its jurisdictional powers, the unifying influence on European states of the European Court's rulings in matters of human rights will be much greater. Representatives of all member countries were active in the making of this convention. Most of them participated in special working groups and committees in the Council of Europe. In the Netherlands, all new legislation in the field of justice is tested against the Convention, which is extremely influential in this respect. Individual European citizens may take a case to the court in Strasbourg, and important judgments have been made on legal procedures in a number of countries, always followed—although sometimes after considerable delay—by legal changes.

X. Hypotheses about Change

Why, first in the United States and then in Europe, have the criminal justice systems as a whole, and juvenile justice in particular, undergone such drastic changes from a welfare model? With respect to the United States, some hypotheses have been advanced by Tonry (2001). One reason might be the belief of many people that the increasingly harsher system is a consequence of the rise in crime. As far as juvenile crime is concerned, there was a substantial rise between 1950 and 1980 in most Western countries, but the bulk of it was nonserious property and petty crime. Furthermore, there is no evidence showing a similar rise in the 1980s and 1990s (see Sec. VI above). An additional hypothesis is that general stability in adult and juvenile crime is the consequence of more severe sanctioning policies. Deterrence and incapacitation are supposed to reduce crime. As far as the Netherlands is concerned, however, police and victimization data show a general annual increase in crime of about 1 percent between 1985 and 1995. Taking into account population increase, changes in recording, and a greater tendency to report offenses to the police, that amounts to only an annual 0.5 percent (Kester and Junger-Tas 1994). The considerable expansion of prisons and youth institutions started in the 1980s when crime was already stabilizing. Moreover, the need for cell capacity is always fluctuating. For example, in 1999 the Dutch minister of justice admitted in parliament that 1,200 prison cells were empty, while later there was again a shortage. Part of that prison capacity has been converted into youth accommodation. American research has long since shown that the manipulation of penalties has little or no effect on crime rates (President's Commission on Law Enforcement and Administration of Justice 1967; Tonry 1995; Howell 1997). The two factors tend to move independently of each other, and increases or decreases in crime have little to do with criminal justice policies.

A different explanation is that the new faith in harsh punishments is a consequence of increased mass media attention to serious, rare, and heavily dramatized crimes. This phenomenon is as frequent in Europe as it is in the United States. As Tonry notes, "We know that ordinary citizens base their opinions on what they know about crime from the mass media and as a result that they regard heinous crimes and bizarre sentences as the norm. They believe sentences are much softer than they are, and they believe crime rates are rising when they are falling. As a result majorities nearly always report that judges' sentences are too lenient" (2001, p. 57). This distorts people's views on crime in general. The media contribute to create a climate of fear in which people believe that crime is fast increasing and that deterrence and retribution are needed to maintain sufficient social control.

An additional problem is that politicians follow the media. They base their political actions on what they see as the public's feelings about the issues figuring in the media. As a consequence they exercise pressure on prosecutors and judges to be firm and pronounce more severe sentences. The latter are not insensitive to the pressure of public opinion and tend also to support more repressive sentencing policies.

These explanations add to our understanding of the actual situation in criminal and juvenile justice, but it seems to me that, at least as far as the Netherlands is concerned, additional factors might be taken into consideration.[8]

For example, Ruller and Beijers (1995), examining trends in the twentieth century, showed that through most of the century crime rates and imprisonment and institutionalization steadily declined in the Netherlands. Not until the 1980s did the rate of imprisonment start to increase. Ruller and Beijers (1995) argue that the main reason for the decline was a slow shift in people's perception of what punishment is sufficiently harsh for a particular crime, in the same way as people's sensitivity to pain and suffering has been increasing. In the Netherlands in the 1850s, prison terms of five years were seen as very severe, but in the 1970s and 1980s, terms of six months and more were considered very harsh punishment. Heightened sensitivity to the amount of suffering deemed necessary to satisfy the need for retribution led to a

---

[8] These tentative explanations may even prove valid for western Europe in general.

systematic reduction in the length of prison terms by several means, such as early release (for good behavior), the suspended sentence, and the power given to the prosecutor to deal with growing numbers of cases out of court.

Gurr (1981, 1989) presented a different hypothesis. He argued that the double decline in crime and imprisonment in the nineteenth and the greatest part of the twentieth centuries is due to the industrial revolution and the development of an industrial economy. The creation of institutions such as schools, factories, and the military, which socialized children and adults into conformity, discipline, and obedience, prepared them to perform their role in the modern economy and state. I think that both explanations have validity and are not mutually exclusive.

My view is that the present trend of meting out more severe punishments to adults and juveniles is related to fundamental changes in the economic, technological, and social makeup of Western society. Three phenomena seem to operate. These are the penetration and pervasive influence of the market economy, changes in the labor market due to technological innovations, and mass immigration.

Western society has long been based on a market economy. However, after World War II and until the end of the 1970s, negative effects on people's lives were cushioned by an elaborate welfare system that gave the state an important interventionist but benevolent role. When, as a consequence of several recessions, this balanced system appeared at risk of collapse, it was gradually dismantled in many, though not all, Western countries. The role of the state declined, and the state withdrew financial support for welfare organizations, education, health, and public housing, expecting private enterprise to take over. Although economic growth increased, there were negative consequences. One consequence is growing social and economic inequality, including a growing class of people living at the margins of society. The breakdown of the welfare system has created a void that is increasingly filled by justice initiatives, such as diversion programs, community sanctions, and local justice bureaus, and prosecutors and police operating at the local neighborhood level. The Scandinavian countries, including Finland, continue to have a strong welfare tradition, and still have low imprisonment rates. Other countries that have not as yet developed a full-fledged punitive justice and control model, such as France and Germany, are also the last continental countries to dismantle their welfare systems. Countries that adopted a more liberal and curtailed welfare system, such as the United Kingdom and the Netherlands, have seen their detention rates skyrocketing.

A second factor is the gradual disappearance of unskilled labor from the economy and the emergence of a strong service sector. The new jobs require considerable training, flexibility, and adaptability to changing circumstances, and high verbal, social, and communication skills. Increasing interdependence among people and institutions requires a controlled environment, reliable and predictable interactions, and a rejection of the use of violence. This is why modern society stresses strong control of emotions, a more deliberate and rational approach to problems, and a strong emphasis on internalized moral norms of behavior. One result is high unemployment rates among those who cannot meet these requirements and increasing marginalization of specific population groups. Furthermore, to the extent that there is a discrepancy between the behavioral requirements of postindustrial society and individual skills to meet them, deviant and delinquent behavior may result.

Finally, mass immigration is a third important factor, both in North America and in western Europe. The United States and Canada have long been immigration countries. In the nineteenth century, most immigrants came from Europe, but since 1950 about 18 million immigrants, most of them of non-European origin, came to the United States. At the same time, Europe received 15 million immigrants, many of whom were recruited as unskilled factory workers (Yinger 1994). Immigration has never stopped, and there is a continuous flow of Third World laborers and asylum seekers to the Western world. The consequences are many. First, it is clear that they will affect the composition of the population. In Holland's big cities, the majority of children younger than fifteen belong to ethnic minorities. Similar trends are apparent in other big European cities, such as Paris and London. Second, changes in the labor market hit these groups particularly hard, with huge unemployment rates as a result. Third, a growing number of segregated and deteriorated city areas are emerging, housing an "underclass" population of mainly, though not exclusively, immigrants (Eisner 1997).

These changes undermine society's stability and social cohesion, producing widespread feelings of insecurity and fear. These feelings are projected on essentially two groups: a loosely defined group of ethnic minorities, including refugees and foreign laborers, and those who threaten social peace and social cohesion to an even higher degree, the deviant and the criminal.

Returning to Gurr's argument, where do we find now the social institutions that should educate and socialize these nonintegrated persons into behavioral conformity, adequate social functioning, and respect for the prevailing value system? The education system, in particular vocational training schools, which should prepare lower-class youths for the labor market and instill in them the necessary behavioral norms and values, has not been able to shift gears and seems to be incapable of meeting the challenge. Big factories have to a considerable extent disappeared. National military conscription, which played a useful role in offering additional training opportunities to unskilled youths, has been replaced by a professional army. The only norm-enforcing system that remains in full force and has the pretension to preserve social peace is the criminal and juvenile justice system. That system is increasingly intervening in people's lives, not just by detaining people, but also by extending its operations and control in the community. To the extent that social unrest, feelings of insecurity, and fear of the future remain prevalent, people will continue to expect the criminal justice system to pacify society and reestablish social cohesion. They will also continue to put pressures on the judiciary to punish and to put away those who are seen as disturbing social peace.

XI. Conclusion

Several conclusions may be drawn. First, there has been a clear shift from thinking in terms of welfare to thinking in terms of rights (Doek 2000). Examples with respect to the position of young people in law include a right of veto of fifteen-year-olds over cases of adoption (if the minor has objections, adoption procedures will be stopped; 1979); the right of twelve-year-olds to be heard by the juvenile judge in civil law procedures where their interests are at stake (e.g., in divorce cases; 1982); the right to complain, and appeal, in cases referring to the rights of furlough, correspondence, use of telephone, and receiving visits in judicial institutions (1984); and, the right to approach the juvenile judge informally with a request about the arrangement concerning parental access in divorce cases (its decision, modification, and termination).

Doek (2000) observes that the most important proposals for review in the 1995 act in reference to adult criminal procedures were the requirement of public hearings for juveniles and the absence of any obligation to appear in court. However, these have not been adopted. Alternative sanctions, however, as an instrument of realizing educational objectives, have been introduced. Although the legal position of juveniles in court has been reinforced in several respects, their welfare remains the ultimate objective of the law. In other words, there has been some shift in the juvenile's position from being an object of rights toward being a subject of rights. The approach clearly is less paternalistic, and there is more of an "equality of arms," but the fundamental welfare orientation of Dutch juvenile justice has been preserved (Doek 2000, p. 31). There is still a long way to go. Some reformers wish to formulate a right of protection and assistance in new legislation (Willems 1999), the establishment of an ombudsperson for children, permanent education programs for members of the youth police, youth prosecutors, and juvenile judges, and a periodic review of those who are placed in an institution on the basis of a civil measure.

It is likely that on the European level there will be a gradual harmonization of family law and other (protective and penal) legislation referring to children and youth, finally resulting in European legal principles and standards. In this respect one may refer to the European Convention on the Exercise of Children's Rights.

It is difficult to predict the future. Will Dutch juvenile (and adult) justice become increasingly repressive, or will there be a reaction to this trend and will conservative cultural forces, which embody traditional social welfare trends, prevail? If we can maintain a reasonable level of prosperity, create a sufficiently accessible labor market, and integrate young ethnic minority members into Dutch society, prospects are that cultural values of collective responsibility and care for delinquent, deviant youth, and children in need of protection, will remain vigorous.

REFERENCES

Anneveldt Commission. 1982. *Revision of the Legislation on Juvenile Justice*. The Hague: Ministry of Justice, Staatsuitgeverij.

Bac, J. R. 1995. "Het nieuwe Jeugdstraf(process)recht door de ogen van een kinderrechter." *Tijdschrift voor Familie- en Jeugdrecht* 17(9):199–201.

———. 1997. "De kinderrechter 75 jaar: Vitaal of terminaal?" *Delikt en Delin-kwent* 27(8):744–57.

Bartels, J. A. C. 1983. "Sanctierecht voor Jeugdigen." *Tijdschrift voor Familie-en Jeugdrecht* 6:105–16.

Boerman, Frank, Wil van Tilburg, and Martin Grapendaal. 2002. *Landelijke Criminaliteitskaart 1999: Aangifte- en Verdachten analyse.* Zoetermeer: Lande-lijk Korps Politiediensten.

Bol, M. W., and J. J. Overwater. 1984. *Dienstverlening: Eindrapport van het Onderzoek naar de vervanging van de vrijheidsstraf in het strafrecht voor volwas-senen.* The Hague: Ministerie van Justitie, Staatsuitgeverij.

Council of Europe. 1989. *Social Reactions to Juvenile Delinquency: Recommenda-tion no. R (87) 20.* Strasbourg: Council of Europe.

Defence for Children International. 2000. *Juvenile Justice: "The Unwanted Child" of State Responsibilities: An Analysis and Commentary of Juvenile Justice in the Concluding Observations of the UN Committee on the Rights of the Child.* Geneva: Defence for Children International.

Dekker, J. J. H. 1985. *Straffen, redden en opvoeden: Het ontstaan en de ontwikke-ling van de residentiële heropvoeding in West-Europa, 1814–1914, met bijzondere aandacht voor "Nederlandsch Mettray."* Assen: Van Gorcum.

Dekker, J. J. H., J. J. Dankers, and C. G. T. M. Leonards. 1997. "Van de Ba-taafse Republiek tot de Kinderwetten: Wezen, boefjes en verwaarloosde kinderen, 1795–1905." In *Wezen en Boefjes: Zes eeuwen zorg in Wees-en Kin-derhuizen,* edited by S. Groenveld, J. J. H. Dekker, and Th. R. M. Willemse. Hilversum: Verloren.

Doek, J. E. 2000. "Minderjarigen in het Recht." *Ars Aequi* 49 (1):24–33.

Eisner, Manuel. 1997. *Das Ende der Zivilisierten Stadt? Die Auswirkungen von Modernisierung und Urbaner Krise auf Gewaltdelinquenz.* Frankfurt and New York: Campus.

Etman, O., P. Mutsaers, and H. Werdmölder. 1993. "Onveiligheid en Allo-chtonen." In *Integrale Veiligheidsrapportage: Achtergrondstudies.* The Hague: Ministerie of Binnenlandse Zaken.

Grapendaal, M., P. P. Groen, and W. van der Heide. 1997. *Duur en Volume: Ontwikkelingen van de onvoorwaardelijke vrijheidsstraf tussen 1985 en 1995* (Length and volume: Trends in unconditional deprivation of liberty be-tween 1985 and 1995). The Hague: Centraal Bureau voor de Statistiek, Wetenschappelijk Onderzoek- en Documentatie Centrum.

Groenveld, S. 1997a. "De Republiek der Verenigde Nederlanden en haar Wezen, 1572–1795." In *Wezen en Boefjes: Zes eeuwen zorg in Wees- en Kin-derhuizen,* edited by S. Groenveld, J. J. H. Dekker, and Th. R. M. Willemse. Hilversum: Verloren.

———. 1997b. "Van late Middeleeuwen tot omstreeks 1572." In *Wezen en Boefjes: Zes eeuwen zorg in Wees- en Kinderhuizen,* edited by S. Groenveld, J. J. H. Dekker, and Th. R. M. Willemse. Hilversum: Verloren.

Gurr, Ted Robert. 1981. "Historical Trends in Violent Crimes: A Critical Re-view of the Evidence." In *Crime and Justice: An Annual Review of Research,* vol. 3, edited by Michael Tonry and Norval Morris. Chicago: University of Chicago Press.

————. 1989. "Historical Trends in Violent Crime: England, Western Europe, and the United States." In *The History of Crime*, vol. 1 of *Violence in America*, edited by Ted Robert Gurr. Newbury Park, Calif.: Sage.

Haan, W. de. 1993. *Beroving van voorbijgangers: Rapport van een onderzoek naar straatroof in 1991 in Amsterdam en Utrecht*. The Hague: Ministry of Internal Affairs.

HALT Nederland. 2000. *Review of HALT Measures, 1992–1999*. Leiden: HALT Nederland.

Hawkins, J. David, and Richard F. Catalano, Jr. 1992. *Communities That Care: Action for Drug Abuse Prevention*. San Francisco: Jossey-Bass.

Howell, James C. 1997. *Juvenile Justice and Youth Violence*. Thousand Oaks, Calif.: Sage.

Huls, F. W. M., M. M. Schreuders, M. H. ter Horst-van Breukelen, and F. P. van Tulder. 2001. *Criminaliteit en Rechtshandhaving 2000*. The Hague: Centraal Bureau voor de Statistiek, Wetenschappelijk Onderzoek- en Documentatie Centrum.

Hulst, H. van, and J. Bos. 1993. *Criminaliteit van geïmmigreerde Curaçaose jongeren*. Utrecht: Onderzoek Kollektief Utrecht.

Junger, Marianne. 1990. *Delinquency and Ethnicity: An Investigation on Social Factors Relating to Delinquency among Moroccan, Turkish, Surinamese and Dutch Boys*. Deventer: Kluwer Law and Taxation.

Junger-Tas, Josine. 1989. "Self-Report Delinquency Research in Holland with a Perspective on International Comparison." In *Cross-National Research in Self-Reported Crime and Delinquency*, edited by Malcolm W. Klein. Dordrecht: Kluwer.

————. 1996. "Youth and Violence in Europe." *Studies on Crime and Crime Prevention* 5(1):31–59.

————. 1997. "Ethnic Minorities and Criminal Justice in the Netherlands." In *Ethnicity, Crime, and Immigration: Comparative and Cross-National Perspectives*, edited by Michael Tonry. Vol. 21 of *Crime and Justice: A Review of Research*, edited by Michael Tonry. Chicago: University of Chicago Press.

Junger-Tas, Josine, Maarten J. L. F. Cruyff, Petra M. van de Looij, and Fred Reelick. 2003. *Etnische minderheden: Maatschappelijke integratie en Anti-sociaal gedrag*. The Hague: SDU Uitgevers.

Junger-Tas, Josine, Marianne Junger, Els Barendse-Hoornweg, and Marianne Sampiemon. 1983. *Jeugddelinquentie: Achtergronden en Justitiële Reactie*. No. 42. The Hague: Ministry of Justice.

Junger-Tas, Josine, and John N. van Kesteren. 1999. *Bullying and Delinquency in a Dutch School Population*. Leiden: E. M. Meijersinstituut.

Junger-Tas, Josine, Ineke Haen Marshall, and Denis Ribeaud. 2003. *Delinquency in an International Perspective: The International Self-Reported Delinquency Study (ISRD)*. New York and The Hague: Criminal Justice Press and Kugler Publications.

Junger-Tas, Josine, and A. A. van der Zee-Nefkens. 1980. *Preventieve hechtenis Minderjarigen*. Den Haag: Ministerie van Justitie, Staatsuitgeverij.

Kester, J. G. C., and Josine Junger-Tas. 1994. *Criminaliteit en Strafrechtelijke reactie: Ontwikkelingen en Samenhangen*. Arnhem: Gouda Quint.

Koens, Theo M. J. C. 1995. "Het nieuwe Jeugdstraf(proces)recht." *Tijdschrift voor Familie- en Jeugdrecht* 18(1):3–8.

Kruissink, Maurits, and Ad A. M. Essers. 2001. *Ontwikkeling van de Jeugdcriminaliteit: Periode 1980–1999.* Onderzoeknotities, no. 2001/3. The Hague: Wetenschappelijk Onderzoek- en Documentatie Centrum.

Laan, Peter H. van der. 1987. *Leerprojecten onderzocht: Eindrapport van het onderzoek Alternatieve Sancties.* The Hague: Coördinatie Commissie Wetenschappelijk Onderzoek Kinderbescherming.

———. 1991. *Experimenteren met Alternatieve Sancties voor Jeugdigen: Een onderzoek naar de invoering en resultaten van alternatieven in het jeugdstrafrecht.* Arnhem: Gouda Quint.

Laan, Peter H. van der, and A. A. M. Essers. 1990. *De Kwartaalcursus en Recidive.* Arnhem: Gouda Quint.

Leest, Judith. 2001. "Recht gedaan, recht gevoeld: Een zorgethisch argument voor herstelrecht." In *De straf voorbij: morele praktijken rondom het strafrecht*, edited by Hans Boutellier, Hart Kunneman, and Judith Leest. Amsterdam: SWP Uitgeverij.

Leonards, Chris. 1995. *De ontdekking van het onschuldige criminele kind: Bestraffing en opvoeding van criminele kinderen in jeugdgevangenis en opvoedingsgesticht 1833–1886.* Hilversum: Verloren.

Lewis, Chris. 2001. "Accreditation Procedures for Offender Programmes." Paper presented at the annual meeting of the European Society of Criminology, September 6–8, Lausanne, Switzerland.

Martinson, R. 1974. "What Works? Questions and Answers about Prison Reform." *Public Interest* 35:22–54.

Mijnarends, E. M. 1999. *Richtlijnen voor een Verdragsconforme Jeugdstrafrechtspleging, 'Gelijkwaardig maar minderjarig.'* Dordrecht: Kluwer Rechtswetenschappelijke publicaties.

———. 2001. "De betekenis van het Internationaal Verdrag inzake de Rechten van het Kind voor het Nederlandse jeugdstrafrecht." *Tijdschrift voor Familie- en Jeugdrecht* 23(11):302–7.

Ministry of Justice. 2002. "Vasthoudend en Effectief: Versterking van de aanpak van Jeugdcriminaliteit" (Perseverant and effective: An improved approach of juvenile crime). Memorandum to Parliament. Den Haag: Staatsuitgeverij en Drukkerij.

Pease, K., S. Billingham, and I. Earnshaw. 1977. *Community Service Assessed in 1976.* Home Office Research Study, no. 39. London: Her Majesty's Stationary Office.

Penders, J. 1980. *Om sijne Jonckheyt.* Utrecht: Rijksuniversiteit Utrecht.

Petersilia, Joan, and Susan Turner. 1990. "Comparing Intensive and Regular Supervision for High-Risk Probationers: Early Results from an Experiment in California." *Crime and Delinquency* 36:87–111.

———. 1991. "Evaluation of Intensive Probation in California." *Journal of Criminal Law and Criminology* 82:610–58.

President's Commission on Law Enforcement and Administration of Justice. 1967. *The Challenge of Crime in a Free Society: A Report.* Washington, D.C.: U.S. Government Printing Office.

Rooy, P. de. 1982. "Kinderbescherming in Nederland." In *Geschiedenis van Opvoeding en Onderwijs*, edited by B. Kruithof, J. Noordman, and P. de Rooy. Nijmegen: SUN.

Rothman, David J. 1990. *The Discovery of the Asylum: Social Order and Disorder in the New Republic*. Rev. ed. Boston: Little, Brown.

———. 1998. "Perfecting the Prison: United States, 1789–1865." In *The Oxford History of the Prison: The Practice of Punishment in Western Society*, edited by Norval Morris and David J. Rothman. New York and Oxford: Oxford University Press.

Ruller, S. van, and W. M. E. H. Beijers. 1995. "Trends in Detentie: Twee eeuwen gevangenisstatistiek." *Justitiële Verkenningen* 21(6):35–53.

Schegget, H. ter. 1976. *Het kind van de Rekening: Schetsen uit de voorgeschiedenis van de Kinderbescherming*. Alphen aan den Rijn: Samsom.

Schreuders, M. M., F. W. M. Huls, W. M. Garnier , and K. E. Swierstra. 1999. *Criminaliteit en Rechtshandhaving*. The Hague: Centraal Bureau voor de Statistiek, Wetenschappelijk Onderzoek- en Documentatie Centrum.

Smelser, Neil J. 1959. *Social Change in the Industrial Revolution: An Application of Theory to the Lancashire Cotton Industry, 1770–1840*. London: Routledge & Kegan.

Social and Cultural Planning Office. 2001. *The Netherlands in a European Perspective*. The Hague: Social and Cultural Planning Office.

Spaans, E. C. 1994. *Appels en Peren -Een onderzoek naar de recidive van dienstverleners en kortgestraften*. Arnhem: Gouda Quint.

———. 1995. *Werken of Zitten: De toepassing van werkstraffen en korte vrijheidsstraffen in 1992*. Arnhem: Gouda Quint.

Tonry, Michael. 1995. *Malign Neglect: Race, Crime, and Punishment in America*. New York: Oxford University Press.

———. 2001. "Why Are U.S. Incarceration Rates So High?" In *Penal Reform in Overcrowded Times*, edited by Michael Tonry. New York: Oxford University Press.

Vlis, Ingrid van der. 2001. *Leven in Armoede: Delftse Bedeelden in de Zeventiende Eeuw*. Amsterdam: Prometheus/Bert Bakker.

von Hirsch, Andrew. 1976. *Doing Justice: The Choice of Punishments; Report of the Committee for the Study of Incarceration*. New York: Hill & Wang.

Wiarda Commission. 1971. *Revision of the Legislation on Child Protection*. The Hague: Ministry of Justice, Staatsuitgeverij.

Willems, J. C. M. 1999. *Wie zal de Opvoeders opvoeden?* Den Haag: TMC Asser.

Wittebrood, K., and M. Junger. 1999. "Trends in Geweldscriminaliteit." *Tijdschrift voor Criminologie* 41(3):250–68.

Woude, A. M. van der. 1985. "Bevolking en Gezin in Nederland." In *De Nederlandse Samenleving sinds 1815: Wording en samenhang*, edited by F. L. van Holthoon. Assen: Van Gorcum.

Yinger, J. Milton. 1994. *Ethnicity: Source of Strength? Source of Conflict?* Albany: State University of New York Press.

Britta Kyvsgaard

Youth Justice in Denmark

ABSTRACT

Denmark, strictly speaking, does not have a juvenile justice system. The age of criminal responsibility is fifteen. Offenders younger than that are dealt with by social welfare authorities. Offenders aged fifteen and older are dealt with in regular criminal courts under the same laws, procedures (with a few exceptions), and circumstances as adults. In practice, the divide is not so sharp. Social welfare authorities can place children in secure institutions, though they seldom do so. Offenders under age eighteen benefit from a number of sentencing policies and options not available for adults. These include shorter sentences, diversion to the welfare authorities, and special sentencing options. Crime rates generally and for young offenders were stable or declining throughout the 1990s. Criminal justice policy generally and concerning young offenders has become increasingly politicized, and tougher laws and policies have been enacted. Owing, however, to the influence of international standards, renewing confidence in rehabilitative programs, and Danish skepticism about incarceration of young offenders, punishments for young offenders in the 1990s did not become markedly harsher, as enforcement of prison sentences declined.

Denmark is small in size and population. It comprises 43,000 square kilometers (twice the size of New Jersey) and has 5.4 million inhabitants. One-fifth live in the capital, Copenhagen, and another 9 percent live in the next three largest cities. Forty-five percent live in cities of under 10,000 inhabitants or in the countryside.

Denmark has long had many small political parties. Minority or coalition governments are the norm. Most governments since the Second World War have been led by Social Democrats. In November 2001, for the first time in seventy years, a right-wing coalition government,

Britta Kyvsgaard is chief of research, Ministry of Justice, Denmark.

which is not dependent on center parties but was able to form an entirely right-wing majority, took office. This has special importance for criminal justice policy. A center party, the Danish Social-Liberal Party, which supports very liberal criminal justice policies, long held the balance of power and resisted right-wing influence. This era has come to an end.

Denmark—like Norway and Sweden—has long been known for its advanced welfare programs. Today, however, many other European countries have caught up with the Scandinavian countries. In the case of Denmark, this results in part from cuts in welfare programs in the late 1970s and the 1980s owing to high unemployment rates. In mid-2002, the unemployment rate was 5.1 percent. Some parts of the welfare program, however, including maternity benefits and leave, have improved in recent years.

The Danish legal system is closely related to those of Norway, Sweden, Finland, and Iceland. This results both from informal, intimate contacts among the Nordic countries and from periods of political unification at various times in history. During the last century, close relationships among the Nordic countries have been maintained through intense cooperation in many fields and endeavors, and not least in relation to legal systems. For many years, until the beginning of the 1990s, a standing Nordic committee worked toward harmonization of penal codes. The affiliation of Denmark (in 1972) and Sweden and Finland (both in 1995) with the European Union (EU) has probably decreased Nordic cooperation, as Norway and Iceland are not members.

The Nordic legal systems bear greater resemblance to the civil law systems of Germany, France, and continental Europe than to the common-law systems of England and the United States (Tamm 1996). The Nordic systems do, however, differ in important respects from those in continental Europe. For instance, they tend to favor pragmatic solutions rather than decisions based strictly upon legal theory, and they exhibit relatively strong confidence in the welfare state. The Nordic legal systems are also characterized by a significant element of corporatism, since they look favorably upon the involvement of interest groups in decision-making processes.

In enacting penal law, legislation provides broad guidelines as opposed to detailed regulation. Government ministries then provide the more precise wording. All legal system officials and practitioners are appointed administratively. There are no political appointees.

As in many other countries, criminal policy has come to play an increasingly central role in partisan and ideological politics, especially during the last decade. Criminal justice policy previously to a high degree was framed by experts and nonpolitical committees. The politicians are now eager to play a much more central role. This has led to a growing number of legal changes aiming at more severe penalties, primarily for violent and sexual offenses.

Compared to criminal justice policy for adults, youth policy is characterized by greater tensions between ideas of punishment and of treatment or prevention. This difference is reflected in the history of youth justice and in current trends. A huge number of crime-preventive measures focus on young offenders and at-risk youth. At the same time, however, recent policies calling for more severe sanctions also apply to young offenders. The contradiction in youth justice is well illustrated by a newly introduced sanction for young offenders that includes both punitive and rehabilitative elements. More frequent and more intense discussions of proposals to lower the minimum age of criminal responsibility are threatening the stability of the youth justice system.

The most distinctive characteristic of Danish youth justice compared with other countries is that it has no separate system for juvenile justice. There are no special courts for young offenders above the age of criminal responsibility, and the status offense is an unknown concept. As in the other Nordic countries, the minimum age of criminal responsibility is fifteen years. Children under this age are handled by the social authorities, and the possibilities of legal system intervention are very limited. Juveniles above the age of criminal responsibility at the time of committing the offense are sentenced in accordance with the same criminal code as adult offenders and in the same courts. A number of special rules, sanctions, and measures aimed at offenders aged fifteen to seventeen, however, result in more lenient, and sometimes different, sanctions for young offenders. With a few exceptions, young adult offenders eighteen to twenty-one years old are treated like adult offenders.

Denmark's system can best be described as overlapping—combined with some special youth sanctions and measures. Young offenders between the ages of fifteen and seventeen are in many respects treated partly in accordance with the system for adult offenders and partly in accordance with the system for offenders under age fifteen, besides being subjected to dispositions and interventions aimed only at young offenders.

The most fundamental policies concerning youth justice are the rules limiting application of the full use of penalties and restrictive measures against juveniles and rules allowing special sanctions and measures. Both historically and at present, the age limits distinguishing the criminally responsible from those not criminally responsible, and young offenders from adult offenders, are of fundamental importance.

In Section I, I discuss the historical evolution of Danish youth justice. In Section II, I offer an overview of the crime situation in the last two decades with special emphasis on crime patterns among children, youth, and young adults in the 1990s. Sections III and IV discuss policies and practices affecting offenders under the age of criminal responsibility, and young offenders aged fifteen to seventeen. Section IV also discusses adult offenders aged eighteen to twenty-one. As youth justice involves both the social and the legal authorities, cooperation between these authorities, and cooperation between the different parts of the legal system, are essential to youth justice. This is discussed in Section V, which also gives an account of increasing efforts to improve this cooperation. In Section VI, I deal with the international conventions that are influencing the Danish legal system and have led to a number of changes concerning, inter alia, child prostitution and child pornography. Recent trends in youth justice and future perspectives are discussed in Section VII. I end by sketching some of the tremendous changes Danish youth justice might face if efforts toward EU harmonization in criminal justice policy are realized.

I. History

Stability is the most pronounced characteristic of the Danish system of handling youth crime over the last 100 years. Changes have been made, of course, but these are reflections of general changes in society and of the development of the welfare state rather than the results of independent and unconventional initiatives. The same is true of developments in child welfare, which mirror changes in views of education of children and the growth of the welfare state. Changes in this area are often familiar because they resemble or revive previously abandoned ideas and policies. Penal ideologies have moved back and forth between classical theory, with its focus on legal rights, and rehabilitative ideas, which focus on treatment-oriented sanctions and discretion. This is illustrated by the emergence of the youth prison system in the beginning of the past century, its closing down in the latter half of the century, and the reemergence of an essentially similar youth sanction at the beginning of the twenty-first century.

The history of youth justice is to a great extent the history of changes in age limits governing the intervention of the penal system in young people's lives. The present age of criminal responsibility, fifteen years, has been influential since the Middle Ages, although it has been an absolute age limit only since 1930 (B. Nielsen 1999).

A. Before the Twentieth Century

Before 1683 there was no minimum age of criminal responsibility for crimes committed against private victims. Children under fifteen years could not, however, except in case of homicide, be prosecuted by the authorities. Civil law suits were possible. If a private victim brought a case to court, the child could in principle be convicted in exactly the same way as an adult. More lenient sanctions, however, seem to have been used for children. Civil lawsuits were uncommon, and in practice fifteen years functioned as the minimum age of criminal responsibility (Løkke 1990).

The Law of 1683 did not change this system except that it introduced a minimum age of ten years for use of harsh punishment for homicide. For children under age ten, punishment for homicide was a fine.

In the late eighteenth century, practices toward offenders paralleled changes in other European countries. The penal system slowly shifted from the use of sporadic and symbolic public executions and cruel corporal punishments to imprisonment (Rømer 1969). Simultaneously, the aim of punishment shifted from general deterrence as the only purpose to multiple aims including reforming the offender. For children, this shift precipitated an increase in the number of prosecutions. In 1789, the age of responsibility for theft was lowered to ten years (Løkke 1990). For the first time, special sanctions for children between ten and fifteen years old were introduced in order to limit the application of harsh sentences to children. Children in this age group could be punished by birching and up to two years imprisonment with hard labor for theft, while children under ten years were not punished in practice.

In the mid-nineteenth century, further steps were taken that limited use of penal sanctions for children and juveniles. Ten years was set as the minimum age of criminal responsibility, while sentencing of children between ten and fifteen years depended on individual evaluations.

Children were to be punished only if they were evaluated to have been sufficiently mature to understand the criminal nature of the behavior (Greve 1996). Special sanctions for offenders fifteen to seventeen years old were introduced for the first time. Charges could be withdrawn if it was adjudged that the child could be reformed by the use of other measures (e.g., placement in a reformatory; Løkke 1990).

B. Child Welfare in the Twentieth Century

By the beginning of the twentieth century, individual assessments of amenability to punishment came to be seen as unsatisfactory and burdensome. In 1905, an absolute age limit of fourteen was introduced. Simultaneously, a child welfare law was introduced, based on the principle that children and juvenile offenders under eighteen years should be educated, not punished (Greve 1996). Child welfare committees were established. Reformatories were established for "erring and wicked children" and for young offenders. The new law gave the welfare committees authority to detain children on the basis of behavioral problems and neglect. The idea for child welfare committees came from Norway, where a similar arrangement was established in 1900 (Dahl 1985). New ideas on criminal policy and treatment of offenders, which emerged in Europe around the beginning of the twentieth century, also influenced policies concerning children and child welfare. These ideas developed from the positivistic school and led to changes in views of the offender and a move away from the classical penal ideology based strictly on ideas about proportionality.

The introduction of child welfare committees resulted not only from new ideas but also from social changes. It has been questioned whether child criminality really increased at that time or whether increasing poverty, especially in the cities, was seen as threatening and disturbing by the middle classes and their philanthropic organizations (Løkke 1990; Lützen 1998). The introduction of child welfare committees thus had two aims: to protect society and to facilitate interventions in poor children's lives.

The introduction of a child welfare system can also be seen as a reflection of the emergence of the welfare state. Modern social legislation began in the late nineteenth century and resulted in the recognition of legitimate demands for welfare support by more and more groups. The obligation of the state to monitor citizens and intervene in cases of child neglect and other social problems is, however, also a part of the welfare state. The child welfare law of 1905 resulted more in increased use of punitive measures than in increased help. Education in reformatories for the purported benefit of the child was the order of the day (Nielsen 1986; Wegener 1986; Løkke 1990; see also Dahl 1985).

In 1933, child welfare became a part of the general social services system. The emphasis on coercion was reduced. Preventive measures to reduce use of detention were given priority. Not, however, until 1958 did child welfare fundamentally come to be seen primarily as help and support rather than coercion. The main idea was and is that the overall view of state interventions in children's lives should be based on family policy and social education. A child is part of a family, and the most important aim of interventions is to help the child function in his or her own home environment. Cooperation with the parents and other social authorities is essential, and interventions must in general be provided on a voluntary basis and not be made compulsory (Wegener 1986).

Positivistic thinking emerging in Europe around the beginning of the twentieth century also affected criminal policy. Although Cesare Lombroso's research has been heavily criticized, ideas that arose from it greatly influenced thinking at that time and increased confidence in the possibilities of rehabilitating offenders. Lombroso's influence also depended upon widespread discontent with the classical penal systems of that time. Time had come for changes, and people were ready to grab new ideas.

Within penal law circles, new ideas spread through the Union Internationale de Droit Pénal, founded in 1888 by Franz von Liszt, the famous German scholar. A similar Danish union was founded in 1899, and the first meetings echoed the new trends in criminal policy (Dansk Kriminalistforening 1900; Garde 1999; Kyvsgaard 2001b).

These developments had a pronounced influence on the new Danish Criminal Code of 1930, which is still in force. The minimum age of criminal responsibility was then raised to fifteen years. The child welfare committees were seen as capable of dealing with fourteen-year-olds (B. Nielsen 1999). This age limit has remained unchanged since then.

The new criminal code introduced a number of special sanctions, which were based on treatment ideas and provided for partly or totally indeterminate sentences. For youth justice, it resulted in a youth prison sentence for juveniles between ages fifteen and twenty-one aimed at educating and training juveniles with criminal proclivities. The youth prison sanction was partly indeterminate—a minimum of one year and a maximum of three years, with extremes of up to four years for read-mitted offenders. The time of discharge was to depend not on the se-verity of the offense but on the juvenile's progress.

To be sentenced to youth prison, the juvenile had to be guilty of an offense that would otherwise result in a prison sentence for an adult offender. Arguments have been made over the extent to which propor-tionality should affect the use of youth prison. An official report from 1959 rejected the idea of further emphasis on proportionality, even though legal usage was in any case far from consistent with propor-tionality principles (Waaben 1962).

The youth prison sentence gave rise to a new type of prison. The ideology implied that juveniles should be educated in healthy sur-roundings. The preamble to the law asserted that "the construction and arrangement of the youth prison will take care that it will be healthy and well situated by a lake or the seashore and with sufficient land so that gardening and agriculture besides different trades can form part of the work which is learned and conducted" (Straffelovs-kommissionen 1917). Before 1930, only maximum-security prisons ex-isted, but during the 1930s and 1940s open prisons without walls and fences were established.

Although the youth prison sanction was meant only for juveniles in need of care and education, it gradually became the principal prison sentence for juveniles. At its peak in 1965, there were three open pris-ons, parts of two maximum-security prisons functioned as youth pris-ons, and 438 juveniles were serving youth prison sentences. This amounted to 85–90 percent of the average daily prison population of prisoners under age twenty-one.[1] Most youth prison sentences, how-ever, concerned offenders eighteen to twenty years old, as offenders under eighteen years generally had their charges withdrawn and were dealt with by child and youth welfare authorities. During the final de-cades of the existence of the youth prison sanction, it was increasingly used for juveniles under eighteen years old.

The youth prison sanction was abandoned in 1973 along with other special sanctions based on treatment ideas. Just as introduction of treatment-oriented sanctions followed international trends, so did

---

[1] The average number of offenders under twenty-one years old serving a prison sen-tence in 1965 is estimated from the number and the length of prison sentences for this age group.

their abolition. While "nothing works" ideas were important in opposition to the treatment ideology elsewhere, ideas of legal rights, fairness, and proportionality were more important in Denmark. Criticism of the indeterminate sentence in Denmark began in the early 1950s, long before publication of Martinson's (1974) article based on the report he wrote with Lipton and Wilks, which was finally published in 1975 (Lipton, Martinson, and Wilks 1975). Criticism was first offered by lawyers and jurists and later on by Norwegian criminologists Vilhelm Aubert, Nils Christie, and Thomas Mathiesen (see, e.g., Christie 1960; Aubert and Mathiesen 1962). Although studies showed high rates of recidivism following youth prison sanctions, criminological debate focused much more on the false analogy between illness and crime drawn by the treatment ideology.

Underlying the debate on indeterminate sanctions were a general criticism of total institutions and a trend toward deinstitutionalization. The work of, among others, Clemmer (1958) and Goffman (1961) had Scandinavian counterparts (e.g., Galtung 1959; Sundin 1970), which influenced discussions not only about prisons but also about other institutions. Later on, ideas about stigmatization and labeling intensified the criticism of total institutions. Criticism of treatment ideology and the indeterminate sentence was involved, but deinstitutionalization was the crucial point.

After the abandonment of the youth prison sanction in 1973, no legislation pertaining only to juveniles and young adults was adopted until 2001, when a new youth sanction, indicating a reemergence of treatment ideas, was introduced. I discuss this below. Criminal justice policy changes since 1973 mostly relate to increased use of community sanctions and measures, and concern age groups other than young offenders.

II. The Crime Situation
During the 1960s and 1970s the number of reported criminal offenses nearly tripled, in significant part because of an increase in youth offending. More recently, this situation has changed, and both the general crime level and youth crime have stabilized. This, however, has not caused the debates and concern about crime to stop. Focus has shifted to specific incidents, specific types of crimes (i.e., violent and sexual offenses), and crimes committed by particular groups, particularly ethnic minorities.

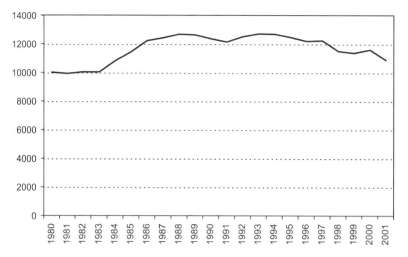

Fig. 1.—Number of reported criminal code offenses per 100,000 population over age fifteen years, 1980–2001. Source: Statistics Denmark, various years.

A. The General Level of Crime

The number of reported offenses has been stable for the last fifteen years, with a slight downward trend in the last few years. The number of reported crimes in 2001 was a bit lower than in 1985 (see fig. 1). The most important explanation for this is a demographic change; the birthrate decreased dramatically from 1966 to 1983, which means there are proportionately fewer young people in high-crime-rate years than in the 1960s and 1970s.

Criminal code offenses include primarily violent offenses, sexual offenses, property offenses, and serious drug offenses. Traffic offenses including drunken driving form part of the Road Traffic Act. Of all reported criminal code offenses, 95 percent are property crimes. Less than 1 percent are sexual offenses, and around 2 percent are violent offenses. In the early 1990s, the number of reported violent offenses increased somewhat but leveled off in the late 1990s. Victimization studies and studies on the inclination to report to the police indicate, however, that the number of violent offenses has been stable or even decreased (Rigspolitichefen 1998; Brink and Sørensen 2001). "Increasing violence" nonetheless has nearly constantly been in focus during the 1990s and has generated a number of political initiatives.

Trends in the imposition of penal dispositions (here including traffic law violations and other special law violations) in the different age

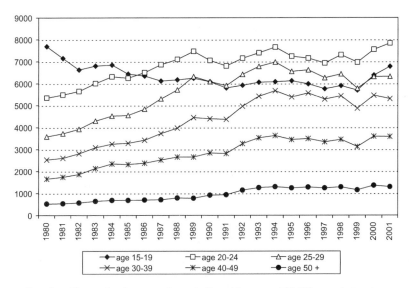

Fig. 2.—Change in the rate of penal dispositions per 100,000 population in age groups, 1980–2001. Source: Statistics Denmark, various years. Note: The rapid growth in the number of dispositions in most age groups from 1991–92 and again from 1999–2000 is caused by increases in the amount size of the fines imposed primarily for traffic law offenses. Until April 2001, the minimum amount for fines to be registered as a disposition was 1,000 DKK. By April 2001, the limit was raised to 1,500 DKK.

groups indicates that offending among persons aged twenty-five and older increased during the 1980s, while offending among juveniles aged fifteen to nineteen decreased. See figure 2. During the 1990s the number of dispositions remained stable for offenders under thirty years old and increased somewhat for offenders over this age.

B. Child Offenders

The number of registered crimes committed by children under age fifteen is probably somewhat unreliable, as crime records are not kept for children. When a child is apprehended for an offense, however, the police draw up a report, and statistics based on this are prepared. Due to problems of reliability, statistics on the number of crimes committed by children are not made public today. Since children cannot be prosecuted, it is not known to what extent children registered for an offense actually committed it.

Table 1 shows the total number of reported crime incidents involving children under fifteen years old during the 1990s. The numbers have fluctuated somewhat, and there is neither a clear upward nor a

TABLE 1

Number of Children Registered by the Police for Having Committed an Offense, by Type of Offense, 1990–2001
(Absolute Numbers)

	1990	1991	1992	1993	1994	1995	1996	1997	1998	1999	2000	2001
Violence	23	45	64	76	54	67	60	63	99	133	163	208
Burglary	741	601	526	336	385	256	240	211	182	108	173	165
Robbery	21	35	25	30	22	22	68	30	39	47	97	75
Joyriding	350	275	252	253	261	261	203	254	230	217	290	246
Shoplifting	674	1,038	1,194	1,374	1,285	1,261	1,344	1,271	1,490	1,550	1,794	1,310
Other offenses	973	993	1,074	1,038	924	927	763	644	798	784	992	959
All offenses except shoplifting	2,108	1,949	2,014	1,732	1,646	1,533	1,334	1,202	1,348	1,289	1,655	1,653
Total	2,782	2,987	3,208	3,106	2,931	2,794	2,678	2,473	2,838	2,839	3,449	2,963
Per 1,000 population	9	10	11	11	10	10	10	9	10	10	12	10

SOURCE.—The national police.
NOTE.—Population is defined as all children ten- to fourteen-years-old.

clear downward trend in crime prevalence among children. However, separate types of offenses, especially violence and to some extent robbery and shoplifting, show a tendency toward an increase, while joyriding and, in particular, burglary have decreased. The table also indicates that the number of children registered for shoplifting heavily influences the total number of registered crimes.

C. Young Offenders

The pattern is about the same for offenders aged fifteen to seventeen, as table 2 shows. Violence, robbery, and shoplifting have increased, while burglary has decreased. Sanctions for shoplifting have increased, especially since 1991–92. This is primarily due to changes in sanctions policy and not to changes in offending rates.[2] The last row in table 2 shows that the number of sanctions and measures per 1,000 population has increased somewhat despite a stable number of dispositions. This, as mentioned above, is due to the decrease in the number of youth (a decrease by 25 percent during the 1990s).

Shoplifting again plays an important role in trends in the number of sanctions and measures for youth. If shoplifting were left out, the number of sanctions and measures per 1,000 population was stable for juveniles during the 1990s, with an upward trend from 2000.

Homicide is rarely committed by young offenders, less than once per year on average. The number of rape cases is shown separately in the table as rapes committed by young immigrants have attracted much attention and significantly influenced the introduction of a new youth sanction.

D. Young Adult Offenders

The crime pattern since 1992 for offenders aged eighteen to twenty years is much more stable than for younger offenders, as table 3 shows. There is no clear pattern of increase for violence and robbery. The downward trend in burglary is pronounced. There is also a marked decrease in the number of shopliftings.

As the last row in table 3 shows, the number of dispositions per 1,000 population increased from 1992 to 1994 and has since then returned to the level at the beginning of the 1990s. The figures reflect a

---

[2] Until July 1991, around half of all charges for shoplifting were dropped and a warning was issued. By July 1, 1991, this practice was changed and instead a fine was imposed. Offenses not leading to a charge are not included in the table.

TABLE 2

Number of Dispositions concerning Criminal Law Offenses among Young Offenders, by Type of Offense, 1990–2001
(Absolute Numbers)

	1990	1991	1992	1993	1994	1995	1996	1997	1998	1999	2000	2001
Violence	271	264	264	380	482	493	424	407	441	482	693	748
Sexual offenses	13	20	21	22	19	34	19	28	19	28	39	23
Rape	2	3	2	2	3	9	0	3	5	6	11	2
Robbery	72	86	61	58	70	86	87	112	110	113	142	152
Burglary	867	716	705	517	534	512	451	434	322	297	299	318
Joyriding	355	259	284	311	333	394	359	405	341	365	340	345
Shoplifting	458	650	1,217	1,294	1,335	1,320	1,315	1,381	1,371	1,210	1,194	1,024
Other offenses	1,987	1,864	1,951	1,962	1,923	2,027	1,790	1,692	1,606	1,430	1,692	1,799
All offenses except shoplifting	3,567	3,212	3,288	3,252	3,364	3,555	3,130	2,871	2,844	2,721	3,205	3,385
Criminal code, total	4,025	3,862	4,505	4,546	4,699	4,875	4,445	4,252	4,215	3,931	4,399	4,409
Per 1,000 population	18	18	21	22	24	26	24	24	25	24	27	26

Source.—Statistics Denmark, various years.
Note.—The number of dispositions includes fine, withdrawal of charge, probation, and prison sentence.

TABLE 3

Number of Dispositions concerning Criminal Law Offenses among Eighteen- to Twenty-Year-Old Offenders, by Type of Offense, 1992–2001 (Absolute Numbers)

	1992	1993	1994	1995	1996	1997	1998	1999	2000	2001
Violence	680	829	1,069	909	858	889	830	862	852	997
Sexual offenses	33	30	33	42	27	34	24	35	33	38
Rape	4	5	3	4	6	7	3	7	4	6
Robbery	119	121	89	110	115	112	115	103	140	133
Burglary	1,108	1,087	958	829	804	662	601	504	474	486
Joyriding	360	434	521	500	540	551	514	452	362	403
Shoplifting	1,139	1,300	1,318	1,110	1,056	1,025	990	985	894	811
Other offenses	3,439	3,801	3,988	3,500	3,400	3,273	3,074	2,941	2,755	2,277
Criminal code, total	6,374	6,757	6,936	6,459	5,938	5,714	5,432	5,131	4,984	5,145
Per 1,000 population	28	31	32	30	29	29	28	27	28	30

Source.—Statistics Denmark, various years.

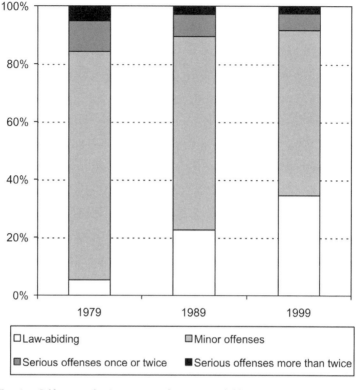

Fɪɢ. 3.—Self-reported crimes among fourteen- and fifteen-year-olds in 1979, 1989, and 1999 (percent). Source: Balvig 2000.

decrease in the number of eighteen- to twenty-year-olds during the 1990s, down 23 percent from 1992 to 2001.

E. Self-Reported Crime

Research on self-reported crime among adolescents (fourteen to fifteen years old) shows declines in both the number of juveniles engaging in crime and the number of juveniles committing serious offenses. The former pattern is especially pronounced (see fig. 3). The studies show that while the number of youth who have committed serious offenses has decreased, the incidence rate is higher because they tend to commit more offenses. Serious offenses include car theft, burglary, and robbery. Minor offenses include, among others, shoplifting, theft of bicycles, and vandalism. The studies thus reveal an increased polarization in crime prevalence and frequency among juveniles. Similar patterns of increased polarization are found in the lifestyles of juveniles and in school life (Kyvsgaard 1992; Balvig 2000).

The decrease in prevalence among juveniles has been explained by demographic changes. Small cohorts face different and better life circumstances than do bigger cohorts and children of large families (Kyvsgaard 1992). The decrease has also been attributed to an increased tendency among youth to focus more on future opportunities and to view crime as risky behavior (Kyvsgaard 1992; Balvig 2000). Finally, intensified crime preventive measures may also have diminished the number of minor thefts (Balvig 2000).

F. Ethnic Minorities

Denmark has long been very homogeneous. Since the 1970s, this has gradually changed. In the mid-1980s, 3.5 percent of the total population had a non-Danish heritage. This number had increased to 7.4 percent in 2000.

Since the beginning of the 1990s, crimes committed by immigrants, especially second-generation immigrants, have attracted considerable attention. Eleven percent of all convicted persons in 2000 had a non-Danish heritage, which amounts to a 47 percent overrepresentation relative to their presence in the population (Kyvsgaard 2002b). For the small group of second-generation immigrants, however, the overrepresentation is more than 100 percent, and for violent offenses it is even bigger. Violence, especially gang-related violence committed by juveniles from ethnic minorities, and so-called group rapes, also committed by foreign juveniles, have attracted considerable attention in the media and overshadowed the fact that most rapes and violent offenses are committed by persons of Danish heritage.

The overrepresentation of ethnic minorities in the crime statistics is largely due to demographic differences and to the poorer social and economical conditions characterizing many non-Danish residents. When differences in gender, age, and socioeconomic status are controlled for, the 49 percent higher prevalence rate among males with a non-Danish background falls to 8 percent (Kyvsgaard 2002a). Moreover, research indicates that ethnic minorities are probably monitored more closely by the police than other groups, as they more often have charges dismissed and more often are arrested without subsequent convictions (Kyvsgaard 2001a). Overrepresentation in the crime statistics might thus also be a result of a higher probability of detection.

III. Reactions toward Child Offenders

The age of criminal responsibility is based on the principle that liability to punishment should depend on the offender's level of maturity. The offender should be able to understand the nature and reprehensibility of the act and to understand and foresee the consequences. Furthermore, in Denmark it is generally believed to be inhumane and unjustifiable to apply harsh and severe sentences to children. The minimum age of criminal responsibility of fifteen years in Denmark means that a child under age fifteen who commits a crime cannot be prosecuted or punished. The legislation and guidelines for measures that can be taken in case of child criminality are presented below.

A. The Police

The police can investigate cases in which children are involved in order to clarify the scope of the crime, to ascertain whether other persons were involved, and to confiscate stolen goods. Children under the age of fifteen who are suspected of a criminal offense may be detained, provided that the conditions for arrest are met and that detention is found necessary in order to clear up the case. Detention may, however, not take place in a jail or a prison. Detained children must be placed in an ordinary office. Detention must be terminated as soon as possible and must not exceed what is absolutely necessary in view of the inquiries. Handcuffs and similar means of force may not be applied.

When a child is detained, a representative from the local social authorities is summoned. The child's parents are also notified. The social authorities of the municipality of the child's residence will be notified if the crime or other circumstances indicate that the child is in need of social care. The social authorities will then decide whether further steps should be taken. In the event of trivial offenses committed by "normal" children, the case is not referred to the social authorities and thus does not lead to social intervention.

B. Social Intervention

Social legislation authorizes a wide range of options that may be used when a child is assessed to be in need of help. It is important to emphasize that the choice of options used—at least in principle—depends only on the situation of the child and not on the seriousness of the crime committed. Proportionality between the seriousness of the alleged offense and the social intervention is thus not relevant, because interventions are supposed to be for the benefit of the child.

Among the options are improvements in the situation of the child, including that the child must regularly attend and participate in a supervised activity such as a sports team, youth club, or educational program. The local authority can also provide practical, educational, or other support in the home, including family therapy. Moreover, a personal adviser or a person who can give the juvenile support can be appointed. In certain cases, financial support can be granted to the parent, for instance, to avoid an out-of-home placement.

Besides these preventive measures, children and juveniles may also be placed in an institution, a foster family, or another approved place of residence. In most cases, this is done with the consent of the parents. In case of denial of consent and when there is an "obvious" risk that the child might suffer severe injuries due to the home situation, the child's abuse problems, criminal behavior, or other adjustment problems, an out-of-home placement can be effected without the consent of the parents. While the social authorities can decide on placements about which the parents agree, placements without the consent of the parents must be brought before a local committee composed of three politicians from the local council, a judge, and a child expert. This committee has the authority to reject the recommendation. If the committee approves the recommendation, the decision can be appealed by the parents. Slightly less than 10 percent of all residential placements are carried out without the consent of the parents.

It is also possible to use secure accommodations—buildings in which the outer doors and windows can be locked constantly—for children and juveniles. The secure institutions fall within the sphere of the social authorities, and the staff have, as with other social institutions for children and juveniles, socioeducational training.

Children and juveniles can be placed in secure accommodations in order to prevent self-inflicted damage or damage toward others. Secure accommodations may also be used when it is essential for making observations and obtaining information needed for further steps, and finally also when the observations demonstrate that it is imperative to implement a treatment in secure surroundings. For children under fifteen years, placements in secure settings are rare occurrences, and they may be held in secure accommodations only for two months. Juveniles over fifteen years may be placed in secure buildings for a maximum of fourteen months. In 2002, secure accommodations existed for eighty-five persons.

Figure 4 shows the number of out-of-home placements for children aged twelve to fourteen years from 1982 to 2000. It is not possible to

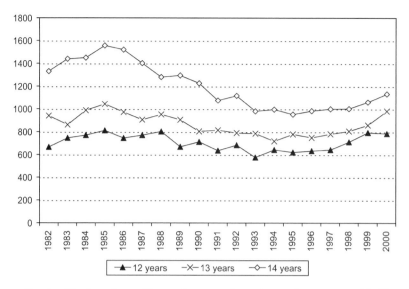

F<small>IG</small>. 4.—Number of out-of-home placements for twelve- to fourteen-year-olds, December 21, 1982, to 2000 (absolute numbers). Source: Statistics Denmark, various years.

say to what extent these measures are initiated due to crimes committed by the children. Crime is seen as a signal of trouble, but interventions are seldom implemented only because of crimes, as other circumstances must also indicate a need of help. Statistics on child welfare do not report the number of measures initiated on the basis of criminality. At the end of 2000, nearly 1,800 boys aged twelve to fourteen were placed outside their homes. This amounts to nineteen per 1,000 population. Placement in foster families is most common. Around one-fourth of the placements are in institutions.

IV. Reactions toward Young Offenders

The ordinary system of penal sanctions applies to juveniles above the age of responsibility. This includes the rules of the criminal code and the provisions of the Danish Administration of Justice Act on criminal prosecution, including investigation, prosecution, and court proceedings. A number of special rules on sentencing apply to offenders under the age of eighteen.

A. The Pretrial Situation

As with child offenders, the police must summon a representative from the local social authorities to attend interrogations of young offenders, but there are no age-specific rules or limitations concerning apprehension. Pretrial detention, that is, arrest exceeding twenty-four hours, is also applicable for young offenders, though substitutes to the normal remand prisons are generally used in these cases. The substitute is the secure accommodations facilities mentioned above.

Solitary confinement is allowed even for young offenders, but recently the practice has become more restricted. The Supreme Court in 1999 stated that it may be used only in quite exceptional cases. Juveniles cannot be held in solitary confinement for more than eight consecutive weeks. Solitary confinement is typically used in case of collusion, that is, when there is risk that the offender will destroy evidence or influence witnesses if not kept totally isolated. In 2001, solitary confinement was used only once for a young offender. A seventeen-year-old suspect charged with robbery was held in solitary confinement for fifteen days.

B. Legal Proceedings

Most young offenders under eighteen years do not go to court; cases typically result in a ticket fine or a withdrawal of charge.[3] Juveniles are dealt with in the same courts as adult offenders, and demands concerning segregation from older offenders are not made. Sittings are ordinarily open to the public, but judges have authority to decide under the circumstances of particular cases that proceedings against offenders under age eighteen should be held behind closed doors.

C. Sentencing

The criminal code includes several provisions that limit use of severe sentences for young offenders. These limitations result from the same principle influencing the limits on responsibility: human beings should not be exposed to harsh and possibly harmful penalties unless their age and maturity are such that they can fairly be deemed responsible adults.

The most important provision limiting the use of punishment for young offenders is section 84 of the criminal code, which provides that punishment prescribed by the code may be reduced if the offender was not yet eighteen at the time of the offense. The provision also includes a general maximum limit for punishment regardless of the offense: the punishment for young offenders may not exceed a prison sentence of

---

[3] Ticket fines are fines handed out by the police and accepted by the offender without going through a court trial.

eight years. It further follows from the criminal code (sec. 81) that re-cidivism should have an effect on sentencing only if the previous crime was committed after the offender had attained the age of eighteen.

Most provisions of importance to youth crime pertain to young of-fenders. One provision, however, includes offenders up to their twenty-first birthday. Section 91 of the criminal code provides that persons under the age of twenty-one can be sentenced to a fine even when the law does not authorize a fine. Originally this provision was motivated by the desire to limit the right of an employer to dismiss apprentices in case of offending. If the offender was sentenced to a fine, dismissal could not take place.

In general, young age is thus seen as an important mitigating cir-cumstance in fixing the sentence.[4] Beyond this, the fundamental princi-ple for sentencing, proportionality, also pertains to young offenders.

D. Sanctions and Measures

Besides the general provisions limiting sentences because of offend-ers' young ages, several special sanctions and measures exist for young offenders.

Withdrawal of charge, which is of special relevance for young of-fenders, is not, formally speaking, a sanction as it is decided by the public prosecutor and not by a court. It must, however, be regarded as a penal disposition; a withdrawal of charge to which conditions are attached functions in many ways like a suspended sentence or, as it is called in many countries, probation.

If the offender has made an unqualified confession, one that can be confirmed from the evidence, the public prosecutor may withdraw the charge on certain conditions. In general, withdrawal of charge is con-ditional upon the offender not committing a punishable act for a pe-riod of up to (normally) three years. If the offender does not comply with this condition, the case can be reopened and a punishment can then be imposed. The same goes for noncompliance with other condi-tions. It is the public prosecutor who decides whether to reopen the case.

There are distinct possibilities of withdrawing charges against sus-

---

[4] There is one exception to this general trend. A recent amendment to the Traffic Act states that if a person drives under influence within two years after having acquired the driving license the penalty will be harsher than for other drunken drivers. In practice, this will mostly apply to persons aged eighteen to twenty (eighteen years is the minimum age for acquiring a driving license).

pects who were under the age of eighteen at the time of the offense. In such cases, conditions must be stipulated, and these can be similar to the measures authorized by social legislation for children under fifteen years old. Conditions may also include payment of a fine or may correspond to the conditions available with a suspended sentence. Among the latter, supervision is a standard condition, which may be combined with other conditions like submission to drug or alcohol abuse treatment. All conditions must be approved by the court.

In 1998, the so-called youth contract was introduced. This is a new type of condition for young offenders. The offender, his or her parents, and the social authorities prepare and sign a contract, which typically obliges the offender to participate in certain activities, for instance, to finish a training program. The contract must be approved by the court. The youth contract was introduced to allow a quicker response in case of crime and to achieve a more perceptible and constructive reaction, as it was felt that withdrawal of charge was too lenient and was perceived by offenders as having no consequences. Noncompliance with the youth contract was thus to be met with a firmer attitude. Noncompliance to conditions, except for the condition of not reoffending, however, seldom leads to formal reactions, let alone a new sanction. The new condition does not seem to have speeded up the response time markedly (Høgelund 1993; Kyvsgaard 2000).

The fine is the most common sanction in Denmark. Fines for young offenders are usually set at lower amounts than for adult offenders. Traffic code offenses generally result in a fine of half the normal amount in case of a young offender. If a fine is not paid, a sentence in lieu in the form of imprisonment may come into play. This, however, does not apply to persons under age eighteen.

Suspended sentence is, in accordance with the general rules for sentencing young offenders, used relatively often, for instance, in cases when a withdrawal of charge is not possible due to serious or repeated offenses. The main condition attached to a suspended sentence is supervision, but offenders may also, as in the case of a withdrawal of charge, be dealt with in ways authorized by social legislation. Supervision is handled by the social authorities if the offender is under eighteen years, and by the Probation Service for older offenders and in case the supervision period exceeds the offender's eighteenth birthday.

Community service is rarely used for criminal code offenses and is not of special interest for young offenders since youth does not facilitate access to community service. Regular restorative justice measures are not now used by the Danish penal system, but an experiment on victim-offender mediation is underway and will probably result in a permanent arrangement. The Danish experiment uses mediation not as an alternative to a sanction but as a supplement to the usual sentence. The judge may take participation in mediation into consideration, but it need not affect sentencing.

It can be argued that the principles underlying restorative justice have long been part of the Danish penal system. The Danish Criminal Code of 1930 in section 84 mentions among mitigating circumstances freely and voluntarily averting the damage caused by the crime, fully restoring the damage caused by the crime, and otherwise freely and voluntarily making efforts to prevent the completion of the crime or to restore the damage caused by it.

Imprisonment may be imposed on offenders under age eighteen at the time of the crime for up to a maximum of eight years. As a result of the restrictions in using severe punishment for young offenders, imprisonment is seldom used, and when it is, alternative ways of serving the sentence must be considered. These include the following.

A 1973 amendment to the criminal code authorizes the possibility of serving a sentence in an alternative way, that is, serving the sentence in an institution or other place outside the prison system. This possibility is now part of the new Act on Enforcement of Sentences. A person may serve the whole or a part of a prison sentence in a hospital, in family care, or in an institution if the person is in need of special nursing or care or in case of other special circumstances like advanced age or bad health. The 1973 amendment is consistent with many prison reforms adopted at that time that aimed at "opening up the prisons" by giving prisoners access to leaves and furlough and by giving the families of the prisoners more opportunities to visit the prisoner in the prison.

The option of permitting someone to serve a sentence in an alternative way was not used before 1978 and until 1988 was used in only a few cases. Since then, and not least due to the ratification of the UN Convention on the Rights of the Child in 1991, the frequency with which young offenders are allowed to serve a sentence in an alternative way has increased. In 2001, it was made mandatory that convicted offenders under eighteen years of age must serve an imposed prison sentence in an alternative way unless particular considerations, such as the dangerousness of the convicted person, argue against it.

The Prison and Probation Service decides about these cases, while the local probation center assists in planning the alternatives. The length of the prison sentence determines the length of the stay in the alternative institution, but there are no limitations on the length of a sentence served alternatively.

During the stay in the institution, the local probation center, which also oversees the fulfillment of obligations by the offender, supervises the young offender. In cases of noncompliance, such as unauthorized departure from the treatment institution to which the person has been committed, the offender can be returned to a prison to serve the sentence.

Parole is widely used. Approximately 80 percent of all inmates with a minimum sentence of three months or more are released on parole, in most cases after having served two-thirds of the sentence but sometimes earlier. There is no special statutory application of parole for young offenders, but it is safe to assume that parole is more frequently used for young offenders than for older ones. Parole may imply supervision, which normally lasts for one year. Young offenders under age eighteen are supervised by the social authorities while the Probation Service handles older offenders. The rules on parole also apply to sentences served in an alternative way.

A new youth sanction, intended for offenders under the age of eighteen, was introduced on July 1, 2001. It was precipitated by a number of serious crimes, mostly rapes, committed by young offenders. Politically these crimes demanded action, particularly because the effectiveness of the existing sanctions was questioned.

The new sanction is different from other sanctions in that it is decided by a judge but is implemented by the social authorities. It consists of three phases, which altogether last two years. It begins with a placement in secure accommodations, followed by a placement in a normal—open—residential institution. Altogether the placements in institutions may not exceed 1.5 years, of which a maximum of one year may be in secure accommodations. The last phase is aftercare or supervision in freedom, the length of which depends on the time spent in institutions. The offender is subject to intensive socioeducational treatment and training during all three phases.

The new youth sanction is meant for young offenders who have committed serious offenses. Like the old youth prison sanction, the principle of proportionality is not applicable even though it is said in the preamble to the amendment that it is expected to be an alternative to prison sentences between one month and 1.5 years. Like the old youth prison sanction, the maximum length of the sanction can be pro-

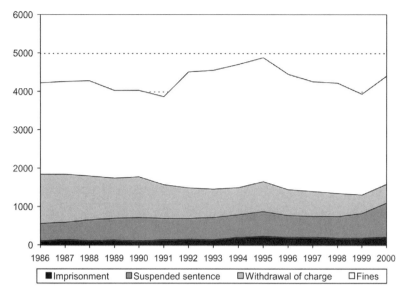

FIG. 5.—Sanctions for criminal code offenses for offenders fifteen to seventeen years old by type of sanction, 1986–2000 (absolute numbers, cumulated). Source: Statistics Denmark, various years.

longed in case of new offenses. The maximum prolongation is six months. And like the old youth prison sanction, the purpose of the new sanction is twofold: to rehabilitate and to incapacitate. The new sanction was imposed approximately fifty times in its first year.

E. Statistics on Sanctions and Measures

Figure 5 shows sentences imposed on Danish youth from 1986 to 2000. Five percent of sanctions for young offenders in 2000 were prison sentences, 20 percent were suspended sentences, 11 percent were withdrawals of charge, and the remaining nearly two-thirds were fines. For offenders over seventeen years, the corresponding figures were 22 percent prison, 21 percent suspended sentences, 5 percent withdrawals of charge, and 53 percent fines. Fines and withdrawals of charge are thus more frequently used for young offenders, and most fines are ticket fines.

Prison sentences imposed on young offenders are shorter than for adults, even though prison sentences for young offenders typically embrace offenses for which the juvenile previously has been given a withdrawal of charge or a suspended sentence. In 2000, the average length

TABLE 4

The Number of Young Offenders (Fifteen- to Seventeen-Years-Old)
Sentenced to Imprisonment and Serving Alternative Sentences,
1991–99

	1991	1992	1993	1994	1995	1996	1997	1998	1999
Sentenced to imprisonment	51	69	70	91	113	105	111	111	89
Serving in an alternative way	10	23	27	44	55	53	58	75	60
Actually imprisoned	41	46	53	47	58	52	53	36	29

SOURCE.—Ekspertgruppen om ungdomskriminalitet 2001.

of the prison sentence was 4.4 months for young offenders compared to 6.5 months for older offenders. No sentence for a juvenile exceeded three years.

The number of prison sentences imposed on young offenders increased somewhat in the 1990s due to both an increase in robberies and violence by juveniles and harsher sentences for violence. Withdrawals of charge have been declining for many years. While 40 percent of all sanctions for offenders under eighteen years in 1980 were withdrawals of charge, this had fallen to 11 percent in 2000. The penal system seems to have lost faith in this sanction even though, as mentioned, an attempt to revive it was made in 1998.

The Prison Service keeps a record of the number of juveniles under age eighteen who have served a prison sentence during a given year. These statistics are not totally comparable with the statistics on the number of youth sentenced to imprisonment. The numbers shown in the Prison Service statistics are somewhat lower. This is because of differences in age at recording time and that some sentences are served during pretrial detention. Table 4, however, gives an impression of the extent to which alternatives to prison are used for young offenders.

The number of juveniles serving prison sentences in an alternative way has increased substantially since the ratification of the UN Convention on the Rights of the Child in 1991. During spring 2001, a combination of imprisonment and the serving of the sentence in an alternative institution was authorized, thereby enabling those who were not allowed to serve a sentence in an alternative way in the first instance to be transferred to an institution outside the prison system

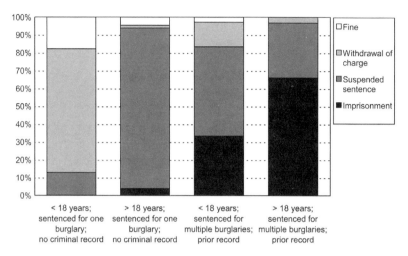

Fig. 6.—Sanctions for burglary in public buildings for offenders under and over age eighteen. Source: Kyvsgaard 2002*a*.

after some time. Service of a sentence in an alternative way was made mandatory in 2001 though exceptions are allowed.

Figure 6 gives a more specific picture of the significance of age in the sanction policy. The figure is based on a study on sentencing in 1996–2000 in which the numbers and types of offenses included in the sentence and previous convictions, if any, are controlled for (Kyvsgaard 2002*a*). The average lengths of prison sentence for burglars sentenced for multiple burglaries and who have a record are forty days and four months, respectively, for persons under and over eighteen years.

Figure 6 illustrates a core characteristic of the Danish system. Young offenders are often sentenced the same way as adults, but the sentences are less severe.

V. Cooperation between Authorities
Cooperation between authorities generally has increased, mostly because of problems and frustrations resulting from earlier failures of integration of efforts of different authorities. The initiative to increase cooperation was taken by the Danish Crime Prevention Council, which was established in 1971. As a major part of its work relates to preventive work among children and young people, it took, in 1975, the initiative to promote cooperation among authorities at the local level in order to combat and prevent crime among children and juve-

niles. The result was the so-called SSP cooperation—among the local School and Recreation Administration (S), the local Social and Health Administration (S), and the local police (P). Today most municipalities (92 percent) have set up a local SSP committee. The type and extent of cooperation vary greatly among municipalities. Some have engaged special staff who work only on crime prevention and have undertaken a wide range of activities and measures. Other municipalities have set up the committee but have taken few initiatives.

The SSP system has led to debate about exchanges of information among the participating authorities. The Administrative Act of 1987 demands professional secrecy between administrative authorities on confidential matters. The central controversy concerns the role of the police and the extent to which they are allowed to make investigative use of information obtained through SSP cooperation. The result was a Solomonic solution: an amendment to the Administration of Justice Act in 1990 stating that exchange of information on individuals may take place when necessary for crime preventive work but that information may not be exchanged in relation to investigation of criminal cases.

A new field for SSP cooperation has recently developed as the scope of cooperation has broadened in order also to focus on crime problems among eighteen- to twenty-four-year-olds. Efforts in this field concentrate on training and job possibilities.

Within the criminal justice system, cooperation between different authorities has long taken place because of overlap in fields of responsibility. The social authorities must be informed and participate whenever the police want to interrogate a person under eighteen years of age, and the police must be able to bring young offenders to the social authorities day and night. The social authorities also must participate in preparation of court cases by evaluating what type of conditions will be suitable in case of a withdrawal of charge or a suspended sentence. Participation is also required in case of a youth sanction. On January 1, 2001, an amendment to the Social Service Act was implemented under which the local social authorities must prepare plans to prevent reoffending in cases of violence or other serious crimes by offenders under eighteen years. Another 2001 amendment requires the plans to be ready within seven days after police documents are received. As the social authorities supervise all offenders under age eighteen, including withdrawals of charge, suspended sentence, and parole, the social authorities report to police in cases of noncompliance with conditions.

Along with the introduction of the new youth sanction, a small survey was conducted on interaction between the police and the social authorities. The survey showed that in many instances the cooperation functioned well but that cooperation could not be characterized as optimal. Municipalities that have worked out procedures and set up a joint council are generally content with cooperation. More and more local initiatives are being taken in order to develop cooperation between authorities and to make it more effective; so, too, with cooperation between the Prison and Probation Service and the social authorities. Cooperation is the new mantra.

In 1998, the Prison and Probation Service introduced guidelines for cooperation with the social authorities. As both parties must prepare a plan of action for the offender/client and as most clients of the Prison and Probation Service also are clients of the social welfare system, it can only make sense to cooperate and to coordinate efforts. As for young offenders, the guidelines recommend that cooperation start early in the course of a criminal career and that plans of action drawn up by the two authorities be harmonized whenever a young offender is facing a prison sentence.

An interim evaluation carried out in 2000 showed that agreements concerning cooperation were drawn up in more than half of the municipalities. A final evaluation is expected in 2003.

VI. International Conventions

International conventions are increasingly influencing national policy. The UN Convention on the Rights of the Child has been important for Danish efforts to diminish the extent to which young offenders serve prison sentences. The UN Convention and other international conventions and agreements have also influenced other legislation regarding children and juveniles.

In order to protect children from sexual exploitation, patronage of prostitutes under the age of eighteen was criminalized in 1999. This was in response to the UN Convention on the Rights of the Child and to the UN congress against commercial sexual exploitation of children held in Stockholm in 1996, which committed governments to take initiatives to combat, inter alia, child prostitution (Lautrup 2002). New laws on child pornography in 1994, followed by an amendment in 2000, broadened the scope of the law on child pornography and increased sentences. This also related to the UN Convention and the Stockholm congress. In 2002, an amendment concerning trafficking in human beings was implemented in order to, inter alia, ratify the Additional Protocol to the UN Convention on the Rights of the Child of 2000. The amendment contains a special provision on trafficking in children with the intent of sexual exploitation.

In 1999 as a result of the Stockholm congress, the International Labor Organization adopted Convention Number 182 concerning the Prohibition and Immediate Action for the Elimination of the Worst Forms of Child Labor. As a direct consequence, Danish law was enacted in 2000 prohibiting the use of children under eighteen years as porn models.

On a general level, cooperation between the Nordic countries on criminal justice policy played an important role during the twentieth century. For many years, a standing Nordic committee worked toward harmonization of penal codes. This effort has also influenced youth justice. In the late twentieth century, Nordic cooperation ceased, and attention focused more on international and European matters. The European Convention on Human Rights, which was incorporated into the Danish Law in 1992, is essential. A white paper *On the Incorporation of Human Rights in the Danish Law* was submitted in 2001, and it proposes also to incorporate into Danish law the International Covenant on Civil and Political Rights, the International Convention on the Elimination of All Forms of Racial Discrimination, and the Convention against Torture and Other Cruel, Inhuman or Degrading Treatment and Punishment (Betænkning no. 1407 2001).

VII. Recent Trends and Future Perspectives in Youth Justice

It is hard to separate recent trends in youth justice policy from prognostications about the future. Many recent trends will probably become more pronounced.

In criminal justice policy, the most distinct recent trend can best be characterized as diversification in relation both to the penal system and to crime preventive initiatives. Especially within crime prevention, there has been an explosion in different types of initiatives and measures. Most are directed at juvenile offending. Chairman Mao's adage about letting a thousand blossoms blossom seems to guide present efforts in youth justice.

As a result of the tendency to diversify, more emphasis is put on measures taken by the social authorities, and the social authorities are to an increasing extent participating in the enforcement of sentences. The tendency in child welfare in recent decades to deinstitutionalize has stopped, and reinstitutionalization is taking place.

This trend, which implies increased differentiation between the juvenile and adult systems, coincides with what might seem a contradictory trend—limitations in the adult justice system on use of one special youth sanction—withdrawal of charge. This, however, must be seen as a result from efforts to increase effectiveness, the guiding principle for current criminal justice policy.

The enormous number of changes in recent years results in part from a change in actors. As in many European countries, criminal justice policy has become a more central issue for politicians, and this influences the rate as well of the types of reforms and legal changes.

To understand recent trends in criminal justice policy, other developments must be taken into account. One is immigration and a focus on crimes committed by immigrants and their descendants. Another is a new moralism, which emphasizes weak victims and the viciousness of crimes toward children and women. Whether the point really is about moralism can, of course, be questioned. Probably it is related to what a Danish historian has described as a swing in our self-knowledge from an offensive to a defensive understanding (Jensen 1998). The narrative of the hero is being replaced by the story of the victim, and the possibility that any of us can be victims is an important underlying theme. Similar ideas are found in Ulrich Beck's book *Risk Society* (1994).

Finally, I touch on what has been called the Europeanization of criminal law. At present the EU has limited influence on national criminal justice policies, but there are advocates of a common criminal law and even of harmonization of sentences.

A. Diversification

The abandonment of treatment ideas in the beginning of the 1970s led to a revival of classicism in countries like Sweden and Finland, now in the form of neoclassicism, while in Denmark it was not succeeded by any formal ideological changes. However, an increased emphasis on alternatives to imprisonment can be seen as a result of rejection of the treatment ideology; the harmful and destructive effects of imprisonment were an important part of this criticism. Thus, in 1975 a Danish committee on alternatives to imprisonment was appointed, thereby keeping abreast of the Council of Europe, which in 1976 recommended increased use of alternatives to imprisonment.

The increased focus on alternatives offered a welcomed extension in the number of sentencing options. After abandonment of treatment-oriented sanctions, the authorized sanctions were limited to fines and suspended and unsuspended prison sentences.

Increased diversity in sentencing options and in the enforcement of sentences accelerated during the 1990s, ironically due to a revival of treatment ideas. The changes during the 1970s left an ideological vacuum, which the focus on alternatives to imprisonment was not entirely able to fill. In this situation, new developments on the international scene were influential, including the decline of the "nothing works" paradigm. Close contacts to Canada caused Denmark to pick up some of the many ideas developed by the Canadian Prison Service and to import some of its programs.[5] In addition, alternatives to imprisonment involving treatment programs have been developed in Denmark, among them treatments for offenders with addiction problems and for sexual offenders.

The new youth sanction is also related to the renaissance of the idea of treatment. While it contains elements of incapacitation, it would not have taken its present form had it not been for knowledge gained from recent research on treatment and crime prevention.

The increasing diversity of the penal system offers the authorities more options and possible interventions tailored to individual offenders. This ambition is linked to growing emphasis on effectiveness in reducing crime through criminal justice system measures. As a Swedish penal law professor has put it, criminal law policy is changing from a defensive to an offensive model, focusing on prevention of crime (Jareborg 1995). Diversity, however, risks making the system less understandable and predictable for offenders and the public and risks more inconsistency in practice. Renewed optimism about possibilities for reducing the crime problem through treatment and interventions is still new, and in coming years more new programs will probably be directed toward specific groups of offenders.

The diversity of crime-preventive programs has increased steadily since the foundation of the National Crime Preventive Council in 1971. Particularly within the last decade, numerous nationwide initiatives have been started. Most focus on violent offenders, but some aim at "unadjusted youth," a loose and undefined concept indicating that crime is not a necessary prerequisite to crime-preventive action. The initiatives primarily concern crime preventive measures and measures relating to public schools, training, housing, and social legislation.

[5] The former commissioner of the Canadian Prison Service, Ole Ingstup, used to be prison director in Denmark.

Efforts to increase reaching-out casework, street work directed toward at-risk-youth, warrant mention. A program that gives a child or an adolescent a "contact-person" has been introduced. This person is always available and can provide support if parents cannot. Various new programs, including a cognitive skills program, have been initiated. It has also been decided that authorities should react quickly to child or juvenile crime, and that the social authorities must promptly contact parents to discuss incidents and whether further efforts by the social authorities are needed. Besides these proposals and initiatives from the government, many local activities have also been launched by local crime prevention committees.

The preventive effect of all these initiatives is not known; neither is it in all instances known to what extent they have been implemented. The initiatives can be compared to a shotgun: some shots inevitably will hit the target. Danish traditions of program evaluation are poor, and evaluations seldom meet such scientific standards as use of control groups.

B. De- and Reinstitutionalization

Deinstitutionalization was a consequence of the changing ideology of child welfare in the 1960s and 1970s. A number of institutions were dismantled, and foster homes were used more often when out-of-home placements were needed. This trend is now shifting; a number of new institutions have been established, and more will be established in 2003 for "unadjusted youth." The number of secure accommodations has recently increased drastically, as have the number of residential placements without the parents' consent—from 4 percent of all placements in 1989 to 10 percent in 1999.

Amendments to social legislation have facilitated placements, and longer placements in secure accommodations have been allowed. In 1997, the maximum period for a stay in secured institutions was increased from two to fourteen months for juveniles over age fifteen. Whereas placement in secure accommodations earlier was typically intended either to prevent self-inflicted damage or for observation, the prolongation of the placement is intended to meet a perceived need for long-term treatment in secure settings. A recent evaluation of treatment in secure surroundings is somewhat skeptical about the need for the arrangement and points to a number of problems (Bonke and Kofoed 2001).

The official reason for the recent increase in institutional place-ments, and the authorization of long-term treatment in secure settings, is increasing problems with "unadjusted juveniles" in general and vio-lent juveniles in particular. The crime problem among juveniles in the 1990s, however, scarcely justifies interventions of this nature. In-stead, the tendency toward reinstitutionalization is a political manifes-tation of efforts at greater effectiveness necessitated by the increasing media preoccupation with crime. The media emphasis on spectacular offenses has, independent of crime trends, influenced the political agenda (Laursen 2001).

Although political initiatives can be seen as emerging from the mass media focus on crime, the specific nature of the interventions can be related to the pendulum movement seen in criminal justice policy areas. Institutional treatment and coercion were tried and rejected earlier in history, but the problems leading to their rejection seem to have been forgotten, and renewed optimism about their potential is spreading.

C. Approaching the Adult Justice System

There is no single direction in Danish youth policy changes. Some components of youth justice that distinguish it most from the adult system, such as the use of social institutions instead of prisons and the new youth sanction, have become more prominent. Other develop-ments, however, have brought youth and adult justice closer together.

Increasing numbers of juvenile offenders are being handled in the criminal justice system just like adults. In the mid-twentieth century, very few young offenders were found guilty and sentenced by a judge. Around 5 percent of all dispositions (except ticket fines) for young of-fenders were convictions in the beginning of the 1950s, and the rest were withdrawals of charge (Straffelovskommissionen 1959).[6] In 2000, the situation was quite different: 77 percent of all dispositions (exclud-ing ticket fines) were convictions, and the rest were withdrawals of charge.

This has not resulted from specific amendments or deliberate youth policy changes but has resulted from general changes in legal usage and criticisms of withdrawals of charge for young offenders. During the 1970s and 1980s, withdrawal of charge was repeatedly criticized for

[6] These figures are for criminal law cases.

being used too often for young offenders and for being ineffective in reducing reoffending. Although the evidence in support of these propositions has been minimal, the criticisms have resulted in a continuous decrease in the number of withdrawals of charge (Vestergaard 1991). Even the attempt to revive the sanction in 1998, by introducing a new condition, did not stop the trend toward decreased use, though use has now stabilized at a low level.

The underlying bases of criticisms of withdrawal of charge were probably changes in child welfare ideology and the trend toward de-institutionalization in the 1960s and 1970s. Before then, many juvenile offenders who were given withdrawals of charge were placed in institutions for rather long periods of time, signaling that action was being taken in consequence of crime. The less perceptible and restrictive interventions and measures that came to be associated with withdrawals of charge may have led many to the seemingly commonsense conclusion that they were less effective.

To what extent this change in youth policy is of real importance to young offenders is hard to say, but the answer is probably that it results in less restrictiveness. In place of withdrawals of charge, juveniles today are given fines or suspended sentences, the former being a less severe sentence and the latter being very similar to withdrawal of charge. The change and its consequences thus also emphasize that special youth measures do not automatically guarantee leniency.

D. Actors

Until recently, criminal policy in Denmark was not a political issue. A former director of the Danish Correctional Service illustrated this in describing a 1968 conversation with a newly appointed minister of justice. The new minister told the director that the change of administration would not affect criminal policy, as that was considered an objective and impartial matter and not a political one (L. Nielsen 1999). Since 1950, most changes to the penal code have been prepared by a standing committee of representatives from the criminal justice system and the universities, and most proposals have been adopted without modification. To the extent that governmental officials influenced the justice system, they tended to have a liberalizing effect, reflecting the liberal tradition of Danish politics more generally. No criminal justice system officials are elected.

This is now changing. As in other countries, criminal justice policy is becoming more important to politicians (Ryan 1999). Criminal justice policy has huge symbolic value because it is believed to preoccupy voters and it is a subject in which politicians can propose what—they say—will be more effective measures.

Politicians act faster than committees, and when a problem enters the political agenda, an immediate solution is expected. Furthermore, politicians to an increasing extent respond to specific celebrated crimes, and such responses nearly always go in one direction—toward more interventions and harsher sentences. An analysis of background to introduction in 1997 of a so-called violence package revealed that a few specific violent incidents were highly significant (Laursen 2001). Similarly, the introduction of the new youth sanction in 2001 resulted from specific crime problems, primarily group rapes. The terms of reference for the committee proposing the sanction start as follows: "Lately we have observed that children and juveniles increasingly commit serious and dangerous offenses, among these street robberies and group rapes" (Ekspertgruppen om ungdomskriminalitet 2001, p. 7).

Moral panics become a greater risk when criminal policy is politicized. Furthermore, there is a risk that solutions will be put forward too hastily. Politicization is undoubtedly a significant cause of the larger number of preventive and restrictive initiatives taken during the last decade. Some proposals are too dramatic and too ambitious, and many professionals see them as dubious. The proposals, however, may be effective in demonstrating vigor as opposed to powerlessness, and they may appeal to common understandings of the nature of crime problems and how to handle them.

Politicization of criminal policy will probably become even more pronounced, which makes predictions about youth justice policy more difficult. One possible scenario is a lowering of the minimum age of criminal responsibility. Proposals to do this have been put forward lately. My guess is that a change is highly likely if and when a very serious and cruel crime is committed by a thirteen- or fourteen-year-old.

E. Immigration

Danish immigration policy is commonly described as the most restrictive in Europe. The general election in November 2001 attracted international attention to Danish attitudes toward foreigners. It is hard to say whether Danes suffer more from xenophobia than others do, but immigration has unquestionably influenced politics considerably. The success of a right-wing party, the Danish Peoples Party, as a result of its hostility toward aliens, has caused other parties to compete on harshness concerning immigration.

Immigration and crime are often associated, and the Danish Peoples Party has linked these issues by coupling "group rapes," a new term in the Danish vocabulary, with immigration. Four incidents of rape committed by groups of young immigrants or second-generation immigrants in 2000 created an outcry in the media and resulted in the appointment of the committee that later proposed the new youth sanction. The number of rapes committed by more than one person was stable for many years though probably the number of rapes committed by three or more males was higher in 2000 than earlier. Whether the political debate occurred in response to the rapes or was related to the ethnic backgrounds of the offenders remains, however, uncertain.

The minister of justice then in power initiated an investigation on sentencing in rape cases, as the sentences for group rape were criticized for being too lenient (Rigsadvokaten 2001). This investigation did not lead to statutory changes, but continued criticism of the comparatively low severity of sentences for rape in Denmark led to the introduction of a bill aimed at substantially increasing prison sentences for rape. The preamble to the bill emphasizes that commission of a rape by more than one offender should be considered a special aggravating circumstance. That bill was not enacted because a general election in November 2001 intervened. The new government, however, enacted a similar bill that took effect in June 2002.

Initiatives to combat crime have also been linked to immigration. The report on unadjusted youth contains another element: integration of immigrants. It is not made explicit, but from the context it is hard not to associate "unadjustment" with immigration, and some of the proposals in the report aim directly at immigrants and their descendants.

In general, the debates on immigration and on criminal policy have had a mutually destructive effect. The focus on crimes committed by persons with foreign ethnic backgrounds has attracted much attention and resulted in demands for harsher punishment and furthermore put emphasis on the problematic elements among immigrants. This pervasive association with crime problems reflects negatively on immigrants and immigration.

F. New Moralism

During the 1970s, criminal justice policy focused on white-collar crime and economic criminality and to a lesser extent on traditional forms of crime. This led to a reduced emphasis on theft and other offenses against property. During the 1990s, attention shifted toward violent and sexual offenses.

These changes result from both international and national influences. Weak victims—children and women—have attracted much attention internationally, which to some extent is due to "globalization" in the spread of child pornography through the Internet and trafficking in human beings. The Social Democrats, being in power during most of the last decade, nominated the 1990s as the "moral decade," and most debates on criminal policy have concentrated on violence and sex offenses.

Extensive mass media coverage has accentuated attention on violent and sexual offenses. The starting point has been specific crimes rather than crime trends, and, even though crime in general is not going up, the media leave the impression of increasing crime problems.

The results include more severe sentences for violent and sexual offenses and criminalization of different forms of behavior related to prostitution and pornography. New moralism is largely old in the sense that the focus is on very traditional types of crimes.

G. Europeanization

Crime control recently has been significantly upgraded as a priority area within the European Union. Especially the "Presidency Conclusions" from the Tampere meeting in 1999, during the Finnish presidency of the EU, is of extreme significance (Tampere European Council 1999).[7] The aim was to develop the EU as an area of "freedom, security and justice." The title of section C is "A Unionwide Fight against Crime." This means "the European Council is deeply committed to reinforcing the fight against serious organized and transnational crime. The high level of safety in the area of freedom, security, and justice presupposes an efficient and comprehensive approach in the fight against all forms of crime. A balanced development of unionwide measures against crime should be achieved while protecting the freedom and legal rights of individuals and economic operators" (Tampere European Council 1999, no. 40).

---

[7] The document, often referred to as "The Tampere Milestones," includes the decision to establish a EU prosecutor unit, the so-called Eurojust.

Among the more specific measures taken in order to combat crime, one is a harmonization of criminal laws: "Without prejudice to the broader areas envisaged in the Treaty of Amsterdam and in the Vienna Action Plan, the European Council considers that, with regard to national criminal law, efforts to agree on common definitions, incriminations and sanctions should be focused in the first instance on a limited number of sectors of particular relevance, such as financial crime (money laundering, corruption, Euro counterfeiting), drugs trafficking, trafficking in human beings, particularly exploitation of women, sexual exploitation of children, high tech crime and environmental crime" (Tampere European Council 1999, no. 48). Since Tampere, harmonization has taken place in the subject areas just described, and the September 11, 2001, attack on the United States has led to further criminalization and harmonization regarding terrorism.

Efforts are under way toward harmonization of criminal law, sentencing, crime prevention, and victim policy. Among the Scandinavian countries, enthusiasm is lower than elsewhere, and the Scandinavians are trying to limit the extent of harmonization. Nevertheless, many feel that the game is up.

If the future brings this kind of EU harmonization, it will affect both the penal system and youth justice. This might produce a total change in Danish—and Scandinavian—youth justice. Separate youth justice systems such as many EU member states have may be the result. Then the contents of this essay will turn into history.

REFERENCES

Aubert, Vilhelm, and Thomas Mathiesen. 1962. "Forbrytelse og sykdom." *Tidsskrift for Samfunnsforskning* 3:169–92.
Balvig, Flemming. 2000. *RisikoUngdom.* Copenhagen: Det Kriminalpræventive Råd.
Beck, Ulrich. 1994. *Risk Society: Towards a New Modernity.* London: Sage.
Betænkning no. 1407. 2001. *On the Incorporation of Human Rights Conventions in Danish Law.* Copenhagen: Ministry of Justice.
Bonke, Jens, and Lene Kofoed. 2001. *Længerevarende behandling af børn og unge i sikrede pladser.* Copenhagen: Socialforskningsinstituttet rapport 01:8.
Brink, Ole, and Villy Sørensen. 2001. "Er voldens mørketal faldende?" *Nordisk Tidsskrift for Kriminalvidenskab* 88:230–39.
Christie, Nils. 1960. *Tvangsarbeid og alkoholbruk.* Oslo: Universitetsforlaget.

Clemmer, Donald. 1958. *The Prison Community.* New York: Rinehart.

Dahl, Tove Stang. 1985. *Child Welfare and Social Defence.* Oslo: Norwegian University Press.

Dansk Kriminalistforening. 1900. *Aarbog 1900.* Copenhagen: Dansk Kriminalistforening.

Ekspertgruppen om ungdomskriminalitet. 2001. *Rapport om ungdomskriminalitet.* Copenhagen: Ministry of Justice.

Galtung, Johan. 1959. *Fengselssamfunnet.* Oslo: Universitetsforlaget.

Garde, Peter. 1999. *Dansk kriminalistforening, 1899–1999.* Special issue of *Nordisk Tidsskrift for Kriminalvidenskab.*

Goffman, Erving. 1961. *Asylums: Essays on the Social Situation of Mental Patients and Other Inmates.* 1st ed. Garden City, N.Y.: Anchor.

Greve, Vagn. 1996. *Straffene.* Copenhagen: Dansk Jurist-og Økonomforbunds Forlag.

Høgelund, Jan. 1993. *Ungdomskontrakter.* Copenhagen: Socialforskningsinstituttet rapport 93:8.

Jareborg, Nils. 1995. "What Kind of Criminal Law Do We Want?" In *Beware of Punishment*, vol. 14, *Scandinavian Studies in Criminology*, edited by Annika Snare. Oslo: Norwegian University Press, Scandinavian Research Council for Criminology.

Jensen, Henrik. 1998. *Ofrets århundrede.* Copenhagen: Samleren.

Kyvsgaard, Britta. 1992. *Ny ungdom?* Copenhagen: Dansk Jurist-og Økonomforbunds Forlag.

———. 2000. "Undersøgelse af ungdomskontrakter." *Rigsadvokaten Informerer* no. 2/2000.

———. 2001a. "Kriminalitet, retshåndhævelse og etniske minoriteter." *Juristen* (2001), pp. 363–73.

———. 2001b. "Strafferetlig ideologi og praksis i det 20. århundrede." In *Skyldig eller sjuk?* edited by Hildigunnur Olafsdottir. NAD-publikation no. 40. Helsinki: Nordiske nämnden för alkohol och drogforskning.

———. 2002a. *Domspraksis, 1996–2000.* Undersøgelse til brug for Straffelovrådet (forthcoming).

———. 2002b. "Notat vedrørende kriminalitet og national oprindelse 2000." Available on-line at http://www.jm.dk.

Laursen, Søren. 2001. *Vold på dagsordenen.* Århus: Magtudredningen.

Lautrup, Claus. 2002. *Evaluering af § 223a.* Copenhagen: Pro-centret.

Lipton, Douglas, Robert Martinson, and Judith Wilks. 1975. *The Effectiveness of Correctional Treatment: A Survey of Treatment Evaluation Studies.* New York: Praeger.

Løkke, Anne. 1990. *Vildfarende børn.* Copenhagen: SocPol.

Lützen, Karin. 1998. *Byen tæmmes.* Copenhagen: Hans Reitzel.

Martinson, Robert. 1974. "What Works? Question and Answers about Prison Reform." *Public Interest* 35:22–34.

Nielsen, Beth Grothe. 1986. *Anstaltsbørn og børneanstalter gennem 400 år.* Copenhagen: SocPol.

———. 1999. "Historien om den kriminelle lavalder." *Social Kritik* 11(62):56–60.

Nielsen, Lars Nordskov. 1999. "Bølger i den kriminalpolitiske udvikling." *Nordisk Tidsskrift for Kriminalvidenskab* 86:261–79.

Rigsadvokaten. 2001. *Rigsadvokatens undersøgelse af udviklingen i strafniveauet i voldtægtssager.* Copenhagen: Ministry of Justice.

Rigspolitichefen. 1998. *Vold på gaden, i hjemmet og på arbejdet: Oversigt over resultater fra voldsofferundersøgelsen 1995/96.* Copenhagen: National Commission of the Danish Police.

Rømer, Harald. 1969. "Retssystemet og fængselsvæsenet udvikling." In *Fængsler og fanger,* edited by Flemming Balvig, Ole Dalå, Svend Poulsen-Hansen, Harald Rømer, and Preben Wolf. Copenhagen: Paludan.

Ryan, Mick. 1999. "Penal Policy Making towards the Millenium: Elites and Populists; New Labour and the New Criminology." *International Journal of Sociology* 27:1–22.

Straffelovskommissionen. 1917. *Betænkning af 9. november 1917.* Blueprint. Printed in Copenhagen.

———. 1959. *Betænkning nr. 232 om ungdomskriminalitet.* Blueprint. Printed in Copenhagen.

Sundin, Bertil. 1970. *Individ, institution, ideologi.* Stockholm: Aldus.

Tamm, Ditlev. 1996. "The Danes and Their Legal Heritage." In *Danish Law in a European Perspective,* edited by Børge Dahl, Torben Melchior, Lars Adam Rehof, and Ditlev Tamm. Copenhagen: GadJura.

Tampere European Council. 1999. "Presidency Conclusions." Also known as "The Tampere Milestones." Proceedings of the European Council meeting, Tampere, Finland, October 15–16.

Vestergaard, Jørn. 1991. "Juvenile Contracting in Denmark: Paternalism Revisited." In *Youth, Crime and Justice,* vol. 12, *Scandinavian Studies in Criminology,* edited by Annika Snare. Oslo: Norwegian University Press, Scandinavian Research Council for Criminology.

Waaben, Knud. 1962. "Straffelovskommissionens betænkning vedrørende ungdomskriminaliteten." In *Nordisk Kriminalistisk Årsbok 1960.* Stockholm: Dansk Kriminalistforening.

Wegener, Morten. 1986. "Sanktioner eller hjælp?" In *Børnekriminalitet,* edited by Benny Lihme. Copenhagen: SocPol.

Carl-Gunnar Janson

Youth Justice in Sweden

ABSTRACT

The age of criminal responsibility in Sweden is fifteen. Offenders under age twenty are dealt with in regular criminal courts. Some special policies apply to young defendants, including waivers of prosecution, restrictions on prison sentences, and handing over offenders to the local social welfare committee. Social welfare committees are responsible for offenders under age fifteen. Compulsory reformatory treatment can be used with permission from the county administrative board. The welfare committee has jurisdiction over nonoffending problem behaviors between ages fifteen and twenty, and over offenders of those ages referred to it by the court. Fifteen is the age of responsibility, and social welfare committees aim to save underage offenders from harmful prison experiences. The youth justice system has largely succeeded in keeping juveniles out of court and practically all out of prison. Delinquency increased in the thirty-year period beginning in the mid-1950s. This increase, and later increases in violence, result from factors outside the youth justice system. Since 1990, rates have declined or stabilized.

Swedish society has changed fundamentally since 1950 from a homogeneous industrial society to a prosperous urban postindustrial society with more choices available to more people. A substantial increase in juvenile delinquency was documented from the 1960s to the end of the 1980s, leveling off in the early 1990s and then reversing slightly in property crimes and possibly increasing somewhat in crimes of violence. The pattern is similar in adult crime. Substantial changes in so-

Carl-Gunnar Janson is professor emeritus, Department of Sociology, Stockholm University. Thanks to Kerstin Söderholm Carpelan, Vickie Sheridan, William R. Smith, and Michael Tonry.

cial structure occurred; most of them arguably had criminological relevance, but only one—immigration—has been shown to be associated with juvenile delinquency.

Among social conditions that might affect juvenile delinquency and, indirectly, adult criminality, the youth justice system should be included, perhaps in interaction with some family or social class conditions. After all, the youth justice system is meant to affect delinquency. However, to trace its consequences, quite another approach than that taken in this essay would be necessary.

The youth justice system's basic idea is that, to the extent a young delinquent needs treatment in a locked institution, the institution should be for young people only, and the goal is individual prevention. A second core idea is that it is desirable, whenever possible, to avoid prosecuting young people in court. These ideas have been successfully maintained even in the face of opposition to the principle of treatment and an insistence on just-deserts policies.

This essay discusses youth justice in Sweden, mostly in the twentieth century. Section I briefly discusses the period before 1900. Section II begins with a description of the 1902 legislation that laid a foundation for the modern system. It then discusses the development of the primary institutions and processes for dealing with serious misbehavior in very young persons. Section III discusses the courts and their relations with local social welfare organizations in dealing with alleged offenders of various age groups: under fifteen, fifteen to seventeen, and eighteen to twenty. This section also describes court procedures. Section IV examines juvenile delinquency as a function of major changes in Swedish society after World War II. The youth justice system has largely succeeded in keeping young offenders out of court and, almost completely, out of prison. However, it is doubtful if major increases in juvenile delinquency can be traced to the youth justice system.

I. Youth Justice before 1900

At the beginning of the twentieth century, Sweden was still mostly a rural, conservative, and authoritarian society in transition. Most cities were small—in 1911 the median town size was 5,200. Until 1866, free-holding peasants had constituted a Fourth Estate of the Riksdag and, at the turn of the century, were still a part of the establishment. Times were ripe for basic changes: the dissolution of the union of Norway and Sweden in 1905, the radical expansion of men's right to vote in

1909, and a general strike in 1909. These changes all occurred without violence.

In this preindustrial society, a large proportion of the population could not manage on their own at one time or another during their life course because of poverty, illness, or old age. Around 1850, the agrarian underclass had grown to almost 40 percent of the total population. The local community's traditional responsibility to take care of its poor was codified in 1847. Some paupers were supported as dependent tenants by private persons, a large proportion were supported at home by the parish, and some were admitted to poorhouses or hospitals. Some foster children lived in orphanages. Orphans and old people were farmed out to the lowest bidder. The number of paupers peaked around 1850. Then industrialization and the transatlantic wave of emigration—the latter culminating in the 1880s and 1890s—relieved some population pressures.

Itinerants were another basic social problem. Unruly groups of beggars of all ages, orphans, homeless vagrants, thieves, and mentally disturbed people roamed the country. For centuries, rules about relations between masters and servants presupposed that all able-bodied members of the serving class had an annual contract with a master unless some privileged position gave them a legally valid defense against charges of vagrancy. Otherwise, they were defenseless and could be put in a workhouse as vagrants. This was somewhat softened in the 1885 Act of Vagrancy, which provided that a person who roved about without trying to earn an honest living and lived in a way that threatened public safety, order, and decency might be sentenced to forced labor for vagrancy by the county administration. This law sided with the viewpoint of the privileged classes and became increasingly controversial. The vagrancy perspective came under almost constant attack. In 1934, all youth below age twenty-one were exempted from the vagrancy law. Gradually it lost most of its relevance in modern society and became a mostly symbolic issue concerning a few maladjusted vagabonds at the margins of society, for whom other—and nonpolitical—approaches were preferred. Enactment of a new Vagrancy Act was delayed until 1965, and it was never applied (Eriksson 1967, pp. 99, 326–34).

Thieves, robbers, and assailants were to be punished: flogged, fined, executed, or sent to hard labor in a workhouse or fort. To be sent to the fort at Marstrand was considered next to the death penalty in severity. Some argued that vagrancy rules applied only to people age fifteen and up, but even so, vagrant parents might bring children with them into workhouses or leave them in orphanages. *Vanartiga* children were frequently sent to the same houses of correction and workhouses as older and hardened offenders.[1] From the 1740s on, children below age seven could not be sentenced to workhouses.

It became clear to enlightened people that living with older and more advanced felons must be harmful to young minds—even or especially to wayward and neglected children. In the 1840s, a parliamentary committee proposed a version of a theory that became popular in the 1960s. It pointed out that a poor and neglected boy might develop a propensity to crime when, after having served his sentence, he found himself excluded from society and "eventually degenerated into a hardened criminal" (Qvarsell 1996, p. 32). Neglected children should instead be placed in special rescue homes to protect them from bad influences and to help them learn good work habits and Christian ways of thinking. A series of private reformatories were created. Råby Rescue Home, near Lund, from 1838, was the first. Prince Carl's Betterment Home in Stockholm was the second, in 1840 (Bolin and Dahlström 1992). The agricultural colony at Hall near Södertälje opened in 1876.[2]

Admission to the rescue homes was controlled by each institutional board, and most rescue homes had waiting lists. Applications for placements could be submitted by local poor-law boards, by local school boards in cases of truancy (after an 1842 law mandated elementary schools at parish level), by city police authorities, and by private citi-

---

[1] From prefix "van-," meaning "mis-," as in "mismanage," or "mal-," as in "malfunction": *vanart* (n.) and *vanartig* (adj.). These are early standard terms for children and young people with severe problem behaviors such as being antisocial, maladjusted, neglected, and strongly delinquent.

[2] The first rescue homes were run by charitable societies. In 1905, when the Acts of 1902 took effect, the first state institution, Bona, was ready. Even at that time the state was unwilling to take the full responsibility for the care of the young but wanted the regional authorities—counties, cities, and parishes—to join charitable societies that were already engaged. As late as in 1937, there were private, regional, and state treatment institutions caring for the young, the state reluctantly letting its share grow. That year, however, in principle, state authorities started to take over the institutional social care of the young. The rescue homes became reformatory schools, differentiated into school homes, *skolhem*, for school-age children from ages seven to fourteen (at this time the age of compulsory school attendance still was only seven years); vocational schools, *yrkesskolor*, for youth beyond school age; and home schools, *hemskolor*, for expecting mothers or mothers with children. Nationalization was not completed until 1950. With the Social Service Act of 1980, responsibility for the reformatory schools was moved to municipalities and county administrative boards. In addition to foster homes, private and small foundations continued to be used for around-the-clock living and care.

zens seeking rescue homes for imprisoned children being pardoned (Bramstång 1964, chap. 6). Most rescue homes had waiting lists. From 1864, young offenders could be sentenced to "general reformatories," but the state did not establish any. In 1873, the law was changed so one could apply to the new agricultural colony at Hall.

In 1896, Norway inaugurated *vergeråd*, a youth court (Eriksson 1967, pp. 154–60). The Swedish government in 1896 appointed the Tvångsuppfostringskommittén (Committee on reformatory upbringing), which in 1898 submitted a report and proposal on the treatment of underage offenders. In 1900, it presented its report and recommendations on "the treatment of vanartade [chronic delinquents] and morally neglected children" (Betänkande och förslag angående vanartade och i sedligt afseende försummade barns behandling [Tvångsuppfostringskommittén, p. 142]). Thus were the foundations laid for twentieth-century institutions.

II. Youth Justice Institutions in the Twentieth Century

In preparing its 1900 report, the Committee on Reformatory Upbringing asked all chairs of school boards to report the number of depraved and morally neglected children. It turned out that 3,516 boys and 1,580 girls—mostly below the age of twelve—were placed in reformatories or orphanages. (The following summary is based mostly on Eriksson 1967, pp. 253–63.) The committee's 1898 and 1900 reports led to passage of fundamental legislation in 1902. This came into force on January 1, 1905, and has defined the Swedish youth justice system since then. It has kept its basic structure while undergoing minor changes to adjust to changing times.

For offenders below age fifteen, all sanctions were removed from the penal code. For young offenders who had reached age fifteen but were not yet age eighteen, punishments were reduced: death sentences or penal servitude for life were changed to penal servitude for six-to-ten years, and penal servitude for a stated time was shortened to half of the shortest time possible for the given offense. In place of prison terms of up to six months or fines, the court could substitute forced reformatory care.

Child welfare committees were created to deal with *vanart*—advanced delinquency or moral neglect—in children below the age of fifteen. The committees were directed to assure that children below age fifteen would receive an adequate education, even when their parents were so unfit or unable to attend to them that special measures were needed to prevent the children from becoming "morally ne-glected," or when the educational means available at home and at school were insufficient. In some cases of *vanart*, a child may be held for education until age sixteen. In every school district there must be a child welfare committee, which may consist of the educational com-mittee. Measures may include cautioning those in charge of the child, warning or caning the child, supervising the home and the child, and—if these measures seem useless—separating the child from the home. The child may be sent to a private home, a children's home, or a refor-matory. In time for the new laws, the national reformatory for boys, Bona, outside Motala, was ready, and the private school for girls, Vie-bäck, near Nässjö, opened the next year.

Concern about high rates of infant mortality, especially among those born out of wedlock, resulted in the increased protection of fosterlings. In some cases, the farmed-out care of infants as fosterlings had turned out to be dangerously inadequate, sometimes even fatal. Prepaid foster expenses could be kept by the foster parent when the baby died. To protect the health and lives of farmed-out infants and children during their first seven years, supervisory parish committees were established. Initially handled as a form of poor relief, this function was later re-framed as a form of child welfare.

The Acts of 1902 expressed early notions of social welfare. They re-flected Enlightenment ideas about the rights that children had to a decent life and an adequate education, even when this conflicted with the rights of parents. As implemented in the child welfare legislation, child and youth care was moved from poor law to social welfare law. Although the Acts of 1902 had much the same philosophical back-ground as contemporaneous legislation in other European countries, including Norway, it differed in rejecting a youth court and in relying instead on "the century-old tradition of common sense and experience of the trusted men in the parish guided by the vicar" (Kumlien 1994, p. 245). The question was whether responses to youthful misbehavior should aim at nurturing or punishment. By turning offenses into *va-nart*—that is, behavior by deprived and morally neglected children—the child welfare committees were defined as agencies of upbringing and education and could on that basis defend the legitimacy of their compulsory powers. The debate indicates that "well-to-do intellectual categories were inclined to force society's poor individuals to increase their social capacities" (Kumlien 1994, p. 241; Björkman 2001, pp. 96–137).

Through the remainder of the twentieth century, the child welfare system underwent almost continuous development, as did judicial procedures for older youth. However, the basic division of responsibilities between social service and judicial institutions remained as outlined in 1902: the social sector was in charge of youth justice up to age fifteen, and responsibility was shared between the systems for youths between ages fifteen and twenty, with gradually increasing judicial involvement as youths' ages increased.

A. Social Welfare Developments

In 1902, legislators paid little attention to the risk that interventions might damage children. Probably members of the upper classes did not see children of the lowest classes as delicate and sensitive. Correspondingly, the poor did not have great expectations of considerate treatment by their betters (Levin 1996, 1997). Not until the 1920s did the child welfare committees take more interest in preventive measures. In 1920, the master's right to flog his subordinates was abandoned. A report in 1921 by a poor-law committee on child welfare led to the 1924 Child Welfare Act. All municipalities—more than 2,000 at that time— were required to establish a child welfare committee of at least five members appointed by the municipal council. It had to include a member of the poor-law board, a clergyman, a schoolteacher, and a physician in the public medical organization (if there was such a person within the municipality). At least one member had to be a woman.[3]

The child welfare committees' authority was gradually extended. They might support education at home by organizing nursery schools and maternity and child-care clinics and might take other preventive measures (both general and individual) to support parents and children. Their authority was extended to include, first, children below age sixteen who were maltreated or seriously neglected by their parents, and whose life and health were thus in danger, or who were in danger of becoming depraved (*vanartiga*); second, children below age eighteen who were so *vanartiga* that setting them right would require special measures; and, third, in 1934, persons between the ages of eighteen and twenty-one who were addicted to a careless, lazy, or vicious way of life, and whose correction required special social measures. For this last age group, the committees were to concentrate on asocial but only

[3] Since 1960, a legal expert member has been required for the child welfare committee.

occasionally criminal activities such as male prostitution; thus, as mentioned earlier, they took over responsibilities from the vagrancy law.

The moralistic vocabulary and the general authoritarian approach were characteristic of their time: even when protecting children from negligence, the committees' purpose was to uphold the social order by putting lower class people right. Not until after World War II did the municipal social service become a part of the social welfare system. In the 1940s, findings in the new behavioral social sciences and their presumed penological applications cumulatively strengthened treatment-oriented attitudes. The new treatment ideas developed in the 1950s were less moralistic and more pragmatically preventive, partly in interaction with changes in the young clientele. The emphasis on avoiding incarceration was strengthened.

In 1970, municipalities were permitted to reorganize their social welfare services into a central social welfare committee instead of separate committees for social welfare, child welfare, and temperance. They might also develop the social welfare organization on a district basis, each district having a social welfare district committee. The central social welfare committee is now mandatory, and from 1991 on the municipalities have been free to organize their social welfare services at will. The social welfare committee itself is a fairly small board of members appointed by the municipality and is staffed by a group of social workers, day-care attendants, preschool teachers, and so on. In 1982, the municipalities and their welfare committees, with the county's administrative boards in backup supervisory roles, took over the responsibility for the institutional treatment of children and the young.

1. *Residential Institutions.* In 1951, the state operated twenty-five reformatory schools with 919 beds. In 1981, the numbers were down to eighteen schools with 497 beds. Table 1 shows the variation in number of pupils taken in charge and the number actually cared for. After peaking in the mid-1960s, the figures went down to less than half of the peak number.

The social welfare organization is not a court and is not primarily concerned with preventing delinquency. Neglected children and children with severe problem behaviors (even if not delinquent) may be taken into social care to save them from destructive influences. Thus, the reformatory schools in table 1 housed neglected and antisocial inmates and those who were both neglected and antisocial. The trends shown in the table reflect the critical view of coerced institutional treatment that became widespread after the late 1960s.

TABLE 1

Annual Number (December 31) of Pupils
Admitted to Reformatory Care, 1951–
1981; Number Taken in Charge and
Number Cared for in School

	Frequency	
Year	Taken in Charge	Cared for in School
1951–52	1,570	699
1953–54	1,422	594
1955–56	1,410	674
1957–58	1,479	737
1959–60	1,575	869
1961–62	1,506	908
1963–64	1,702	972
1965–66	1,718	888
1967–68	1,683	848
1969–70	1,625	750
1971–72	1,547	705
1973–74	1,217	542
1975–76	973	454
1977–78	786	424
1979–80	766	428
1981	746	413

Sources.—Statistics Sweden 1952, table 273;
1955, table 284; 1957, table 285; 1960, table 267;
1963, table 288; 1972, table 294; 1980, table 324; and
1984, table 355.

By the 1950s, reformatory school clientele were becoming more difficult to handle. Because reformatory care was used as a last resort when all other attempts had failed, the remaining clients became progressively more antisocial and difficult to manage. Serious delinquency doubled in the fifteen- to eighteen-year-old group, became qualitatively more serious, and reached its highest level at age fourteen within the twelve- to seventeen-year-old category. In the 1920s, crime rates had been highest among twenty-one- to twenty-five-year-olds. In the 1930s, the highest crime rates were in the eighteen- to twenty-year-old group. In the 1940s, the peak was in the fifteen- to seventeen-year-old group (Bolin 1992a, pp. 73–74).

Tables 2 and 3 show the main reasons indicated by social welfare

TABLE 2

Boys Admitted to Reformatory School: Main Reasons for Measures Taken (Percent)

Behavioral Problem	1953	1954	1955	1956	1957	1958	1959	1960	1961	1962	1963	1964	1965	1966	1967	1968	1969	1970	1971	1972	1973	1974	1975	1976	1977	1978	1979	1980	1981
Incorrigibility	49	47	43	25	18	16	16	12	8	9	12	12	10	8	6	6	54	50	46	45	47	45	48	50	53	55	56	50	43
Car theft	6	6	7	17	24	30	35	35	39	40	49	50	51	49	44	39	22	16	14	11	11	7	8	12	15	14	11	14	13
Damage																													
Other property crime	72	72	80	72	79	85	88	90	88	86	91	93	92	91	87	82	77	76	72	74	75	74	75	73	73	74	74	77	77
Violence, assault	4	4	3	4	5	5	6	7	11	16	27	29	30	31	26	22	25	23	22	18	18	17	17	20	28	30	30	29	25
Abuse of alcohol				6	11	11	16	20	24	25	36	39	41	40	43	46	29	28	27	25	23	25	28	31	33	31	30	28	23
Abuse of thinner																	22	21	22	22	23	23	22	20	20	14	12	10	10
Abuse of drugs																	25	27	31	30	30	27	22	22	17	15	17	23	23
Sexual misbehavior, prostitution	2	1	2	5	6	6	5	5	5	6	7	7	5	5	3	2	1	2	1	0	0	0	0	1	1	1	1	1	1
Shy of working	1	1	1	3	6	9	8	10	10	11	27	39	38	34	38	36	33	29	25	18	16	14	14	17	17	17	10	8	5
Truancy, school problems	5	4	7	14	20	23	21	19	17	16	29	33	31	26	30	25	23	23	21	19	22	20	22	17	24	23	10	8	5
Absconding																	38	39	34	29	29	25	27	28	31	35	20	18	13
Other	5	3	2	2	3	3	4	4	5	5	5	6	4	5	3	3	24	19	12	8	7	5	4	5	5	3	3	3	2

SOURCES.—Blomberg and Grunewald 1964, p. 22; Statistics Sweden 1964, table 282; 1968, table 288; 1971, table 289; 1972, table 293; 1979, table 314; 1981, table 323; 1983, table 354; Socialstyrelsen 1982–89.

NOTE.—Category "shy of working" includes "vagrancy."

TABLE 3

Girls Admitted to Reformatory School: Main Reasons for Measures Taken (Percent)

Behavioral Problem	1953	1954	1955	1956	1957	1958	1959	1960	1961	1962	1963	1964	1965	1966	1967	1968	1969	1970	1971	1972	1973	1974	1975	1976	1977	1978	1979	1980	1981
Incorrigibility	60	65	61	34	28	20	19	19	13	13	14	12	12	12	9	9	3	3	3	3	4	3	4	6	7	7	3	8	3
Car theft	0	0	0	2	3	3	4	3	2	3	4	5	4	4	4	3	5	4	3	2	3	2	2	2	7	3	2	4	5
Damage																													
Other property crime	27	27	25	30	32	33	36	39	35	36	42	46	45	43	39	36	31	31	24	22	22	18	22	32	29	29	30	29	27
Abuse of alcohol				6	12	15	19	24	29	32	40	41	40	40	44	50	36	36	34	29	31	33	36	38	40	41	47	45	41
Abuse of thinner																	9	11	11	12	14	16	16	17	15	17	17	15	16
Abuse of drugs																	49	49	57	59	58	58	53	54	57	57	60	51	48
Prostitution, sexual misbehavior	42	41	49	49	50	55	55	52	52	55	53	54	24	25	51	49	43	34	17	13	12	11	11	13	15	14	16	18	21
Shy of working	5	5	4	6	14	32	42	49	47	55	69	81	85	84	82	79	36	33	33	28	24	19	20	17	13	11	9	8	3
Truancy, school problems	3	3	5	11	20	19	20	13	13	13	25	33	35	33	38	33	16	18	22	24	28	34	37	38	34	35	37	34	30
Absconding																	73	71	68	62	59	55	60	58	61	57	58	56	53
Other	0	1	0	1	1	1	1	1	2	2	1	1	2	2	2	1	5	4	6	4	4	4	3	3	3	1	1	1	1

SOURCES.—Blomberg and Grunewald 1964, p. 22; Statistics Sweden 1964, table 282; 1968, table 288; 1971, table 289; 1972, table 293; 1979, table 314; 1981, table 323; 1983, table 354; Socialstyrelsen 1982–89.

NOTE.—Category "shy of working" includes "vagrancy."

committees for placing juveniles in reformatory care in 1953–81. Categories were changed in 1969, mostly to make them more specific. Abuse of alcohol was used beginning in 1956. Since more than one main reason may be given, column totals may exceed 100 percent, making the sum a kind of delinquency index for the group of reformatory pupils. The psychologists Dick Blomberg and Karl Grunewald (1964) examined data from 1953–62, surveying the causes why reformatory students were admitted and finding indications of strong changes in the recruitment of clients. In 1953, general problems of upbringing were important for almost 50 percent of the boys and almost 60 percent of the girls. In 1962, the corresponding figures were down to 9 and 13 percent, respectively. In 1953, other contributing factors accounted for a total of 95 percent among boys and 77 percent for girls. Among boys, "other property offenses" characterized 72 percent. Among girls, 27 percent were property offenses, and 42 percent were prostitution and promiscuity. All other categories comprised less than 10 percent each. In 1962, the total percentage of contributing causes had increased to well over 200 for both genders, indicating more versatile antisocial patterns—other property offenses were recorded for almost all, car thefts for almost half, alcohol abuse for one in four, and there were also assaults, truancy, other school problems, and vagrancy for boys. For girls, the major behaviors were prostitution, promiscuity, vagrancy, and other property offenses; alcohol abuse, truancy, and other school problems were also common.

Between 1962 and 1968, the sum of percentages reached the 300 level among boys, with car thefts characterizing 50 percent, other property crimes 90 percent, alcohol abuse well over 40 percent, violence 30 percent, and vagrancy almost 40 percent. Among girls, vagrancy characterized 85 percent, and prostitution, promiscuity, and alcohol abuse reached 50 percent.

In 1969, delinquency percentages for boys were 373 percent and were 306 percent for girls; the percentages ended in 1980 and 1981 in sums of 254 and 259 percent, respectively. In the thirteen years, the picture was mixed. Some behaviors showed persistently high rates—such as car theft, other property crime, and alcohol abuse for boys, and abuse of alcohol and drugs, truancy, other school problems, and running away for girls. Other behaviors showed decreasing figures: damage, abuse of thinner, vagrancy, truancy and other school problems, running away, and possibly abuse of drugs for boys; prostitution, promiscuity, and vagrancy for girls.

2. *The Social Service Act (Socialtjänstlagen).* Social care in a welfare society is an individual right rather than an obligation to society. In 1968, the minister of social affairs appointed a parliamentary committee, which was given extensive instructions concerning the social institutions and conditions of appropriate care. The committee reported in 1977 (Socialutredningen 1977).

Under the Social Service Act of 1980 (Socialtjänstlagen [SoL]), which took effect in 1982 (Ottoson 1992, pp. 202–7; Söderholm Carpelan 1994, pp. 8–10), the social welfare committee has an ambitious set of preventive and caring responsibilities for children and young persons. Its purpose is to work—if possible in close cooperation with parents—for safe and good living conditions for children and youth; to promote in children a balanced personality development and favorable physical and social development; to provide protection to those who are at risk of developing adversely; and, if this is in their best interest, to provide care and upbringing outside of the home. Activities include setting up nursery schools and youth recreation centers, in cooperation with the family, and providing individually designed support for children and young persons. The committee should supply both family homes where children and parents could be cared for together and foster homes for children and young persons who need to live outside their parental home.

The assistance that is offered, according to SoL, is always voluntary. Special acts in force from 1982 made it possible under special circumstances to use coercive intervention when children or young people were in need of care or protection.[4]

The new legislation specified four kinds of responsibilities for the care of children and the young, including institutional care. Three responsibilities—care, costs, and treatment—fell on the municipalities and their social welfare organizations. As to the fourth responsibility, the municipalities were expected to cooperate with one another for resources when they were needed, but mainly the counties' administrative boards were brought in both to provide treatment resources and, in a supervisory role, to report to the government.

---

[4] The Care of Young Persons Act (LVU) makes it possible under special circumstances to use coercive intervention when children and young persons are in need of protection. Paragraph twelve of LVU says that there shall be special homes for young persons who need treatment under especially close supervision. These homes are generally referred to as "paragraph-twelve homes." There were also special treatment homes for adult substance abusers (*Lagen om Vård av Missbrukare* [LVM]).

In January 1983, there were eighteen reformatories with 568 clients in residence. By the end of the year, that number had risen to 833. The total number of youths in care at any time was 1,769. The number of reformatories increased from eighteen to thirty-four in the 1980s, but the number of placements remained about the same, as older institutions reduced their number of places, and the new ones were allowed to accept not more than ten clients at a time. These institutions belong to three broad types (Söderholm Carpelan 1994, pp. 10–11).

First, "assessment and acute assistance institutions" are mostly small with short placement times to investigate and suggest treatment, often offering alternatives to reformatories. Second, "treatment centers with residential facilities" are small, mostly unlockable places, often with treatment times of a year or more. "Traditional institutions" are usually large facilities like those of the 1950s, with four or five wards and thirty to forty clients, with locked assessment and acute wards as well as open wards and even halfway units. Sometimes young clients start in the acute and observation ward, then move to a closed ward, then to an open ward, and finally to the halfway unit.

Operating according to diverse principles and having widely varying resources, the programs, philosophies, and results of the institutions varied and became controversial. There were several ways in which homes were not operating satisfactorily: little collaboration between social welfare service and child mental welfare service, too little proximity to children's homes, social workers spending too much time calling around and hunting out places for clients, and little general knowledge of the number and location of available places and of the total situation.

A government bill in 1989–90 on revising the legislation governing the handling of children at extreme risk concluded that the care of the most vulnerable youth—teenage girls, immigrants, and youth with early signs of mental disturbances—was inadequate in terms of both the number of available places and the quality of care. The bill emphasized the need for differentiation and regional coordination. In 1991, the Riksdag put the paragraph-twelve homes back under state authority. In 1993, the National Board of Institutional Care (Statens institutionsstyrelse [SiS]) was established and began operating the paragraph-twelve homes on April 1, 1994.[5]

---

[5] The SiS was also put in charge of the LVM homes. Addicts below age twenty might be taken care of within LVU.

B. The Judicial Youth Justice System

Beginning in 1938, investigations of and discussions about a thorough legal reform of youth justice took place in the Commission on Penal Law (Strafflagberedningen) under the chairmanship of Karl Schlyter (1879–1959) and, somewhat later, within the ministry of justice. The commission's final report in 1956 was provocatively titled Protective Act (*Skyddslag;* Strafflagberedningen 1956). Work on legal reforms continued and was summarized in a governmental bill Criminal Code (*Brottsbalk*), which was passed by the Riksdag in 1962 and took effect in 1965, finally replacing the Penal Act of 1864. Since then several changes of the 1965 code, including whole chapters, have been made.

A recurring theme was a fear that appearing in court might be detrimental to young defendants. Anticipating the eventual statutory changes, prosecutors as early as 1944 were authorized to desist from prosecuting young confessed offenders between the ages of fifteen and seventeen (and, in special cases, offenders below age twenty) and hand them over to the social welfare committee, if the measures to be taken by the committee were considered appropriate.

In the first postwar decades, biological and hereditary explanations of crime were generally discredited. Instead, considerations of social factors came to the fore. Social engineering was envisioned as a tool for building a welfare society. There was optimism about the ability to change young offenders into law-abiding citizens. The intense work under Karl Schlyter on the new Preventive Act (Strafflagberedningen 1956) had a strong flavor of individual prevention. Schlyter was an outspoken proponent of the idea that being in prison would harm juveniles. In 1934, he had published a pamphlet "Avfolka fängelserna!" (Depopulate the prisons! Eriksson 1967, pp. 23–25). He did not believe in deterrence or "general prevention" (Andenaes 1952) as a treatment method. At a meeting of the Criminal Law Committee, when his law colleagues began to discuss general prevention, Schlyter is reported to have risen and said: "I am an old and tired man. I should not be upset. I will take a break, while you gentlemen go on discussing a thing that does not exist" (Bolin 1992*b*, p. 193).

The treatment-oriented jurisprudence had great hopes for the new social sciences. In 1956, an empirical study of young delinquents was organized under the ministry of justice. It included a large and prominent staff of sociologists, including Gösta Carlsson, psychologists, psychiatrists, and statisticians. The empirical results were published in the

1970s in five reports on "young offenders" (*Unga lagöverträdare*). A series of hearings with experts on juvenile delinquency was held between January 1957 and April 1959, and the evidence was summarized and commented on by a task force (Justitiedepartementet 1959). The interest in institutional treatment was obvious, as it was in the report of a 1969 committee on treatment research in criminology (Justitiedepartementet 1973). The latter also designed a research project on strengthened noninstitutional care in a district and proposed the creation of a Crime Prevention Council (BRÅ) with a research unit and a grant-giving research council. Finally, a task force, the 1971 drafting committee on treatment of offenders, reported their conclusions (Justitiedepartementet 1972).

Penal legislation focuses on the lower classes of society, and it may not be far-fetched to see the penal reforms from the 1930s onward as elements of social welfare reforms: "The ideology that carried the Swedish social welfare reforms in the 1930s also characterized the penal policy. The efforts that then, and (to a lesser extent) later came up, testified to a strong sympathy with that part of the population which were labeled criminals and were subjected to punishment. Penal policy was directed towards designing sanctions so as to diminish the damage of the punishment and to provide the offender care that increased chances for social adjustment" (Nelson 1968, p. 129).

The reform policies enacted in 1952, following the recommendations of Schlyter's committee, represented an enlightened opinion, but increased juvenile delinquency, including car thefts and dissipated behavior, sometimes seemed to provoke "the general sense of justice," which in legal parlance tends to stand for a general popular conservatism in penal matters (Qvarsell 1996, p. 46). Alcohol consumption increased among young people after the ration-book system for wine and spirits was abandoned in 1955. In 1965, a new middle-strength beer became popular among the young and remained so until it was prohibited in 1977. By that time, drug use had become sufficiently widespread among young people to compete with juvenile drinking as a major problem. What angered general law-abiding citizens most in the early postwar years, however, was car thefts for joyriding.

Taking a car for joyriding had been impossible during the war years because of a lack of gasoline. The use of a private car required a special charcoal pan to produce carbon monoxide for fuel. It would take about half an hour to get the car started. After the war, a car was often the owner's most precious possession.

In the good years of the first postwar decades, the number of registered passenger cars increased rapidly, from some eight per 1,000 population in 1945 to thirty-six in 1950, eighty-seven in 1955, 159 in 1960, 283 in 1970, and 347 in 1980. For some time, the proportion of cars stolen kept pace with the number of cars registered: 0.3 per 1,000 inhabitants in 1950, 2.4 in 1960, 4.0 in 1970, and 4.1 in 1980 (for a general discussion of car thefts, see Justiedepartementet [1959, pp. 193–208]). In 1956 in Stockholm, 3.3 cars were stolen per 1,000 inhabitants and twenty-nine were stolen per 1,000 cars, as against sixteen per 1,000 cars in Oslo, and well below ten per 1,000 cars in both Helsinki and Copenhagen (Blomberg 1960, p. 73). In 1959, about 80 percent of new passenger cars—and some 60 percent of all registered passenger cars—had wheel locks or other theft-prevention devices.

After angry complaints that "nothing happens" to young offenders, a new 1964 law (*Lag om unga lagöverträdare*) outlined to police and prosecutors how to handle cases involving young offenders. A new form of nonprison sentence (probation) was made available. Acts in 1988 advised prosecutors to be in closer contact with the social welfare committee, and good behavior was added as a criterion for escaping prosecution. Acts in 1995 advised less delay in case handling, only exceptional remissions of prosecutions to recidivists, and more frequent presence by parents and social workers during interrogations.

In 1990, the number of stolen cars per 1,000 registered passenger cars in Sweden reached its temporary maximum of twenty-one, and in 1991 the number of stolen cars per 1,000 inhabitants peaked at 8.8. Thus, car thefts continued but had lost much of their central position in opinion, even in the calls for law and order that appeared each election.

Sweden was affected in the 1970s and 1980s, like most of the Western world, by a shift toward negative attitudes about coercion and institutional care. This was not inconsistent with the ideas behind Swedish law reforms, although a minimum number of coercive institutions were thought necessary for the successful treatment of clients needing therapy. Somewhat later, Martinson's pessimistic conclusion that "nothing works" (1974) became the state of the art. Not until the late 1990s was an optimistic message heard again (Loeber and Farrington 1998).

However, if interventions by the authorities were seen as being intrinsically harmful, creating problems rather than solving them, this would change attitudes radically. The version of labeling theory that became influential within the social sciences—particularly in sociology and social work—did just that. The popular version taught in undergraduate sociology courses fitted in beautifully with the radical critical ideology of the times (Becker 1963; Goffman 1963; Börjeson 1966; Rubington and Weinberg 1971; Lundén and Näsman 1973). Other parts of the model were left implicit. A further simplified version flooded the media. Basically, the popular version exaggerated five elements of the labeling model and then applied it to a less relevant area.

The exaggerations concerned the generality of primary deviations, the possibility that those who hold power can label at will, the correlation between resources and the risk of being labeled, how little it takes for a label to stick, and the personal and social consequences of being labeled. These assumptions were capped by the view that the labeling of children and the young occurred mainly within formal institutions, such as the judicial system, the social services, and the educational system. If so, the policy implication appeared almost inevitable: to protect clients from being labeled, a conscientious social worker must keep them away from the police, courts, and social welfare committees.

In the 1980s, this version of labeling theory began to lose some of its influence (see also Lundström and Vinnerljung 2001). It had been severely criticized (Gove 1975; Janson 1977; Knutsson 1977). It was, of course, quite possible to be strongly critical of the labeling theory of the 1970s and find other versions that were quite useful, particularly versions focusing on preschool-age labeling in primary groups. Similarly, it is not necessary to adhere to the popular version of labeling theory to be critical of prison as juvenile therapy.

A criminal-policy task force of the Crime Prevention Council suggested that principles of justice and proportionality between crime and punishment should be applied in the criminal courts without regard to the perpetrator's personal need for therapy (BRÅ 1977). This "neo-classical" approach became influential and was taken up by, among others, the 1979 Commission on Imprisonment, which stated that incarceration is no more effective in reducing recidivism than is nonincarceration and that long prison terms do not work better than short ones (Fängelsestraffkommittén 1986, p. 30).[6] The commission's pro-

---

[6] One of the commission's references was Bengt Börjeson's well-made but controversial dissertation (1966), an ex-post facto study showing significantly higher recidivism among young prisoners than among nonprisoners, even after extensive controls for selection. Börjeson's data have been further analyzed, which has made the picture somewhat more complicated (Dalteg 1990, pp. 91–92). However, the most crucial problem

posed system of sanctions aimed at increased predictability and uniformity, lower levels of sanctions generally, and keeping sanctioning decisions independent of both individual and general preventive considerations. Instead, the sanction should reflect how severe and reprehensible the criminal act had been (Fangelsestraffkommittén 1986, p. 20). That is, the punishments should follow a system of "just deserts" (von Hirsch 1976; Jareborg and von Hirsch 1984). The just-deserts sanctions came into force in 1989.

The just-deserts approach caught the attention of the Juvenile Delinquency Committee, which observed that "the previously so vividly discussed question, whether ideas of general prevention or of individual prevention should determine the courts' selection of sanctions and estimations of punishment, now is considered rather uninteresting. Instead interest has focused on the offenses and their just deserts" (Ungdomsbrottskommittén 1993, p. 209). This is a reminder that the treatment needs alone should not define society's responses to an offense. In its final report, the Juvenile Delinquency Committee reached the tough conclusion that the practice of referring a young offender to the social authorities for care should be abandoned because it was inconsistent with the notion of a connection between sanction and offense. The committee proposed that special supervision be moved from the social authorities to the courts as a new sanction. A more severe sanction than suspended sentence and probation, special supervision for young offenders would be set for at least six months and not more than two years. This may be interpreted as an attempt by the judiciary to take back some of the authority it had lost to the social sector.

However, the new social democratic government balked, wanting to leave the social services in charge of the care and protection of the young. According to its Proposition 1997/98:96, the practice of the court referring cases to the social services would be retained, but a new form of referral to the social sector also was introduced, "youth custody" in lockable spaces for a period between two weeks and four years, as decided by the court according to the seriousness of the offenses. This would apply to offenders between fifteen and seventeen years of age who were sentenced before reaching age eighteen. The new sanction would not completely substitute for prison for its age group, but

probably is whether the inevitable errors in controls are related to the unrecorded selection of offenders during court procedures.

only in exceptional cases would it be possible to sentence someone of this age to prison (Government Bill Proposition 1997/98:96, pp. 156–62). The Riksdag accepted the proposition, and the new Act of Youth Custody (LSU 1998; *Om verkställighet av sluten ungdomsvård* [Act number 603 instituted in 1998]) took effect on January 1, 1999. The custody was to be carried out by the SiS (LSU 1998, sec. 3) in cooperation with the social welfare committee (LSU 1998, sec. 4). It must start in a lockable unit, but as soon as possible the youth in custody should get an opportunity to stay under more open conditions (LSU 1998, sec. 14), even outside the institution if suitable (LSU 1998, sec. 18).

C. The Institutional Care System from the 1990s

The transfer of the responsibility for managing some young offenders from local social welfare committees back to state authority was much against the tide in 1993. In the early 1990s, problems with a rapidly growing national debt developed from a financial crisis into a general depression. From 1.6 percent unemployed in 1990, unemployment rose to 8.2 percent in 1993. In the 1991 parliamentary election, the social-democratic government fell and was replaced by a conservative-liberal government. For both ideological and practical reasons, the new government cut public-sector spending and shifted to a market-oriented policy. In the 1994 election, the social democrats came back. The unemployment rate remained high, until it started a slow downward turn, but it still remained somewhat above the goal of 4 percent in 2001.

During the prolonged economic crisis, most municipalities were in fiscal difficulties and may not have been averse to being relieved of a responsibility that still remained anchored in the local social welfare organization. Qvarsell (1996) surmised that local politicians felt uneasy about some treatment policies within the youth justice system and were neither able nor inclined to justify them to their voters. It was especially embarrassing when the media revealed that social welfare committees, as a last resort, sent some of their worst cases to be crew members on cruises to the West Indies or the Mediterranean.

The SiS (Statens institutionsstyrelse 2001) has remained in charge of all social welfare youth treatment institutions. All social welfare treatment programs are planned and run in close cooperation with the appropriate social welfare committee. Thus, as the relevant legislation provides that "if the Social Welfare Committee has decided that a young person shall stay in a [paragraph-twelve home], the SiS must find a place for him in such a home" (1990 Care of Young Persons

[Special Provisions] Act [*Lagen om vård av unga*, often referred to as LVU], par. 12, pt. 2). The main legal framework, in addition to general social services legislation, is two acts concerning institutional social care administered by SiS, the latest versions of LVU, and the significant new act from 1998 (LSU).

According to LVU, care should be provided to young persons vulnerable to health and developmental risks that result from defective home conditions or their own behavior. This applies to young people below the age of twenty. On the social welfare committee's request, the county administrative court may decide to place someone into institutional care. The essential condition is that the young person's health or development is in jeopardy. If the situation is deteriorating too quickly, so that there is no time for a formal decision, the committee itself—or its chairman or a specially assigned member—may decide that the young person must be taken in charge immediately. In 2000, this happened in half of all admissions. Special homes must be maintained for young persons who need treatment under especially close supervision because of their own behavior. As already mentioned, such special homes are specified in the twelfth paragraph of the LVU and are generally referred to as "paragraph-twelve homes." In 1994, there were thirty-four homes for young patients in coercive LVU care and a few voluntary patients, according to SoL.

In 2000, 1,133 young persons were enrolled for treatment. This was 10 percent more than in 1994. Nine percent of the entries were based on SoL, the others on LVU. Thirteen percent were below age fifteen, 74 percent were ages fifteen to seventeen, and 13 percent were age eighteen or above. The lengths of stay varied between one month and three years, with an average of ten months. The demand for lockable spaces increased from 51 percent of the cases in 1994 to 63 percent in the year 2000.

Table 4 shows SoL and LVU cases annually for 1990–2001; for LVU, cases arising from social factors and from behavioral problems are recorded separately. Cases arising from both social and behavioral factors are included among the behavioral cases. The few behavioral cases under SoL are not included.

The table suggests that the extent to which SiS took part in social intervention exclusively to protect children and youth from negligence and harmful factors in their social environment was largely constant through the 1990s, and that treatment motivated at least partly by antisocial behavior increased slowly. However, if there was an increasing

TABLE 4

Frequency: Children and Young Persons in Care according to SoL or LVU per 1,000 Population, 1990–2001

Year	SoL, Ages 0–17 Twenty-Four-Hour Care Outside Home Total	LVU, Taken in Charge, Ages 0–20 Total	Due to Social Condition	Due to Own Behavior Problem	LVU Care, Ages 0–20 Total	Due to Social Condition	Due to Own Behavior Problem	Total Due to SoL + LVU
1990	1.53	.41	.26	.15	.37	.22	.15	1.82
1991	1.53	.47	.34	.13	.37	.22	.15	1.83
1992	1.88	.52	.34	.18	.45	.30	.16	2.25
1993	2.00	.60	.37	.23	.48	.28	.20	2.39
1994	2.10	.63	.38	.25	.54	.32	.21	2.54
1995	2.18	.64	.38	.26	.54	.31	.23	2.60
1996	2.38	.62	.34	.28	.52	.28	.24	2.78
1997	2.32	.61	.31	.31	.50	.25	.25	2.71
1998	2.25	.62	.30	.32	.53	.27	.26	2.66
1999	2.40	.69	.32	.37	.55	.24	.31	2.82
2000	2.36	.70	.33	.38	.57	.27	.31	2.81
2001	2.40	.71	.32	.38	.53	.24	.30	2.82

Source.—Socialstyrelsen 2002, table 2.

Note.—LVU = *Lagen om vård av unga* (1990 Care of Young Persons [Special Provisions] Act); SoL = *Socialtjänstlagen* (Social Services Act of 1980); if care is due to both social factors and own behavior, the care is classified as due to own behavior.

correlation between antisocial behavior and living conditions (or belief in such a correlation), the role of protection may also have increased at least slightly. In fact, however, there were few of such mixed interventions.

III. Interactions within the Youth Justice System between the Social Welfare System and the Judicial System

The youth justice system consists of the two interacting parts: the social service system for children and young people, and the courts insofar as they define and mete out sanctions on youth.

A. Coming of Legal Age

If crime is defined as a violation of a law that is subject to sanctioning, even minors—persons below the age of fifteen—and insane persons may commit crimes. Sanctions may include the imposition of a punishment by the judiciary, the surrender of the perpetrator to the care of social or medical authorities, or the forfeiture of property or rights.

However, according to Swedish law, no legal sanctions may be imposed for acts committed by persons under age fifteen, except possibly forfeiture under special circumstances (according to chap. 32 of the Penal Code). Thus, the age of responsibility is fifteen. Coming of legal age at fifteen is part of the transition into full legal adulthood. It is the first major step in the process after reaching compulsory school age at seven. Film censorship sets fifteen as the age limit between movies for adults only (and for children accompanied by their parents) and universal showing. At age eleven, children can watch some movies only if accompanied by their guardians. Between fifteen and seventeen, a young person may not, except under special circumstances, be sentenced to prison but must be referred to the institutional care facilities of the social welfare authorities.

From age fifteen on, one may drive an autobike, have sexual intercourse with someone of age fifteen and older, and get married with parental consent. At age sixteen, compulsory school age ends, and one can obtain a driving license for light motorbikes and cross-country scooters. The list of entitlements from age eighteen is longer: to sign contracts, for example, to buy on an installment plan; to obtain an ordinary driving license; to buy beer and tobacco at food shops; to visit hangouts unsuitable for younger persons, for example, pool rooms and porn shops; to get married without parental consent; and to vote in municipal, county, and parliamentary elections and referenda. Finally, at age twenty, supervision and social care by social authorities must end, and one can buy hard liquor in liquor shops.

Despite the many steps involved in coming of legal age, it takes some ingenuity to identify a status offense in the Swedish justice system. Several activities are prohibited for minors and underage persons, but there are no legal sanctions against the young perpetrators, so technically these acts are not offenses. A minor sneaking in to see an adult movie, driving an autobike, or having sexual intercourse may concern the social authorities. A police officer may take the autocyclist off the road, but legal sanctions—except forfeiture—apply only to persons of legal age. The person operating the movie theater may be fined for letting the minor in, and the adult sexual partner may go to prison. Pimping is an offense, but prostitution is not.

Correspondingly, there is no legal sanction against the seventeen-year-old who buys liquor in the liquor shop or privately—except that the liquor may be confiscated—but the manager of the shop may be fined, although this is unlikely. If the driver of a car is only seventeen, he or she may be punished for driving without a license, just as any fifty-year-old driver without a license would. Hence, none of these violations is a status offense. One may say that Swedish law does not recognize status offenses of minors. If there are no sanctions in the penal system if the offender is a minor—that is, below age fifteen—what may happen to him or her?

B. Below Age Fifteen

Suspected offenses by a minor may be observed by constables on the beat, may be reported to the police, or may be reported directly to the social authorities by private persons, shops and other businesses, schools, and other public units. When this happens, the constable may talk with the youngster without reporting the incident. In more serious situations—criminally or in terms of child welfare—the police are expected to report and take various precautions to protect the minor. A social worker should be alerted, parents should be contacted and asked to take the child home, or the child should be driven home in an unmarked car. If a hearing is necessary, for instance, to learn the role of possible older co-offenders, or when the alleged offense had been reported to the police, parents and a social worker must be present. Then the case is closed with the police as far as the minor is concerned and is handed over to the social welfare committee of the young person's hometown or home district.

The social welfare system offers three kinds of support: support to community structure by taking part in local social community planning; general support by providing social services to special populations, such as children, the elderly, and the disabled; and individual support by caring for specific individuals and families, such as social assistance allowances for needy individuals and families, for addicts, and for children and young persons with problems.

In 2000, a large number of children and young persons, most below age twelve, were subject to various SoL measures, such as being assigned a contact person or family, receiving need-tested personal support, or being subjects of structured noninstitutional care programs. At some time in the year 2001, 13,925 clients received SoL care. Of these, 3,662 were ten to fourteen years old; 4,230 were fifteen to seventeen years old; and 3,056 were eighteen to twenty years old (Socialstyrelsen 2002, table 14).

Young offenders and delinquents may be placed in an institution for treatment, according to the LVU. In the year 2000, this occurred to 226 LVU clients in the age category ten to fourteen, of whom 105 were placed in so-called special homes (Statens Institutionsstyrelse 2001). Table 5, for 1982–89 and 1994–97, gives the age distribution of LVU pupils in social care. The first part includes only children in care because of their own behavior. Since interventions by the social authorities are not legal sanctions, they may affect children below age fifteen. The second and third parts include interventions other than those resulting from the pupils' own behavior, such as parental negligence. Here the proportions of children under age fifteen are larger, even when children under ten are left out.

C. Ages Fifteen to Seventeen

From ages fifteen to twenty, sanctions are decided by the courts. Police officers on the beat, however, see many things that are not reported. The decision not to report can be made on the spot when the infraction is insignificant and when an admonition seems sufficient. Even when a report is written, remission can be given in retrospect for minor traffic violations and disturbances of the peace. To avoid a court process for minor offenses, an administrative process may be substituted. The simplest are the parking tickets handed out by traffic supervisors and tickets given by police for violations of the Road Traffic Act. In addition, a prosecutor may send an order of summary punishment as a paying-in form. If the alleged offender pays the stated amount,

TABLE 5

Percentage Distribution of LVU Pupils in Care due to Behavior
Problems

| Year | Ages | | | No. of Pupils |
	10–14 (%)	15–17 (%)	18–20 (%)	
1982*	5	58	37	972
1983*	6	53	41	767
1984*	7	49	44	674
1985*	8	46	46	622
1986*	8	42	50	656
1987*	7	44	49	689
1988*	5	42	53	716
1989*	5	37	58	809
1994**	12	61	27	347
1995**	15	63	22	373
1996**	10	59	31	411
1997**	10	58	32	429
1998***	18	68	14	1,225
1999***	22	67	12	1,229
2000***	13	74	13	1,133

Sources.—Statistics Sweden 1991; Socialstyrelsen 1982–89, table 47; 1995–97, table
1A; 1995:11, 1996:11, 1997:11, 1998:12; Statens Institutionsstyrelse 2001, table 3:11.
    Note.—LVU = Lagen om vård av unga (1990 Care of Young Persons [Special Pro-
visions] Act); SiS = Statens Institutionsstyrelse (National Board of Institutional Care);
SoL = Socialtjänstlagen (Social Services Act of 1980).
    * On December 31.
    ** New cases within the year.
    *** Age distributions of SoL and LVU pupils in care of SiS.

this means that he has confessed to an offense, and the case is closed.
If he refuses to pay, his case may be dismissed or reopened. Thus, the
alleged offender may end up in court after all. Summary punishment
is frequent in the fifteen- to seventeen-year-old age group.
    In taking persons into custody, the police must proceed with cau-
tion. There are strict rules about use of service revolvers. All spent bul-
lets must be accounted for. Preventing an escape by firing is not permitted. It is still true that "a policeman firing his gun is still front-page
news" (Janson and Torstensson 1984, p. 201). For investigating alleged offenses, the police and the district attorney's office are organized into divisions—traffic, theft, fraud, violence, and so on. For-

mally, district attorneys (DAs) are in charge, but in practice investigations are run by the police except in serious or otherwise complicated cases, at least until a promising suspect is found. The police may hold a person for up to six hours for questioning, after which the officer in charge may hold him for another six hours after telling him that he is a suspect with the right to legal counsel. For those who cannot afford legal fees—that is, for almost all suspects of "traditional" offenses—that counsel is paid for by public funds.

In most cases the suspect is released, but he cannot be released on bail, as there is no bail concept in Swedish law. Economic means should not make a difference to the law. If, however, there are substantiated grounds to believe the suspect committed an offense that could result in imprisonment for at least a year, and there are good reasons to believe that the subject, if released, would abscond, destroy evidence, or remain criminally active, the DA may within five days obtain a court order for the suspect's detention (arrest) for no more than fourteen days. If the investigation has not been completed at the end of this period, the DA may ask the court for another period of detention. Suspects younger than eighteen are arrested only under very special circumstances. Instead, they may be temporarily placed under the jurisdiction of the social welfare committee. Of 1,190 suspects who were arrested in 2001, only eight were under age eighteen (Kriminal-vårdsstyrelsen 2002, tables 5.4 and 5.5).

If the evidence against a suspect is considered sufficient for conviction, court proceedings should be opened. However, if further measures are not called for, the DA may refrain from prosecuting a minor for an offense punishable by fines only. A confession is a necessary condition for a decision not to prosecute. The same holds for the application of the Act of 1964 (Wallén 1979)—and later versions of that Act—regarding handing over cases of under-eighteen offenders to the social authorities, when the DA accepts the measures to be taken by them—if no indictment is made—as appropriate. The case is then filed and included in the statistics report. "Appropriate measures" by the social authorities might include parental action, supervision, or social care. Young offenders on leave or on the run from reformatory schools, other social institutions, prisons, or mental institutions are usually sent back without taking the roundabout route through the court.

A Swedish trial is not a competition between two parties, one winning and the other losing. Proceedings are not adversarial. There is little adversarial eloquence. Rather, it is an inquisitorial system in which all involved should try—to put it somewhat naively—to find out what really happened. The prosecution must give the defense access to all evidence and documents and try to find supplementary information asked for by the defense. The DA cannot plea-bargain or offer legal immunity to prosecution witnesses.

Procedural rules are not very strict, and restrictions on permissible evidence are few. The defendant is not placed under oath and may change or withdraw any statement at any time. Still, there are few surprises, especially when the defendant is young. The violation is often admitted, and the points of disagreement concern what section of the penal code to apply and possible mitigating circumstances. Proceedings follow the same rules whether or not the defendant has pleaded guilty and are open to the public except when the court decides on closed doors out of consideration for the defendant or a victim. There are no verbatim minutes. The report of the proceedings contains documents, petitions, and the court's reasoned decision and is open to the public insofar as it pertains to proceedings in open court.

Compared with an adversarial system, the Swedish court system assigns a more limited role to the defense counsel since there is less room for a spirited defense. There are no public defenders and no star pro bono defenders. Instead, the defendant may ask for any lawyer, however famous, and as far as possible the court will try to honor his request, assigning at least a roughly equivalent counselor, whose bill will be paid from public funds, usually without question. By tradition, suing for damage is rare, damages are small, and lawyers are less numerous and less prominent socially, politically, and economically than in the United States—although recently the media seem to be somewhat more interested in them.

Court proceedings are chaired by a judge. Minor cases are decided by one judge, but in other cases the court consists of one judge and a panel of five lay assessors, with four of them constituting a quorum. The judge is a career official with a university legal education and relevant experience, as is the DA. The assessors are nominated by the municipal council's political parties and are elected by the council. They serve for six years, often working with the same judge in the same panel, are paid a fee, and may be reelected until age seventy. The tradition of the lay assessor panel goes back to the Middle Ages, when it consisted of trusted local citizens.

The judge and the panel decide both guilt and sanctions. Deliberations are very free and take place in private. The decisions are made by vote—the judge first and then the assessors—and need not be unanimous. If four out of five or three out of four assessors disagree with the judge, the judge is overruled. If appealed, this kind of outcome stands a better-than-average chance of being reversed. Whether or not unanimous, the verdict is announced by the judge.

Swedish prison sentences tend to be short. In 1998, 30 percent of all sentences were two months or less, 63 percent were for a year or less, and 83 percent were for less than two years (BRÅ 1998, table 5.11). A prisoner receiving a sentence of between two months and a year would be conditionally discharged after serving two-thirds of that sentence. A life sentence usually means ten years. As to young offenders, there are special restrictions: a prison sentence for a person below age eighteen requires "extraordinary" justification, and a person below age twenty requires "special" justification. Prisoners below age twenty serve their time in special prisons separate from adult prisoners.

Cases in which the court suspects the offender is not mentally responsible are set aside. In these cases sentencing is postponed until a psychiatric investigation has been carried out, which should take no more than six weeks but is often delayed beyond that, while the defendant remains in custody. Depending on the result, the offender will be either sentenced or handed over to medical authorities. All court sentences may be appealed.

A young defendant found guilty could be fined, with the fine perhaps assessed on the basis of his daily income. This is the most frequent sentence. Only very exceptionally would he be sentenced to prison. A conditional sentence would be more likely, but not as likely as the defendant being referred to the social welfare committee. Probation is possible but only if it is found more appropriate than handing over the defendant to the committee. A qualified form of probation, contract care, may be considered when the abuse of habit-forming drugs seems to be a major factor and the offender has declared himself or herself willing to go through treatment.

Beginning in 1990, there have been experiments—expanded to the whole country in 1993—with community service. As a condition of receiving probation instead of prison, the defendant must accept a specified kind of unpaid work for a specified time between forty and 200 hours. Similarly, when the court entrusts offenders below age twenty-one to the social welfare committee, the court may require them to carry out remedial work that is directly related to the offense. Since

1999, the court has had the option to sentence young offenders between the ages of fifteen and seventeen to closed institutional treatment operated by the social services agencies for a specified time (LSU). This may be for as little as fourteen days and as much as four years without release on parole. This sanction ranks in severity below prison but above probation and conditional sentence.

Table 6 shows sentences given to offenders ages fifteen to seventeen in selected years. There are few prison sentences, even if prison sentences in combination with probation are included. Waivers of prosecution and other surrenders to the social services not part of the new youth custody system remain frequent, although it may be too soon to see the effects of the new sanction on the court's sentencing. A detailed and penetrating analysis can be found in Kühlhorn (2002).

Only recently has probation been combined with secondary conditions. In a 2001 personal communication, Eckart Kühlhorn pointed out to me that the sum of the three cohorts of fifteen-, sixteen-, and seventeen-year-olds is an overestimation of the persons at risk of being sentenced according to the restrictive rules applying to minors, since both the offense and the sentence should fall within the three-years interval.

D. Ages Eighteen to Twenty

When the suspect is age eighteen but not yet twenty-one, he is not considered quite grown up and is still somewhat protected by his youth. His likelihood of being arrested and placed in detention is greater than it is for younger offenders. The possibility of having the charge against him withdrawn is much less than it is for younger offenders. It takes more for social care to be a viable alternative. In exceptional cases, when the social committee's arrangements appear especially apt, as when the offender is already in social care, the same procedure may be applied even if the offender has turned eighteen years old but is not yet twenty-one. The proscriptions against imprisonment are not as strong as for younger offenders, and the court sentence of youth custody in a special home for young people is only rarely available after age eighteen. From 1938 to 1980, the courts might sentence a youth in this age group to youth prison for at least one and at most four years, with release decided without appeal by a special youth-prison commission. Table 7 contains figures for the eighteen- to twenty-year-old age group corresponding to figures in table 6.

TABLE 6

Court Dispositions of Offenders in the Age Category 15–17 Years, Selected Years

	1979	1980	1981	1991	1992	1996	1997	1998	1999	2000	2001
Population ages 15–17	347,000	361,000	371,000	322,000	309,000	304,000	302,000	299,000	298,000	307,000	318,000
Number of defendants	21,293	21,930	23,387	17,447	16,048	15,216	14,947	14,672	11,848	12,074	12,029
Prison	22	27	39	22	47	25	33	15	3	1	3
Psychiatric treatment						2	2	3	3	3	3
Probation	93	85	117	183	190	237	204	164	129	143	132
Prison				20	16	18	12	1	1	5	5
Voluntary treatment						2	2				1
Community service						12	10	9	5	10	13
Conditional sentence	104	122	127	278	267	156	145	141	115	133	117
Youth custody									58	94	85
To social service	668	736	791	1,239	1,146	1,991	1,956	1,980	1,972	2,194	2,178
Community service									235	392	416
Extended sentence	22	15	17	72	69	100	65	56	24	32	43
Fined	2,204	2,275	2,143	2,032	2,425	2,405	2,147	2,200	2,125	2,210	2,171
Not prosecuted	7,546	7,435	8,537	6,868	5,496	4,479	4,188	4,084	2,894	3,046	2,871
1964 act						4,099	3,780	3,655	2,522	2,437	2,236
In social care						11	1	68	42	70	30
Other						369	407	351	330	509	605
Summary Fines	10,634	11,235	11,616	6,753	6,408	5,821	6,207	6,029	4,525	4,218	4,426

Sources.—Statistics Sweden 1980, table 372; 1981, table 371; 1982–83, table 369; 1986, table 371; 1988, table 374; 1993, table 400; 1994, table 390; 1998, table 385; 1999, table 390; BRÅ 2000:12, table 4.6; 2001:12, table 4.6; 2001:16, table 4.6; 2002:13, table 4.6.

TABLE 7
Court Dispositions of Offenders Ages Eighteen to Twenty, Selected Years

	1979	1980	1981	1991	1992	1996	1997	1998	1999	2000	2001
Population ages 18–20	321,000	320,000	339,000	345,000	343,000	303,000	302,000	304,000	304,000	302,000	300,000
Number of defendants	25,040	25,615	26,623	17,829	16,791	10,304	11,233	11,347	10,421	10,701	10,333
Prison	1,183	1,170	1,240	785	954	744	730	783	606	707	733
Psychiatric treatment						10	16	12	18	20	15
Probation	1,280	1,443	1,469	1,062	1,036	1,102	1,133	1,133	993	983	1,087
Prison						93	94	113	68	103	98
Voluntary treatment						41	42	29	39	33	47
Community service						229	232	238	256	208	223
Conditional sentence	1,521	1,675	1,726	2,215	2,095	1,166	1,107	1,122	1,204	1,268	1,310
Community service									317	399	455
Youth custody									11	21	17
To social service	291	321	355	206	196	183	194	250	216	217	239
Community services									11	41	28
Extended sentence	839	842	879	644	500	529	435	472	305	261	280
Fined	5,244	5,206	5,196	3,265	3,450	1,888	1,801	1,712	2,066	1,920	1,833
Not prosecuted	2,239	2,187	2,296	1,341	1,271	733	914	896	725	1,268	1,086
1964 act						98	123	112	68	99	89
In social care						15	21	22	23	11	87
Other						617	770	758	634	1,158	990
Summary fine	12,443	12,771	13,462	8,311	7,289	3,949	4,903	4,967	4,277	4,036	3,373

SOURCES.—Statistics Sweden 1980, table 372; 1981, table 371; 1982–83, table 369; 1986, table 371; 1988, table 374; 1993, table 400; 1994, table 390; 1998, table 385; 1999, table 390; BRÅ 2000:12, table 4.6; 2001:12, table 4.6; 2002:13, table 4.6.

IV. Juvenile Delinquency after 1950

In the fifty years from 1950 to the twenty-first century, there were extensive changes in Swedish society and its population, and in adult crime and juvenile delinquency. There were also changes in youth justice, although its basic principles remained much the same. Family, economic, educational, and ethnic conditions affect juvenile delinquency and adult crime. It is natural to presuppose that penal policy has a penological effect. For such a connection to be demonstrated, however, it must overcome the presumably strong influences of social changes.

A. Crime Change

Tables in the *Statistical Yearbook* for 2001 (Statistics Sweden 2001) show recidivism rates by age (table 471) and sentence (table 472) after three years for seven cohorts of offenders from 1973 to 1985. Lower and upper numbers of cohort members in each row of age or sanctions vary from small to very large—from 222 to 60,537 for lower bounds and from 305 to 75,685 for upper bounds. Recidivism rates were highest for the youngest offenders and decreased steadily with age. By sentence the rates were highest in the youngest category, that is, among offenders handled within the social services, whereas fines and conditional sentences had the lowest rates. Generally, the variation in rates between kinds of sentences suggests selection of offenders by age and severity. This may illustrate a need for looking behind the sentence in policy analyses. Table 8 shows relapses within one year in 1991–99 cohorts of young male offenders and all offenders for various sanctions. Even here some effects of selection by age and severity of offenses can be traced.

Table 9 gives the number of reported offenses per 100,000 population for every fifth year from 1950 for selected offense categories. Drug abuse peaked in 1980, and drunken driving had a plateau between 1975 and 1990. With a few early inversions, the other offenses tended to increase to 1990 or later. Increases in the 1950s tended to accelerate in later decades. Reported offenses, however, are an imperfect measure of the incidence of crimes. Victims' inclination to report and authorities' inclination to record may change over the period, for instance, because of an increased sensitivity to violence or because violence is becoming more lethal, or both.

Clearance rates, in table 10, are calculated as percentages of the

TABLE 8

Relapses within One Year in 1994–99 Cohorts of Young Offenders by Sentences (Percent)

Sentence and Ages	No. of Relapses	N	Percent
Prison:			
15–17	48	99	48
18–20	1,075	2,976	36
All	17,460	61,848	28
Probation:			
15–17	299	1,027	29
18–20	1,075	4,271	25
All	4,206	22,006	19
Voluntary treatment instead of prison:			
15–17			
18–20	70	212	33
All	953	6,090	16
Community service:			
15–17	10	62	16
18–20	253	1,511	17
All	520	3,712	14
Probation with prison:			
15–17	25	68	37
18–20	169	519	33
All	623	1,817	34
Supervision with electronic control:			
15–17			
18–20	27	506	5
All	439	11,327	4

Source.—Kriminalvårdsstyrelsen 2000, chap. 7.

numbers of offenses in the year.[7] The picture emerging from the table tends to be the reverse of the picture of table 9: clearances declined as numbers of reported offenses increased. Thus, the number of undetected crimes increased through the period, except during short intervals. The main reasons for this are that the increase in reported offenses was not matched by an equal increase in the number of police investigators and that, in some cases, investigators were diverted to other tasks or released (Ahlberg 2002). The number of cleared cases per investigator remained about equal.

[7] A case is considered cleared if it led to prosecution, summary fines, or a waiver of prosecution; the offender is found to be below fifteen years of age; the investigation is closed without a suspect; or the case is found not to be an offense.

TABLE 9
Reported Offenses per 100,000 of Mean Population, Every Fifth Year from 1950

Year	Total	Offenses against Life and Health	Assault	Rape	Theft	Car Theft	Robbery	Drug Abuse	Drunk Driving
1950	2,784	120	106	5	1,578	N.A.	3	0	49
1955	3,357	135	118	5	2,254	N.A.	4	0	125
1960	3,982	131	116	7	2,729	244	6	2	170
1965	5,801	167	151	8	3,694	397	12	10	213
1970	8,157	247	228	9	4,874	402	19	196	212
1975	9,221	282	263	9	5,709	448	29	258	265
1980	11,170	320	297	11	6,228	413	41	715	261
1985	12,195	411	383	12	7,413	539	46	431	237
1990	14,240	504	475	16	9,650	882	70	310	298
1995	12,982	647	616	19	7,759	659	65	323	193
2000	13,694	696	663	23	7,934	912	101	365	196
2001	13,390	701	668	23	7,495	675	96	365	203

Sources.—BRÅ 2000:12, table 1.1; 2002:13.
Note.—N.A. = Not available.

TABLE 10
Clearance Rates (as Percentages), Every Fifth Year from 1950

Year	Total	Offenses against Life and Health	Assault	Rape	Theft	Car Theft	Robbery	Drug Abuse	Drunk Driving
1950	58	N.A.	91	74	34	N.A.	48	140	92
1955	43	N.A.	88	77	25	N.A.	65	60	88
1960	43	81	80	68	26	32	53	66	83
1965	31	80	59	65	19	22	42	45	67
1970	41	65	64	56	21	34	38	83	93
1975	37	61	62	55	19	33	34	81	90
1980	38	63	63	52	17	27	29	90	89
1985	35	54	53	40	17	17	25	96	86
1990	30	50	50	39	13	12	19	91	81
1995	25	44	44	37	12	11	20	73	78
2000	26	47	47	40	10	9	13	75	89

Sources.—BRÅ 2000:12, table 2.1; 2002:13. Drug abuse: according to Narkotikaförordningen (the drug ordinance) 1950–83; from then on according to Narkotikastrafflagen (the drug act) sec. 5A.

Note.—N.A. = Not available.

Clearance rates vary among offenses. Ahlberg (2001, pp. 11–12) distinguishes three kinds of crimes that tend to have different rates. First, in "hunt-and-catch" offenses, there is an identified suspected perpetrator when the deed is reported, usually by the police officer. Such "self-clearing" offenses—traffic offenses, drug abuse, or shoplifting—recorded by the police have very high clearance rates, which have not gone down much. Second, in "interaction" offenses, such as assault, physical intrusion, or molesting, the victim can often describe the offender, making for fairly high clearance rates, which have had about average decreases. Third, offenses without offender-victim interaction, such as thefts and vandalism, which constitute two-thirds of reported offenses, are increasingly difficult to solve as resources become scarcer. Serious crimes, such as homicide, rape, bank robbery, and aggravated assault, are given high priority even though they are difficult to solve.

B. Estimating Juvenile Delinquency

The general trend in reported crimes in Sweden from 1950 is easy to describe in bold strokes (even if somewhat controversial in details): from 1950 to 1960 the increase in offenses was slow, but thereafter it was clear and steady until the 1990s, after which crime rate variations have stayed on the same level (Ahlberg 2001; Westfelt 2001). To move from reported crime trends to total crime trends, one needs a set of assumptions about unreported crimes. Generally, the numbers can be seen as functions of the "situation" in which the crime is committed— in terms of spatial or social circumstances of perpetrator and victim, and the kind of offense (fairly simple or very elaborate), according to context and criminological inclination.

The trends for reported youth offending are more difficult to know since this requires knowledge of the age of the offenders. This places another set of unknowns in our way. One way around this is to look for alternative approaches. Self-reports are the first. These are well-established, although they have problems of their own: biased nonresponse and retrospective data (Janson 1990). There are several modern Swedish self-report studies with modern questionnaires and satisfactorily low nonresponse rates (much less nonresponse than is accepted in U.S. sociology). The problem lies in the 1950s–70s; there are few early low-nonresponse studies samples (Elmhorn 1969; Olofsson 1971; Sarnecki 1989; Ward 1998). It is difficult to make strict comparisons with later self-reports, regardless of the quality of the early studies. For instance, Birgitta Olofsson's dissertation (1971) had a cohort sample of

549 boys who were in the ninth form of the comprehensive school of the medium-sized city of Örebro. In May 1968, she collected data on thirty self-report items and experienced a nonresponse rate of only 5 percent. In addition, 6 percent of the cohort had left school before the ninth form. From other data collected in the longitudinal project of which the self-report study was a part, it was known that many of these dropouts were more delinquent than those responding. Ward's study (1998) refers to a cohort of children in the ninth form of comprehensive school in the same city—but in 1996 with a 12 percent nonresponse rate and almost the same questionnaire. This is ideal for a comparison between juvenile delinquency in 1968 and 1996. The main results are that in 1996 fewer boys commit crime, but those who do are more active than their counterparts in 1968; further, in 1996, those fewer boys who start committing crime run a greater risk of continuing and of being caught by the police (Ward 1998, p. 54).

Unfortunately, one cannot hope for corresponding comparisons of time points within the thirty-year period between 1968 and 1996. For a variety of reasons, victim studies would not solve the comparison problem satisfactorily.

Jan Ahlberg (1996*b*) has presented an interesting approach. Annual statistics are available on persons—specified for age, sex, and type of offense—who are suspected of being the perpetrator of a given offense, and for how many reported offenses this was the case. Comparing these figures with the annual number of offenses reported and cleared up may be used to estimate the risk of being apprehended during the year. If so, annual numbers of apprehended persons may be corrected so as to give the same risk of apprehension, say, to all fifteen- to nineteen-year-old offenders, considering the offender's criminal involvement. Starting in 1975 with thefts—except shoplifting—by fifteen- to nineteen-year-old suspects, Ahlberg calculated the reported annual numbers of apprehended fifteen- to nineteen-year-old offenders so as to contain an equal number of apprehended offenders, given the clearance rates and estimated degree of offenders' criminal activity. The adjusted number for 1990 was 47 percent higher than the 1975 value. Then the adjusted numbers decreased to 25 percent above the 1975 value (Ahlberg 1996*b*, p. 199). Corresponding adjustments as to crimes of violence resulted in some slight decrease in juvenile offending until 1981 and, from there, an accelerating increase until the end of the period, which may partly result from an increase in reporting. Finally, other offenses are analyzed, assuming the same decreases in clearance rates for all other offenses. The composite estimated curve suggests an increase in juvenile offending between 1975 and 1990 of 25 percent. During the same period, reported offenses increased by 60 percent. The discrepancy might be accounted for by an underestimation of the increase in juvenile offending and an actual increase in the number of offenses per offender (Ahlberg et al. 1996*b*, p. 202).

Ahlberg's results are controversial. Filipe Estrada (1999) used the same approach with slightly different assumptions and reached other results. Granath and Lindström (2000) used prosecuted and suspected cases and concluded that recorded juvenile delinquency has not increased after 1980 and that recently reported juvenile offending shows a decrease in car thefts, other thefts, and traffic violations but increases in assaults, violence, damage, and shoplifting (Granath and Lindström 2000, pp. 11–13).

C. Sociological Factors in Juvenile Delinquency

In 1950, the Swedish population reached seven million people, of whom 66 percent lived in metropolitan places. Of the economically active population, 25 percent worked in agriculture, fishing, and forestry and 46 percent worked within manufacturing, construction, and mining. In 1999, the population had grown to almost nine million, of whom 84 percent lived in urban places. Agriculture and related branches of industry employed only 2 percent of the economically active population. Manufacturing employment had decreased to 26 percent, as Sweden had proceeded from being an industrial to being a postindustrial society.

This development brought profound social changes, of which several are criminologically relevant. For instance, good times tend to be good also for illegal activities. In good times, some goods such as new cars make attractive targets for property crimes, as do movable goods that are light in weight but have a heavy price, such as many electronic gadgets. In the terms of Marcus Felson's routine activity approach (Cohen and Felson 1979; Clarke and Felson 1993; Felson 1994), dangerous situations multiply. When much money is around, opportunities for business transactions abound, and people are often away from home traveling to work and spending time in entertainment areas, attractive targets multiply. When business is slow, targets tend to be fewer, less attractive, and more cautious. Furthermore, minorities may be disproportionately hit by unemployment and spending cuts. With increasing segregation, more run-down neighborhoods, and schools deprived of resources to take care of pupils with special needs, bad times can be especially hard for minority young people. Both strong variations in reported offending and in business cycles are well mapped for the fifty-year period.

In the 1950–90 period, the Swedish unemployment rate was almost always below 3 percent, except in the earliest years and for some years in the 1980s. Juvenile delinquency and adult criminality wriggled upward. In the late 1980s, the deregulation movement led to a crisis in the real estate and banking businesses, which, combined with a rapidly growing national debt, developed into a general economic depression during the first years of the 1990s (Ortmark 2000). From unemployment rates of 1.6 percent in 1990 and 3.0 percent in 1991, the rates rose to 5.2 percent in 1992 and 8.2 percent in 1993, well above any previous unemployment rate in the postwar period. Cutbacks were introduced and continued for several years. About this time, juvenile delinquency and adult criminality stopped going up.

Interactions within the family have key roles in socialization theory. In the 1950–99 period, family structures changed, and intergenerational interactions within families changed with them. In 1950, 76 percent of Swedish families consisted of married cohabiting spouses, of whom 55 percent had at least one child. Of wives, 86 percent were housewives, while 23 percent of females were economically active. Thirteen percent of the families had female heads. In 1999, cohabiting spouses constituted 39 percent of families, but both spouses were working in 23 percent of these families, and 75 percent had at least one child. Families headed by single women now made up 33 percent of families. Nineteen percent of them had at least one child.

In 1950, ninety-eight out of 1,000 live births were out of wedlock. In 1999, the rate had risen to 553 (for a somewhat similar but belated U.S. development, see Hacker [2002]). The time sequence of getting married, cohabiting, and having children became open to choice.

A third factor that should be noted is the use of alcohol and narcotics. Since 1971, the Center for Education on Alcohol and Narcotics has monitored the use of alcohol and narcotics according to self-reports (Guttormsson and Svensson 1997). After high ever-used frequencies in the 1970s, by the end of the 1980s the use of narcotics showed much lower frequencies than ever reported in the series of studies. Drug users had become older, and few young persons seem to have been newly recruited. Since then, self-reported use has again increased but perhaps has become more rave-party oriented.

A fourth important change was immigration. Sweden and the other Nordic countries generally have more often imported than exported ideas and competence. Urbanization and industrialization started late in Sweden, around 1850, but proceeded fast. Also around 1850, the huge European, mostly transatlantic, flow of emigration started to stream out of Sweden. It culminated in 1880–93 and subsided after the first years of the twentieth century; the 1930s was the first decade with a small immigration surplus. Sweden at that time was an ethnically homogeneous country with a homogeneous culture, albeit with some regional variations.

Since 1945, Sweden has been a country of immigration. A sometimes heavy inflow of immigrants and refugees has produced the ethnically heterogeneous population of 2003. However, the process has been gradual, and at least during the first decades after World War II, the population retained much of its ethnic and cultural homogeneity. The great transition to a "multicultural" society came with the influx from the Middle East and other non-European countries in the 1980s.

During World War II and at its end, Sweden received about 200,000 temporary immigrants, most of whom returned to their home countries.[8] In 1954, a common Nordic labor market was established. Starting in the 1950s, non-Nordic labor force immigrants were brought in, but after 1972, with a few exceptions, only family members of those already in Sweden were admitted. Labor force immigration peaked in the boom years of 1969–70, when 142,000 persons entered. Among them were 80,000 Finns, of whom about 45,000 returned home in the next few years. By 1985, around 450,000 Finns had entered, including family members. Of these, some 280,000 eventually returned to Finland.

A policy of integration rather than assimilation was established during the 1970s. In 1976, noncitizen immigrants who had been living in the country for at least three years were given the right to vote in local elections. Since 1977, children of foreign-born parents have received

---

[8] Including approximately 70,000 Finnish children evacuated during the 1939–40 Finnish-Russian-Winter War; some 43,000 members of the Norwegian resistance; some Danish Jews escaping from deportation in 1944; about 31,000 Norwegian, Danish, and Jewish prisoners of German camps, such as Ravensbruck, during spring 1945 by "The White Buses"; and about 30,000 refugees from the Baltic States, many of whom settled in Sweden.

some teaching in their mother tongues. Rules of naturalization were generous, especially between the Nordic countries. In the 1980s, an average of about 20,000 immigrants yearly became Swedish citizens, some 60 percent of them from non-Nordic countries. In the mid-1980s, the first Swedish mosque of some size was founded in Malmö, and recently an impressive mosque was opened in central Stockholm.

In the 1970s, about half of the immigrants came from non-Nordic countries, almost all from European countries. From the 1950s, refugees were received from several European countries and, after 1974, from Chile. In the 1980s, most new non-Nordic arrivals were refugees or their close relatives; in the second half of the decade more than half came from non-European countries. In 1980, noncitizens comprised 5 percent of the population, almost 3 percent from the Nordic countries. Adding foreign-born Swedish citizens would increase the immigrant part of the population to 8 percent, of whom 43 percent were Finnish and 16 percent were from other parts of Scandinavia. Five percent of the Swedish labor force were non-Swedish citizens, of whom about half were Nordic citizens. At the end of 1986, those born abroad and noncitizens together constituted 10 percent of the Swedish population, with half coming from the Nordic countries.

In 1993, there were 61,900 immigrants; in 1994, 83,600; and in 1999, 49,800. Of the 1999 group, 22,300 were Nordic citizens; 21,700 were close relatives of refugees; and 5,600 were refugees who were granted residence permits as quota refugees, by UN convention, or on humanitarian grounds. Another 2,600 asylum applicants were rejected. Other categories were accepted as adopted children, as visiting students, or for labor market reasons.

In 1999, Sweden had 8.86 million inhabitants, of whom 7.88 million were born in the country and 982,000 were born abroad: 280,000 in the Nordic countries; 323,000 in other European countries; 53,000 in Africa; and 159,000 in the Middle East (including Iran). Of those foreign-born, 582,000 were Swedish citizens, whereas 87,000 of the Swedish-born population were citizens of other countries. The foreign-born population and the non-Swedish citizens add up to 1.07 million, or 12 percent, of the inhabitants in Sweden.

In some contexts, second-generation immigrants—all children born in Sweden in a family with at least one foreign-born parent, whether or not they are Swedish citizens—should be counted as equivalent to foreign-born immigrants. Culturally, religiously, and socioeconomically, these children form a mixed category—and include members of the royal family. The size of the category in 1985 has been estimated at 8 percent and has increased since then. In his sample of 16,886 ninth-year students for self-report studies in 1995, 1997, and 1999, Jonas Ring (2000) found 21 percent of students who had at least one parent born abroad, whereas Tommy Andersson (2000), in his 1999 stratified sample of 4,498 Stockholm and Malmö junior and senior high school students, found 23 percent who had at least one parent born abroad. Similarly, Knut Sundell's sample of 4,756 Stockholm students in the last year of comprehensive school in the year 2000 held 22.5 percent first- and second-generation immigrants (Sundell 2001, pp. 98–101).

The percentage of immigrants is higher in the three metropolitan areas than elsewhere and is twice as high in the Stockholm area as in the country as a whole. Metropolitan ethnic segregation is increasing and seems recently to have reached U.S. levels, but with the ethnic ghettos in the suburbs and upper-middle-class areas in the central city. The ghetto areas are not dominated by a single immigrant group but are ethnically heterogeneous, with a large number of languages represented in the population. United States–type street gangs with turfs have not yet developed (Klein 1995, chap. 8), although there are tag gangs. The ethnic heterogeneity of immigrant neighborhoods may tend to make young groups less ethnically homogeneous (Sarnecki 2001, chap. 9). Perhaps group membership will be selected more according to the standing of immigrant categories in the neighborhood.

On arrival, the refugees are housed in municipalities that have agreed to receive them while their applications for residence permits are being processed. This might take some time and is a trying period of insecurity. Equipped with the permanent permit, the refugee may live anywhere in the country, and many move to a metropolitan area despite serious housing shortages. If a permit is denied, this may lead to media-covered local protests, for instance, by neighbors or classmates of the refugee family's children. Often, the refusal will be reconsidered, or sometimes the refugees will go into hiding in sanctuaries, abetted by nuns, vicars, or other morally upright people.

It is not always that magnanimous. A few municipalities have refused to receive permit-seeking refugees. In the 1991 election, a new party critical of large-scale immigration obtained parliamentary seats but disintegrated before the 1994 election. Opinion polls indicate considerable disapproval of large-scale immigration, with supporters only in some municipality councils, mostly in the south. However, the general attitude of the authorities and the media remains positive toward Swedish society's increased diversity. Both politicians and mainstream media emphasize that a multicultural society should be seen as an advantage—better many-sided than one-sided—and that immigrants are a resource rather than a problem. To receive refugees is seen as an obligation. Explicit criticism of immigration policy runs the risk of being interpreted as racist, and any incident seen as an act of racism is strongly condemned.

Behind the discontent with the heavy immigration, especially of non-Europeans, are two perceptions. First, it is expensive. Labor force immigrants pay more taxes than they receive benefits, but refugees cost the country a lot. Helping refugees in need is, of course, not intended to be profitable in the short run, but some feel that Sweden has taken on more than its share. Second, immigrants have a higher propensity to crime than the general population. Both of these claims appear to be ideologically incorrect simplifications of the situation.

The steady rise in offending until, say, the mid-1970s cannot be more than marginally attributed to the new population heterogeneity. In the period 1985–89 and in 1993, both first- and second-generation immigrants were found to be overrepresented among offenders, although native-born Swedes had committed the majority of offenses (Ahlberg 1996a). Generally, second-generation immigrants had lower rates than immigrants of the first generation.

Finns in Sweden had higher crime rates than Finns in Finland, but generally labor force immigrants differed only slightly from Swedish natives of the country. A cohort study of 15,117 Stockholmers born in 1953 and living in the Stockholm area in 1963 included 1,236 members (8.2 percent) who were born abroad or were born in Sweden to a mother who was born abroad. Their educational records were almost the same as those for the whole cohort (Janson 2000, 2002). The rate of delinquency participation was slightly higher than for the entire cohort or for Swedish members alone, one-third higher, say, for the children with "immigrant background," with Finns on the top (Martens 1994). The higher rates of offending by immigrants as a whole emerge in several later studies on larger and less specialized data, such as Peter Martens's extensive summary (1997) and Ahlberg's statistical analysis (Ahlberg 1996a). Compared with the cohort study, both Martens and Ahlberg identify smaller proportions of early labor force immigrants and their families and correspondingly more non-Nordic immigrants and refugees and their families, as well as larger total proportions of immigrant populations. Increased numbers of immigrants offending at the same higher rates contribute more to the overall level of offending than did smaller numbers. However, both Ahlberg (1996a) and Martens (1997) found higher rates of reported offending by immigrants than in the longitudinal study. For those born abroad, Martens calculated offending rates in 1985–89 that were at least twice the general population rate for homicide, rape, robbery, and shoplifting (Ahlberg 1996a, table 8, pp. 41–42; Martens 1997, table 7, p. 223). Neither Martens's nor Ahlberg's figures refer to juveniles exclusively.

Granath and Lindström (2000) base their analyses of juvenile sanctions on a sample of 2,846 court cases from 1993 and 1998 in four judicial districts. An analysis of differences between young immigrants and others showed slight tendencies to sentence immigrants more often and waive prosecution less often (Granath and Lindström 2000, table 6). Disaggregating by offense and taking account of lower levels of confessions by immigrant shoplifters—who were thus not eligible for waiver of prosecution—reduced the differences further (Granath and Lindström 2000, table 10). Granath and Lindström's study gives little support to claims that sentencing practices account for the overrepresentation of immigrants among known offenders. Most likely, most immigrant groups and minorities face some bias in sanctioning policy but also have at least slightly higher propensities to delinquency than do the general population (McDonald 2002).

Knut Sundell (2001) carried out self-report studies of drug and high-risk behavior of 16,226 students in Stockholm in 1993, 1996, 1998, and 2000. In his sample for the year 2000, of 4,756 students—after an 11 percent nonresponse—he recorded 1,071 immigrants, around 22 percent among both boys and girls. The immigrant boys had stolen a bike or a motorbike, robbed someone, carried a weapon, and been involved in a fight more often than Swedish boys, who had pilfered and wantonly destroyed property more often. Immigrant girls had more frequently robbed someone and been involved in fights than Swedish girls, who had more often pilfered and been victimized (Sundell 2001, pp. 98–102).

Tommy Andersson (2000) has data from 1995 and 1999 in Stockholm and Malmö for "youngsters who rob youngsters." The numbers of such street robberies of personal valuables—cell phones, watches, money, and so on—were not very high even when it was popular among robbers, and only about every second robbery was reported. For those reported, the offender rate among immigrant boys was about 5.5 times the population rate.

Jonas Ring (2000) analyzed three waves of self-reports of sixteen- to seventeen-year-old high school students in 1995, 1997, and 1999. With less than 9 percent nonresponse in the first two waves and 15 percent in the third wave, the number of interviewees was 8,622 boys and 8,252 girls. In general, the results are in line with what has been conjectured from studies of reported offenses: some decrease of juvenile property offenses. Ring noted low frequencies but more incidents in 1999 than in the earlier years (Ring 2000, table 4, p. 45). In his report, immigrants are not conspicuous—perhaps according to Crime Prevention Council policies—but one can see that they appear somewhat more frequently in the two highest-risk categories (Ring 2000, table 4, app.). Immigration, thus, appears to have had an impact on the level of offending and to changes in it from, say, the 1970s, even if we do not know what mechanisms have been at work.

It is easy to overestimate the direct effects of penal policy on deviance, especially when parts of the youth justice system are commonly seen as missing opportunities to stop delinquency with tougher interventions. The Commission of Penal Law (as Nelson noticed [1968, p. 135]) offered a remarkable paragraph warning against overestimating the likely effects of interventions.

> Society's penological interventions aim at protecting society and its members from criminality by preventing crime. Hence its legislation should if possible primarily attempt to produce efficient measures of crime prevention. In creating its proposed bills the Commission of Penal Law has aimed at meeting this demand, considering actual conditions and paying attention to legal rights and the demands of humanity.
>
> However, it must be emphasized that the possibilities of penal policy to prevent crime in many ways are limited and that the presence of crimes does not depend only on, or even substantially on, shortcomings in the penal legislation. It is a misconception, when many—probably because the penological intervention is the only social action that has the single purpose to prevent crime—seem to think that by reforming the sanction system one might stop an increase in the number of offenses. This goes against all experience. And it seems obvious that the extent to which people commit crimes depends on an interaction among a great number of factors that between themselves are very different. Some of them encourage offending, others deter from crime. Thus, it is unreasonable to assume that one might succeed, through one

single factor, the penological intervention, to control people to complete obedience to the law. (Strafflagberedningen 1956, p. 28)

REFERENCES

Ahlberg, Jan. 1996a. *Invandrares och invandrares barns brottslighet* (Offenses by immigrants and children of immigrants). Report 1996:2. Stockholm: BRÅ.

———. 1996b. "Ungdomsbrottslighet" (Juvenile delinquency). In *Brottsutvecklingen 1994* (Crime trends 1994). Report 1996:4, edited by Jan Ahlberg. Stockholm: BRÅ.

———. 2001. *Brottsutvecklingen i Sverige, 1998–2000* (Crime trends in Sweden, 1998–2000). Report 2001:10. Stockholm: BRÅ.

———. 2002. *Varför har brottsuppklaringen minskat?* (Crime clearance and efficiency). Report 2002:4. Stockholm: BRÅ.

Andenaes, Johannes. 1952. "General Prevention—Illusion or Reality." *Journal of Criminal Law, Criminology, and Police Science* 43:176–98.

Andersson, Tommy. 2000. *Ungdomar som rånar ungdomar* (Youth who rob other youth). Report 2000:6. Stockholm: BRÅ.

Becker, Howard. 1963. *Outsiders: Studies in the Sociology of Deviance*. New York: Free Press.

Björkman, Jenny. 2001. *Vård för samhällets bästa* (Care for the sake of society). Stockholm: Carlsson.

Blomberg, Dick. 1960. *Den svenska ungdomsbrottsligheten* (Swedish juvenile delinquency). Stockholm: Natur och kultur.

Blomberg, Dick, and Karl Grunewald. 1964. *Behandlingsforskning vid ungdomsvårdsskolorna* (Research on treatment at the reformatory schools). Report 1964:24, Stockholm: Statens Offentilga Utreningar (SOU).

Bolin, Lars. 1992a. "Från tukthus till ungdomsvårdsskola" (From penitentiary to reformatory). In *Från tukthus till behandlingshem* (From penitentiary to treatment home), edited by Lars Bolin. Stockholm: Allmänna Barnhuset.

———. 1992b. "En verksamhet i takt med tiden" (An activity in tune with time). In *Från tukthus till behandlingshem* (From penitentiary to treatment home), edited by Lars Bolin. Stockholm: Allmänna Barnhuset.

Bolin, Lars, and Arne Dahlström. 1992. "Kronologisk sammanställning" (Chronological list). In *Från tukthus till behandlingshem* (From penitentiary to treatment home), edited by Lars Bolin. Stockholm: Allmänna barnhuset.

Börjeson, Bengt. 1966. *Om påföljders verkningar* (On the consequences of sanctions). Stockholm: Almqvist & Wiksell.

BRÅ. 1977. *Nytt straffsystem* (New punishment system). Report 1977:7. Stockholm: BRÅ.

———. Annual 1998–2002. *Årlig Kriminalstatistik* (Annual criminal statistics). Stockholm: BRÅ.

Bramstång, Gunnar. 1964. *Förutsättningarna för barnavårdsnämnds ingripande mot asocial ungdom* (Conditions of child welfare committee's interference with asocial youth). Lund: Gleerup.

Clarke, Ronald V., and Marcus Felson. 1993. "Introduction: Routine Activity, and Rational Choice." In *Routine Activity and Rational Choice*, vol. 5, *Advances in Criminological Theory*, edited by Ronald V. Clarke and Marcus Felson. New Brunswick, N.J.: Transaction.

Cohen, Lawrence, and Marcus Felson. 1979. "Social Change and Crime Rate Trends." *American Sociological Review* 44:588–605.

Dahlström, Arne. 1992. "Ungdomsvård i förändring" (Youth care in change). In *Från tukthus till behandlingshem* (From penitentiary to treatment home), edited by Lars Bolin. Stockholm: Allmänna barnhuset.

Dalteg, Arne. 1990. "Avancerade unga lagöverträdare" (Advanced young offenders). Ph.D. dissertation, University of Lund, Department of Psychiatry.

Elmhorn, Kerstin. 1969. *Faktisk brottslighet bland skolbarn* (Actual delinquency among school children). Report 1969:1. Stockholm: SOU.

Eriksson, Torsten. 1967. *Kriminalvård: Idéer och experiment* (Treatment of offenders). Stockholm: Norstedt.

Estrada, Filipe. 1999. "Ungdomsbrottslighet som samhällsproblem" (Juvenile delinquency as societal problem). Ph.D. dissertation, Stockholm University, Department of Criminology.

Fängelsestraffkommittén (Imprisonment committee). 1986. *Påföljd för brott* (Sanctions for offenses). Report 1986:14. Stockholm: SOU.

Felson, Marcus. 1994. *Crime and Everyday Life: Insights and Implications for Society.* Thousand Oaks, Calif.: Pine Forge.

Goffman, Erving. 1963. *Stigma: Notes on the Management of Spoiled Identity.* Englewood Cliffs, N.J.: Prentice-Hall.

Gove, Walter, ed. 1975. *The Labelling of Deviance.* New York: Wiley.

Granath, Sven, and Peter Lindström. 2000. *Påföljdssystemet för unga lagöverträdare* (The sanction system for young offenders). Report 2000:7. Stockholm: BRÅ.

Guttormsson, Ulf, and Daniel Svensson, coordinators. 1997. *Alkohol- och narkotikautvecklingen i Sverige* (Trends in alcohol and drug use in Sweden). Report 97. Stockholm: Folkhälsoinstitutet (Institute for Public Health); Centralförbundet för alkohol- och narkotika upplysning (Center for Education on Alcohol and Narcotics).

Hacker, Andrew. 2002. "How Are Women Doing?" *New York Review* (April 11), pp. 63–66.

Janson, Carl-Gunnar. 1977. *The Handling of Juvenile Delinquency Cases.* Project Metropolitan Research Report no. 7. Stockholm: Stockholm University, Department of Sociology.

———. 1990. "Retrospective Data, Undesirable Behaviour, and the Longitudinal Perspective." In *Data Quality in Longitudinal Research*, edited by David Magnusson and Lars R. Bergman. Cambridge: Cambridge University Press.

———. 2000. "Project Metropolitan." In *Seven Swedish Longitudinal Studies*, edited by Carl-Gunnar Janson. Stockholm: FRN.

————. 2002. "Swedish Society and Stockholm: The Cohort and Its Context." In Sheilagh Hodgins and Carl-Gunnar Janson, *Criminality and Violence among the Mentally Disordered: The Stockholm Metropolitan Project.* Cambridge: Cambridge University Press.

Janson, Carl-Gunnar, and Marie Torstensson. 1984. "Sweden." In *Western Systems of Juvenile Justice*, edited by Malcolm W. Klein. Beverly Hills, Calif.: Sage.

Jareborg, Nils, and Andrew von Hirsch. 1984. *Påföljdsbestämning i USA* (Estimating sanctions in the United States). Report 1984:4. Stockholm: BRÅ.

Justitiedepartementet. 1959. *Ungdomsbrottslighet* (Juvenile delinquency). Report 1959:37. Stockholm: SOU.

————. 1972. *Kriminalvård* (Treatment of offenders). Report 1972:64. Stockholm: SOU.

————. 1973. *Kriminologisk forskning* (Criminological research). Report 1973: 35. Stockholm: SOU.

Klein, Malcolm W. 1995. *The American Street Gang: Its Nature, Prevalence, and Control.* New York: Oxford University Press.

Knutsson, Johannes. 1977. *Labeling Theory: A Critical Examination.* Report no. 3. Stockholm: BRÅ.

Kriminalvårdsstyrelsen (National prison board). 2000. *Fångvårdens redovisning om återfall* (Reports on relapses). Norrköping: Kriminalvårdstyrelsen.

————. 2002. Kriminalvårdens Officiella Statistik 2001 (National Prison Board Official Statistics 2001). Norrköping: Kriminalvårdstyrelsen.

Kühlhorn, Eckart. 2002. "Sluten ungdomsvård" (Youth custody). In *Rättsliga reaktioner på de ungas brott före och efter införandet 1999* (Judicial sanctions on youth delinquency before and after its introduction in 1999). Report no. 5. Stockholm: SiS.

Kumlien, Mats. 1994. *Uppfostran och straff* (Upbringing and sanction). Uppsala: Uppsala University.

Levin, Claes. 1996. "Barnen mellan straff och behandling" (Children between punishment and treatment). In *Vård av ungdomar med sociala problem* (Treatment of young people with social problems), edited by Bengt-Åke Armelius, Sven Bengtsson, Per-Anders Rydelius, Jerzy Sarnecki, and Kerstin Söderholm Carpelan. Stockholm: Liber.

————. 1997. *Ungdomar i tvångsvård* (Adolescents in coerced treatment). Report no. 2. Stockholm: SiS.

Loeber, Rolf, and David P. Farrington. 1998. "Conclusions and the Way Forward." In *Serious and Violent Juvenile Offenders: Risk Factors and Successful Interventions*, edited by Rolf Loeber and David P. Farrington. Thousand Oaks, Calif.: Sage.

Lundén, Ann, and Elisabet Näsman. 1973. *Stämplingsprocessen* (The labeling process). Stockholm: Prisma.

Lundström, Tommy, and Bo Vinnerljung. 2001. "Omhändertagande av barn under 1990-talet" (Taking care of children in the nineties). In *Välfärdstjänster i omvandling* (Welfare service in transformation), edited by Marta Szebehely. Report 2001:52. Stockholm: SOU.

Martens, Peter L. 1994. "Criminal and Other Antisocial Behaviour among

Persons with Immigrant and Swedish Background—a Research Note." In *Studies of a Stockholm Cohort*. Project Metropolitan Research Report no. 39. Stockholm: Stockholm University, Department of Sociology.

———. 1997. "Immigrants, Crime, and Criminal Justice in Sweden." In *Ethnicity, Crime, and Immigration: Comparative and Cross-National Perspectives*, edited by Michael Tonry. Vol. 21 of *Crime and Justice: A Review of Research*, edited by Michael Tonry. Chicago: University of Chicago Press.

Martinson, Robert. 1974. "What Works? Questions and Answers about Prison Reform." *Public Interest* 10:22–54.

McDonald, William. 2002. "Immigrant Criminality: In the Eye of the Beholder?" Paper presented at European Society of Criminology Annual Conference, September 2002, Toledo, Spain.

Nelson, Alvar. 1968. "Den svenska kriminalpolitiken" (The Swedish penal policy). In *Sociala avvikelser och social kontroll* (Social deviances and social control), edited by Joachim Israel. 2d ed. Stockholm: Almqvist & Wiksell.

Olofsson, Birgitta. 1971. *Vad var det vi sa! Om kriminellt och konformt beteende bland skolpojkar* (I told you so! On criminal and conforming behavior among schoolboys). Stockholm: Utbildningsförlaget.

Ortmark, Åke. 2000. *Ja-sägarna* (The yes men). 3d ed. Stockholm: Wahlström & Widstrand.

Ottoson, Ivan. 1992. "Socialtjänstutredningen" (The social service report). In *Från tukthus till behandlingshem* (From penitentiary to treatment home), edited by Lars Bolin. Stockholm: Allmänna barnhuset.

Qvarsell, Roger. 1996. "Ungdomars brottslighet och samhällets vård" (Juvenile delinquency and societal care). In *Vård av ungdomar med sociala problem* (Treatment of adolescents with social problems), edited by Bengt-Åke Armenius, Sven Bengtsson, Per-Anders Rydelius, Jerzy Sarnecki, and Kerstin Söderholm Carpelan. Stockholm: Liber.

Ring, Jonas. 2000. *Stöld, våld och droger bland pojkar och flickor i årskurs nio* (Theft, violence, and drugs among boys and girls in ninth form). Report 2000:17. Stockholm: BRÅ.

Rubington, Earl, and Martin S. Weinberg. 1971. *The Study of Social Problems: Six Perspectives*. 2d ed. New York: Oxford University Press.

Sarnecki, Jerzy. 1989. "Self-Reported and Recorded Data on Drug Abuse and Delinquency on 287 Men in Stockholm." In *Cross-National Research in Self-Reported Crime and Delinquency*, edited by Malcolm W. Klein. Dordrecht: Kluwer Academic.

———. 2001. *Delinquent Networks: Youth Co-offending in Stockholm*. Cambridge: Cambridge University Press.

Schlyter, Karl. 1934. *Avfolka fängelserna!* (Depopulate the prisons). Stockholm: Tiden.

Socialstyrelsen (National Social Welfare Board). 1982–89. *Socialvård* (Social care). Stockholm: Socialtjänst.

———. 2001. *Insatser för barn och ungdom, 1992–98* (Measures for children and youth 1992–98). Stockholm: Socialstyrelsen.

———. *Insatser för barn och ungdom 2001* (Children and young persons subjected to measures 2001). Report 2002:7. Stockholm: Socialstyrelsen.

Socialutredningen. 1977. *Socialtjänst och socialförsäkringstillägg* (Social service and national security additions). Report 1977:40. Stockholm: SOU.

Söderholm Carpelan, Kerstin. 1994. "The Institutional Care of Young People in Sweden during the 20th Century: From the State to Local Authorities and Back." Paper presented at the conference "Child Welfare: Reviewing the Framework," Shetland Islands, June 1994. Unpublished manuscript. Stockholm: Statens Institutionsstyrelse.

Statens Institutionsstyrelse (SiS, National Board of Institutional Care in Sweden). 2001. *Årsbok 2001 Verksamheten vid Statens institutionsstyrelse* (Annual report 2001, National Board of Institutional Care in Sweden). Stockholm: SiS.

———. 2002. *Årsbok 2002 Verksamheten vid Statens institutionsstyrelse* (Annual report 2002, National Board of Institutional Care in Sweden). Stockholm: SiS.

Statistics Sweden. Annual 1952–2001. *Statistisk Årsbok för Sverige* (Statistical yearbook of Sweden). Stockholm: Statistics Sweden.

Strafflagberedningen. 1956. *Skyddslag* (Protective act). Report 1956:55. Stockholm: SOU.

Sundell, Knut. 2001. *Stockholmsungdomars drog- och riskbeteenden* (Young Stockholmers' drug and risk behaviors). Report 2001:2. Stockholm: Administration of Social Service, Fou Unit.

Tvångsuppfostringskommittén. 1900. *Betänkande och förslag angående vanartade och i sedligt afseende försummade barns behandling* (Report and proposition on treatment of chronic delinquent and morally deprived children). Stockholm: Justitiedepartementet.

Ungdomsbrottskommittén (Commission on juvenile crime). 1993. *Betänkande angående Reaktion mot ungdomsbrottslighet* (Sanctions against juvenile crime). Report 1993:35. Malmö: SOU.

von Hirsch, Andrew. 1976. *Doing Justice: The Choice of Punishments. Report of the Committee for the Study of Incarceration.* 1st ed. New York: Hill & Wang.

Wallén, Per-Edwin. 1979. *Svensk straffrättshistoria, Del 2* (History of Swedish penal law, part 2). 2d ed. Stockholm: AWE/Gebers.

Ward, Martin. 1998. *Barn och brott av vår tid?* (Children and crime by our time?). M.A. thesis. Stockholm University, Department of Criminology.

Westfelt, Lars. 2001. *Brott och straff i Sverige och Europa* (Crime and punishment in Sweden and Europe). Report no. 5. Stockholm: Kriminologiska Institutionen.

Hans-Jörg Albrecht

Youth Justice in Germany

ABSTRACT

Youth justice policies in Germany, except for three years under the Nazi regime, have been remarkably stable. The governing premise has been the desirability of directing responses to crimes by children, youth, and—often—young adults toward sanctions that foster prosocial development. Young offenders are dealt with by specially designated judges in the crime court. The age of responsibility is fourteen. A considerably larger percentage of young offenders receive some confinement, but Germany has the lowest youth incarceration rate in Europe. A variety of special sanctions apply to young offenders, and maximum prison sentences are much lower than for adults. Recent regimes have stressed procedural protections, strengthened victims' rights, and introduced mediation and restitution. Overall, though, despite media and public support for more repressive policies, continuing stability is likely.

The German Youth Court Law (*Jugendgerichtsgesetz*), like its counterparts in Europe and North America, is a child of the nineteenth century. Its emergence is linked to modernity, industrialization, and urbanization, and also to recognition of youth as a social and legal category fostered by social, psychological, and pedagogical sciences. A new category of policy—youth policy—was born. From the very beginning, its justification was the need to protect the young from corrupting effects assumed to be exerted by the adult world (including its criminal justice system).

In the early 1920s, a lengthy debate ended with enactment of special laws and institutions for juvenile offenders and children in need of care and supervision (Oberwittler 2000). In 1923, the German Youth Court Law took effect. The Youth Court Law made profound changes in dealing with young offenders and provided a distinctive legal framework for criminal acts committed by juveniles ages fourteen to seven-

Hans-Jörg Albrecht is director and scientific member, Max Planck Institute for Foreign and International Criminal Law, Freiburg.

teen. Before that, juvenile offenders ages twelve to seventeen fell under the jurisdiction of the adult system, although a minority led to mitigated penalties (Eisenberg 1995). That general approach to juvenile crime and juvenile delinquency—although sometimes heavily criticized—has persisted into the twenty-first century. German policy continues to be based on the view that children and juveniles should be treated differently from adults, and the reason for this is founded on the aim of educating and reforming young offenders.

The Youth Court Law was the first significant result of rehabilitative thinking in modern German criminal legislation. The idea of rehabilitation had been expressed by the "modern school of criminal law," which rejected the classical doctrine of punishment and use of punitive sanctions in favor of behavior-modifying rehabilitative measures. The leading figure, Franz von Liszt, put it this way, as part of a crime control program called the *Marburger Programm* (Marburg program): "If a juvenile commits a criminal offense and we let him get away with it, then the risk of relapse in crime is lower than the risk we face after having him punished" (Liszt 1905, p. 346). That demonstrated, he concluded, the dramatic failure of punitive responses to crime if prevention of crime and safety of society were the primary goals to be pursued. Liszt's statement became the most widely cited phrase in the field of criminal justice policy throughout the past century. It never lost its popularity and became a powerful symbol of a liberal, welfare-oriented approach not only to youth and youth crime but to crime problems in general. The empirical basis for this approach was as weak then as it is today. However, the approach fit well into the emergence of a society based on rationality and cost-benefit thinking and a conception of social welfare as a basic task of the state.

The development of the modern school of criminal law coincided partly with emergence of the "youth court movement" (a sister movement to the child-saving charitable organizations of North America and Great Britain), which also stressed the importance of rehabilitating juvenile offenders, diverting young offenders from the adult system, and providing professional and specialized services for young offenders. The movement also pointed to the need for a distinctive system of justice for juvenile offenders, which was then conceived as a system of education. The youth court movement relied heavily on the thinking of the North American child-saving movement and on North American experiences with juvenile courts. The development of an industrialized society and the emergence of the modern metropolis led to the perception that youth problems were caused by the failure of families, neighborhoods, and society at large to exert proper control over the young. Children of the laboring classes and the *Lumpenproletariat* (the dangerous classes of the nineteenth century) became the primary target of the youth protection movement and ultimately of the youth laws at the beginning of the twentieth century (Voss 1986; Fritsch 1999; Schüler-Springorum 2001). The youth court movement formed part of the general political movement promoting the creation of a welfare state, social security, and a new balance between labor unions and employers. Statutory changes were followed by changes in practice. In 1908, Frankfurt became the first German city to establish a special court department for juvenile offenders. The first juvenile prison opened in 1911.

One year before enactment of the Youth Court Law, the Youth Welfare Law (*Jugendwohlfahrtsgesetz*) of 1922 had taken effect. It was aimed at juveniles under the age of civil responsibility, which then commenced at age twenty-one (today age eighteen), in need of care and education. The German youth laws derived from fundamental beliefs that underlie new youth laws in virtually all Western juvenile justice systems—that juveniles differ from adults psychologically and physiologically and in their social status due to stress and conflicts arising during the transitional developmental period from childhood to adulthood (Empey 1982; Klein 1984). The belief prevailed that juvenile crime indicates the need for legal intervention because of young offenders' social and psychological status.

Juvenile criminal and welfare laws partition youth problems by separating young offenders from otherwise endangered children and juveniles. Both approaches were based on the idea that failures of parents in raising their offspring and providing adequate education puts the responsibility on the state to provide public education, organized either by youth departments or by the juvenile criminal court. The basic difference is in how young people are identified. Admission to the criminal justice system and the juvenile criminal court requires suspicion and indictment of a criminal offense. Public prosecution services are the gatekeepers. Admission to the juvenile welfare system, by contrast, requires establishing the need for care and education of a child or a juvenile with no minimum age requirement. However, juvenile welfare law does not extend beyond age eighteen, while juvenile criminal law (as is explained later) extends to young adults (ages eighteen to twenty).

Here is how this essay is organized. Section I, building on the introduction, surveys the major statutory enactments and changes that shaped youth systems for children, youth, and young adults in the twentieth century. Section II describes the current system and shows how it reflects an amalgam of values that derive from adult criminal law and youth welfare law. Sections III and IV describe young peoples' recent crime rates and survey the explanations for them that have been offered. Section V discusses the disproportionate role in crime trends of young immigrants, including non-German-speaking ethnic Germans from the former Soviet Union. The special situation of these groups is also discussed in later sections. Section VI describes, separately, procedures for handling alleged crimes by children (ages fifteen to seventeen), youth (ages eighteen to twenty), and young adults (ages twenty-one to twenty-five). Section VII describes sanction patterns for the three age groups. Section VIII discusses recent unsuccessful proposals for changes and concludes that broad stability is likely to continue for many years to come.

I. Juvenile Criminal Law Reform

Youth Court Law amendments in 1943, 1953, and 1990, with one exception, have consistently advocated and implemented the principle of education and reduction in the punitive impact of juvenile criminal justice (Kerner 1990). A partial setback occurred in 1943. Under the influence of German fascism, an amendment concerning juvenile felons introduced the possibility of the transfer of juvenile offenders age sixteen and older to adult criminal courts with adult criminal penalties, including the death penalty (Kerner and Weitekamp 1984). The age of criminal responsibility was lowered to twelve for serious crimes. This law, in force for three years, was abolished immediately after World War II as part of the general cleansing of fascist ideology from the legal system. Amendments in 1953 brought important changes in authority to sentence young adults as juveniles and to place juvenile offenders under probation supervision on suspension of a youth prison sentence. The most recent amendment, in 1990, abolished the indeterminate sentence of youth imprisonment, widened diversion and victim-offender mediation, and introduced important restrictions on pretrial detention, among other changes. No further changes were made during the 1990s despite a vocal debate on asserted needs to amend both juvenile criminal law and child welfare law. These debates were triggered by media coverage of seemingly uncontrollable child career criminals, juvenile immigrant offenders, and youth violence (particularly hate violence).

The 1923 Youth Court Law exempted children up to the age of thirteen from criminal responsibility. The range of criminal sanctions was expanded to include so-called educational measures besides prison sentences. Sentencing rules were adjusted to the goal of education. The Youth Court Law explicitly stated that prison sentences were to be used only if educational measures were assessed to be insufficient to respond to juvenile offenders' needs. A dogma was introduced that still prevails today: a youth prison sentence represents the course of last resort to implement education within the juvenile justice system. In 1923, for the first time in German criminal law history, judges were given the option, but only for juveniles, to suspend a prison sentence and replace it with probation. Special procedural rules for juvenile offenders restricted the principle of legality, allowed for expediency in prosecution decisions, and prohibited public juvenile trials.

The Youth Court Law Amendment of 1943 provided for a third category of juvenile sanctions called "disciplinary measures," one example being short-term detention (labeled as "arrest") not exceeding four weeks. However, short-term imprisonment for juveniles was abolished completely, and the minimum prison sentence was set at three months. Prison sentences in the Youth Court Law were renamed "youth imprisonment." However, the change in names was not merely a formal act but made youth imprisonment independent from the range of (prison) penalties provided for adults. A separate and uniform set of minimum and maximum youth prison sentences, justified by the offender orientation of juvenile criminal sanctions, was established. Suspended youth prison sentences were abolished.

The Youth Court Law Amendment of 1953 reintroduced suspended prison sentences and established probation services. More important was the placement of young adults (ages eighteen to twenty) under the Youth Court Law regime. Finally, the minimum youth prison sentence was set at six months.

A principled debate took place in the 1960s and 1970s on whether to place juvenile delinquents completely under the regime of welfare laws and welfare administration, thereby abolishing juvenile criminal law. In particular, the *Arbeiterwohlfahrt* (Labor Welfare, a labor union associated organization) in 1970 proposed an "Extended Juvenile Welfare Law" that would have treated juvenile criminals mainly as juveniles in need of care and supervision and subjected them entirely to the regime of juvenile welfare law (Arbeiterwohlfahrt Bundesverband e.V. 1970). The Ministry of Youth, Family, and Health contributed a draft "Juvenile Law" guided by the idea of restricting punitive sanctions to those ages sixteen and seventeen while using welfare measures for offenders ages fourteen and fifteen (Bundesministerium für Jugend, Famile und Gesundheit 1973). It was during this period that Germany came closest to abolishing juvenile criminal law and replacing it with a "Youth Welfare Law" or a "Law for Youth in Conflicts." However, the reform dynamic, driven by the student movement and new liberal and welfare-oriented policies implemented by the Social Democratic liberal government in office since 1969, faded out without leaving significant traces. One reason was strong resistance by criminal justice professionals, who made a compromise impossible (Schaffstein and Beulke 1995, p. 30).

The last Youth Court Law amendment, in 1990, brought fewer changes than many expected. These included some consolidation of diversion, decarceration, and depenalization policies that had been changing juvenile court practice since the late 1970s. The last symbol of purely rehabilitative detention—the indeterminate youth prison sentence—was abolished; in practice, however, it has never played a numerically significant role. Decarceration was expanded by introducing social training courses, supervision and support orders, and victim-offender mediation (and restitution) in place of short-term confinement, and by expanding the scope of existing alternatives such as community service. Finally, pretrial detention was restricted, allowing detention prior to trial for juveniles under age sixteen only if foster care is not available. To implement this policy, the juvenile court aide was directed to provide a report containing mandatory information on the need for detention and the unavailability of alternative sanctions. The 1990 Youth Court Amendment extended a paradigm shift away from prison and toward community-based sanctions and social work-based measures that had been under way since the end of the nineteenth century (Oberwittler 2000, p. 332).

Throughout its history, juvenile criminal law has sought to distance itself from adult criminal law. Three approaches—diversion, depenalization, and decarceration—were influential in shaping youth criminal policy and juvenile justice practice (and eventually became important for the adult criminal justice system; see, e.g., Kerner 1990).

Why? The reasons point to general politics, ideological concepts, and professional interests working together and building coalitions in favor of a distinctive juvenile criminal justice system.

Diversion, depenalization, and decarceration fit well into the general welfare approach (*Sozialstaat*) that emerged during the second half of the nineteenth century (Bismarck's social welfare legislation was the first visible sign of this powerful movement that came to dominate German [and European] society for most of the twentieth century). The Marburg program set up by Franz von Liszt stressed the damaging effects of adult criminal penalties (then almost exclusively prison sentences) when applied to juvenile offenders. Liszt's vision came much closer to social welfare measures in giving up the prison-based approach of traditional criminal law. Liszt's idea that imprisonment should be reserved for a small group of offenders assessed to be in need of extensive rehabilitation programs, to be administered during long prison sentences and aimed at reducing risks of relapse in crime, represented a clear call for alternatives to imprisonment for all other offenders. However, other offenders ought to fall within the regime of alternatives to imprisonment (fines and welfare measures designed to support delinquents rather than punish them).

Liszt's proposals lacked a convincing theory that could explain both the evident failure of traditional criminal law and criminal sanctions in terms of individual prevention and why the alternative that would replace it would be more effective. The rise of the social work professions and their insertion into the criminal justice system (as probation officials, juvenile and adult court aides, prison social services providers, and in various charitable organizations) occurred during the twentieth century. Their motivation to support ex-convicts and juveniles at risk strengthened the welfare approach and enlarged mistrust toward criminal law and criminal justice. These conflicting interests continue to characterize the relationship between the justice system and welfare professionals in juvenile criminal justice.

The 1960s experienced a strong move against conservative policies in general, bringing social democratic and liberal parties into office and setting the stage for a change in politics away from preservation of conservative values toward the establishment of equal treatment and equal chances across social classes and segments. This included establishing equal opportunities in education and training for deprived youth. Equal-opportunity policies fit well with analyses that painted Western and capitalist societies as discriminating against working-class youth, especially through existing juvenile justice practices. Such reasoning fell on fertile ground. Ulrike Meinhof, one of the leading figures of the Red Army Faction, published an influential book in 1971, *Bambule* (Meinhof 1971), that described the deplorable conditions in *Fuersorgeerziehungsheimen* (a euphemistic term for prison-like foster homes for troubled youth, children in need of care, young delinquents, and young criminals). They were portrayed not only as a breeding ground for serious criminals but also as a symbol of repression of working-class youth. Criticism of this type of closed foster homes (which had always been places of detention for delinquent children) ultimately led to their almost complete abolition. In 1990, the new child welfare law stressed the voluntary nature of all welfare services for children and juveniles and the need to restrict foster care to open homes.

Paralleling these developments, labeling theory gained momentum in sociology and rapidly emerged as a leading theoretical framework for juvenile criminal justice practitioners. Labeling theory generally became the most influential theory in German criminal justice. It fit well with social welfare policies, provided legitimacy to a policy of equal opportunities, and was warmly received by social work practitioners. Labeling theory enabled probation officers and social workers to justify a strong distinction between criminal law control and the professional support provided by their own professions and underlined the appropriateness of a social work-based approach. Labeling theory thus provided a plausible theoretical basis for Franz von Liszt's modern school of criminal law and its move away from imprisonment as the paradigm of criminal sanctions.

II. Reconciling Adult Criminal Law and Youth Welfare Law

The Youth Court Law focused on educational and rehabilitative needs of juvenile offenders. German juvenile justice, however, was never dominated by a social welfare model and never adopted more than marginal traces of welfare and social support. Throughout the twentieth century, the idea prevailed that punishment and education could be reconciled within the framework of juvenile justice. Strict separation between juvenile offenders and children and juveniles in need of care and education can be observed throughout the history of juvenile laws. Voices were repeatedly raised in favor of a unified welfare approach to delinquent children and juveniles. But juvenile criminal law never deviated far from general criminal law. It remained bound to the rule of law with respect to the criminal offense statutes that triggered juvenile-criminal-justice-based intervention and to a compromise between punishment and education. However, this compromise was mostly rhetorical, for though policies of diversion and decarceration were successfully implemented, punitiveness was not replaced by welfare or education but only made less severe. Thus, the juvenile justice system always remained a subsystem in the general criminal justice system.

The German criminal justice system classifies individuals into four categories according to age. The onset of criminal responsibility since 1923 is age fourteen (German Criminal Code, sec. 19). But as criminal law assumes that full criminal responsibility is the product of a fully completed process of socialization and moral development, a distinct system of juvenile criminal justice should respond to offenses committed by juveniles (Kaiser 1993*a*). Section 3 of the Youth Court Law demands proof that a juvenile offender was mature enough to be aware of the wrongfulness of an illegal act and was capable of behaving according to such awareness. Criminological research shows, however, that juvenile court practices do not comply fully with section 3 but routinely assume criminal responsibility of juvenile offenders (Ostendorf 1997, sec. 3). This can be observed even for the most serious criminal charge (murder) and in convictions resulting in the most serious youth prison sentence of ten years (see Schulz 2001, p. 316). Full criminal responsibility commences at age eighteen. Young adult offenders (ages eighteen to twenty) are treated as adults and therefore are presumed to be fully responsible; however, under certain conditions, young adults may be prosecuted as if they were juveniles (Youth Court Law, sec. 105). Sections 3 and 105 acknowledge that the concept of adolescence requires flexibility because of variations in maturation, social and moral development, and integration into the adult world.

Children up to age thirteen and juveniles ages fourteen to seventeen who are defined to be in need of care and education are handled by youth welfare departments set up under the Youth Welfare Law (now *Kinder- und Jugendhilfegesetz*). Although youth problem behavior in general does not justify juvenile court proceedings, a criminal offense committed by a child may be used as an indicator for the need of care and education. Public youth welfare is generally understood to be a last resort, with private youth welfare having priority over public interventions.

The links between the Youth Court Law and the Youth Welfare

Law can be seen in overlapping of measures that may be imposed for a criminal offense, initiated on the basis of welfare considerations. However, these measures have always been of minor importance in practice. The Youth Court Law requires judges to have specialized (psychological and sociological) knowledge of youth and, as a general rule, also to be appointed as a family judge (*Vormundschaftsrichter*) responsible for applying juvenile welfare law in the family court. Despite such statutory requirements, juvenile judges and prosecutors seldom have such specialized knowledge but are recruited mainly from among newcomers to criminal justice. Specializing in juvenile justice often creates obstacles for a career in criminal justice professions (Adam, Albrecht, and Pfeiffer 1986).

A. The Definition of Juvenile Crime

The definitions of juvenile crimes do not differ from those of adult crimes. Juvenile criminal procedures may be initiated only if there is sufficient reason to believe that a juvenile has committed a criminal offense. The same standards apply as in adult criminal procedures. Age at the time of the offense is key to the definition of juvenile crime. The same basic rules must be followed for adults and juveniles when establishing criminal responsibility. The differences lie in the type and range of penalties that may be imposed. Procedural rules for juvenile prosecution, courts, and trials also differ. Unlike other justice systems, especially in North America, German laws do not provide for status offenses.[1] Nor does the Youth Court Law allow waivers of juvenile rights or transfer of juvenile offenders to adult courts.

To the contrary, young adults ages eighteen to twenty may be transferred to the juvenile justice system from the adult court. Although there are no youth-specific behaviors that trigger juvenile justice measures, there is an ongoing debate over whether offense definitions should be adapted to distinctive aspects of the lives and lifestyles of young people. For example, offenses such as fraud or forgery and certain aggravating circumstances make sense in judgments about adult behavior but, it is said, may be too complicated to be understood fully by a fourteen- or fifteen-year-old (Ostendorf 1992). Similarly, some juvenile behaviors, such as taking items belonging to opposing soccer fans, are said to be triggered by expressive motivations and not to re-

---

[1] However, conversely, youth protection laws do define criminal offenses that can be committed only by adults.

flect the instrumental considerations at the center of offenses such as robbery or theft.

B. The Principle of Education

The major difference between juvenile and adult criminal law is in their general orientations of sentencing. The offense itself is the focus of adult criminal law; sentencing should reflect the seriousness of the offense, personal guilt, and special and general prevention. Youth criminal law focuses on the offender and adopts special prevention as the sole sentencing goal. This creates an ambivalence that, from the view of equality in sentencing, is obvious when demanding a judge or prosecutor to consider factors, such as school achievements, family background, and the like, in imposing sanctions. Youth criminal law under the Youth Court Law targets education and rehabilitation of the young offender. Although a juvenile is held legally responsible for a crime (mens rea must be proven), the primary goals are education and rehabilitation. The emphasis is not on the offense or its seriousness but on the offender and his or her needs.

This orientation has led to controversy about the relationship between punishment and education (see Oberwittler 2000). It began shortly after the enactment of the Youth Court Law and continues today. Before enactment of the Youth Court Law in 1923, the modern school of criminal law pushed for a rehabilitative system. Supporters of the punishment approach expressed fear that criminal law in general would be undermined (Heinz 1992, p. 123). The wording of the Youth Court Law, however, is inconsistent. With respect to sanctions, the term "educational measure" is used in conjunction with the term "punishment" (*Jugendstrafe*). This allows for diverse interpretations, depending on whether the criminal offense or educational needs are emphasized.

The adoption of the principle of education and disregard for general prevention, general deterrence, and seriousness of the offense as guides in sentencing does not mean that the principle of proportionality must not be applied. The principle of proportionality (*Verhältnismäßigkeit*) is derived from the German Constitution. It requires that the educational measure chosen be sufficient to reach the goal that is sought, be the least severe measure among several equally suited to attain that goal, and be proportional to the goal to be achieved. This principle sets an upper limit to legal intervention in juvenile criminal cases, thus boiling down educational needs and their possible impact to what is seen to be proportional (from the viewpoint of the seriousness of the offense). Thus, while any disposition must be proportional to the offense, it must also be guided by the goal of education.

The meaning of "education" is at the center of an ongoing debate. Streng (1994), among others, suggests that its meaning in the context of juvenile criminal law should not go beyond the prevention of individual relapse into crime. Any meaning aimed at altering motivation for norm compliance, attitudes, and general behavior patterns is likely to violate constitutional rights (of the juvenile offender and his or her parents) and overestimates the capabilities of any justice system.

Although juvenile criminal law has, since enactment, been called an offender-based system, the sanctions imposed and executed in practice suggest a miniature model of adult sentencing. This can be demonstrated when looking at the sanctions most widely imposed: community service and pecuniary sanctions. Their use can be explained by their easy conversion into the basic currency of criminal sanctions, that is, time.

New research, based on the Freiburg Cohort Study (see Grundies, Höfer, and Tetal 2002), demonstrates that sentencing for juveniles is not different from that for adults when looking at sentencing careers or the individual course of sentences. Both are characterized by escalation and the strong influence of prior convictions and the type and extent of prior penalties (Höfer 2002).

Figure 1 shows average offense seriousness and average sentencing severity for juvenile offenders adjudicated and sentenced repeatedly. Variance in sentencing severity over time is explained by prior convictions and offense seriousness. The extent to which variance in severity can be explained through offense seriousness and prior convictions contrasts starkly with the individualized and personalized sentencing that should—according to the law—be guided by the goal of education. In particular, prior convictions lead to escalation in sentencing, with increases in severity being particularly pronounced in the beginning of a career in criminal convictions. That is why, over the course of a juvenile criminal career, the gap between offense seriousness and sentencing severity becomes larger. Prior convictions thus lead to a dynamic of their own (Hering 1993).

Moreover, recent changes pay special attention to the victim, compensation, and victim-offender reconciliation in juvenile justice, thereby evidently supporting the offense- and seriousness-based response to juvenile offenders. Consideration of the victim and his or her

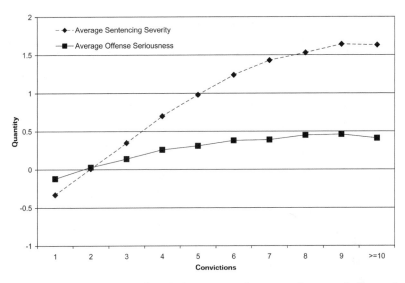

Fɪɢ. 1.—Average severity of criminal sentences and average seriousness of offenses of persistent juvenile offenders. Source: Höfer 2002.

needs in terms of restitution fits comfortably with a view that is guided not by education but by offense seriousness and general prevention as the ultimate goals.

III. Youth Crime

Youth violence and gang-related violence have preoccupied media and politics since the 1950s, when "mass-event-related" violence in connection with large gatherings (such as football games), "rockers," and motorcycle gangs first emerged as political issues. Youth behavior has been at the center of attention ever since, including drug use in the 1960s, student movements and public order problems (including terrorism) in the 1970s, youth movements in the 1980s that resorted occasionally to violence, and, finally, youth violence in the 1990s.

The discussion in the 1990s extended to school violence, hate and bias-related violence, juvenile drug use, and uncontrollable children and youth. Typical of the latter category is a young boy called "Mehmet," born in Germany but of Turkish descent and—for policy makers certainly a rare gift—displaying all important aspects of the juvenile crime problem: immigration, violence, and a career in crime. Mehmet committed sixty criminal offenses before age fourteen and continued offending thereafter, which resulted in a sentence of youth imprisonment and a deportation order (which was enforced immediately).

Bavaria proposed an amendment to the Law on Foreign Nationals that would allow the expulsion of child and juvenile chronic offenders (Bundesrat Drucksache 620/98, 25/6/98; Gesetzesantrag des Freistaates Bayern, Entwurf eines Gesetzes zur Änderung des Ausländergesetzes). It was rejected by the Federal Council and withdrawn. In a time of rising rates of juvenile crime, some immigration authorities feel the need to expel and deport criminal children and juveniles of foreign descent and nationality (and also parents for not properly supervising and restricting their offspring). In 1998, Bavarian immigration authorities issued expulsion orders in four cases involving foreign children and juveniles (of which two also affect parents who have been ordered to leave). The Bavarian authorities argue that these children are chronic offenders who commit a disproportionate share of serious crimes. Information was channeled from police to immigration authorities on eight foreign juveniles and young adults belonging to a group of eighty-seven chronic offenders allegedly responsible for half the crimes committed by this age group in Munich (*Süddeutsche Zeitung*, Friday, June 5, 1998, p. 19). Political and media debates during the 1990s pointed to young immigrants, violent offenders, young career criminals, and chronic child offenders who cannot be controlled by use of conventional juvenile welfare and juvenile justice measures and for whom secure detention, deportation, or other safety-producing instruments are said to be called for.

Longitudinal analyses of youth crime in Germany can be based on police statistics and court statistics. Police statistics contain information on suspects (and offenses), while court information systems collect data on convicted and sentenced offenders. In German criminal procedure, the finding of guilt and sentencing are not split into two decisions but are instead produced in a single decision. Moreover, unlike in some other countries, German police statistics count suspects, not arrested offenders. Suspicion does not necessarily lead to an arrest. Police may arrest a suspect under conditions that do not permit proper identification on the spot, or police may initiate placement in pretrial detention, which must be requested by the public prosecutor and ordered by the court within forty-eight hours. But in most criminal cases a formal arrest is not made.

Longitudinal self-report studies and victimization surveys are not available for the Federal Republic of Germany. However, a multitude

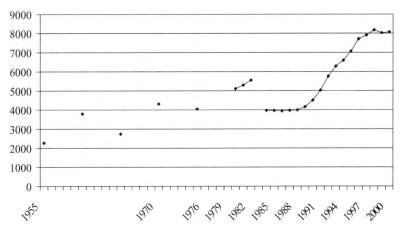

F<small>IG</small>. 2.—Juvenile offender rates 1955–2000, suspects ages fourteen to seventeen (per 100,000). Note.—1984 multiple counts of suspects have been omitted; until 1992, data refer to the west of Germany; from 1993 on, data cover the whole of Germany; rates are inflated as population statistics do not account for parts of foreign groups (e.g., illegal immigrants) that are counted among the suspects. Source.—Bundeskriminalamt, various years 1955–2000.

of local self-report studies have been carried out that only rarely allow cross-sectional or longitudinal comparative perspectives (H.-J. Albrecht 1998). That is why all serious assessments of developments and trends in youth crime are based on police crime statistics.

As figure 2 demonstrates, a considerable increase in juvenile suspects occurred during the 1960s and 1970s. During the mid-1980s these figures stabilized, but the end of the decade and the beginning of the 1990s were marked by another increase. This continued until the end of the 1990s, when it leveled off. Parallel trends can be observed in most Western European countries (Kaiser 1989; Pfeiffer 1998).

Demographic changes led to a considerable decrease in the proportions of child, juvenile, and young adult suspects in the total population of suspects. While juveniles accounted for approximately 15 percent of all suspects in 1980, their share dropped to 9.5 percent in 1991. Children accounted for 6.3 percent of all suspects in 1980 and 4.4 percent in 1991. During the same period, the proportion of young adult suspects (ages eighteen to twenty) decreased from 13.5 percent to 10.2 percent. However, during the 1990s the proportions of children, juveniles, and young adults increased again (due to a post–World War II baby boom echo and immigration) and stood in 2000 at 6.4 percent

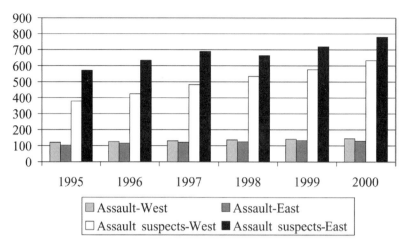

FIG. 3.—Rates of aggravated assault and juvenile assault suspects (per 100,000) in the west and east of Germany. Source: Bundeskriminalamt 1995, 2000.

for children, 12.9 percent for juveniles, and 10.8 percent for young adults. The increase in juvenile offender rates over the last five decades resulted largely from an enormous increase in rates of petty theft, particularly shoplifting.

As figure 2 shows, the 1990s were a period of rapid changes in youth crime. This coincided with German reunification, abolition of border controls in the Schengen space, and normalization of border controls between Eastern and Western Europe. Data for the east of Germany are available from 1993 onward. In eastern Germany, there was an increase in crime in general and especially in juvenile crime. The trend since reunification is toward convergence with rates in the west. However, crime rates among the young in eastern Germany for some offenses far exceed those in the west. Rates of suspects for assault and robbery in the east have skyrocketed, although they remain slightly below those in the west. Figure 3 shows aggravated assault trends for the second half of the 1990s. Some argue that young people in the east are far more exposed to risks thought to contribute to crime and therefore are far more involved in crime—particularly street crime and car theft (Frehsee 1995; Kerner and Sonnen 1997, p. 342). Police and the public in the east may also still differ from the west in control styles and crime reporting patterns. Another hypothesis is that children and juveniles in the east are far more visible than in the west because the infrastructure of specially designated places for juveniles is only slowly catching up

TABLE 1

Changes in Number of Cases of Suspects between 1987 and 2000
(German Suspects Only)

	Cases		
Crime	1987	2000	Trend
Total	3,477	7,258	→
Street robbery	25	141	↓
Assault	104	346	↑
Fraud	258	590	↑
Public order offenses	140	390	↑
Vandalism	500	247	↑
Burglary	90	121	↓
Shoplifting	1,138	2,089	↓
Drugs (total)	91	877	↑
Possession of cannabis	69	597	↑
Arson	21	55	↑

→ = Constant.
↑ = Upward trend.
↓ = Downward trend.

with the west. Another hypothesis, not yet examined closely, is that extended group activities (which produce more suspects for a single criminal offense) are more common.

Times series of police data on juvenile crime for the period 1987–2000 reveal trends in juvenile crime that deserve careful analysis and observation (see table 1). However, they do not justify ongoing attempts in the 1990s by conservative politicians, media, and criminologists to construct juvenile crime and juvenile violence as a critical social problem that warrants tougher criminal juvenile law responses. The increase in rates of juvenile suspects (ages fourteen to seventeen) is confined to street robbery, assault, shoplifting, vandalism, and drug offenses. Police records make clear, however, that aggravated forms of robbery (bank robbery, robbery of shops, etc.) are rarely committed by juveniles, and there are no indications of changes over the last decades. As regards assault, such offenses occur in public places and among juveniles themselves. With respect to drugs, the substantial increase is due to possession of cannabis and also ecstasy. Hard drugs and drug trafficking, however, evidently do not contribute to increased drug offense rates among juveniles. The increase in fraud consists mainly of fare dodging.

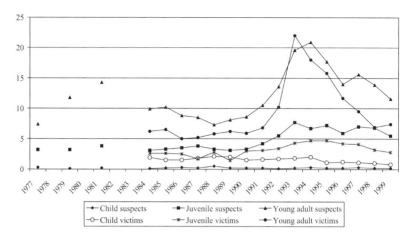

Fig. 4.—Murder suspects and victims (per 100,000), 1977–1999. Source: Bundes-kriminalamt 1995, 2000.

Thus, the substantial increases in rates and absolute numbers can be explained mostly by increases in crimes that take place in public, in groups, and against other juveniles, and are of low seriousness (see Albrecht 1998).

Serious crimes, especially violent crimes, are rare events among younger age groups. Figures 4–7 show the (relative) trends in murder, robbery, and aggravated assault figures during the last two decades for

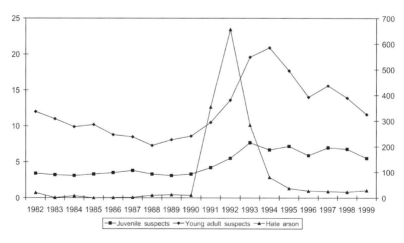

Fig. 5.—Trends in hate arson and juvenile/young adult murder rates. Sources: Bundesverfassungsschutz, various years, 1982–99.

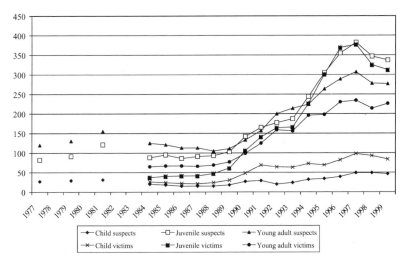

Fig. 6.—Robbery suspects and victims, per 100,000. Source: Bundeskriminalamt 1995, 2000.

children (ages eight to thirteen), juveniles (ages fourteen to seventeen), and young adults (ages eighteen to twenty). Regarding murder and robbery, clear distinctions can be made between children and juveniles, as a group, and young adults. Young adults are more heavily involved in serious crimes than are children and juveniles, for whom theft ac-

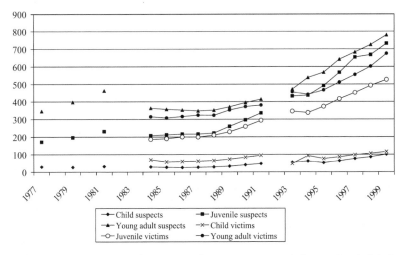

Fig. 7.—Aggravated assault suspects and victims, per 100,000. Source: Bundeskriminalamt, various years 1995–99.

counts for a large proportion of crime. The peak in murder suspects that emerged during the 1990s for juveniles and young adults may tentatively be explained by two things. First were the shootings and killings taking place at the German-German border prior to reunification, which have been investigated and prosecuted since the beginning of the 1990s (cases involving young adults as suspects [former East German soldiers] and as victims [trying to cross the German-German border]). Second is the case of arson committed by throwing Molotov cocktails into houses of refugees, which often is prosecuted and sentenced as attempted or completed murder (particularly after the case of Mölln, where several Turkish citizens were killed by fire caused by a Molotov cocktail; see Neubacher 1999).

Whether an intent to kill must be proven in the case of juvenile or young adult arsonists who preyed on homes of refugees or asylum seekers has been controversial (see, e.g., Frommel 1994). Criminal courts ultimately decided to apply the murder statute. Trends in the number of young murder suspects and in the number of arsons linked to hate motivations (and having asylum and refugee homes or homes of immigrants as targets) are displayed in figure 5. Significant changes occurred around 1992–93. The increase in the number of arsons (data collected by intelligence services, or *Bundesverfassungsschutz*) correlates strongly with the increase in the number of young murder suspects. The German criminal justice system evidently responded to the increase in hate arson by treating them as attempted or completed murder. This contributed to the increase in the number of young murder suspects.

Robbery, shown in figure 6, increased during most of the 1990s, due mostly to street robbery and confined mostly to incidents among peers. The increase was most pronounced for street robberies involving small losses (Pfeiffer et al. 1998). Police data show no change between 1987 and 2000 in the rate of street robberies (these cases usually involve taking bags from elderly people caught off guard; this is classified as robbery by German criminal courts).

Trends in the rates of child, juvenile, and young adult victims of violent crime parallel offender rates in these age groups, suggesting a considerable degree of overlap between offender and victim roles. Research on self-reported crimes and victimization revealed that juveniles and young adults ranking very high on scales of self-reported crime also have the highest risk of being victimized by their own peers (Villmow and Stephan 1983).

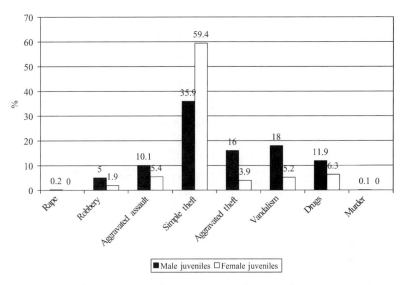

Fɪɢ. 8.—Offense structure of crimes committed by juveniles, 1999 (percent)

Figures 8 and 9 illustrate the structure of crimes committed by juveniles and young adults. Property and nonviolent crimes outweigh other offense types among female offenders. Female juveniles' share of police-recorded crime was 21 percent in 1999; for female young adults, 18 percent. There has been no qualitative change in female crime; the proportion of female crime has, however, increased somewhat during recent decades (see Albrecht 1987a).

The general structure of crimes committed by male juveniles is shaped by theft and criminal damage. Serious violent offenses and drug offenses play a minor role. Drug offenses become more important for young adults (and even more so in the adult population). Figure 8 shows considerable proportions of aggravated theft (which includes burglary), but robbery and other violent offenses are significantly less serious than those of young adults and adults (Dölling 1992).

Official crime data suggest that criminal behavior may represent rather normal behavior for young people, even in terms of police-recorded crime and court dispositions. Estimates of the prevalence of criminal convictions are that one-third of males have a criminal record by age twenty-four (Kaiser 1988). Analysis of four birth cohorts' data (1970, 1973, 1975, and 1978 cohorts) from Baden-Wurttemberg show that approximately 15 percent of males of German descent have been

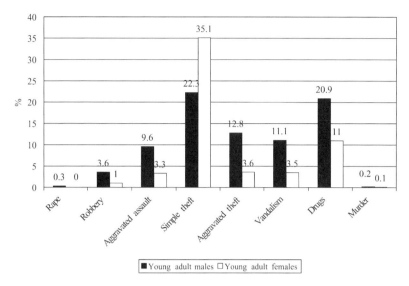

Fig. 9.—Offense structure of crimes committed by young adults, 1999 (percent)

suspected of a crime at least once by age seventeen (see also Karger and Sutterer 1988; Grundies 1999). The corresponding rates for immigrant male youth and ethnic Germans (immigrants from the former Soviet Union; for details, see Grundies [2000]), born in 1978, are about 40 percent (see fig. 10).

The cohort study on crime and delinquency and court dispositions both demonstrate "overcriminalization" and a related need for depen-

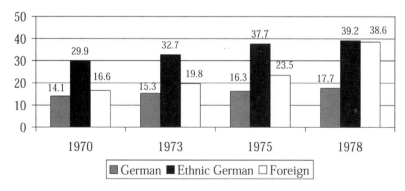

Fig. 10.—Activities of community prevention councils (percent). Source: Data from the birth cohort study conducted at the Max Planck Institute for Foreign and International Criminal Law, Freiburg.

alization (or decriminalization) among young people. Such overcriminalization undermines the preventive and norm stabilizing effects of criminal law. Popitz, a German sociologist, argues: "If a norm is applied rarely, the 'teeth' of the norm cannot bite anymore; if applied too often, the 'teeth' may also lose their capacity to bite. There must be a balance. The basic function of criminal law can be achieved only if people believe that it is uncommon to break the law. If everybody breaks the law, lawbreaking is facilitated" (1968, p. 3).

IV. Conflicting Explanations

Increases in officially recorded crime have received much attention and remain controversial. Several positions can be identified.

First, some argue that children and juveniles constitute a growing menace to society and require strong preventive and (partially) repressive actions (Stümper 1973; Böhm et al. 1997; Pfeiffer et al. 1998). Violent crime receives special attention.

Second, some argue that the increase in youth crime is exaggerated by the media, police, and politicians. The increase results from heightened police attention to children and juveniles and from a general increase in the efficiency of police crime investigation (P.-A. Albrecht and Lamnek 1979; P.-A. Albrecht 1993, 2001).

Third, some argue that youth crime did increase but due mainly to an increase in crime of a nonserious nature, which should not be overdramatized (Steffen 1979; Heinz 1997; Kerner and Sonnen 1997; Elsner, Steffen, and Stern 1998).

Research on the causes of juvenile crime carried out in the 1950s and 1960s pointed to broken families, bad parenting, school problems, and unemployment (Villmow and Kaiser 1974). Self-report results since the mid-1960s indicate a shift from etiological concepts to labeling theory, leading to new perspectives on juvenile delinquency and delinquency prevention. The finding that delinquent behavior is ubiquitous while official criminal law-based interventions concentrate on only a small proportion of those who could be targeted supports two ideas. First, juvenile crime in general represents normal behavior. Second, juvenile criminal behavior by itself is not sufficient to justify public intervention in education or punishment pursuing the goal of rehabilitation.

From these perspectives, prevention discriminates against marginal and deprived youths and risks deepening disintegrative processes. In-depth studies of the relationship between undetected and known crime reveal that the assumption of ubiquity of crime holds true only for petty or trivial offenses, while commission of serious and repeated criminal offenses is restricted to a small group. Nonetheless, the argument was decisive in designing youth criminal policies in the 1970s and 1980s.

Conclusions drawn from these studies supported the view that a juvenile offense is not a signal requiring official intervention and public education. Longitudinal research shows that as many as 70 percent of juvenile offenders are one-time offenders (Krüger 1983; Grundies 1999), suggesting that prevention efforts should rely heavily on nonprosecution and diversion rather than on youth prisons and other punitive measures. Decision makers should refrain from using social deprivation as a guiding criterion in juvenile court decision making. The 1980s therefore saw an increasing use of diversion and community-based measures, such as community service, social training courses, and, most recently, restitution, conflict mediation, and reconciliation. Informal sanctions and informal systems of control as represented by the family, peer groups, and schools currently outweigh formal systems of control. As a result, there is renewed criminological interest in family, school, religion, and employment as decisive elements in the prevention of juvenile delinquency (H.-J. Albrecht 1991). This corresponds to a shift in theoretical thinking about juvenile delinquency and its prevention from stress and labeling theories to control theories of juvenile crime (Kaiser 1993a).

Research has turned to the question of how large-scale changes in the roles and functions of the family, school, and religion in postindustrial societies relate to changing patterns of juvenile crime. The potential of the family, school, and neighborhood to provide bonds between juveniles and society has diminished steadily, it is said. However, it is also argued that probably nothing has changed in terms of behavior patterns of juveniles, but, instead, systems of informal control have broken down and exposed children and juveniles to formal control systems for behavior that would have been handled informally in the past. Increases in assault rates for young people must be understood, therefore, as reflecting not only changes in behavior patterns of young people but also changes in societal and institutional sensitivity toward violence (Elsner, Steffen, and Stern 1998). Both explanations point to a common prevention perspective: strengthening the roles of the community, neighborhood, family, and school in handling problem behavior. Community crime prevention approaches and programs have

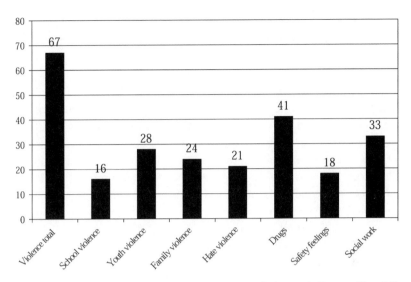

Fig. 11.—Activities of community prevention councils (percent). Source: Obergfell-Fuchs 2001.

spread rapidly since the beginning of the 1990s, focusing on youth and youth-related problems with particular emphasis on violence (see fig. 11).

These research findings suggest that formal interventions do not make a difference with respect to exiting from criminal lifestyles, but, on the contrary, formal interventions add to juvenile offenders' difficulties in adjusting to societal demands. Current research focuses on the feasibility of replacing formal juvenile court responses with restitution and victim-offender reconciliation schemes. Restitution and victim-offender mediation receive strong support outside and inside the criminal justice system (Schöch 1992). Surveys confirm the acceptance of restitution by the public and by the victims (Sessar 1992).

V. Problem Groups and Particular Risks

In the 1980s, two subgroups of juvenile delinquents received considerable attention in German research: foreign and immigrant minority youth and chronic juvenile offenders. The observation that substantial portions of police-recorded crime and self-reported delinquent acts can be linked to a disproportionately small group of juveniles (Krüger 1983; Karger and Sutterer 1988; Grundies 1999) has led to a growing interest in identifying early signs of chronic offending. As Günther Albrecht (1990) concludes, however, it is not possible to convert the retrospective findings on high-rate juvenile offenders into ethically and economically feasible prospective prevention strategies.

Minority juveniles are also targeted for preventive reasons. The most important group numerically is Turkish. Official crime rates among certain ethnic and foreign minority groups are two to four times greater than for the majority group (H.-J. Albrecht 1987*b*, 1997; Karger and Sutterer 1990). Time series data demonstrate clear trends that might be interpreted as the result of changes in behavior patterns of second and third generations and of changes in migration patterns. Disproportionate involvement of foreign minority members in police-recorded crimes can be observed especially in the eighteen-to-twenty age bracket. In 1999, 27.6 percent of suspects were foreign minority members (19.8 percent of all juvenile offenders and 18 percent of children; Bundeskriminalamt 2000). Michael Walter (1995) suggests that demographic characteristics may account for the increase in crime participation among foreign populations. The number of foreign suspects was inflated by the influx of asylum seekers, peaking in 1993, and decreased considerably as a result of subsequent significant changes in asylum laws. In North Rhine-Westphalia between 1984 and 1993, the crime rate among young foreigners more than doubled (from 6,651 to 13,614 cases), while the increase among young Germans was from 4,075 to 5,038. Conversely, between 1984 and 1993, the crime rate among guest workers and immigrant workers did not change much (Bundeskriminalamt 1995). A tentative explanation is that first generation immigrants experience improved living conditions, housing, medical care, and so on, which outweighed existing differences between minority and majority groups (Kunz 1989; H.-J. Albrecht 1997).

Most self-report surveys do not include ethnic or foreign minorities, but samples are regularly drawn from the resident German youth population (H.-J. Albrecht 1988). Evidence from those surveys that do include immigrant minority youth is not conclusive. Self-report research from the city of Bremen in the 1980s concluded that foreign juveniles were not more involved in delinquency and that foreign juveniles appeared remarkably conformist (Schumann et al. 1987; H.-J. Albrecht 1997). Self-report surveys in the 1990s show higher crime participation rates of certain minority and immigrant youth (H.-J. Albrecht 1998). This could reflect changes in immigration patterns and increasing problems of marginalization among certain segments of immigrant and ethnic minority youth (see, e.g., Grundies [2000] on immigrant ethnic German youth).

As society segments along ethnic lines, the lowest segments are filling up with immigrant groups most likely to be affected by unemployment, bad housing, poverty, poor education, and lack of vocational training. The central research questions, which in the 1960s and 1970s highlighted class, crime, and justice issues, are being replaced by ethnicity and crime. Crime and delinquency among minority youth should be explained by the same theories applied to the majority group (Kube and Koch 1990). Although bonding theories fit the sensitive situation of second- and third-generation immigrants (e.g., Turkish juveniles) who live between two distinct cultures, this creates conflicts between traditional norms valued by parents and the values and norms of the peer group (Mansel and Hurrelmann 1993).

Economic recession in the 1970s, exposing the young to unemployment, revived interest in links between youth unemployment and youth crime (Münder et al. 1987; Kaiser 1993b). Despite considerable increases in unemployment rates among juveniles and young adults, the proportion of those unemployed and suspected of committing a criminal offense decreased. These diverging trends do not suggest a causal relationship between these variables at the microlevel but point to a reinforcing effect of unemployment. Youth gangs attracted scientific attention in the late 1970s in connection with soccer hooliganism (Heitmeyer and Peter 1988; Kersten 1993). In the 1990s, after German reunification, the problem of right-wing extremist violence toward immigrants and other minorities committed by groups of juveniles and young adults arose (Viehmann 1993). Most bias-motivated violent offenses were and continue to be committed by juveniles or young adults: 70 percent of offenders fall into the age bracket of fourteen to twenty years, and only 3 percent are thirty or older (Bundesamt für Verfassungsschutz 2000). Part of the hate violence is linked to youth subcultures, such as skinhead groups, that are concentrated in the east of Germany (where more than half of violence-prone skinheads live; just one-fifth of the population at large lives in the east) (Bundesamt für Verfassungsschutz 2000, p. 25). However, the proportion of bias-motivated violence of all violent crimes committed by youth is small. Furthermore, most interethnic violence obviously is not linked to racism or hate but to conventional triggers of violent behavior (Solon 1994).

In recent years youth violence has been targeted as a pressing social and policy problem. Demands for "get tough" approaches to right-wing juveniles conflict with educational demands put forward by the Youth Court Law. The solution lies in the conception of youth violence. Youth violence may be conceived as indicative of anomie and social disintegration (following rapid social and economic changes produced by German unification) or as part of a broader violence-prone political radicalism backed up by extremist political parties. Youth violence may, from a conservative view of society, be conceived as the result of a permissive society that displays violence and sex on television and the Internet to even the young (Glogauer 1991). Finally, youth violence may be conceived as a specific transitional phenomenon of male youth associating in gangs (Kersten 1993). Depending on these conceptions, youth violence against foreign and ethnic minorities may be the product of social turmoil, representing hate crimes and therefore deserving repressive action, or indicative of surface changes in ordinary violent gang activities. However, the prevalent approach in explaining youth violence toward minorities involves the traditional frustration-aggression hypothesis (Bliesener 1992; Rommelspacher 1993).

The mass media, especially television, have received particular interest. It is widely assumed that the presentation of violence on video and television (facilitated by easy access to video and television) contributes considerably to youth violence (Glogauer 1991; Jung 1993a). Such assumptions are not, at least so far, supported by scientific evidence.

VI. Juvenile Criminal Law and Juvenile Criminal Proceedings

Criminal prosecution in Germany begins with investigation of the crime by police. Police have no discretionary power to dismiss criminal cases (e.g., such as after cautioning the juvenile) but must refer every suspect to the public prosecutor's office. Without a formal indictment by the public prosecutor's office, no juvenile case may be brought before the juvenile criminal court. However, recently the position of police in diversion procedures has been strengthened. Police in some jurisdictions are now empowered to initiate the conditions required to dismiss (or not prosecute) a case. Police thus influence who will be diverted and who will not.

After criminal proceedings have been initiated, investigators gather information on personal and social circumstances relevant for evaluating the personality of the juvenile offender and the choice of sanction (Youth Court Law, sec. 43). Immediately after initiation, the juvenile court aide (*Jugendgerichtshilfe*) must be notified. A social worker investigates the personal and social circumstances of the juvenile offender in order to provide the court with information on the appropriate sanction. The court aide has the right to be present during trial. The juvenile court has no discretion in admitting the social inquiry report. The court must hear the report in order to comply with the general procedural rule that any evidence relevant to the finding of guilt and the appropriate sentence must be heard (Laubenthal 1993). Except for the parents of the juvenile offender, court hearings are not open to the public (including the media).

In recent years, the position of the victim has been strengthened. The victim may not only be present during the trial but may also act as joint plaintiff (*Nebenklage*). A series of victim's rights were added to the Code of Criminal Procedure in a major criminal law reform in 1987 (among them the rights of access to court files and to be informed about the outcomes of the criminal trial). At present, these rights do not exist in juvenile court proceedings (see Schaal and Eisenberg 1988). Debate is under way on whether the goal of juvenile justice—that is, education—justifies restricting the victim's rights (H.-J. Albrecht 2002).

The right to appeal is restricted for juvenile offenders. Unlike adults, juvenile offenders must choose between two options: a full retrial or review of their case on legal grounds. Adult offenders may have their cases reviewed twice.

Pretrial detention is restricted in juvenile proceedings. For juvenile suspects ages fourteen to fifteen, risk of escape in order to justify pretrial detention may only be assumed when the juvenile has made an attempt to escape or has no permanent place of residence (Youth Court Law, sec. 72 II). None of the reasons valid for adult offenders justify pretrial detention for juvenile offenders. In addition, the court, in deciding on pretrial detention, must consider whether it is sufficient to place the juvenile offender in a foster home. If a juvenile offender is placed in pretrial detention, the court aide must be informed (Youth Court Law, sec. 72a) to ensure that all relevant information is available, including on possible alternatives such as foster care. Juvenile pretrial detention must be organized in a way that favors education. As a consequence, a juvenile offender placed in a pretrial detention center is obliged to work.

TABLE 2

Short-Term Detention as an Instrument to Enforce Educational
Measures (Hamburg, 1991–94)

	1991	1992	1993	1994
Disposition total	3,086	2,795	2,939	2,534
Community service	417	397	476	388
Fine	454	312	458	424
Supervision order	187	158	231	226
Restitution	86	124	105	123
Combination	214	170	47	26
Orders that can be enforced by "arrest"	1,358	1,161	1,317	1,187
N arrest	7	8	10	12
Arrest in %	.5	.7	.8	1.0

SOURCE.—Hinrichs 1996, p. 59.

A. Criminal Penalties

Each offense in the German Penal Code carries a minimum and a maximum range. The penalty ranges, however, do not apply to juvenile offenders. The Youth Court Law contains a separate system of three categories of sanctions or measures.

1. *Educational Measures.* Educational measures cover a range of orders. Educational measures should, according to section 10 of the Youth Court Act, have a positive impact on the behavior patterns of juvenile offenders in securing and enhancing conditions of socialization. A catalogue of orders is annexed to section 10. These include community service, participation in social training courses, participation in victim-offender mediation, participation in traffic education, supervision by a social worker, and attendance at vocational training. The assistance provided by the Children and Youth Welfare Law may include placement in a home or a foster family. Table 2 provides data on the use of short-term detention to enforce educational measures (noncompliance can result in short-term detention).

This type of enforcement is rarely used. The power to enforce educational measures through short-term detention has provoked a debate on whether the order to do community service violates the German Constitution (which prohibits forced labor outside the prison system). The procedure, however, was upheld recently by the Constitutional Court.

2. *Disciplinary Measures.* Disciplinary measures are the second cat-

egory (*Zuchtmittel*, Youth Court Law, sec. 13). These are divided into three subcategories. First is cautioning by the juvenile judge. This is a formal verdict that is registered in the criminal record. Second is fulfilling certain conditions (e.g., paying a fine), doing community service (the maximum number of hours is not prescribed but is limited by the principle of proportionality), compensating the victim of the offense, and making a formal apology to the victim. Third, the most severe, is short-term detention (*Jugendarrest*), which may last for up to four weeks or be imposed during weekends or spare time. Short-term detention means placement in a special unit separated from the youth prison.

3. *Youth Imprisonment.* Under section 17 of the Youth Court Law, youth imprisonment is, strictly speaking, the only juvenile criminal penalty. Although official records provide for two separate court information systems, for juvenile sanctions and for adult sanctions, a verdict of youth imprisonment is registered in the adult criminal record when a juvenile reaches age eighteen. All other juvenile measures are recorded only in juvenile records, which are accessible only to the prosecution services and the court system. All aspects of access to information on prior records are regulated in the Law on the Federal Register of Judicial Information (*Bundeszentralregistergesetz*), which is guided by the goal of reducing the stigma of prior criminal convictions.

The minimum sentence for youth imprisonment is six months, the maximum, five years. For offenses for which the Criminal Code provides a maximum term of adult imprisonment of more than ten years, the maximum youth imprisonment may not exceed ten years. The minimum six-month term of imprisonment (in adult court the minimum is one month) is based on the belief that treatment and education of a juvenile offender are efficient only if a minimum term of secure placement is available. As with adult criminal law, a sentence of youth imprisonment may be suspended if the juvenile offender is low-risk and the sentence does not exceed one year. A juvenile offender serving youth imprisonment may be paroled after having served one-third of the sentence (sec. 88, Youth Court Law) while the minimum term for adults is one-half.

B. The Choice among Sanctions

The focus in choosing among different types of measures is on educational needs. Section 5 of the Youth Court Law says that disciplinary measures may be applied only if educational measures are insufficient to respond to the educational needs displayed by the juvenile offender. Moreover, section 17 II states that juvenile imprisonment may be imposed only if educational or disciplinary measures are insufficient to educate the juvenile offender or if the seriousness of the crime requires criminal punishment. The wording reflects the ambivalence (education versus punishment) embedded in the system of juvenile sanctions. Youth imprisonment may be imposed either as a consequence of the necessity to educate the juvenile offender and to respond to negative habits indicated by the offense committed or as a result of the seriousness of the offense and guilt. Although the primary goal is education, section 17 II makes it clear that the legislature had in mind cases where educative reasons alone are insufficient to explain a prison sentence of up to ten years (e.g., when the lack of obvious psychological and social deficits and a serious criminal offense would lead to a measure not consistent with the seriousness of the crime). General prevention and general deterrence are behind section 17 II's allowance of resort to imprisonment for serious crimes. A recent study of youth court decisions imposing imprisonment of ten years demonstrates that virtually all were justified by, inter alia, the seriousness of the crime (Schulz 2001).

C. Young Adults and Sentencing

People ages eighteen to twenty are presumed to be adults and may be tried and sentenced according to adult criminal law. But, as a general rule, section 105 of the Youth Court Law requires that a young adult be adjudicated and sentenced as a juvenile under the following circumstances: first, if a psychological evaluation reveals that the young adult offender shows a typical youthful personality in terms of intellectual and emotional maturity; or, second, if the offense involves typical juvenile misbehavior in type, circumstances, or motives.

Virtually all adolescent offenders adjudicated for serious offenses are sentenced under the Youth Court Law. An exception involves traffic offenses. A substantial fraction of adolescent traffic offenders are processed through the adult criminal justice system.

The proportion of young adults tried and sentenced as juveniles has increased steadily. Figure 12 shows the proportions sentenced as juveniles broken down by offense categories. On average, slightly more than 60 percent of all young adults are sentenced as juveniles. Virtually all young adults are sentenced as juveniles for robbery (corresponding rates can be observed for first- and second-degree murder). An expla-

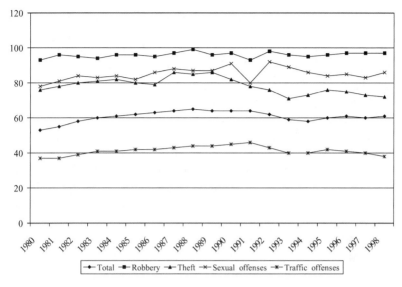

Fig. 12.—Young adults adjudicated and sentenced as juveniles (percent). Source: Statistisches Bundesamt 1980–98.

nation of the considerable variation in referring young adults to juvenile courts is the reluctance of judges to impose high minimum penalties on young offenders or adult offenders. The minimum penalties are one year for robbery, five years for aggravated robbery, two years for rape, and five years to life for murder. The penalty for first-degree murder is mandatory life imprisonment; however, the German High Court tolerates deviation from life imprisonment if the circumstances demand a mitigated sentence.

The system of juvenile justice and the practice of treating young adults as if they were juveniles recently came under pressure from the enormous increase in bias-motivated violent crimes committed by juveniles and young adults. The debate on how to use juvenile criminal law for young adults centers on three suggestions.

First is the abolition of the choice available today with respect to young adults and the legal difference between juveniles and young adults. Young adults of eighteen to twenty years should, according to this view, be treated as juveniles. Second is the amendment of section 105 of the Youth Court Law to reduce significantly the number of young adults adjudicated and sentenced and to make this option an exception to a presumption that young adults should be sentenced as adults (motion of the Christian Democratic Party of April 12, 2000, BR-Drucksache 14/3189). Third is to remove young adults completely from the adult system, expand the regime of juvenile criminal law to offenders under eighteen, but cut by half the minimum and maximum penalties available for adult offenders (such a system has been adopted in Austrian juvenile criminal law).

The German system for young adult offenders is a youth-specific system that falls between a juvenile welfare system and adult criminal justice. Besides a welfare approach to juvenile delinquency and problem behavior, a justice approach to juvenile crime that can be extended to young adults is feasible. Because transitional periods have been prolonged and entrance into the adult world has been made more difficult, failure to respect the differences between young adults and adults risks failure of adequate justice for young adult offenders.

D. Decision Making in the System

Unlike common law systems in which the prosecutor has full discretion to decide whether to file an indictment, German prosecution of juveniles is based on the principle of legality. As a general rule, the public prosecutor is obliged to file a charge in every case where there is reasonable evidence that the offender has committed a crime. Nonetheless, important exceptions permit dismissal of cases concerning petty offenses on opportunity grounds (Code of Criminal Procedure, sections 153 and 153a). Even more important are the exceptions made in the Youth Court Law.

In proceedings against a juvenile offender, the prosecutor may dismiss the case on the same grounds as would justify dismissal in adult proceedings, that is, when the offense is a minor or trivial misdemeanor and the personal guilt of the offender is negligible. In addition, section 45 of the Juvenile Court Law empowers the prosecutor to dismiss any case if an adequate educational measure has been carried through by some other institution or by individuals such as teachers, parents, or other relatives. If the prosecutor has filed a formal charge, the judge may dismiss the case (with the concurrence of the prosecutor) on the same reasons mentioned above (Youth Court Law, sec. 47). This type of diversion was considerably extended during the 1980s on the rationale that the average juvenile does not need education and the attention of the juvenile court but will grow out of crime and stay out of crime if diverted. The German parliament has explicitly adopted this position in the Youth Court Law amendment of 1990 and thus

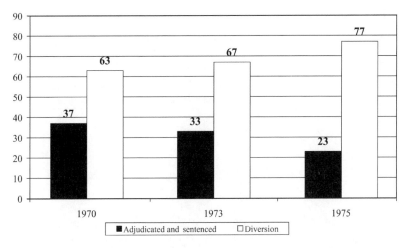

Fɪɢ. 13.—Proportions of diversion (nonprosecution) of first-time theft offenders ages fourteen to fifteen in birth cohorts 1970, 1973, and 1975.

supported the idea that juvenile court procedures leading to adjudication and formal sentencing should be a last resort.

VII. Juvenile Justice Practice

Despite the increase in the number of offenders during the 1960s and 1970s, there was only a slight increase in adjudication and sentencing rates. But during the 1980s, conviction and sentencing rates declined substantially from approximately 1,500 juvenile offenders per 100,000 youth per year at the end of the 1970s to slightly more than 1,000 in 1990 (Heinz 1990b). The rate increased again during the 1990s to around 1,200 per 100,000 in 1998 (still well below the 1970s). Research on public prosecutors' decision making revealed that dismissals of juvenile cases are frequent and that every second juvenile offender has his or her case dismissed (Heinz 1989, 1990b). Diversion by the prosecutor has become a major dispositional alternative. Figure 13 shows the significant increase in the use of diversionary practices for first-time shoplifters over a period of some five years. The growing use of nonprosecution, in a context of rising crime rates, led in the second half of the 1990s to conflicts between police and the judiciary, with police complaining that the judiciary and prosecution services fail to enforce the criminal law (see Braasch et al. 1997).

Strong arguments have been made to require victim-offender mediation as a prerequisite for dismissals. A considerable number of victim-

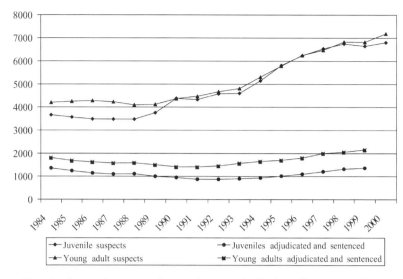

FIG. 14.—Rates of suspects and rates of sentenced offenders (all criminal offenses)

offender mediation schemes have been evaluated positively, although strong evaluation designs are rare and minor offenders are the predominant target (H.-J. Albrecht 1990). The pronounced increase in juvenile and young adult suspects has not been followed by a corresponding increase in adjudication and sentencing. Rates of adjudication and sentencing are stable. This means that most of the increase in police-recorded juvenile crime is dealt with by way of nonprosecution or dismissals by the public prosecutor (Heinz 1997, p. 291).

The proportion of cases receiving the most severe disposition (youth imprisonment) remained fairly stable in the 1970s at approximately 8 percent of all youth court dispositions. Even though the number of juvenile suspects increased steadily during the 1980s and 1990s, the youth imprisonment rate decreased to some 6 percent of dispositions (see fig. 14). The average length of incarceration increased slightly. Conversely, there has been a marked increase in the number of educational measures requiring community service and social training. This trend reflects growing support within the system for community-based responses while short-term detention (*Jugendarrest*) continues to be in decline (from 24 percent in 1976 to 18 percent in 1998). Approximately half of the sentences of juvenile imprisonment are of one year or less, and some 64 percent of all youth prison sentences are suspended. Long prison sentences are very rare. Between 1987 and 1996,

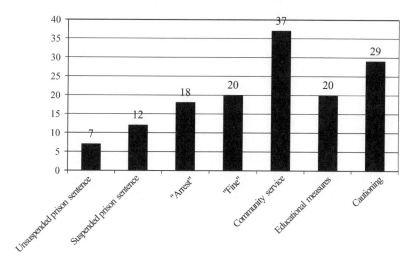

Fig. 15.—Distribution of juvenile criminal sanctions, 1999 (percent). Note.—Totals more than 100 percent because educational and disciplinary measures can be combined. Source: Statistisches Bundesamt 2001.

seventy-four juveniles and young adults were sentenced to the maximum ten-year term of youth imprisonment (Schulz 2001). These sentences have been imposed almost exclusively for murder and on young adults (Schulz 2001, p. 313).

Measures can be combined, except for short-term detention ("arrest") and a suspended prison sentence. Prosecutors and judges sometimes argue that there are certain advantages in imposing a suspended sentence while letting a juvenile taste what prison is like. As the Youth Court Law explicitly forbids this practice, there are allegations that practitioners sometimes abuse pretrial detention to achieve the same result. Current reform proposals call for allowance of short detention combined with a suspended prison sentence. There does not, however, seem to be enough political support to attract a majority vote in the Federal Parliament.

Figure 15 gives some insight into juvenile and young adult sentencing in 1999. Sentencing options are not equally used. Judges appear to have distinct preferences. Immediate detention (unsuspended youth prison sentence and arrest) is imposed on some 25 percent of juveniles and young adults convicted. Fines, community service, and cautioning are widely and routinely used. These sentencing options are attractive because of their easy convertibility. Other options, such as restitution and social training courses, do not play a major role.

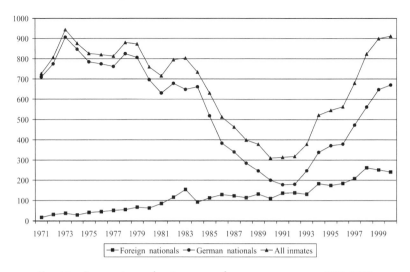

FIG. 16.—Inmates in youth prisons, ages fourteen to seventeen, 1971–2000

A. Correctional Supervision

Rates of incarceration of juvenile and adolescent offenders fell steadily from the late 1960s until the beginning of the 1990s (from approximately forty per 100,000 in 1961 to ten per 100,000 by 1989). In the 1990s, rates increased for juveniles ages fourteen to seventeen, standing on March 31, 2000, at twenty-five per 100,000. A corresponding decline and increase can be observed in prisoner rates for young adults (ages eighteen to twenty) and for twenty-one- to twenty-five-year-olds. Prison rates for adults age twenty-six and older remained fairly stable throughout the 1970s and 1980s but have—as with younger age groups—increased considerably during the 1990s (see fig. 16). With the beginning of the new millennium, the increase seems to be leveling off. Between 2000 and October 2001, there was a slight decrease. The increase in the youth prison population reflects the increase in the number of adjudicated and sentenced juveniles. There is evidently not a significant change in sentencing practices, but a stable application leads automatically to more youth prison sentences and hence to more youth prison inmates.

Very few female offenders are detained in youth prisons. As of March 31, 2000, thirty-one sentenced female juveniles ages fourteen to seventeen were detained in the whole of Germany.

The age structure in youth prisons shown in figure 17 suggests re-

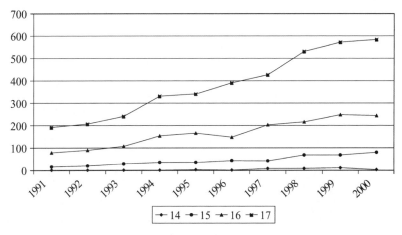

Fig. 17.—Trends in age structure among juvenile prison inmates

luctance in use of imprisonment for fourteen- and fifteen-year-olds. Most of the increase in the 1990s resulted from more sixteen- and seventeen-year-olds entering youth prisons.

The ratio of juvenile pretrial detainees to juvenile prisoners throughout the 1980s and 1990s was 1:1. The corresponding ratio for young adults was 1:2 and for adults 1:4. This occurs despite the statutory requirement that pretrial detention be used only in cases where there is reason to believe that the juvenile offender either will not attend the trial or will receive a long youth prison sentence. The disproportionate use of pretrial detention for juvenile offenders may result from a strategy of using pretrial detention as a short, sharp shock immediately after the offense has been committed or as a means of crisis intervention (Gebauer 1987; Heinz 1987, 1990a).

Despite the decrease in youth imprisonment during the 1970s and 1980s, the proportion of juveniles placed under some type of judicial control has increased considerably since the 1960s. The rate climbed from 200 per 100,000 in 1965 to 400 per 100,000 in 1989. In a context of expanded use of intermediate sanctions such as probation and parole, imprisonment has changed from a means of immediate physical control to a last resort, thereby backing up the credibility of sanctions based on supervision and control outside the prison. The greater elasticity of probation and parole and the restriction of prison use to a symbolic level are supported by changes in criteria for revoking probation. In the 1960s, the offender population on probation was low risk

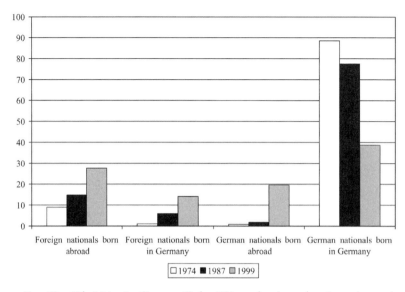

Fɪɢ. 18.—Ethnicities in German (Baden-Württemberg) youth prisons (percent).
Source: Walter 2000.

(as measured by prior record) and had a limited need for control (no
prior record and a stable work record were preconditions). Since the
mid-1970s, the target group for probation is people who were formerly
sent to prison.

The recent sharp increase in juvenile imprisonment is only partly
due to the increase in the number of foreign nationals (as can be seen
in fig. 17). A separate factor since the beginning of the 1990s is the
emigration of ethnic Germans from the former Soviet Union (and presenting all characteristics of immigrants in terms of language, cultural,
and economic marginalization). Figure 18, presenting data on changes
in the Baden-Wurttemberg's youth prison system, indicates a dramatic
decrease in the proportion of German nationals born in Germany and
a corresponding increase in the proportion of German nationals born
abroad (a reasonable proxy for ethnic Germans from the former Soviet
Union).

The disproportionate presence of foreigners is equally pronounced
in juvenile pretrial detention. Depending on the region, foreign youth
comprise up to 57 percent of the youth inmate population. Enormous
differences in rates of young prisoners may be observed in Western
Europe. The rate of imprisoned young offenders (up to twenty-one

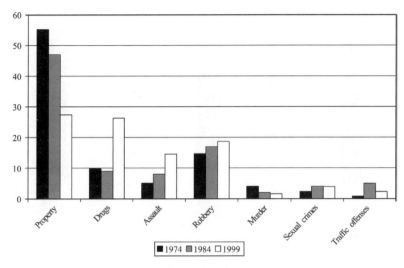

FIG. 19.—Types of criminal offenses in the Baden-Württemberg youth correctional system. Source: Walter 2000.

years of age) varied in the 1980s between approximately thirty per 100,000 (Italy, Netherlands, and Greece) and approximately 300 (England and Wales).

Further changes in the youth prison system emerge from figure 19. The structure of offenses changed considerably during the last twenty-five years. Property offenses lost their predominant role, and drugs, assault, and robbery replaced simple and aggravated forms of theft. Figure 20, comparing time served by German and foreign nationals, demonstrates changes linked to the changing ethnic composition of youth prison populations. Foreign nationals serve significantly less time than German nationals due to a policy that reduces imprisonment in exchange for immediate deportation.

B. Problems in Sentencing Juvenile Offenders

Reliance on the principle of education in the juvenile justice system is accompanied by disparate decision making in that disadvantaged youth are more likely to be sentenced to intensive types of sanctions. Further problems currently being discussed include differences in treatment between the juvenile and adult justice systems and the enormous regional variations in dispositions in juvenile cases.

Criminological studies reveal that juvenile judges make considerably more use of sanctions involving deprivation of liberty than do adult

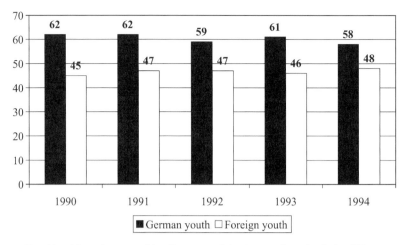

Fɪɢ. 20.—Mean time served by German and foreign youth in the Baden-Württemberg youth correctional system. Source: Walter 2000.

judges (Heinz 1990*b*). While unconditional prison sentences amount to only 5 percent of all adult offenders sentenced, the rate for juveniles sentenced to an unconditional term of youth prison or to short-term detention is approximately 25 percent, even though the average seriousness of juvenile crimes is well below that for adult crimes. Juvenile offenders are thus treated more harshly than their adult counterparts (which is explained by the prevailing belief that placement in secure detention will lead to favorable rehabilitative outcomes; Heinz 1992). Differential treatment can be observed with respect to the length of prison sentences. The average juvenile prison sentence is longer than adult prison sentences for comparable offense categories (Pfeiffer 1991).

Studies on decision making show considerable regional variation with respect to the disposition of juvenile offenders, which cannot be explained by differences in characteristics of offenses or offenders (Heinz 1990*c*). These styles of juvenile justice reflect differing court traditions. Equal treatment is difficult to attain when decision making is based on the principle of education.

C. Does the Youth Prison Meet the Promise of Education and Rehabilitation?

Pessimistic assessments prevail on the effects of treatment in juvenile correctional institutions. Although studies based on strong research designs are scarce, there is no reason to believe that focusing on the offender's vocational skills or other treatment options produces lower recidivism rates. Differences in rates of recidivism between differentially treated groups are usually small and may reflect preexisting differences between the groups treated (Geissler 1991). In general, the possibly positive effects of treatment or support offered in youth prisons are probably outweighed by negative influences of imprisonment and the prison subculture. Evaluations of dispositional alternatives in the juvenile justice system can take advantage of natural variation in decision making between different juvenile court districts. The results support the conclusion that different juvenile measures have similar effects in terms of rates of recidivism and the general toll of juvenile crime (Heinz 1990c). Variation in the intensity of intervention is not associated with juvenile criminal behavior or with juvenile crime. Other Western European countries rely on different policies vis-à-vis juvenile crime and juvenile offenders but face similar crime and delinquency problems (Kaiser 1989).

VIII. The Future of the German Juvenile Justice System

Reformers have shifted from advocating a unified juvenile welfare law to retention of a separate criminal law for juvenile and young adult offenders. This coincides with growing distrust of rehabilitation and education as major goals of juvenile welfare and juvenile criminal justice and with growing demands for punitiveness from the political system and the parliament. In the 1970s and early 1980s, juvenile law reform focused on rehabilitation and treatment based on a youth welfare approach. The 1980s and 1990s can be characterized as emphasizing the need to grant juvenile offenders the same procedural and trial rights that adult offenders receive. The 1990 amendment to juvenile court law brought some important changes, but some critical issues were not touched. The indeterminate youth prison sentence was abolished and the position of intermediate sanctions was strengthened.

Moreover, with victim-offender mediation, a new perspective has been introduced that places less weight on the offender's person and more on the effects of the offense on the victim and society. However, Parliament did not abolish short-term detention or amend the conditions for imposing youth imprisonment. Recent proposals for youth law amendments suggest that decriminalization and diversion will continue to be among the prominent topics of reform (DVJJ-Kommission zur Reform des Jugendstrafrechts 1992; Zweite Jugendstrafrechtskommission 2002). However, at the beginning of the twenty-first century, public discourse focuses on perceived increases in juvenile crime and an intensifying political debate on safety. Conservative political parties and mainstream public opinion call for a more repressive approach to juvenile and young adult offenders, even to criminal children. In 2000, several proposals were introduced that would bring about significant changes to youth legislation if accepted by the Federal Parliament.

The Christian Democratic Party/Christian Social Union introduced a proposal that was supported in part by various German states (BR-Drucksache 14/3189 as of April 12, 2000). It proposes to make adjudication and sentencing of young adult offenders as juveniles exceptional; to introduce sentencing powers that allow combination of short-term detention (up to four weeks) with a suspended sentence of youth imprisonment; to increase maximum imprisonment for young adults if they are sentenced as juveniles to fifteen years; to introduce a new supervision order that allows tight control of free movement of juveniles; to authorize the family courts or youth court to impose restrictive (and punitive) orders (such as participation in a social training course, victim-offender mediation, and community service, as well as restrictions in visiting places or meeting other persons) that correspond to the powers authorized in Youth Court Law as a response to juvenile crime;[2] and, to strengthen powers of family courts to respond to parents who have allegedly failed to supervise and control their delinquent or criminal offspring.

So far, however, there is little sign that such proposals will be successful. Among juvenile justice professionals and most political parties represented in the Federal Parliament, the conviction prevails that experience with separating the juvenile from the adult criminal system has, in general, been positive and does not justify major changes.

The stability of the general structure of the juvenile justice system could also be observed during the deliberations and in the outcomes of the German Law Day 2002 (Deutscher Juristentag 2002). In the general criminal law section, the question "Is German juvenile justice still up to date?" (Ist das deutsche Jugendstrafrecht noch zeitgemäß?) was discussed. The general report submitted for discussion (H.-J. Albrecht 2002) proposed complete abolition of education as the major

---

[2] Criminal responsibility of children—although statutorily not established—would be introduced by way of switching labels in the Children and Youth Support Law (*Kinder- und Jugendhilfegesetz*).

goal of juvenile justice and replacement with a system based upon a youth-adjusted proportionality principle based solely on seriousness of crime. The report also proposed to reduce the range of educational and disciplinary measures and prison sentences to two categories of penalties (community-based and imprisonment) in order to enhance uniformity and reduce disparity in sentencing. However, the votes demonstrated clearly the legal profession's preference for the principle of education and for a system of sentencing and sanctions based upon a range of sentencing options and consideration of educational needs of juvenile offenders (Deutscher Juristentag 2002). Proposals to keep the minimum age of criminal responsibility at fourteen years and to include young adults completely in the juvenile justice systems received wide support, as did a proposal to grant victims of crime in juvenile procedures the same rights they have in adult criminal trials. In general, the debate's results demonstrate remarkably strong support for education as the basic justification of separating juvenile and adult criminal law and a strong preference among legal professionals to restrict punitive responses when dealing with juveniles. The results also demonstrate growing concern for crime victims' rights and support for eliminating procedural disadvantages (compared to adult criminal procedural law).

The basic structure and the major elements of the juvenile justice system will not change in the foreseeable future. The German juvenile justice system will continue to be characterized by stability and slow processes of change as it has been for the last 100 years.

REFERENCES

Adam, Hansjörg, Hans-Jörg Albrecht, and Christian Pfeiffer. 1986. *Jugendrichter und Jugendstaatsanwälte in der Bundesrepublik Deutschland.* Freiburg: Max-Planck-Institut für Ausländisches und Internationales Strafrecht.
Albrecht, Günther. 1990. "Möglichkeiten und Grenzen der Prognose 'krimineller Karrieren.'" In *Mehrfach Auffällige, mehrfach Betroffene: Erlebnisweisen und Reaktionsformen,* edited by Deutsche Vereinigung für Jugendgerichte und Jugendgerichtshilfen. Godesberg: Forum.
Albrecht, Hans-Jörg. 1987a. "Die sanfte Minderheit. Mädchen und Frauen als Straftäterinnen." *Bewährungshilfe* 34:341–59.
———. 1987b. "Foreign Minorities and the Criminal Justice System in the Federal Republic of Germany." *Howard Journal of Criminal Justice* 26:272–88.

————. 1988. "Ausländerkriminalität." In *Fälle zum Wahlfach Kriminologie, Jugendstrafrecht, Strafvollzug,* 2d ed., edited by Heike Jung. Munich: Beck.

————. 1990. "Kriminologische Perspektiven der Wiedergutmachung." In *Neue Wege der Wiedergutmachung im Strafrecht: internationals strafrechtlich-kriminologisches Kolloquium in Freibrug i. Br.,* edited by Albin Eser, Günther Kaiser, and Kurt Madlener. Freiburg: Max-Planck-Institut für Ausländisches und Internationales Strafrecht.

————. 1991. "Bilan des connaissances en République fédérale d'Allemagne." In *Les politiques de prévention de la délinquance à l'aune de la recherche,* edited by Philippe Robert. Paris: L'Harmattan.

————. 1993. "Ethnic Minorities: Crime and Criminal Justice in Europe." In *Crime in Europe,* edited by Francis Heidensohn and Michael Farrell. London: Routledge.

————. 1997. "Ethnic Minorities, Crime, and Criminal Justice in Germany." In *Ethnicity, Crime, and Immigration: Comparative and Cross-National Perspectives,* edited by Michael Tonry. Vol. 21 of *Crime and Justice: A Review of Research,* edited by Michael Tonry. Chicago: University of Chicago Press.

————. 1998. "Jugend und Gewalt." *Monatsschrift für Kriminologie und Strafrechtsreform* 81:381–98.

————. 2002. *Ist das deutsche Jugendstrafrecht noch zeitgemäß?* Munich: Beck.

Albrecht, Peter-Alexis. 1993. *Jugendstrafrecht: ein Studienbuch.* 2d ed. Munich: Beck.

————. 2001. *Gegenreform im Jugendstrafrecht wider jede wissenschaftliche Einsicht.* Paper presented to a Parliamentary hearing, Berlin, May 9.

Albrecht, Peter-Alexis, and Siegfried Lamnek. 1979. *Jugendkriminalität im Zerrbild der Statistik: e. Analyse von Daten u. Entwicklungen.* Munich: Juventa.

Arbeiterwohlfahrt Bundesverband e.V., ed. 1970. *Vorschläge für ein erweitertes Jugendhilferecht. Denkschrift der Arbeiterwohlfahrt zur Reform und Vereinheitlichung von Jugendwohlfahrtsgesetz und Jugendstrafgesetz.* Schriften der Arbeiterwohlfahrt, no. 22, 3d ed. Bonn: Arbeiterwohlfahrt.

Bliesener, Thomas. 1992. "Psychologische Hintergründe der Gewalt gegen Ausländer." In *Ausländer im Jugendstrafrecht: Neue Dimensionen,* edited by DVJJ-Regionalgruppe Nordbayern. Erlangen: Deutsche Vereinigung für Jugendgerichte und Jugendgerichtshilfen.

Böhm, Alexander, H. Helmrich, J. Kraus, F. Krause, R. Schmidt, J. Schwarte, and H.-D. Schwind. 1997. *Jugendkriminalität—Herausforderung für Staat und Gesellschaft.* Sankt Augustin, Germany: Konrad Adenauer Stiftung.

Braasch, Hans-Joachim, K. Köhn, K. Kommoß, and O.-H. Winkelmann. 1997. *Der Gesetzesungehorsam der Justiz.* Lübeck: Schmidt-Römhild.

Bundesamt für Verfassungsschutz. 2000. *Verfassungsschutzbericht 1999.* Berlin: Bundesamt für Verfassungsschutz.

Bundeskriminalamt. Various years, 1982–2000. *Polizeiliche Kriminalstatistik.* Wiesbaden: Bundeskriminalamt.

Bundesminister für Jugend, Familie und Gesundheit, ed. 1973. *Diskussionsentwurf eines Jugendhilfegesetzes.* Bonn: Bundesministerium für Jugend, Familie und Gesundheit.

Bundesverfassungsgericht. 1991. *Neue Juristische Wochenschrift* 44:1043.

Bundesverfassungsschutz. Various years, 1982–99. *Verfassungsschutgherichte.* Berlin: Bundesminiserium des Inneren.

Deutsche Vereinigung für Jugendgerichte und Jugendgerichtshilfen (DVJJ)-Kommission zur Reform des Jugendkriminalrechts. 1992. "Für ein neues Jugendgerichtsgesetz." *DVJJ-Journal* 1-2:4–39.

Deutscher Juristentag. 2002. *Die Beschlüsse des 64: Deutschen Juristentages.* Berlin: Deutscher Juristentag.

Dölling, Dieter. 1992. "Die Bedeutung der Jugendkriminalität im Verhältnis zur Erwachsenenkriminalität." In *Grundfragen des Jugendkriminalrechts und seiner Neuregelung,* edited by Bundesministerium der Justiz. Godesberg: Forum.

Eisenberg, Ulrich. 1995. *Jugendgerichtsgesetz: mit Erläuterungen.* 6th ed. Munich: Beck.

Elsner, E., W. Steffen, and G. Stern. 1998. *Kinder-und Jugendkriminalität in München.* Munich: Bayerisches Landeskriminalamt.

Empey, LaMar Taylor. 1982. *American Delinquency: Its Meaning and Construction.* Rev. ed. Homewood, Ill.: Dorsey.

Frehsee, Detlev. 1995. "Sozialer Wandel und Jugendkriminalität." *DVJJ-Journal* 3-4:269–78.

Fritsch, Markus. 1999. *Die jugendstrafrechtliche Reformbewegung (1871–1923): die Entwicklung bis zum ersten Jugendgerichtsgesetz unter besonderer Berücksichtigun der Diskussion über die Altersgrenzen der Strafmündigkeit.* Freiburg: Edition Iuscrim.

Frommel, Monika. 1994. "Alles nur ein Vollzugsdefizit? Warum die Strafjustiz nicht angemessen auf die Gewaltverbrechen gegen Auslaender reagiert." *DVJJ-Journal* 1:67–68.

Gebauer, Michael. 1987. *Die Rechtswirklichkeit der Untersuchungshaft in der Bundesrepublik Deutschland.* Göttingen: Schwartz.

Geissler, Isolde. 1991. *Ausbildung und Arbeit im Jugendstrafvollzug: Haftverlaufs-und Rückfallanalyse.* Freiburg: Max-Planck-Institut für Ausländisches und Internationales Strafrecht.

Glogauer, Werner. 1991. *Kriminalisierung von Kindern und Jugendlichen durch die Medien.* 2d ed. Baden-Baden: Nomos.

Grundies, Volker. 1999. "Polizeiliche Registrierungen von 7-bis 23jährigen. Befunde der Freiburger Kohortenuntersuchung." In *Forschungen zu Kriminalität und Kriminalitätskontrolle am Max-Planck-Institut für Ausländisches und Internationales Strafrecht in Freiburg i.Br.,* edited by Hans-Jörg Albrecht. Freiburg: Max-Planck-Institut für Ausländisches und Internationales Strafrecht.

———. 2000. "Kriminalitätsbelastung junger Aussiedler: Ein Längsschnittvergleich mit in Deutschland geborenen jungen Menschen anhand polizeilicher Registrierungen." *Monatsschrift für Kriminologie und Strafrechtsreform* 83:290–305.

Grundies, Volker, Sven Höfer, and Carina Tetal. 2002. *Basisdaten der Freiburger Kohortenstudie: Prävalenz und Inzidenz polizeilicher Registrierung.* Freiburg: Edition Iuscrim.

Heinz, Wolfgang. 1987. "Recht und Praxis der Untersuchungshaft in der Bundesrepublik Deutschland: Zur Disfunktionalität der Untersuchungshaft gegenüber dem Reformprogramm im materiellen Strafrecht." *Bewährungshilfe* 34:5–31.

———. 1989. "Jugendstrafrechtsreform durch die Praxis—Eine Bestandsaufnahme." In *Jugendstrafrechtsreform durch die Praxis*, edited by Bundesministerium der Justiz. Bonn: Burg.

———. 1990*a*. "Die Jugendstrafrechtspflege im Spiegel der Rechtspflegestatistiken: Ausgewählte Daten für den Zeitraum 1955–1988." *Monatsschrift für Kriminologie und Strafrechtsreform* 73:210–76.

———. 1990*b*. "Gleichheit vor dem Gesetz in der Sanktionspraxis? Empirische Befunde der Sanktionsforschung im Jugendstrafrecht in der Bundesrepublik Deutschland." In *Kriminologie und Strafrechtspraxis: Tagungsberichte des kriminologischen Arbeitskreises*, vol. 7, edited by H. Göppinger. Tübingen: Aktuelle Probleme der Kriminologie.

———. 1990*c*. "Mehrfach Auffällige—Mehrfach Betroffene: Erlebnisweisen und Reaktionsformen." In *Mehrfach Auffällige, mehrfach Betroffene: Erlebnisweisen und Reaktionsformen*, edited by Deutsche Vereinigung für Jugendgerichte und Jugendgerichtshilfen. Godesberg: Forum.

———. 1992. "Abschied von der 'Erziehungsideologie' im Jugendstrafrecht? Zur Diskussion über Erziehung und Strafe." *Recht der Jugend und des Bildungswesens* 40:123–43.

———. 1997. "Jugendkriminalität zwischen Verharmlosung und Dramatisierung." *DVJJ-Journal* 3:270–93.

Heitmeyer, Wilhelm. 1995. *Gewalt: Schattenseiten der Individualisierung Jugendlicher aus unterschiedlichen Milieus*. Munich: Juventa.

Heitmeyer, W., and J. I. Peter, eds. 1988. *Jugendliche Fußballfans: Soziale und politische Orientierungen, Gesellungsformen, Gewalt*. Munich: Juventa.

Hering, E. 1993. *Mechanismen justizieller Eskalation im Jugendstrafverfahren*. Pfaffenweiler, Germany: Centaurus.

Hermanns, J. 1983. *Sozialisationsbiographie und jugendrichterliche Sanktionspraxis*. Freiburg: Max-Planck-Institut für Ausländisches und Internationales Strafrecht.

Hinrichs, Klaus. 1996. "Weisungen auf Auflagen brauchen keinen Zwang durch Jugendarrest." *DVJJ-Journal* 1:59–63.

Höfer, Sven. 2002. *Sanktionskarrieren—eine Analyse der Sanktionshärteentwicklung anhand von Daten der Freiburger Kohortenstudie*. Freiburg: Edition Iuscrim.

Jung, H. 1993*a*. "Massenmedien und Kriminalität." In *Kleines Kriminologisches Wörterbuch*, 3d ed., edited by Günther Kaiser et al. Heidelberg: Müller.

———. 1993*b*. "Täter-Opfer-Ausgleich: Anmerkungen zu seiner Bedeutung für das Rechtssystem." *Monatsschrift für Kriminologie und Strafrechtsreform* 76:50–56.

Kaiser, Günther. 1988. *Kriminologie*. 2d ed. Heidelberg: Müller.

———. 1989. "Jugenddelinquenz im internationalen Vergleich." In *Jugend und Kriminalität*, edited by Innenministerium Baden-Württemberg. Stuttgart: Innenministerium Baden-Württemberg.

———. 1993*a*. "Jugendstrafrecht." In *Kleines Kriminologisches Wörterbuch*, 3d ed., edited by Günther Kaiser et al. Heidelberg: Müller.

———. 1993*b*. *Kriminologie*. 9th ed. Heidelberg: Müller.

Karger, Thomas, and Peter Sutterer. 1988. "Cohort Study on the Development of Police-Recorded Criminality and Criminal Sanctioning." In *Crime and Criminal Justice: Criminological Research in the Second Decade at the Max Planck Institute in Freiburg*, edited by Günther Kaiser and Isolde Geissler. Freiburg: Max-Planck-Institut für Ausländisches und Internationales Strafrecht.

———. 1990. "Polizeilich registrierte Gewaltdelinquenz bei jungen Ausländern." *Monatsschrift für Kriminologie und Strafrechtsreform* 73:369–83.

Kerner, Hans Jürgen. 1990. "Jugendkriminalrecht als 'Vorreiter' der Strafrechtsreform? Überlegungen zu 40 Jahren Rechtsentwicklung in Rechtsprechung, Lehre und Kriminalpolitik." *DVJJ-Journal* 133:68–81.

Kerner, Hans Jürgen, and Bernd-Rüdeger Sonnen. 1997. "Jugendkriminalität und Jugendstrafrecht." *DVJJ-Journal* 158:339–45.

Kerner, Hans Jürgen, and Elmar Weitekamp. 1984. "The Federal Republic of Germany." In *Western Systems of Juvenile Justice*, edited by Malcolm W. Klein. Beverly Hills, Calif.: Sage.

Kersten, Joachim. 1993. "Das Thema Gewaltkriminalität in kulturvergleichender Sicht." *DVJJ-Journal* 1:18–26.

Klein, Malcolm W., ed. 1984. *Western Systems of Juvenile Justice*. Beverly Hills, Calif.: Sage.

Krüger, Horst. 1983. "Rückfallquote: rund 30%." *Kriminalistik* 37:326–29.

Kube, Edwin, and Karl-Friedrich Koch. 1990. "Zur Kriminalität jugendlicher Ausländer aus polizeilicher Sicht." *Monatsschrift für Kriminologie und Strafrechtsreform* 73:14–24.

Kunz, Karl-Ludwig. 1989. "Ausländerkriminalität in der Schweiz—Umfang, Struktur und Erklärungsversuch." *Schweizerische Zeitschrift für Strafrecht* 106:373–92.

Laubenthal, Klaus. 1993. *Jugendgerichtshilfe im Strafverfahren*. Cologne: Heymanns.

Liszt, Franz von. 1905. "Die Kriminalität der Jugendlichen." In *Strafrechtliche Aufsätze und Vorträge*, vol. 2, edited by Franz von Liszt. Berlin: Guttentag.

Mansel, J., and K. Hurrelmann. 1993. "Psychosoziale Befindlichkeit junger Ausländer in der Bundesrepublik Deutschland." *Soziale Probleme* 4:167–92.

Meinhof, Ulrike Marie. 1971. *Bambule: Fürsorge für wen?* Berlin: Wagenbach.

Münder, J., F. Sack, Hans-Jörg Albrecht, and H. J. Plewig. 1987. *Jugendarbeitslosigkeit und Jugendkriminalität*. Neuwied, Germany: Luchterhand.

Neubacher, Frank. 1999. "Die fremdenfeindlichen Brandanschläge nach der Vereinigung." *Monatsschrift für Kriminologie und Strafrechtsreform* 82:1–15.

Obergfell-Fuchs, Joachim. 2001. *Kommunale Kriminalitätsprävention*. Freiburg: Max-Planck-Institut für Ausländisches und Internationales Strafrecht.

Oberwittler, Dietrich. 2000. *Von der Strafe zur Erziehung? Jugendkriminalpolitik in England und Deutschland (1850–1920)*. Frankfurt: Campus.

Ostendorf, Heribert. 1992. "Ansatzpunkte für materiell-rechtliche Entkrimi-
nalisierungen von Verhaltensweisen junger Menschen." In *Grundfragen des
Jugendkriminalrechts und seiner Neuregelung*, edited by Bundesministerium
der Justiz. Godesberg: Forum.

———. 1997. *Jugendgerichtsgesetz: Kommentar*. 4th ed. Cologne: Heymanns.

Pfeiffer, Christian. 1991. "Wird nach Jugendstrafrecht härter bestraft?"
Strafverteidiger 11:363–70.

———. 1998. "Juvenile Crime and Violence in Europe." In *Crime and Justice:
A Review of Research*, vol. 23, edited by Michael Tonry. Chicago: University
of Chicago Press.

Pfeiffer, Christian, I. Delzer, D. Enzmann, and P. Wetzels. 1998. *Ausgrenzung,
Gewalt und Kriminalität im Leben junger Menschen*. Hannover: Deutsche Vereinigung für Jugendgerichte und Jugendgerichtshilfen.

Popitz, Heinrich. 1968. *Über die Präventivwirkung des Nichtwissens*. Freiburg:
Soziologisches Institut.

Rommelspacher, Birgit. 1993. "Männliche Jugendliche als Projektionsfiguren
gesellschaftlicher Gewaltphantasien: Rassismus im Selbstverständnis der
Mehrheitskultur." In *Lust auf Randale: Jugendliche Gewalt gegen Fremde*, edited by Wilfried Breyvogel. Bonn: Dietz.

Schaal, Hans-Jürgen, and Ulrich Eisenberg. 1988. "Rechte und Befugnisse
von Verletzten im Strafverfahren gegen Jugendliche." *Neue Zeitschrift für
Strafrecht* 8:49–53.

Schaffstein, Friedrich, and Werner Beulke. 1995. *Jugendstrafrecht: eine systema-
tische Darstellung*. 12th ed. Stuttgart: Kohlhammer.

Schöch, Heinz. 1992. *Empfehlen sich Änderungen und Ergänzungen bei den stra-
frechtlichen Sanktionen ohne Freiheitsentzug?* Munich: Beck.

Schüler-Springorum, Horst. 2001. "Hundert Jahre Jugendgerichtsbarkeit." In
Grundfragen staatlichen Strafens: Festschrift für Müller-Dietz, edited by Guido
Britz. Munich: Beck.

Schulz, Holger. 2001. "Die Höchststrafe im Jugendstrafrecht (10 Jahre)—eine
Urteilsanalyse. Zugleich ein Beitrag zur kriminalpolitischen Forderung
nach Anhebung der Höchststrafe im Jugendstrafrecht." *Monatsschrift für
Kriminologie und Strafrechtsreform* 84:310–25.

Schumann, Karl F., C. Berlitz, H.-W. Guth, and R. Kanlitzki. 1987. *Jugendkriminalität und die Grenzen der Generalprävention*. Neuwied, Germany:
Luchterhand.

Sessar, Klaus. 1992. *Wiedergutmachen oder strafen: Einstellungen in der Bevölker-
ung und der Justiz*. Pfaffenweiler, Germany: Centaurus.

Solon, Jochen. 1994. "Jugendgewalt in München—Ausdruck deutscher Frem-
denfeindlichkeit oder unvermeidbare ethnische Konflikte." *Der Kriminalist*
26:73–79.

Statistisches Bundesamt. Various years, 1980–98. *Strafverfolgung*. Wiesbaden:
Statistisches Bundesamt.

———. 2001. *Stratuenfolgungsstatistik*. 1999. Wiesbaden: Statistisches Bundesamt.

Steffen, W. 1979. *Kinder-und Jugendkriminalität in Bayern*. Munich: Landeskriminalamt.

Streng, F. 1994. "Der Erziehungsgedanke im Jugendstrafrecht." *Zeitschrift für die Gesamte Strafrechtswissenschaft* 106:60–92.

Stümper, A. 1973. "Die kriminalpolitische Bewertung der Jugendkriminalität." *Kriminalistik* 27:49–54.

Viehmann, H. 1993. "Was machen wir mit unseren jugendlichen Gewalttätern?" *DVJJ-Journal* 1:26–29.

Villmow, Bernhard, and Günther Kaiser. 1974. "Empirisch gesicherte Erkenntnisse über Ursachen der Kriminalität." In *Verhütung und Bekämpfung der Kriminalität: ressortübergreifende Planung*, edited by der Regierende Bürgermeister von Berlin, Senatskanzlei, Planungsleitstelle. Berlin: Senatskanzlei, Planungsleitstelle.

Villmow, Bernhard, and Egon Stephan. 1983. *Jugendkriminalität in einer Gemeinde: Eine Analyse erfragter Delinquenz und Viktimisierung sowie amtlicher Registrierung*. Freiburg: Max-Planck-Institut für Ausländisches und Internationales Strafrecht.

Voss, Michael. 1986. *Jugend ohne Rechte*. Bremen: Campus.

Walter, Joachim. 2000. "Jugendstrafvollzug: Was hat sich getan? Was könnte getan werden?" In *Landesgruppe Baden-Württemberg in der DVJJ: Entwicklungen und Perspektiven in der Jugendstrafrechtspflege*. Heidelberg: INFO.

Walter, Michael. 1987. "Der Strafverteidiger im Jugendkriminalrecht." In *Verteidigung in Jugendstrafsachen*, edited by Bundesministerium der Justiz. Bonn: Burg.

———. 1993. "Jugendrecht, Jugendhilfe, Jugendschutz." In *Kleines Kriminologisches Wörterbuch*, 3d ed., edited by Günther Kaiser et al. Heidelberg: Müller.

———. 1995. *Jugendkriminalität*. Stuttgart: Boorberg.

Zweite Jugendstrafrechtskommission. 2002. *Vorschläge für eine Reform des Jugendstrafrechts*. Hannover: Deutsche Vereinigung für Jugendgerichte und Jugendgerichtshilfen.

Julian V. Roberts

Public Opinion and Youth Justice

ABSTRACT

Surveys conducted over the past twenty years in several English-speaking countries reveal that most members of the public subscribe to a number of misperceptions about juvenile crime and justice. Regardless of actual trends, significant majorities believe youth crime to be increasing, and most people have quite negative views of youth courts. The public display considerable ambivalence with respect to juvenile justice. While strong majorities favor punishing violent juveniles with the same severity as adults, there has always been considerable support for rehabilitation. There is a clear consensus among scholars that public concern about youth crime, particularly violent crime, has been a driving force behind reforms that facilitated the transfer of accused juveniles to adult criminal court and made penalties harsher for offenders sentenced in youth court.

Although juvenile delinquency has long been a cause of concern for the public,[1] in the 1990s juvenile crime became the single most discussed criminal justice issue in Western nations. This is particularly true in the United States where, as Crews and Montgomery note, "juvenile violence was (and is) the criminal justice issue foremost in the

---

Julian V. Roberts is professor of criminology in the Department of Criminology, University of Ottawa. I am grateful to the editors of this volume as well as the following individuals for comments on an earlier draft of this essay: Francis Cullen, Loretta Stalans, Jane Sprott, and Peter Carrington.

[1] Gilbert (1986) notes that there was widespread public concern about juvenile delinquency in America in the 1950s: "A large portion of the public thought that there was a delinquency crime wave" (p. 77). Writing in 1967, Boss noted, "Juvenile delinquency is a problem which has exercised the mind of a great many people for a great many years" (p. 8). In the same year, a survey of Americans found that when asked to identify spending priorities, juvenile delinquency was the second-most-often cited issue (Louis Harris and Associates 1968).

minds of the American people" (2000, p. xiii). In Britain, Canada, and Australia, murders by youthful offenders have likewise continued to focus public attention on and generate public anxiety about youth violence.

The explanations for this rise in the visibility of youth crime vary from country to country but include an increase (or perceived increase) in the volume and seriousness of juvenile offending, particularly violent offending; increased media coverage of juvenile crime and justice stories, especially high-profile murders by juveniles; the presence of a "get tough" lobby of politicians and criminal justice practitioners (such as police organizations); the existence of populist politicians, or a government that uses juvenile justice reforms to enhance its electoral prospects; the use of polls that provide little information about the subject. These are the most obvious causes, but there are others involving structural changes in most Western nations in the 1990s that have spawned or facilitated the emergence of punitive sanctions and expressive justice with respect to all kinds of offenders (see Bottoms 1995; Garland 2001). Not surprisingly, perhaps, juvenile justice systems in most countries (but especially the United States) became a target for reform as politicians sought to respond to rising juvenile crime rates and address growing public apprehension about juvenile crime.

The reforms in the United States generally made the juvenile justice systems more punitive, by facilitating the transfer of violent juvenile offenders to adult criminal court and enhancing penalties for juveniles sentenced in youth court (see Snyder and Sickmund 1995). Almost fifty states passed legislation in the mid-1990s facilitating the transfer of juveniles to adult criminal courts. Over the same period, sixteen states added or modified statutes requiring mandatory minimum periods of custody for certain violent juvenile offenders. Many states have modified or removed confidentiality provisions pertaining to juvenile court proceedings and increased the severity of sentencing options in juvenile courts (see Sickmund, Snyder, and Poe-Yamagata 1997). Fully forty states in recent years have housed juveniles convicted in adult courts among adult prisoners (Amnesty International 1998).

These changes have meant that the border between juvenile and adult justice in the United States became less distinct in the 1990s, particularly for juveniles accused of crimes of violence. Many of these changes had a disproportionate effect upon visible minority youth, who in the mid-1990s were already significantly overrepresented in custodial populations (Sickmund, Snyder, and Poe-Yamagata 1997). Over two-thirds of juvenile defendants transferred to adult court in 1998 were African-American (Tonry 1995; Bureau of Justice Statistics 1998; Mauer 1999; Soler 2001; Correctional Association of New York 2002; Cullen and Wright 2002).

In reviewing juvenile justice developments, Zimring concluded that "the 1990s have witnessed the broadest and most sustained legislative crackdown ever on serious offenses committed by youth within the jurisdictional ages of American Juvenile Courts" (1999, p. 260). This opinion is shared by other juvenile justice scholars (e.g., Bazemore and Umbreit 1995; Feld 1998). As several contributors to this volume make clear (e.g., Junger-Tas, in this volume) these changes are most evident in, but not restricted to, the United States.

It is clear from research conducted in several jurisdictions that public knowledge of trends in juvenile crime and justice is poor. It is equally apparent that this regrettable state of affairs can be attributed to inaccurate media coverage of these issues. The youth crime stories that appear in the news media often involve violence and, frequently, lethal violence. The mass killings perpetrated by juveniles in the United States and Germany, as well as homicides committed by very young children, have received widespread and intense media attention, and this has had an impact on public anxiety about juvenile crime and attitudes toward juvenile justice. Opinions on the appropriate response to juvenile crime tend to be influenced by knowledge about the scope of the problem.

Opinion polls reveal that the public in most Western nations assign a high level of importance to responding to juvenile crime, particularly serious violent crime. These same polls seem to suggest that a highly punitive public exists in all Western nations. However, as with other issues in criminal justice, such as attitudes toward the death penalty, the whole story seldom emerges from surveys that ask simple questions and that provide little or no context. Unfortunately, it is the opinion poll findings that influence politicians and policy makers. As will be seen over the course of this essay, considerable consensus exists that opinion polls have encouraged governments to introduce a number of "get tough" policies with respect to juvenile offending. In the United States in particular, the youth court has been under sustained attack, and this movement has been driven by the perception that the public favor much tougher justice for juveniles.

The "real story" about public opinion and youth crime emerges from a wealth of additional research that qualifies the image of a highly punitive public. Public support for punitive sentencing policies is restricted to a very small category of the most violent juveniles. In addition, there is considerable support for rehabilitation as a goal of the juvenile justice system. When given the chance to consider the age of a juvenile offender or his or her social background, people use this information to come to a judgment about the appropriate justice response. The public also display considerable enthusiasm for policies and dispositions that keep juvenile offenders out of prison. Research of this kind circulates in scholarly periodicals but fails to make its way into the mass media or to the attention of politicians.

Public opinion does not shift overnight. Accordingly, responding to public anxiety and misperceptions about juvenile justice will require a concerted effort. The first step involves educating the public about the true nature of juvenile crime trends. This will not be easy, as any public legal education initiative will perforce be transmitted through the media. Nevertheless, no government has ever made a systematic and serious attempt to come to grips with the problem of public misperception in this vital area of justice. It is high time that such a step was undertaken. The indications from the limited research in the field are that public views are amenable to change and that educating the citizenry will have important benefits. However, this is only one side of the equation. It will also be necessary to increase the volume and quality of research into juvenile justice and the views of the public. There is no need for another national poll that asks respondents whether juveniles who commit serious crimes should be treated as adult offenders. What is needed is more careful research that employs "informed" samples of the public. Finally, a much better bridge needs to be constructed between this latter kind of research and politicians and individuals in government who devise crime policies. Until this occurs, juvenile justice legislation will continue to reflect, or worse, be driven by, an inaccurate representation of public attitudes to youth crime.

This essay examines public attitudes to juvenile justice and explores the link between the views of the public and the evolution of juvenile justice policies in a number of Western countries. Establishing the nature and strength of the relationship is far from easy; politicians and policy makers may advert to the views of the public, but they seldom cite community sentiment as the primary or even partial justification for specific iniatives. Moreover, even if penal policies are driven by public pressure, it is difficult to establish a direct causal chain from public opinion to specific juvenile justice legislation. Nevertheless, there is considerable indirect evidence that public concern about rising youth crime rates and dissatisfaction with the youth court response have stimulated a number of changes and has created a climate conducive to the promulgation of more punitive juvenile justice policies. In this essay I explore public opinion about juvenile crime and justice, and the influence that community views have upon politicians. The emphasis is on the United States, Canada, and the United Kingdom. Most of the public opinion research has been conducted in these countries.

Section I of this essay summarizes research on public knowledge of crime and justice trends with respect to juveniles. Polls in several Western countries reveal that the public hold a distorted view of the magnitude (and nature) of the juvenile crime problem. Thus the public believe that juvenile crime rates are constantly rising, and they overestimate the recidivism rates associated with juvenile offenders. Section II reviews findings from research exploring public opinion regarding the justice system's response to juvenile crime. The public have little faith in their juvenile justice system, seeing the system as excessively lenient. Indeed, some surveys have found that many people regard youth court as a cause of, as much as a response to, juvenile crime, which is seen as a consequence of lax sentencing patterns. This is a manifestation of a broader public belief in a syllogism that links harsher sentencing to declining crime rates. In Section III, I review the relationship between specific juvenile justice policies and community views and evaluate the extent to which policies and programs may have arisen in response to public pressure. I draw upon specific examples from several Western nations. The experience in a number of jurisdictions suggests that policies have been introduced to address public anxiety rather than respond to rising juvenile crime rates or to the results of systematic research in criminal justice, an increase in violent offending by juveniles, or widespread reporting of an increase in offending. In Section IV, I propose two strategies to improve the level of debate surrounding the future of juvenile justice.

I. Public Knowledge of Trends in Juvenile Crime and Justice

Establishing the nature of public knowledge is critical to any description of public opinion. As with other areas of criminal justice, most people in the United States, the United Kingdom, and Canada have inaccurate views of juvenile crime and justice trends.

A. Knowledge of Juvenile Crime Trends

Research in several jurisdictions has demonstrated that most people subscribe to a number of misperceptions about juvenile crime trends (see also Schwartz 1989; Roberts and Stalans 1997; Roberts et al. 2002). As with perceptions of crime by adults, public views of juvenile crime and justice are systematically distorted in the direction of seeing the problem as being worse than it is. Some specific findings illustrate the seriousness of the problem.

First, it is clear that people tend to overestimate the volume of crime for which juveniles are responsible. Mattinson and Mirrlees-Black draw upon the 1998 British Crime Survey (BCS). They demonstrate that many people believed that crime was committed "mainly by juveniles" even though only one offender in ten is a juvenile according to official statistics. Over half the sample held the view that adults and juveniles accounted for equal proportions of crime (Mattinson and Mirrlees-Black 2000). Similarly, a 1996 survey of California residents found that 60 percent of respondents believed that juveniles were responsible for most of the violent crime recorded by the police, although official statistics reveal that only 13 percent of violent arrests involved juveniles (Dorfman and Schiraldi 2001). According to McCord, Widom, and Crowell (2001) juveniles accounted for 16 percent of violent Index crimes in 1998.

Although no survey has addressed public perceptions of the kinds of crimes committed by juveniles, it seems likely that people overestimate the seriousness and proportion of juvenile crime involving violence. Research has demonstrated such misperceptions of adult crime (see Roberts and Stalans 1997), and similar biases undoubtedly exist with respect to juveniles. Most Americans would probably be surprised to learn that three-quarters of juvenile arrests are for less serious non-Index crimes (McCord, Widom, and Crowell 2001).

Estimates of changes in crime rates are also at odds with the patterns emerging from police reports and victimization surveys. Two-thirds of respondents to the 2000 British Crime Survey held the view that juvenile crime rates in the United Kingdom had increased within the previous two years when in reality they had declined (Mattinson and Mirrlees-Black 2000). Almost three-quarters of the public believed that the number of female young offenders had increased, when in fact this number had also fallen (Mattinson and Mirrlees-Black 2000). Similarly, fully four out of five Canadians held the opinion that youth crime rates had escalated over the previous five years; these rates had actually

TABLE 1

Public Perceptions of Changes in Youth Crime Rates

Jurisdiction (Source)	Year of Survey	Percent of Respondents Believing Youth Crime Rates Have Increased Significantly within Previous Year or Recent Years*
Canada (Ekos Research Associates 2000)	2000	71
Canada (Earnscliffe Research and Communications 2000)	1999	76
United States (Soler 2001)	1999	62
United States (Dorfman and Schiraldi 2001)	1998	62
Canada (Environics Canada 1998)	1998	89
England and Wales (Mattinson and Mirrlees-Black 2000)	1998	66
United States (Soler 2001)	1995	84
North Carolina (Doble Research Associates 1995a)	1995	85
Oklahoma (Doble Research Associates 1995b)	1995	90
Canada (Environics Canada 1998)	1994	91
United States (Schwartz 1992)	1991	62
California (Steinhart 1988)	1988	82
United States (Krisberg and Austin 1993)	1982	87

* The wording used varies slightly from poll to poll; see specific citation for further details.

been stable or declining (Earnscliffe Research and Communications 1999).

More recently, there has been a slight decline in the percentage of Americans who believe that youth crime rates are rising; nevertheless, in 1999, almost two-thirds of the public still held this view (Soler 2001). Finally, a similarly pessimistic view emerges when the public is asked about future crime trends. Sixty percent of the Canadian public believed that there would be more youth crime in the next few years (Earnscliffe Research and Communications 2000), even though official youth crime rates in Canada had experienced eight years of decline at the time that this poll was conducted (Logan 2001).

Table 1 summarizes findings from representative surveys conducted over the past few years. The table reveals considerable consistency in the public's response to this question. Since juvenile crime rates have declined or remained stable in many jurisdictions in recent years, this table also demonstrates that perceptions of crime trends are independent of actual changes in rates, a phenomenon with parallels at the adult level (Roberts and Stalans 1997). These studies all employed a representative survey of the public; similar trends, however, emerge from smaller-scale qualitative research such as use of focus groups (e.g., Earnscliffe Research and Communications 1999).

Politicians tend to respond to these poll findings as though they have just revealed a new crime problem. Members of the public respond the same way when asked about crime trends at the adult and juvenile level: crime always seems to be on the increase. The same pattern emerges with respect to adult crime (see Roberts et al. 2002). Fully twenty years ago (in 1982), almost nine out of ten Americans believed that juvenile crime was increasing at an "alarming" rate (Krisberg and Austin 1993). Even earlier, when a 1963 Gallup poll asked Americans to identify the top problem facing their community, juvenile delinquency headed the list (McIntyre 1967).

Similar trends emerge when members of the public are asked to estimate juvenile rates of specific offenses: most Canadians (77 percent according to one survey; see Doob et al. [1998]) believe that the number of homicides involving young offenders has been increasing when analysis of homicide rates reveals that this is not true (see Doob and Sprott, in this volume, fig. 3). Dorfman and Schiraldi (2001) report similar trends for shootings in American schools: almost three-quarters of respondents to an NBC poll believed that a school shooting in their community was "likely," a view that is in considerable contrast to the actual incidence of such tragedies.

People tend to make overly pessimistic public projections about future offending. This finding emerges from surveys that explore public expectations of juvenile offender recidivism. The public (at least in the United States) hold the view that young offenders are very likely to reoffend; one survey found that 20 percent of the sample believed that juvenile offenders were "almost certain" to reoffend, and half believed that juvenile offenders would "probably" reoffend (Soler 2001). These perceptions are not sustained by actual recidivism rates. Snyder (1988), for example, notes that high recidivism rates are associated only with a relatively small percentage of juveniles; most young people referred to youth court do not return. The British public are probably unaware that two years after having been cautioned, almost 90 percent of youths had stayed out of trouble (Nacro 2001).

The trends with respect to public estimates of crime rates are important to consider when evaluating public attitudes to sentencing. A number of studies have demonstrated that members of the public see a clear link between crime rates and sentencing severity. Many people believe that an inverse relationship exists between the two. The latest demonstrations of this come from surveys conducted in Scotland and Canada. In the Scottish poll, over half the sample agreed with the statement "the tougher the sentence, the less likely an offender is to commit more crime" (Hutton 2002). In Canada, when asked to identify the most significant factor producing crime, a "lenient criminal justice system" headed the list (Ekos Research Associates 2000).

Public perceptions of rising juvenile crime rates have fueled a more general attitude that regards contemporary youth as being worse than previous generations, presumably because they appear to be committing more, or more serious, crimes. Another example of this tendency can be found in a recent survey of Canadians in which almost half the sample agreed with the statement "youth crime is worse than when I was young." Only 8 percent of the respondents disagreed with the statement (Earnscliffe Research and Communications 2000).[2] Most Canadians believe that youth crime has become more serious as well as more prevalent in recent years. However, this perception is also at odds with reality: systematic examination of youth court statistics in Canada suggests youth crime has not become more serious in recent years (Doob and Sprott 1998).

B. Knowledge of Juvenile Justice

The trends with respect to public perceptions of youth crime are mirrored by responses to surveys that explore public knowledge of the juvenile justice system. Although people tend to have strong views about juvenile justice, they know little about their juvenile justice systems. In Canada, after new youth justice legislation was passed in 1984, three-quarters of the public admitted that they had not heard of the new act (Angus Reid Group 1984). A decade later, almost half the polled public stated that they were still not familiar with the youth justice system (Decima Research 1993). Most recently, at the height of

---

[2] The perception that the problem is worse may be accurate for respondents who grew up in the 1950s and 1960s, before crime rates began to escalate. However, younger respondents also held this perception. Frontline workers, such as police officers and youth court workers, generally express a different opinion with respect to this issue. For example, police officers in the United Kingdom frequently note that young offenders are far more sophisticated with respect to their legal rights and that it is common to find eleven-year-olds asking for legal counsel.

the debate surrounding the introduction of sweeping reform legislation, few Canadians had, or even claimed to have, any real knowledge about the forthcoming act (Earnscliffe Research and Communications 1999). Sprott (1996) posed a number of questions about the juvenile justice system in Canada and found quite low levels of awareness. For example, the overwhelming majority was unaware of the transfer provisions in effect. Similar results emerge from the limited literature on public knowledge of juvenile justice in the United States.

As is the case with most public views of crime, these inaccurate perceptions about youth crime and justice can be traced to the news media. Juvenile crime has placed high on the media agenda for many years now as a result of the rising crime rates in the 1980s, the succession of homicides involving juveniles beginning with the murder of James Bulger in 1992, and the mass murders committed in 2002 by a student expelled from a school in Germany. Numerous content analyses of the news media reveal that youth crimes reported in the media are much more likely to involve violence, guns, and collective offending than cases in court. Youth crime stories are highly discrepant with the reality, and this appears to be the case in most Western nations (e.g., Sprott 1996; Buttrum 1998; Dorfman and Schiraldi 2001).

II. Public Opinion Regarding Juvenile Justice Policies

Surveys from several countries demonstrate that most members of the public hold negative views of their juvenile justice systems. The principal cause of public dissatisfaction appears to be the perception of excessive leniency (see Doob, Marinos, and Varma 1995; Triplett 1996; Sprott 1998). However, this simplistic finding fails to do justice to the complexity of public attitudes to juvenile crime. A reading of public opinion based on polls is quite different from what emerges from more refined research. And despite the critical tone of public attitudes, particularly to violent juveniles, there is still a bedrock of support for rehabilitation.

A. Views of Juvenile Justice

The 1998 British Crime Survey included a number of questions on public perceptions of juvenile courts in England and Wales. Only 14 percent of respondents believed that these courts were doing a good job. Performance ratings were lower for juvenile courts than for any other component of the criminal justice system (Mattinson and Mirrlees-Black 2000, p. 23). The principal cause of dissatisfaction is a perception of excessive leniency on the part of youth court judges. Six out of ten respondents were of the opinion that youth court sentences were too lenient (Mattinson and Mirrlees-Black 2000). Surveys in the United States have routinely found that the public think juvenile sentencing is too lenient (e.g., Hart 1998). When asked to identify factors causing violent crime by juveniles, 70 percent of respondents in the United States identified lenient treatment by youth courts as being "mainly to blame" (Bureau of Justice Statistics 1991, table 2.5). This result reflects an important shift in public opinion. When the public was asked to identify the causes of juvenile crime in a 1967 poll, only 5 percent chose "courts too lenient" as a response (Louis Harris and Associates 1968).

Canadians are equally critical of their juvenile justice system. A nationwide survey conducted in 1997 found that seven out of ten respondents reported having little or no confidence in the Young Offenders Act (Angus Reid Group 1997). As with England and Wales, the youth justice system attracted the lowest confidence ratings, lower even than the prison and parole systems (Angus Reid Group 1997).[3] Once again, the source of the dissatisfaction is public perception of sentencing patterns. In 2000, a nationwide study found that over three-quarters of the public believed that sentences imposed in youth court were not severe enough (Earnscliffe Research and Communications 2000). Sprott (1998) reports that almost 90 percent of respondents to another survey in Canada believed that sentences for juvenile offenders were too lenient. This is higher than the percentage of the public who believe that sentences in adult court are too lenient.

Table 2 summarizes trends in public perceptions of youth court sentencing. As with perceptions of juvenile crime rates, there is considerable consistency over time and across the jurisdictions in which this question has been posed. And once again, there are parallels at the adult level; in recent years, the majority of the public in the United States, the United Kingdom, Canada, and Australia have held the view that sentences imposed on adults are too lenient (Roberts and Stalans 1997). These findings suggest that a shift has occurred over recent decades. In 1964, only 20 percent of Americans believed that juvenile court was very lenient (Parker 1970).

The trend emerging from table 2 should not be taken as evidence

---

[3] Thus only 4 percent of the sample was very confident in the YOA; in comparison, 37 percent of the sample had this degree of confidence in the police (Angus Reid Group 1997).

TABLE 2

Public Perceptions of Youth Court Sentencing

Jurisdiction (Source)	Year	Percent Sample Agreeing That Youth Court Sentences Are Too Lenient
England and Wales (Mattinson 2002)	2000	75
Canada (Earnscliffe Research and Communications 2000)	2000	76
Canada (Earnscliffe Research and Communications 1999)	1999	75
England and Wales (Mattinson and Mirrlees-Black 2000)	1998	76
Canada (Environics Canada 1998)	1998	68
Ontario, Canada (Doob et al. 1998)	1997	77
Tennessee (Hart 1998)	1996	81
Canada (Environics Canada 1998)	1994	78
Alberta, Canada (Baron and Hartnagel 1996)	1993	77
Canada (Environics Canada 1998)	1988	79
United States (Opinion Research Corporation 1982)	1982	78

that the public are purely punitive in their responses to juvenile crime. Questions of this kind, which the public answer by thinking of the most serious cases, elicit a punitive response. As I show in a later section, public opinion is far more sophisticated than these polls would suggest. However, it is the poll results summarized in table 2 that attract the attention of the media and appear to drive the political agenda for reform.

Why is the public so antipathetic toward youth court sentencing? The public may not be responding simply to perceptions of escalating juvenile crime rates or media coverage of individual spectacular crimes. There is probably also a reaction to the mitigated sentences imposed in youth court and reported by the news media. It seems clear that the most controversial sentences described by the media are often imposed in cases of serious violence committed by juvenile offenders near the upper age limit of the juvenile justice system. These are the kinds of cases for which, in the eyes of the public, mitigated punishments are hardest to justify. For members of the public who often focus on the offense, rather than on the offender, this "discounting" seems inappropriate, and this leads to calls for more frequent transfers. Applied to the lower reaches of the age of criminal responsibility, this leads many people to support the criminalization of behavior committed by children ten years or younger; there is clear resistance to the notion that a crime can be committed without an individual being criminally responsible.

In Canada, the penalty for juveniles convicted of murder has been amended on several occasions, becoming harsher each time. These amendments have not followed an increase in the volume of homicide cases involving juvenile accused. Doob and Sprott (in this volume, fig. 3) demonstrate that the number of youth charged with a homicide offense has remained stable over a considerable period of time (1974–2000). The pressure to increase the maximum penalty appears to have come from politicians reflecting a public opinion that the penalty originally available in youth court for juveniles convicted of first-degree murder (three years) was simply too discrepant from the adult penalty (life imprisonment with a period of twenty-five years without parole). The public perceived this gap as being too great, and politicians were quick to act.[4]

Public knowledge of related issues may explain some of the resistance to mitigated punishments. Although seldom explored by pollsters, it is clear that most people lack much awareness of the developmental psychology that is relevant to the punishment of juvenile offenders. One of the justifications for a separate youth justice system, and for mitigated punishments, is that juveniles are less culpable because they are less able to fully appreciate the significance of their actions. Most people see matters otherwise. Thus, fully half the respondents to a nationwide survey in Canada agreed with the statement that twelve-year-olds "know exactly what they are doing when they commit a crime" (Earnscliffe Research and Communications 2000). This naive perception carries implications for juvenile justice systems.

Serious crimes committed by juveniles elicit an ambivalent response from the public. The seriousness of the crime provokes a desire to punish; the youthfulness of the offender generates a natural human reaction to temper the severity of the sanction. It seems clear that the

---

[4] One possible problem arising from a large discrepancy between the penalty for murder imposed on adults and juveniles is that people may assume that sentences for all crimes follow the same pattern and that this may contribute to the perception that youth court sentencing is generally very lenient. Comparisons between sentences imposed on adults and juveniles reveal that sentencing patterns are much closer than many people realize (see Sanders 2000).

public become more opposed to discounted sentencing for juveniles as the age of the offender or the seriousness of the offense increases.[5] Indeed, for the most serious crimes, people probably see no justification for according any mitigation to the offender. The seriousness of murder appears to swamp any sympathy for the offender that is elicited by the presence of mitigating factors such as age. Although the maximum penalty for first-degree murder imposed on juveniles in Canada is currently ten years' imprisonment, nearly nine out of ten Canadians are of the opinion that the sentence should be life imprisonment without parole for twenty-five years, the term imposed on adult offenders (Gallup Canada 1999).

Most people believe that for murder the penalty for juveniles should be the same as the penalty for adults. At least that is the result that emerges from general questions on polls. However, it would be interesting to conduct more detailed and careful research on this issue comparable to research that has explored attitudes toward capital punishment in the United States. A number of such studies have shown considerable support for capital punishment in response to a general question, but once people are asked to consider specific cases, the percentage favoring the death penalty declines significantly (see Cullen, Fisher, and Applegate [2000] for a review).

Part of the explanation for this phenomenon is that people answering such questions generally envision the worst possible cases (involving recidivists) rather than the typical cases sentenced by the courts. Members of the public also tend to focus on aggravating rather than mitigating factors. The existence of a long record carries more weight than the absence of previous convictions. In order then to understand where the public stand with regard to the penalty for murder, it is necessary to do more than simply ask them whether it should be the same as that which is imposed on adults. This kind of research has never been conducted.

Public attitudes are complex in nature and origin. Clearly the news media play an important role in shaping public perceptions of the scope of the problem. But people are likely to have more direct contact

---

[5] This can be demonstrated by examining the question from another direction. The 1991 National Juvenile Crime Survey conducted by the Survey Research Center at the University of Michigan's Institute for Social research asked the public whether they supported equal sentencing for juveniles and adults "no matter what the crime." In response, 62 percent of the sample rejected the proposition, suggesting that people are sensitive to the nature of the crime in question. (Summary data tables are available from the author.)

with juveniles, unlike other specific groups of offenders (such as drug offenders or sex offenders), and this should not be overlooked. Unsurprisingly perhaps, when asked to sentence a juvenile convicted of a serious violent crime who is also a relative, the public oppose the use of custody by an overwhelming margin (see Steinhart 1988). Many members of the public are also parents, and this may explain some of the ambivalence that characterizes public reaction to youth crime. People are far more likely to have contact with a young offender than an adult offender. This is borne out by systematic research; almost two-thirds of the polled public stated that they personally knew a young person who had been charged or convicted of a criminal offense (Earnscliffe Research and Communications 2000).

This finding helps to explain the punitive response to the most serious cases of youth violence and the widespread support for alternative sanctions for the vast majority of juvenile offenders, to which I return later in this essay. In addition, unlike issues such as sex offending, there is a considerable constituency of youth advocates who provide the public with alternative responses to youth crime. It would be a mistake to discount this source of information just because it does not have the immediacy or prevalence of news stories.

The portrait emerging from this review is of an uninformed and punitive public. This image—based on poll findings—is the one usually transmitted by the media and accepted by politicians. It is the punitive and anxious public that guides juvenile justice reform on the political level. But there is more to the story than this; moving beyond poll findings brings us to a rather different understanding of public reaction to juvenile crime.

B. Public Attitudes toward Juvenile Justice: The Real Story

Experts agree that many "get tough" juvenile justice policies constitute a political response to public opinion or perceptions of public opinion. Are politicians right to believe in a punitive public? At the adult level, a growing body of empirical research suggests that politicians overestimate the punitiveness of the public, as well as the electoral benefit that accrues from promoting tough penal policies (Roberts et al. 2002; Roberts 2003). The same may be true at the level of juvenile justice as well. Public attitudes toward the punishment of juveniles are marked by considerable ambivalence, but there has always been strong support for rehabilitation and for alternative punishments when considering juveniles. Indeed, public opinion in Western nations can be construed as tolerant of juvenile offending until the offending involves extreme repetition, violence, or the use of firearms or drugs, at which point the public favors a much more punitive model.

This can be demonstrated by surveys that ask whether juveniles should be sentenced with the same severity as adults. When asked about juveniles in general, 66 percent of respondents to a survey conducted by Schwartz, Abbey, and Barton (1990) rejected punishing adult and juvenile offenders with equal severity. However, when the public is asked to consider violent offenders, the trend is reversed in all surveys on the subject. A poll conducted in 2000 found that almost the same percentage (65 percent) of the public favored imposing the same treatment; less than one-quarter favored more lenient treatment (Bureau of Justice Statistics 2002, table 2.58). This bifurcation in public views is not new; a decade earlier almost exactly the same percentage (68 percent) of the public responded in this fashion (Bureau of Justice Statistics 1995, table 2.51).

The simultaneous support for punishment and prevention repeatedly emerges from the survey literature. According to a 1998 poll, fully four out of five Canadian respondents favored increasing the severity of sentences for violent youth, but almost as many (77 percent) supported increasing the number of social programs for young people (Environics Canada 1998). In Canada, fully 85 percent of the public favored amending the Young Offenders Act to permit juvenile offenders to be eligible for adult sentences but only if they are charged with a serious violent offense (Angus Reid Group 1998). Similar levels of support for adult-level sanctioning emerge when referring to selling drugs (e.g., Mears 2001) or recidivist juvenile offenders; fully 83 percent favored treating recidivist offenders the same as adult offenders (Bureau of Justice Statistics 1995, table 2.54; see also Golay 1997).

There is also a substantial body of literature that has shown that although the public favors "adult" sentencing, the public is nevertheless highly sensitive to age as a mitigating factor. A recent ABC News poll found that the percentage of Americans supporting the "equal sentencing" principle declined steeply for juveniles aged fifteen years and younger (Roper Center 2001). Respondents were asked at what age juveniles convicted of a violent crime should be sentenced as adults; 62 percent stated age fifteen or higher, but only 11 percent chose age fourteen (Roper Center 2001). Similarly, Stalans and Henry (1994) and Feiler and Sheley (1999) have demonstrated that the age of the juvenile offender exercises an important influence over public preferences regarding the transfer of juveniles to criminal court. Even when the juvenile has been convicted of a serious violent crime, the public appear less likely to favor criminal than juvenile court processing. These studies—which qualify the finding that the public favor transferring juveniles convicted of violent offenses—underline the importance once again of using vignettes with more information than simple poll questions.

Why do the public wish to treat certain categories of offenders with the same severity as adults? Little research has addressed the question, but part of the explanation must lie in public perceptions of deserved punishment. Many people subscribe to a view of offending that places limited emphasis on offender characteristics. If crime seriousness alone determines the sentence, there should be no discount for youth. However, doubts about the effectiveness of rehabilitation programs may also underlie public opposition to differential sentencing; if rehabilitation is not possible, adult-style punishment may represent the only real alternative.

A Gallup survey conducted in the United States in 1994 revealed the extent of public skepticism with regard to attempts to rehabilitate juvenile offenders. Respondents were told about criminal justice programs that emphasize rehabilitating juvenile offenders and were asked the following question: "How successful would you say these programs have been at controlling juvenile crime?" Almost three-quarters of the public (72 percent) believed that the programs had been "not at all" or "not very" successful (Bureau of Justice Statistics 1995, table 2.52). Sprott (1998) found a similar pattern of results with a sample of Canadians. She explored the nature of public opposition to a separate youth justice system, which many people have speculated is founded on a desire to simply punish juveniles. However, support for imprisoning young offenders was related to perceptions that alternative sanctions were ineffective. Doob (2000) found widespread public skepticism about community service orders. Many people believed that these orders are seldom actually completed, and this belief nourishes public support for imprisonment. To the extent, then, that rehabilitative programs and alternative sanctions are successful, there is clearly a need to communicate this information to the public.

C. Support for Rehabilitation

Another manifestation of the public's ambivalence with respect to punitive responses is its support for rehabilitation. The American public has steadfastly supported rehabilitation as a goal of youth court sentencing over the past twenty years. In 1982, three-quarters of the public favored rehabilitation over punishment in youth court (Opinion Research Corporation 1982). Five years later the same result emerged (Steinhart 1988). A decade after the first poll, approximately the same level of support existed—78 percent of respondents felt that the primary purpose of juvenile court should be to treat and rehabilitate rather than to punish (see Schwartz 1992). Rehabilitation as a sentencing goal received significantly more support than punishment from respondents to the National Crime and Justice Survey (Gerber and Englehardt-Greer 1996). (For adult offenders, the opposite was true [see also Doob 2000].)

The Building Blocks poll found the strongest support for rehabilitation—90 percent of the respondents aligned themselves behind prevention rather than incarceration (Soler 2001). Thus, American support for the rehabilitation of juvenile offenders has not wavered in the face of escalating juvenile crime rates, a series of high-profile murders (and mass murders) by juveniles, populist media coverage of the juvenile crime problem, and a plethora of punitive reforms across the country.[6] Support for rehabilitation is not restricted to the American public. Doob (2000) reports strong support for rehabilitation as the purpose of sentencing juveniles in Canada.

Public support for alternatives to adult processing remains strong even in the face of rising juvenile crime rates (or perceptions of rising rates). Krisberg and Austin (1993), for example, note some interesting findings from a poll in California. Most respondents believed that juvenile crime rates were escalating rapidly. Nevertheless, the public also strongly endorsed rehabilitation as the goal of juvenile court, favored less severe sentences for juveniles, and strongly opposed the practice of housing juveniles with adult prisoners. Although the public tend to favor treating adults and juveniles similarly when serious violent crime is involved, there is, and has always been, strong public support for separating juveniles and adults in different facilities. Over twenty years ago, an American poll found that only 5 percent of respondents favored using the same facilities (Knowles 1980). Support for this basic position has not wavered since.

---

[6] For similar evidence of the American public's support for juvenile rehabilitation, see Cullen, Golden, and Cullen 1983; Gerber and Englehardt-Greer 1996; Moon, Sundt, Cullen, and Wright 2000; Cullen and Wright 2002.

D. Public Support for Alternatives to Imprisonment

The research on sentencing alternatives contains some surprises for politicians who believe that the public oppose alternatives. While custody plays a central role in public reactions to crime, alternatives are frequently very acceptable. This has been demonstrated repeatedly in the literature at the adult level (e.g., Doble 2002; Roberts 2002) and appears equally true with respect to juveniles. Despite the findings from general polls that reveal support for harsher sentencing, most people adhere strongly to a restraint-based policy with regard to the use of imprisonment. For example, 71 percent of Canadians agreed that young offenders should "only be sent to prison as a last resort" (Moore 1985).

When members of the public are asked to sentence juvenile offenders described in scenarios, the results reveal considerable support for alternative sanctions. A recent demonstration of this phenomenon comes from Canada. Tufts and Roberts (2002) analyzed data from a national survey in which respondents were asked to sentence juvenile offenders described in brief scenarios. Public sentencing preferences were then compared to sentences actually imposed in youth courts. The study is significant from two perspectives. First, the sentences favored by members of the public were generally of comparable severity to the court patterns, a finding consistent with earlier research (e.g., Parker 1970). For example, when asked to sentence a repeat juvenile burglar, 55 percent of the public endorsed the imposition of a custodial term, while the actual incarceration rate in youth court for this type of offender was 50 percent.

The second important finding pertains to the acceptability of alternative sanctions. Participants who in the first instance favored imprisoning the juvenile offenders were then asked a subsequent question: "If a judge sentenced the offender to one year of probation and 200 hours of community work, would that be acceptable?" If public support for prison is strong, it seems unlikely that many respondents would find the community-based alternative acceptable as a substitute. In fact, approximately half the participants responding to four juvenile crime scenarios stated that they would find the alternative sanction acceptable as a replacement for custody. Indeed, in the scenario that had attracted the highest degree of support for custody (a repeat juvenile burglar), half the subjects who had favored sentencing the offender to prison nevertheless found the alternative sanction acceptable. Even when the offense involved a juvenile convicted of assault and with previous convictions, 49 percent still found the community-based sentence acceptable (see Tufts and Roberts 2002, table 1).

It is worth contrasting the opinion poll findings ("sentencing is too lenient") with findings from research in which respondents have more time to consider more information before expressing their views. This exercise has been repeatedly undertaken with respect to adult offenders (see Doob and Roberts 1988), and it is even more important to undertake at the level of juvenile justice. As with public opinion with respect to the punishment of adult offenders, research has demonstrated that public attitudes change following the provision of information (see Roberts and Stalans 1997).[7]

Awareness that public views of juvenile justice sentencing are complex and change in response to information is generally restricted to the scholarly community. Politicians do not have the time, or perhaps the interest, to seek out this kind of research. Opinion polls that pose simple, short questions, on the other hand, can generate clear, yet potentially misleading answers within a very short space of time. As well, opinion polls by survey organizations routinely attract the attention of the news media; publication of academic research escapes the attention of the media and the public. Until the findings from more refined research permeate the political conscience, it is the political construction of public attitudes that must be considered when evaluating influences on juvenile justice policy.

Public interest in alternatives emerges clearly from research by Doob (2000). This study also illustrates the importance of offering respondents a choice between competing options. Members of the public were asked to choose between two strategies: building more prisons for juveniles or sentencing more offenders to alternatives to imprisonment. Support for the alternatives was particularly strong: 79 percent of the sample chose alternatives over prison (Doob 2000).

There is little doubt that serious violent crime by juveniles provokes a punitive reaction from the public. However, the public make a clear distinction between violent crime and other forms of offending and also distinguish between the juvenile and adult systems of justice. The political discourse surrounding juvenile justice reform appears to have focused primarily on the punitive aspects of public reaction and to have ignored the public's support for rehabilitation over punishment for the vast majority of juvenile offenders.

---

[7] A good example of this phenomenon can be found in research by Covell and Howe (1996).

E. Influences on Public Attitudes to Juvenile Crime and Justice

Public attitudes and opinions necessarily depend on public knowledge. People who know more about a subject, and have a nuanced understanding of it, tend to have more complex views than people who lack knowledge or possess only fragmentary knowledge. Not many people know much about the juvenile justice system, and their knowledge tends to be filtered through the mass media and often involves notorious cases.

1. *News Media.*   It is a truism that news media coverage of crime conveys a distorted portrait of the cases being processed by the courts. However, there is evidence that the distortions are worse for juveniles than for adults. In Canada, Sprott (1996) found that coverage of youth crime in the newspapers was heavily skewed toward violence—one-quarter of the court cases but over 90 percent of news stories involved violent crimes. Dorfman and Schiraldi (2001) summarized recent media trends in America that demonstrate the same finding (see also Feld 1995, pp. 982–86; Buttrum 1998). Dorfman and Schiraldi (2001) also found that the volume of crime coverage bore little relationship to actual crime trends; the number of crime stories increased while actual crime rates were falling. There is little doubt that media coverage of juvenile crime in the 1980s and 1990s transformed the discourse surrounding juvenile justice. And, as researchers such as Estrada (2001) demonstrate, it is not only the English-language countries in which this transformation took place. Estrada documents an abrupt shift in the treatment of juvenile violence in the Swedish media at about the same time.

The link between media coverage of youth crime and public over-estimates of juvenile crime rates is clear enough,[8] but there is also evidence that coverage of juvenile crime in the media may affect public reaction to youth justice by promoting an offense-based view of sentencing. This is significant because the existence of a separate youth justice system, and of mitigated punishments for juvenile offenders, is founded upon recognition that the offender's age affects his degree of culpability—young people are less culpable than adults who commit the same acts. However, if we focus on the crime alone, there is likely

---

[8] Dorfman and Schiraldi note that crime coverage in the news in America did not reflect actual crime trends. They also document the ways in which the news media provide extreme distortions of juvenile crime. They conclude, "Rather than informing citizens about their world, the news is reinforcing stereotypes that inhibit society's ability to respond effectively to the problem of crime, particularly juvenile crime" (2001, p. 20).

to be less awareness of the importance of an offender characteristic such as age. If members of the public adopt a sentencing perspective based on the offense alone, they are likely to oppose mitigated punishments for juveniles and criticize youth courts for imposing such penalties. Sprott's 1996 analysis of news media coverage of youth crime stories demonstrated that the focus was on the seriousness of the crime, including the impact on the victim. Viewed through this lens, news consumers are less likely to support the existence of youth court or the imposition of mitigated punishments.

One cause, then, of the public support for the aphorism "a crime is a crime" (with its corollary that punishments should not vary according to the age of the offender) is probably news media emphasis on the offense at the expense of factors related to the offender, such as age. In addition, this may also fuel public demands for lowering the lower age limit of criminal responsibility, as the argument is the same: if behavior constitutes a crime when the offender is, say, twelve years old, how does this change when the individual is eleven? This reasoning underlies public support for lowering age limits. Knowledge of the issue plays a role here as well. People know too little about alternative social welfare responses, including placement in secure institutions, to children below the age of criminal responsibility who commit crimes. Many members of the public assume that if the criminal justice system is not activated, the child will be free to continue offending. This view has been encouraged by media coverage of children making statements that appear to confirm the public's assumption.

The public is encouraged by media coverage of youth crime to draw general inferences about young people on the basis of specific incidents. The news media contribute to this generalization effect in a number of ways. Specific incidents are seen as representing a general decline in moral standards. The tragic case of a young immigrant who was killed in South London in 2001 is a good example. When the youths charged with the crime were acquitted, the media were quick to draw several lessons. One was that the criminal justice system was no longer capable of convicting the guilty. Another encapsulated the failed prosecution and related it to the entire country, using the headline "Damning Verdict for the Savage Society" (*Sunday Times* 2002).

Finally, it is significant that the only two juvenile justice provisions with which the Canadian public appear to have any familiarity are the ones most often discussed by the media. Research has shown that people know about the Young Offenders Act's prohibition of the publication of young offenders' names (Earnscliffe Research and Communications 1999). As well, almost all respondents (93 percent) in the survey reported by Doob, Marinos, and Varma (1995) were aware that accused juveniles could be transferred to adult court. This too, is a provision that has been repeatedly reported in the news media. These findings demonstrate the ability of the media to educate the public.

2. *Role of High-Profile Crimes Involving Juvenile Offenders.* High-profile incidents and the subsequent media attention to a specific form of youth crime—usually involving firearms—may also help to promote a more generalized response to adolescence; the public sees these incidents as extreme examples of a more general shift in adolescent behavior.[9] There is also a tendency to see tragedies such as the James Bulger murder in England as representing a new departure for youth crime, although many historical precedents of murders by children exist (see Radzinowicz 1948). Such cases spawn advocacy movements and provide an individual face for the movement to reform the system.

Almost every jurisdiction, with the exception of New Zealand, has witnessed a crime of this nature. In Canada, the tragic and near-fatal assault by a group of young offenders on another juvenile provided much impetus to the critique of the youth justice system and helped to attract almost half a million signatures to a petition to make sentences harsher. In Denmark, rapes by immigrant youth led to calls for a new, harsher penalty for juveniles. Britons have read about a number of murders committed by juveniles, including, of course, the killing of James Bulger, that attracted headlines around the world. Not surprisingly, these tragedies have played a role in stimulating media coverage of juvenile justice and thereby raising levels of public concern about violent crime involving juveniles (see Greenwood et al. 1983). As Schwartz notes, "In too many instances, policies [are] developed in response to one or two particularly heinous acts by young people, acts that are the exception rather than the rule" (1992, p. ix). One American example of these "single event drivers" is the murder of a British tourist by four teenagers in Florida. The crime generated widespread criticism of the youth justice system when it became known that one of the accused had had many previous contacts with the justice system (see Rossum 1999). Any crime by an offender with a prior conviction is likely to be seen by the public as a preventable failure of the

---

[9] The media coverage of these cases is understandable. A Canadian case involving teenage girls in British Columbia concerned a crime committed by a gang against a vulnerable victim who had been abused in the past. The crime also appeared to be racially motivated. "Blaming" the media for devoting many stories to such a crime seems naive; it shocked and therefore fascinated the nation.

system. Similarly, a drive-by shooting in Ottawa, Canada, led to vociferous calls for the system to do something about teenage gangs, although, this tragic crime aside, there was no evidence of any increase in gang activity. The killing in British Columbia of a young girl by a gang of teenagers composed largely of other girls led to much media commentary and public concern about "girl gangs."

In the state of New York, public outrage over the case of Willie Bosket, who in 1978 murdered two subway riders, provoked a swift political response. The incident sparked widespread media coverage and public condemnation of the juvenile justice system in which Bosket had spent considerable time. The case became a paradigm example of the system being blamed for failing to deter or rehabilitate with fatal consequences for the public (see Butterfield 1995). The New York state legislature passed the 1978 Juvenile Offender Law, which lowered the age of criminal responsibility to thirteen for murder and fourteen for other violent crimes. This piece of legislation meant that thirteen-year-olds were to be tried in adult court and thereby be at risk of imprisonment (see Singer 1996).

3. *Relationship between Knowledge and Opinion.* Public misperception of juvenile crime trends also exercises an influence over opinions toward juvenile justice policies. Stalans (2002) observes that attitudes to criminal justice issues are clearly affected by public information relevant to the attitude. This phenomenon has also been demonstrated in several countries with regard to juvenile justice. Sprott (1998), for example, demonstrated an association between public opposition to a separate justice system for juveniles and knowledge of a number of juvenile justice issues. People opposed to a separate youth justice system overestimated the recidivism rates of young offenders and were more likely to believe (erroneously) that youth crime rates were rising and that the number of youth charged with murder had increased. Moreover, the punitive attitude (in this case, opposition to a separate youth justice system) was also associated with skepticism about elements of the youth justice system; opponents of a separate system were significantly more likely to believe that young offenders would fail to complete community service ordered by the court. Further research is necessary to determine if these associations reflect causal relationships. If they do, the lesson is clear—dispelling some of the myths about juvenile crime (and the juvenile justice system) will promote public confidence in the youth justice system and bolster support for a separate youth justice system.

The same relationship between knowledge and opinion has been demonstrated with respect to the British public. British Crime Survey respondents who were least well informed about juvenile crime statistics held the most negative views about the juvenile justice response to crime. Specifically, those people who knew the least about juvenile crime trends were significantly more likely to rate the juvenile justice system as too lenient and significantly more likely to rate juvenile courts as doing a bad job; only one-quarter of the most knowledgeable respondents, but over half of the least knowledgeable, believed that juvenile sentences were too lenient (Mattinson and Mirrlees-Black 2000, fig. 4.4).

These associations between knowledge levels and the valence of attitudes to the juvenile justice system suggest that improving public knowledge of juvenile crime and justice trends will also change attitudes to the system and improve public levels of confidence.[10] Many people who support policies such as statutory transfers to criminal court are unaware of the full implications of the policies on juveniles. If provided with more information, they are likely to reconsider their views. For example, while many people favor treating juveniles convicted of violent crimes as adults, they simultaneously (and strongly) oppose detaining juveniles with adult offenders, although that is a natural consequence of the "equal treatment" philosophy. Knowles (1980), for example, found that fully three-quarters of the public favored housing juveniles in separate facilities. In addition, the public has little concrete awareness of some of the consequences of particular juvenile justice policies. How many people, for example, know that juveniles detained with adult prisoners are far more likely to be assaulted than juveniles housed with other juveniles (Correctional Association of New York 2002)?

Finally, it is not just lack of knowledge of the juvenile justice system that influences public attitudes to youth justice policies. The public often lacks awareness of the alternatives to juvenile justice, as well as the limits on the ability of the juvenile justice system to adequately respond to youth crime. Parallels exist at the adult level. One of the principal reasons for public support of harsher sentencing for adults is the wide-

---

[10] It is also possible that people with the least knowledge differ in some important way from the more knowledgeable individuals. For example, they may have more confidence that the youth justice system can control crime rates, or it may be that they are simply less liberal and more inclined to support punitive policies. If this is the case, increasing levels of knowledge may have little impact in terms of changing attitudes.

spread perception that the sentencing process can achieve important reductions in crime rates. The public see the sentencing process as a crime control mechanism and are generally surprised to learn of the important limitations on the ability of that system to effect reductions in aggregate crime rates.

At the juvenile level, people are insufficiently aware of the alternative crime prevention strategies that exist. A clear example of this relates to public support for lowering the age of criminal responsibility. When Canadians were asked simply whether they favor lowering the age limit (currently at twelve years), fully three-quarters of the sample responded affirmatively (Angus Reid Group 1998). However, when given alternative response strategies, public support for criminalizing the behavior of ten-year-olds declined to less than one-quarter of the sample. Highlighting for the public the limited ability of the criminal justice system to reduce juvenile crime rates may help to diminish public support for harsh juvenile justice policies.

To summarize, public opinion research demonstrates that the public are very critical of the juvenile justice response to youth crime; youth court dispositions are seen as being too lenient, hence the support for provisions that mandate or permit transfer of accused juveniles to adult court. This climate of public disenchantment provides the context for juvenile justice reform. Policies that make the system harsher are likely to attract the support of the public, and this will have electoral consequences for the individual or government sponsoring the reform. On the other hand, policies that seem to make the system more lenient or statements of support for the status quo are likely to result in public excoriation of the policies and their sponsors by the public and the news media.

III. Relationship between Public Opinion and Juvenile Justice Policies

These findings set the stage for any consideration of the role of public opinion in juvenile justice policy formation. Most Western governments have been confronted with a public that believes that juvenile crime rates are constantly increasing and that the criminal justice response is inadequate and a cause of rising crime. Confronted with such perceptions, it is hard to imagine any government failing to respond. Indeed, ignoring public views would be seen as an abdication of responsibility. It is the nature of the response that is open to question.

A considerable volume of research has addressed the question of whether punitive criminal justice policies at the adult level represent a response to rising crime rates. Scholars are in agreement that rising crime rates do not directly drive criminal justice reforms (e.g., Garland 2001; Tonry 2001; Zimring 2001; Roberts et al. 2002). This conclusion would also appear applicable to the youth justice field. There are examples of escalating youth crime rates that were not followed by specific reforms and examples of reforms that have followed a period of stable crime rates. One issue that has attracted attention in most Western jurisdictions concerns the minimum age of criminal responsibility.

The lower age limit of the juvenile justice system varies considerably in Western nations, but regardless of the actual age, most jurisdictions have faced demands to lower the limit of criminal responsibility. This is even true in jurisdictions like England and Wales, where the age limit (ten) is lower than in many other countries. When calls to lower the age of criminal responsibility are made, they are seldom sustained by systematic data pertaining to changes in "crime" rates involving children younger than the limit. High-profile cases have played a role. This is certainly true in the United States (see Schwartz 1992, p. 221). In England, much coverage was devoted to a juvenile who had committed many crimes while still under the age of criminal responsibility, while in Canada, an eleven-year-old car thief was the subject of considerable publicity after he bragged in national media interviews that he would steal cars until he was twelve years old.

Unquestionably, juvenile justice in the United States has become more punitive in recent years. In his recent review, Feld (2001) notes that between the years 1992 and 2000, almost half the states took steps to facilitate the transfer of juveniles accused to criminal court. In 2001, the National Research Council Panel on Juvenile Crime concluded, "During the past decade, juvenile crime legislation and policy have become more punitive and have blurred the lines between juvenile and adult justice systems. Movement in this direction is increasing" (McCord, Widom, and Crowell 2001, p. 4; see also Snyder and Sickmund 1995; Mears 1998). What has caused this movement toward more punitive policies? Is it a reasonable response to escalating crime rates or a political response to public pressure?

The panel in the United States concluded that "in response to public concern over crime, particularly violent crime committed by children and adolescents, almost all states have now made changes to their juvenile justice systems" (McCord, Widom, and Crowell 2001, p. 162). There also seems to be near unanimity among English-language scholars that public pressure has been responsible, in whole or part, for many juvenile justice reforms in recent years. Appendix A provides quotations that are illustrative of the consensus among scholars regarding the role of public opinion in influencing youth justice policies. Finally, the volume of public opinion surveys conducted by governments and that focus on juvenile justice is a testament to the importance ascribed to community views. The Canadian government has commissioned a wealth of research, much of it focused on public perceptions of the government in this area, and on public reaction to specific legislative proposals. For example, one report contained a series of questions that explored whether specific reforms would change respondents' level of confidence in the new law (see Earnscliffe Research and Communications 2000).

Documenting the influence of public opinion in the evolution of juvenile justice policy is akin to attempting to demonstrate something that is at once obvious to all observers yet is ultimately not provable. Politicians seldom introduce legislation and cite public opinion as the cause. Far more often legislative preambles cite the seriousness of the problem and the understandable public concern that has arisen. However, public opinion demonstrably affects penal policy in many areas of criminal law, so there appears little reason to believe that juvenile justice policy making will be impervious to political pressure driven by public anxiety about the problem. Indeed, since the polls suggest that youth crime, particularly involving violence, is of greater concern to the public than most other criminal justice issues, the relationship between policy making and public opinion may be particularly close. If it is difficult to establish that a specific piece of legislation arose in direct response to public pressure, the link between public concern and political action can occasionally be detected in specific pieces of legislation as well as in the statements made by politicians. Examples from the United States, Canada, and Australia are illustrative.

A. The United States

In the United States, one of the sponsors of the Violent and Repeat Juvenile Offender Act of 1997 explained, "People are expecting us to do something about these violent teenagers. We've got to move on this" (cited in Schiraldi and Soler [1998], p. 591). Unlike the Canadian statute of 2003, which was an amalgam of liberal and punitive elements (see Doob and Sprott, in this volume), the American act proposed a number of measures in which the emphasis was on increasing the severity of punishment.

A referendum in California in 2000 led to the ratification of Proposition 21 by almost two-thirds of voters. This legislation introduces a number of punitive changes to the juvenile justice system. For example, it requires adult trials for juveniles as young as fourteen years of age if they have been charged with one of a list of enumerated offenses. In addition, the statute transfers from judges to prosecutors the unfettered discretion to decide whether a juvenile accused should be tried as an adult. The legislation also restricts the authority of judges to refer juveniles for treatment or probation (rather than incarcerate them). Ironically, the referendum was held at a time when the state's rates of juvenile arrests had declined significantly—the number of felony arrests declined by 30 percent and the number of homicides by fully 50 percent over the period 1990–98.

The California experience is telling because it illustrates a phenomenon seen repeatedly around the world—even though crime rates have been declining for almost a decade, this has not slowed the pace of populist legislation. Indeed, proponents of tough, populist legislation appear to ignore the declining crime rates and continue to justify their policies by reference to the volume of juvenile crime. Thus, although, as noted, California's crime rate dropped 30 percent between 1990 and 1998, the former governor who sponsored Proposition 21 was still able to talk about "high rates of juvenile and gang-related violence."[11]

Reference has already been made to the case of Willie Bosket in New York. It had consequences for waiver legislation in that state. That incident sparked widespread media coverage and public condemnation of the juvenile justice system in which Bosket had spent considerable time. Finally, the influence of media coverage and public concern about a specific incident was instrumental in provoking punitive juvenile justice legislation in the state of Massachusetts (see Sasson 2000).

Research demonstrates that some of the U.S. policy changes exceed the desire of the public to "get tough" with juveniles. For example, automatic statutory transfers to adult court may go further than the public desire, creating an inconsistency between community sentiment and the practice of the system. Stalans and Henry (1994) showed that most members of the public prefer processing juveniles accused of killing abusive parents in youth court; the public are sensitive to mitigating factors such as childhood abuse. Additional evidence of excessive punitiveness (in comparison to the views of the public) comes from a

[11] Governor Pete Wilson quoted in Associated Press interview with Martha Mendoza, March 3, 2000.

survey reported by Schiraldi and Soler (1998). They explored public reactions to provisions of the Violent and Repeat Juvenile Offender Act of 1997. The results indicated little support for the provisions, even though, as noted earlier, the act was portrayed by proponents as a response to public expectations. For example, the act allows individual states to detain juveniles in facilities where they will have constant contact with adult prisoners. When asked about the mixing of adult and juvenile offenders, over two-thirds of the public disagreed with the housing of juveniles with adult offenders. Schiraldi and Soler concluded that "polling data on the Violent and Repeat Juvenile Offender Act of 1997 show strong public opposition to some of its most important elements" (1998, p. 599).

B. Canada

In Canada, in her first major public address as minister of justice, the minister who introduced sweeping reforms to the juvenile justice system affirmed the relevance of public views to legislative action. Minister McLellan dismissed the declining violent crime rates involving juveniles by noting that "the statistics that demonstrate that violent crime is on the decline are irrelevant if Canadians still feel unsafe. . . . If people think violent crime is an increasing problem, then there is a problem that we have to address" (Department of Justice Canada 1997, p. 2). She proceeded to note that "violent youth crime demands a strong response" and then related the reforms directly to public views by citing a national survey that found that seven in ten Canadians have no confidence in the Young Offenders Act (Department of Justice Canada 1997, p. 6). Other members of the government echoed the minister's position in statements during parliamentary debates. Steve Mahoney, M.P., noted that "we want to try to increase public confidence in the youth justice system" (Hansard 2001).

The minister subsequently introduced a new statutory framework for the juvenile justice system with further reference to the views of the public: "The new Act is built on the values that Canadians want in their youth justice system" (Department of Justice Canada 2001, p. 2). The implication was clear—the previous act was inconsistent with those community values, and this justified, in part, the reforms. Doob and Sprott (in this volume) take the view that the tougher provisions of the new act "appear to have been designed to placate public opinion" (p. 213).

C. Australia

An Australian state (the Northern Territory) introduced one of the most punitive youth justice laws in recent years, a mandatory sentence of imprisonment for young offenders with previous convictions for a relevant property offense. This mandatory sentencing law (since repealed) had been denounced by academics, youth justice workers, and even Amnesty International, whose spokesperson noted that the mandatory sentencing laws had resulted in jail terms for young offenders for stealing "a bottle of cordial, a packet of crisps" (Christie 2001). The issue of mandatory sentencing for juveniles attracted widespread attention following the suicide of a fifteen-year-old aboriginal offender while in custody as a result of a mandatory sentence of imprisonment. In March 2000, a parliamentary committee released a report following its inquiry into the mandatory sentencing legislation relating to juveniles (Senate Legal and Constitutional References Committee 2000).

Australia's first mandatory sentencing laws (passed in 1992) were aimed specifically at juvenile offenders. These laws followed on the heels of intense public pressure to do something about repeat juvenile offenders. Twenty thousand angry protestors had marched to the legislative assembly to complain about the leniency of the juvenile justice system. In the Northern Territory, the government followed the American lead and introduced the "one strike" laws that eventually generated a heated debate in 2000 on the future of Australia's mandatory sentencing laws. Although the new laws specify that juvenile offenders must have at least one prior conviction, many juveniles had records of minor offending. Accordingly, the number of young juveniles sent to detention under the new mandatory laws for trivial property offenses started to rise. When one of these young offenders committed suicide in prison, the issue of mandatory sentencing assumed national importance and attracted widespread international condemnation (see Cunneen and White 1995; Alder and Hunter 2000).

The Northern Territory prime minister noted approvingly the widespread public support for mandatory sentencing for juveniles. He stated, "It shows [the public] want sentencing to reflect community attitudes" and "the poll figures justify the government's decision to stand firm against a campaign to scrap the Territory's laws" (Burke 2000). The "poll" to which the minister referred was in fact nothing more scientific than an invitation by a newspaper for readers to send in their views on mandatory sentencing; systematic surveys of the public on this issue tell a rather different story about the strength of public support for mandatory sentence laws involving juveniles (see Roberts 2003).

D. England and Wales

Finally, with respect to England and Wales, the success of the Labor party in the 1997 election was due in part to its ability to shed the image of a party being "soft" on crime. A central element of the party's electoral platform reflected this tougher tone and focused on the need to revisit the balance between the welfare needs of juvenile offenders and the protection of society (see Rutherford 1999). Once in power, the tenor of government rhetoric continued to emphasize a shift toward a more punitive response to juvenile crime. As noted by Bottoms and Dignan (in this volume), the Home Secretary, in introducing the 1998 Crime and Disorder Act, talked of the "excuse culture" that permeated the youth justice system in England and Wales, language that would resonate well with the more punitive elements of the British public.

E. Summary

The sequence of events giving rise to juvenile justice reforms may correspond to the following pattern. The perception of disproportionate increases in juvenile offending (relative to adult crime), accompanied by a small number of extraordinary cases, attracts intense media attention to the issue. This coverage inflames public opinion and results in changes in public ratings of the seriousness of the youth crime problem, in overestimates of youth crime rates, and in misperceptions of changes in those rates over time. Public views then fuel community dissatisfaction with the youth court system as people search for an explanation of rising youth crime—particularly in a period of relative prosperity. The public's criticism of youth justice is amplified and conveyed to politicians by the media. Acting out of a genuine desire to respond to a perceived problem, or out of a more malign form of penal populism, politicians then introduce legislative reforms that make the juvenile justice system more punitive. The political reaction is based on an interpretation of public opinion derived from opinion polls and more imperfect methods that, to a degree at least, misrepresent the views of the public. Politicians then offer the public what they appear to seek: harsher responses to juvenile crime. Making these solutions salient may itself move the public toward punitive responses.

The news media, the public, and populist politicians thus create an atmosphere in which responses to youth crime are sought and found principally in the direction of criminal justice. Attention is focused on the justice system, and little discussion centers on schools or community systems. The issue of juvenile justice is placed within a punishment-oriented framework; alternative responses are only seldom or fleetingly considered.

A strong, albeit circumstantial, case can therefore be made to support a link between public concern about juvenile crime and punitive sentencing policies. The strength of the link may vary from jurisdiction to jurisdiction but appears present everywhere. In a democratic society, it would be strange if there were not some connection between public views of juvenile justice and legislative reforms. The danger of course is that public pressure, or public concern arising from misperceptions of crime trends, provokes excessively punitive reforms that undermine the principles of juvenile justice, threaten the existence of an autonomous court system, and may, ultimately, be inconsistent with the views of the public.

F. Moderate Reforms

In evaluating the plausibility of the proposed model, it is equally important to explain the examples that run counter to this explanation. In Canada, for example, although there has been intense pressure on the federal government to replace the Young Offenders Act with a much tougher statute, the Youth Criminal Justice Act is not a highly punitive reform.[12] Indeed, as Doob and Sprott (1999; in this volume) have noted, the Youth Criminal Justice Act contains a number of proposals that will in all probability reduce the use of custody as a sanction in Canada's youth courts. Doob and Sprott argue that the government was able to pursue this route in part through the judicious representation of the bill as a tough measure.

The Canadian experience suggests that it may be possible for a government to resist the public and political pressure if the conditions are propitious. The federal government enjoyed a very substantial Parliamentary majority at the time the youth justice legislation was intro-

[12] One explanation for the fact that the Canadian reforms were not as punitive as some American examples involves the time it takes reform proposals to become legislation in Canada. Twenty-three years elapsed between the creation of a departmental committee and the year in which the Young Offenders Act came into effect. If legislators have more time to consider potential legislation, they may be less inclined to support populist, punitive provisions.

duced and debated. In addition, a number of punitive policies that attracted public support were rejected by the government. For example, almost three-quarters of the public endorsed lowering the minimum age of criminal responsibility from twelve years of age to ten (Angus Reid Group 1998).[13] Polls revealed that close to eight in ten Canadians favored publishing the names of young offenders convicted of violent crimes; neither proposal was adopted by the government in its reform legislation.

Finally, the experience with respect to juvenile justice in New Zealand also illustrates the changes that are possible in the absence of punitive precipitants, including public pressure. This country did not experience significant increases in juvenile crime rates or shifts in the percentage of juvenile crime involving violence. Maxwell and Morris (2002) note that while the number of violent incidents increased over the 1990s, it was less, not more, marked for juveniles. These researchers add, "The increases in violent offending do not represent any significant change in the percentage of juveniles involved in violence" (Maxwell and Morris 2002, p. 201; see also Morris, in this volume).

These trends were confirmed by other sources of data as well. It is perhaps no coincidence that, absent the kind of pressures found in the United States, the New Zealand juvenile justice reform legislation moves away from rather than toward a punitive model. The 1989 Children, Young Persons and their Families Act, 1989, as the name implies, places the emphasis on encouraging families to participate in adjudications involving their children. As well, the act stresses the importance of diversion and the need for the least restrictive sentencing alternatives (see Maxwell and Morris 2002). It is hard to imagine such a statute being adopted in the United States.

Appendix B summarizes the conditions that appear to generate a punitive response from the public. These factors have been more present in America, where the most punitive juvenile justice reforms have taken place, and least present in countries such as New Zealand, where juvenile justice policies continue to stress rehabilitation and, more recently, principles of restorative justice that are antithetical to punitive policies such as legislative transfers and mandatory sentences.

IV. Responding to Public Pressure

How can the juvenile justice system respond to public and political pressure to move closer to an adult court model for juveniles? Two

[13] Although, as noted, the percentage drops dramatically when respondents are given an alternative (see Sprott and Doob 2000).

strategies suggest themselves: increasing the level of public knowledge and improving the methods used to determine the nature of public opinion.

A. Public Legal Information

One strategy that has been successfully employed at the adult level involves providing the public with better information. Chapman, Mirrlees-Black, and Brown (2002), for example, report the findings from a randomized experiment in which people were given information about the sentencing process. After having been informed about sentencing patterns, people tended to have more positive perceptions of sentencers. Earlier in this essay, I documented the misperceptions that many people have of the juvenile justice system. A clear opportunity exists therefore to improve the image of the youth court, by educating the public. This proposal has been made repeatedly in the literature but has yet to be implemented on a wide scale.

Examining the poll findings reveals a certain stasis with respect to public knowledge and opinion; people believe crime rates are increasing regardless of actual trends and constantly express their dissatisfaction with youth court sentencing and the youth justice system generally. This is true for adult crime (see Cullen, Fisher, and Applegate 2000, fig. 2) and also for juvenile justice. The static nature of public opinion is curious, since almost all jurisdictions, including moderate European countries, such as Holland (see Junger-Tas 1999), have toughened various aspects of their juvenile justice systems. This finding appears to have escaped the attention of politicians who have put the cart before the horse. They have introduced reforms to respond to public concern and public perceptions of rising crime rather than attempting to clarify the situation for the public.[14] Clearly, the juvenile crime problem, particularly when it involves violence or guns, is not a matter of public perception alone; much more, however, could be done to place the issue in more historical and cross-jurisdictional perspective.

In addition to educating the public about juvenile crime—the volume and the nature of juvenile offending—it is also important to convey to the public the justification for having a separate juvenile justice system that imposes mitigated punishments. Many members of the public regard the more lenient dispositions in youth court as examples

---

[14] One reason for this is that there is a political price to be paid for telling the public that their crime perceptions are distorted, particularly when key professionals, such as police chiefs, contest the assertion that levels of crime are not rising (see Roberts et al. 2002).

of unprincipled indulgence on the part of youth court judges. People need to understand the justification underlying the juvenile sentencing "discount," the same way that they need to understand the imposition of less severe sentences to reflect other sentencing principles (such as the first offender discount). Some members of the public probably believe diminished penalties for juveniles are a relatively new innovation associated with the shift toward a rehabilitative model of justice. These people need to be reminded that the age of the offender has for centuries been considered a mitigating factor, even during periods in which sentences generally have been highly punitive, even barbaric, by today's standards (see Radzinowicz 1948; Junger-Tas, in this volume).

A greater effort also needs to be made to focus the public's attention on aspects of juvenile justice that do not readily spring to mind. Most of the criticism of juvenile courts focuses upon their leniency. From this springs support for tougher responses to youth crime. However, as Mark Soler (2001) points out, there are other issues that need addressing and that would appeal to the public if made salient. Members of the public are very sensitive to the issue of fairness in sentencing. Racial disparity in the administration of the death penalty for adults has undermined public support for capital punishment in a number of states. Knowing of the disproportionate involvement of minority youth in juvenile courts may well result in attitude change.

We need more experimental explorations of the effects of information on attitudes. Several studies have shown significant shifts. Others show more limited movement. In a study reported by Smith (2001), respondents who had expressed support for capital punishment for juveniles convicted of murder were given information about the abolitionist trend with regard to the death penalty. Specifically, they were informed that only three other countries executed juveniles. After hearing this information, the percentage in favor of executing juveniles declined, but only by a small margin (from 34 percent to 30 percent). However, this short message may not have been sufficiently engaging for respondents. We need to know more about the factors influencing public attitudes toward such a critical issue.

Beyond the level of principle, social science research may well have a role to play in this debate. The public may not be aware of research that has demonstrated that juvenile offenders are more amenable to rehabilitation, less culpable than adult offenders for the same criminal behavior, and less sensitive to deterrent threats than adults (see Woolard, Fondacaro, and Slobogin 2001). Nor are they aware of the wealth of research that reveals that many juvenile offenders "age out" of an offending pattern; knowing this may increase public support for less intrusive interventions in the lives of young people who come into (temporary) conflict with the law. Conveying information of this kind may well make some people reconsider the offense-based perspective on juvenile offending that justifies adult punishments and a low age limit of criminal responsibility.

Finally, there may be a lesson from the public opinion literature on alternative sanctions at the adult level. Addressing public support for punitive responses to juvenile offending may best be achieved by identifying the consequences of alternative dispositions for juveniles and also the compensatory elements of these sanctions. Many people support incarceration because they believe that the alternative is probation, and they have little faith that probation conditions are either stringent or well supervised. As well, the idea that offenders may make compensation to the victim carries great appeal at the adult level and is the most important source of support for community sanctions (Roberts 2002). If these elements (impact on the offender, compensation for the victim) are made salient in the context of juvenile justice, there may be less support for incarceration. The public also need to be made aware of alternative programs such as juvenile drug courts that promote treatment with the support of the juvenile's family.

Changing public attitudes toward juvenile justice will require more than simply the provision of information. Statistical information will not sway people whose support for transfer to adult court or the death penalty is founded upon more visceral and emotional grounds. However, there is considerable evidence that the punitive element of public response to juvenile crime is not driven by fear. For example, although Canadians appear to be as concerned or more concerned about youth crime than people in other countries, less than one Canadian in ten admits to being very worried about becoming a victim of a crime by a young person (Earnscliffe Research and Communications 2000). Improving public knowledge of juvenile crime and justice is a necessary, even if insufficient, condition for better juvenile justice policy development. The public may not be swayed by the findings of systematic research that refutes some of the more punitive justice policies; however, the proliferation of better information may well undermine the position of populist politicians.

B. Improve the Quality of Public Opinion Research

Improving the sophistication of research on public opinion would help significantly. As with other areas of criminal justice, politicians derive their image of the public's view from a variety of sources, of which the most important is the conventional public opinion poll. There is, of course, a place for opinion poll research as a means of determining the general tenor of public views. For generating information representative of the public, such surveys have no equal. But their deficiencies, in terms of the amount of time and information at the disposal of the respondent, are by now well documented (e.g., Roberts and Stalans 1997; Cullen, Fisher, and Applegate 2000).

They tend to generate an interpretation of the public that overemphasizes the punitive nature of public views; people are most severe toward offenders, adult or juvenile, when asked questions such as "what penalty is appropriate for a juvenile who uses a gun to commit robbery?" These kinds of surveys must be supplemented by additional research in which the depth of the attitude toward, say imprisonment, is plumbed by asking about specific cases and by giving the respondent more information. This is not simply an attempt to create an atmosphere in which the subject in the study will sympathize with the defendant; it is an attempt to generate an informed participant. Judges in common-law jurisdictions consider a wide range of mitigating and aggravating factors and have at their disposal a complex array of sentencing tools. How appropriate, then, is it to simply ask the public whether a juvenile convicted of robbery should go to prison?

A number of alternatives to the standard survey approach exist. One possible alternative is the deliberative poll approach that has been employed (with respect to criminal justice) on only one occasion (see Fishkin 1995; Hough and Park 2002). The deliberative poll attempts to combine the depth of a qualitative analysis with the generalizability of a representative poll. A representative sample of the public attends a day- or weekend-long seminar at which they receive information about the issue. Questions are posed both before and after the educational sessions to determine whether specific opinions reflect uninformed views or top-of-the-head reactions. This research innovation carries its own dangers as a device to measure public opinion, not the least of which is the difficulty of balancing the information available to the respondents to ensure that it does not degenerate into an exercise in propaganda (see Hough and Park 2002). Nevertheless, the concept is worthy of further exploration and may be useful, if only to demonstrate that public attitudes are flexible and responsive to evidence-based communications.[15]

---

[15] One source of information about juvenile justice that is not subject to the potential criticism that it is manipulative is material about practices in other jurisdictions.

Issues such as public support for transfer to adult court need to be explored much more carefully than has been the case to date. Polls that explore this question tend to focus the respondent's attention on the seriousness of the crime rather than the consequences of transfer. This methodology distorts responses by creating an appetite for transfer. When asked if a juvenile accused of a violent crime should be transferred, most people will respond affirmatively. But respondents need to be given information about the consequences of transfer in terms of the treatment of the juvenile and the likelihood of reoffending.

Fagan (1995) has demonstrated that juveniles transferred to criminal court were more likely to reoffend. If the public were aware of this finding, support for statutory transfer would decline. Asking about issues such as transfer without providing sufficient context and information to the respondent creates a distorted view of public opinion and can only have a deleterious impact on juvenile justice policy. Few members of the public realize that, depending on the state in which they are sentenced, juveniles sentenced as adults may incur several long-term legal consequences, such as loss of their franchise, or their conviction may become a matter of public record (see Young and Gainsborough 2000).

Finally, there is considerable need to expand the range of research on public attitudes to juvenile justice to include other Western, and non-Western nations. This essay has perforce concentrated on three English-speaking jurisdictions. Several of the principal findings with respect to public knowledge may be generalizable to other Western nations, but in the absence of systematic research, this remains an as-yet-unfounded inference. The danger with the present state of affairs is that our conception of public opinion is based on a very small number of jurisdictions. Regrettably this lends the literature a somewhat parochial tone. Only when we have a broader sampling of countries will it become possible to draw a truly international portrait of public attitudes and to establish the features of public opinion common to people in many nations. The International Crime Victimization Survey is one useful point of departure. The inclusion of questions addressing juvenile offending would be a good first step toward a truly comparative analysis of public opinion toward juvenile crime and juvenile justice.

Cross-national surveys have shown that there is considerable international variation in sentencing preferences involving adults. The same is probably true for juveniles (see Mayhew and van Kesteren [2002] for comparisons), although this has yet to be demonstrated empirically.

Among Western nations, American attitudes tend to be most punitive. Perhaps the most telling example of this relates to the death penalty. Although polls exaggerate the extent of public support, significant numbers of Americans favor capital punishment (see Moon, Wright, Cullen, and Pealer 2000). Almost half the American public (44 percent) support the execution of twelve-year-olds convicted of murder (Moon, Wright, Cullen, and Pealer 2000). Pluralities of these magnitudes with respect to this issue do not exist outside the United States.[16]

Comparative public opinion research would permit greater application of the "best practices" principle in juvenile justice. The American public generally favors the transfer of juveniles near the upper age limit of juvenile justice, albeit with qualifications. In Germany (see Albrecht, in this volume), according to section 105 of the Youth Court Law, young adults (eighteen to twenty years old) are sentenced as juveniles, if certain criteria are met. Over the past few years, although U.S. juvenile justice policies have hardened, the proportion of adult offenders tried and sentenced as juveniles in Germany has actually increased. Knowing that this policy does not appear to have provoked widespread public outcry in that country may encourage other jurisdictions to consider such procedures.

APPENDIX A

Examples of the Consensus Regarding the Impact of Public Opinion on Juvenile Justice Policies

"Citizens and politicians perceive a significant and frightening increase in youth crime and violence. A desire to 'get tough' . . . provides political impetus to transfer some young offenders . . . and to strengthen the sanctioning powers of juvenile courts" (Feld 1995, p. 966).

"Fear of violent juvenile crime and a sense of frustration . . . are fueling major changes in juvenile justice. If unchecked, these changes could culminate in the elimination of a separate and distinctive justice system" (Bazemore and Umbreit 1997, p. 5).

"Because of the perceived rise in juvenile crime, especially violent crime, state legislatures have proposed, and in some cases, passed, legislation that would dramatically alter the juvenile courts and/or the juvenile justice system" (Weisheit and Culbertson 1985, p. 28).

---

[16] Unfortunately, the only international survey that permits comparisons across a wide range of countries (the International Crime Victimization Survey) asks about public sentencing preferences in response to an adult offender only (see Mayhew and van Kesteren 2002).

"One of the major responses from politicians and juvenile justice professionals to public pressure to 'do something' about the juvenile crime problem was to formalize and expand the practice of committing youth to detention centers" (Schwartz 1989, p. 59).

"Growing public sentiment over the problem of juvenile crime has resulted in an administrative focus on 'toughening' and rationalizing the sanctions for serious offenders" (Guarino-Ghezzi and Kimball 1986, p. 419).

"While concern about youth crime has historically been great, the intense public reaction in the late 1970s has generated a major shift in the basic premises of the juvenile justice system" (Fagan, Kansen, and Jang 1983, p. 91).

"Reacting to juvenile justice has become a political opportunity for governors and legislators, and a marketing opportunity for the mass media" (Guarino-Ghezzi and Loughran 1996, p. 1).

"Public pressure prompts tougher laws" (Winterdyk 1997, p. 158).

Similar statements can be found elsewhere in the literature (see Greenwood et al. 1983, p. xiii; Schwartz 1992, p. 214; Mears 1998, p. 443; Zimring 1998, p. 111; Redding 1999, p. 2; Corrado, Cohen, and Odgers 2001, p. 28; Hoffman and Summers 2001, p. xvi; Myers 2002, p. 5; Doob and Sprott, in this volume).

APPENDIX B

Conditions That Enhance the Punitiveness of the Public

An increase in violent offending by juveniles, or widespread reporting of an increase in offending

Distorted media coverage of the volume and seriousness of juvenile crime

The conflation of images of guns, drugs, and violence with young persons in the news media

The occurrence of major tragedies that receive considerable attention from the news media and that are cited as exemplars of a general "youth crime problem"

News media coverage of apparently novel forms of offending involving youth (e.g., "swarming")

Juvenile sentencing provisions that create a very wide, and possibly unacceptable, gap between the punishments imposed on adults and juveniles

The existence of populist politicians, or a government that uses juvenile justice reforms to enhance its electoral prospects

Pressure on governments to appear tough in an election campaign or in the run up to an election

The use of polls that provide little information about the subject and that invite a punitive response

An aging population.[17]

REFERENCES

Albrecht, H-J. In this volume. "Youth Justice in Germany."

Alder, C., and N. Hunter. 2000. "Australia." In *Teen Violence: A Global View*, edited by A. Hoffman and R. Summers. Westport, Conn.: Greenwood.

Amnesty International. 1998. *Betraying the Young: Human Rights Violations against Children in the U.S. Justice System*. New York: Amnesty International.

Angus Reid Group. 1984. *Canadians' Attitudes toward the Justice System*. Toronto: Angus Reid Group.

———. 1997. *Crime and the Justice System*. Ottawa: Angus Reid Group.

———. 1998. *Canadians' Attitudes toward Changes to the Young Offenders Act*. Ottawa: Angus Reid Group.

Baron, S., and T. Hartnagel. 1996. "'Lock 'em up': Attitudes toward Punishing Juvenile Offenders." *Canadian Journal of Criminology* 38:191–212.

Bazemore, G., and M. Umbreit. 1995. "Rethinking the Sanctioning Function in Juvenile Court: Retributive or Restorative Responses to Youth Crime." *Crime and Delinquency* 41:296–316.

———. 1997. *Balanced and Restorative Justice for Juveniles: A Framework for Juvenile Justice in the 21st Century*. Washington, D.C.: U.S. Office of Juvenile Justice and Delinquency Prevention.

Boss, P. 1967. *Social Policy and the Young Delinquent*. London: Routledge & Kegan Paul.

Bottoms, A. 1995. "The Philosophy and Politics of Punishment and Sentencing." In *The Politics of Sentencing Reform*, edited by C. Clarkson and R. Morgan. Oxford: Clarendon.

Bottoms, A., and J. Dignan. In this volume. "Youth Justice in Great Britain."

Bureau of Justice Statistics. 1991. *Sourcebook of Criminal Justice Statistics, 1990*. Washington, D.C.: Bureau of Justice Statistics.

———. 1995. *Sourcebook of Criminal Justice Statistics, 1994*. Washington, D.C.: Bureau of Justice Statistics.

———. 1998. *Juvenile Felony Defendants in Criminal Courts*. Washington, D.C.: Bureau of Justice Statistics.

———. 2002. *Sourcebook of Criminal Justice Statistics, 2000*. Online edition: http://www.albany.edu/sourcebook/.

Burke, D. 2000. "Australians Support NT Laws." Press release, March 8, 2000.

---

[17] A number of studies (e.g., Schwartz, Guo, and Kerbs 1993) have demonstrated that people over fifty years of age hold more punitive views of youth justice issues.

Butterfield, F. 1995. *All God's Children: The Bosket Family and the American Tradition of Violence.* 1st ed. New York: Knopf.

Buttrum, K. 1998. "Juvenile Justice: What Works and What Doesn't!" In *Juvenile Crime and Juvenile Justice: Toward 2000 and Beyond,* edited by C. Alder. Griffith, ACT: Australian Institute of Criminology.

Chapman, B., C. Mirrlees-Black, and C. Brown. 2002. *The Effect of Providing Information on Public Attitudes to the Criminal Justice System.* London: Home Office.

Christie, M. 2001. Reuters Report, October 19, 2001.

Corrado, R., I. Cohen, and C. Odgers. 2001. "Canada." In *Teen Violence: A Global View,* edited by A. Hoffman and R. Summers. Westport, Conn.: Greenwood.

Correctional Association of New York. 2002. "Juvenile Justice Project Fact Sheet." Available at www.correctionalassociation.org/juvenile_fact.html.

Covell, K., and R. Howe. 1996. "Public Attitudes and Juvenile Justice in Canada." *International Journal of Children's Rights* 4:345–55.

Crews, G., and R. Montgomery. 2000. *Chasing Shadows: Confronting Juvenile Violence in America.* Upper Saddle River, N.J.: Prentice-Hall.

Cullen, F., K. Golden, and J. Cullen. 1983. "Is Child Saving Dead? Attitudes toward Juvenile Rehabilitation in Illinois." *Journal of Criminal Justice* 11:1–13.

Cullen, F., B. Fisher, and B. Applegate. 2000. "Public Opinion about Punishment and Corrections." In *Crime and Justice: A Review of Research,* vol. 27, edited by M. Tonry. Chicago: University of Chicago Press.

Cullen, F., and J. Wright. 2002. "Criminal Justice in the Lives of American Adolescents: Choosing the Future." In *The Changing Adolescent Experience: Societal Trends and the Transition to Adulthood,* edited by J. Mortimer and R. Larson. New York: Cambridge University Press.

Cunneen, C., and R. White. 1995. *Juvenile Justice: An Australian Perspective.* Melbourne: Oxford University Press.

Decima Research. 1993. *Report to the Department of Justice Canada.* Ottawa: Decima Research.

Department of Justice Canada. 1997. "Minister of Justice Delivers First Major Public Address on Justice Issues." News release, August 23, 1997. Ottawa: Department of Justice Canada.

———. 2001. "Minister of Justice Reintroduces Youth Criminal Justice Act." News release, February 5, 2001. Ottawa: Department of Justice Canada.

Doble, J. 2002. "Attitudes to Punishment in the U.S.: Punitive and Liberal Opinions." In *Changing Attitudes to Punishment: Findings from around the Globe,* edited by J. V. Roberts and M. Hough. Cullompton, U.K.: Willan.

Doble Research Associates. 1995*a. Crime and Corrections: The Views of the People of North Carolina.* Englewood Cliffs, N.J.: Doble Research Associates.

———. 1995*b. Crime and Corrections: The Views of the People of Oklahoma.* Englewood Cliffs, N.J.: Doble Research Associates.

Doob, A. N. 2000. "Transforming the Punishment Environment: Understanding Public Views of What Should Be Accomplished at Sentencing." *Canadian Journal of Criminology* 42:323–40.

Doob, A., V. Marinos, and K. Varma. 1995. *Youth Crime and the Youth Justice System in Canada: A Research Perspective.* Toronto: University of Toronto, Centre of Criminology.

Doob, A. N., and J. V. Roberts. 1988. "Public Punitiveness and Public Knowledge of the Facts: Some Canadian Surveys." In *Public Attitudes to Sentencing: Surveys from Five Countries,* edited by N. Walker and M. Hough. Cambridge Studies in Criminology, 59. Aldershot, Hants, England: Gower.

Doob, A., and J. Sprott. 1998. "Is the 'Quality' of Youth Crime Becoming More Serious?" *Canadian Journal of Criminology* 40:185–94.

———. 1999. "Canada Considers New Sentencing Laws for Youth: A Sheep in Wolf's Clothing." *Overcrowded Times* 10(2):1, 5–11.

———. In this volume. "Youth Justice in Canada."

Doob, A., J. Sprott, V. Marinos, and K. Varma. 1998. *An Exploration of Ontario Residents' Views of Crime and the Criminal Justice System.* Toronto: University of Toronto, Centre of Criminology.

Dorfman, L., and V. Schiraldi. 2001. "Off Balance: Youth, Race and Crime in the News." Building Blocks for Youth. Available at www.buildingblocksforyouth.org/media/media.html.

Earnscliffe Research and Communications. 1999. *Youth Justice Survey.* Ottawa: Earnscliffe Research and Communications.

———. 2000. *Public Opinion Research into Youth Justice and the Youth Criminal Justice Act.* Ottawa: Earnscliffe Research and Communications.

Ekos Research Associates. 2000. *Canadian Attitudes towards the Prevention of Crime.* Ottawa: Ekos Research Associates.

Environics Canada. 1998. *Focus on Crime and Justice.* Ottawa: Environics Canada.

Estrada, F. 2001. "Juvenile Violence as a Social Problem: Trends, Media Attention, and Societal Response." *British Journal of Criminology* 41:639–55.

Fagan, J. 1995. "Separating the Men from the Boys: The Comparative Advantage of Juvenile versus Criminal Court Sanctions on Recidivism among Adolescent Felony Offenders." In *Serious, Violent and Chronic Juvenile Offenders: A Sourcebook,* edited by J. Howell, B. Krisberg, J. Hawkins, and J. Wilson. Thousand Oaks, Calif.: Sage.

Fagan, J., K. Kansen, and M. Jang. 1983. "Profiles of Chronically Violent Juvenile Offenders: An Empirical Test of an Integrated Theory of Juvenile Delinquency." In *Evaluating Juvenile Justice,* edited by J. Kluegel. Beverly Hills, Calif.: Sage.

Feiler, S., and J. Sheley. 1999. "Legal and Racial Elements of Public Willingness to Transfer Juvenile Offenders to Adult Court." *Journal of Criminal Justice* 27:55–64.

Feld, B. 1995. "Violent Youth and Public Policy: A Case Study of Juvenile Justice Reform." *Minnesota Law Review* 79:965–1128.

———. 1998. "Juvenile and Criminal Justice System's Responses to Youth Violence." In *Youth Violence,* edited by M. Tonry and M. Moore. Vol. 24 of *Crime and Justice: A Review of Research,* edited by Michael Tonry. Chicago: University of Chicago Press.

———. 2001. "Race, Youth Violence, and the Changing Jurisprudence of Waiver." *Behavioral Sciences and the Law* 19:3–22.

Fishkin, J. 1995. *The Voice of the People: Public Opinion and Democracy.* New Haven, Conn.: Yale University Press.

Gallup Canada. 1999. "Canadians Want a Strict Young Offenders Act." *Gallup Poll* 59(23).

Garland, D. 2001. *The Culture of Control: Crime and Social Order in Contemporary Society.* Chicago: University of Chicago Press.

Gerber, J., and S. Englehardt-Greer. 1996. "Just and Painful: Attitudes toward Sentencing Criminals." In *Americans View Crime and Justice: A National Public Opinion Survey,* edited by T. Flanagan and D. Longmire. Thousand Oaks, Calif.: Sage.

Gilbert, J. 1986. *A Cycle of Outrage: America's Reaction to the Juvenile Delinquent in the 1950s.* New York: Oxford University Press.

Golay, M. 1997. *Where America Stands.* New York: Wiley & Sons.

Greenwood, P., A. Lipson, A. Abrahamse, and F. Zimring. 1983. *Youth Crime and Juvenile Justice in California: A Report to the Legislature.* Santa Monica, Calif.: Rand.

Guarino-Ghezzi, S., and L. Kimball. 1986. "Reforming Justice by Geography: Organizational Responses to the Problem of Juvenile Crime." *Law and Policy* 8:419–36.

Guarino-Ghezzi, S., and L. Loughran. 1996. *Balancing Juvenile Justice.* New Brunswick, N.J.: Transaction.

Hansard. March 26, 2001. Available from www.parl.gc.ca.

Hart, T. 1998. "Causes and Consequences of Juvenile Crime and Violence: Public Attitudes and Question-Order Effect." *American Journal of Criminal Justice* 23:129–43.

Hoffman, A., and R. Summers, eds. 2001. *Teen Violence: A Global View.* Westport, Conn.: Greenwood.

Hough, M., and A. Park. 2002. "Attitudes to Crime and Punishment: The Results of a Deliberative Poll." In *Changing Attitudes to Punishment: Findings from around the Globe,* edited by J. V. Roberts and M. Hough. Cullompton, U.K.: Willan.

Hutton, N. 2002. *What the Scottish Public Think about Crime and Punishment.* Glasgow: University of Strathclyde, Centre for Sentencing Research.

Junger-Tas, J. 1999. "Juvenile Delinquency: What to Do? The Case of the Netherlands." *Federal Sentencing Reporter* 11:248–54.

———. In this volume. "Youth Justice in the Netherlands."

Knowles, J. 1980. *Ohio Citizen Attitudes concerning Crime and Criminal Justice.* 2d ed. Akron: Ohio Statistical Analysis Center, Office of Criminal Justice Services.

Krisberg, B., and J. Austin. 1993. *Reinventing Juvenile Justice.* Newbury Park, Calif.: Sage.

Logan, R. 2001. "Crime Statistics in Canada, 2000." *Juristat* vol. 21, no. 8. Ottawa: Statistics Canada, Canadian Centre for Justice Statistics.

Louis Harris and Associates. 1968. *The Public Looks at Crime and Corrections:*

Report of a Survey Conducted for the Joint Commission on Correctional Manpower and Training in November, 1967. Washington, D.C.: Joint Commission on Correctional Manpower and Training.

Mattinson, J. 2002. Personal communication to, and available from, the author.

Mattinson, J., and C. Mirrlees-Black. 2000. *Attitudes to Crime and Criminal Justice: Findings from the 1998 British Crime Survey.* London: Home Office.

Mauer, M. 1999. *The Race to Incarcerate.* New York: New Press.

Maxwell, G., and A. Morris. 2002. "Juvenile Crime and Justice in New Zealand." In *Juvenile Justice Systems,* edited by N. Bala, H. Snyder, and J. Paetsch. Toronto: Thompson Educational.

Mayhew, P., and J. van Kesteren. 2002. "Cross-National Attitudes to Punishment." In *Changing Attitudes to Punishment: Findings from around the Globe,* edited by J. V. Roberts and M. Hough. Cullompton, U.K.: Willan.

McCord, J., C. Widom, and N. Crowell, eds. 2001. *Juvenile Crime, Juvenile Justice.* Washington, D.C.: National Academy Press.

McIntyre, J. 1967. "Public Attitudes toward Crime and Law Enforcement." *American Criminal Law Quarterly* 6:66–81.

Mears, D. 1998. "Evaluation Issues Confronting Juvenile Justice Sentencing Reforms: A Case Study of Texas." *Crime and Delinquency* 44:443–63.

———. 2001. "Getting Tough with Juvenile Offenders." *Criminal Justice and Behavior* 28:206–26.

Moon, M., J. Sundt, F. Cullen, and J. Wright. 2000. "Is Child Saving Dead? Public Support for Juvenile Rehabilitation." *Crime and Delinquency* 46:38–60.

Moon, M., J. Wright, F. Cullen, and J. Pealer. 2000. "Putting Kids to Death: Specifying Public Support for Juvenile Capital Punishment." *Justice Quarterly* 17:663–84.

Moore, R. 1985. "Reflections of Canadians on the Law and the Legal System: Legal Research Institute Survey of Respondents in Montreal, Toronto and Winnipeg." In *Law in a Cynical Society? Opinion and Law in the 1980s,* edited by D. Gibson and J. Baldwin. Calgary: Carswell Legal Publications.

Morris, A. In this volume. "Youth Justice in New Zealand."

Myers, W. 2002. *Juvenile Sexual Homicide.* New York: Academic Press.

Nacro. 2001. *Youth Crime Briefing: Public Opinion and Youth Justice.* London: Nacro.

Opinion Research Corporation. 1982. *Public Attitudes toward Youth Crime.* Report for the Hubert H. Humphrey Institute of Public Affairs. Minneapolis: Hubert H. Humphrey Institute of Public Affairs.

Parker, H. 1970. "Juvenile Court Actions and Public Response." In *Becoming Delinquent: Young Offenders and the Correctional Process,* edited by P. Garabedian and D. Gibbons. Chicago: Aldine.

Radzinowicz, L. 1948. *A History of English Criminal Law and Its Administration from 1750: The Movement for Reform, 1750–1833.* New York: Macmillan.

Redding, R. 1999. "Legal, Psychological, and Behavioral Outcomes." *Juvenile and Family Court Journal* 50(Winter):1–19.

Roberts, J. V. 2002. "Public Attitudes to Community-Based Sanctions." In

Changing Attitudes to Punishment: Findings from around the Globe, edited by J. V. Roberts and M. Hough. Cullompton, U.K.: Willan.

———. 2003. "Public Opinion and Mandatory Sentences of Imprisonment: A Review of International Findings." *Criminal Justice and Behavior* (forthcoming).

Roberts, J. V., and L. Stalans. 1997. *Public Opinion, Crime, and Criminal Justice.* Boulder, Colo.: Westview.

Roberts, J. V., L. S. Stalans, D. Indermaur, and M. Hough. 2002. *Penal Populism and Public Opinion: Lessons from Five Countries.* Oxford: Oxford University Press.

Roper Center. 2001. ABC News Poll. Accession Number 031694. University of Connecticut Public Opinion Online.

Rossum, R. 1999. "Juvenile Justice Professionals: Opponents of Reform." In *Juvenile Delinquency in the United States and the United Kingdom*, edited by G. McDowell and J. Smith. New York: St. Martin's.

Rutherford, A. 1999. "The New Political Consensus on Youth Justice in Britain." In *Juvenile Delinquency in the United States and the United Kingdom*, edited by G. McDowell and J. Smith. New York: St. Martin's.

Sanders, T. 2000. "Sentencing of Young Offenders in Canada, 1998/99." *Juristat* vol. 20, no. 7. Ottawa: Statistics Canada, Canadian Centre for Justice Statistics.

Sasson, T. 2000. "William Horton's Long Shadow." In *Crime, Risk and Insecurity: Law and Order in Everyday Life and Political Discourse*, edited by T. Hope and R. Sparks. London: Routledge.

Schiraldi, V., and M. Soler. 1998. "The Will of the People? The Public's Opinion of the Violent and Repeat Juvenile Offender Act of 1997." *Crime and Delinquency* 44:590–601.

Schwartz, I. 1989. *(In)justice for Juveniles: Rethinking the Best Interests of the Child.* Lexington, Mass.: Lexington Books.

———. 1992. "Juvenile Crime-Fighting Policies: What the Public Really Wants." In *Juvenile Justice and Public Policy: Toward a National Agenda*, edited by I. Schwartz. New York: Lexington Books.

Schwartz, I., J. Abbey, and W. Barton. 1990. *The Perception and Reality of Juvenile Crime in Michigan.* Ann Arbor, Mich.: Center for the Study of Youth Policy.

Schwartz, I., S. Guo, and J. Kerbs. 1993. "The Impact of Demographic Variables on Public Opinion regarding Juvenile Justice: Implications for Public Policy." *Crime and Delinquency* 39:5–28.

Senate Legal and Constitutional References Committee. 2000. "Inquiry into the Human Rights (Mandatory Sentencing of Juvenile Offenders) Bill 1999." Commonwealth of Australia. Available at www.aph.gov/senate/committee/legcon_ctte/mandatory.

Sickmund, M., H. Snyder, and E. Poe-Yamagata. 1997. *Juvenile Offenders and Victims: 1997 Update on Violence.* Washington, D.C.: National Center for Juvenile Justice.

Singer, S. 1996. *Recriminalizing Delinquency: Violent Juvenile Crime and Juvenile Justice Reform.* Cambridge: Cambridge University Press.

Smith, T. 2001. *Public Opinion on the Death Penalty for Youths.* Chicago: University of Chicago, National Opinion Research Center.

Snyder, H. 1988. *Court Careers of Juvenile Offenders.* Washington, D.C.: U.S. Department of Justice, Office of Juvenile Justice and Delinquency Prevention, National Institute for Juvenile Justice and Delinquency Prevention.

Snyder, H., and M. Sickmund. 1995. *Juvenile Offenders and Victims: National Report.* Washington, D.C.: U.S. Department of Justice, Office of Justice Programs, Office of Juvenile Justice and Delinquency Prevention.

Soler, M. 2001. "Public Opinion on Youth, Crime and Race: A Guide for Advocates." Available at www.buildingblocksforyouth.org.

Sprott, J. 1996. "Understanding Public Views of Youth Crime and the Youth Justice System." *Canadian Journal of Criminology* 38:271–90.

———. 1998. "Understanding Public Opposition to a Separate Youth Justice System." *Crime and Delinquency* 44:399–411.

Sprott, J., and A. N. Doob. 2000. "Bad, Sad, and Rejected: The Lives of Aggressive Children." *Canadian Journal of Criminology* 42:123–33.

Stalans, L. 2002. "Measuring Attitudes to Sentencing." In *Changing Attitudes to Punishment: Findings from around the Globe,* edited by J. V. Roberts and M. Hough. Cullompton, U.K.: Willan.

Stalans, L., and G. Henry. 1994. "Societal Views of Justice for Adolescents Accused of Murder." *Law and Human Behavior* 18:675–96.

Steinhart, D. 1988. *Public Attitudes on Youth Crime.* Washington, D.C.: National Council on Crime and Delinquency.

Sunday Times. London, April 28, 2002, p. A15.

Tonry, M. 1995. *Malign Neglect.* New York: Oxford University Press.

———. 2001. "Symbol, Substance, and Severity in Western Penal Policies." *Punishment and Society* 3:517–36.

Triplett, R. 1996. "The Growing Threat: Gangs and Juvenile Offenders." In *Americans View Crime and Justice: A National Public Opinion Survey,* edited by T. Flanagan and D. Longmire. Thousand Oaks, Calif.: Sage.

Tufts, J., and J. V. Roberts. 2002. "Sentencing Juvenile Offenders: Comparing Public Preferences and Judicial Practice." *Criminal Justice Policy Review* 13: 46–64.

Weisheit, R., and R. Culbertson, comps. 1985. *Juvenile Delinquency: A Justice Perspective.* Prospect Heights, Ill.: Waveland.

Winterdyk, J., ed. 1997. *Juvenile Justice Systems: International Perspectives.* Toronto: Canadian Scholars' Press.

Woolard, J., M. Fondacaro, and C. Slobogin. 2001. "Informing Juvenile Justice Policy: Directions for Behavioral Science Research." *Law and Human Behavior* 25:13–24.

Young, M., and J. Gainsborough. 2000. *Prosecuting Juveniles in Adult Court: An Assessment of Trends and Consequences.* Washington, D.C.: Sentencing Project.

Zimring, F. 1998. *American Youth Violence.* New York: Oxford University Press.

———. 1999. "The 1990s Assault on Juvenile Justice: Notes from an Ideological Background." *Federal Sentencing Reporter* 11:260–61.

———. 2001. "Imprisonment Rates and the New Politics of Criminal Punishment." *Punishment and Society* 3:161–66.

Lode Walgrave

Restoration in Youth Justice

ABSTRACT

Except in New Zealand, restorative justice programs and values remain at
the fringes of Western youth justice systems. Restorative justice shows
potential for gaining a much larger role. Research shows that programs
typically gain higher levels of victim and offender satisfaction than
traditional approaches, achieve impressively high rates of completion of
offenders' agreed obligations, and take better account of victims',
offenders', and community interests. Research evidence on reoffending
rates and on community effects points toward positive outcomes and does
not point toward worse outcomes than existing justice system approaches.
Restorative justice is more amenable to incorporating procedural fairness
and proportionality than are rehabilitative juvenile justice approaches.
Nearly every Western justice system incorporates restorative justice
programs and values for some young offenders, typically for less serious
offenses, but there is no reason why they need be limited to young
offenders or minor crimes.

Youth justice systems all over the world are under pressure from an
ongoing debate on the balance between treatment and punishment in
the response to youth crime. The discussion is repetitive and dead-
locked. The main reason is the limitation in possible alternatives. The
emergence of restorative justice may open new possibilities.

In the 1980s, restorative justice was barely known. According to Van
Ness and Strong (2002), the phrase was launched by Eglash (1977).
The ideas it encompassed circulated then among a few practitioners
and academics, who seemed to ground their vision on nostalgic and
utopian ideas and on a few experiments of anecdotal significance only.
Much has changed since then. Restorative justice has become a source

Lode Walgrave is professor of law and director of the Research Group Juvenile Criminology, Katholieke Universiteit Leuven, Belgium.

of renovating practices and empirical evaluation, a central issue in theoretical and policy debates, and a ubiquitous theme in juvenile justice and criminal justice reforms worldwide.

Restorative practices have been inserted in different degrees into most systems of responding to crime, especially youth crime. In the maximalist ambition of some advocates, this is a step toward full-fledged systemic restorative responses to crime. Others consider the maximalist option far too ambitious. They see restorative justice as a basis for diversions or alternate sanctions, do not believe that restorative practices can be applied to serious crimes, and are skeptical about the possibilities of combining restorative practices with legal safeguards.

This essay examines this discussion. It first considers why existing juvenile justice systems are under criticism. This section indicates problems and criticisms to which any reform of juvenile justice must find satisfying responses. The restorative justice option is then presented in the second section, which outlines both its potential and the unanswered questions. The third section brings together the ideas developed in the first and the second sections, describing how restorative practices have been included in existing juvenile justice systems and exploring the potential of the restorative justice approach. The conclusion reflects on the conditions on which the further incorporation of restorative ideas in juvenile justice systems will depend.

I. The Treatment Model
The legal history of juvenile justice began at the turn of the last century with the establishment of Chicago's Juvenile Court in 1899. Two decades later, most states and countries in North America, in Europe, and all over the world had separate jurisdictions and laws for children who committed an offense (Dünkel and Meyer 1986; Mehlbye and Walgrave 1998; Winterdyk 2002). These new systems resulted from profound social and cultural changes. Developments in medical and social sciences and industrialization supported widespread beliefs in social development and in the solubility of social and personal problems. This influenced both the conceptualization of juvenile misconduct and social reactions to it. An instrumentalist approach emerged, based on ideas about "the best interests of the child." Most new responses to youth crime focused more on treatment, reeducation, or rehabilitation—on the welfare of the young offender—than on determining ap-

propriate punishments for offenses. Two kinds of justifications were advanced.

First, children and adolescents were viewed as less able to understand the wrongfulness of their act, which reduced their guilt. As a consequence, they deserved no, or reduced, punishment. Complete absence of understanding is assumed for children under a certain age, who are therefore not punished but referred to the welfare system. Many systems currently fix the age threshold at twelve, some at much lower ages. Others do not provide for punishment before sixteen or in principle even eighteen (as in Belgium). If punishable, children and adolescents receive less severe punishments. In Italy or in France, for example, the maximum possible punishment for juveniles is a fixed proportion of the maximum that can be imposed on adults, because of the *excuse de minorité* (excuse of minority; Mehlbye and Walgrave 1998).

Second, offending by children and adolescents was seen as an indication of adverse socialization, which could be corrected. Children and adolescents were seen as more malleable by treatment or reeducation, and this opportunity should be taken. The main function of the juvenile justice system should be the social integration of the offender. "It was to focus on the child or adolescent as a person in need of assistance, not on the act that brought him or her before the court. The proceedings were informal, with much discretion left to the juvenile court judge" (McCord, Spatz Widom, and Crowell 2001, p. 154). The Belgian director general of the Administration for Youth Protection observed that there is "no need anymore to be puzzled by the circumstances or coincidences that have brought the child before the judge rather than before a psychiatrist" (Huynen 1967, p. 202).

Juvenile justice systems built on these beliefs were seldom challenged until the end of the 1960s. By then, economic expansion had slowed and appeared to add to human alienation and to produce harmful ecological side effects. The social and cultural consensus gradually lost its hegemonic power. In juvenile justice, the consensus about the pursuit of the best interest of the child weakened, along with belief in the clinical sciences. Children's rights and related movements sought procedural reforms of the juvenile justice systems.

Things continued to change after the 1960s. Economic, demographic, social, and cultural changes led to more migration, greater diversity, increasing urbanization, less tolerance, and greater insecurity. Youth crime changed in type and in volume. The rehabilitative approach came to seem naive. These developments led to four clusters of criticism, which will be the four main touchstones in our reflections on the potentials of restorative justice later in this essay.

A. Effectiveness

The emergence of juvenile justice was a triumph of instrumental thinking about responses to crime. It was believed that treatment-oriented courts could help endangered youths become conforming and useful citizens. From the beginning of the twentieth century, clinical and sociological research was undertaken on juveniles, known by the courts as "delinquents," in order to "unravel juvenile delinquency" (as in the title of the volume by Glueck and Glueck [1950]). Social work, educational programs, and clinical treatments sought to correct the deviant development of youthful offenders (Rothman 1980; Walgrave 1993). Juvenile justice served as a laboratory for scientific and treatment activities on youthful offending, which dominated criminology though the 1960s.

In the 1960s and 1970s, severe criticisms emerged. The courts and treatment programs appeared to be biased by social and ideological prejudices to the disadvantage of the poor and ethnic minorities (Platt 1969; Chamboredon 1971; Schur 1973; Lascoumes 1977; Schlossman 1977). Evaluations of treatments did not produce encouraging results (Bailey 1966; Greenberg 1977; Sechrest, White, and Brown 1979; Cornejo 1981). Some studies pointed to negative results, which were explained mostly through labeling theory. As a result, many programs sought to divert juveniles from court procedures (Lemert 1971). Diversion, however, appeared often to lead to net widening and to leave court interventions untouched (Albrecht and Ludwig-Mayerhofer 1995; McCord, Spatz Widom, and Crowell 2001, pp. 167–76).

Pessimism about treatment programs has become more nuanced in the past two decades. A series of metaevaluations known as "what works research" offers a more complicated picture than the blunt "nothing works" (Martinson 1974). These studies suggest that under some conditions (proper staff training and expertise, proper implementation and assessment), some programs work (Whitehead and Lab 1989; Palmer 1991; McGuire and Priestley 1995; Lipsey and Wilson 1998).

Cognitive-behavioral programs such as behavioral therapy, relaxation techniques, or social skills trainings, for example, produce partly positive outcomes, estimated by some as a 10–12 percent reduction of reoffending (McGuire and Priestley 1995). Programs that promote structure and taking personal responsibility appear to be more effective than others. However, it is difficult to generalize these conclusions. First, the studies measure only quantifiable aspects of the interventions and seldom include context-oriented interventions, such as community building and its influences on social environment. Second, the evaluations are carried out mostly on experiments in optimal conditions: strong research designs, pioneering enthusiasm, charismatic leaders, and unusually good cooperation from police and the judiciary. The step toward routine practices generally seriously reduces the gains of the evaluated programs. Third, the metanalyses also reveal a great range of problems that underlie different crime patterns, requiring a diversity of appropriate treatment programs. A treatment-oriented system thus requires diagnostic capacities for matching young people to appropriate programming. The feasibility of such capacity is still to be demonstrated. Finally, the "what works" analyses do not address fundamental questions about the ethical acceptability of lengthy and intensive restrictions of liberty, which often seem disproportionate to the modest seriousness of the offenses committed, and which are of doubtful efficiency.

Questions thus remain on the generalizability of treatments, on how far the judicial setting helps or hinders these programs, and on how programs can be combined with adequate legal safeguards. That specific treatment programs work for specific groups does not mean that the rehabilitation-oriented juvenile justice system as a whole is effective.

The challenge for restorative justice is twofold. It must develop its own effectiveness criteria, including the interests of victims and communities, and it must achieve effects on offenders that are not worse than those of existing rehabilitative programs.

B. Legal Safeguards

"Because the judge was to act in the best interest of the child, procedural safeguards available to adults . . . were thought unnecessary" (McCord, Spatz Widom, and Crowell 2001, p. 154). As long as a consensus ideology on child raising prevailed, legal safeguards were displaced by clinical diagnosis and confidence in the juvenile court judge's attachment to commonly held beliefs. Critical criminology and the antipsychiatry movement, however, exposed cultural and socioeconomic bias in the clinical evidence and commonly held beliefs. Juvenile courts widened the net of social control, which was especially detrimental to the most disadvantaged parts of the population (Platt 1969; Schur 1973; Van de Kerchove 1976–77; Lascoumes 1977). The U.S. decision *In re Gault* (387 U.S. 1 1967) focused awareness on a need for greater legal safeguards for children. *Gault* resonated far beyond U.S. borders (van Sloun 1988; Kaiser 1997).

Children's rights movements launched the "4 D's" slogan (decriminalization, diversion, due process, and deinstitutionalization; Empey 1976). International organizations promoted conventions and basic principles regarding dealing with children in general and in court. The United Nations Standard Minimum Rules for the Administration of Juvenile Justice (1985) are now widely seen as a crucial guide. The so-called Beijing Rules provide a series of clear statements about minimum standards for judicial interventions against juveniles (Doek 1994). But they reflect a fundamental ambivalence. For example, it is easy to state that the judicial reaction "should be in proportion to both the offender and the offense" (statement 5.1), but it is far from evident in practice how to achieve both proportionalities. And it is unclear how to "allow appropriate scope for discretion at all stages of proceedings" (statement 6.1) and to assure "the principles of fair and just trial" (statement 14.1). These rules are what is called in French a *mystification du language* (Van de Kerchove 1976–77), a pleasing rhetoric that hides its lack of feasibility.

"In practice, there was always a tension between social welfare and social control—that is, focusing on the best interests of the individual child versus focusing on punishment, incapacitation, and protecting society from certain offenses. This tension has shifted over time and has varied significantly from jurisdiction to jurisdiction, and it remains today" (McCord, Spatz Widom, and Crowell 2001, p. 154). This tension is inevitable because juvenile justice jurisdictions try to combine what cannot be combined satisfactorily. Basing sentencing on the needs of the offender rather than on the characteristics of the offense inevitably erases enforceable limits on judicial intervention. The judgment is passed in view of achieving resocializing aims in the future and is less (or not) based on available checkable characteristics of the offense committed. This "prospectiveness" in the reaction to juvenile crime (van Sloun 1988; Feld 1993) and its extension with preventionist ambitions make the juvenile justice system "unsatiable" (Braithwaite and Pettit 1990) because needs for treatment and prevention are infinitely large. Traditional legal safeguards are hard to combine with it. They are based on retrospection, looking backwards to the offense, as a yard-stick for measuring the permissible degree of restriction of freedom.

Some writers argue for reaffirming procedural rights for juvenile of-fenders by adhering to traditional principles of penal justice. Some would abolish the separate youth court and subject all who commit of-fenses, juveniles and adults, to the same punitive criminal justice sys-tem. The offender's youth would be no more than a mitigating factor (Feld 1999a). While the aim is to preserve the rights of young offend-ers by requiring the observance of procedural safeguards, it risks greater punitiveness. The question for restorative justice will be whether it can provide better legal safeguards without greater punitive-ness. Can legal safeguards be uncoupled from a punitive criminal jus-tice approach?

C. Harsher Responses to Youth Crime

An authoritative Belgian lawyer once obtained general approval for the proposition that the child "has one right only, being the right to be educated, and one duty only, being the duty to be docile in the hands of his educator" (Dabin 1947, p. 13). Since then, the image of childhood and adolescence has fundamentally changed from depen-dent and vulnerable to autonomous and responsible (Verhellen 1989; Meeus et al. 1992). Children and adolescents have more room in which to determine their own lives and more rights to claim respect for their options and interests. This emancipatory view, of course, is also ap-plied to youthful offending. Juveniles who commit offenses increas-ingly are seen not as helpless objects in need of reeducation or treat-ment but as persons who are accountable for their misbehavior. This may be seen in the increasing tendencies toward both restorative re-sponses and greater punitiveness.

This is especially true of juvenile crime that is patterned, organized, premeditated, and violent. The media contributes to the dramatization of urban juvenile crime and creates the image of "young predators," dangerous individuals who are uncontrollable threats to our posses-sions and our lives (Singer 1996). In such a climate, the need for risk management becomes apparent and inevitably is mixed with a retribu-tive just-deserts approach. Added to the just-mentioned (partial) failure of the treatment model, it provides arguments for stricter, harsher, and more incapacitative responses to youth crime—more referrals to adult courts; more and longer detention; and legislation allowing severer and longer sentences (Feld 1999a; McCord, Spatz Widom, and Crowell

2001). Although this is most evident in the United States, it can be observed in most countries (Schüler-Springorum 1999; see also most country chapters in this volume).

However, no valid empirical evidence supports the belief in the crime-preventive effectiveness of harsher punishments. The effectiveness of punishment for improving public safety has never been demonstrated, either through general deterrence (Lab 1992; Sherman 1993; Nagin 1998) or through individual treatment (Lipsey 1995; McGuire and Priestley 1995). Moreover, the a priori position that crime must be punished is ethically questionable (Fatić 1995; Keijser 2000; Walgrave 2003), because it is increasingly clear that censuring crime may also proceed through alternative processes and procedures oriented toward reparation.

Neither the consequentionalist nor the retributivist arguments justify a return to greater punitiveness. Punishment may incapacitate some violent offenders, but the need for incapacitation applies only to a very reduced minority of offenders. Penal procedures may offer decent legal safeguards to arrested juveniles, but they may not be the only way to offer such safeguards.

D. Victims' Needs and Interests

Victims' movements since the 1970s have heavily criticized the criminal justice system. Criminal procedure is focused on assessing the criminal act and culpability and on defining the penalty. Victims are often (mis)used as witnesses in the criminal investigation and then left alone with their grievances and losses (Wright 1999). Many undergo secondary victimization by the criminal justice system (Shapland, Willmore, and Duf 1985). This is also true in youth courts.

The rehabilitative view of youth justice may be detrimental to victims' interests. To protect the young, judges sometimes screen the offender from the victim's anger and claims for restitution or compensation based on the concern that these would be too severe and too hard. Under pressure from victims' movements, the relation between the victim and criminal justice is under reassessment almost everywhere (Goodey 2000). Efforts are under way to improve the experiences of complaining victims at many levels and in many places (Crawford and Goodey 2000).

One spin-off is increasing experimentation with victim-offender mediation and conferencing, educative programs with special attention to victimization, judicial compensation, and restitution orders. In their limited versions, these experiments remain subordinate to rehabilitation or punishment rationales. Only less serious crimes are usually referred to mediation programs, thereby excluding victims of serious crimes who may need them the most. These experiments, however, are among the most vigorous foundations for the redevelopment of restorative justice.

II. Restorative Justice

Restorative justice is deeply rooted in "human thought grounded in traditions of justice from the ancient Arab, Greek, and Roman civilizations . . . the restorative approach of the public assemblies of the Germanic peoples . . . Indian Hindus . . . and ancient Buddhist, Taoist, and Confucian traditions" (Braithwaite 2002, p. 3). The fall of the ancient versions of restorative justice coincided with the establishment of central power, transforming crime from a wrong done to another person into a transgression of the king's law (Weitekamp 1999). The restorative response model reemerged during the 1980s and became an important factor in practice and policy in the 1990s.

It is difficult to delimit restorative justice because its impetus comes from multiple origins (Faget 1997; Van Ness and Strong 2002). The victims' movements claimed an expanded role and demanded outcomes that were more focused on reparation (Peters and Aertsen 1995; Young 1995). Feminist movements drew attention to feminine aspects of primary and secondary victimization (Harris 1990). Critical criminology emphasized the negative effects of the criminal justice system and its inability to assure peace in social life. Many adherents of restorative justice consider it an alternative to criminal justice as a whole (de Haan 1990; van Swaaningen 1997) or to juvenile justice more specifically (Walgrave 1995; Bazemore and Walgrave 1999). Communitarians advocate the revival of community as the organic resource of informal mutual support and control, seeing communities as means and ends for restorative justice. Part of communitarianism is rooted in indigenous emancipation movements (Corrado and Griffiths 1999) or in religion (Zehr 1990).

Given its diverse roots and current forms, it is not surprising that restorative justice appears somewhat confused. It is now a complex domain, covering a wide realm of practices. It is a challenging subject for legal and normative reflection and debate and a fruitful field for theorizing and empirical research. Restorative justice is also a social movement of believers. Adding to the confusion are apparently similar movements under banners like transformative justice, relational justice, community justice, peacemaking justice, and the like. All express a general tendency that I call here "restorative justice."[1]

Only recently have practitioners and researchers recognized a fundamental commonality underlying most versions of mediation, conferencing, and circles. Unsurprisingly, no generally accepted definition of restorative justice exists (McCold 1998). Based on an earlier definition by Bazemore and myself (1999, p. 48), by restorative justice I mean "an option on doing justice after the occurrence of a crime which gives priority to repairing the harm that has been caused by that crime."

This clearly is outcome-based. Most "restorativists" prefer a process-based definition (Zehr 1990; Boyes-Watson 2000; McCold 2000). Marshall's often-quoted definition is typical: "Restorative justice is a process whereby all the parties with a stake in a particular offense come together to resolve collectively how to deal with the aftermath of the offense and its implications for the future" (1996, p. 37). Marshall does not require that the outcome be restorative (and not purely punitive or rehabilitative, for example) and excludes initiatives that may lead to restorative outcomes without parties coming together (as in victim support). In my view, restoration is the goal, and voluntary processes are means only, though crucial ones. Process-based definitions confuse the means with the goal and limit the possible means to achieve (partial) restoration. Deliberative processes appear to hold the highest potentials for achieving restoration, but if voluntary agreements cannot be accomplished, coercive obligations in pursuit of (partial) reparation must be encompassed in the restorative justice model.

This section comments on three basic elements in the definition I offered: harm (Sec. II*A*), restoration (Sec. II*B*), and doing justice (Sec. II*C*). It examines the socioethical foundations of restorative justice (Sec. II*D*) and draws conclusions on its practical feasibility (Sec. II*E*).

A. Harm

A focus on repairing harm and not on what should be done to the offender is the key to understanding restorative justice and is what distinguishes it from punitive and rehabilitative justice approaches. That is why it is presented as another paradigm (Zehr 1990; Bazemore and Walgrave 1999; McCold 2000). It offers a distinctive "lens," in Zehr's

---

[1] The presentation of restorative justice in this essay thus cannot but be my personal view. In some respects, as I try to make clear, it deviates from "mainstream" restorative justice options.

term, for defining the problem caused by crime and for solving it. Crime is defined by the harm it causes and not by its transgression of a legal order. The primary function of responses to it should be neither to punish nor to rehabilitate the offender but to set the conditions for repairing as much as possible the harm caused. Restorative justice thus can go a long way without an offender involved. If the offender is not caught, while the harm caused is assessed, (partial) justice can be done by trying to repair or compensate the victim and by restoring public assurance that the crime is not acceptable. However, as we shall see, it remains important to involve the offender in formulating the aftermath of the offense.

1. *Limits to the Harm Considered.*   Harm includes the material damage, psychological and relational suffering by the victim, social unrest and community indignation, uncertainty about legal order and about authorities' capacity to assure public safety, and the social damage the offender causes to himself.[2]

The only limitation is that the harm considered by the restorative process must be that caused by the particular offense. This positions restorative justice as a reactive option, "a way of responding to crimes which have been already committed" (Johnstone 2002, p. 19). Not all restorative justice adherents would accept this limitation. Some writers believe that restorative processes should address underlying causes of offending (Masters and Roberts 2000). Some conditions, like social exclusion or psychological problems of the offender, are not caused by the offense but may be among its causes. In my view, including offenders' broader needs in the restorative justice reaction is a dangerous option. It blurs the contrast with the rehabilitative approach and risks shifting from a harm-focused to an offender-focused program (Braithwaite 1999). It would also degrade the victim into being a tool in service of the offender's rehabilitation and not recognize the victim as a party on his own. Problems and needs of the offender are important elements in the search for reasonable restorative outcomes, but they are not the subject of the restoration itself.

The offender is not involved primarily because something must be done to him, but because this will serve the goal of restoration. Positive influences on the offender are a secondary objective only. The kind and amount of obligation is decided primarily by the needs of reason-

---

[2] The male form is used as the general form. This is done not to be politically incorrect, but as a practical solution to a practical problem.

able restoration, not by needs for adequate treatment or proportionate punishment.

2. *From Collective Harm to Intrusion upon Dominion.*   Restorative justice addresses more than the harm to the individual victim. It is not limited to settling a tort according to civil law but deals with crimes, which are also public events, traditionally dealt with by criminal law. It is difficult to come to grips with this public aspect of crime-caused harm (Thorvaldson 1990; Van Ness 1990; Walgrave 1999). Distinctions between "communities of care" and the broader community (Braithwaite and Daly 1994), or among "affected communities," "local communities," and "society" (McCold 2000), do not resolve the problem.

What makes an offense a collective or public event? A burglary, for example, is a private and a public affair. Restitution of or compensation for the individual victim's losses could be private, to be arranged by civil law. But there is also a public side. We all are concerned that authorities intervene and try to make things right. The particular victim stands as an example of risks all citizens face. If the authorities do nothing, it hurts all citizens' trust in their right to privacy and property.

This leads to a crucial concept: "dominion," as introduced by Braithwaite and Pettit (1990) in their "republican theory of criminal justice." Dominion can be understood as the set of assured rights and freedoms. "Freedom as non-domination" (or dominion)[3] is the mental and social territory in which we freely move, guaranteed by the state and the social environment. The assurance of rights and freedoms is crucial.[4] "I know that I have rights, I know that the others know it, and I trust that they will respect it." I am assured only if I trust that my fellow citizens and the state will take my rights and freedoms seriously. Only then can I fully enjoy my mental and social territory.

That assurance provides the crucial distinction between the social concept of "freedom as non-domination" and the liberal concept of

---

[3] In later publications, "dominion" has been renamed as "freedom as non-domination." It may make it easier to oppose it to the liberal concept typified as "freedom as non-interference," but I see no other advantage in complicating the wording. I therefore use the "old" term, "dominion."

[4] See also what Putnam (1993) called "trust" in social capital. Social capital is defined as "features of social organization such as trust, norms and networks, that can improve the efficiency of society by facilitating coordinated actions" (1993, p. 167). Trust is crucial. Putnam does not limit trust to "thick trust" based on strong ties with family, friends, and close neighbors. The strongest social capital lies in the generalized trust based on weak ties with social organizations and the generalized other. It is this trust that constitutes our assurance of rights and freedoms.

"freedom as non-interference." In the latter, the rights and freedoms of the individual citizen end where the rights and freedoms of the other citizen begin. Rights and freedoms are conceived as a stable given, which must be divided as justly as possible among citizens. Every other citizen is a possible interferer in my freedom and a rival in my struggle to expand my freedom. In the republican view, on the contrary, rights and freedoms are a collective good. "Dominion" is not a stable given but a value to be promoted and expanded by individual and collective action. The other citizen is an ally in trying to extend and mutually assure dominion as a collective good.

In this theory, crime is an intrusion upon dominion, and especially on the assurance of rights and freedoms. The burglary does not diminish the existing legal rights of privacy and property, but the extent to which the victim and his fellow citizens are assured that these rights are respected and taken seriously. Public intervention after a crime is primarily needed to enhance assurance by communicating the authorities' public disapproval of the norm transgression and by responding through their action in view of restoration. It makes clear that authorities take dominion seriously. The intervention reassures the victim, the public, and the offender of their set of rights and freedoms. Involving the offender in these actions, if possible, is important because it demonstrates the responsibilities and enhances the restorative impact of the action. Voluntary cooperation by the offender is more effective to restore assurance, but only if it is backed by public institutions. The assurance comes not primarily from the individual offender's repentance and apologies, but from the authorities' determination to take the assured set of rights and freedoms seriously.

B. Ways of Restoration

Different processes may lead to a restorative outcome, but not all processes are equally appropriate for it. The main distinction is between voluntary processes and coercive procedures.

1. *Deliberative Restoration.* Most suitable are processes that consist of voluntary deliberation between the victim and the offender, the main stakeholders. Many deliberative processes are known today (McCold 2001; Morris and Maxwell 2001), including mediations between the individual victim and offender, most of which are face-to-face, but some intermediated by a go-between (Umbreit 1994; European Forum 2000); various forms of conferencing in which the victim and offender are supported by their communities of care, some of

which also include participation by police or community representatives (Hudson et al. 1996; Masters and Roberts 2000; Daly 2001; Dignan and Marsh 2001); and sentencing circles, in which the local indigenous community as a whole is a part of the meeting on the occasion of a crime in its midst (Lilles 2001). Such sessions may happen once only or consist of a series of meetings.

Well-conducted restorative processes offer a powerful sequence of moral and social emotions and exchanges like shame, guilt, remorse, empathy, compassion, support, apology, and forgiveness in the offender, the victim, and other participants (Braithwaite 1989; Braithwaite and Mugford 1994; Maxwell and Morris 1999; Walgrave and Braithwaite 1999; Harris 2001). This "encounter" (Van Ness and Strong 2002) may lead to a common understanding of the harm and suffering caused and to an agreement on how to make amends. It may enhance the willingness of the offender to fulfill these agreements. It may lead to satisfaction of the victim, reintegration of the offender, and restored assurance of rights and freedoms in society. Such a sequence is of course the ideal, which is often far from being fully achieved. Even the claimed voluntariness to participate may be seriously reduced by social pressure or subtle threat (Boyes-Watson 2000).

Some identify restorative justice with such processes. Regardless of its outcome, they claim that the process itself has the most powerful restorative impact. However, this may push the difference between process and outcome too far. Why would such a process be more restorative? Because the expressions of remorse, compassion, apology, and forgiveness promote feelings of respect, peace, and satisfaction? These feelings are outcomes, even if they are not explicitly written down in the final agreement. Thus, it seems impossible to evaluate restorative processes without taking account of the restorative outcomes they explicitly or implicitly promote.

The agreement after such processes may include a wide range of actions like restitution, compensation, reparation, reconciliation, and apologies. They may be direct or indirect, concrete or symbolic. The degree of the offender's willingness to undertake such actions is crucial. It expresses his understanding of the wrong committed and his willingness to make up for it. For the victim, it means the restoration of his citizenship as a bearer of rights, and possibly also a partial material redress. For the larger community, it contributes to assurance that the offender takes rights and freedoms seriously and will respect them in the future. Even the offender's agreement to undergo a treatment has a restorative meaning that expresses his recognition of a problem that he wants to resolve in accordance with his social environment.

2. *Imposed Restoration.* There will always be cases in which voluntary processes cannot be achieved or are judged to be insufficient. Pressure or coercion on the offender must then be considered. According to the maximalist view of restorative justice, these coercive interventions also should serve restoration (Claassen 1995; Walgrave 2000*a*; Dignan 2002). In a constitutional democracy, coercion may only be exerted through a judicial procedure, but these procedures can be oriented to obligations or sanctions with a restorative significance. Examples are material restitution or compensation to the victim, paying a fine to the benefit of a victims' fund, or community service. Although these judicially imposed obligations can have an explicit restorative meaning (Wright 1996; Dignan 2002; Walgrave 2003), their restorative impact will be reduced. Restorative justice is not a black-and-white option. Between the fully restorative processes and the not-at-all-restorative reactions, degrees of restorativeness exist (McCold 2000; Dignan 2002; Van Ness 2002).

Enforced restorative sanctions, imposed according to judicial procedures and as a result of assessed accountability for the consequences of offending, seem to leave few or no differences between such sanctions and traditional punishments (Daly 2000; McCold 2000; Johnstone 2002). There are, however, essential differences (Walgrave 2000*a*, 2001, 2003).

First, punishment is a means in the eyes of law enforcement, and it is "morally neutral." It does not issue any message about the moral value of the enforced law itself. For example, in some political regimes, punishment is used to enforce very criticizable or even immoral laws. Restoration, on the contrary, is a goal, and different means can be chosen to achieve it. Moreover, the goal of restoration itself expresses an orientation toward the quality of peaceful social life, which is an intrinsic moral orientation. The a priori position that crime has to be punished is thus counterproductive as a means for achieving restoration.

Second, "punishing someone consists of visiting a deprivation (hard treatment) on him, because he supposedly has committed a wrong" (von Hirsch 1993, p. 9). The pain is intentionally inflicted. An obligation aimed at restoration may be painful but is not inflicted with the intention to cause suffering. It may be a secondary effect only (Wright 1996). Painfulness in punishment is the primary yardstick, while painfulness in restorative obligations is a secondary consideration only.

Third, intentional infliction of pain "involves actions that are generally considered to be morally wrong or evil were they not described and justified as punishments" (Keijser 2000, p. 7). Retributivist and instrumentalist justifications of criminal punishments (von Hirsch 1998) do not convincingly demonstrate the need for systemic punishment. The a priori position that crime must be punished is itself dubious from an ethical standpoint. Thorough exploration is thus needed regarding alternative ways to express blame, to favor repentance, and to promote social peace and order (Fatić 1995).

Restorative justice proponents claim that their approach is more promising in that respect. Deliberative processes, if possible, or imposed obligations in view of restoration, if necessary, make more sense. Acts are criminalized because they cause victimization and disturb public life; the social reaction should thus primarily aim at redressing the victimization and the disturbance. Restorative justice is also socially more constructive: it does not respond to harm caused by the offense by inflicting further harm on the offender, which after all "only adds to the total amount of harm in the world" (Wright 1992, p. 525), but by aiming at repair of the harm caused. Finally, restorativists consider it ethically more acceptable to aim at (imposing) restoration than deliberately to inflict pain.

C. Doing Justice

Restorative justice not only is about restoration, it is also about justice. The notion of "justice" has two meanings here. One is justice as the outcome of an ethical evaluation; the other is justice as respecting legal rights and freedoms.

1. *Ethical Justice.* "Justice" refers to a feeling of equity, of being dealt with fairly, according to a moral balance of rights and wrongs, benefits, and burdens. In retributive justice, this balance is achieved by imposing suffering on the offender that is commensurate to the social harm he caused by his crime. In restorative justice, the balance is restored by taking away or compensating the suffering and harm caused by the crime. Restorative justice then aims at achieving "procedural fairness" (Tyler 1990) and satisfaction (Van Ness and Schiff 2001) for all parties involved. Victims feel that their victimization has been taken seriously and that the compensation and support are reasonably in balance with their sufferings and losses. Offenders experience that their dignity has not unnecessarily been hurt and that they are given the opportunity to make up for their mistake in a constructive way.

All participants, including the community, feel reassured that rights and freedoms are taken seriously by fellow citizens and the authorities.

The best way to guarantee that losses are well-understood and the methods of reparation are adequate is to leave the decision to those with a direct stake: victims, offenders, and others directly affected. "Justice" is what those concerned experience as such. This bottom-up approach is crucial in restorative justice and contrasts with the top-down approach of the criminal justice system.

However, the state cannot withdraw completely. If it did, it would leave the parties alone to find a solution. State authorities would not guarantee respect for rights and freedoms and, thus, would not assure dominion. To give assurance, the state must guarantee that everything possible will be done to respect and restore the intruded-on dominion. In a voluntary restorative deliberation, the state must be present at least in the background to assure that the deliberation takes place and results in an acceptable outcome, to guarantee the power balance in the deliberation, and to provide an opportunity to the parties to leave the deliberative process and turn to the traditional judicial response if one of them feels that their interests are not adequately acknowledged in the deliberative process. That way, the state's rule of law percolates into restorative justice (Braithwaite and Parker 1999). Authorities demonstrate that they take dominion seriously not only with regard to the victim's rights and freedoms but also as a guarantor of the offender's rights and as a safeguard for the collectively assured set of rights and freedoms.

2. *Legal Justice.* Justice also encompasses legality. Restorative justice means that the processes and their outcomes respect legal safeguards (Van Ness 1996, 2000; Trépanier 1998; Walgrave 2000*b*; Dignan 2002). Legal safeguards protect citizens not only against illegitimate intrusions by fellow citizens but also by the state. This is obvious in coerced interventions, but it applies also in voluntary settlements. Participation may not be imposed. Agreements must be accepted by the parties and be reasonable in relation to the seriousness of the harm and to the parties' accountability and capacities. How to make sure rights are observed is a matter of debate among restorative justice proponents. Some rely fully on the potentials of communities (Pranis 2001) and try to reduce state control over restorative processes to a strict minimum out of fear of the state's power to invade the process and undo its informal, humane, and healing potentials. Others try

to find a balanced social and institutional context, which allows maximum space for genuine deliberative processes but also offers full opportunities for all parties to appeal to judicial agencies if they feel not respected in the process.

In a coercive procedure, all legal guarantees must be observed. In a traditional criminal justice procedure, safeguards like legality, due process, and proportionality are evident. The rights that they protect should be protected in coercive restorative interventions as well (Ashworth 1993; Warner 1994). However, as these principles are meant for a punishment-oriented system, it is not obvious that they should be applied unchanged in a system premised on restoration (Walgrave 2000*b*). The main function is different, the actors are partly different, and the social and judicial context is different. Contrary to the traditional top-down approach, a restorative system should allow ample space for a bottom-up approach. The role of the state must be limited to its core functions and be oriented to enhancing the opportunities for settling the aftermath of a crime constructively (Declaration of Leuven 1997). The rule of law must not only percolate down into restorative justice, as stated above, but restorative justice must also bubble up into the rule of law (Braithwaite and Parker 1999).

Thinking about a legal context that combines maximum space for deliberative conflict resolution with complete legal safeguards is only beginning (Walgrave 2002*c*; von Hirsch et al. 2003). Braithwaite speaks of "responsive regulation": "law enforcers should be responsive to how effectively citizens or corporations are regulating themselves before deciding whether to escalate intervention" (2002, p. 29). In Braithwaite's view, intervention after a crime should be planned according to a "regulatory pyramid," in which persuasion, or restorative processing, is the foundation, and incapacitation of "incompetent or irrational actors" is at the top. "What we want is a legal system where citizens learn that responsiveness is the way our legal institutions work. Once they see the legal system as a responsive regulatory system, they know there will be a chance to argue about unjust laws. . . . The forces of law are listening, fair and therefore legitimate, but also are seen as somewhat invincible" (Braithwaite 2002, p. 34).

Such an ideal presupposes responsible citizens in a society in which the state is at the service of the community or the communities. It is far from being achieved at the moment. That brings us to the next subsection.

D. Social Ethics

Restorative justice is more than a technical model of how to respond to crime. It is an ideal of justice in an idealized society. Concern for the broader quality of social life is the inspiring source of restorative justice.

The community occupies a focal position in restorative rhetoric (Bazemore and Schiff 2001). The priority of restoring harms caused by crime necessarily draws attention to social unrest suffered by the community. Restorative interventions require a minimum of "community": the victim and the offender must feel a minimal common interest. However, community as a concept poses great problems (Crawford 1996; Crawford and Clear 2001; Pavlich 2001; Walgrave 2002a). First, the "community" concept suggests a difference between what community is and what it is not, as if it were an ontological territorial or mental "area." It is hard to find the limitations. Community is too vague a concept to characterize and delimit a part of social reality adequately. Second, building on communities for developing restorative responses to crime, as many restorativists do, presupposes its general availability, which is far from being evident. It is difficult, for example, to mobilize community in the settlement of a street robbery in the city where the victim and offender live miles from each other and belong to completely different social networks. Third, leaving community as the loose concept that it is now makes it vulnerable to misuses and excesses. Community may contain "the seeds of parochialism which can lead . . . to atrocious totalitarian exclusions" (Pavlich 2001, p. 58), as has recently been demonstrated by ethnic wars and purges.

Skepticism about the concept of community need not result in rejection of the ideals communitarians promote: social unity, harmonious living based on shared values and beliefs, and mutual commitment. Most communitarians promote social ethics and values, not areas, as suggested by the community notion. "Community" is a container for ethical and social values. They should be unpacked from their container. While rejecting community as the container, "communitarianism" may be a useful label for a socioethical movement. It refers to the pursuit of a utopian social life in which the distinction between society and community is meaningless, because the collectivity would be governed in view of individual and collective emancipation in which autonomy and solidarity are not seen as opposed but as mutually reinforcing. Collective life would draw its strength not from top-down rules enforced by threat, coercion, and fear, but from bottom-up motivation based on trust, participation, and support. Elsewhere I have tried to show that such a view promotes social-ethical "guidelines" like respect, solidarity, and active responsibility and that these guidelines are better achieved through restorative justice than through the traditional criminal justice approach (Walgrave 2002*a*, 2003).

The communitarian option goes far beyond regulatory models of criminal justice. It penetrates how people interact and try to settle conflicts in everyday life (Wachtel and McCold 2001). It is implemented in problems in school contexts (Ahmed 2001) and in neighborhood conflicts (Peper and Spierings 1999). Its deliberative philosophy also applies to world peacemaking (Braithwaite 2002).

In a communitarian ideal, the state must act responsively. The state must respond to the reality of social life in order to serve the quality of that social life. The same communitarian ideal also substantiates the concept of "dominion" as the set of assured rights and freedoms to be promoted by the state. Dominion can be considered a formalization of the communitarian ideal into a political theory. The communitarian utopia can be achieved only if the state acts responsively in view of assuring and expanding dominion. Inversely, the assurance of rights and freedoms is achieved only to the degree that citizens accept active responsibility for respect and solidarity.

E. Empirical Evaluation

Sometimes, brilliant ideas are unrealistic or evolve into being terrible practices. An increasing stream of empirical research explores the extent to which restorative aspirations are achieved in reality.

1. *Methodological Issues.* The evaluation of interventions is precarious. It is difficult to compose appropriate control groups, to isolate and measure adequate evaluation criteria, and to prove the link between programs and observed outcomes. Much restorative justice research suffers from serious methodological shortcomings. Many evaluated practices are limited in scope or are carried out in exceptionally favorable circumstances. They seldom include process evaluations of the procedural quality of the practice. Despite these problems, several surveys of empirical evaluations suggest that restorative practices hold great promise. In general, projects for juveniles appear to achieve better results than those for adults.

2. *Results.* As there are many publications presenting empirical data, it is impossible to refer to all of them at every statement. I there-

fore draw on some of the available surveys (Braithwaite 1999; Schiff 1999; Umbreit 1999; Kurki 2003; McCold 2003) and concentrate on initiatives for juveniles.

Most programs find a majority of victims are willing to participate in mediation or in a conference. The variation in the proportion (between 90 percent and 32 percent, with an average of 60 percent; Umbreit 1999) depends, among other things, on the kind and seriousness of crime or on the way that the victims are invited to participate. The reasons for nonparticipation usually relate to its futility, like not wanting to spend another evening discussing the offense, not finding it worth investing more time, or last-minute cancellations. Maxwell and Morris (1996) found that only 4 percent of the refusals to participate in conferences were for principled or emotional reasons. Participation by juvenile offenders is very high, reaching a participation rate of between 87 percent and 92 percent (as in Hartmann and Stroezel 1996). Most surveys indicate agreement rates of over 80 percent, although some programs achieve much lower rates (as in Aertsen and Peters 1998).

Compliance with agreements is achieved in a great majority of cases, reaching more than nine out of ten, if partial compliance and compliance with difficulties are included (as in Hartmann and Stroezel 1996). The same figures apply for successful completion of community service for juveniles (Geudens 1996; Schiff 1999). Whereas the seriousness of the crime appears to be a complicating factor in all this, very serious crimes have been successfully dealt with through mediation or conferencing. New Zealand's experience, described by Allison Morris (in this volume), is illustrative. The first conclusion therefore must be that restorative responses are realistic, reaching more kinds of crimes and more serious crimes than originally expected.

All comparisons of victims' experiences find that victims who participated in a mediation or a conference had greater satisfaction than victims who were involved in traditional responses to crime. They say that they are better informed and supported, experienced more respect and equity, and appreciated the emotional opportunities (see, among others, Strang and Sherman 1997; McCold and Wachtel 1998; Strang 2002). The material restitution or compensation is considered important to them but is not as crucial as the emotional benefits. Even when the process does not lead to an agreement, the majority of victims still are more satisfied than those involved in a traditional judicial procedure. A small minority of victims feel worse after a restorative process.

This minority always is smaller in the restorative process group than in the justice system group.

During and after restorative interventions, offenders better understand the reason for the intervention than they do after a traditional juvenile justice procedure. They express feelings of "procedural justice" (Tyler 1990), feeling more fairly treated and seeming better able to accept the outcome of the process. More than after a traditional court session, offenders express respect for police and for the law and say that they will stop further offending (as in Sherman and Strang 1997). Research on recorded reoffending mostly reveals less recidivism in the "restorative justice group," but the differences are not always statistically significant. There is no research pointing to more reoffending.

The effects of the intensive use of restorative interventions on local communities and public safety have not been systematically researched (Kurki 2003). This might be because, except for New Zealand, restorative justice practices have not been implemented so extensively that one might expect observable changes in the community at large, or because it is difficult to construct measures of the impact of restorative justice on public life. Communitarian rhetoric proposes that restorative justice should be beneficial to the community and public life in general, and no data available so far lead to opposite conclusions.

Samples of lay respondents in several countries have presented options for responding to several crimes. A majority prefer responses that promote or allow for reparation. Sessar concludes that "the conception of the public's strong punitive sentiments is a myth" (1999, p. 301). Professional respondents, on the contrary, are more comfortable with traditional criminal justice responses and, thus, stick to their own approach.

3. *Conclusions.* Available data do not indicate that the ambitions of restorative justice proponents are unfeasible or counterproductive. Victims, offenders, and their communities mostly do come together and do reach constructive agreements, which are carried out reasonably well. Involved parties generally express higher degrees of satisfaction than they do with traditional approaches, and reoffending risks are mostly lower, and certainly not higher. Variations in outcomes depend on several variables. The seriousness of the crime is one of them, but even the most serious crimes can be dealt with restoratively. Another is the technical quality of the methodology in monitoring the restorative process. There are no indications that social life and public security are

adversely affected by restorative practices, and the public appears to support their implementation.

This optimistic summary must be accepted cautiously. The research results are provisional only and need expansion and improvement, strong methodologies for monitoring restorative interventions must be developed, and much theoretical and normative work is still to be done.

Even in the best possible circumstances, however, a purely restorative approach to all crimes will never be workable. Concerns for public safety, very recalcitrant offenders, and unreasonably vindictive victims may raise insuperable difficulties and oblige the use of other approaches, as set out in Braithwaite's "regulatory pyramid" (Braithwaite 2002; see also Dignan 2002; Walgrave 2002*b*). Indeed, the restorative justice option does not mean that all crimes, in all circumstances, must be dealt with restoratively. The restorative option should be the first to be considered, but it must sometimes be completed or replaced by other intervention models.

III. Restorative Foundations for Juvenile Justice?

Restorative justice appears to hold great potential generally, but particularly concerning juvenile justice. Here I examine the penetration of restorative approaches into the existing juvenile justice systems and then discuss how restorative justice might address the criticisms of juvenile justice, as mentioned in the first section of this essay.

A. Restorative Practices in Existing Youth Justice Systems

Many essays in this volume describe versions of victim-offender mediation, family group conferencing, and community service. Most were introduced by the end of the 1970s or at the beginning of the 1980s. Originally, they were seldom based explicitly on restorative justice premises but were offered with different rationales, such as providing diversions to unburden the traditional system, offering additional opportunities for victims, or providing more effective rehabilitation programs. The idea of restoration was, and often still is, secondary. The schemes nevertheless suggest how practices with a restorative dimension can be implemented in a legal context.

The brief survey here below is based on the chapters in this volume, and on two surveys, one by Miers (2001), who describes restorative practices in thirteen European countries, Australia, Canada, New Zealand, and the United States, and another by Schelkens (1998), who surveys restorative models in juvenile justice in the European Union, Norway, and Switzerland.

Restorative practices have been incorporated differently into the juvenile justice systems of the Anglo-Saxon countries, which are based on common-law principles, and European continental countries, which are based on civil law principles. Both models have important consequences for ways in which restorative justice practices can develop. Common-law regimes impose less strict procedural and sentencing rules. The police and the judiciary have considerable discretionary power, and large margins are provided for community input and debate. Victims and other community members play a role in the settlement, and there is room to experiment outside or at the margins of the judiciary. It is therefore no coincidence that most restorative justice experiments have emerged in common-law countries.

The legality principle that dominates the civil law systems on the European continent prescribes strict legal rules and allows a limited scope only for exercise of discretion. In principle, the police only record offenses and must refer every case to the public prosecutor, a professional judge who oversees the criminal investigation and decides whether to prosecute. The input of nonprofessional citizens is limited. This results in less flexible systems that are less permeable to innovation but offer solid grounds for safeguarding legal rights. As a consequence, it is Europeans especially who raise procedural and jurisprudential questions about restorative practices, most of which were "invented" in the Anglo-Saxon countries.

1. *Common-Law Countries.*   Morris's essay on New Zealand (in this volume) makes clear that the Children, Young Persons and Their Families Act (1989) provides ample space for restorative practices in dealing with youth crime. At the police level, cautioning often includes restitution or community service. The act is, however, most original in its inclusion of family group conferences, which must be offered for all young offenders (including multiple recidivists) and for all offenses, except for murder and manslaughter. The youth court judge cannot impose any measure or sanction unless a family group conference has been tried. New Zealand is therefore often represented as the "beacon" country with the most far-reaching restorative justice system for juveniles.

Nevertheless, there is no guaranteed priority for restorative approaches. The explicit governing principles of the act do not give priority to restoration. Rehabilitative aims are at least as important. In current practice, family group conferences appear to be inclusive and participatory, which is an important condition for implementing restorative justice, but not every family group conferencing process aims to achieve restoration. Morris's essay clearly indicates that participation by victims is limited and that many family group conferences aim at rehabilitation rather than at restoration. Implementing restorative justice thus needs not only a legal context but also the development of adequate strategies for quality control.

Several Australian states have incorporated conferencing in their juvenile justice legislation, but always as a diversionary program, leaving more serious youth crime to the traditional proceedings. The conferencing models and processes are different from those in New Zealand (Strang 2001; Power 2002).

Anthony Bottoms and Jim Dignan's essay (in this volume) shows that England and Wales were in 1982 among the very first countries to provide court-ordered community service as a sanction for young offenders. From the mid-1980s, many stand-alone mediation initiatives existed. In the Crime and Disorder Act (1998), juvenile justice legislation in England and Wales now authorizes restorative responses in mainstream reactions to youth crime. Police in preprosecution stages are explicitly encouraged to use restorative ideas in reprimands and final warnings in order to make them more meaningful and effective. The Youth Offender Teams for first-time convicted juveniles appear to function in a way that resembles restorative conferencing principles and pursued outcomes. For multiply convicted offenders, youth courts can impose orders with a restorative orientation, including reparation orders, action plan orders, and conditions of supervision orders.

At first sight, English police reprimands and warnings and the Youth Offender Teams bear resemblance to what happens in New Zealand. There are, however, crucial differences. First, the police interventions and the teams are explicitly addressed to nonserious offenders, whereas family group conferences in New Zealand apply to all offenders, with the exceptions of murder and manslaughter. Thus, the English programs are diversionary, whereas the restorative practices in New Zealand have penetrated much deeper into the "hard-core" response to youth crime. Second, though the Youth Offender Teams may be more inclusive and participatory than a traditional court session, the final decisions are taken by the panel, not by the participants. The participatory philosophy underlying restorative justice is thus far less achieved than in the New Zealand family group conferences in which the participants have the decisive power.

The situation in the United States is less clear and more disparate.[5] As of 1998, some twenty states included restorative ideas in the purpose clauses of their juvenile justice legislation. The United States offers an impressive number of local restorative justice initiatives by private agencies (Miers 2001; Bazemore and Schiff 2002). Mediation, conferencing, restitution, and community service are used in preprosecution stages by police or on referral by prosecutors, and there are also informal diversionary dispositions and postdispositional programs. Court-ordered restitution or community service is common in U.S. juvenile justice (Schneider 1986; Bazemore and Maloney 1994). It is, however, not always clear what that means in practice. Community service is often used in a clearly punitive way. Referrals to mediation or conferencing in many states are sporadic and are for the most part limited to minor offenses and first offenders. Many states seem more inclined to punitive responses to youth crime than to exploiting the new opportunities opened by restorative justice.

Through the victim-offender reconciliation program in Kitchener, Ontario (1974), Canada is one of the pioneering countries in restorative practices. Such practices have spread across the country (Miers 2001). Some are influenced by aboriginal populations who seek to reestablish traditional ways of dealing with crime and conflicts in their communities, and who inspired the emergence of "circles" as participatory, inclusive deliberation models (Jaccoud 1998). Nonetheless, Canadian federal youth criminal justice legislation is not very explicit on restorative issues, as Anthony Doob and Jane Sprott's essay (in this volume) demonstrates. In 1984, the Young Offenders Act highlighted the possibility of referral to diversion programs such as community service or restitution. The 1995 amendments allude to holding young offenders accountable to the victim and to society through noncustodial dispositions, which may be understood as an implicit reference to restorative values. The latest Youth Criminal Justice Act (2001), which allows for and encourages the use of community-based sentences and alternatives to the justice system for youth who commit nonviolent offenses, includes possibilities for several restorative practices. Moreover,

---

[5] Many thanks to Gordon Bazemore for additional information.

conferences are a possibility at all stages. These conferences are not, however, clearly defined and may in practice operate like the English Youth Offender Teams, the New Zealand family group conferences, or some other conferencing model; they may also take a completely different shape. They could operate in restorative ways, but this is far from assured. Earlier diversion programs remain in place. The several provinces will probably implement the new act differently. Quebec is likely, as it was before 2001, to make more use of nonjudicial and noncustodial approaches, based on its more rehabilitative traditions. Relatively well-developed mediation practices may shift in a more rehabilitative direction and lose their original restorative perspective (Charbonneau 1998).

Common-law countries thus use many discretionary methods to divert less serious offenders from formal prosecution. Police discretion appears to be crucial. Some laws explicitly favor voluntary restoration through processes like mediation or conferencing. Others merely allow for it. Court orders of restitution or community service are possible. How these programs are used in practice depends on local traditions, on available agencies, and on the social and cultural climate.

2. *Civil Law Countries.* Throughout Europe, an earlier emphasis on rehabilitation has been replaced by a greater attention to holding young offenders accountable. This has been done through stricter sentences and through more pressure for victim reparation and community compensation.

In a number of countries, including Germany, France, Italy, Austria, and Spain, mediation and community service are regulated in one single statutory paragraph (Schelkens 1998). The most extensive seems to be in Germany, described by Hans-Jörg Albrecht (in this volume). Since 1990, the public prosecutors office has been able to divert young offenders from prosecution if educational measures are accepted voluntarily, to refer cases to youth court under a "simplified procedure" if the juvenile admits the offense, or to follow a normal procedure. In either of the less formal tracks, "educational measures" include community service, reparation, victim-offender mediation, and making apologies. "Disciplinary measures" may be imposed only by the youth court but may include the same possibilities. Short-term detention may be used to enforce educational measures. Youth imprisonment, the only youth punishment in the strict legal sense, can be converted into probation, for which community service or victim restitution are possible conditions.

Other countries regulate community service, mediation, or both separately. Belgium, Luxembourg, the Netherlands, Portugal, and Switzerland allow youth court orders to community service. In Scandinavian countries, community service is a possible court order for young adult offenders (but excluding juveniles under the age of sixteen). As described by Josine Junger-Tas (in this volume), community service in the Netherlands has had a statutory basis since 1994. Within the "HALT-projects," police can order and monitor up to twenty hours of community or reparative work for "nonserious" offenders, if they and their parents agree. The public prosecutor can divert young offenders from prosecution if they agree to carry out community service for up to forty hours. The youth court judge can also order community service as an alternative to a traditional punishment. The maximum amount now is 200 hours.

Victim-offender mediation is seldom separately regulated. Standalone experiments have been carried out in several countries, often on cases referred by a few public prosecutors in specific judicial districts (Weitekamp 2001*a*). Conferencing experiments have been underway in Belgium and the Netherlands since 2001. Most cases are first offenders of low or moderate seriousness. Only the Belgian conferencing experiment seems to focus on serious and repeat young offenders (Vanfraechem 2002). The relation between these experiments and the system is very variable, depending on individuals (Miers 2001).

Altogether, community service appears to be well established in the juvenile justice systems on the European continent. Although not explicitly a restorative measure, the restorative logic of community service in Europe appears from its inclusion as an alternative to mediation and from the comments on the legislation. Junger-Tas, for example, indicates that the emergence of "work-projects" in the Netherlands constitutes "more emphasis on demanding compensation and reparation of the harm to the victim, be it the private person or the community" (1988, p. 25).

Mediation is statutorily authorized only in a few countries, but the extent of the practice differs. Norway, Germany, and Austria are among the most "mediating" countries in the world (Miers 2001). The extent to which legal regulation differs has much to do with the intrinsic characteristics of community service and mediation. The latter is essentially voluntary and informal. Community service can be coercively imposed and, therefore, presents a greater need for legal safeguards.

Three principal rationales have been offered (Schelkens 1998). First, the offender must take responsibility for his deeds (which seems to depart from the traditional treatment philosophy). Second, he must make up for his misbehavior toward the victim and the community (which does relate to the restorative justice philosophy). Third, purely punitive sanctions, especially prison, should be avoided (a shift away from simple retributive responses). Thus, the restorative approach has influenced the ways that juvenile justice systems respond to youth crime. Its practice, however, is unequally spread, even within a same country. In Germany, for example, some judicial districts make intensive use of mediation, while others use it scarcely at all (Weitekamp 2001a). It often depends on individual police officers, public prosecutors, and judges and also on the availability of local agencies to monitor the restorative actions.

The current state of affairs is not really satisfying. Mediation, conferencing, and community service are now mostly located in juvenile justice systems that are not grounded on a restorative philosophy. Restorative practices are seen as complements to punitive or rehabilitative responses, or are reinterpreted as alternative punishments or treatments. This raises two problems. First, it undervalues the potential of restorative justice, and, second, it makes them vulnerable to conventional criticisms of the punishment and the treatment paradigms. The second objection suggests that restorative justice has the intrinsic qualities to escape these criticisms. Is that so? If restorative justice were seen as a full-fledged paradigm and grounded a coherent systemic response to youth crime, would such a system better address problems than traditional juvenile justice systems?

B. Restorative Justice as a Response to Juvenile Justice Critics

This subsection explores whether a restorative justice system could resist better the criticisms against the existing juvenile justice systems mentioned earlier. Could a restorative juvenile justice system be more effective than existing systems? Can restorative justice principles be reconciled with essential legal safeguards? Can restorative responses offer a credible response to serious and patterned youth crime? Can they better meet victims' needs and rights?

1. *Effectiveness.* The evaluation research described earlier supports optimism. Restorative justice interventions do work and produce outcomes more satisfying than the outcomes of punitive or purely rehabilitative interventions. They are more satisfying to victims and their

communities of care, and no evidence suggests that restorative practices are less effective at achieving public safety than traditional treatment or punitive responses.

In principle, this should be justification enough for implementing restorative justice. Restorative justice indeed shifts its goals, from offender rehabilitation in traditional juvenile justice to broader restoration in restorative justice. But in these paragraphs on effectiveness, we compare effectiveness on offenders of both the rehabilitative and restorative responses.

In Section II, I assigned the offender in two roles in restorative justice. He is a "tool" in the restorative effort, because his voluntary cooperation considerably enhances the restorative quality of the disposition. He is also an objective, because his reintegration is part of the broader restoration in view.

Restorative justice should not encompass offender treatment as a primary aim. That would risk shifting back into the traditional rehabilitative approach, with its neglect of legal safeguards and lesser attention to the harm and suffering of the victim and the community. However, aiming at the offender's reintegration is not contradictory to restorative goals (Bazemore 1999; Bazemore and O'Brien 2002). Empirical evidence confirms that restorative actions have more positive effects on juvenile offenders than do traditional juvenile justice treatment programs. There are three reasons for this.

First, restoration can remediate the harms that the offender did to himself by his crime (e.g., social exclusion and stigmatization) if he takes the opportunity to repair the consequences of his offense and expresses his willingness to conform. Mediation and conferencing offer opportunities for the offender to explain himself, be confronted, and understand the consequences of the offense. All this happens in a context of respect and support. The opportunity to atone is close at hand, and the chances that it will be taken are greater than in any other responses to crime. Reacceptance and reintegration are also more probable (Braithwaite and Mugford 1994; Maxwell and Morris 2001). Through performing community service, the juvenile can express his willingness to cooperate and thereby prevent further social exclusion or stigmatization. These are all possibilities for the offender to "make good" his personal life experience, which, according to Maruna (2001), is a crucial element in desisting from crime.

Second, mediation, conferencing, and community service have educative potentials that go beyond the traditional treatment or punishment responses. Within the framework of restorative justice, attention can be paid to needs of the offender. Mediation is set up primarily to benefit the victim, but the methodology also allows concern for the needs of the offender and for his social integration. Community service compensates symbolically for the harm caused, but it offers constructive elements for the offender through, for example, networking, learning experiences, and social identity building (Bazemore and Maloney 1994; Bazemore 1999).

Third, restorative justice processes can help the offender (and his family) become aware of social, relational, and psychological problems. The conversation in the conference, for example, may make clear that drug use is a serious problem or that family conflicts have been dysfunctional to the education of children, and it may lead families to accept or seek voluntary welfare assistance. Many conference agreements include such elements (Warner-Roberts and Masters 1999).

2. *Legal Safeguards.*   In practice, mediation or conferencing is often carried out in a rehabilitative framework. They may lead to far-going interventions that would be highly suspect from a retributivist standpoint (Feld 1999*b*, Groenhuysen 2000). "Educative" community services may be ordered that are disproportionate to the seriousness of the harm caused or to the crime *tout court* (Walgrave and Geudens 1996). Such anomalies result from philosophical and theoretical confusion. Restorative practices are often isolated from their theoretical foundations and simply inserted into a rehabilitative juvenile justice system.

Basically, restorative justice has better potential to respect legal safeguards than does rehabilitative justice. Its focus on the harm is retrospective and thus more appropriate than a focus on the needs of the offender. Harm already caused by the crime is a more controllable yardstick for the intervention than are the offender's future needs (Walgrave and Geudens 1996).

This kind of retrospectivity is common to the retributivist approach to crime, but, as I described earlier in the essay, crucial differences between restorative justice and retributive punishment subsist. A justice system primarily oriented toward doing justice through restoration would have some commonalities and some crucial differences with the traditional criminal justice system (see also Walgrave 2002*b*). Both express clear limits to social tolerance, hold the offender responsible for his behavior, and, if necessary, use coercion.

The limits of social tolerance are clear, because the intervention is based on the offender's behavior. In retributive justice, the seriousness of the crime is the yardstick for deciding the proportionate punishment. In restorative justice, the seriousness of the harm serves as the criterion for gauging the maximum of reasonable restorative effort.

Holding the offender responsible is essential to both punitive and restorative approaches. Both also can take account of personal and social circumstances. The amount of punishment or compensation will depend on personal capacities to understand and material resources, degrees of premeditation, and social and situational circumstances. Such elements can be considered more thoroughly in deliberative conditions but are also crucial in judicial sentencing. Restorative justice thus addresses the two crucial questions in traditional sentencing: have the facts and the degree of guilt been established (Ashworth 1986)?

Sentencing in view of restoration raises a third question: How can the sanction contribute maximally to restoration? This question is not asked in retributive justice, because of the a priori option for punishment, and because it is not prospective. Restorative justice aims at restoring the harm and is therefore prospective also. Again, voluntary deliberative processes are more adequate to assess the harm and consider possible reasonable reparation, but the question should also be central in judicial proceedings. Restorative justice is thus retrospective and prospective at the same time (Duff 2001).

Judicial procedures incorporating restorative values would therefore deviate from traditional criminal procedures in several respects.

First, restorative justice procedures should at all stages allow easy exits into informal crime regulations. Diversion is obligatory wherever possible. The decision to prosecute must be justified with concrete arguments and not occur simply because the law has been broken.

Second, restorative justice procedures must allow opportunities for input by victims and others affected by the crime. This is crucial in defining the kind and amount of harm and in finding the best possible restorative outcome. However, these actors must not be given any decisive power.

Third, criminal investigation should focus not only on establishing the facts and guilt but also on defining the harm, suffering, and social unrest caused by the offense. It should also explore possible ways for negotiation, and thus for "diversion," and for restorative sanctions if diversion is not possible.

Fourth, the sanction should not tie the seriousness of crime to a proportionate punishment. It should tie the seriousness and kind of harm to the maximum reasonable restorative effort.

3. *Application to Serious Offending.* Most restorative practices are used for less serious cases. Statutory language often mentions seriousness thresholds and excludes severe offenses from restorative dispositions.

Several reasons have been offered for why restorative responses are inappropriate for serious youth crime. It is said that people who commit serious crimes cannot benefit from a restorative process because they respond only to punishment and deterrence. Such a position reflects a naive view of the etiology of crime, as if crime seriousness expresses the offender's social callousness. Many who commit very serious offenses appear to be sensitive to social influence, feel deep remorse, and are prepared to work to undo what they have done.

From a retributive standpoint, serious crimes should result in punishment. Mild misbehavior might be left to restorative processes, but the serious offenses are "unforgivable" and warrant a proportionately hard treatment (von Hirsch 1993; Duff 2001). Earlier in the essay, I already rejected this position. However, offending, and particularly serious offending, must meet with a public reaction if dominion is to be restored, and this response may include coercion. In my view, these coercive interventions should be imposed primarily for restoration and not primarily to make the offender suffer. How the voluntary and coercive interventions relate to each other has been elaborated in several publications. Braithwaite accepts deterrence and punishment in the response to the calculating "nonvirtuous" offenders (Braithwaite 2002, pp. 31–34), but he does not link this to the seriousness of the offense. Others do not see a place for punishment in the strict sense of the word and speak of restorative sanctions (Walgrave 2000*a*; Dignan 2002).

More specifically, victims and their intimates may continue to support retributive responses. People often refer to the feelings of the victims to justify (harsh) punishments. I describe this later but here point out that this position may be based on a myth. It is not at all evident that most victims of serious crimes want punitive responses. Practical experiences, as in New Zealand and elsewhere, show that many victims of serious crimes, even parents of murdered victims, agree to participate in a restorative process when it is proposed realistically. In any case, victims' wishes should not determine what happens. Moreover, the objectives of the judicial processes are broader than satisfying the individual victims and their families. In addition, research discussed earlier shows that victims, including victims of serious crimes, are more satisfied and at peace and feel more respected after participating in a restorative process than after being involved in a traditional penal justice procedure.

Some argue that fewer risks can be taken with those who commit serious crimes, because their possible reoffending is more likely to involve serious revictimization. In serious cases, the aim of restoration would have to be overruled by public safety concerns. This point must be taken seriously. Restorative justice proponents increasingly accept the need for incapacitation of "incompetent or irrational actors" who commit serious crimes (Braithwaite 2002, pp. 31–34; Dignan 2002). Restorative ambitions must be subordinated to the need for public safety. In such cases, the opportunities and the quality of possible restoration will be reduced, but restorative justice is not completely ruled out. Increasingly, experiments in prisons aim at restoration within closed facilities (Aertsen 1999; Umbreit, Bradshaw, and Coates 1999; Hartmann 2003).

Many questions remain on when and how incapacitation must be given priority. These questions are not asked in traditional criminal justice, because punishment through imprisonment overlaps with incapacitation. The principled priority given to restoration is confronted with its limits when incapacitation is needed for preserving public security. How to define these cases? By a return to the old and severely criticized concept of "dangerousness"? How could this be combined with the need for legal safeguards, including legality and proportionate maximum?

All in all, no principled or empirical arguments seem to justify excluding offenders and victims of serious youth crimes from restorative interventions. On the contrary, there are reasons to believe that especially serious crimes should be dealt with as much as possible in a restorative way.

If the paradigm shift toward restorative justice is taken seriously, the amount of harm and suffering caused by a crime is a reason to favor restorative actions. Victims of serious crimes and communities where these crimes occurred are hurt more than by trivial offending. They are more in need of reparation. Although it may seem more difficult to achieve effective reparative actions after a serious crime, it violates restorative justice principles to exclude victims of such crimes from the possible benefits.

Certainly after a serious crime, offenders must be confronted with their responsibility. Pure rehabilitative responses do not do this sufficiently. Punitive reactions do confront offenders with the consequences of their conduct but do this poorly. Responsibility in traditional criminal justice only means accepting the punishment. That is a passive, retrospective form of responsibility. Restorative justice confronts the youthful offender directly and extends his responsibility to future-oriented "active responsibility" (Braithwaite and Roche 2001). The offender must contribute to the resolution of the problem created by his behavior. If he does not do so voluntarily, coercion may be imposed.

Restorative justice is not a soft option. Traditional procedures make the confrontation indirect, impersonal, and filtered through ritual. Restorative processes are personal, direct, and often emotional. For the offenders, being confronted directly with the suffering and harm caused and with the disapproval of beloved persons (as in family group conferences) is a deeply moving burden. Apologizing in front of others can be hard and humiliating. Experiencing the pressure to make up for the harm is hard to cope with. The offender is brought to feel intensely a mixture of unpleasant emotions like shame, guilt, remorse, embarrassment, and humiliation (Braithwaite and Mugford 1994; Maxwell and Morris 1999; Walgrave and Braithwaite 1999; Morris 2000; Harris 2001). These feelings can have an enduring impact on the offender's further life. Agreements often require serious and unpleasant commitments and demanding time investments. Some offenders experience victim-offender mediation and compliance with the agreements, a kind of "double punishment" (Schiff 1999; Daly 2000). Court-ordered community services are experienced as being serious sanctions (Schiff 1999).

Therefore, restorative justice can also respond credibly to serious offending. The only practical limit is the risk of serious reoffending. It is not now known where this limit lies nor how it should be implemented. After all, the experience with systemic restorative responses to youth crime is limited. Other than the general practice in New Zealand, only a few isolated experiments are known today. Research suggests that restorative justice has a much broader scope than is widely believed in mainstream thinking.

4. *Respect Victims' Interests and Needs.*   It may seem self-evident that restorative justice responses meet victims' needs better than does traditional juvenile justice. The relation between victims' views and restorative justice is, however, more complicated than that. The rights-focused victim advocates, for example, strongly oppose victims' interests to those of the offenders (Strang 2002, chap. 2). They focus on strengthening the rights of the victims in the traditional criminal justice procedure in part by diminishing consideration and protections for the offender. In their view, the more offenders are approached in a constructive, respectful way, the less respect is shown for the victims.

That oppositional approach is losing its impact (Weitekamp 2001*b*; Strang 2002). Victims increasingly understand that they have much to lose in the criminal justice system. They are often used as witnesses in court but are then left alone with their losses and grievances. Giving priority to punishing the offender impedes victim restoration, because the offender undergoing punishment has little opportunity for reparative actions. Monetary compensation ordered by the court does not appear to provide peaceful relief to victims. Victims in traditional criminal justice often experience secondary victimization (Dignan and Cavadino 1998; Gendreault 2001).

Despite their contrasting roles and originally contradictory views on the criminal incident, both victims and offenders have interests in a constructive settlement of the conflict and in the social peace it may facilitate. Victims are mostly more satisfied if they participate in a constructive dialogue with the offender (Strang 2002, pp. 49–61). Victims appreciate communicative opportunities, often more even than material compensation. After victimization, many victims suffer from continuing anger, uncertainty, and anxiety, based on a stereotyped image of a "monstrous criminal" and on the fear that he will repeat his victimization. In mediation or conferencing, the human contact in a secure environment reassures most victims, because of the respect and support they experience, because they observe the offender as a human being who is embarrassed by what he has done, and because they feel that apologies and other reparative acts express the offender's understanding of the wrong committed and his willingness not to reoffend.

However, some victims' concerns must be taken seriously. I mentioned that restorative justice envisions a broader concept of harm, surpassing the individual victim and including broader unrest in social life and even prejudices caused to the offender. Some fear that the victim may lose out in this broadened conception of harm and that respect for his interests and needs may be subordinated. This risk is especially acute in the juvenile justice context, where the rehabilitative tradition is strong. Mediation or conferencing experiments in such contexts may adopt a treatment perspective and subordinate the victim's interests (Davis, Boucherat, and Watson 1988; Young 1989). Sometimes social pressure is exerted on the victim to participate, to be "moderate" in his claims, or to accept agreements primarily based on the offender's treatment needs. The victim's story may be used as a "pedagogical means" to motivate the offender for treatment rather than to understand genuinely the victim's suffering in view of determining appropriate reparative actions. Secondary victimization occurs when such pressure happens.

Taking these problems seriously is no reason to abandon or delimit the restorative approach. On the contrary, it must be clear that abusing the victim is contrary to restorative principles. Such deviations must be prevented by strengthening the links between practices and principles. Restorative justice's purpose is to restore, and secondary victimization is unacceptable.

IV. A Look toward the Future

Restorative justice holds great promises for the future of juvenile justice. It offers benefits to victims, communities, and offenders, and it opens prospects for addressing problems with predominately rehabilitative juvenile justice systems. Restorative justice is more effective, even for reintegrating offenders. Its clear normative approach and its retrospective aspects provide stronger criteria for applying legal safeguards. The appeal to the offender's personal responsibility seems more adequate for responding to serious crime, and victims are better off with restorative responses than with rehabilitative or punitive ones. Moreover, restorative justice does not so far provoke destructive consequences for public safety, and it has good intrinsic potentials for public law enforcement.

Many countries have turned to restorative schemes in their juvenile justice systems, in order to make young offenders accountable, to benefit victims, and to avoid a shift toward purely punitive approaches. How far this development will go is unclear. In its most ambitious vision, the restorative justice movement can be compared with the children's justice movements of the end of the nineteenth century. If that is correct, within a few decades restorative justice will replace the predominant treatment approach and become the mainstream response to youth crime.

Others are skeptical and believe that it will remain only one of the possible reactions to youth crime. Juvenile justice would then develop a "three track model." Children and adolescents whose responsibility is considered slight, because of their age or obvious incapacity, would be referred to welfare institutions, operating outside of the judicial system but possibly under judicial supervision. Most children and adolescents would be considered able to take responsibility and would increasingly be invited (under pressure) to cooperate in voluntary restorative processes or be subjected to judicial sanctions with a restorative meaning. Adolescents who are considered serious offenders and at risk for serious reoffending would receive penal sanctions, with a mixed rationale of incapacitation and of punishment. They would experience inflictions of pain for the sake of pain. The crucial question is how the three tracks will relate to each other, and especially how far the restorative track will reach. It will depend on several conditions.

A. Finding a Balanced Relation between Restorative Justice and the Law

I have discussed the legal position of the parties involved in restorative processes, the relation between informal processes and the formal judicial system, the possibility of using coercion, the balance of attention between victims' harm and the public interest, and interactions among restoration, rehabilitation, and punishment. All concern the relation between the bottom-up approach crucial to restorative justice philosophy and practice and the top-down procedures that seem essential for regulation in a democratic constitutional state. In their experimental stage, restorative practices can afford some *flou artistique* with regard to legal safeguards, because they are limited in scope and are carried out by reformers whose personal moral authority suggests that serious violations of participants' legal rights are unlikely.

The more restorative justice evolves into a kind of mainstream response, however, the more urgent it is to reflect on how to insert it into an adequate legal frame. Without neglecting the communitarian dream of many restorative justice advocates, there is an increasing need to look for ways in which to implement restoration in the real world. Legal formalism must not intrude on the restorative process, but the process must take place in a legalized context.

An intrinsic tension surfaces. The participatory philosophy of restorative justice, which aims at maximum openness for informal dialogue and process, is difficult to combine with the need for formalization and legalization. The terms of the debate are somewhat different in common-law and civil law countries, but the basic issues are the same: how to juxtapose informal processes with formal procedures, how to rely on communities while living in organized states, how to combine creativity and richness in the bottom-up approach with the clarity and strictness of the top-down approach, and how to complement priority for voluntariness and compliance with possible coercion. If restorative justice is taken seriously, the legal safeguards of the punitive systems cannot just be reproduced. Due process, legality, equality, a right of defense, the presumption of innocence, and proportionality may be irrelevant or be applied differently. Perhaps other legal principles must be constructed that are more appropriate for the restorative perspective.

The restorative justice literature on these questions is not large. The vast majority of publications so far characterize restorative justice as another approach to crime, describe the different models, and try to find out whether restorative practices "work," for what kind of cases, and under what conditions. Now that it is generally accepted that "it does work," that its appeal is deeper and its scope is larger than just a few techniques, and that attempts are being made to insert restorative practices into mainstream systems of responding to crime, the relation between the traditional options for doing justice and the restorative option must be explored thoroughly. Skeptics doubt that restorative justice can ever be combined with decent legal standards and, therefore, would keep it at the margins of the social response to crime (Ashworth 1993; von Hirsch 1998; Feld 1999b). Among restorative justice proponents, different positions are held by so-called "diversionists," "maximalists," and "purists." The debate is now getting into its stride (Braithwaite 2002; Walgrave 2002c; Van Ness 2003; von Hirsch et al. 2003) and is one of the decisive themes for the defining of the possible scope of restorative justice in the future.

B. Developing Good Practice

The expansion of restorative principles will also depend on the quality of the practices themselves. Conferences strongly differ. Mediators have different ways of working with victims and offenders. These differences matter. How the process is monitored often has decisive impact on the outcome and the degree of restoration. How victims and offenders are invited, guided, and monitored and how community service is monitored make an important difference in victims' satisfaction and offenders' motivations and integration.

The experience with restorative processes and with facilitating and achieving compliance with reparative agreements is relatively recent. It is not just a version of social work. Bringing victims and offenders together and facilitating dialogue and negotiation is quite different from counseling offenders, supporting victims, or visiting a family in trouble. Designing and monitoring the execution of restorative community service is not the same as doing casework with a young probationer or controlling school attendance. Many practitioners initially proceeded tentatively, based on their own experience and intuition, ad hoc exchanges with colleagues, a few available guidelines, and their grounding in restorative principles. Increasingly they can ground their work on programmatic guides and standards (see, e.g., Declaration of Leuven 1997; Wachtel and Wachtel 1997; Balanced and Restorative Justice Project 1998; Umbreit 2001), which are based on extensive experience and provide general guidelines.

Restorative practice has improved drastically, leading to greater confidence and broader implementation. This is, paradoxically, a threat, as it may lead to routinized "fast food" practices (Umbreit 1999) with weak methodological underpinnings. There is a need for ongoing attention to the quality of what is done under the label "restorative justice," and for further development of a methodology for guiding restorative processes. A good methodology is not a detailed sequence of "tricks" but must offer orientations to see possible problems and advice on choosing well-considered options based on intensive experience and a balanced view of what restorative justice can and cannot achieve, and under what conditions.

The evolution of restorative practice will require a permanent interaction between reflexive practitioners and evaluative research. That will improve processes and outcomes, thereby leading to more satisfaction among participating victims, offenders, and communities of care; extending the scope of restorative justice to more difficult and more serious cases; and gaining credibility among professionals and the public. Good methodology is one of the basic preconditions for the expansion of restorative values in juvenile justice systems.

C. Developing Good Normative and Explanatory Theory

Most restorative experiments occur in institutional settings that are not based on restorative principles. Traditional juvenile justice or criminal justice systems predominate, practicing their treatment- or punishment-oriented responses. The traditional systems deliver mainstream responses and act as the gatekeepers to possible restorative practices, which are considered as exceptions, often even as favors. The success of these practices is judged by the gatekeepers according to criteria that are not really restorative. They value, for example, mediation because it may influence offenders, or they accept conferencing because it may include the family in the reeducative process, while appreciating that the "hard-core justice business" is relieved from less serious cases. Genuine restorative values are neither recognized nor valued. It is difficult for restorative justice practitioners to challenge this view, because they depend on the judicial gatekeepers for the survival of their programs.

Isolated practices run great risks. Paradoxically, the greatest threat to restorative justice may be the thoughtless enthusiasm of policy makers, police, magistrates, judges, and social workers who want to integrate a few techniques into traditional rehabilitative or punitive justice systems. A taste of mediation, a bit of conferencing, or a pinch of community service are added to the system without questioning fundamental principles. The pioneering spirit risks getting lost and being replaced by routinized but uncommitted attitudes. Practices would be stripped from personal commitment and deteriorate into pure technique, as "fast food" restorative practices (Umbreit 1999) ornamenting systems that would essentially remain unchanged. This would cost restorative justice its potential and reduce it to a limited additional opportunity.

Avoiding such deterioration requires permanent theorizing. Restorative justice is a lively field of reflection with different and opposing views. Despite some basic common understandings, there is no generally accepted basic theory of restorative justice.[6] And such a theory is not what is needed. Rigid definitions and rules would limit developments. On the contrary, permanent debate provokes permanent reflection and increasing awareness. Ongoing normative theorizing must reflect on the essentials of restorative justice and be self-critical. It must make explicit why it would in principle be better than both the retributive or rehabilitative models of responding to crime, what ethical conditions must be fulfilled, and how restorative practices should

---

[6] It must be remembered that the version presented here is also not completely as it would be presented by all restorative justice experts.

be combined with decent legal safeguards. Some such issues have been raised in this essay, but the options presented are not definitive and not the only possible options. It is the reflection and debate itself that keeps the field sensitive to essentials that must be preserved in relation to the traditional systems. Besides normative theorizing, more descriptive and explanatory theory is needed to improve the quality of the restorative fieldwork. Theory is needed to inspire experiments, to explain why it works, and to orient evaluative research (as in Bazemore and O'Brien [2002]).

The technicité of restorative justice may not be isolated from its theoretical and socioethical foundations. Together with developing methodology, ongoing theoretical and socioethical reflection must point to the essentials of restorative justice, bundle and interpret experience, and build reference models to comment on and orient the practices, which altogether form the best possible counterforce to avoid restorative justice's absorption into the traditional modes of responding to crime.

D. "Zeitgeist" and Strategy

Restorative justice is an ideal of justice, grounded on a set of social and ethical beliefs and values. Its potential is embedded in broader social and political developments. Developments in juvenile justice are a matter of criminal justice policy, which depend not only on practical and scientific qualities and options but even more on the cultural and political climate. In almost all Western countries, crime problems are exploited commercially by dramatizing media and boosted through populist rhetoric by some politicians, which together lead to simplistic attitudes among much of the public. Many observers typify the social climate as being intolerant of deviancy and inclined to repressive measures against offending. If that is true, the chances that restorative responses will be generally accepted and promoted are reduced.

However, reality is more nuanced. The media and the public represent different views and opinions. Simplistic repressive outcries may sound the loudest, but it is far from evident that they really are the mainstream (Roberts and Hough 2002). There is an increasingly widespread understanding that purely repressive responses do not offer satisfying solutions and lead to escalation in problems (Messner and Rosenfeld 1994; Skolnick 1995; Tonry 1995). Awareness is growing that simply boosting repressiveness is leading crime policy to a dead end, with more imprisonment, greater human and financial costs, less ethics, and less public safety. Moreover, many explorations of public attitudes toward crime show results that are not unfavorable to restorative responses (see, e.g., Wright 1989; Sessar 1999). If alternate reactions to crime are presented realistically, many respondents favor reparation. Such preferences are noted for all types of crimes, including serious crimes.

There is no reason to be too pessimistic about the future of restorative justice, particularly in the juvenile context. "Public opinion" is neither monolithic nor deterministic but can be influenced. Restorative justice advocates have a strong case. They may have a deep influence on future developments, if the case is presented well. This is partly a matter of strategy (Walgrave and Bazemore 1999; Johnstone 2002; Van Ness and Strong 2002). First, the full potentials of restorative justice practice and vision must be exploited as much as possible. This will improve the intrinsic quality of the restorative programs. But besides that, specific efforts must be made to get the story out to policy makers, professionals, the judiciary, and the public. If these actors are informed realistically about what can be achieved, and what cannot, they will more easily be persuaded to try restorative approaches.

E. A Final Question

My final question is provocative, but it emerges from the theoretical options described. If restorative justice became predominant, would there be any fundamental reason for maintaining a separate juvenile justice system? After all, restorative justice focuses on the harm and suffering to be repaired, and not on treatment or punishment for the offender. Does it then logically make sense to retain separate models of criminal justice for adults and for minors? It does not matter to a victim whether he has been burglarized or beaten up by a sixteen-year-old boy or a twenty-one-year-old young adult. The harm must be repaired, and the offender must contribute to this reparation. The "reasonableness" may be different in degree, but not intrinsically different.

The acceptance of a separate justice system for juveniles, apart from the adults' system, is never a self-evident option. If intrinsic qualities of a category of offenders justify the maintenance of a separate system, there are no fundamental reasons not to invent other systems for the elderly, for females compared with males, or for immigrants compared with natives. These categories of people also show some systematic differences in life experiences and prospects, in their interpretations of needs and deeds. Like adults, children are entitled to legal safeguards and, therefore, need a system that focuses on the offense or on its consequences. Conversely, adults' criminality is an expression of specific life circumstances, and adults also should be treated with respect and in a way that is as little destructive as possible of their future life chances. Guilt and culpability are not linked to a specific age threshold but develop gradually. Age is only one indicator of differences and often not the decisive one.

Keeping a separate juvenile justice system may be a provisional strategic option for the present, because it will prevent youthful offenders from being subjected to the greater punitiveness of adult criminal justice, and because the public more generally accepts restorative experiments for juveniles than for adults (Bazemore and Walgrave 1999). That is why I reject the current proposals to abolish juvenile justice (as in Feld 1993). But if restorative justice became predominant, this strategic argument would disappear. Both juvenile and adult offenders would have to contribute to reparation and would be treated respectfully, respecting as much as possible dominion for them as well.

REFERENCES

Aertsen, Ivo. 1999. "Mediation bei schweren Straftaten—auf dem Weg zu einer neuen Rechtskultur" (Mediation in serious crimes: A pathway to a new legal culture?). In *Mediationsverfahren: Horizonte, Grenzen, Innensichte*, edited by Christa Pelikan. Baden-Baden: Nomos.

Aertsen, Ivo, and Tony Peters. 1998. "Mediation and Restorative Justice in Belgium." *European Journal on Criminal Policy and Research* 6:507–25.

Ahmed, Eliza. 2001. "Shame Management: Regulating Bullying." In *Shame Management through Reintegration*, edited by Eliza Ahmed, Nathan Harris, John Braithwaite, and Valerie Braithwaite. Cambridge: Cambridge University Press.

Albrecht, Günther, and Wolfgang Ludwig-Mayerhofer, eds. 1995. *Diversion and Informal Social Control*. Berlin: de Gruyter.

Ashworth, Anthony. 1986. "Punishment and Compensation: Victims, Offenders and the State." *Oxford Journal of Legal Studies* 6:86–122.

———. 1993. "Some Doubts about Restorative Justice." *Criminal Law Forum* 4:277–99.

Bailey, W. 1966. "Correctional Outcome: An Evaluation of 100 Reports." *Journal of Criminal Law, Criminology and Police Sciences* 57:256–60.

Balanced and Restorative Justice Project. 1998. *Guide for Implementing the Balanced and Restorative Justice Model: Report*. Washington, D.C.: U.S. Department of Justice, Office of Justice Programs, Office of Juvenile Justice and Delinquency Prevention.

Bazemore, Gordon. 1999. "After Shaming, Whither Reintegration: Restorative Justice and Relational Rehabilitation." In *Restorative Juvenile Justice: Repairing the Harm of Youth Crime*, edited by Gordon Bazemore and Lode Walgrave. Monsey, N.Y.: Criminal Justice.

Bazemore, Gordon, and Dennis Maloney. 1994. "Rehabilitating Community Service: Toward Restorative Service Sanctions in a Balanced Justice System." *Federal Probation* 58(1):24–35.

Bazemore, Gordon, and Sandra O'Brien. 2002. "The Quest for a Restorative Model of Rehabilitation: Theory-for-Practice and Practice-for-Theory." In *Restorative Justice and the Law*, edited by Lode Walgrave. Cullompton, U.K.: Willan.

Bazemore, Gordon, and Mara Schiff. 2002. *Understanding Restorative Conferencing: A Case Study in Informal Decision-Making in the Response to Youth Crime: Final Report*. Washington, D.C.: U.S. Department of Justice, National Institute of Justice.

Bazemore, Gordon, and Mara Schiff, eds. 2001. *Restorative Community Justice: Repairing Harm and Transforming Communities*. Cincinnati: Anderson.

Bazemore, Gordon, and Lode Walgrave. 1999. "Restorative Justice: In Search of Fundamentals and an Outline for Systemic Reform." In *Restorative Juvenile Justice: Repairing the Harm of Youth Crime*, edited by Gordon Bazemore and Lode Walgrave. Monsey, N.Y.: Criminal Justice.

Boyes-Watson, Carolyn. 2000. "Reflections on the Purist and the Maximalist Models of Restorative Justice." *Contemporary Justice Review* 3:441–50.

Braithwaite, John. 1989. *Crime, Shame, and Reintegration*. Cambridge: Cambridge University Press.

———. 1999. "Restorative Justice: Assessing Optimistic and Pessimistic Accounts." In *Crime and Justice: A Review of Research*, vol. 25, edited by Michael Tonry. Chicago: University of Chicago Press.

———. 2002. *Restorative Justice and Responsive Regulation*. Oxford: Oxford University Press.

Braithwaite, John, and Kathleen Daly. 1994. "Masculinities, Violence, and Communitarian Control." In *Just Boys Doing Business? Men, Masculinities, and Crime*, edited by Tim Newburn and Elizabeth Stanko. London: Routledge.

Braithwaite, John, and Stephen Mugford. 1994. "Conditions of Successful Reintegration Ceremonies: Dealing with Juvenile Offenders." *British Journal of Criminology* 34:139–71.

Braithwaite, John, and Christine Parker. 1999. "Restorative Justice Is Republican Justice." In *Restorative Juvenile Justice: Repairing the Harm of Youth Crime*, edited by Gordon Bazemore and Lode Walgrave. Monsey, N.Y.: Criminal Justice.

Braithwaite, John, and Philip Pettit. 1990. *Not Just Deserts: A Republican Theory of Criminal Justice*. Oxford: Oxford University Press.

Braithwaite, John, and Declan Roche. 2001. "Responsibility and Restorative Justice." In *Restorative Community Justice: Repairing Harm and Transforming Communities*, edited by Gordon Bazemore and Mara Schiff. Cincinnati: Anderson.

Chamboredon, Jean-Claude. 1971. "La délinquance juvénile: Essai de construction d'objet" (Juvenile delinquency: Trying an object construction). *Revue Française de Sociologie* 12:335–77.

Charbonneau, Serge. 1998. "Restorative Justice Trajectory in Québec: 360 Degrees in the Last 20 Years." In *Restorative Justice for Juveniles: Potentialities, Risks and Problems for Research*, edited by Lode Walgrave. Louvain: Leuven University Press.

Claassen, Ron. 1995. "Restorative Justice Principles and Evaluation Continuums." Paper presented at National Center for Peacemaking and Conflict Resolution, Fresno, Calif., May.

Cornejo, Juan. 1981. *Le problème de l'efficacité et de l'évaluation des interventions de prévention de la délinquance* (The problem of efficiency and of evaluating the interventions in view of preventing delinquency). Louvain-La-Neuve, Belgium: Ecole de Criminologie U.C.L.

Corrado, Ray, and Curt Griffiths. 1999. "Implementing Restorative Youth Justice: A Case Study in Community Justice and the Dynamics of Reform." In *Restorative Juvenile Justice: Repairing the Harm of Youth Crime*, edited by Gordon Bazemore and Lode Walgrave. Monsey, N.Y.: Criminal Justice.

Crawford, Adam. 1996. "The Spirit of Community: Rights, Responsibilities and the Communitarian Agenda." *Journal of Law and Society* 2:247–62.

Crawford, Adam, and Todd Clear. 2001. "Community Justice: Transforming Communities through Restorative Justice?" In *Restorative Community Justice: Repairing Harm and Transforming Communities*, edited by Gordon Bazemore and Mara Schiff. Cincinnati: Anderson.

Crawford, Adam, and Jo Goodey, eds. 2000. *Integrating a Victim Perspective within Criminal Justice: International Debates*. Aldershot: Ashgate.

Dabin, Jean. 1947. *Le contrôle de la puissance paternelle en droit Belge* (The control over paternal power in Belgian law). Brussels: Larcier.

Daly, Kathleen. 2000. "Revisiting the Relationship between Retributive and Restorative Justice." In *Restorative Justice: Philosophy to Practice*, edited by Heather Strang and John Braithwaite. Aldershot: Ashgate.

———. 2001. "Conferencing in Australia and New Zealand: Variations, Research Findings and Prospects." In *Restorative Justice for Juveniles: Conferencing, Mediation and Circles*, edited by Allison Morris and Gabrielle Maxwell. Oxford: Hart.

Davis, G., J. Boucherat, and D. Watson. 1988. "Reparation in the Service of Diversion: The Subordination of a Good Idea." *Howard Journal* 27:127–34.

Declaration of Leuven. 1997. "On the Advisability of Promoting the Restorative Approach to Juvenile Crime." Issued on the Occasion of the First International Conference on Restorative Justice for Juveniles, Louvain, Belgium, May.

de Haan, Willem. 1990. *The Politics of Redress: Crime, Punishment, and Penal Abolition*. London: Unwyn Hyman.

Dignan, James. 2002. "Restorative Justice and the Law: The Case for an Integrated, Systemic Approach." In *Restorative Justice and the Law*, edited by Lode Walgrave. Cullompton, U.K.: Willan.

Dignan, James, and Mick Cavadino. 1998. "Which Model of Criminal Justice Offers the Best Scope for Assisting Victims of Crime?" In *Support for Crime Victims in a Comparative Perspective*, edited by Ezzat Fattah and Tony Peters. Louvain: Leuven University Press.

Dignan, James, and Peter Marsh. 2001. "Restorative Justice and Family Group Conferences in England: Current State and Future Prospects." In *Restorative Justice for Juveniles: Conferencing, Mediation and Circles*, edited by Allison Morris and Gabrielle Maxwell. Oxford: Hart.

Doek, Jaap 1994. "The Juvenile Court: An Endangered Species?" *European Journal of Criminal Policy and Research* 1:42–56.

Duff, R. Antony. 2001. *Punishment, Communication, and Community*. Oxford: Oxford University Press.

Dünkel, Frieder, and Klaus Meyer. 1986. *Jugendstrafe und Jugendstrafvollzug: Stationäre Massnahmen der Jugendkriminalrechtspflege im Internationalen Vergleich* (Juvenile punishments and procedures: Residential measures in juvenile justice from an international comparative perspective). 2 vols. Freiburg: Max-Planck-Institut für Ausländisches und Internationales Strafrecht.

Eglash, A. 1977. "Beyond Retribution: Creative Restitution." In *Restitution in Criminal Justice*, edited by Joe Hudson and Burt Galaway. Lexington, Mass.: Heath.

Empey, L. T. 1976. "The Social Construction of Childhood, Delinquency and Social Reform." In *The Juvenile Justice System*, edited by Malcolm W. Klein. Beverly Hills, Calif.: Sage.

European Forum for Victim-Offender Mediation and Restorative Justice, ed. 2000. *Victim-Offender Mediation in Europe: Making Restorative Justice Work*. Louvain: Leuven University Press.

Faget, Jacques. 1997. *La médiation: Essai de politique pénale* (Mediation: An essay on penal policy). Ramonville Saint-Agne, France: Erès.

Fatić, Aleksandar. 1995. *Punishment and Restorative Crime-Handling: A Social Theory of Trust*. Aldershot: Avebury.

Feld, Barry C. 1993. "Criminalizing the American Juvenile Court." In *Crime and Justice: A Review of Research*, vol. 17, edited by Michael Tonry. Chicago: University of Chicago Press.

———. 1999a. *Bad Kids: Race and the Transformation of the Juvenile Court*. New York: Oxford University Press.

———. 1999b. "Rehabilitation, Retribution and Restorative Justice: Alternative Conceptions of Juvenile Justice." In *Restorative Juvenile Justice: Repairing the Harm of Youth Crime*, edited by Gordon Bazemore and Lode Walgrave. Monsey, N.Y.: Criminal Justice.

Feld, Barry C., ed. 1999c. *Readings in Juvenile Justice Administration*. New York: Oxford University Press.

Gendreault, Arlène. 2001. "La victimisation secondaire" (Secondary victimization). In *Dictionnaire critique des sciences criminelles* (Dictionary of criminal sciences), edited by D. Jolivet, G. Lopez, and S. Tzitzis. Paris: Dalloz.

Geudens, Hilde. 1996. *De toepassing van de Gemenschapsdienst in het kader van de Belgische Jeugdbescherming* (The implementation of community service in Belgian juvenile justice). Louvain: Katholieke Universiteit Leuven, Onderzoeksgroep Jeugdcriminologie.

Glueck, Sheldon, and Eleanor Glueck. 1950. *Unraveling Juvenile Delinquency.* New York: Commonwealth Fund.

Goodey, Jo. 2000. "An Overview of Key Themes." In *Integrating a Victim Perspective within Criminal Justice: International Debates*, edited by Adam Crawford and Jo Goodey. Aldershot: Ashgate.

Greenberg, David F. 1977. "The Correctional Effects of Corrections: A Survey of Evaluation." In *Corrections and Punishment*, edited by David F. Greenberg. Beverly Hills, Calif.: Sage.

Groenhuysen, Mark. 2000. "Victim-Offender Mediation: Legal and Procedural Safeguards: Experiments and Legislation in Some European Jurisdictions." In *Victim-Offender Mediation in Europe: Making Restorative Justice Work*, edited by the European Forum for Mediation and Restorative Justice. Louvain: Leuven University Press.

Harris, M. 1990. "Moving into the New Millennium: Towards a Feminist Vision of Justice." In *Criminology as Peacemaking*, edited by Harold E. Pepinsky and Richard Quinney. Bloomington: Indiana University Press.

Harris, Nathan. 2001. "Shaming and Shame: Regulating Drink-Driving." In *Shame Management through Reintegration*, edited by Eliza Ahmed, Nathan Harris, John Braithwaite, and Valerie Braithwaite. Cambridge: Cambridge University Press.

Hartmann, Arthur 2003. "Restorative Justice in Prison?" In *Repositioning Restorative Justice*, edited by Lode Walgrave. Cullompton, U.K.: Willan (forthcoming).

Hartmann, Arthur, and Holger Stroezel. 1996. "Die Bundesweite TOA-Statistik" (Statistics on victim-offender mediation in Germany). In *Täter-Opfer-Ausgleich in Deutschland* (Victim-offender mediation in Germany), edited by Dieter Dölling, Dieter Banneberg, Arthur Hartmann, Elke Hassemer, Wolfgang Heinz, Susanne Henninger, Hans-Jürgen Kerner, Thomas Klaus, Dieter Rössner, Holger Stroezel, Petra Uhlmann, Michael Walter, Michael Wandrey and Elmar Weitekamp. Bonn: Bundesministerium der Justiz.

Hudson, Joe, Allison Morris, Gabrielle Maxwell, and Burt Galaway, eds. 1996. *Family Group Conferences: Perspectives on Policy and Practice.* Annandale, New South Wales: Federation; Monsey, N.Y.: Willow Tree.

Huynen, Simonne. 1967. "De nouveaux horizons pour la protection de la jeunesse" (New prospects for youth protection). *Revue de Droit Pénal et de Criminologie* 47:183–202.

Jaccoud, Mylène. 1998. "Restoring Justice in Native Communities in Canada." In *Restorative Justice for Juveniles: Potentialities, Risks and Problems for Research*, edited by Lode Walgrave. Louvain: Leuven University Press.

Johnstone, Gerry. 2002. *Restorative Justice: Ideas, Values, Debates.* Cullompton, U.K.: Willan.

Junger-Tas, Josine. 1988. "Veranderingen in het gezin en reacties op delinquent gedrag" (Changes in family and reactions to offending behavior). *Justitiële Verkenningen* 14:7–30.

Kaiser, Günther. 1997. "Krise und Zukunft des Jugendstrafrechts" (Crisis and future of the juvenile penal law). In *Entwicklungstendenzen und Reformstrategien im Jugendstrafrecht im Europäischen Vergleich* (Developmental tendencies and strategies for reform in European juvenile justice systems), edited by Frieder Dünkel, Anton van Kalmthout, and Horst Schüler-Springorum. Mönchengladbag: Forum Verlag Godesberg.

Keijser, Jan Willem de. 2000. *Punishment and Purpose: From Moral Theory to Punishment in Action.* Amsterdam: Thela Thesis.

Kurki, Leena. 2003. "Evaluating Restorative Practices." In *Restorative Justice and Criminal Justice: Competing or Reconcilable Paradigms?* edited by Andrew von Hirsch, Julian V. Roberts, Anthony E. Bottoms, Kent Roach, and Mara Schiff. Oxford: Hart.

Lab, Steven P. 1992. *Crime Prevention: Approaches, Practices, and Evaluations.* 2d ed. Cincinnati: Anderson.

Lascoumes, Pierre. 1977. *Prévention et contrôle social: Les contradictions du travail social* (Prevention and social control: The contradictions of social work). Geneva: Médecine et Hygiène, Collection Déviance et Société.

Lemert, Edwin M. 1971. *Instead of Court: Diversion in Juvenile Justice.* Chevy Chase, Md.: National Institute of Mental Health, Center for Studies of Crime and Delinquency.

Lilles, Heino. 2001 "Circle Sentencing: Part of the Restorative Justice Continuum." In *Restorative Justice for Juveniles: Conferencing, Mediation and Circles,* edited by Allison Morris and Gabrielle Maxwell. Oxford: Hart.

Lipsey, Mark. 1995. "What Do We Learn from 400 Research Studies on the Effectiveness of Treatment with Juvenile Delinquents?" In *What Works: Reducing Reoffending: Guidelines from Research and Practice,* edited by James McGuire. Chichester, N.Y.: Wiley.

Lipsey, Mark, and D. Wilson. 1998. "Effective Intervention for Serious Juvenile Offenders." In *Serious and Violent Juvenile Offenders: Risk Factors and Successful Interventions,* edited by Rolf Loeber and David P. Farrington. Thousand Oaks, Calif.: Sage.

Martinson, R. 1974. "What Works? Questions and Answers about Prison Reform." *The Public Interest* 35:22–54.

Marshall, Tony. 1996. "The Evolution of Restorative Justice in Britain." *European Journal of Criminal Policy and Research* 4:21–43.

Maruna, Shadd. 2001. *Making Good: How Ex-Convicts Reform and Rebuild Their Lives.* Washington, D.C.: American Psychological Association.

Masters, Guy, and Ann Roberts. 2000. "Family Group Conferencing for Victims, Offenders and Communities." In *Mediation in Context,* edited by Marian Liebmann. London: Kingsley.

Maxwell, Gabrielle, and Allison Morris. 1996. "Research on Family Group Conferences with Young Offenders in New Zealand." In *Family Group Conferences: Perspectives on Policy and Practice,* edited by Joe Hudson, Allison Morris, Gabrielle Maxwell, and Burt Galaway. Annandale, New South Wales: Federation; Monsey, N.Y.: Willow Tree.

————. 1999. *Understanding Reoffending: Final Report.* Wellington: Victoria University, Institute of Criminology.

————. 2001. "Family Group Conferences and Reoffending." In *Restorative Justice for Juveniles: Conferencing, Mediation and Circles,* edited by Allison Morris and Gabrielle Maxwell. Oxford: Hart.

McCold, Paul. 1998. "Restorative Justice: Variation on a Theme." In *Restorative Justice for Juveniles: Potentialities, Risks and Problems for Research,* edited by Lode Walgrave. Louvain: Leuven University Press.

————. 2000. "Towards a Holistic Vision of Restorative Juvenile Justice: A Reply to the Maximalist Model." *Contemporary Justice Review* 3:357–414.

————. 2001. "Primary Restorative Practices." In *Restorative Justice for Juveniles: Conferencing, Mediation and Circles,* edited by Allison Morris and Gabrielle Maxwell. Oxford: Hart.

————. 2003. "A Survey of Assessment Research on Mediation and Conferencing." In *Positioning Restorative Justice,* edited by Lode Walgrave. Cullompton, U.K.: Willan (forthcoming).

McCold, Paul, and Ted Wachtel. 1998. *Restorative Policing Experiment.* Pipersville, Pa.: Community Service Foundation.

McCord, Joan, Cathy Spatz Widom, and Nancy A. Crowell, eds. 2001. *Juvenile Crime, Juvenile Justice.* Washington, D.C.: National Academy Press.

McGuire, James, and Philip Priestley. 1995. "Reviewing 'What Works': Past, Present and Future." In *What Works: Reducing Reoffending: Guidelines from Research and Practice,* edited by James McGuire. Chichester, N.Y.: Wiley.

Meeus, Wim, Martijn de Goede, Willem Kox, and Klaus Hurrelmann, eds. 1992. *Adolescence, Careers, and Cultures.* Berlin: de Gruyter.

Mehlbye, Jill, and Lode Walgrave. 1998. *Confronting Youth in Europe: Juvenile Crime and Juvenile Justice.* Copenhagen: AKF Forlaget.

Messner, Steven F., and Richard Rosenfeld. 1994. *Crime and the American Dream.* Belmont, Calif.: Wadsworth.

Miers, David. 2001. "An International Review of Restorative Justice." Crime Reduction Research Series no. 10. London: Home Office.

Morris, Allison. 2000. "Shame, Guilt and Remorse: How to Understand and Justify Moral Emotions in the Context of Juvenile Justice." Paper presented at the symposium "Punishing Children," Utrecht, June 8–9.

Morris, Allison, and Gabrielle Maxwell, eds. 2001. *Restorative Justice for Juveniles: Conferencing, Mediation and Circles.* Oxford: Hart.

Nagin, Daniel S. 1998. "Deterrence and Incapacitation." In *The Handbook of Crime and Punishment,* edited by Michael Tonry. Oxford: Oxford University Press.

Palmer, Ted. 1991. "The Effectiveness of Intervention: Recent Trends and Current Issues." *Crime and Delinquency* 37:330–46.

Pavlich, George. 2001. "The Force of Community." In *Restorative Justice and Civil Society,* edited by Heather Strang and John Braithwaite. Cambridge: Cambridge University Press.

Peper, Bram, and Frans Spierings. 1999. "Settling Disputes between Neighbours in the Lifeworld: An Evaluation of Experiments with Community Mediation." *European Journal on Criminal Policy and Research* 7:483–507.

Peters, Tony, and Ivo Aertsen. 1995. "Restorative Justice: In Search of New Avenues in Judicial Dealing with Crime." In *Crime and Insecurity in the City*, vol. 1, edited by Cyrille Fijnaut, Johan Goethals, Tony Peters, and Lode Walgrave. The Hague: Kluwer International.

Platt, Anthony M. 1969. *The Child Savers: The Invention of Delinquency*. Chicago: University of Chicago Press.

Power, Patrick. 2002. "Restorative Conferences in Australia and New Zealand." Ph.D. dissertation, University of Sydney.

Pranis, Kay. 2001. "Restorative Justice, Social Justice and the Empowerment of Marginalized Populations." In *Restorative Juvenile Justice: Repairing the Harm of Youth Crime*, edited by Gordon Bazemore and Lode Walgrave. Monsey, N.Y.: Criminal Justice.

Putnam, Robert D. 1993. *Making Democracy Work: Civic Traditions in Modern Italy*. Princeton, N.J.: Princeton University Press.

Roberts, Julian, and Mike Hough, eds. 2002. *Changing Attitudes to Punishment: Public Opinion, Crime and Justice*. Cullompton, U.K.: Willan.

Rothman, David J. 1980. *Conscience and Convenience: The Asylum and Its Alternative in Progressive America*. 1st ed. Boston: Little, Brown.

Schelkens, Wim. 1998. "Community Service and Mediation in the Juvenile Justice Legislation in Europe." In *Restorative Justice for Juveniles: Potentialities, Risks and Problems for Research*, edited by Lode Walgrave. Louvain: Leuven University Press.

Schiff, Mara. 1999. "The Impact of Restorative Interventions on Juvenile Offenders." In *Restorative Juvenile Justice: Repairing the Harm of Youth Crime*, edited by Gordon Bazemore and Lode Walgrave. Monsey, N.Y.: Criminal Justice.

Schlossman, Steven L. 1977. *Love and the American Delinquent: The Theory and Practice of "Progressive" Juvenile Justice, 1825–1920*. Chicago: University of Chicago Press.

Schneider, Anne L. 1986. "Restitution and Recidivism Rates of Juvenile Offenders: Results from Four Experimental Studies." *Criminology* 24:533–52.

Schüler-Springorum, Horst. 1999. "Juvenile Justice and the 'Shift to the Left.'" *European Journal on Criminal Policy and Research* 7:353–62.

Schur, Edwin M. 1973. *Radical Nonintervention: Rethinking the Delinquency Problem*. Englewood Cliffs, N.J.: Prentice-Hall.

Sechrest, Lee, Susan O. White, and Elizabeth D. Brown, eds. 1979. *The Rehabilitation of Criminal Offenders: Problems and Prospects*. Washington, D.C.: National Academy of Sciences.

Sessar, Klaus. 1999. "Punitive Attitudes of the Public: Reality and Myth." In *Restorative Juvenile Justice: Repairing the Harm of Youth Crime*, edited by Gordon Bazemore and Lode Walgrave. Monsey, N.Y.: Criminal Justice.

Shapland, J., J. Willmore, and P. Duf. 1985. *Victims in the Criminal Justice System.* Aldershot: Gower.

Sherman, Lawrence. 1993. "Defiance, Deterrence and Irrelevance: A Theory of the Criminal Sanction." *Journal of Research in Crime and Delinquency* 30:445–73.

Sherman, Lawrence W., and Heather Strang. 1997. "Restorative Justice and Deterring Crime." RISE (Restorative Justice in Australia) Working Papers no. 4. Canberra: Australian National University.

Singer, Simon I. 1996. *Recriminalizing Delinquency: Violent Juvenile Crime and Juvenile Justice Reform.* Cambridge: Cambridge University Press.

Skolnick, Jerome H. 1995. "What Not to Do about Crime: The American Society of Criminology 1994 Presidential Address." *Criminology* 33:1–15.

Strang, Heather. 2001. *Restorative Justice Programs in Australia: A Report to the Criminology Research Council.* Available online at www.aic.gov.au/crc/reports/strang. Last accessed March 6, 2003.

———. 2002. *Repair or Revenge: Victims and Restorative Justice.* Oxford: Oxford University Press.

Strang, Heather, and Lawrence W. Sherman. 1997. "The Victim's Perspective." RISE (Restorative Justice in Australia) Working Papers no. 2. Canberra: Australian National University.

Thorvaldson, Sveinn. 1990. "Restitution and Victim Participation in Sentencing." In *Criminal Justice, Restitution and Reconciliation,* edited by Burt Galaway and Joe Hudson. Monsey, N.Y.: Criminal Justice.

Tonry, Michael. 1995. *Malign Neglect: Race, Crime, and Punishment in America.* New York: Oxford University Press.

Trépanier, Jean. 1998. "Restorative Justice: A Question of Legitimacy." In *Restorative Justice for Juveniles: Potentialities, Risks and Problems for Research,* edited by Lode Walgrave. Louvain: Leuven University Press.

Tyler, Tom R. 1990. *Why People Obey the Law.* New Haven, Conn.: Yale University Press.

Umbreit, Mark S. 1994. *Victim Meets Offender: The Impact of Restorative Justice and Mediation.* Monsey, N.Y.: Criminal Justice.

———. 1999. "Avoiding the 'McDonaldization' of Victim-Offender Mediation: A Case Study in Moving Toward the Mainstream." In *Restorative Juvenile Justice: Repairing the Harm of Youth Crime,* edited by Gordon Bazemore and Lode Walgrave. Monsey, N.Y.: Criminal Justice.

———. 2001. *The Handbook of Victim Offender Mediation: An Essential Guide to Practice and Research.* San Francisco: Jossey-Bass.

Umbreit, Mark S., William Bradshaw, and Richard Coates. 1999. "Victims of Severe Violence Meet the Offender: Restorative Justice through Dialogue." *International Review of Victimology* 6:321–44.

Van de Kerchove, Michel. 1976–77. "Des mesures répressives aux mesures de sûreté et de protection: Réflections sur le pouvoir mystificateur du language" (From repressive measures to safety and protection measures: Reflections on the mystification power of language). *Revue de Droit Pénal et de Criminologie* 57:245–79.

Vanfraechem, Inge. 2002. "Implementing Conferencing in a Legalistic Country." From a session presented at "Dreaming of a New Reality," the Third International Conference on Conferencing, Circles and other Restorative Practices, Minneapolis, August 8–10, 2002. Available at www.restorative-practices.org/pages/mn02_vanfraechem.html. Last accessed March 6, 2003.

Van Ness, Daniel W. 1990. "Restorative Justice." In *Criminal Justice, Restitution and Reconciliation*, edited by Burt Galaway and Joe Hudson. Monsey, N.Y.: Criminal Justice.

———. 1996. "Restorative Justice and International Human Rights." In *Restorative Justice: International Perspectives*, edited by Burt Galaway and Joe Hudson. Monsey, N.Y.: Criminal Justice.

———. 1999. "Legal Issues of Restorative Justice." In *Restorative Juvenile Justice: Repairing the Harm of Youth Crime*, edited by Gordon Bazemore and Lode Walgrave. Monsey, N.Y.: Criminal Justice.

———. 2002. "The Shape of Things to Come: A Framework for Thinking about a Restorative Justice System." In *Restorative Justice: Theoretical Foundations*, edited by Elmar Weitekamp and Hans-Jürgen Kerner. Cullompton, U.K.: Willan.

———. 2003. "RJ City." Available online at www.restorativejustice.org.

Van Ness, Daniel W., and Mara Schiff. 2001. "Satisfaction Guaranteed? The Meaning of Satisfaction in Restorative Justice." In *Restorative Juvenile Justice: Repairing the Harm of Youth Crime*, edited by Gordon Bazemore and Lode Walgrave. Monsey, N.Y.: Criminal Justice.

Van Ness, Daniel W., and Karen Heetderks Strong. 2002. *Restoring Justice*. 2d ed. Cincinnati: Anderson.

Van Sloun, Theo. H. J. G. 1988. *De Schuldvraag in het kinderstrafrecht* (The question of guilt in children's penal law). Arnhem: Gouda Quint; Deventer: Kluwer.

Van Swaaningen, René. 1997. *Critical Criminology: Visions from Europe*. London: Sage.

Verhellen, Eugeen. 1989. "A Strategy for a Fully Fledged Position of Children in Our Society." In *Ombudswork for Children: A Way of Improving the Position of Children in Society*, edited by Eugeen Verhellen and Frans Spiesschaert. Louvain: Acco.

von Hirsch, Andrew. 1993. *Censure and Sanctions*. Oxford: Clarendon.

———. 1998. "Penal Theories." In *The Handbook of Crime and Punishment*, edited by Michael Tonry. New York: Oxford University Press.

von Hirsch, Andrew, Julian V. Roberts, Anthony E. Bottoms, Kent Roach, and Mara Schiff, eds. 2003. *Restorative Justice and Criminal Justice: Competing or Reconcilable Paradigms?* Oxford: Hart.

Wachtel, Ben, and Ted Wachtel, eds. 1997. *Real Justice Training Manual: Coordinating Family Group Conferences*. Pipersville, Pa.: Piper's Press.

Wachtel, Ted, and Paul McCold. 2001. "Restorative Justice in Everyday Life: Beyond the Formal Ritual." In *Restorative Justice and Civil Society*, edited by Heather Strang and John Braithwaite. Cambridge: Cambridge University Press.

Walgrave, Lode. 1993. "The Making of Concepts on Juvenile Delinquency and Its Treatment in the Recent History of Belgium and the Netherlands." In *History of Juvenile Delinquency: A Collection of Essays on Crime Committed by Young Offenders, in History and in Selected Countries*, vol. 2, edited by Albert Hess and Priscilla F. Clement. Aalen, Germany: Scientia.

———. 1995. "Restorative Justice for Juveniles: Just a Technique or a Fully Fledged Alternative?" *Howard Journal* 34:228–49.

———. 1999. "Community Service as a Cornerstone of a Systemic Restorative Response to (Juvenile) Crime." In *Restorative Juvenile Justice: Repairing the Harm of Youth Crime*, edited by Gordon Bazemore and Lode Walgrave. Monsey, N.Y.: Criminal Justice.

———. 2000*a*. "How Pure Can a Maximalist Approach to Restorative Justice Remain? Or Can a Purist Model of Restorative Justice Become Maximalist?" *Contemporary Justice Review* 3:415–32.

———. 2000*b*. "Restorative Justice and the Republican Theory of Criminal Justice: An Exercise in Normative Theorizing on Restorative Justice." In *Restorative Justice: Philosophy to Practice*, edited by Heather Strang and John Braithwaite. Aldershot: Ashgate.

———. 2001. "On Restoration and Punishment: Favourable Similarities and Fortunate Differences." In *Restorative Justice for Juveniles: Conferencing, Mediation and Circles*, edited by Allison Morris and Gabrielle Maxwell. Oxford: Hart.

———. 2002*a*. "From Community to Dominion: In Search of Social Values for Restorative Justice." In *Restorative Justice: Theoretical Foundations*, edited by Elmar Weitekamp and Hans-Jürgen Kerner. Cullompton, U.K.: Willan.

———. 2002*b*. "Restorative Justice and the Law: Socio-Ethical and Juridical Foundations for a Systemic Approach." In *Restorative Justice and the Law*, edited by Lode Walgrave. Cullompton, U.K.: Willan.

———. 2003. "Imposing Restoration Instead of Inflicting Pain: Reflections on the Judicial Reaction to Crime." In *Restorative Justice and Criminal Justice: Competing or Reconcilable Paradigms?* edited by Andrew von Hirsch, Julian V. Roberts, Anthony E. Bottoms, Kent Roach, and Mara Schiff. Oxford: Hart.

Walgrave, Lode, ed. 2002*c*. *Restorative Justice and the Law*. Cullompton, U.K.: Willan.

Walgrave, Lode, and Gordon Bazemore. 1999. "Reflections on the Future of Restorative Justice for Juveniles." In *Restorative Juvenile Justice: Repairing the Harm of Youth Crime*, edited by Gordon Bazemore and Lode Walgrave. Monsey, N.Y.: Criminal Justice.

Walgrave, Lode, and John Braithwaite. 1999. "Schaamte, Schuld en Herstel" (Shame, guilt and restoration). *Justitiële Verkenningen* 25:71–81.

Walgrave, Lode, and Hilde Geudens. 1996. "The Restorative Proportionality of Community Service for Juveniles." *European Journal of Crime, Criminal Law and Criminal Justice* 4:361–80.

Warner, K. 1994. "Family Group Conferences and the Rights of the Offender." In *Family Conferencing and Juvenile Justice: The Way Forward or Misplaced Optimism?* edited by Christine Alder and Joy Wundersitz. Canberra: Australian Institute of Criminology.

Warner-Roberts, Ann, and Guy Masters. 1999. *Group Conferencing: Restorative Justice in Practice.* St. Paul: University of Minnesota, Center for Restorative Justice and Mediation.

Weitekamp, Elmar. 1999. "History of Restorative Justice." In *Restorative Juvenile Justice: Repairing the Harm of Youth Crime*, edited by Gordon Bazemore and Lode Walgrave. Monsey, N.Y.: Criminal Justice.

———. 2001*a*. "Mediation in Europe: Paradoxes, Problems and Promises." In *Restorative Justice for Juveniles: Conferencing, Mediation and Circles*, edited by Allison Morris and Gabrielle Maxwell. Oxford: Hart.

———. 2001*b*. "Victim Movement and Restorative Justice." Keynote address presented at the Fifth International Conference on Restorative Justice for Juveniles, Louvain, Belgium, September 16–19.

Whitehead, Ted, and Steven P. Lab. 1989. "A Meta-analysis of Juvenile Correctional Treatment." *Journal of Research in Crime and Delinquency* 26:276–95.

Winterdyk, John A., ed. 2002. *Juvenile Justice Systems: International Perspectives.* Toronto: Canadian Scholars' Press.

Wright, Martin. 1989. "What the Public Wants." In *Mediation and Criminal Justice: Victims, Offenders, and Community*, edited by Martin Wright and Burt Galaway. London: Sage.

———. 1992. "Victim-Offender Mediation as a Step toward a Restorative System of Justice." In *Restorative Justice on Trial*, edited by Heinz Messmer and Hans-Uwe Otto. Dordrecht: Kluwer Academic.

———. 1996. *Justice for Victims and Offenders: A Restorative Response to Crime.* 2d ed. Winchester: Waterside.

———. 1999. *Restoring Respect for Justice.* Winchester: Waterside.

Young, Marlene. 1995. *Restorative Community Justice: A Call to Action.* Washington, D.C.: National Organization for Victim Assistance.

Young, R. 1989. "Reparation as Mitigation." *Criminal Law Review* 1:463–72.

Zehr, Howard. 1990. *Changing Lenses: A New Focus for Crime and Justice.* Scottdale, Pa.: Herald.

Author Index*

* The letters *t* and *f* following a page number denote a table or figure, respectively.

Subject Index